Walter Lippmann
and the
American Century

(Newsweek Photo by Vytas Varaitis)

Walter Lippmann and the American Century

by
RONALD STEEL

Vintage Books
A Division of Random House
New York

Many of the *New Republic* articles quoted are contained in *Early
Writings* by Walter Lippmann and are reprinted by permission of
Liveright Publishing Corporation. Copyright © 1970 by Liveright
Publishing Corporation.

Quotations from:

—*Public Opinion* by Walter Lippmann, copyright 1922, renewed
1951 by Walter Lippmann, are reprinted by permission of
Macmillan Publishing Co., Inc.

—Lippmann's columns in the *Washington Post* are reprinted with
the *Post's* permission.

A portion of this book has appeared in *Esquire*.

Library of Congress Cataloging in Publication Data
Steel, Ronald.
Walter Lippmann and the American century.
Bibliography: p.
Includes index.
1. Lippmann, Walter, 1889–1974. 2. Journalists—
United States—Biography. I. Title.
PN4874.L45S8 1981 070'.92'4 [B] 81-40077
ISBN 0-394-74731-3 AACR2

Manufactured in the United States of America

To
Dori Lewis

Philosophies . . . are the very soul of the philosopher projected, and to the discerning critic they may tell more about him than he knows about himself. In this sense the man's philosophy is his autobiography; you may read in it the story of his conflict with life.

— *Walter Lippmann*
in the *New Republic*, July 17, 1915

Contents

Part Two: 1931–1974

The Name That Opened Every Door

Once you touch the biographies of human beings, the notion that political beliefs are logically determined collapses like a pricked balloon.

— *A Preface to Politics,* 1913

WALTER LIPPMANN began his career in the halcyon days before the First World War, when human progress seemed unlimited and inevitable, when poets danced in the squares and science promised a life of leisure and abundance for all. He ended it with the trauma of Vietnam, the shame of Watergate, and rioters running through the streets. His career spanned a century, a century during which the American empire was born, matured, and began to founder, a time that some have called, first boastfully, then wistfully, the American Century.

As a small boy in the 1890s, Walter Lippmann shook hands with President McKinley, was formally presented to Admiral Dewey, and rapturously cheered Theodore Roosevelt on his return from San Juan Hill. He studied at Harvard with Santayana, took tea with William James, worked as a legman for Lincoln Steffens, debated socialism with Bernard Shaw and H. G. Wells, was in Belgium when the Germans invaded and at the House of Commons when Britain declared war in 1914. For a time he worshiped Theodore Roosevelt, and when he was twenty-five TR pronounced him to be the "most brilliant young man of his age in all the United States."[1] He was one of the founders of the *New Republic* and among the "movers and shakers" who sounded the trumpet for a cultural and social revolution in America before the First World War. He became the *eminence grise* to Woodrow Wilson's own alter ego, Colonel House, and was a key member of the secret organization that produced the territorial part of the Fourteen Points.

Enthusiastically supporting the war to make the world "safe for democracy," Lippmann bitterly denounced the peace that within a generation spawned an even more terrible conflict. He became editor of the greatest newspaper of its day, Pulitzer's *World,* the voice of America's liberal conscience. High in a tower above Park Row, protected from clanging telephones and clamoring reporters by a shield of secretaries, for more than nine years he penned the biting editorials that first made him a national figure. None of these editorials were signed and few are remembered today. For the devoted readers of the *World,* they needed no signature, for they bore their own special stamp.

Yet Lippmann was anything but anonymous. When he traveled, as he did a part of every year, and in great style, he conferred with heads of state. Often they sought him out, eager for the privilege of being interviewed by a man who commanded so many faithful and influential readers. His was, as a colleague once said, "the name that opened every door."[2] On a trip to Greece in the mid-1950s, for example, he jotted in his private engagement book: "Saw the King, the prime minister, etc — the usual people." For him they were. Eschewing scoops and scorning planted "leaks," which he thought unworthy of a serious commentator, he ruminated on the meaning of events in a column that was required reading in every chancery, foreign office and editorial room.

For nearly forty years his syndicated column appeared in the leading newspapers of the United States and throughout the world. When he went into semiretirement in 1967 it was as though an institution had suddenly ceased to exist. Three generations had been led through the maze of political affairs by Walter Lippmann. He was not always right and he was not universally popular. His rare gaffes — such as his early dismissal of Franklin D. Roosevelt as a well-meaning playboy — were memorable. His occasional enmities — such as his bitter feud with Lyndon Johnson over the Vietnam War — were monumental.

Readers turned to Lippmann, not for solutions, but for dispassionate analysis. He had a marvelous ability for simplifying the complex. His extraordinary success was due to two qualities: a mind that could plunge through the miasma of contention to grasp the essence of a situation, and a superbly lucid literary style. He had an intellect of a sort that is rarely attracted to journalism. He could have been a philosopher, a professor of history or even, as he once wistfully reflected, a mathematician. At college he had been Santayana's assistant, and his classmate John Reed had hailed him as a future President of the United States.

But Lippmann would be neither a politician nor a professor. Just a few weeks before he was to have received a master's degree in philosophy he left Harvard to work on a new socialist newspaper in Boston. Nor was he ever seriously tempted by government work after his painful experience with politicians during the First World War. Why did he flee academia? Partly because he feared such a career would insulate him from the "real" world he yearned to join. He loved the glamour and excitement of being part of that world. Yet a political life, particularly if it meant running for office, was out of the question for a man who so distrusted emotionalism and so detested insincerity. He enjoyed being famous and influential, but he preferred to analyze power rather than to exercise it. So he chose a career that combined involvement and detachment in a mixture peculiarly his own. He was, as he once described himself, a man who led two lives, one of books and one of newspapers, each feeding the other. The combination made him unique and gave his voice an unparalleled authority.

Lippmann was proud of being a journalist. He took younger colleagues under his wing. He listened to what they had to say rather than pontificating at them. They were, for a man who worked alone, his city room. The only advice he ever gave them was to avoid the dangers of "cronyism" — of getting so close to a politician that a journalist would lose his objectivity. It had happened to him. He got too close to Theodore Roosevelt, and was badly burned by Woodrow Wilson. For a moment he was captivated by John F. Kennedy, and later fell under the spell of Lyndon Johnson's beguiling ways, until the spell was shattered by the Vietnam War.

Influence was Lippmann's stock-in-trade; was what made him a powerful public figure. That influence was tangible, but hard to measure. He commanded no divisions, but he did have an enormous power over public opinion. This in turn gave him a power over Presidents, politicians and policymakers. They did not, by any means, always do what Lippmann advised. But they listened to him and sought his support — and they learned not to take his opposition lightly. Lippmann commanded a loyal and powerful constituency, some ten million of the most politically active and articulate people in America. Many of these people literally did not know what they ought to think about the issues of the day until they read what Walter Lippmann had said about them. A politician could ignore that kind of power only at his own risk.

Lippmann had a reputation for being a man of Olympian detachment — a Jove prone to hurling thunderbolts, but too scrupulous to descend into the political fray. That reputation, like so many others, bore only a scant relation to reality. In fact, he had promoted a good many men for public office, and had actively worked to defeat others. Sometimes he operated in print, at other times behind the scenes in ways that would have astounded his readers, had they known. He was an Olympian, with his correct public manner and his firm moral sense, but he was assuredly not detached.

His editorials for the New York *World* helped prevent an American invasion of Mexico, and his secret negotiations made possible a settlement between the revolutionary Mexican leaders and the Vatican. He wrote political speeches for John W. Davis, Al Smith, Dwight Morrow and Newton D. Baker. Later he prepped Wendell Willkie and Dwight

Eisenhower for the presidency, conspired with the Dulles brothers, and counseled Kennedy and Johnson. His ivory tower was equipped with a swift-moving elevator.

Walter Lippmann was without doubt the nation's greatest journalist. His was, as Van Wyck Brooks once said, the "most brilliant career ever devoted in America to political writing." But he was also a moralist and a public philosopher. In effect there were two Walter Lippmanns: the man who put out a weekly magazine, a daily newspaper, and finally a syndicated column without ever missing a deadline, and the man who retreated to his "pool of silence" to speculate on a "longer past and a longer future."[3]

Essentially a man of reason — an Enlightenment rationalist in an age of hot ideologies and global crusades — Lippmann was also buffeted by passions. The lean, stony face, the finely chiseled mouth, the gray-green eyes flecked with violet gave only a hint of a man who, in his late forties, was caught in a tempestuous love affair that drove him to the edge of despair. He was an emotional man who could keep those emotions under control only through an iron will.

The last years marked a strange capstone to Lippmann's work. Instead of bowing out gracefully as the elder statesman of American journalism, he became involved in the most vituperative fight of his career. Outraged by the destructiveness and the obsessions of the Vietnam War, he turned bitterly against the administration — one whose highest echelons were staffed by those who admired and flattered him. He became emotionally involved in the war, and in the struggle that was dividing America into armed camps.

When he was nearly eighty Walter Lippmann regained the fervor of his youth. He turned his back on the conservatism he had espoused during the 1930s and on the intellectual detachment with which he had viewed the follies of the late 1940s and the 1950s. The war in Vietnam had rekindled his sense of outrage. It was perhaps his finest hour.

Throughout his long life Lippmann engaged in an unending search, one that led him to socialism, to political activism, to skepticism, to stoical detachment, to economic conservatism, to cold war criticism, to social liberalism, and finally to emotional revulsion against what he viewed as imperial ambitions. He wanted his country to pursue its own high ideals, and never tired of reminding his readers of them.

He was a teacher rather than a preacher. He knew, as he once wrote, that if the moralist "is to deserve a hearing among his fellows, he must set himself this task which is so much humbler than to command and so much more difficult than to exhort: he must seek to anticipate and to supplement the insight of his fellow men into the problems of their adjustment to reality."[4]

Even though a part of Lippmann was tempted to retreat from the world, to build "walls against chaos," he fought that temptation. He challenged himself, grappled with his demons, and deliberately pursued a career that forced him into the political thick of battle, did not allow him to withdraw from a fight, and exposed him every day to his enemies. That took a special kind of courage for a man who shunned personal contention.

What saved him from withdrawal was a conviction that politics mattered, that men could live a life of reason, and that those with special gifts or understanding had a responsibility to do what they could to illuminate the path. "The hallmark of responsible comment is not to sit in judgment on events as an idle spectator, but to enter imaginatively into the role of a participant in the action," he once wrote in appreciation of a renowned newspaper editor. "Responsibility consists in sharing the burden of men directing what is to be done, or the burden of offering some other course of action in the mood of one who has realized what it would mean to undertake it."[5]

Intellectually Lippmann was engaged in the battle, emotionally he stood apart. This gave an unresolved tension to his work and to his life. He was a complex man — far more so than he appeared to those who knew him only from the sublimely self-assured tone of his articles. Spirits were fighting within him, spirits he never fully subdued and whose warring claims he never quite resolved. Like H. G. Wells, of whom he wrote so admiringly as a young man,

he seemed to be buffeted from both sides, challenged by his dreams, which revolted at the compromises of reality, and assaulted by reality which denounced the emptiness of all dreams.

He seemed to spend himself in that struggle — the severest that a man can face; and he seemed to win by a constant renewal of effort in which he refused to sink either into placid acceptance of the world, or into self-contained satisfaction with his vision.[6]

Lippmann was, in a sense, "an antediluvian, a survivor from the time before the wars and revolutions of this century . . . born and raised in one epoch and living and working in another," as he once said of himself. "Nothing in my childhood prepared me for the violent and bewildering times in which I was to live and for the radical changes which have occurred in the human condition."[7] A man whose childhood had been spent learning Latin and Greek by gaslight and riding a goat cart in Central Park lived through the revolutions of psychoanalysis, bolshevism and fascism, nuclear fission, and frenzied nationalism. He spent his life trying to understand those revolutions and to help his countrymen make their "adjustment to reality."

Part One

1889–1931

◄ 1 ►

The Only Child

Our life is managed from behind the scenes; we are
actors in dramas we cannot interpret. Of almost no decisive event can we say: this was of our own choosing.
— *Drift and Mastery*, 1914

WALTER LIPPMANN was brought up to be a gentleman. His wealthy
parents sent him to the finest schools and, from the time he was
six, took him to Europe on annual cultural excursions. He knew his way
around Paris and London, Carlsbad and St. Moritz, St. Petersburg and
Berlin long before he ever saw Philadelphia or Coney Island.

Born in the comfort of his parents' home on Lexington Avenue in
New York City on September 23, 1889, he was four years old during
the Panic of 1893, and not yet nine when the United States fought its
"splendid little war" with Spain. Like most boys, he was a fervent pa-
triot, indignant at the perfidious Spaniards who kept Cuba in bondage
and stood in the way of America's manifest destiny. This patriotism was
fortified by his maternal grandfather, Harris Baum, who had fled Berlin
after the Prussians suppressed the liberal uprising of 1848, and, following a sojourn in England, had settled in New York. Baum taught him,
as Lippmann later recounted, that "wherever the American flag was
planted, there tyranny must disappear."[1]

During the summer of 1898, when with his parents at the resort town
of Saratoga Springs, where New Yorkers of all classes retired to test the
waters and bet on the horses, he met his first authentic hero. There on
the veranda of that great, and now demolished, gingerbread palace, the
Grand Union Hotel, his father introduced him to Admiral George
Dewey, fresh from his destruction of the Spanish fleet in Manila Bay. A
few days later he went to a great open-air rally where he heard a stubby
little man with glasses give a speech that moved him to a state of excitement he could never forget or quite understand. Theodore Roosevelt, returned from the battle of San Juan Hill and running for governor of New

York, was working the crowd. He bellowed, he gesticulated, and he left eight-year-old Walter Lippmann — along with a good many grown men and women — shaken. Lippmann became, as he said, "an unqualified hero-worshiper." Roosevelt was for him "the image of a great leader and the prototype of Presidents. . . . I should have to say," he admitted years later, "that I have been less than just to his successors because they were not like him." [2]

Lippmann never lost his admiration for men of daring and determination. He liked them to be strong, but they also had to have a redeeming vision and a sense of democratic values. In men like Theodore Roosevelt and Woodrow Wilson, later in Winston Churchill and Charles de Gaulle, he saw leaders who could express the inarticulate needs of their people, help them subdue unnameable fears and paralyzing doubts. The capacity to act "upon the hidden realities of a situation in spite of appearance is the essence of statesmanship," he once wrote. [3]

That he should have admired Theodore Roosevelt is not surprising; millions of Americans did. That he should have kept that faith throughout his life says something about the kind of qualities Roosevelt embodied and the kind of man Lippmann was. TR, for all his bombast, was an intellectual, a reformer, a doer, a man of vast and barely contained energies. He knew what he wanted and moved the earth to get it. Lippmann responded to that.

In one of his early books, written when he was only twenty-three and still open enough to reveal his anxieties, he spoke of what he called the "inner history of weakness, of what disappoints us in leaders, the timidity of thought, the hesitancy and the drift." In these cases imagination and will are often blinded by "constructed evils," he wrote. "We falter from childhood amidst shames and fears, we move in closed spaces where stale tradition enervates, we grow hysterical over success and failure, and so by surrounding instinct with terror, we prepare the soul for weakness."

The appeal of Theodore Roosevelt for men like Lippmann was that he had conquered those constructed evils. As a child Lippmann had known some evils. One of the family maids, a superstitious and devout Irish girl, had told him she had read the predictions of an astronomer that the end of the world was at hand. He must pray for forgiveness before the day of judgment. Impressionable enough to be frightened by such stories, he also had a child's fear of ghosts and the dark. Alone in his room at night, he had no way to allay those fears other than by an act of will. Later he recounted how he had laid his fears to rest one night in what was "undoubtedly the most heroic event of my life." Confronting the ghost, he got out of bed, turned on the light, "identified the ghost with the lace curtain, went back to bed, turned on the light once more, made sure that the ghost *was* the curtain, and felt immeasurably happier."[4]

He told the story to illustrate how people were crippled by irrational fears of the unknown. But it revealed something more: not just the danger of "bogeys," as he called them, but the crucial role that reason played in his life. Reason was the light that dispelled darkness, turned ghosts into lace curtains, allowed men to confront and conquer the dark. Reason became a kind of religion. Even though he later came to admire the order and community of what he termed "higher religion," he continued to put his trust in reason rather than in mystery, in works rather than in faith. And he continued to look for men who could see beyond the "bogeys" and "constructed evils," for great leaders who could direct the passions of lonely men in crowds and guide them toward higher paths. From the time he was a child he sought out these men.

He did not find them at home. His father was a kind and decent man, eager to provide luxuries for his son and proud of his accomplishments. But Jacob Lippmann was not the sort of man to inspire either adulation or dislike. He was a benign presence, generous but ineffectual. His wife, Daisy, dominated him, thereby inducing in Walter an anger toward his father he could never fully admit, even to himself. His disappointment and irritation took the form of a studied indifference. Rather than rejecting or struggling with his father, he simply ceased to take him seriously. When Jacob died of cancer in 1927, after a protracted and painful illness, Walter showed tender feeling but no sorrow. "I couldn't wish him to live more of the contracted and miserable existence which remained to him," he wrote Judge Learned Hand.

When I received word of his death I was relieved. And then suddenly it seemed I forgot what he had been for two years and remembered him clearly as he once was. He was a very kind man with a kind of sweet humility and an unfailing good humor. He had so far as I knew no ambitions and no anxieties of any kind for himself, even when he knew that he was hopelessly ill.

We were never very intimate, but affectionately friendly; he always let me do whatever I wanted to do, even when he did not understand it, because he trusted me very much. When something I did got the obvious sort of recognition he felt justified and was happy about it in a way which I had to pretend often to share.[5]

The death of his father, which Freud has described as the most poignant moment of a man's life, did not appear to touch Walter deeply — or at least not in any way he could admit.

Fathers are not so easily discarded. Walter found his in a succession of strong leaders whom he greatly admired, and in a variety of older men to whom he became attached, men of strong character and personal warmth, such as Justice Oliver Wendell Holmes, political theorist Graham Wallas, Judge Learned Hand, art historian Bernard Berenson, presidential counselor Edward M. House and cabinet official Newton D. Baker. From the beginning he was drawn to men of purpose and daring. While some boys filled their rooms with baseball bats and pictures of athletes, he decorated his with a bust of Napoleon and an engraving of the emperor's retreat from Moscow — and, as an aesthetic touch, the prow of a gondola and a reproduction of a fresco in the Sistine Chapel.

Other heroes were closer at hand. One was his teacher. At Dr. Julius Sachs's School for Boys on 59th Street just off Fifth Avenue — where he prepared for college on a rigorous program of history, classics and mathematics — Walter fell under the spell of his geography instructor, Fred Thompson. A good-looking, easygoing, athletic young man who also coached the school football team, "Fritz" became a model of assertiveness and masculinity for a boy too much confined to a household of women. He also inspired a fascination with geography that was later to dominate his pupil's view of foreign policy.

Their association continued even after Fritz went to Amherst College to teach history and Lippmann set off on his own career. "In most respects he was the human being to whom I was the closest," Lippmann later confessed. "He was my first friend, my first teacher, in all the improbable things a father," he told Thompson's widow on his mentor's death in 1935.[6] To a boy who had rejected his own father, Fritz Thompson, with his warm laugh, his easy arm around the shoulder, his pleasure in games and fellowship, played a vital role.

Fritz was one of the Gentile anomalies of Walter's school, an institution for children of the German-Jewish establishment run with Teutonic rigor by Dr. Sachs. The Sachs School for Boys, and its upper-level extension, the Sachs Collegiate Institute, served as a training ground for the great Jewish families of New York. Because of its high standards, the school also attracted rich Catholics who did not want their children to mingle with the poor Irish in the parochial schools. The demanding curriculum, designed to produce cultivated young gentlemen who at the age of sixteen would be ready to enter either business or Harvard, included eleven hours of Greek and five of Latin each week. Walter, together with his neighbor and closest friend, Carl Binger, entered the Sachs school in September 1896, just a few days short of his seventh birthday.

Although predominantly Jewish in enrollment, the Sachs school was entirely secular in spirit. In this sense it was the perfect complement to the prestigious temple where the rich German Jews worshiped — the palace of reason and moderation known as Emanu-El. The symbol of Reform Judaism in America, Emanu-El — then located at Fifth Avenue and 43rd Street, before its move uptown — was hailed on its opening in

1870 by the *New York Times* as "the first to stand forward before the world and proclaim the dominion of reason over blind and bigoted faith." As such, it turned its back on a ritualistic Orthodox Judaism — with its evocations of European ghettos and medieval cabalas — and sought to assimilate Jews into the mainstream of American life by "modernizing" Judaism. In surroundings more resembling a church than a synagogue, women in hats and men without them worshiped together.

The fashionable members of the Emanu-El congregation, like many of their Protestant brethren, had been brought up to think of religion more as a social convention or an act of bonding than as an expression of piety. Instead of ushering its young men into the congregation by the ancient rite of bar mitzvah, Emanu-El granted them "confirmation." Walter was confirmed in May 1904 at fourteen. His religious instruction had been scant; his religious faith was minimal. In this sense he was like most German Jews of his class and background. Their Judaism was inherited rather than affirmed, and many sought to transmute their heritage into something less obtrusive, less "foreign."

Emanu-El also symbolized the desire of the German Jews to seal themselves off from their unassimilated brethren on the Lower East Side. The immigration waves that began in the 1870s had brought hundreds of thousands of Jews to New York, most of them refugees from the massacres and pogroms of eastern Europe. Impoverished, clinging to the ghetto for support, often socialist in their politics, these immigrants were distressingly foreign to the cultivated German Jews. The loud and abrasive newcomers, it was said uptown, gave Jews a bad name. A form of Jewish anti-Semitism developed. The rabbi of Emanu-El praised his congregation for having shed the "shackles of medievalism" and for being "no longer Oriental." Being Oriental became a euphemism for being a Russian or Polish Jew. The *American Hebrew* echoed the sentiments of its uptown readers in declaring that the "assimilation between Orientalism and Americanism . . . will never take place."[7]

The Lippmanns shared this aversion to "Orientalism" and, although they could hardly be compared to the princely Schiffs, Warburgs and Loebs, considered themselves a part of New York's Jewish society. Nearly every summer they made a tour of Europe, once taking Walter as far as St. Petersburg and Moscow. As befit those proud of their German culture, they crossed on the Hamburg-Amerika Line and took the waters at Baden-Baden, Carlsbad or Marienbad. During intervals between such excursions the Lippmanns escaped New York City's summer heat at Saratoga or at that stretch of the Jersey shore known as the "Jewish Newport."

They had not always been so grand. Walter's mother, Daisy Baum, had been born in a modest wooden house with a garden and a picket fence on 84th Street just off Third Avenue. Jacob, as a child, had lived even more modestly, on West 22nd Street in the Chelsea district. Harris Baum had started out his career in America as a wholesale meat merchant, while Jacob's father, Louis Lippmann, was a garment manufacturer.

As a young man Jacob worked with his father and his two brothers, Henry and Leopold, in the family business. The shop took up two floors of a commercial building at Fourth and Prince streets, in what is now called the SoHo district: one floor for sales and display, the other for cutting and sewing the garments. Theirs was one of the first clothing firms to use machines for cutting. The business prospered, providing the brothers with a handsome, though not spectacular, living.

Real money came into Jacob's life after the death of Daisy's father. Harris Baum had branched beyond the meat business into real estate. He had made some smart investments in downtown tenements and uptown apartments, and by the time he died was extremely well off. He left all his money to his wife, and on her death to Daisy. This enabled the Lippmanns to move first to a comfortable town house at 123 East 79th Street, and then to a grander one at 46 East 80th Street. It also permitted Jacob to retire from the clothing business and to engage in more gentlemanly pursuits, such as travel, the appreciation of fine art, and leisurely meals at good restaurants. His waist, along with his artistic sensibilities, expanded considerably.

Jacob and Daisy rarely spent an evening at home, unless they were entertaining friends. Their life was a constant round of concerts, plays and dinner parties. Every summer, when New York social life tapered off, they would go to Europe for the spas and museums. Walter always accompanied them, along with Daisy's mother, who lived with the Lippmanns after Harris Baum's death. They were a contented family, sure of their place in society: Jacob, florid and a bit stout from a life of overindulgence, good-natured, easy to please, a bit weak-willed; Daisy, a dazzling moth, high-spirited, elegantly turned out, a graduate of Hunter College at a time when few women aspired to higher education; Mrs. Baum, earthy and fun-loving, cultured and at home in three languages, though not at all intellectual, doting on her only grandchild; and Walter, the prize possession, coiffed, groomed, overprotected, and left too much on his own.

Walter was neither particularly unhappy nor rebellious, although sometimes a bit lonely as an only child. He was coddled by his grandmother, whom he adored; indulged by his father, whom he considered weak; and ignored by his mother, whom he came to dislike. Obedient and well-mannered, he did his homework, had a professional shampoo every week, and took the piano lessons that Daisy imposed upon him.

Daisy loved music and was an accomplished pianist; Walter developed an aversion to music — a feeling he was never able to overcome no matter how many concerts he attended.

Walter grew up in a gilded Jewish ghetto. Virtually everyone he knew was wealthy, Jewish and of German background. His earliest and closest friends, the Binger brothers, Carl and Walter, came from a family like his. They drove their goat carts together in Central Park, were confirmed at Emanu-El, went to the same school, and thought of themselves as part of a cultural and social elite. Unlike the immigrant Jews on the Lower East Side, they did not feel cut off from the mainstream of American culture. Indeed, they were eager to be a part of it, and believed the path lay through assimilation. This meant submerging rather than affirming their Jewishness, relegating it to a small and unimportant part of their identity. For them Judaism was not a matter of pride or a question to be discussed, but an infirmity that could be rendered innocuous, perhaps unnoticeable, by being ignored. Assimilationist Jews like Lippmann and the Binger brothers married Gentiles and lived most of their adult lives in a largely Gentile social world. Theirs was a time when young intellectuals were inspired by a cultural cosmopolitanism that ignored or actively tried to eliminate ethnic differences. If assimilation was not the highest goal, it was at least a necessary way station on the road to a universal society.

But assimilation demanded a price. It meant being cut off from one's origins and trying to fit into a society where one was never fully secure. However cosmopolitan one's friends, or the world one traveled in, there were always moments when anger or passion might break the bonds of civility. Demagoguery and mass emotions were as threatening to the Jews of the Diaspora as to the Negroes of the American South. Civility, reason, respect for the law were valued by all civilized men, but perhaps particularly by the assimilated Jew, who had historical reason to feel threatened by a breakdown of the social order.

If Walter lived in a Jewish world, he was never fully of it. He was a young man whose interests knew no ethnic boundaries, and whose ambitions would not be limited by them. He had no intention of being confined to a gilded ghetto, to its materialism, its political conservatism, its narrowness, and its exclusive Jewishness. Born to privilege, living in a home where the arts were respected and enjoyed, admired by his teachers and well liked by his schoolmates, he had every reason to believe that he could be whatever he wanted. His father thought he should be a lawyer, and his debate coach, Arthur Garfield Hays, urged him to go to Columbia Law School after Harvard. But the law had little appeal for him. His sights were set on something more aesthetic, more elevated and humanistic. He would be an art historian. This taste was formed partially by Jacob, who escorted his son through the Metropolitan on Sunday afternoons and through the great museums of Europe during the summers, and who had collected prints of paintings in a huge scrapbook that he showed Walter on winter nights. The taste was inspired even more directly from Walter's reading of the aesthetic and social criticism of John Ruskin.

The Stones of Venice and *Seven Lamps of Architecture* had snared him in Ruskin's vision of a social order where political reform and aesthetic purity went hand in hand. From Ruskin he acquired the tastes of a Victorian puritan, admiring the clean lines of preclassical Greek, Romanesque and early Gothic architecture, and deploring as vulgar all secular art, including that of the Renaissance. The perfect model of a prim, adolescent aesthete, he echoed his master in deploring the corruption of the modern age.

During the summer of his junior year at Sachs, accompanying his parents on their annual wanderings around Europe, he haunted art museums with a single-minded dedication. While Jacob and Daisy strolled through the Tuileries and lingered at the Café de la Paix, he took to spending his afternoons at the Louvre. There, one afternoon as he was inspecting Cimabue's *Madonna and Child* with the concentration of an appraiser, he was approached by a fashionably dressed American lady and her young companion. The lady, who introduced herself as Mrs. Gardner of Boston and her companion as Matthew Pritchard of the Simmons College art faculty, had seen him often at the museum and thought it curious that such a young man would spend so much time looking at paintings. As they fell into conversation she was immediately taken with his intelligence and charm, and offered to guide him through the galleries, which she obviously knew very well. Over the next few weeks they met frequently, with Mrs. Gardner explaining the pictures and their history. When they parted she gave him her address in Boston, and urged him to visit her when he enrolled at Harvard.

Walter was not nearly so naive as his cherubic face seemed to indicate. Within a few days after arriving in Cambridge in the fall of 1906, he took the trolley across the Charles River to the pink Italianate villa on the Fenway. There Isabella Stewart Gardner received him wearing a long velvet gown very much like the one in which she had posed for the famous portrait by John Singer Sargent that adorned her remarkable palazzo. She showed him her collection of paintings, one of the finest in the world, and explained that it had been formed with the aid of Bernard Berenson. Later Berenson would come to play an important part in Lippmann's own life.

Walter had already developed a taste for the world beyond books and paintings, and particularly beyond that of the Sachs school and Temple Emanu-El. Isabella Stewart Gardner offered a glimpse of that world — a world he would soon make his own. As he began his studies at Harvard in September 1906, still a few days short of his seventeenth birthday, he had no doubt that he would become an art historian, pursuing, with Ruskin as his model, the pleasures of an art poetic in inspiration and reformist in spirit.

Unfortunately, he had less interest in aesthetics than he had imagined, and it was not long before he replaced Ruskin with other heroes. But then many things at Harvard turned out to be different — and not always agreeably so — than he had imagined.

◂ 2 ▸

Harvard '10

Gentlemen, the future President of the United
States!

— John Reed, introducing Lippmann, 1908

WHEN he arrived in Cambridge in the fall of 1906, Walter was
ready, or so he thought, to launch his new life as a Harvard gentleman. He came prepared with several trunks of clothes, including half
a dozen tailored suits cleverly cut to conceal his chubbiness, two tennis
rackets and several dozen indispensable books. He was not intimidated
by Harvard. Sachs, after all, had a tradition of turning out Harvard-
bound men, and had prepared him to handle any academic challenge he
was likely to meet.

What it had not — what it could not have — prepared him for was
the social challenge. He thought he would scale the social peaks at Harvard as easily as he had at Sachs. But he had not realized quite how
many Harvards there were, and how little they overlapped. There was a
Harvard of athletes; a Harvard of the scholars intent on graduate school;
of the good-time boys who would later be selling bonds on Wall Street
or State Street; of the privileged young men from proper families, with
their social clubs like Porcellian and the A.D., who perfunctorily sat in
on an occasional class; of outsiders searching for kindred souls; and of
rebels eager to defy authority.

For quarters, Walter was assigned a single room in Weld Hall, one of
the dingiest dormitories in the Yard. It had neither running water nor
central heating. A small fireplace provided the only warmth, and the
nearest bath was at the gymnasium two blocks away. But Carl Binger
had a room just one floor below, and it was not long before Walter
made new friends in class or over meals at Memorial Hall and Randall
Hall. There he met a good many upperclassmen, for one of the innovations of President Charles W. Eliot had been to put all the undergrad-

uates together in the Yard rather than segregating freshmen in separate dormitories.

By the time Lippmann entered Harvard the legendary Eliot was nearing the end of his forty-year tenure as president of the university. A man of awesome energies, Victorian integrity, and an unshakable faith in science and progress, "a little bit like God walking around," as Lippmann later said of him,[1] Eliot had come to Harvard in 1869, when there were only 563 students in the college. On his departure in 1909 there were nearly 2,000. He sought out the best scholars, gave them academic freedom, inaugurated the free elective system for undergraduates, and developed the university into a college surrounded by a cluster of autonomous professional schools. The elective system, which opened the intellectual resources of the university to undergraduates, was a liberating draft for those who could handle it. Students were encouraged to strike out on their own. One of the purposes of a Harvard education, Eliot told the 605 entering freshmen of Lippmann's class, was "to allow each man to think and do as he pleases."

Some of the students took advantage of that freedom, rebelling — at least for a time — against convention, and even against the university itself. "There was talk of the world, and daring thought, and intellectual insurgency; heresy has always been a Harvard institution," John Reed wrote of his college days. "Students themselves criticized the faculty for not educating them, attacked the sacred institution of intercollegiate athletics, sneered at undergraduate clubs so holy that no one dared mention their names."[2] Yet the undergraduates were not so daring as they thought. Rebellion was also part of the Harvard tradition. Experimentation and free thought, not indoctrination, were the goals of the Harvard education under Eliot. "Our undisciplinables are our proudest product," the philosopher William James declared at a commencement dinner.

For intellectually curious boys like Walter the atmosphere was exciting. "At Harvard class distinction counts for nothing," he reported to the boys back at Sachs in an article for the school magazine. "Men of all types and purposes are thrown together in dormitory, dining hall and on the athletic field . . . the scientific student is expected to know poetry, and the aesthete is generally interested in physics."[3] Green freshmen may have been thrown together with seasoned upperclassmen in dormitories and dining halls, but strong class distinction persisted at Harvard. The richer undergraduates shunned the Yard for the spacious new private dormitories on Mount Auburn Street, the "Gold Coast," as it was called because of its comparative magnificence. Private social clubs dominated most undergraduate activities and closed their doors to those considered "unsuitable." Rough was the path and narrow the gate that led to the acme of Harvard social life: the final clubs. In their sophomore year, athletes, men of social distinction, hard workers, such as editors of the *Crimson* and the *Lampoon,* and the managers of the major athletic teams were chosen for the three "waiting clubs." From these a handful of the elect gained admission to the prestigious final clubs.

Since one path lay through athletics, Walter, eager to make the grade socially, entered the competition for manager of the freshman track team. When he won the post of second assistant manager, he thought he was in the running for the waiting clubs. But the clubs were not interested in Jews, or for that matter in those who did not "fit"— who were from public high schools or the hinterlands, or were obviously intellectual, or in some way "odd." Rejection was part of the game. This rejection made some boys, like Walter's friend David Carb, feel worthless, while it inspired others, like John Reed, to a personal awareness of social injustice. By the end of his freshman year, Walter, realizing he was not going to make the clubs, dropped out of the athletic circle and concentrated on the intellectual side of Harvard.

Taking advantage of the system of free electives, he sought out the star professors: Hugo Münsterberg and Edwin B. Holt in psychology, George Lyman Kittredge and Barrett Wendell in English, Irving Babbitt in French literature, George Santayana in philosophy. During his first three years he took seven courses in philosophy, five in languages (Latin, French and Italian), three in English and comparative literature, three in economics, and one each in history and government — but not a single course in mathematics or the sciences. The work was not hard — Sachs had prepared him well — and he spent most of his time reading in the library. By the end of his third year, with mostly A's and a few B's, he made Phi Beta Kappa and had enough credits to graduate, but decided to stay on for a fourth year to do advanced work in philosophy.

This easygoing academic schedule left him with a good deal of free time for writing and for late-night bull sessions in the Yard. Above all it allowed him to wander through College Library. Having been saturated in the classics at Sachs, he set out to devour modern social critics like Ibsen, Shaw and Wells, and novelists like Hardy, Meredith, Galsworthy and Kipling. These writers seemed to speak a new language, promising liberation from the inherited privilege, outmoded social conventions, and moral smugness of the Victorian world. Caught up in the spirit of these critics he memorized whole paragraphs from Wells's *Tono-Bungay* and *The New Machiavelli,* and read passages from Shaw's *Man of Destiny* to his friends. Their fervor aroused him to flights of indignation: "Ibsen and Shaw have shown us with perfect truth that morality is not respectability, that the Life Force is above marriage laws, that society is against the individual," he wrote Lucile Elsas, a New York girl with whom he was conducting a shy romance. "We have seen that the curse of great fortunes is the degradation of the poor, that social position is built upon the slum.'' Naturally, the duty of those who had seen the light was to lead the way. ''In the work of uplifting we cannot do too much.''[4]

While his social conscience burgeoned, Walter also hovered on the fringes of aestheticism. The Celtic revival was afoot, and like many literary-minded undergraduates he savored the poems of Yeats, Synge and Dunsany. Joining the Circolo Italiano, he studied Dante. This led, naturally, to a passion for Swinburne, and late in the evenings he would recite to his friends lines like ''The lilies and languors of virtue and the roses and raptures of vice'' — though he himself focused more on the lilies. In the spirit of the day he staunchly proclaimed the need to embrace the world, advising Lucile that salvation lay in ''saying with Nietzsche, 'Yes, to the universe . . . then and only then are we divine and immortal.' ''[5]

Yea-saying was very much in vogue at Harvard at the time, and it did not take Walter long to find a circle of men eager to talk about rapture, joy, beauty and the life-force. Besides his oldest friend, Carl Binger, he drew close to Ernest Westcott and to Kenneth Hunter; to Dave Carb and Lee Simonson, the star pupils of George Pierce Baker's ''47 Workshop'' in playwriting; to a Hindu prince named Gupta, who followed him around like a spaniel and quoted his remarks as though they were graven on stone; to the poet Paul Mariett, who died of cancer before graduation; and to troubled Alfred Kuttner, whose interest in psychiatry first made Lippmann aware of Freud.

While none of these men fitted into the clubman's Harvard — being either odd, Jewish or improperly connected — they were part of an extraordinary group. Walter's class of 1910 was probably the most illustrious Harvard ever produced, including not only journalist John Reed, but T. S. Eliot, already writing poems while in training for the freshman track team; Robert Edmond Jones, who transformed American stage design; Hans von Kaltenborn, later a well-known radio commentator; Bronson Cutting, who would become a senator from New Mexico; Heywood Broun, Lippmann's colleague on the New York *World* in the 1920s; and the promising poet Alan Seeger, who died in the First World War. Just ahead of the Class of '10 came the literary triumvirate of Edward Sheldon, Van Wyck Brooks and John Hall Wheelock; just after, the poet Conrad Aiken.

They wrote plays and poems, edited the literary and political magazines, and argued long into the night. Lippmann's room at Weld Hall became a place for them to sit around the fire while drinking beer, reading poetry, and speculating on their professors and the meaning of life. ''It has been such a wild time,'' Walter wrote Lucile after one of these sessions; ''metaphysics, Socialism, art theories, Schopenhauer, a vitality in religion — every night till late in the morning and then dissatisfaction and bed." Lest she get the wrong idea, he told her that "dissatisfaction is the price we pay when we're young for vision . . . it is better never to see and to realize, than to see and realize and not transcend the vision." Their ideal, he explained, was "to build a citadel of human joy upon the slum of misery . . . to give the words 'the brotherhood of man' a meaning." [6]

One way to bring about such a lofty ambition was through the pen. Writing seemed as natural to Walter and his friends as arguing at the dinner table. Barrett Wendell used to tell them — on the assumption that they would all one day be authors — that in writing a book they must be sure it opened and ended well, but that the parts in between did not matter so much. To tighten his prose style Walter signed up in his sophomore year for the advanced composition course taught by Charles Copeland. "Copey," as he was known to admirers and detractors alike, had attracted and trained some of Harvard's best writers. A former actor and a biographer of Edwin Booth, he loved to perform. He would summon his students to his office to have them read aloud from their papers. Retiring to a sofa he would close his eyes, and as the terrified student read, he would shout out, "Awkward!" or "Purple prose!"

Walter's leanings toward the purple were knocked out and stomped upon by Copey, and he soon became one of his teacher's pets. One time as he was reading a paper, Copey shouted at him: "Lippmann, put in the margin, 'Your pen drips vitriol.' " Copey knew no higher compliment. Not everyone responded to Copey's brutal methods, fey manners, and obvious favoritism for the talented and the handsome. Some found him shallow and mean-spirited. But Lippmann learned a lot during those nerve-racking sessions at Hollis Hall, where, as he later wrote in tribute to Copey, "you began to feel that out of the darkness all around you long fingers were searching through the layers of fat and fluff to find your bones and muscles." [7]

In college magazines like the *Monthly* and the *Illustrated,* Lippmann put into practice what he had learned from Copey. In typical Harvard fashion, he devoted one of his first published articles to an attack on a professor. Barrett Wendell, an Anglophile defender of gentility, had written a book called *The Privileged Classes,* in which he charged that true culture had been debased by mass taste. Such elitism offended Lippmann's liberal scruples. The simple workingman, he wrote in retort, "has gone on genially producing houses he will never enter except to repair them, producing food while his own children go to school unfed; building automobiles so that fashionable ladies may take their Teddy Bears out for an airing in Newport." [8]

Such bold words lifted the hearts of all lovers of social justice. Among them was William James. Bored in his retirement and restless after the publication of his great work *Pragmatism* the previous year, the sixty-six-year-old philosopher was always on the lookout for new ideas and new people. An iconoclast by nature and a Whitmanesque democrat by temperament, he was suspicious of whatever was hallowed, and willing to give any theory a respectful hearing. He assumed that there must be a grain of truth in everything. Barrett Wendell's cultural absolutism was obviously the antithesis of everything he believed in. Nothing gave him greater pleasure than to see snobs like Wendell shot down, even by supercilious undergraduates.

In characteristically impromptu fashion, James decided to congratulate the young author in person. Early one fall morning in 1908, the nineteen-year-old Lippmann responded to a knock on his door at Weld Hall and found the white-bearded philosopher on the other side. "I'm William James," he said, as though he were not a living institution to every Harvard student. "I thought I'd drop by and tell you how much I liked that article on Wendell." Recovering from his stupefaction, and quick, as always, to seize upon an opportunity, Lippmann suggested that they take a little walk together through the Yard. They chatted of cultural fossils like Wendell, the bright promise of socialism, and the lectures James was preparing to give the following year on pluralism. The philosopher, impressed by Lippmann's charm and intellectual curiosity, suggested he come to tea.

The invitation became a weekly ritual. Every Thursday morning at eleven Lippmann crossed the Yard to take tea with James and his wife at their house on Irving Street. Conversation ranged over politics, religion, ethics, whatever struck James's fancy. Lippmann responded eagerly to the philosopher's passion for social reform, commitment to experimentation, abhorrence of dogma, and deep sense of personal morals. His talk with James, he wrote his parents after their first meeting, was "the greatest thing that has happened to me in my college life."[9]

William James was a liberating influence on an entire generation. Man, he declared in words that ardent youths like Lippmann took to heart, must "live today by what truth he can get, be ready tomorrow to call it a falsehood." Rejecting all dogma, except, of course, his own dogma of iconoclasm, he exalted skepticism to a philosophical principle. In place of the gloomy Social Darwinism of Herbert Spencer, or the ephemeral Idealism of Josiah Royce, he preached experimentation, pluralism and action. Downgrading intellectualism, he exalted will over reason, and urged his young disciples to give up logic "fairly, squarely, and irrevocably," substituting for it "reality, life, experience, concreteness and immediacy."

As a young man eager to remake the world and kick over the constraints of an inherited Victorian cosmology, Lippmann was drawn to idol-smashing. James provided an intellectual justification. This alone made him a culture hero. Through his writings, and even more through his weekly conversations over tea, James aroused in his young follower an interest in science and experimentation, persuaded him that religion could be reconciled with science by the standards of empiricism, and evoked realms of consciousness beyond everyday experience. In his first book, written a few years later, Lippmann was echoing James when he proclaimed that "no moral judgment can decide the value of life, no ethical theory can announce any intrinsic good."[10] The philosopher taught him some lessons he never forgot. One was meliorism, the belief that things could be improved but never perfected. Another was practicality — that men had to make decisions without worrying about whether they were perfect: "We must choose, whether we will it or not, and where all is doubt," as Lippmann later wrote. James also taught him discipline — that every writer should set down at least a thousand words a day, whether or not he felt like it, even whether or not he had anything to say.

James's openness to new ideas, his warm character, his life-embracing optimism revealed how philosophy could help enrich human life. Even though Lippmann later strayed far from his mentor's pragmatic iconoclasm, he never lost his admiration for this gentle and kindly man. When James died in the summer of 1910, Lippmann, just out of college, eulogized him in his first signed article as a journalist. James, he wrote, was a man who "listened for truth from anybody, and from anywhere, and in any form, from Emma Goldman, the pope or a sophomore; preached from a pulpit, a throne or a soap-box." He was "perhaps the most tolerant man of our generation."[11]

If James taught Lippmann to open his mind to new ideas, others, less fatherly and far less gentle, also had a powerful effect on him. One was Irving Babbitt, the *enfant terrible* of the French department. Brandishing the battered, but still unbowed, standard of classical humanism, Babbitt vitriolically denounced the modern vices — materialism, science and naturalism. "There are tastes that deserve the cudgel," he would cry out to the delight of his students, scattering notes and bits of paper stuck in the books from which he indignantly quoted. Above all, Babbitt detested Romanticism, believing that its self-righteous anti-intellectualism and its mindless assumption that all men were innately good debased all cultural and moral standards.

Most undergraduates looked on Babbitt as an anachronism, one of the characters the university had provided for their amusement. Yet on some he made an indelible impression. T. S. Eliot was one, and in a different way, so was Lippmann. At first Lippmann detested Babbitt's Tory conservatism. Like most young men he admired Rousseau, believed that "the people" really were good and were corrupted by soci-

ety, and that their "general will" should be obeyed. Babbitt undermined that faith. He showed how the supreme values of Western
civilization had been built by men with a vision of excellence who were
willing to defy the corrupt tastes and the fleeting passions of the common people, how the substitution of will and instinct for reason could
wipe away the thin veneer of civilization and leave men naked to their
own brute passions, how democracy itself rested on restraining the
power of the majority. The young Lippmann resisted this, found it offensive, elitist, antimajoritarian. But a decade later he was a good deal
closer to Babbitt than to James.

Harvard's other great influence on Lippmann was George Santayana.
A Catholic freethinker who valued religion aesthetically rather than as a
guide to morality, he was a prolific writer of exquisite sensibilities who
had been teaching in the Philosophy Department since the year of Lippmann's birth. During that time Santayana had made an impressive reputation and a great many enemies. He had little time for colleagues whom
he considered intellectually feeble, and even less for Boston society.
But he had devoted disciples, for he was a superb teacher whose subtle
mind was complemented by a compelling classroom presence and a poetic literary style.

Though he had come to America from Spain as a child and had taken
his degree in philosophy at Harvard under Royce and James, Santayana
claimed he was American only "by long association," and he took a
certain pride in his distance. "I see by my little Spanish paper that President Taft isn't very popular," he once told Lippmann. By temperament
and by choice he was estranged from both Spain and his adopted land.
"A man's feet should be planted in his country," he said, "but his eyes
should survey the world." Alien everywhere, Santayana's mind wandered across the continents and the centuries, his sharp tongue demolishing academic pedantry and the cultural colonialism of what he
mockingly called "the genteel tradition."

There was a physical fascination about the man that was hard to pin
down. Lippmann once described him as "resembling Leonardo's Mona
Lisa with a little pointed beard," while Max Eastman thought him
"dangerously fascinating" with eyes like Milton's Satan.[12] Dangerous
or not, the undergraduates found him mysterious and exotic. Always
elegantly dressed, often with piqué vest, spats, and suede gloves, he
would stand at the lectern, stare into space, and, never once glancing at
a note, give lectures that could have been printed verbatim. He seemed
a visitor from another shore, always "gazing over our heads as if looking for the sail that was to bear him home," in Lee Simonson's words.
Soon it did. In 1912 he retired from Harvard at the age of forty-nine and
spent the forty remaining years of his life in Europe, first in Oxford,
then in Rome. There he produced some of his most important works,

including the four-volume *Realms of Being,* a three-volume autobiography, and a novel.

Lippmann first encountered Santayana in 1907, during the fall of his sophomore year, when he signed up for the introductory course in Greek philosophy. The experience was disturbing. With his devastating wit, precise turn of phrase, and corrosive intellect, Santayana challenged most of the nineteenth-century shibboleths of progress and moral uplift that Lippmann had grown up believing. In their place he offered a neo-Platonic naturalism, positing that everything man experiences comes from nature and has a potential to develop toward an ideal end. With his poetic sensibility and gift for language, he described the goal of man's existence as a struggle for excellence, an effort to capture the harmony and beauty of the human spirit.

At first Lippmann resisted Santayana's subtly insinuating philosophy. But soon he was overwhelmed by it. While still in the introductory course he plunged into Santayana's five-volume *Life of Reason,* published just a few years earlier. During his third year he struggled between the rival visions of Santayana and James, but soon fell under the Spaniard's spell. Abandoning any thought of becoming an art historian or, as his family still hoped, a lawyer, he concentrated on philosophy, taking every course Santayana offered — some of them virtual tutorial sessions. One course, which Santayana was using as a testing ground for his book *Three Philosophical Poets,* made such an impression on Lippmann that he organized his third year around it, reading Lucretius in Latin, Dante in Italian, and Goethe's *Faust* in German.

The philosopher had drawn his star pupil into his net, enlisting him as a dinner companion on forays into Boston, making him an audience for malicious remarks about his colleagues. He had irrevocably demolished Walt Whitman for Lippmann by pointing out the poet's "corrupt desire to be primitive." Nor was he more charitable to James, whose philosophy he compared to the Polish constitution: if a single vote were cast against the majority, nothing could be enacted. Dismissing James's experimental pragmatism as "romantic cosmology" (James had described Santayana's doctoral thesis as "the perfection of rottenness"), he observed with caustic accuracy that it would depress James to have to confess that any important question was finally answered. If he squirmed at such gibes, Lippmann nonetheless found Santayana intellectually irresistible. Having finished his course work in three years, he decided to stay on at Harvard for a fourth year to work on a master's degree when the Spaniard offered him the post of assistant in his introductory philosophy course.

They made a curious combination: the fine-boned philosopher with his burning dark eyes, noble brow, and quizzical smile; the eager pupil whose quick intelligence and passionate idealism shone in a face still round and a bit unformed. Superficially they were worlds apart, Lippmann all intensity and indignation faced with the inequities of society, Santayana bemused by the human condition, preferring to pass his leisure in the company of handsome athletes rather than with colleagues or Boston matrons.

There was no drawing close to Santayana. "Aloofness and facile contempt were his defects," wrote Bertrand Russell, "and because of them, although he could be admired, he was a person whom it was difficult to love." Yet Santayana struck a powerful chord in Lippmann. From Santayana the poet he learned the importance of writing gracefully as well as clearly; from Santayana the humanist he learned to value the classical virtues of measure and restraint. It was Santayana who steered him away from the Idealism of Josiah Royce and from the experimental pluralism of William James, Santayana who instilled in him a striving for excellence as the highest goal of a life guided by reason. "Our lives must be given over to the most beautiful ones, for beauty alone, physical or intellectual or spiritual, has the power of completeness," an impressionable Walter wrote Lucile in phrases turned from Santayana. "Beauty alone is immortal, not skin-deep as cynics say, because fullness is the essence of immortality." [13]

Except for the exuberant books of his early youth, Lippmann's works bear the imprint of Santayana's search for a reality beyond experience, one rooted in neo-Platonic "essences," eternal values, and a "detached contemplation of earthly things," as Santayana himself described it. While James's praise of instinct and experimentation, his war against dogma and abstract intellectualism, captured the imagination of the young Lippmann, Santayana's doctrine that the "function of reason is to dominate experience," and his fear that excessive democracy would establish a tyranny of the majority, "the most cruel and unprogressive of masters," proved more enduring. Lippmann came to see James's pragmatism, with its moral relativism and its belief that truth was to be made rather than found, far less compelling than Santayana's search for absolute moral values that could be reconciled with human experience. "I love James more than any very great man I ever saw," he wrote Bernard Berenson a decade after leaving Harvard, "but increasingly I find Santayana inescapable."

In Santayana's emotional detachment Lippmann also saw a quality he recognized in himself. The year after he left Harvard he wrote a sketch of Santayana, perceptive in its judgment, but as revealing of the student as of the teacher. "The serenity and aloofness of Santayana shut him out of the rank of prophets," wrote the twenty-one-year-old Lippmann.

You feel at times that his ability to see the world steady and whole is a kind of tragic barrier between him and the common hopes of ordinary men. It's as if he saw all forest and no trees. He filled active souls with a sense of the unbridge-able chasm between any ideal of perfection and the squeaky, rickety progress of human affairs. There is something of the pathetic loneliness of the spectator about him. You wish he would jump on the stage and take part in the show. Then you realize that he wouldn't be the author of *The Life of Reason* if he did.

"For it is a fact," Lippmann added, perhaps more revealingly than he realized, "that a man can't see the play and be in it too."[14]

When he wrote those lines Lippmann did not feel he had to choose between being a spectator and being a participant. He wanted to see the play and be in it too. It took him somewhat longer to realize that to "see the world steadily and whole" was as much a matter of temperament as of choice.

◄ 3 ►

A Friend of the Masses

I long to . . . reach some small portion of the
"masses" so that in the position not of a teacher but of
a friend, I may lay open real happiness to them.
— To Lucile Elsas, c. 1908

THE subtle lure of Santayana's neo-Platonic essences was rudely
shattered for Lippmann during the spring of his second year at Harvard. A week before Easter 1908 a fire ravaged the slums of the nearby
city of Chelsea, leaving thousands homeless. He joined a brigade of
Harvard students who volunteered to help the victims. Although he had
spent some time working with underprivileged children at Hale House, a
Boston settlement, this was his first experience with poor people. The
working class had been an abstraction: anonymous janitors, policemen,
shop clerks. As he roamed the smoldering tenements he saw poverty for
the first time as a human reality.

On returning to the Yard he began to relate what he had seen to the
social criticism he had been reading. Shaw's plays and Wells's novels
took on a different meaning. Until then his social concern had been sentimental and literary. Now he began to question the system that produced such inequality. He began to relate it to socialism. The subject
was daring even at Harvard and unthinkable in the social world he had
come from, a world in which, as he later wrote, the name of a Democrat
like Grover Cleveland "was uttered with monstrous dread in the household," and where William Jennings Bryan was "an ogre from the
West."[1] He read *The Communist Manifesto* and some of Karl Marx's
shorter essays, but disliked the emphasis on class struggle and felt that
inciting the masses to mob action was not a desirable way to bring about
a better society. Like most children of the Progressive era, he wanted to
make society more equitable, not turn it upside down.

In search of reform without revolution, he found what he wanted in
the British Fabians. Organized in the 1880s by Beatrice and Sidney

Webb, the Fabian Society had attracted an impressive group of writers and intellectuals, including H. G. Wells and George Bernard Shaw. Preaching moderation, emphasizing education, and confining their membership to a small group of the "enlightened," the Fabians took just enough of Marx to be modern, while eliminating everything that threatened social stability. Convinced that nothing constructive could be done by the masses, they favored the creation of a small core of selfless leaders — what Wells had called a "new mass of capable men" — mostly scientists and engineers with a "strong imperative to duty." Subordinating their appetites to the service of the state, these men and women would surmount the inefficiency and prejudices of popular democracy. Fabianism appealed to intellectuals like Lippmann because it so perfectly expressed the desire of the middle-class reformer to "level up" rather than to "level down," to transform the poor into contented bourgeois rather than to seize the state apparatus, and to put power in the hands of an intellectual elite.

Lippmann burrowed into the stacks of College Library, devouring the Fabian texts: the Webbs' *Industrial Democracy* and *Report on the Poor Laws,* the novels of Wells, the political essays of Shaw and H. N. Hyndman. From these he delved into the futurist classics: William Morris's *News from Nowhere,* Thomas More's *Utopia,* and Edward Bellamy's *Looking Backward.* After hearing a talk on socialism at Faneuil Hall he had been "walking on air all day," he told Lucile. "Isn't it a thing great enough to make you feel like getting down on your knees and worshipping man to find that in the center of American conservatism . . . people are today discussing the fundamental errors of our government?" A week later he announced his conversion. "I have come around to socialism as a creed," he told Lucile. "I do believe in it passionately and fearlessly — not that all men are equal, for that is a misapplication of democracy — I believe that the people must express themselves in an organized society where religion is the dynamic."[2] The young convert's questioning of equality was characteristically Fabian, as was the equating of religion with Justice, Progress and Efficiency.

His social conscience aroused by the Chelsea fire and his intellect engaged by the Fabian tracts, Lippmann worked closely with a socialist discussion group at Harvard. In March 1908 he and eight undergraduates had formed the Socialist Club to consider, according to its manifesto, "all schemes of social reform which aimed at a radical reconstruction of society." The group unanimously elected Lippmann, its organizer and most effective debater, as president. In its first official action the club applied for a charter from the Intercollegiate Socialist Society (ISS), a coordinating body founded by Clarence Darrow and Jack London in 1905.

The budding Fabians set up a reference library in Hiram Moderwell's dormitory room, and every other week held meetings to discuss papers written by the members on equality and injustice. "If anyone taking a bird's eye view of Cambridge at one o'clock in the morning were to see five or six groups of excited Harvard men gesticulating wildly on various street corners," Lippmann wrote in an article for a school magazine, "let him know that the Socialist Club held a meeting that evening." In addition to gesticulating wildly, the young socialists also invited speakers such as Lincoln Steffens, the muckraker journalist; Florence Kelley, head of the National Consumers' League and a pioneer of the women's movement; Morris Hillquit of the Socialist party; James MacKaye, author of *The Economy of Happiness;* and such local writers as Charles Zueblin and B. O. Flower. William James extended his blessing, while George Santayana and Ralph Barton Perry came to speak. For Harvard, where the annual Hasty Pudding show was still the leading undergraduate activity, the Socialist Club was a daring iconoclasm. "He who listens carefully enough," Lippmann wrote in an effort to tantalize his fellow students, "will hear at Harvard heresies about private property which ten years ago would have been denounced by the public press as leading straight to atheism, to free love, and all the other horrors that terrified ignorance can conjure up."[3]

Not content to debate issues, the young socialists challenged the university to stop exploiting ill-paid workers, permit women speakers, and offer full credit for a course in socialism. They even reached beyond Harvard Square, drawing up a socialist platform for municipal elections and introducing bills into the state legislature. Their aim was to overcome what Lippmann described as the "suffocating discretions, the reservations, and the bland silence" of college life. Fired by his new faith, he helped found the Social Politics Club, joined the Debating Club and the Philosophical Club, wrote for the political *Harvard Illustrated,* edited by his classmate Kaltenborn, and for the more literary *Harvard Monthly,* then under the direction of Edward Eyre Hunt — his socialist "comrade."

He became part of a group of rebel agitators whose aim, in John Reed's words, was "to make undergraduates take sides, grow angry, to split the university in sides on every question." "I'm very happy," Walter wrote Lucile of his work at the Cambridge Social Union, "because it gives me an opportunity of working in the exact field I long to — to reach some small portion of the 'masses' so that in the position not of a teacher but of a friend, I may lay open real happiness to them."[4]

As he developed confidence in himself as a writer, he turned out a stream of articles for the school magazines extolling the superiority of socialism, decrying the commercialism of college athletics, and defending the women's movement. "They are unladylike, just as the Boston Tea Party was ungentlemanly, and our Civil War bad form," he wrote of the suffragettes. "But unfortunately in this world great issues are not won by good manners." He even took on A. Lawrence Lowell, who had succeeded Charles W. Eliot as president of Harvard in 1909, for decreeing that freshmen could no longer live in the same buildings as upperclassmen. This, he charged, discriminated in favor of the opulent private dormitories on Mount Auburn Street and meant "the grouping of men by the amount of rent they are willing to pay, by fashion or tradition . . . the reproduction at Harvard of the same social stratification which exists in the world."[5]

Although the Socialist Club had fifty members by the fall of 1909, most undergraduates remained indifferent to the great political issues. "We move in a political darkness," Lippmann complained in the *Monthly*. "We fail to grasp the overwhelming duties that freedom imposes on the individual; our consciences are not social; we are 'hopelessly private persons.' " There was nothing wrong in being dissatisfied, he told the undergraduates, but it was "decidedly ridiculous for young men to be 'conservative,' for it means that they will probably be 'stand-patters' — when they grow older. Men who are 'orthodox' when they are young are in danger of being middle-aged all their lives." He even tried to activate younger boys. "Join the sleepy political clubs and wake them up," he wrote in an article for his old school paper. "Make them count for what they ought to count in college life. . . . You will do your studying eagerly because it will seem to have a connection with interesting and important events."[6]

Eager to make that connection himself, he did not confine his socialist activities to Harvard. As an effective public speaker, his delivery refined from years of training as a debater, he was greatly in demand at other socialist clubs, and was often called on by the Intercollegiate Socialist Society. When the ISS held its first convention in New York early in 1910, Lippmann was a featured speaker. Later that year he joined the executive committee and toured other campuses to give pep talks.

As an apostle of socialism, Lippmann was excited to discover that Graham Wallas, one of the original Fabians, would be at Harvard in the spring of 1910 to teach a seminar in politics. Unlike academic political scientists, Wallas had written political tracts, addressed mass meetings, and even run for office on the Labor party ticket. He was also a bit of a renegade. Having been a guiding director of the Fabian Society, he had dramatically resigned in 1904 following a quarrel with the Webbs. To undergraduates who had only read about such distant and dramatic personalities, the chance to come into contact with one was irresistible. In his last term at Harvard Walter, with considerable anticipation, joined six other students in signing up for Wallas's seminar.

The fiery British radical turned out to be a shy and diffident man, given to jotting down notes on little bits of paper and stuffing them into his pockets whenever an idea came to mind. "Rather slovenly, slightly pedantic," in H. G. Wells's description, he was also a noble-spirited teacher, and behind the bland demeanor lay a subtle and original mind. Two years earlier, with the publication of his book *Human Nature in Politics,* Wallas had set off a small furor by contending that politics, like human life, was an essentially irrational phenomenon. People made political judgments, not by a judicious weighing of the facts and their probable consequences, but as they made other judgments — through instinct, prejudice and habit. The trouble with political science, he argued, was that it refused to take human nature into account, preferring to examine statistics.

For Lippmann, who had been taught that politics was about constitutions, elections and legislative committees, Wallas's approach was a revelation. Demonstrating that principles and institutions meant little unless based on human motivation, Wallas taught him to look suspiciously on political scientists who could, in the scathing words Lippmann himself later used, talk about "the national will of America as if it were a single stream of pure water which ran its course through silver pipes laid down by the Constitutional Fathers." A pioneer in social theory, Wallas nonetheless never took his analysis into realms of the unconscious. He had no inkling of how Freudian psychology might be applied to politics: that lay for Lippmann himself to do. But Wallas did blaze a path, and deserved credit, as Lippmann wrote a few years later, for having "turned the study of politics back to the humane tradition of Plato and Machiavelli — of having made man the center of political investigation."[7]

Wallas left two other legacies to Lippmann. First was the view that modern man lived in a "great society" where the environment was so large as to be virtually invisible. Such a concept — though Wallas himself never fully explored it — threw into doubt the assumption that men could know their environment and make intelligent political judgments about it. This was a theme Lippmann himself was to elaborate so disturbingly a dozen years later in *Public Opinion.* Wallas also induced in the young Lippmann a skepticism about the socialism to which they both professed allegiance. Having broken with the Fabians, Wallas was not at all sure that socialism was the only path to reform. Nor was his student. "Socialism stands or falls by its fruits in practice," Lippmann wrote that spring of 1910 at Harvard. "If it can be shown that public enterprise, where tried under democratic conditions, fails to produce a beneficent effect on the health, happiness and general culture of a community, or that private enterprise is more beneficent, then the socialist case collapses. And good riddance to it." More the words of a meliorist and a liberal than of a socialist militant.

That germ of skepticism was planted by Wallas, and fell on fertile soil. "The man who diverted me more than anyone else was Graham Wallas himself," Lippmann later explained of his lapse from socialism. "He began more and more, gradually, slowly and patiently to explain to me his doubts as to how it would work, and the inability of man to administer a great society."[8] Wallas detailed his doubts four years later in *The Great Society,* the book he was formulating at Harvard and that — in a striking testimony to the impact his student had made upon him — he dedicated to Lippmann.

Lippmann impressed Wallas the way he had impressed James and Santayana and so many of his teachers. He had an ability to ask the right questions, to go to the heart of a matter, to challenge his teachers without impertinence. With his charm, his talent for writing, his ingratiating manner and appearance, he clearly seemed marked for a brilliant future. His articles for the college magazines and his leadership of the Socialist Club had made him a well-recognized figure. Once when he came as a guest to the Western Club, a gathering place for undergraduates from what Barrett Wendell referred to as "the wilds of Ohio" and beyond, John Reed jumped to his feet, made a sweeping bow, and announced, "Gentlemen, the future President of the United States!" There were smiles and laughs, but not of disbelief. Reed himself summed up Lippmann's promise in a poem he wrote a few years after college:

> Lippmann, — calm, inscrutable,
> Thinking and writing clearly, soundly, well;
> All snarls of falseness swiftly piercing through,
> His keen mind leaps like lightning to the True;
> His face is almost placid — but his eye —
> There is a vision born to prophecy!
> He sits in silence, as one who has said:
> "I waste not living words among the dead!"
> Our all-unchallenged Chief![9]

A Chief for some, but not for all. Although attractive, well liked, and an outstanding achiever, he had not been invited to join the *Crimson,* the Signet Society, or the elite social clubs. He was, as his friend Lee Simonson, also a Jew, had written of discrimination at Harvard, "an outsider as that term is understood in college life."[10] Since he could not be an insider at Harvard, he would become a brilliant outsider. The decision to form the Socialist Club in the spring of 1908 was a step in that direction. He took a more explicit step during his final term when he joined a group of radical undergraduates in attacking Harvard's holy of holies, the Institute of 1770. This organization was the nerve center of the clubman's Harvard. Each spring the Institute chose some hundred-odd sophomores for the prestigious waiting clubs. By tradition, clubmen dominated the social activities of the college — athletics, the theater, the *Crimson* — and filled most of the class offices.

Trouble had been brewing for some time between the clubmen in the private dormitories on Mount Auburn Street and the social rejects in the Yard. In the spring of 1910 a group of students challenged the right of the Gold Coast clubmen to control the class offices. Plunging into the fight, Lippmann had the Debating Club schedule an open meeting on the question of "The Yard and the Street." Interest was so intense that eight hundred men jammed the lecture hall — a third of the student body. After several men had spoken, Lippmann stepped to the podium and gave a tough, impassioned speech, accusing the Institute of splitting the university into factions and of imposing social snobbery on the freshmen. When he finished, the hall was still. It was, as John Reed wrote, "as if a sacrilege had been spoken."[11] Students shook Lippmann's hand and said they thought he was right. His speech was not wasted. After a bitter fight, the Yard men asserted their numerical strength and captured most of the class offices.

Although it was a striking victory, Lippmann never wrote about the incident, nor did he ever again seriously challenge a system of discrimination that excluded people on the grounds of race or religion. Whatever pain his exclusion from the clubman's Harvard gave him, it was buried too deep for him to speak of it openly. Later he became an Overseer of the university, a director of its Nieman Fellowship, and one of Harvard's most honored alumni; the token Jew at such fashionable clubs as the Metropolitan in Washington and the River in New York; and was courted by many who had hardly deigned to speak to him as a student. But the memory of a hurt was there. At his twenty-fifth class reunion he told the widow of a classmate that her husband was one of the first Gentiles who had been kind to him.

Although Lippmann never spoke directly about discrimination and the club system, a few years after leaving Harvard he wrote an article spoofing a fictitious clubman he called Albert the Male. "After many nights of worry and a rather strenuous campaign conducted by his mother," he wrote sarcastically, Albert managed to get into the right club. "I saw something of Albert in those days when we were freshmen together, and he was always cordial when we were alone. In public he did not know me so well, and there were times in the month before his election when he did not know me at all." Election to the club was all that mattered: "Albert could have lost his degree and laughed about it with the feeling of a good loser, but the club he required to give meaning to his life."

The article was Lippmann's belated revenge against the Alberts, people who had hurt him more than he was willing to admit. He could not hate Albert as the evil accomplice of an exploiting class. Rather, he saw him as "a charming, well-mannered, unconscious snob, who knows nothing of men outside his class, an uneducated, untrained and shut-in person who has been born to power by the accident of wealth." [12] It was a fair assessment, and perhaps also a bit of sour grapes. But unlike friends such as Reed, Lippmann was never a radical who wanted to overthrow the ruling class. His method was to find, on his own terms, a secure place within it.

Lippmann was not by nature an outsider. His anger never led him to emphasize his Jewish heritage and become a Zionist, like his friend Felix Frankfurter or Louis D. Brandeis. Instead, the experience of discrimination led him to put even greater emphasis on assimilation as an answer to anti-Semitism. He believed that acceptance lay in identification with the values and style of the white Protestant majority. If being an outsider had led him to socialism, so later, when he ceased to be an outsider, he also ceased to be a socialist.

Through his work with the Socialist Club, Lippmann came into contact with a number of Boston reformers, including a sometime Congregational minister named Ralph Albertson. A ladies' man and bon vivant, Albertson had come to Boston after the dissolution of his utopian colony in Georgia. Installing his family in a spacious house in Jamaica Plain, he dabbled in the ministry, laid plans for a socialist newspaper, and became involved in a municipal improvement project known as Boston — 1915. After an invitation to speak at the Socialist Club, Albertson returned the favor by asking its members to come out to his house for food and drink on Sunday afternoons. Albertson loved an audience, enjoyed the company of young people, and delighted in potential suitors for his three adolescent daughters by a previous marriage. The boys often teased Faye — blond, still a bit ungainly at fifteen, but already showing signs of the beauty she would become — for having a crush on Walter. Sunday afternoons at Jamaica Plain became a habit for the little band of socialists and freethinkers. There they discussed egalitarianism, smoked cigarettes, drank beer, and plotted the socialist paradise they were sure would soon be born.

During Lippmann's senior year at Harvard Albertson sold his house and moved his family to a farm outside West Newbury, about forty miles north of Boston. Although the clergyman was often away, attending to various professional and extramarital interests in the city, his absence did not prevent the boys from spending weekends at what they called "the Farm." The chief attraction was not the country air, but Albertson's second wife, Hazel, only a few years older than the boys themselves. Earthy, fun-loving, clever, she was their sister, their companion, their unattainable seductress. As her friend Mabel Dodge later said of her, she was, "on a high level indeed, a superior flirt."[13] At the rambling farmhouse on the banks of the Merrimack, Hazel and her three stepdaughters, her four small children by Ralph, and the Harvard boys — Walter, Carl Binger, Samuel Eliot Morison, Kenneth MacGowan, Lee Simonson, Gerard Henderson, Ernest Westcott and Ted Behre — formed a loose-knit, affectionate family.

Hazel became for Walter the sister he never had; he confided in her as he was never able to confide in his friends. Hazel was a life-force, a spirited heroine in a Wells novel. She gave Walter the affection he felt he never had from his mother, helping him to overcome the shyness and defensiveness that made him stand apart. Teasing him as no one else dared, she called him "Buddha"— partly because he was still pudgy, more because of the impression he already gave of serene detachment. She also dared to call him on what many considered to be his hypercritical and superior attitude. Once, at a time when he was feeling particularly pleased with himself, she pointedly warned him against his tendency to "skim along in a glorified fashion on the surface of things and . . . become utterly self-satisfied."

This was not the first time he had received such a complaint. A few years earlier Lucile Elsas had chided him for giving her a "little sermon," and reminded him that "some of us are not so entirely sure of ourselves as you are." And Lucile warned him against idealizing people. "You think me much finer, much bigger, much better, than I really am," she wrote the eighteen-year-old Lippmann. "You believe that I should stand and sing on mountain peaks. . . . It is not true! The altitude would prove too high! The sun would be too strong and bright! I almost feel when I have said that I should ask you to forgive me!" She sensed that by idealizing others he would inevitably be disappointed in them.[14]

On Sunday afternoons at the Farm, Walter talked earnestly with Hazel about his future. He no longer cared for the path he had set out upon. Art history seemed a dilettante's occupation, and law school inconceivable. He was on his way to a master's degree in philosophy and, as Santayana's favorite, had the way to academic success paved for him. But he was bored with academic life and had no desire to immerse himself in the Harvard graduate school, which Santayana had contemptuously dismissed as a "normal school for future professors." He was tired of studying ideas and preparing for life. He wanted to plunge into the world of action.

His work on the college magazines and discussions with journalists like Lincoln Steffens had convinced him that writing was what he did best, and that through it he would make his mark. While assisting Santayana, running the Socialist Club, attacking the Institute of 1770, and writing for campus magazines, he also was working part-time for Ralph Albertson. Through connections with the Boston — 1915 civic program the clergyman had got financial backing for a weekly paper he called the *Boston Common*. Albertson was the publisher; Charles Zueblin, the editor. Neither knew much about journalism, but their reformist hearts were in the right place. Needing a reporter, they asked Lippmann to join the staff.

Before accepting Albertson's offer, Lippmann decided to test it out on Lincoln Steffens, and to see if by chance the great muckraker had anything better to suggest. "The most important consideration for you selfishly," Steffens responded to Lippmann's query, was not whether the paper would be a success, but "whether the editor who will be your instructor is a wise man and a good journalist."[15]

The men on the *Common* were not particularly wise or good journalists. But they did have a job to offer, and Lippmann decided to seize the opportunity. In May 1910 he wound up his work as Santayana's assistant, moved out of Weld Hall, and boarded the trolley to begin his career as a cub reporter.

◄ 4 ►

Muckrakers and Socialists

I have a splendid little collection of letters informing
me that I have "botched" my political career.

— To Graham Wallas, July 31, 1912

THE *Boston Common* was both a high-minded and a cheery paper.
Espousing a moderate Progressivism in the form of public ownership of utilities and railroads, it promised its readers to be "optimistic as
a matter of habit." Such a sunny approach to politics was quite appropriate to the paper's sponsor, the Boston — 1915 reform movement,
organized by department-store philanthropist Edward A. Filene, and
supported by such eminent citizens as Richard Dana, Louis D. Brandeis, Robert Treat Paine and Charles Cabot. These men wanted reform:
it was good for business, good for the city's image and good in itself.
They were eager to expose corrupt politicians and the more shameful
malefactors of privilege. It did not, of course, occur to them to make
any fundamental changes in the economic structure — a structure that
served them well, and whose workings they so conspicuously represented.

Lippmann had signed on enthusiastically, feeling that for all its good
government ("goo-goo," as cynics said) liberalism, the paper would
give him valuable journalistic experience. It did not work out that way.
Albertson, despite his earlier involvement with *Twentieth Century Magazine,* knew little about putting out a weekly paper, and Charles Zueblin, the dashing socialist orator-about-town, knew even less. Lippmann
soon grew discouraged. "I have been with the paper since the beginning," he wrote Lincoln Steffens toward the end of May 1910, after
only a few weeks on the job, "and I see clearly that it would be a
serious waste of time on my part to stay with it after the summer." His
boss, he complained, had a one-sided notion of fairness "identical with
the baldest statement of facts . . . any attempt to find the meaning, or
the tragedy, or the humor of the story is rigorously edited out as an

expression of opinion which belongs only in the editorial columns. The result is that I sit all day in the office, reading newspaper clippings, and trying to restate the facts as colorlessly as possible. . . . The work is so mechanical that I am learning nothing. I might as well be attached to a clipping bureau.''[1]

Lippmann was doing more than complaining; he was angling for a job. He had first met Steffens in the fall of 1908 when the journalist was in Boston at Filene's invitation, alerting the citizens to the corruption around them and admonishing them, with his peculiar brand of Christian Socialism, to open their hearts to goodness. During that year he had lectured at Harvard several times, twitting the students for letting their teachers make decisions for them. Lippmann, not one to let a great man pass by, cornered Steffens with earnest questions about corruption in high places.

A professional gadfly who had won a national reputation for his exposés of municipal graft, Steffens had graduated from the University of California at Berkeley the year that Lippmann was born, sampled German universities for a few years, then returned to New York to become one of the great journalists of the day. His book *Shame of the Cities,* based on a study of corruption he had written for *McClure's* magazine in 1902 and 1903, responded to and helped push a wave of civic reform. Yet he was no ordinary do-gooder. In his sardonic way, he enjoyed shocking people by insisting that everyone was corrupt, the good people no less than the sinners. The only way to salvation, he maintained, lay through confession and Christian redemption.

Steffens knew everybody, from reform politicians like Tom Johnson of Cleveland and Brand Whitlock of Toledo, Ohio, to the bosses at Tammany Hall. He spoke their language. Although well traveled and educated, Steffens was quite devoid of intellectual pretense. He loved to talk, to shock the innocent, to indulge in paradoxes. If anyone epitomized the era of the muckraker — its high-minded indignation, its low-level search for sensationalism, its earnest exposés for mass-circulation magazines — it was Steffens.

''What I have dreamed of doing is to work under you,'' Lippmann wrote Steffens that May from Boston. ''Can you use me in your work? There is no position I should go at with more eagerness, because there is no kind of work that appeals to me as much as yours does.'' Money, he added, ''does not happen to be an important consideration for me at the present time. Opportunity to work and learn is the thing I am looking for.''[2]

Lippmann's letter could not have come at a better moment. Bored with the semiretirement he had sunk into after his year in Boston, Steffens had joined the editorial staff of *Everybody's* magazine to do a new series of investigative articles. This time he would analyze financial power, as he had earlier focused on municipal corruption. He needed a young reporter to help him. And he also wanted to prove one of his pet theories: that a bright young man could learn to be a good journalist, even if he never covered night court or wrote obituaries. Steffens made a bet with his editors. "Give me an intelligent college-educated man for a year," he told them, "and I'll make a good journalist out of him."

Now Steffens was ready to try his experiment. "I was going to look for a man something like you," Steffens responded to Lippmann's letter, explaining his bet with the editors of *Everybody's* and warning that the job was less glamorous than it sounded. "My assistant would have to put in a lot of time getting stuff for me and typewriting and doing a whole lot of menial labor," he warned. "But my present subject is interesting: . . . It would amount for you to making an investigation of the business and the politics of Wall Street under my direction. You would have to learn to investigate. But all the while I would be trying to get you ready to go and do likewise for yourself." The pay was low, only fifteen dollars a week, but opportunities to learn were unlimited. "I'll try to be square with you, but I want you very, very much."[3]

Hiring Lippmann was no snap decision. When Steffens first started thinking about an assistant, he asked around Harvard, as he later related, for "the ablest mind that could express itself in writing." Three names came up and after a bit of discussion everyone agreed on one. "I found Lippmann, saw right away what his classmates saw in him," Steffens recounted. "He asked me intelligent, not practical, questions about my proposition. . . . He caught on right away. Keen, quiet, industrious, he understood the meaning of all that he learned; and he asked the men he met for more than I had asked for. He searched them; I know because he searched me, too, for my ideas and theories."[4]

Lippmann did not care about the pay. He had an allowance from his parents and was willing to live simply. Meeting with Steffens in Riverside, Connecticut, he liked what he found, quit his job on the *Boston Common,* and early in July 1910 moved into a small room at a club around the corner from Steffens's house. Aside from an assistant, Steffens also wanted a companion, someone he could go fishing with in the afternoons to get out of the house where his chronically ill wife, Josephine, lay slowly dying.

Through the summer and fall, and most of the following winter, Lippmann worked with Steffens on the investigation of financial power. The series, which Steffens called "It," was meant to be a continuation of Tom Lawson's famous exposé of Wall Street manipulations, but delving deeper into the structure of the business world. Lippmann was Steffens's legman. Commuting between lower Manhattan and Riverside, burrowing through financial reports and interviewing scores of people from stockbrokers to messenger boys, traveling through the East and Middle West to Washington, Chicago, Kansas City and Cleveland, Lippmann gathered his data. On these trips, and at Steffens's side in New York, he met some of the leading figures in the Progressive movement, men like Francis Heney, the California prosecutor; Rudolph Spreckels, the sugar-trust liberal; Fremont Older, the crusading San Francisco editor; Tom Johnson, the retired reform mayor of Cleveland, and his successor, Newton D. Baker; and the writer-politician Brand Whitlock. After a few months of fact gathering, Lippmann drew up a detailed report showing the secret arrangements between New York banks and the major financial houses on Wall Street.

"We were looking not for the evils of Big Business, but for its anatomy," Lippmann later explained. Steffens had made a "bold and brilliant guess" that running a business was like running a city. "We found that the anatomy of Big Business was strikingly like that of Tammany Hall: the same pyramiding influence, the same tendency of power to center on individuals who did not necessarily sit in the official seats, the same effort of human organization to grow independently of legal arrangements." At the end of the trail was the great banking house of J. P. Morgan, which controlled some forty banks. The economic life of the country was organized by small groups of men, "making short work of all legal formulae, and exercising sovereignty regardless of the little fences we erect to keep it in bounds."[5] The material Steffens and Lippmann unearthed helped trigger the Pujo Committee investigations, which in turn paved the way for the attempt to control the giant banks through the Federal Reserve Act of 1913.

By the time Lippmann joined Steffens, the great days of the muckraking era were over. Muckraking had been based on the populist strain of Progressivism — essentially a rural and small-town revolt against the big city and big business. The Populist-Progressive movement directed its anger at the industrial trusts, the city political bosses, and the robber barons beyond the reach of the law. This loose and disparate coalition of reformers believed that men were essentially good and that a just society could be legislated into existence. To do this they sought wider public participation through such electoral changes as initiative, referendum and recall, the regulation or public ownership of utilities, and the destruction of the urban political machines.

The muckraking journalists were the watchdogs of this movement. Exposing the corruption of political machines, detailing the stranglehold of the giant corporations, crying shame on the cities where immigrants and blacks were exploited, these journalists roused the middle-class conscience and made reform a mass movement. Through mass-circulation magazines they transformed scattered discontent into a national crusade. Such magazines as *McClure's* — which featured Ida Tarbell's famous series on the Standard Oil Trust, Ray Stannard Baker's account of the

Colorado mine strike, and Lincoln Steffens's report on city government — attracted a wide audience avid for tales of graft and corruption. At ten or fifteen cents a copy, these journals reached millions of readers. Though the muckrakers' criticisms ran deep, their solutions were shallow. Dedicated to a preindustrial form of capitalism, they celebrated the virtues of the small entrepreneur, free competition, and equal opportunity for all. They were quite baffled by the new forms of industrial organization, and their impulse was to preach against it — hence their frequent appeals for confession and redemption, as though a change of heart would eliminate exploitation and privilege. Only the socialists, with their big-city base, looked beyond the mere symptoms of corruption toward a fundamental change in the social system. Eventually Steffens himself adopted this view, moving left until he ended up in the 1930s among the communists.

Steffens had made his reputation on paradox, extolling the party boss over the "goo-goo" reformer, arguing that the common man was just as corrupt as the monopoly capitalist or the Tammany politician. To prove his point he decided, in December 1910, to show that Riverside's neighbor, prosperous, civic-minded Greenwich, was as corrupt as any place in the nation. The Greenwich elders took up his challenge and arranged a town meeting for him to detail his charges. The press was, of course, alerted — by Steffens himself — and on the appointed night the hall was packed with people who had come to watch Steffens try to prove the inconceivable. New York reporters scurried for front-row seats, prepared to give blow-by-blow accounts of how the great man had made a fool of himself.

But Steffens had done his homework. He had assigned Lippmann to burrow through town records and interview people for evidence of shady dealings. He had also hired a black gardener to hang around street corners and eavesdrop on conversations. When the great night came around, Steffens was ready. As he stood on the rostrum explaining to a skeptical crowd how corruption could infect even the cleanest town, an attentive Lippmann — described by the press as "an admiring young man with glasses and an imposing collection of documents" — drew a diagram of corruption on a blackboard. The audience shifted uneasily as Steffens explained how the people themselves had sanctioned a system that gave special privileges to banks and big business. Properly chastened, the audience dutifully passed a resolution declaring that Greenwich was indeed as corrupt as any town in the country. Steffens concluded the meeting with a sermon, telling the somewhat incredulous gathering that "the remedy of all these things is Christianity."[6]

Although Lippmann was then "an admiring young man," he later grew critical of Steffens's evangelical side and his intellectual laziness. "He enjoyed his own somewhat paradoxical style and the writing of articles in that style more than he did the task of trying to collect facts, analyze them, and read hard, difficult books about the facts,'' Lippmann later said. While Steffens was ''a man of great sweetness of character and kindness to people, he didn't work hard, he became increasingly a kind of Christian anarchist saint, detached from the realities of the world.'' One who seriously proclaimed that crooks were more honest than good men and that the path to honest government lay through emulating Jesus was ''too whimsical for a permanent diet.''[7] Nonetheless some of Steffens rubbed off on Lippmann: his skepticism about the inherent goodness of the average man, his belief that corruption was an inherent part of the system, his insistence on uncluttered declarative writing, his emphasis on intelligence, his admiration for strong leaders, and his faith in science.

While doing research for Steffens, Lippmann kept up his ties with the Intercollegiate Socialist Society, spoke at college chapters to recruit new members, and in late December 1910 attended the annual ISS convention in New York. Over the Christmas holidays delegates from twelve colleges assembled at the Greenwich Village studio of Helen Phelps Stokes, a socialite sympathetic to the cause. Among the large group were Upton Sinclair, a fire-breathing young journalist; Morris Hillquit, one of the more sober party officials; Edwin Markham, a well-known writer; Jessica Finch, mistress of a fashionable girls' school; and as star attractions, a socialist member of the German Reichstag and a survivor of the Paris Commune of 1870. At the final dinner concluding the activities, Lippmann spoke to the delegates on ''The Place of College Men and Women in the Socialist Movement.'' With cautious practicality he warned that students could be frightened away by ''too radical talk and by mannerisms and habits of the typical agitators.'' Of all the things that Harvard disliked, he pointed out, bad taste was one, and the propaganda therefore ''must be carried on in good taste.'' Even though Harvard's social conscience was growing, he warned, ''we must not outrage it.''[8]

The first articles in the *Everybody's* ''money power'' series rolled off the press in September 1910, just in time to mark Walter's twenty-first birthday. Jacob and Daisy, who were off touring Europe, found a copy of the magazine at Brentano's in Paris and sent Walter their congratulations on the ''excellent and interesting'' study, which they were ''quite sure will appeal to the intelligent reading public.'' Although Jacob thought anyone to the left of President William Howard Taft a dangerous radical, he praised his son's article as ''clearly and concisely written, free of sophistry, and easily understood.''[9]

Lippmann had done his job well, and Steffens was ready to collect on his bet. When William James died in the summer of 1910 Walter had written a tribute to the philosopher that Steffens had submitted to the ed-

itors under his own name. After the article was set in type, he revealed
that the real author was his young cub. Steffens had proved that he
could turn an untrained reporter into a polished journalist. In this case
he had had a head start. Lippmann was a good writer when he came to
the magazine, but was even better when he left. A year with Steffens
had taught him some rules that he never forgot: that whatever he said
had to be solidly based on the facts, that he should know exactly what
he wanted to say before he sat down to write, and that, as he later said,
"if I wrote a paragraph about a fire down the street, I must write it with
as much care as if that paragraph were going down in one of the an-
thologies."

Lippmann may not have gained a great deal intellectually from Steffens, but he learned something important about tolerance for human foi-
bles and a bemused acceptance of life's absurdities. He also learned
how to please the men he admired. "You often asked me whether the
year had been worthwhile," he wrote Steffens when they had finished
the series.

Lord, if I could tell you and make you believe it. You'd know then why "Everybody who knows you loves you." You gave me yourself and then you ask
me whether it has been worthwhile. For that I can't write down my thanks. I
shall have to live them. Whenever I understand a man and like him, instead of
hating him or ignoring him, it'll be your work. You've got into my blood, I
think, and there'll be a little less bile in the world as a result. . . . You gave
me a chance to start — you know what that means to a fellow who has an indifferent world staring him in the face.[10]

If the world was not exactly "indifferent" to Lippmann, neither was
it beating a path to his door. With the money-power series completed,
Steffens went off to England in the spring of 1911, leaving Lippmann at
Everybody's in what he called "a dreary little job as sub-editor."
Muckraking was passing out of fashion, and the editors had no real assignment for him. Restless working as "first reader of manuscripts and
the sorter-out of jokes for a funny column," as he later said, he started
writing on the side for the socialist monthly the *International,* and the
socialist-anarchist *Masses.* He also kept up his ties with the ISS, and
joined the Liberal Club. The club, still in its respectable uptown phase,
was less liberal than its pretensions, as he discovered when he unsuccessfully put up for membership W. E. B. DuBois, the Harvard-
educated black scholar who was his "comrade" on the board of the socialist *New Review.*[11] Not until the following year, when it moved down
to Greenwich Village, did the club shed some of its prejudices.

Although Lippmann considered himself a socialist and a radical, his
militancy was tempered by a strong sense of practicality. In the signed
editorial notes he wrote every month for the *International,* from August

1911 to July 1912, he castigated those "simple-minded socialists" who believed that labor could do no wrong and capital no right, that "all conflicts between them resolve themselves into conspiracies and persecutions by rich men of poor men." Nor did he have any use for violence. "You cannot plan a civilization on a heated powder mine," he wrote of the labor bombing of a newspaper plant in Los Angeles. "You cannot rearrange industrial processes, lay out cities, solve the problems of food and work, devise uses for leisure, breed finer strains of men, on a battlefield." Not only was there nothing doctrinaire about Lippmann's socialism, there was not even much that was particularly socialist. When party militants promoted Eugene V. Debs, hero of the Pullman strike, for President, Lippmann leaned toward the moderate governor of New Jersey, Woodrow Wilson. "It is of more far-reaching importance that men should become liberal-minded than that they should believe in a radical creed," he wrote.[12]

What attracted Lippmann to socialism was not a fiery passion for justice and equality, as was the case with his friend John Reed, but an impatience with how badly society was managed. The Fabians, with their statistics, their elaborately detailed programs, and their emphasis on leadership from the top, were far more in key with his own temperament than the well-meaning "goo-goo" reformers or the bomb-throwing labor militants. Society had to be organized, plans drawn up, the "scientific method" invoked. "We cannot afford to start a crusade against every pimple on the face of American optimism," he complained in an attack on the "sentimental" reformers.[13]

Lippmann wanted reform, what he called a "radical constructive program," but he believed it had to come from the top, free from meddling by the masses or by do-gooders. His work with Steffens had eroded whatever lingering faith he may have had in the wisdom of the common man. It was part of the "cult of democracy," he charged, "to assume that the people have all the virtues and then pretend, when they don't exhibit them, that it is somebody else's fault." Political democracy was "not so much a way of expressing the wisdom people have, as it is a way of enabling them to get wisdom." Such suspicion of proletarian enthusiasms was more in line with the view of big-city Progressives than with that of American socialists, who, as Lippmann complained, downgraded leadership, exalted the masses, and held as a dogma "to which all are expected to subscribe, that initiative springs anonymously out of the mass of the people."[14]

Such iconoclasm failed to rattle his fellow socialists, many of whom shared his suspicion of the masses. As an editorialist for journals like the *International* and the *Call*, Lippmann was much in demand as a speaker and writer of tracts, and many predicted a brilliant future for him within the party. When the party faithful gathered shortly after

Christmas 1911 at Jessica Finch's elegant finishing school for the annual ISS convention, Lippmann was one of the leading younger members of a movement that seemed the wave of the future. Socialist mayors ran thirty-three American cities, and Eugene V. Debs was preparing to carry the party banner for the presidency.

Among the new breed of socialist politicians was the Reverend George Lunn, a mild-mannered reformer who had just been elected mayor of Schenectady, New York, on a "good government" ticket. Lunn, being inexperienced in politics and shaky on socialism, was looking for a bright young man whom he could take to Schenectady as an assistant. Hillquit introduced him to Lippmann, who knew even less than Lunn about politics, but had a bagful of theories about socialism that he wanted to try out, and was bored at *Everybody's*. Lippmann asked Lunn a few practical questions about the kind of work he would be doing and decided to give it a try. He and Lunn exchanged a comradely handshake in one of Jessica Finch's empty classrooms and he went home to 80th Street to pack a few shirts and some books. When the new mayor took office on New Year's Day, 1912, Lippmann was already stationed at his desk, just outside Lunn's door.

At the beginning it was all very exhilarating. John Macy, another young socialist, who was married to Annie Sullivan, the teacher of Helen Keller, worked at Lippmann's side, and promised to enlist his wife's former pupil — herself an ardent socialist — to serve on the welfare board. Charles Steinmetz, the engineering genius of General Electric, helped them plan strategy, and prominent socialists from New York came by to lend support. As Lunn's aide, Lippmann wrote speeches, drafted bills for the city council, met with ward bosses and union officials, and fed stories to journalists. After two months on the job he reported approvingly to the readers of the *Masses* that "an enormous amount of dust has been removed, and a great many rusty joints oiled."

But once the dust was removed, Lunn did not do much else. He knew he had been elected not because the voters embraced socialism but because they wanted to get rid of the scoundrels in office. In his inaugural address he had admitted that "we cannot abolish the capitalist system in Schenectady."[15] Afraid to alienate the moderates, Lunn decided to please the public by providing more services, such as playgrounds, cheap ice and coal, and milk inspection. The moderates were appeased, but the socialists began to feel they had been cheated. They expected Lunn to take over the utilities and streetcars, to challenge the power structure. When he proved more timid than they had imagined, they accused him of being an opportunist.

Lippmann prodded Lunn to move more boldly, but the mayor could not be budged. Finally, after four months of frustration, Lippmann gave up. He had no patience for politicians, and even less for ward heelers, union officials, and favor-seeking voters. He had had his taste of practical politics, and did not much like what he saw. The whole experience had been disillusioning: the voters were unripe for socialism, the mechanics of government were tiresome. "The petty vexations pile into mountains," he wrote of his political apprenticeship, "distracting details scatter the attention and break up thinking, while the mere problem of exercising power crowds out speculation about what to do with it . . . constant speech-making turns a man back upon a convenient little store of platitudes."[16] His irritation was as much with the voters and with the whole mechanism of government as with Lunn's lapses from socialist doctrine. Having tried practical politics and found it not to his liking, he elevated his dislike to a matter of principle.

In defending his sudden departure from Schenectady he put the blame on Lunn. The mayor, he charged, was not a dedicated socialist. Having gone over to the attack, he struck at Lunn's weakest point. The mayor's administration, he wrote in the New York *Call,* a socialist weekly, was paralyzed by "timidity of action, the lack of a bold plan, a kind of aimlessness." Instead of paving the path for socialism, it was content with mere reform — "a sharp object lesson in what always results when we turn from education to politics, when we seek to win votes rather than to make converts." Sounding a radical note, he warned that socialists could not be mere reformers: "Reform under the fire of radicalism is an educative thing; reform pretending to be radicalism is deadening."[17]

This line of attack was ironic, considering Lippmann's own skepticism about socialist doctrine. But it had the desired effect. His blast set off a new schism in the ranks. Morris Hillquit, as spokesman for the moderates, accused Lippmann of being unrealistic: the party could not drag people further toward socialism than they were willing to go. Some of the militants, he predicted, "will sooner or later sober up; others will quit the uninteresting Socialist movement in disgust." Lippmann was unmoved. Socialists should not play it safe, he retorted the following week; those who sought to be "shrewdly good should come out flatly for the biggest truth they see . . . nothing but that will save them from little successes, from the self-stultification that comes of a gumshoe morality." Comrades had to distinguish between "socialist power and the external clap-trap of victory."[18] For months the debate echoed in the *Call* and the other socialist journals, with the firebrands supporting Lippmann and the more cautious defending Mayor Lunn.

Lippmann returned to New York City in May 1912, the taunts of socialist regulars like Hillquit ringing in his ears. He felt defensive, and yet convinced he had done the right thing in leaving Schenectady. "I fought as hard as I could within the 'organization' without any result," he wrote Graham Wallas. "When I saw that the policy and program were settled . . . I resigned and attacked the administration. This brought down upon me the wrath of the leaders. My analysis was ignored, but I was the subject of the most careful and bitter attention for several weeks." Lippmann was unrepentant. "The whole affair is very objective to me," he insisted. "I have a splendid little collection of letters informing me that I have 'botched' my political career. But as the only interest a 'career' would have is the chance to understand politics a little more directly, I really feel elated that mine was so compressed that I can already look back upon it." [19]

It was not long before even the most patient socialists became disenchanted with what was happening in Schenectady. John Macy, who had replaced Lippmann as the mayor's assistant, resigned at the end of the summer, taking with him his wife and Helen Keller. Even Hillquit eventually resigned his post on the mayor's staff, along with Ben Henry, star writer for the pro-socialist *Schenectady Citizen.* Ultimately the party expelled Lunn and he switched over to the Democrats, with whom he had a happy and continuing career.

At twenty-two Lippmann already had a good deal to look back on: two months as a cub reporter in Boston, a year with Steffens, a column on politics in the *International,* four months in Schenectady, some practical experience in politics, an expanding number of contacts, and a pile of clippings to show that his voice was being heard. Since 1909 he had been a registered member of the Fabian Society, carrying his card and paying his one pound sterling annual dues. He was militant socialist, or so he thought. But the experience at Schenectady had led him to wonder whether the people would ever be ready for the great social changes that seemed so necessary, whether in fact, as he wrote caustically, "soap and socialism" were "middle-class fads."

The socialists blamed "special privilege" for their failures, but as Lippmann later wrote, "it always seemed that we were like Peer Gynt struggling against the formless Boyg — invisible yet everywhere — we were struggling with the unwatered hinterland of the citizens of Schenectady." Already he was concerned by the "great dull mass of people who just don't care," by a tyrannical public opinion. "No financial power is one-tenth so corrupting, so insidious, so hostile to originality and frank statement," he complained of his experience on *Everybody's,* "as the fear of the public which reads the magazine. For one item suppressed out of respect for a railroad or a bank, nine are rejected because of the prejudices of the public." The public's "prejudices" were to trouble him increasingly.

Nearly four decades later, his friend Bernard Berenson commented on this impatience with the public. "The trouble, if any, with Walter Lippmann is that he tends to treat politics as a series of problems almost geometrical, and fails to take into sufficient account that politics consists not merely of abstract good and evil, but chiefly of the human material engaged, whether as executors or public,'' Berenson wrote in his diary. ''Ever so much that would be feasible and rational with reasonable beings is anything but possible with inertia, tropism for the immediate advantages, and impulsive greed. They play havoc with the proposals of the noblest legislators, and dispose according to their fundamental urges. In Walter Lippmann again and again I have felt an impatience with such considerations, and indignation with 'the fools' who would not attend his behests.''[20] That impatience was there from the start.

The events of the winter and spring of 1912 had been dispiriting, and by June Lippmann was eager to get away from New York. His parents had gone off to Europe, leaving him in the house with the maids, and the city was oppressive with summer heat and socialist polemics. Shortly after he had returned from Schenectady, Mitchell Kennerley, a brash young Anglo-Irishman who had just set up his own publishing house, urged him to write a short book on politics. Lippmann decided he might as well give it a try. Enlisting his Harvard friend Alfred Booth Kuttner as a companion, he set off for the Rangeley Lakes in the backwoods of Maine, hoping to put together a little book of heretical thoughts.

◄ 5 ►

A Little Iconoclasm

It was a happy time, those last few years before the
First World War. The air was soft, and it was easy for
a young man to believe in the inevitability of progress,
in the perfectability of man and of society, and in the
sublimation of evil.

— Biographical fragment, 1959

Lippmann was eager to write a book, but was not quite sure how to get
at what he wanted to say. He had read a lot about politics, and
most of it had left him dissatisfied. The year with Steffens had shattered
his faith in reformers and the experience in Schenectady had soured him
on socialism. He knew that something was wrong with the way people
had been taught to think about politics. Wallas had made him realize
how futile it was to squeeze human beings into intellectual molds, to
base laws on abstract notions of right and wrong rather than on how
people actually thought and behaved. His mentor seemed to him on the
right track in emphasizing the irrational elements of political behavior
rather than parliaments and constitutions. "I have been writing what
may be a small book — at least a series of essays," he wrote Wallas in
July, "and no small part of it is aimed at popularizing your *Human Nature in Politics.*"[1]

As Lippmann put together his essays, laying out what he had learned
in his work with Steffens and the socialists, he talked over his ideas
with his cabin mate. Alfred Kuttner was an agreeable companion, book-
ish, complaisant, and with a keen mind. Although he had little interest
in politics, preferring to write poetry and literary criticism, he had some
interesting insights. Kuttner had been forced to drop out of college several times as a result of mental depression. When traditional doctors
proved unable to help, he put himself in the hands of A. A. Brill, a disciple of Freudian psychoanalysis, then just beginning to be known in the
United States. Fascinated by the new discipline, with its unfamiliar

terms of "libido," "superego" and "repression," Kuttner read everything he could by Freud. Since virtually nothing had been translated into English, Kuttner set out, under Brill's guidance, to translate the master's classic *Interpretation of Dreams*.

Thus it was that in a cabin in the backwoods of Maine in the summer of 1912 Kuttner was putting into English theories that would transform the way people thought about their unconscious, while a few feet away Lippmann was trying to figure out why politics so often seemed contrary to human behavior and needs. Around the fire at night, as Kuttner explained what Freud meant by words like "taboo" and "sublimation," Lippmann glimpsed a new analytical tool. Since politics was a system of social interaction, it had to be governed by the same forces that governed other social behavior. The link seemed obvious, but no one had ever made the connection. Freud offered liberation, not only from the prison of Herbert Spencer's Social Darwinism, but also from a Progressivism that saw man climbing ever upward to perfection. Freud's analysis of the unconscious showed why reason alone could not explain human behavior and at the same time suggested how emotions could be channeled by reason. This is what Wallas had glimpsed but not quite grasped.

"Are you in your new book making much use of the Freudian psychology?" Lippmann wrote Wallas. "I have been studying it with a great deal of enthusiasm for several months now, and I feel about it as men might have felt about *The Origin of Species!* . . . I went back and read some of James with a curious sense that the world must have been very young in the 1880s." Lippmann could hardly contain his enthusiasm. "The dream interpretations, the book on wit, the aesthetics, the child psychology, do for the first time in any psychology I know furnish a picture of human nature in the act, so to speak, of creating and expressing the character. . . . Its political applications have hardly begun, though there are a few stray articles here and there."[2] Freud was just what Lippmann needed to give his book a novel twist. Excitedly he raced through the chapters, injecting Freudian terms into his discussion of politics.

He returned to New York at the end of the summer with a completed manuscript in hand. One of the first people he looked up was Lincoln Steffens, back from his wanderings in Europe after the death of his invalid wife, and now living in the same Washington Square rooming house as his protégé John Reed. "Lippmann dined with me last night," Steffens reported to a friend, "and he is in a bully state of mind." He had good reason to be. Mitchell Kennerley had snapped up the book and was planning to serialize parts of it in three successive issues of his magazine, the *Forum*. Not bad for a man just turned twenty-three.

Going over the revised page proofs that fall, Kuttner wrote Lippmann of his excitement at finding it "intellectually so wide open." Although he had heard Lippmann sketch out the argument of the book, he was delighted at the daring of the phrasing and the inexorable flow of the logic. "I keep thinking of the types of men that will collide with it, and their utter bewilderment; their anxiety to follow you in one point and feel themselves clear of it, only to be caught up by their unconscious prejudice even as they complacently turn the page."

The book came out in the spring of 1913 to the sort of reviews that turn an author's head: "The ablest brief book of its kind published during the last ten years"; "the quality of a fine mind cutting sharply under its problem and fertilizing it to new issues"; "one of the most energetic, resourceful iconoclasts who ever turned to browse in the field of American politics." One reviewer even went so far as to predict that "a few years hence, academic discussions in political economy may be very generally punctuated with the explanatory clause: 'as Lippmann says.' "[3]

Sparely, even elegantly, written, the book was an intellectual potpourri, stuffed with nearly everything Lippmann had learned at college and after. Beginning with John Dewey's blueprint for social change and Herbert Croly's "New Nationalism," he had added James's celebration of experience, Bergson's intuition, Nietzsche's affirmation of the will, Wells's scientific utopianism, and, of course, a heavy dose of Freud. He had written, not a systematic theory, but, as he called it, *A Preface to Politics*. It was a young man's book that raised more questions than it explored, and showed Lippmann's receptivity to new ideas rather than any coherent philosophy. Later he half-mockingly said it covered "pretty nearly all human problems." But for all its thinness, it was taut, perceptive and iconoclastic. Copey had taught him to hone down his prose to lean, graceful sentences, and Steffens had drilled into him the need to stick to the facts.

In nine gracefully turned short chapters Lippmann assaulted virtually the entire catalogue of traditional Progressivism: electoral reform, the two-party system, muckraking, trust-busting, free competition. Corruption flourished because the laws failed to take human nature into account; political machines existed because they provided a service the voters needed. "Tammany," he declared in words that shocked a good many Progressives, "has a better perception of human need, and comes nearer to being what a government should be, than any scheme yet proposed by a group of 'uptown good government' reformers." Where traditionalists on the Left extolled the wisdom of the people, Lippmann questioned the tyranny of popular majorities and called for the scientific expertise of a class of managers. "No moral judgment can declare the value of life," he proclaimed in an echo of William James. "No ethical theory can announce any intrinsic good." Creeds were to be distrusted. "Tradition is nothing but a record and a machine-made imitation of the habits that our ancestors created."

Heady stuff indeed. *A Preface to Politics* exalted the faith of the young radicals in scientific management, their openness to emotion and experience, their admiration of leadership, their rejection of nineteenth-century morality, and their contempt for the cautious reformism of the small-town Progressive. Lippmann managed to capture the energies of an era just discovering cubism and symbolism, psychoanalysis and syndicalism. He became a spokesman for a generation that found not only pleasure but a moral imperative in denying the wisdom of its elders.

The book's originality, however, lay not in its undergraduate idol-smashing but in its application to politics of Freud's theories of personality. "Instead of trying to crush badness we must turn the power behind it to good account," Lippmann wrote in an attack on laws against prostitution and adultery. Detaching such concepts as "taboo," "repression," and "sublimation" from their strict Freudian context, he gave them a new interpretation and made them the key to his theory of politics. "Instead of tabooing our impulses, we must direct them." People had to be provided with "civilizing opportunities" for satisfying their needs and desires. Most laws, like those against drinking or sex, tried to prohibit and punish human drives rather than redirect them toward better goals. Sublimation provided the key for "supplying our passions with civilized interests."

Lippmann's novel interpretation of Freud's concepts soon reached Vienna. The master's British disciple, Ernest Jones, reviewed the book in the Freudian journal *Imago,* and declared that while books about politics "have, as a rule, little claim to the attention of the psychoanalyst," Lippmann's could be "recommended most heartily as an impressive attempt to apply modern psychological knowledge and insight to the problems of sociology and political science." What interested Lippmann was not so much Freud's methods of psychiatric treatment as the liberating effect of the theory of the unconscious on social thought. "When I compared his work with the psychology that I studied in college, or with most of the material that is used to controvert him," he wrote of Freud in 1915, "I cannot help feeling that for his illumination, for his steadiness and brilliancy of mind, he may rank among the greatest who have contributed to thought."[4] A few years later in Vienna Lippmann actually met Freud, who invited him to a meeting of the Psychoanalytic Society, and introduced him to Adler and Jung.

Lippmann used Freud's work imaginatively, though not as wisely as he might have done had the ideas been more familiar. His prescription for "sublimating" the evils of giant trusts by channeling them to social uses was fanciful, as he later recognized. Also, in emphasizing the role of unconscious he came close to extolling irrationalism for its own sake. Graham Wallas, somewhat upset by Lippmann's foray into the irrational, mildly chided his former student. Lippmann took the lesson to heart, and by 1914 had dropped Nietzsche and Bergson by the wayside. He also discarded any lingering sentimentality about socialism. While urging justice for the "voiceless multitudes who have been left to pass unnoticed," he now castigated many of his fellow socialists as "interested pedants of destiny," and saw in centralized government "the germs of that great bureaucratic tyranny which Chesterton and Belloc have named the Servile State." Rejecting the Marxist analysis of capitalism, he was left with an approach to socialism as expedient as it was eclectic. "We shall feel free to choose among alternatives, to take this much socialism, insert so much syndicalism, leave standing what of capitalism seems worth conserving." This was not socialism; it was a fruit salad. Small wonder that Lippmann was criticized by socialist militants, or that within two years he would leave the party altogether.[5]

Rather than being a socialist tract, *A Preface to Politics* was a hymn to Bull Moose progressivism phrased in the language of Greenwich Village radicalism. It had been written during the very summer that Theodore Roosevelt, having been denied renomination by the Republicans, had formed his own renegade Bull Moose party. Lippmann trooped to the colors, proclaiming TR "the working model" for an ideal American statesman. Just as TR's challenge to the prevailing economic order was one of style more than of substance, so Lippmann's book was less an attack on an inequitable social system than an assault on the arbiters of a dying Victorian culture. As such it was a perfect expression of the revolt against what Santayana had contemptuously called "the genteel tradition." Appearing in the spring of 1913, it coincided with a flood of cultural experimentation.

To young radicals like Lippmann the world was waiting to be reborn, and a beneficent providence had put the tools in their hands. "The fiddles are tuning up all over America," wrote the young critic Van Wyck Brooks. Restless men and women flocked to the narrow streets of Greenwich Village to express themselves and seek out kindred souls. Their political journal was the *Masses,* which, under the freewheeling direction of Max Eastman and John Reed, playfully declared it would "do as it pleases and conciliate nobody, not even its readers." Their theater was the Provincetown Playhouse, which had just moved to New York from Cape Cod to put on experimental plays by the unknown Eugene O'Neill. Their art gallery was Alfred Stieglitz's 291 Fifth Avenue, where Matisse and Cézanne had their first American showings, where young native experimentalists like Marsden Hartley and Georgia O'Keeffe exhibited, and where photography became an instrument of art. Their restaurant was Polly's on MacDougal Street, where over spaghetti and cheap wine they could argue all night about psychoanalysis and socialism. "It seems as though everywhere, in that year of 1913, barriers went down and people reached each other who had never been in touch before," remembered Mabel Dodge, hostess to the cultural revolution. "There were all sorts of new ways to communicate, as well as new communications." Everything seemed possible; the only enemies were tradition and timidity.

Whether they believed in salvation through Marx, like the frolicsome editors of the *Masses,* or through poetry, like Harriet Munro and Amy Lowell, or through family planning, like Margaret Sanger, the young radicals loved to argue and express themselves in ways designed to shock the complacent. "We live in a revolutionary period and nothing is so important as to be aware of it," Lippmann summed up. "The dynamics for a splendid human civilization are all about us."[6]

If a cultural movement can be said to have an official beginning, this one was launched in February 1913 at the Sixty-ninth Regiment Armory in New York. There Americans saw for the first time the wild colors of European fauvism, the geometrical reductions of the cubists, the strange visions of the expressionists. Theodore Roosevelt spoke for many when he said that he preferred the Navajo rug in his bathroom, but he also recognized that something important was afoot. The Armory show, Mabel Dodge told Gertrude Stein, was the most important event to have happened in America since 1776.

Although she never penned a political tract or created a work of art, Mabel Dodge was at the center of American cultural experimentation in the years just before the First World War. Rich, shrewd, forever sniffing after new trends, she had discarded two husbands by her early thirties and had grown bored with her art-littered villa in Tuscany, where she had steeped herself in European culture and collected such adornments as Gertrude and Leo Stein. Returning to New York in 1912, she rented an apartment at 23 Fifth Avenue, on the fashionable northern fringe of Greenwich Village, painted the woodwork white, installed crystal chandeliers, laid down a white bearskin rug, and set out to meet the luminaries of the radical scene. "I wanted in particular to know the Heads of things," she explained. "It was not dogs or glass I collected now, it was people. Important people." Her qualifications were quite sufficient: money, insatiable curiosity, and the ability to draw people out. There was something about her, Max Eastman said, "that creates a magnetic field in which people become polarized and pulled in and made to behave very queerly. Their passions become exacerbated, they grow argumentative; they have quarrels, difficulties, entanglements, abrupt and violent detachments. And they like it — they come back for more."[7]

Putting her unfocused energies to work, she assembled a microcosm of the American cultural revolution: anarchists Emma Goldman and Alexander Berkman; poets Edwin Arlington Robinson and George Sylvester Viereck; socialist aristocrat William English Walling; militant labor organizer Bill Haywood of the Industrial Workers of the World, or Wobblies, as they were better known; progressives Lincoln Steffens, Frederick Howe and Amos Pinchot; reformers Margaret Sanger and Frances Perkins; artists Marsden Hartley, Andrew Dasburg and Jo Davidson; sentimental radical Hutchins Hapgood, who roamed the Bowery for noble drunks; novelist Carl Van Vechten, who brought jazz musicians down from Harlem; editors Max Eastman and Floyd Dell of the anarchist *Masses;* and a sprinkling of society ladies seeking titillation.

Wobblies and suffragettes, socialists and family planners, vers-librists and cubists, they flowed in and out of Mabel's spacious white rooms, relishing argument, the abundant liquor, and the cold chicken at midnight. Hers was a place, Lincoln Steffens recalled, for "poor and rich, labor skates, scabs, strikers and unemployed, painters, musicians, reporters, editors, swells; it was the only successful salon I have ever seen in America."[8] Steffens and Hutchins Hapgood had helped Mabel organize her salon, suggesting that instead of merely letting people talk at random she ought to set a theme. This was the beginning of her celebrated Evenings: the Anarchist Evening, the Psychoanalytic Evening, the Journalist Evening, the Family Planning Evening.

One of the people Steffens brought round to meet Mabel and help get her Evenings rolling was his young assistant from *Everybody's* — already coming to be known as a polemicist, freethinking socialist, and author of great promise. Charmed by Lippmann, Mabel found the well-mannered, carefully dressed young man "thoroughly free intellectually . . . 'Harvardized,' well-bred and in possession of himself. There was no incontinence there, no flowing sensuality," she later wrote of him. "Rather a fine poise, a cool understanding, and with all the high humor in the world shining in his intelligent eyes."

Lippmann was the centerpiece of her "younger generation" — a Harvard contingent that included his sidekick, Alfred Kuttner; Lee Simonson, who had already been to Paris and been admitted into the charmed circle of Gertrude and Leo Stein; Robert Edmond Jones, who began his revolution of American stage design in a tiny room in the back of Mabel's apartment; and the impetuous young poet and journalist John Reed. Mabel, who was attracted to energy even more than to intelligence, was irresistibly drawn to the lanky, tousle-haired Reed. She found the former Hasty Pudding thespian, now turned anarchist-revolutionary, exactly what she needed to fill in the space between her Evenings. Reed soon took to spending the nights at 23 Fifth Avenue. But he was a tenuous conquest and Mabel had a good deal of trouble keeping her young lover in tow. She would often turn to Lippmann for advice. In the well-tailored suits that made him seem less stocky and a bit older, and with his habitual air of bemused detachment, he struck her as "remarkably certain in his judgments, sure of them, and very definite in his speech as well as his outline." Once he advised her that while she could appear almost anywhere in public with Reed, she could not expect to live at the White House. "That's just what I want!" she exclaimed. "Well, you can't," Lippmann laughed.

Lippmann and Mabel Dodge were a study in contrasts: he self-controlled and intellectual, she impetuous and instinctive. Yet they had a sympathetic attraction. He admired her vitality, even while despairing of her disorganized mind; she was impressed by his intelligence and self-possession. Like their mutual friend Hazel Albertson, she affectionately called him Buddha. "Walter was big and rather fat," she recalled with some exaggeration, "but he had . . . intellectualized his fat so that it shone a little." Mabel depended on him to bring some order to the chaos of her salon and of her life. "I don't think Walter ever realized how strongly he figured in my fantasies," she wrote later. "Like most women, all my life I had needed and longed for the strong man who would take the responsibility for me and my decisions. . . . Walter seemed to be about the only person I knew that I could really look up to."[9]

What she needed from him was a sympathetic ear for an unending cascade of problems with lovers, anarchists and decorators, and one who might bring some order to her Evenings. At his suggestion she invited A. A. Brill to talk about psychoanalysis, and although a few rowdy guests hooted at such concepts as infantile sexuality and disrupted Lippmann's determined efforts to conduct a discussion after the talk, it was nonetheless a historic evening. Mabel's salon was one of the first places in America where Freudian analysis was discussed before a general audience. There, Brill recalled, "I met radicals, litterateurs, artists and philosophers, some of whom have influenced the trends of our times in no small way." The session had a powerful effect on many present. Even Steffens, the professional skeptic, had his assumptions shaken. "I remember thinking how absurd had been my muckraker's description of bad men and good men and the assumptions that showing people facts and conditions would persuade them to alter them or their own conduct," he later wrote.

Mabel was so impressed that she decided to be psychoanalyzed by Brill. Lippmann, who futilely tried to bring her down to earth, was not enthusiastic. "You haven't anything the matter with you except that you haven't enough education to carry your wisdom," he told her. "You've got enough endowment to run all of Greenwich Village half a century, and experience enough to supply a regiment, and all that's wrong with you is that your categories aren't any good. They remind me of a Fourth Avenue antique shop."[10]

Not only did Mabel's categories bother Lippmann, but so did her penchant for throwing disparate people together to see what would happen. For one Evening she invited Big Bill Haywood, the Wobbly leader, to argue the case for violent revolution. Emma Goldman, the earth mother of anarchism, and her comrade-lover, Alexander Berkman, recently released from jail after trying to assassinate steel magnate Henry Clay Frick, were to flank Big Bill on the Left, and young William English Walling, a wealthy litterateur who had established his credentials by going to Russia and meeting Lenin, on the socialist Right. The good-natured crowd that had gathered in Mabel's elegant living room for fireworks was quickly disappointed. Big Bill, a bit worse for drink, had trouble distinguishing the Wobbly position from that of the anarchists; Goldman gave a schoolmarmish lecture; and Walling treated them both with snide condescension. Lippmann desperately tried to salvage the Evening by lobbing sympathetic questions at Haywood. But the Wobbly leader seemed more interested in the adoring young society ladies gathered around his chair, and mumbled unintelligibly. "They talk like goddam bourgeois!" shouted Hippolyte Havel, the anarchist cook at Polly's restaurant.

Lippmann had little patience for such carryings-on. Backed by Kuttner and Simonson he urged Mabel to give some shape to her Evenings. "You have a chance to do something really inventive here," he told her. "Do try to make something of it instead of letting it run wild. Weed it out and *order* it." Although order was not her strong point, Mabel tried. Under the prodding of the Harvard contingent she issued a manifesto announcing that henceforth the Evenings would have "a more definite direction, there would be standards of ability, parliamentary rule, invitations!"

The invitations, however, did not extend to the working press. Once reporters discovered that Mabel's Evenings made good copy, they infiltrated her salon, disguised as society socialists in tuxedos or labor organizers in overalls. At one Evening, as Emma Goldman and Alexander Berkman were discussing unemployment, Lippmann spotted a group of strangers. "This is a private meeting," he said, pushing them toward the door. "The Press is not invited." The next day the papers titillated their readers with accounts of ladies in evening gowns, "men with long, black, flowing locks who say they are anarchists," tweed-wearing members of "social uplift movements," and a "heavy-set young man" who said that the gathering was for the discussion of social problems and that "positively nothing should be published about it."[11]

Although Lippmann soon grew impatient with the theatrics, the superficiality, and the ineffectiveness of the discussions, he was caught up for a time in the excitement of the radical movement. When Frank Tannenbaum, a young Wobbly, was sentenced to prison for bringing the homeless into fashionable churches for refuge, Lippmann marched behind the black flag of the anarchists in a parade on Fifth Avenue, and, along with Haywood, Goldman, Berkman, Steffens and Hapgood, spoke at a mass meeting in Union Square. During that same spring of 1913 he went out to Paterson to talk to the striking textile workers and hear the Wobblies argue doctrine with socialists and anarchists. It was at Paterson that Upton Sinclair thought he had glimpsed the dawn of American revolution, and there that John Reed, with his genius for self-promotion, managed to get himself thrown in jail while doing a story on the strike.

Reed, fired by what he had seen, organized a mammoth pageant reenacting the key events of the strike: the police intervention, the funeral of a worker killed by policemen, and strike meetings punctuated by rousing choruses of the "International." Bobby Jones designed the sets in the manner of a Gordon Craig extravaganza, while Lippmann, Kuttner and Eddy Hunt — joined by Mabel, Steffens and Margaret Sanger — helped organize. On the day of the great event — June 7, 1913 — thousands of strikers took the ferry across the Hudson from Paterson and marched through the streets of New York to Madison Square Garden. It was a glorious event — although unfortunately it cost more to produce than it earned for the strike fund.

During all his heady activity Lippmann commuted between the Upper East Side and the Village. Dining with his parents in a stuffy Victorian house, and drinking with Reed, Steffens and Eastman in Mabel's salon, Lippmann oscillated between two cultures that winter and spring of 1913, unable to cut loose from the first, or to embrace the second. The comfort and the radical conversation were both important. A part of him wanted to join the crowd, to feel simple emotions without being self-conscious. "Human statistics are illuminating to those who know humanity," he wrote in one of the many throwaway phrases in his *Preface to Politics*. "I would not trust a hermit's statistics of anything." Yet another part of him held back. This was the Lippmann who grew impatient with the chaos of Mabel's life and disdainful of those, like Hutchins Hapgood, who wandered the Bowery looking for wisdom among the drunks. He was a seeker, but for him experience had to be strained through a very fine intellectual sieve. From childhood he had learned to protect himself by rejecting the things that might cause pain. Behind his cynicism and humor was a person always on guard against some obscure hurt.

This contrast between the warmth, even the sentimentality, of Lippmann's emotions and the cold intellectualism that so often overtook him was captured in a few deft lines by his friend John Reed:

> . . . But were there one
> Who builds a world, and leaves out all the fun —
> Who dreams a pageant, gorgeous, infinite,
> And then leaves all the color out of it —
> Who wants to make the human race, and me,
> March to a geometric Q.E.D. —
> Who but must laugh, if such a man there be?
> Who would not weep, if Walter L. were he?

Lippmann did not really want anyone to march to a geometric Q.E.D. But neither could he march with the crowd, or lose his head in an argument. "Walter was never, never going to lose an eye in a fight," Mabel Dodge said in comparing him to the one-eyed Bill Haywood. "He might lose his glow, but he will never lose an eye."[12] It was his nature to mingle cautiously, to test the waters, to dip in and out. He was a smiling, gracious figure, someone in the group but never totally of it, always on the edge, ready to withdraw. Where others plunged, he analyzed.

His friends admired him and when they were in trouble he gave generously of his time and energies. During his senior year, one of his Harvard friends, Paul Mariett, was stricken with cancer. Lippmann went to visit him nearly every day during the last months of his illness, and as a memorial put together and helped pay for a volume of Mariett's poems. Because he was strong, many looked to him for support. Another college friend, David Carb, dedicated a play to him. "I like to feel that you who had faith and enthusiasm for my first real thought on paper own it with me," Carb wrote him. "It has been tremendous, that faith — the most encouraging thing that has ever come to me. And it will last. Through whatever I may do hereafter, your vision of life will run. Your enthusiasm for knowledge." Carb saw a kindred spirit in Lippmann, one equally susceptible to hurt, but with a different way of handling it. "You and I, Walter do not suffer from the same things," Carb wrote him in the winter of 1913. "Your pain is rarely personal. Mine is only that. And so I spend much of my time trying to anticipate it or trying to excuse those who inflict it. Our sensitivenesses are antithetical. When your flesh has been scourged you become taut, Spartan and rebellious; and when mine has been lacerated I slink away to prevent people from seeing the pain. You stiffen, I collapse, and that's the difference, emotionally, between us."[13] Lippmann's tautness, the emotional distance that he put between himself and others, was, as Carb perceptively observed, a form of self-protection. Others felt it, too, although they could not understand it quite as well as Carb.

One of those most puzzled by it was Lucile Elsas. All through Walter's first three years at Harvard he had bombarded her with letters exalting Socialism, Beauty and Joy, mostly in that order. During vacations he took her to dances and parties, and it was assumed, by him at least, that they were sweethearts. Yet he never openly showed any sign of his affection, never even kissed her. Lucile's interest waned, and in 1910 she married a man a few years older than Walter and very different in temperament — the stylish publisher and founder of the Modern Library, Horace Liveright.

Walter was furious when he heard the news and never forgave Lucile. Although he went to the wedding, he refused to kiss the bride, turning from her with the remark, "It's too late now." Two years later, in the spring of 1912, she tried to heal the breach by inviting him to drop by to see her new baby. The invitation came just as he was breaking with the socialists at Schenectady. Some of his disappointment with Mayor Lunn may have colored his reaction to Lucile's invitation, but his response was cool. "In asking me to your house you make the situation very difficult for me," he replied. "What can possibly come of a visit? You and I have grown hopelessly apart, and you know as well as I that there is no retracing of the way." When she urged him to let bygones be bygones, he responded defensively, charging that she had the "most amazing capacity for being perfectly sure that all the nobility and humanity are with you to put to shame my smallness and hypocrisy." It was the end of their relationship. Rarely did their paths cross. Once, years later, when they were on the same pier in New York harbor, he studiously ignored her — or so she believed.[14]

When he felt rejected, Lippmann defended himself by casting the offending person from his life. His self-protectiveness, however much it may have enabled him to "see the world steadily and whole," was for him, as for Santayana, a "tragic barrier between him and the common hopes of ordinary men." He wanted to share those common hopes, to draw close to the people he cared for, to show the affection he often felt, but it was not easy. His emotions took the form of a generalized idealism. "What do you love, Walter?" Mabel Dodge asked him one day. "The living world," he responded in a flash. A noble answer, but an abstract and even evasive one. He who loves the whole world often has trouble with the ornery individuals who compose it.

If Lippmann was not much of a democrat, he was an ardent idealist. He spun visions of a better world. Even Hutchins Hapgood, who was a bit jealous and thought him smug, found him in those months before the war "full of youthful hope for society." Lippmann's ideas were changing rapidly. He had indulged himself in what he had called "some necessary iconoclasm." Now he wanted to try something more constructive. In May, as plans for the Paterson pageant moved into high gear, he decided that he must get away and put his ideas on paper. Was there, he wrote Graham Wallas, some inn "where the country is fine, the swimming good, and where one can play tennis, all at a moderate cost?"[15] There was, at the village of Woking, in Surrey. On June 5, 1913, two days before the glorious Paterson pageant was to take place, Lippmann gathered Kuttner in tow and sailed for England.

◄ 6 ►

Reputation

A writer on public affairs can't pretend to despise reputation, for reputation is not only flattering to the vanity,
it is the only way of meeting the people you've got to
know in order to understand the world.

— Diary, July 5, 1914

WHILE in Surrey at the inn of moderate cost Wallas had found,
Lippmann worked furiously on his new book, breaking off only
for afternoon swims and sets of tennis. Every week or so he and Kuttner
took the train to London for a play, a tour through the bookshops, and
tea with Wallas and his friends. There he met the writers whose works
had impressed him in college. There, too, he found his own sort, cultural radicals out to remake the world — men like Van Wyck Brooks,
who had been at Harvard a few years earlier and was working on the
book that launched his literary career, *America's Coming of Age*. "It
was really fine to meet you," Lippmann wrote Brooks that summer. "I
want very much to have it a beginning, for I do feel about America as
you do, and I do want to establish communication with those of us who
are young enough to be working on the same puzzles and trying to see
into the same fog."[1]

Returning to New York in late October, after a hiking tour of the
Swiss Alps with Kuttner, Lippmann found himself a bit at loose ends.
Occasional articles for the *New York Times* and the socialist *New Review*
hardly gave him the kind of audience he wanted. As he was pondering
his next move, he received an unexpected invitation to lunch at the
Players, a fashionable club for men of arts and letters, from Herbert
Croly, whom Lippmann had never met, but who had greatly influenced
his view of politics.

Croly had become a national figure a few years earlier with the publication of his powerful polemic, *The Promise of American Life*. Combin-

ing the passion of a reformer and the rectitude of a moralist he had attacked the mainstays of old-style Progressivism, with its Jeffersonian dogma of free competition, its preference for weak central government, and its philosophy of laissez-faire. The shibboleth of "equal opportunities for all, special privileges for none," he had declared, merely rewarded the strong, who, under a laissez-faire system, would always exploit the weak. Only a strong central government could control and equitably distribute the benefits of industrial capitalism. Croly parted company with the Populist strain of Progressivism by arguing that the inequities of American life could never be rectified by weakening federal power, by mechanical electoral reforms such as referendum and recall, by breaking up the efficient trusts, by coddling the small businessman at the expense of the consumer, or by imagining that good government was that which governed least.

Big Business was here to stay, Croly argued. It could not be wished out of existence by those nostalgic for a happier day when every man could aspire to his own little shop. For this reason the Sherman Anti-Trust Act, which sought to deal with the evils of monopoly by breaking up giant corporations into more "competitive" units, seemed to him outdated, inefficient and futile. The power of industry could be held in check only by an even greater power representing the good of the entire commonwealth — that is, a strong central government. And for government to do its job properly, Croly insisted, to avoid becoming the tool of special-interest groups, it must be guided by a strong and farsighted leader. This formulation enchanted Theodore Roosevelt, who saw it as an elaboration of some of his own sketchy ideas, and who, in his fire-breathing speech at Osawatomie, Kansas, in the summer of 1910, explicitly embraced Croly's "New Nationalism."

Lippmann's own *Preface to Politics* — with its call for strong leadership, big government, and regulated monopolies operating in the public interest — had been influenced by Croly. To receive a lunch invitation from such an influential man was a singular honor. It was also a puzzlement, and as he rode the trolley down to Gramercy Park, Lippmann wondered how he should handle this unusual opportunity. Entering the clubroom, with its red brocade and its portraits of actors in theatrical poses, he spotted Croly sitting in a corner. The older man — Croly was then in his early forties — awkwardly shook his young guest's hand and led him into the dining room. After a few stiff remarks about the weather, the painfully shy Croly came to the point.

He and some others were about to start a new magazine, Croly explained. It would appear every week, cover politics and the arts, and spread the ideas of a "constructive nationalism." The money would come from Willard Straight and his wife, Dorothy — she a Whitney and the beneficiary of many millions in Standard Oil royalties, he a

Morgan banker who had done a stint at the American consulate in Manchuria and who, having helped spread the virtues of capitalism and Christianity in pagan China, was now eager to prepare Americans for their international responsibilities. "Use your wealth to put ideas into circulation," Straight had told his wife. "Others will give to churches and hospitals." At first the Straights had thought of setting up a school in Washington to train young people for the diplomatic service, but after reading Croly's book, decided that what the country needed most was a magazine espousing the New Nationalism — edited, of course, by Croly himself.

Croly persuaded the Straights to put up enough money to publish the magazine for four years, and also to forgo any veto over editorial content. With the magazine's financial security assured, he began rounding up a staff. He needed someone who could write fast and well, who had vague socialist sympathies but could be counted on to be "responsible," and who was young and ambitious enough to work hard without complaint. He had been impressed by *A Preface to Politics,* and when he met Lippmann realized that this was a man he could work with easily. He made his bid across the lunch table. The new magazine, with its links to Roosevelt, its financial freedom, and its Bull Moose Progressivism, offered Lippmann great possibilities. It would put him in touch with influential people and give him a forum far beyond that of the socialist true believers. At sixty dollars a week the salary was more than adequate. Lippmann accepted on the spot.

Croly was delighted by his acquisition. "Lippmann, as you say, is an interesting mixture of maturity and innocence," he wrote Judge Learned Hand. "The *Preface to Politics* is an astonishing book for a fellow three years out of college to write, but no matter how he turns out as a political philosopher he certainly has great possibilities as a political journalist. I don't know where I could find a substitute with so much critical versatility. I had him down here for a few days and tested him out all along that line. He does not know quite as much as he might, but he knows a lot, and his general sense of values is excellent." Lippmann, Croly added, "has real feeling, conviction and knowledge to give a certain assurance, almost a certain dignity to his impertinence, and of course the ability to get away with the impertinent is almost the best quality a political journalist can have." It was an impertinent journal they were planning to put out. "We'll throw a few firecrackers under the skirts of the old women on the bench and in other high places,"[2] Croly promised.

To help throw his firecrackers Croly assembled an eclectic staff: Walter Weyl, a maverick muckraker whose book *The New Democracy* put him somewhere between the socialists and the Roosevelt Progressives; Francis Hackett, who had created the imaginative book supplement of the *Chicago Evening Post;* Philip Littell, an old friend from Harvard who would do a weekly book column; and a young Vassar graduate, Charlotte Rudyard, as editorial assistant. Learned Hand, then a federal judge for the southern district of New York, and later for the powerful second circuit court, offered advice and an occasional editorial note. Hand, an old friend of Croly and his summer neighbor in the artistic enclave of Cornish, New Hampshire, brought along one of his favorite disciples: Felix Frankfurter, a thirty-one-year-old Viennese immigrant, then teaching at Harvard Law School. He soon spread himself over the entire magazine, writing articles, furnishing legal advice, and joining in editorial conferences. To round out the staff Croly later added two young economists, George Soule and Alvin Johnson.

The magazine was a model of looseness, designed on the theory, Lippmann later explained, that "none of its editors wished to do much editing, that none of them would remain at a desk very long, and that there would be a place on the board for men who were not wholly organizable." Although Lippmann was awesomely organized, the system allowed him to write his articles at home and do occasional pieces for other journals. During his first two years on the magazine he contributed regularly to the socialist monthly *Metropolitan,* and managed to write a book on foreign policy. The relaxed atmosphere meant, he said, that "an incorrigible free-lance could dip in for a while to edit or to shape policy, and dip out again without upsetting everybody and everything."[3]

While there was a fledgling staff and an assured income from the Straights, the magazine still had no name. Croly wanted to call it the *Nation,* but there already was one — a journal fallen into amiable respectability since the crusading days of Edwin Godkin and not yet revitalized by Oswald Garrison Villard. As second choice they settled on the *Republic,* although vaguely dissatisfied with its Platonic overtones. Halfway through the planning stage they discovered that a Boston politician, "Honey Fitz" Fitzgerald, grandfather of a future President, was already publishing a *Republic* for Democratic party faithfuls. Reluctantly, and with what Lippmann described as a "positive dislike for the suggestion of utopianism," they added the word *new.* Thus the *New Republic* was christened. The title, as it turned out, was not a bad one for a journal addressed to the public-spirited elite that H. G. Wells had once called the "New Republicans."

Determined to have a handsome as well as an influential magazine, Croly spent an entire year experimenting with type designs and pasting up dummy issues. The result was a clean, striking format that became a model for journals in its field. To ensure the staff's comfort the

Straights bought a four-story brick town house owned by Croly at 421 West 21st Street between Ninth and Tenth avenues, next door to a home for wayward girls and across the street from a theological seminary. There they installed a book-lined library with deep leather chairs and the latest journals from England and the Continent, a kitchen where a French chef prepared lunches, and a paneled dining room where the editors could entertain prominent visitors. It was all very clubby and far removed from the stains of printer's ink. "The vision I have of *The New Republic* will, I fear, set angel Dorothy back some hundreds of thousands of dollars," Croly wrote Learned Hand, ". . . but she will get a little education for her money and so will I and so, I hope, will you and the others." Angel Dorothy was indeed generous, never using her wealth to control editorial policy even though the magazine — except briefly during the First World War — always ran a deficit. For forty years the Straight family subsidized the *NR* at an average cost of some $100,000 a year.

Strong-minded and incorruptible, Croly knew what he wanted. "We shall be radical without being socialistic," he declared, "and our general tendency will be pragmatic rather than doctrinaire."[4] Some skeptics questioned how radical a magazine could be with a Wall Street financier as angel and a bevy of corporation lawyers, executives and judges as guiding lights. The answer was, not very. These men were progressives in the Roosevelt mold — believers in strong leadership, civic responsibility, regulation of Big Business, and greater sympathy toward labor and the poor. Reform was their way of heading off more disruptive change.

Lippmann could not have been more pleased with the magazine and his new colleagues. He had a prestigious job with a good salary, could write about what mattered to him and work closely with influential men. "We're starting a weekly here next fall," he wrote Van Wyck Brooks early in the winter of 1914, "a weekly of ideas — with a paid-up capital — God save us — of 200,000. The age of miracles, sir, has just begun." Explaining that the substance would be "American, but sophisticated and critical," he urged Brooks to contribute articles and to think of himself as "one of our group." The magazine's objective was to "infuse American emotions with American thought" — to be, in other words, a vehicle of cultural nationalism. "We have no party axe or propaganda to grind," he underlined. "We shall be socialistic in direction, but not in method, or phrase or allegiance. If there is any word to cover our ideal, I suppose it is humanistic, somewhat sharply distinguished . . . from humanitarianism." Its humanism would consist of having a "real sense of the relation between the abstract and the concrete, between the noble dream and the actual limitations of life." His hope, he told Brooks rather solemnly, was that every part of the paper would be "vivid with the humor and insights and sounds of American life, and yet imaginative enough to point through them to a more finely disciplined and what Wells calls a more spacious order of living."[5]

While seeking that "more spacious order of living," Lippmann was meeting different people from those he had known as a muckraker and socialist. Some were rich, many were eminent — very few were radical. They were progressive in a patrician way, with a sense, like Theodore Roosevelt's, of *noblesse oblige*. Through Steffens, Lippmann had met reformers like Tom Johnson, Fremont Older and Jane Addams. Now Croly and the Straights opened the door to a world of high finance and national politics. Through them he met, not only Learned Hand, but Louis D. Brandeis, the future Supreme Court justice; Ogden Mills, the Republican politician who later became Hoover's secretary of the treasury; and the lawyer George Rublee, who provided an entrée to Woodrow Wilson.

Lippmann cultivated these people for what they could teach him and for their ability to advance his career. Influence, he now believed, rested not on trying to convert the masses, but on reaching the people whose opinions mattered. The radicals, he felt, lived in a small world of plots, promises and hyperbole. He would break out of the constricting circle of the *Masses* and the *Call*, away from the true believers and professional agitators.

Later the great would seek him out. At twenty-four he sought them out. In his quiet way he was an exceedingly ambitious young man who used his intelligence and charm to cultivate older men: Learned Hand and Oliver Wendell Holmes, Jr. — later Colonel House and Newton Baker. He challenged them, as he had Steffens, and provided them with an engaging, even idealized, version of their younger selves. In the talented young essayist — intense, precocious, a bit shy — they found a disciple worthy of their own estimate of themselves.

Among those he cultivated there was none he admired more than Theodore Roosevelt. TR was his model of what a statesman should be, "the first President who shared a new social vision," as he had written in his book. However curious such enthusiasm may seem to generations that remember Roosevelt as a jingoist who played toy soldier in Cuba and stole Panama from Colombia to build his canal, he was a hero to progressives. For all his bombast and pugnacity, his obsession with shooting animals and demonstrating his virility, Roosevelt was a reformer and an intellectual — a man who wrote history books, defied convention by inviting blacks to the White House and appointing a Jew to his cabinet, laid the groundwork for the welfare state, set up the national park system, and shocked conservatives by declaring that private property was "subject to the general right of the community to regulate its use to whatever degree the public may require it." Roosevelt, Lippmann wrote many years later,

was the first President who knew that the United States had come of age — that not only were they no longer colonies of Europe, and no longer an immature nation on the periphery of western civilization, but that they had become a world power. He was the first to realize what that means, its responsibilities and its dangers and its implication, and the first to prepare the country spiritually and physically for this inescapable destiny. . . . The first President who realized clearly that national stability and social justice had to be sought deliberately and had consciously to be maintained . . . that once the period of settlement and easy expansion had come to an end, the promise of American life could be realized only by a national effort. . . . Theodore Roosevelt began the work of turning the American mind in the direction which it had to go in the Twentieth Century.[6]

Roosevelt, who became President at age forty-two in 1901, when McKinley was assassinated, was reelected to office three years later, but stepped aside in 1908 for his protégé, William Howard Taft. By 1912 TR was ready to return to the White House. But Taft, having grown to like the place, refused to step down, and the Republican party bosses, who considered TR to be troublesome and even dangerously radical, gave the nomination to Taft. In a fury Roosevelt stomped out of the convention, taking his followers with him, and formed his own Bull Moose party. "We stand at Armageddon and we battle for the Lord," he told an ecstatic gathering, and millions joined the crusade. "Roosevelt bit me and I went mad," the Kansas publisher William Allen White later said, speaking for many progressives. Lippmann too went a little mad when he heard TR speak at Madison Square Garden in the fall of 1912. Although he later fell out with Roosevelt, as he did with most of the great leaders he admired, he never quite ceased to be, as he said, "an unqualified hero-worshiper." More than sixty years later he told a friend that of all the Presidents he had known — and he personally knew twelve — only one was lovable, "Teddy Roosevelt, and I loved him."

Although TR fought a brilliant campaign, capturing 700,000 more votes than the incumbent Taft on the regular Republican ticket, he lost the three-cornered race to Woodrow Wilson. To revive his spirits he went off to the Amazon, where he shot crocodiles and contracted jungle fever. He also read a good many books, including *A Preface to Politics,* whose cheeky iconoclasm and lavish praise for himself so impressed him that he wrote a note of congratulation to the author. Lippmann was overwhelmed. "You can readily see from my book that it owes a great deal to you," he pointed out to TR, "and for that reason I was very eager to have your opinion of it."[7]

Delighted as he was to receive TR's praise, Lippmann even more wanted to meet the great man, which he finally did in the spring of 1914. Roosevelt, having returned to New York somewhat the worse for wear after his Brazilian escapade, invited Lippmann and Felix Frankfurter to breakfast at the Harvard Club. He was, he confided to his eager admirers, thinking of running against Wilson in 1916, but there were many issues to brush up on. First of all he needed to work out a position on the labor question. Labor and management were at each other's throats, and the country was being paralyzed by strikes, lockouts, and police brutality. In West Virginia the United Mine Workers were locked in battle with company guards, while in Colorado a strike against the Rockefeller-owned mines had ended in the "Ludlow massacre" of miners and their families. Lippmann, who had written a good deal about the labor problem, volunteered to draft a position paper for Roosevelt. TR rose from the breakfast table, grasped Lippmann's hand in a viselike grip, and told him that they were now partners in a common cause. As Lippmann left the Harvard Club and walked out into the clamor of the streets, he felt he had crossed another frontier.

A few weeks later he retreated to Maine to work on TR's labor plank and do some proofreading. It was now mid-May and his colleagues at the *NR* were drifting off to their summer homes: Croly and Philip Littell to New Hampshire, Weyl to Woodstock, New York. They would begin publication in November. From his retreat at Sebasco, in the Maine woods, Lippmann put together a labor platform for TR, advising him to support a minimum wage and to endorse organized labor "with all its crudities" as the best hope for industrial democracy. Like Roosevelt, Lippmann was pro-labor because he believed that strong unions would prevent violence and anarchy. Only through a powerful labor movement, he told TR, could America avoid a "class structure imperiled by insurrection."

The memo he put together for TR was, in effect, an abridged version of the chapter on the labor movement he had just written for his new book — the one he had begun the previous summer in England and had decided to call *Drift and Mastery*. "It is labor organized that alone can stand between America and the creation of a permanent, servile class," he had written. "The effort to build up unions is as much the work of pioneers as the extension of civilization into the wilderness. The unions are the first feeble effort to conquer the industrial jungle for democratic life." Such an effort, he recognized, would not always be peaceful. "Men are fighting for the beginnings of industrial self-government. . . . No wonder they despise the scab. He is justly despised. Far from being the independent, liberty-loving soul he is sometimes painted, the scab is a traitor to the economic foundations of democracy."[8] Lippmann's views on labor, radical enough in the context of the times, were only one of the striking pronouncements that gave such impact to *Drift and Mastery* when it appeared a few months later.

In self-imposed isolation in the woods, Lippmann spent most of the month of June putting the finishing touches on the book. "I spend my days reading proof," he wrote Learned Hand, "which is worse than testimony, writing out what I think about socialism, and reading a history of the French revolution. I also chop wood twice a day and kill mosquitoes."[9] By the end of June he had finished his corrections and was ready to take off for Europe to round up writers for the *New Republic*, to garner whatever laurels he could for *A Preface to Politics*, just published in England, and to take a walking tour of the Swiss Alps.

On July 2, 1914, after spending an evening at Coney Island with Judge Hand and Francis Hackett, he boarded the S.S. *Baltic* for Europe. "The place lacks sexual interest," he confided to his diary about the amusement park. The week-long crossing allowed a rare moment of introspection. "Indolence and the dislike of self-consciousness have kept me from writing a diary," he confessed in an early entry. "I dislike diaries that consist of soliloquies before the infinite. And, moreover, things that happen to me and my feelings about them are not so precious that they need be recorded in detail." Nevertheless, he continued,

I have regretted often that I had not set down the fresh impressions of many conversations, meetings, men, things seen. The talks long ago with Pritchard who opened up painting to me, my contact with William James in the last two years of his life, with Santayana, with H. G. Wells, with Graham Wallas, John Hobson, with scores of literary men, politicians, agitators here and abroad — I should not like to lose them. I should like to recall long conversations through the night with Kenneth Hunter and Felix Cole, walks over the mountains or through Brittany with Alfred Kuttner and Lee Simonson. I should like to preserve the rich texture of memory — Moscow and Norway, Ireland and the Riviera — blue and gold days on the Merrimack, long horseback rides through the Berkshires, the beach at the Lido . . .

He was ending one phase of his life: he had drawn away from the radicals, left free-lance journalism for a regular job, switched from a loose socialism to a left-wing progressivism, and exchanged his downtown friends for a new set of uptown ones. He still thought of himself as a radical, but an independent and "responsible" one. Intellectually he was feeling his way. His two books, as he confided to his diary on the ship that July, were "both prolegomena — terribly inadequate, I realize. I put them out as preliminary sketches, and I never claimed much for them. But they not only crystallize and state. They have opened up the experience I must have if I'm to work them out." Experience was the key to reputation, and on that all else hinged. "A writer on public affairs can't pretend to despise reputation," he added significantly, "for reputation is not only flattering to the vanity, it is the only way of meeting the people you've got to know in order to understand the world."[10]

Lippmann's key to meeting people was Graham Wallas. No sooner had he set down his bags at Garland's Hotel behind the Haymarket than he went out to Highgate to see his old mentor. Wallas had just brought out a new book, the one he had been working on when Lippmann first met him at Harvard four years earlier. He called it *The Great Society*, by which he meant the wider world beyond the confines of the city-state, and a moral community free from both bourgeois materialism and socialist collectivism. Wallas had been so influenced by Lippmann's comments in the politics seminar at Harvard that he not only dedicated the book to his former student, but began it with an open letter to Lippmann. As his earlier work had been an argument against nineteenth-century intellectualism, Wallas noted, *The Great Society* was intended as "an argument against certain forms of 20th century anti-intellectualism." Intimating that Lippmann had gone a bit overboard in extolling the irrational in his first book, Wallas gently suggested that this approach might "be of some help when you write that sequel to your *Preface to Politics* for which all your friends are looking."

Lippmann was naturally flattered by this remarkable tribute from a teacher thirty years his senior. "I had no idea that you had in mind to do for me what you have done," he wrote Wallas on receiving an advance copy of the book. "Nothing that has ever come to me has meant so much as this chance to be identified a little with your work. I know what form you want my gratitude to take — you wrote it on the copy of *Human Nature in Politics* which you gave me when you were at Harvard — to be 'truth's pilgrim at the plough.' I'll keep that faith," Lippmann promised, "and while I know I've done nothing to deserve such a gift, I can take it as a pupil from his teacher."

Although Lippmann later strayed far from the socialist enthusiasm that had originally drawn him to Wallas, he remained attached to his mentor for more than twenty years. "He was the greatest teacher I have ever known," Lippmann wrote Audrey Wallas upon her husband's death in 1932. "I owe everything to him that enables me to understand at all the human problems of the Great Society, and I have for him a loving gratitude which is boundless. I should rather be known as a pupil of Graham Wallas than any other way, and no one can ever take that title away. But he was more than a teacher to me, the kindest, richest human being of my life."[11]

Through Wallas, Lippmann met the guiding members of the Fabian Society: Beatrice and Sidney Webb, George Bernard Shaw, and most memorably H. G. Wells. One of England's most prolific and successful writers, a father of science fiction and a utopian socialist, Wells had by that time made his break with the Fabians, lampooning the Webbs maliciously in his *New Machiavelli,* just as he had also sharpened his claws on Wallas. But to a generation of young idealists, Wells was a prophet. With him, Van Wyck Brooks recalled, "one felt that the nineteenth century had at last come to an end and a century of hope and adventure had opened. . . . Under the spell of this great myth-maker, young people saw themselves as no longer creatures of the past but as creators of the future."

Ever since college Lippmann had been in awe of this man who called for scrapping an outdated old order and building a "new republic" that superior men and women — his "intellectual samurai" — would direct for the good of all. Now at last Lippmann found himself in the hazy smoking room of the National Liberal Club, with its crowded little tables where men sat talking in all the accents of the British Empire, face to face with the writer he had so long admired. They spoke of literature and politics, with Wells switching without pause from abstract theory to malicious gossip about the Fabians. Shyly Van Wyck Brooks came up to be introduced, and later wrote of being "almost too excited to speak in the presence of this red-faced man with his shrill asthmatic voice, a half-cockney squeak, pouring forth words like a freshet in spring and looking as if he was on the point of a fatal stroke of apoplexy even as he stood there."[12]

Finding Lippmann engaging and remarkably mature for his years, Wells introduced him to some friends: Arnold Bennett, G. K. Chesterton, Hilaire Belloc and Frank Harris. He also introduced Lippmann to his latest mistress, a lovely young woman named Cecily Fairfield, but who preferred to be known as Rebecca West, after an Ibsen heroine. An enchanted Lippmann signed her to write cultural articles from London for the *New Republic* on whatever subject interested her. In addition he rounded up promises of articles from Wells, Wallas, Alfred Zimmern, Bernard Shaw, James Bryce, Hugh Walpole, John Hobson, and H. N. Brailsford. To keep tabs on British politics and culture, he hired S. K. Ratcliffe, former editor of the *Statesman of India,* to be the *NR*'s official correspondent at a salary of one thousand dollars a year. Even for a magazine so self-consciously "nationalistic" as the *NR,* there seemed nothing inappropriate about relying heavily on British contributors — who furnished a quarter of the magazine's signed articles during the first year of publication. Culture, after all, was supposed to be international, and the fight against ossified thinking and entrenched privilege knew no national boundaries.

Like many Fabians and young intellectuals, Lippmann spent a good deal of time at Dan Rider's bookshop on St. Martin's Lane. Rider, the

London agent of Lippmann's publisher, Mitchell Kennerley, introduced him to the writers, famous and aspiring, who dropped by his shop to browse and have a cup of tea. "Lippmann is a great boy," Rider told Van Wyck Brooks. "He gets more into a day than the whole population of England. His timetable is worked out with the regularity of a railroad." Rider took him to see Fisher Unwin, who had published *A Preface to Politics* in England and who told him that the book had not sold well. "I couldn't seem to care," Lippmann wrote in his diary on July 13, "maybe because England is unreal to me. But rather because I am tired of the *Preface*." Tired or not, he was pleased when Unwin decided to publish the new book, *Drift and Mastery*.

It was a summer for making contacts: Geoffrey Dawson, editor of *The Times;* Wickham Steed, a well-known journalist; John Hobson, a critic of imperialism; Ezra Pound, whom he found an "unhealthy, neurotic, infinitely conceited person and pretentious to the point of exasperation"; Lytton Strachey, who was "very odd-looking"; and above all Beatrice and Sidney Webb. Tireless pedants, inveterate snobs, incessant moralizers, the Webbs had single-mindedly and with no material reward devoted their lives to uplifting the unworthy poor and penetrating the capitalists from within. Wells's delicious parody of them, written after he had tried and failed to take over the Fabian Society, had made not the slightest dent in their supreme self-confidence. They knew what they wanted, which was to have the "nicest people" — another version of Wells's "social engineers" — run society on sound principles. They were very dubious about the Labor party, preferring instead to bore from within through the two elite institutions they had founded: the *New Statesman* and the London School of Economics. However ludicrous they seemed to detractors, they were fearless and dedicated. Lippmann had pulled a few strings to be invited to their home on Grosvenor Road.

One afternoon in July 1914 the maid ushered him into a bare, white and not particularly tasteful room where he was warmly greeted by Sidney Webb, "an absurdly small man with a large puffy, hairy head, a curious beak-like nose, long capable hands," as he recorded in his diary on July 14. They talked of the *New Republic,* Wilson's bungling in Mexico, Graham Wallas's new book, and the nasty gibes that the ungrateful Wells had made against them. "Mrs. Webb was perhaps a little too frankly open-minded, yet it was magnanimous," Lippmann wrote, finding in them "a real desire to avoid quarrels," and even an appreciation of Wells. "They seem to stand there as the two pillars of socialist morality — with no gratuitous rebellion, a disciplined, socialized, humane and endlessly useful couple. I came away angry at the slurs that it is so fashionable to cast upon them."

A few days after his encounter with the Founding Couple, Lippmann joined Wallas for a train trip to the Lake District, where the Fabians were holding their annual summer school. At the village of Keswick, Lippmann found himself in a summer camp populated by a hundred-odd Fabians of all ages and appearances: "a dozen or so young university graduates and undergraduates, another strain of middle-class professionals, a stray member of Parliament or a professor, a bevy of fair girls — and the remainder — a too large remainder — elderly and old nondescript females, who find the place lively and fairly cheap," in Beatrice Webb's tart description.[13]

Despite the hangers-on, the conference promised to be stimulating. The young G. D. H. Cole was trying to snatch the organization away from the Webbs and dedicate it to guild socialism. The Cole group dreaded the all-powerful State inherent in the Webbs' version of collectivism, and wanted the workers to run the factories. At Keswick they went on a rampage, singing revolutionary songs in the village square, heckling the speakers at the discussion groups, and ostentatiously walking out when called to order. Preaching salvation through a general strike, the Cole group "sat in the back of the room and sneered" at the calls to discipline by "Shaw, Webb and the old gang in the front, reasonable, kind, open-minded," Lippmann noted in his diary on July 20.

After the meeting Lippmann walked back to the hotel with Bernard Shaw and talked with the dramatist on the doorstep for nearly an hour. Lippmann had never got over his undergraduate awe of the author of *The Man of Destiny,* and now wanted to get Shaw's view of Freud and the new theories of psychoanalysis. Shaw was not in the least interested, preferring instead to discuss motor cars, of which he had a particularly handsome example — a glittering sports model in which he had arrived dramatically at the conference. Before turning in for the night, Shaw gave Lippmann and some others who had gathered during their conversation a little demonstration of his gift for mimicry — a gift he had recently turned to advantage in *Pygmalion,* the great hit of the current London theater season. Lippmann asked if it were true that one could really discover where people came from by their speech, as Henry Higgins had done. "Of course," Shaw replied. "I can identify anybody from any county in Ireland," at which point he launched into a multivoiced conversation with himself in a variety of accents. The little band of socialists who had gathered on the doorstep cheered his virtuoso performance.

The next day Lippmann did encounter someone who wanted to talk about Freud. On the train back to London he found himself in a carriage with Leonard Woolf. They soon fell into a conversation that never flagged until they reached London hours later. "I do not think I had a premonition of his future eminence," Woolf later wrote of his young traveling companion. "But I liked him very much as a man and felt him to be both intelligent and sensitive." Woolf was struck by how intimate their conversation became, particularly once they discovered that they shared a fascination with Freudian psychology. "There are few things more unexpected and more exciting than suddenly finding someone of intelligence and understanding who at once with a complete frankness will go with one below what is the usual surface of conversation and discussion,"[14] Woolf wrote, giving a glimpse of the impression the young Lippmann made on others: one of intensity, perception, maturity, and frankness. They never met again until the mid-1930s, when the London hostess Sybil Colefax brought them together. They then found they had little to say to each other. His work in England finished, Lippmann prepared for a fortnight's hike in the Swiss mountains. It never crossed his mind that events taking place in the Austro-Hungarian Empire that summer — the assassination of Archduke Ferdinand at the end of June, the Austrian ultimatum to Serbia in late July, the Russian threat to declare war if Austria attacked Serbia, the danger that Germany, France and Britain might be forced to honor their alliances — could affect his vacation. Nor, to be sure, had it impressed the distinguished figures he had heard debate the virtues of syndicalism, denounce capitalism and imperialism, deplore the class system, and advocate the freedom of India and Ireland.

On July 27, as the French ordered mobilization in support of their alliance with Russia, Lippmann crossed the Channel with a friend from Harvard, Harold Stearns. When he arrived in Brussels on the twenty-ninth he discovered that Austria had declared war on Serbia, Germany was threatening to come in on Austria's side, and Russia was warning that it would protect the Serbs. "War in Europe impending," Lippmann scrawled in his diary. "Panic in Brussels. Run on banks. Collapse of credit." No one seemed to know what was happening. "My own nervousness has taken the form of an uninterrupted purchase of newspapers," he wrote Wallas. "The railroad stations are crowded with angry, jostling people, carrying every conceivable kind of package. On the train from Ostend yesterday I found it somewhat dangerous to speak German . . . I am making straight for Switzerland tonight."[15] He never got there. At the station they told him the border was closed. Anxiously he turned back to England, traveling all night on the boat train. In London the next morning, shaken and exhausted, he went straight to the Wallases, who put him to bed in their guest room.

The date was August 1. Germany had refused a plea to respect the neutrality of Belgium. That afternoon Paris and Berlin ordered a general mobilization. A few hours later Germany declared war on Russia. The unthinkable had happened. A dynastic imbroglio in the decaying

Austro-Hungarian Empire had triggered a war engulfing Europe. The next morning as the news came through, Lippmann sent a letter to Frankfurter:

> Dear Felix,
>
> This isn't a very cheerful day to be writing to you. It's an hour since we learned that Germany has declared war against Russia. We shall hear of France later in the day, no doubt. Wallas and Hobson, Gilbert Murray, Hobhouse and the others are at work trying to stir up liberal feeling, but it's a toss up. We sit and stare at each other and make idiotically cheerful remarks. And in the meantime, so far as anyone can see now, nothing can stop the awful disintegration now.
>
> Nor is there any way of looking beyond it: ideas, books, seem too utterly trivial, and all the public opinion, democratic hope and what not, where is it today? Like a flower in the path of a plough.
>
> Petitions are being signed. We shall march in Trafalgar Square this afternoon, and the madness is seizing us all, so that taking war as we do, there is something which makes me feel like getting at the throat of Germany . . .
>
> There is nothing to "see" except anxious people buying thoroughly censored news dispatches — you feel this money panic, but all anyone can do is to wait and wait. Jack Reed was bored at the battle of Torreon. I can understand it now. There is the worst event in the world hanging over our heads and all we can do is to read once in twenty-four hours a two-line Reuters telegram entirely surrounded by journalese.[16]

In Trafalgar Square on August 2 Lippmann heard Keir Hardie and H. N. Hyndman speak to an enormous antiwar crowd, sprinkled with a few people who booed and sang "God Save the King." "I was overcome with a general feeling of futility," he wrote in his diary that night, "a sense that fighting had to be, and the sooner the better." The next day he was again at the National Liberal Club, with Sidney and Beatrice Webb, Norman Hapgood of *Harper's Weekly,* Ratcliffe and Zimmern. The Webbs seemed suddenly irrelevant. "We don't form opinions on foreign affairs," Beatrice said. "We don't know the technique." Later he met John Hobson, who had just come from hearing the foreign secretary, Sir Edward Grey, declare that Britain would come to the aid of France. "We're fighting for the barbarization of Europe and the revenge of France," Hobson said bitterly.

The following day, Tuesday, August 4, Britain mobilized and sent an ultimatum to Germany. That night, as Lippmann waited with a group of Fabians on the terrace of the House of Commons, Parliament declared war. On the fifth Lippmann received a telegram from his parents, who had been traveling in Central Europe: they were safe in Switzerland. The suspense was over. "I began to enjoy understanding again, having recovered from the personal worry and the stupefaction," he wrote that day in his diary. The sudden reality of war shook the sanctity of his world and made him realize how little he knew. "My own part in this is to understand world politics, to be interested in national and military affairs, and to get away from the old liberalism which concentrates entirely on local problems. We cannot lose all that, but see now that all our really civilized effort is set in a structure of hard necessities." It was his initiation to a lifelong preoccupation with foreign affairs.

While some of his pacifist friends denounced the declaration of war, and others railed against the Germans, Lippmann calmly drew up a list. "I want to begin organizing my impressions of the war," he wrote on August 5: "1) How it came to me; 2) Sources of information; 3) Conjecture of causes; 4) Evidence of the crisis in daily life; 5) Relation to other problems; 6) Persons in organization; 7) Looking forward to a settlement." It was the end of his diary.

Lippmann lingered on in London as the young Englishmen with whom he had played tennis that summer eagerly volunteered. Few were ever to return. At the end of August his parents arrived penniless from Geneva, having been unable to cash their traveler's checks. On September 16 he had a farewell dinner with the Wallases, never dreaming that it would be four years before they would meet again. "The *Adriatic* has not yet gone, and I feel as if I were saying goodbye," Wallas wrote in a note he sent to the ship. "In all the dreary waste of life and livelihood, I like to think of you yourself, young and splendidly equipped, and determined to get some meaning and purpose into the organized life of mankind."[17]

A week later Lippmann was back in New York, the shock of the war beginning to fade behind him.

"Agitation Isn't My Job"

A man has to make up his mind what his job is and
stick to that. I know that agitation isn't my job.

— To Upton Sinclair, May 6, 1914

LIPPMANN got back to New York just in time to help with the last frantic efforts of getting the *New Republic* into print. The lamps burned late on West 21st Street all through October as he, Croly, Weyl and the others whipped copy for the first issue into final shape and smoothed out the technical details of publishing and distribution. "The preliminary work on the paper has been tremendously hard," Lippmann wrote Wallas in late October, just a week before publication. "I begin to see somewhat more clearly why administrators have not time to think, and why people who think often can't administer." [1]

The first issue came out November 7, 1914, three months into the war that none of the editors had remotely contemplated. "Who cares to paint a picture now, or to write any poetry but war poetry, or to search the meaning of language, or speculate about the constitution of matter?" Lippmann asked in his debut editorial. But he was sure the answer was not American involvement in the war. "The final argument against cannon is ideas. . . . For while it takes as much skill to make a sword as a ploughshare, it takes a critical understanding of human values to prefer the ploughshare." [2] The advice was reasonable, but the editors had no idea whether anyone was listening. The magazine was designed to jostle its readers, "to start little insurrections in the realm of their convictions," in Croly's words. But there were only nine hundred names on the initial mailing list, and most of those were friends. Would anyone buy a magazine designed for well-educated reformers? Lippmann went to New Haven for the Harvard-Yale game in late November and spent most of the afternoon, his companion Freda Kirchwey recalled, scouring the newsstands for copies of the magazine. But the *New Republic* caught on; within three months it was selling twenty-five hundred copies a week, and by the end of the war in late 1918, more than forty thousand.

The formula was clever and the timing good. Without being radical, the magazine was just far enough left of the liberal consensus to be stimulating. It attracted liberals who felt that government had a responsibility to ensure a modicum of economic and social justice, and who applauded restrained experimentation in the arts. Moderation and social responsibility were the *NR*'s watchwords. A forum for the most serious and original minds writing in English, it featured in the first year articles by Charles Beard, John Dewey, James Harvey Robinson, George Santayana, Ralph Barton Perry, Lincoln Colcord, Theodore Dreiser, and the young critics Van Wyck Brooks and Randolph Bourne. The *NR* also reached across the Atlantic, bringing in such contributors as H. G. Wells, Norman Angell, Harold Laski, James Bryce, George Bernard Shaw and Graham Wallas — plus the regular London correspondents, S. K. Ratcliffe, H. N. Brailsford and Rebecca West. The arts section, under Francis Hackett's direction, offered space to such little-known poets as Amy Lowell, Conrad Aiken, Alan Seeger, Edwin Arlington Robinson and Robert Frost, whose "Death of a Hired Man" first appeared in the *NR*. Lippmann did a good turn for his Harvard chums by inviting Lee Simonson to write on painting, Hiram Moderwell on music, Alfred Kuttner on psychoanalysis, Kenneth MacGowan on movies, and John Reed on the miseries of the downtrodden.

Buoyed by the high quality of its writing and the firm hand of its editors, the *NR* maintained a delicate balance between the aggressive and the conciliatory, the practical and the visionary. While tending toward solemnity, it took its responsibilities seriously, and produced some of the best editorial and critical writing in America. Justice Oliver Wendell Holmes was one of the first subscribers; so was nineteen-year-old Edmund Wilson. Theodore Roosevelt thought it bully. Charles Beard and John Dewey were eager contributors. What attracted such disparate types was a political outlook that combined the more attractive aspects of progressivism with an elitist emphasis on intellect and leadership.

Such an approach was particularly appealing to Roosevelt, who looked — with encouragement from the editors — on the journal as his own personal stepping-stone back to the White House. Croly, Straight and Lippmann flattered him, seemed to share his views on domestic reform, urged him to run for President again, and filled the early issues of the *NR* with articles extolling his virtues.

Pleased with the eminently sensible line the magazine was taking, TR invited Croly, Weyl and Lippmann to his home at Oyster Bay in late November 1914 for dinner and the night. In the Great Trophy Room, where he had entertained many statesmen and artists, he showed them the animals he had shot on his trip to Africa and had had mounted, and a photograph of himself reviewing a military parade with the kaiser. In a loquacious mood, TR rattled on for hours, talking about his trip, the war, and the brilliant future progressivism would have under his leadership. TR was "as fresh as a daisy at two in the morning," Lippmann recalled, "Walter Weyl alert as ever, and Croly dozing in his chair." Several times Lippmann moved to rouse Croly but TR stopped him. "No, no," he said, "let him be," and then continued his monologue unperturbed. Finally even TR wound down and let his guests go to bed. "I spent last night at Oyster Bay with Roosevelt and loved him more than ever," Lippmann reported to Mabel Dodge.[3]

Lippmann's romance was delirious, but rested on a shaky foundation. Admitting no independence, it could endure only so long as he was willing to remain uncritical. The limits of his adoration were soon tested. The magazine was hardly a month old when the editors had their first quarrel with Roosevelt. The issue was Wilson's decision to pick a fight with the Mexican military junta over a trivial incident in Veracruz harbor. Wilson, wanting to teach the Latins "to elect good men," had tried to topple the junta and later even sent American troops across the border in pursuit of Pancho Villa's men. Roosevelt had no quarrel with the intervention; he merely wanted more of it. And he blamed Wilson, as Lippmann later commented, for every sin committed by Villa's forces, from the general's drunkenness to "personal responsibility for the rape of nuns in Mexico."

The men at the *NR,* who never approved of Wilson's intervention in the first place, thought their hero had gone a bit too far. Convinced that Roosevelt had responded so violently not because of events in Mexico but because of his hatred for Wilson, they felt they must tap him on the knuckles. In December 1914 they admonished him for making a "brutally unfair attack" on the President, and described it as "an example of the kind of fighting which has turned so many of his natural admirers into bitter enemies."[4]

Roosevelt did not take kindly to criticism. He flew into a rage, accusing the editors of "personal disloyalty" and dismissing them as "three circumcised Jews and three anemic Christians." A wounded Croly tried to explain to Roosevelt that they had made "merely the same kind of criticism which candid friends continually pass upon one another, and that we had no idea that any question of loyalty or disloyalty could be raised by it." But Roosevelt was not so easily appeased. "He reproached us bitterly and never forgave us," Lippmann recalled.

Despite the quarrel with TR, the early days on the *New Republic* were a happy time for Lippmann. Open, enthusiastic, optimistic, he was receptive to everything around him and eager to remake the world. "He certainly is in fine fettle these days," Bobby Rogers, one of his Harvard friends, wrote Mabel Dodge in the autumn of 1914. "Whether it is the book or a regular job or the responsibility of finishing up the incomplete work of the Creator, I don't know. But I have never seen him happier or nicer."[5]

The book Bobby Rogers referred to was, of course, the one Lippmann had been working on since the summer of 1913, *Drift and Mastery*. Its publication, coinciding with the launching of the magazine, added impressively to his reputation. Critics found it a more mature work than *A Preface to Politics*. Theodore Roosevelt, writing before the quarrel over Mexico, compared it favorably to James Bryce's *American Commonwealth* and declared: "No man who wishes seriously to study our present social, industrial and political life can afford not to read it through and through and ponder and digest it." Randolph Bourne, perhaps Lippmann's only equal among the young social critics, described it as "a book one would have given one's soul to have written." It dealt with the problem of the age: "what to do with your emancipation after you have got it." Even the demanding Justice Holmes found it "devilishly well-written, full of articulation of the impalpable and unutterable, discussing labor with insight, touching the absurd Sherman Act with Ithuriel's spear, not without the superstitions of a young comeouter as to capital, and quoting foolish things about the Court — altogether a delightful fresh piece of writing and thinking."[6]

Drift and Mastery was as brashly self-confident as the *Preface to Politics* had been, but solider in substance. Gone was the exuberant celebration of experience for its own sake, the exaltation of intuition, the downgrading of reason. In their place was an emphasis on scientific management and rational blueprints for organizing society. Nietzsche's yea-saying had been supplanted by Frederick W. Taylor's time-and-motion studies. Having inserted Freud into politics in his first book, Lippmann now extracted him. Bergson's *élan vital* and Sorel's "creative myth" fell unnoticed by the wayside, and even James's disorderly world "full of variety and spontaneous creation" seemed messy and inadequate. After earlier dismissing logic, Lippmann now decried the "widespread attempt to show the futility of ideas" — a fair complaint, but one that could have been directed most pointedly against his own *Preface to Politics*.

If nothing else, *Drift and Mastery* showed Lippmann's intellectual flexibility, his willingness to jettison old ideas as soon as new ones were at hand. While some may have considered it evidence of a lack of conviction, it reflected the fact that he had put his iconoclasm behind him. Whereas the battle had earlier been against an outmoded tradition, it was now against aimless drift. "Those who went before inherited a conservatism and overthrew it; we inherit freedom and have to use it." The old battles had been won: "The sanctity of property, the patriarchal family, hereditary caste, the dogma of sin, obedience to authority — the rock of ages, in brief, has been blasted for us. . . . The battle for us does not lie against a crusted prejudice, but against the chaos of a new freedom.''

The announcement was undoubtedly premature. For many, the old gods were still secure and the new freedom more a slogan than a reality. Yet Lippmann had captured a mood that permeated the radical movement: the future was there for the making. The tool, he now decided, was not instinct or emotion, but scientific method. By this he meant purposeful activity, conscious planning, vision tamed by practicality, and above all, a common discipline. ''Rightly understood science is the culture under which people can live forward in the midst of complexity, and treat life not as something given but as something to be shaped.'' There was a good deal of John Dewey in this, even more of Theodore Roosevelt: science at the service of culture. Through social and economic reform it would be possible, Lippmann declared with the faith of a social engineer, to ''create in the country a life that shall be really interesting.'' The goal was not mere efficiency, or even equality, but that dream of the cultural radical, ''to use the political state for interesting and important purposes.''

Drift and Mastery marked Lippmann's break with both muckrakers and socialists. ''If anyone really desired that kind of proof,'' he wrote scathingly of the muckrakers' accumulation of data on the perfidious practices of businessmen and politicians, ''a few German scholars, young and in perfect health, should be imported to furnish it.'' He also had little use for the muckrakers' insistence that corporate power be broken up and competition restored. This was the logic behind the Sherman Anti-Trust Act. Lippmann followed Croly and Roosevelt. He argued that the ills of society could not be blamed on industrial concentration. Big Business was being made the scapegoat for the ''feverish fantasy of illiterate thousands thrown out of kilter by the rack and strain of modern life.'' The answer was public control, not a return to a more primitive industrial structure of unrestricted competition.

Second, Lippmann maintained that something dramatic had happened within the very structure of capitalism. The giant corporation, with its thousands, and even millions, of shareholders, was not ''owned'' by anybody, except in the most technical sense. Those who ostensibly ''owned'' the company, the shareholders, had no effective control over it. Control was exercised by highly skilled managers. ''The trust movement is doing what no conspirator or revolutionist could ever do,'' he declared; ''it is sucking the life out of private property.'' By pointing out the divorce of ownership from control, Lippmann anticipated the detailed study Berle and Means were to make twenty years later.[7]

Lippmann had developed a theory that allowed him to circumvent the conflict between capitalism and socialism. If the modern corporation had "sucked the life" out of private property, then the socialist argument had become irrelevant. Business was already "nationalized" through dispersed ownership, and corporate managers were more interested in the public good than in private profit. Or so his logic dictated. But ownership was not as divorced from control as he assumed — a fact that became clearer as banks gained effective control of corporations. Nor did corporate managers have the sense of public responsibility — or the lack of interest in amassing private fortunes — that he believed. Lippmann, as one critic later wrote, "looked at carnivorous teeth and called them herbivorous." His argument was logical, but abstract.[8]

In discovering the divorce of management from ownership, and in subjecting the modern corporation to political control, Lippmann found the justification for his final break with the socialists. It had been coming for some time. Early in 1913 he had written articles urging the socialists to cooperate with progressives — quite the opposite of what he had been arguing in 1912 at Schenectady. By the time he joined Croly he had abandoned the ideological basis of socialism and replaced it with a Wellsian vision of an elite of enlightened managers who would run society along scientific grounds for the public good.

"The winter of 1914 is an important change for me," he had confided to his diary while en route to Europe that summer. "Perhaps I have grown conservative. At any rate I find less and less sympathy with the revolutionists — with English Walling and Max Eastman — and an increasing interest in administrative problems. I come definitely nearer to the Progressives." In the pages of *Drift and Mastery* he made clear that the break was total, dismissing Marxist theorists as "interested pedants of destiny," and the American socialist movement as a "great citadel of dogma almost impervious to new ideas." For him socialism had now become irrelevant. "I have not been able to convince myself that one policy, one party, one class, or one set of tactics, is as fertile as human need," declared the young man who only two years earlier had walked away from Schenectady in disgust with the cautious reformism of the "shrewdly good."[9]

Reform was now Lippmann's credo, and its instruments were to be professionalism, science, and social control. "We propose to subject nature to our purposes, to make it measure up to our values," he had written in a magazine article while working on *Drift and Mastery*. "We shall use all science as a tool and a weapon. And that is what we propose to do with moralities and institutions — use them as instruments of our purpose." Echoing Croly and Theodore Roosevelt, Lippmann urged social reform through a government-sponsored "war against poverty." This was necessary not only on humanitarian but also on political grounds. "You can't build a nation out of Georgia crackers, poverty-stricken negroes, the homeless and helpless of the great cities,'' he observed. ''Before you can begin to have democracy you need a country in which everyone has some stake and some taste of its promise.'' That meant strong labor unions. ''Without unions industrial democracy is unthinkable. Without democracy in industry . . . there is no such thing as democracy in America.'' In this plan there was no place for Woodrow Wilson's brand of progressivism, with its emphasis on trust-busting, individualism, limited government, and glorification of the small entrepreneur. Wilson's ''New Freedom'' was a nostalgic reversion to the nineteenth century, ''a freedom for the little profiteer, but no freedom for the nation from the narrowness, the poor incentives, the limited vision of small competitors.'' To Wilson's comment that every American aspired to be head of some ''small but hopeful business,'' Lippmann scornfully replied that the ''intelligent men of my generation can find a better outlet for their energies than in making themselves masters of small businesses.''[10]

Lippmann made a telling argument in scoring Wilson for trying to restore nineteenth-century competition to a world dominated by technology and mass markets. Yet Wilson's practice turned out to be more flexible than his preaching, and William Allen White was not amiss when he called the New Freedom and the New Nationalism about as different as Tweedledum and Tweedledee.

If Lippmann was weak on prescription and shaky on economic analysis, he had a sure feel for the modern sensibility. Other books have called for new policies to deal with the impact of industrialization. Croly's was one of them, Weyl's another. Most have been forgotten. What made Lippmann's book unique was the way he caught the poignancy of a world moving too fast for ordinary men. ''All of us are immigrants spiritually,'' he wrote in a celebrated passage.

We are all of us immigrants in the industrial world, and we have no authority to lean upon. We are an uprooted people, newly arrived, and *nouveau riche*. As a nation we have all the vulgarity that goes with that, all the scattering of soul. The modern man is not yet settled in his world. It is big. The evidence is everywhere: the amusements of the city; the jokes that pass for jokes; the blare that stands for beauty, the folklore of Broadway, the feeble and apologetic pulpits, the cruel standards of success, raucous purity. We make love to ragtime and we die to it. We are blown hither and thither like litter before the wind. Our days are lumps of experience.

The condition that Lippmann described, the tension between reason and emotion, was affecting his own life, taking him ever farther from his downtown friends. Although a part of him had responded to the passions and casual living arrangements of the radicals, he had never been one of them. From the beginning he had been a visitor in Bohemia. For a while he floated between the two worlds. But now that he had cast his lot with Croly and the Bull Moose Progressives, he was no longer interested in socialist polemics. He stopped going to Intercollegiate Socialist Society meetings and writing for radical journals. When Upton Sinclair urged him to get more actively involved in causes, he begged off. "A man has to make up his mind what his job is and stick to that," he explained. "At least I know that agitation isn't my job. . . . Each of us can do only a little, and he ought to try to do what he can do best."

It was a wonder that Sinclair was still speaking to him. A few years earlier Lippmann had written a devastating portrait of the socialist militant, describing even his best work, such as the muckraking study of the meat-packing industry, *The Jungle,* as being "products of his hate." Sinclair, he wrote, with that vitriolic pen Copey had noticed at Harvard, was "forever the dupe of his own sincerity, imagining that the intensity of his feeling is a substitute for a clear-eyed vision of fact." A man forever complaining of being misunderstood, "his self-pity amounts almost to a disease, distorting his sense of life, pandering to a fussy, trivial egotism, obliterating all humor, exalting the prig, and turning his artistic production into a monotonous whine."[11] No one could be more devastating than Lippmann when he let himself go. Later he would hold his pen in check; now he gave it free rein.

The radicals were beginning to annoy him, just as he was beginning to disappoint them. Few were more critical of Lippmann's lapse from radicalism than John Reed. Although the two men had never been close in college — Reed was too busy as song leader of the football team and thespian in the Hasty Pudding reviews to bother much with socialism — they had drawn close in New York when Reed moved to Greenwich Village, under Lincoln Steffens's watchful eye, to embrace bohemianism and the world revolution. As roving correspondent for *Metropolitan* magazine and coeditor of the *Masses* with Max Eastman, he rode with Pancho Villa's army against dictator Huerta's troops and reported the battle of Torreón. His articles, later put together in the book *Insurgent Mexico,* made him an overnight hero of the Left. This was the kind of writing Lippmann admired — raw, direct, passionate — even though it was a far cry from his own style. "It's kind of embarrassing to tell a fellow you know he's a genius," Lippmann wrote Reed when the Mexico pieces began appearing. "I can't begin to tell you how good the articles are . . . I want to hug you, Jack. If all history had been reported as you are doing this, Lord — I say that with Jack Reed reporting begins. Incidentally, of course, the stories are literature, but I didn't realize that till afterwards, they were so alive with Mexico and with you."[12]

But when Reed came back from Mexico he was distressed to find Lippmann working for a magazine financed by Wall Street and promoting the warmongering Roosevelt. Nor did he much like the patronizing remarks about radicals in *Drift and Mastery*. When they got together, Reed, hot-tempered and impolitic, told Lippmann he had no business being involved with "that crowd" and that he sometimes sounded as if he had gone over to the other side. Nettled, Lippmann responded with a biting, but perceptive, portrait of Reed for the *NR*, describing him as one who exemplified the *Masses* view of life.

He assumed that all capitalists were fat, bald and unctuous, that reformers were cowardly or scheming, that all newspapers are corrupt. . . . He made an effort to believe that the working class is not composed of miners, plumbers, and workingmen generally, but is a fine statuesque giant who stands on a high hill facing the sun. He wrote stories about the night court and plays about ladies in kimonos. He talked with intelligent tolerance about dynamite, and thought he saw an intimate connection between the cubists and the I.W.W. He even read a few pages of Bergson.

Reed, Lippmann explained, "did not judge, he identified himself with the struggle, and gradually what he saw mingled with what he hoped. Whenever his sympathies marched with the facts, Reed was superb. . . . But where his feelings conflicted with the facts, his vision flickered." Reed, he pointed out, had "no detachment and is proud of it. By temperament he is not a professional writer or reporter. He is a person who enjoys himself."

Lippmann hit the mark all too well. But his critique also revealed something about the critic: a person who did not identify himself with the struggle, who did judge, who valued detachment. Although Reed was understandably put off by Lippmann's condescension, his resentment soon blew over, and the two men remained friends for a time. But they were traveling in opposite directions: Reed toward a conviction that redemption lay in revolution; Lippmann toward reform and an attachment to men of influence and power. A few months later, in the spring of 1915, Lippmann severed his ties with the Socialist party, while Reed went off to Russia to report the war on the eastern front.[13]

Their short-lived friendship was more a matter of timing than of temperament. It would be hard to think of two people more dissimilar. Lippmann was calm, contemplative, hypersensitive, withdrawn, disliking personal confrontation, intellectually self-assured and mature while barely past his adolescence; Reed was impetuous, emotional, forever in search of challenge, chasing after adventure the way some men do after money, or women, or the perfect wave — the "playboy of the revolution," as Upton Sinclair called him.

In January 1915, nine months after his quarrel with Reed, Lippmann had an encounter with Isadora Duncan that confirmed all his doubts about the political frivolity of most radicals. The dancer, just back from

Russia with a bevy of little girls, had persuaded Mabel Dodge to help her find a public arena where she could perform. Having considered, then reluctantly rejected, the Harvard stadium and the Yale Bowl, the two women decided that one of New York's armories would be ideal. Mabel, for whom Lippmann always had a soft spot, induced him to use his influence on the city's young reform mayor, John Purroy Mitchel. A meeting was set up at Isadora's curtain-festooned loft, which she referred to as her Temple of Beauty and Art, and her friends, more simply as the Ark.

The mayor arrived shortly after lunch, with Lippmann and Alfred Kuttner on hand to moderate. "The Buddha-like curves of Walter's face had the heightened lights they took on when he was exhilarated and amused," Mabel recounted in her reconstruction of the incident. "His slightly exophthalmic eyes bulged and shone. He generally managed to wear his dark serges with a certain distinction and he did on this day. His clothes looked elegant and clear cut, but having the significance of another world than this one he was in."

The mayor, a tall, thin young man, gripped his hat nervously and seemed reluctant to enter the room. Isadora had expected someone more prepossessing, but recovering quickly, she swept forward with outstretched hands and invited Mitchel to join her on a narrow velvet settee. The mayor flushed and moved quickly to the nearest wooden chair. Visibly disappointed, Isadora began to pout. Instead of having the little girls dance, as she had promised, she began haranguing the mayor on the fate of a "poor woman" in jail for murdering her children. The ills of society could be cured, she assured him, if the family were abolished and free love allowed to reign. The mayor, his eyes growing wide, began to sweat. Suddenly he lurched from his seat, muttered something about an appointment, and fled to his waiting car and the safety of City Hall.

Lippmann gathered the faithful Kuttner in tow and slipped out of the Ark. "I'm utterly disgusted," he wrote Mabel from the library of the Harvard Club. "If this is Greece and Joy and the Aegean Isles and the Influence of Music, I don't want anything to do with it. It's a nasty, absurd mess." For him it was more than an embarrassing scene: it was a lesson. "I went into this because, like a damn fool, I deluded myself into thinking that we could have one spot of freedom and beauty," he told Mabel. "I should have known better. Those spots exist only in the imagination we weave about performers like Miss Duncan. I should have known better than to be dazzled into a short cut to perfection — there are none, and Isadora is not the person to show the way."[14]

Two years later he wrote an amusing account of the incident — Lippmann could be very funny when he let his imagination play — in which he described a "solemn afternoon at her studio when vision and reality almost touched hands,'' and where Mayor Mitchel ''was to be struck mad by a vision of beauty and that we were all to dance on Fifth Avenue.'' The object of his gibe, however, was not so much Isadora as the kind of ''archaic moralist . . . who tells men to be good, be true, be beautiful, and forgets to say how.'' It was those ''writers in the *Masses* who are fond of saying: that pile of stones would look better if it were on top of that mountain, and having indicated this desirable conclusion, go home to dinner.'' He had grown tired of the ''dilettante rebel, he who would rather dream ten dreams than realize one, he who so often mistakes a discussion in a café for an artistic movement, or a committee meeting for a social revolution.'' It was, he complained, ''a form of lazy thoughtlessness to suppose that something can be made of nothing, that the act of creation consists in breathing upon the void.''[15]

Working in a world of practical men and of compromises with the ideal, he had become repelled by what he called the ''eccentricity and the paradox, the malice and the wantonness of the iconoclast.'' Many radicals, he had charged in *Drift and Mastery,* seemed in rebellion not against an unjust system but ''against something within themselves,'' distraught by ''conflicts in their souls,'' their revolt an ''endless pursuit of what their own disharmony will never let them find.'' Whom could he have meant by the ''specialist in rebellion'' if not the anarchists with whom he had marched up Fifth Avenue, the playful revolutionaries at the *Masses,* the parlor socialists at Polly's restaurant, the ''movers and shakers'' who had gathered at Mabel Dodge's gilded apartment to denounce the bourgeoisie? These had been his friends, but he was drawing away from them. ''I find less and less sympathy with revolutionists,'' he had written in his diary in the summer of 1914, ''. . . and an increasing interest in administrative problems and constructive solutions.''

Lippmann was never a serious iconoclast, and soon outgrew his early rebelliousness. While he felt things deeply, he shunned open display of emotion. Easily bored, in discussion he often seemed emotionally detached and, if he found his listener uninteresting, condescending. This irritated some of the radicals. ''If you sometimes will go down to the Bowery and see the Booze victims,'' Hutchins Hapgood, who spent a good deal of his time searching for wisdom in unlikely places, wrote Mabel Dodge, ''you will see another way in which God manifests himself. God doesn't manifest himself *at all* in Walter Lippmann.'' But then Hapgood was annoyed because Lippmann considered him a sentimentalist and a bore.[16]

Yet what seemed coldness or a sense of superiority was really defensiveness — the hallmark of a certain kind of person, as Lippmann himself had suggested in another context. Woodrow Wilson's chilly exterior, he had written in a perceptive portrait of the President, was not due to insensibility, but rather ''to extreme sensitiveness, to a thin skin rather than a thick one." Wilson, he explained, "cannot 'let himself go,' not because he lacks feeling, but because he is not robust enough to withstand the strain of allowing himself to feel too deeply." Though such a man feels for human liberty and "real people," Lippmann continued, these feelings have been "transplanted into terms of the mind, they have become ideas, and it is to these ideas far more than to actual men and women that his emotions go out." Perceptive as an analysis of Wilson, the portrait was even more revealing of Lippmann himself. The sensitivity that made him vulnerable also provided the psychological insight that lent such richness to his writing.

In an essay on John Dewey, written in the summer of 1915, he speculated freely on Dewey's argument that philosophies should be made to fit each man's needs and purposes. Defending this approach as merely an expression of how people actually lived, he quoted Dewey's statement that "every living thought represents a gesture made toward the world, an attitude taken to some practical situation in which we are implicated." To this observation Lippmann made a more interesting comment of his own: "We may add that the gesture can represent a compensation for a bitter reality, an aspiration unfulfilled, a habit sanctified. In this sense philosophies are truly revealing. They are the very soul of the philosopher projected, and to the discerning critic they may tell more about him than he knows about himself. In this sense the man's philosophy is his autobiography; you may read in it the story of his conflict with life."

Nowhere is the story of Lippmann's "conflict with life" more apparent, for those willing to read between the lines, than in the essays he wrote during his first two years on the *New Republic* and in the monthly column he did for *Metropolitan* magazine for a year beginning in September 1914. There he was making his own "gesture to the world," alternately hopeful and pessimistic, practical and romantic. He mused over the carnage of war and the cheapness of life at home as well as on the battlefields. "Every city is full of women whose lives are gray with emptiness, who sit for hours looking out of the window, who rock their chairs and gossip, and long for the excitement that never comes," he wrote just before Christmas 1914. "Our cities are full of those caricatured homes, the close, curtained boarding houses to which people come from the day's drudgery to the evening's depression, the thousands of hall bedrooms in which hope dies and lives the ghost of itself in baseball scores and in movies, in the funny page and in Beatrice Fairfax, in purchased romance and in stunted reflections of the music-hall." This was Lippmann the moralist.[17]

Lippmann could be playful even when being serious. Deploring the dreamers who believed that earnest wishes could bring about utopia, he wrote: "One of the loveliest utopias I ever knew was of sunburnt philosophers playing with shells on a coral island written by a friend of mine living in Washington Square who wished he could spend the winter in Bermuda. It filled him with passionate revolt to think that Manhattan was not a coral island peopled with lithe, brown naked bodies of laughing philosophers. Well, it filled him with revolt, and left Manhattan otherwise unchanged.'' Utopia required work, he argued. Man was beginning to realize that ''he cannot live unless he lives against something, that hope is dull unless its edges are sharpened on fact . . . that we are so irretrievably beings who want and struggle that the only utopia we can endure is the process of making it.''

The modern utopia had to be built on ''a life of vision,'' he argued, ''not merely a life and a vision.'' Vision could be translated into fact only by dealing with the real world, by realizing that politics was not an affair ''set in spacious halls of white marble inhabited by dignified men in purple togas,'' but a struggle where idealism had to be tempered by realism. The difference between realists and idealists lay in the ''capacity for appreciating the immense gap of blue inane which separates earth from heaven, and in the realist's unwillingness to assume that men have angel wings.'' Lippmann never believed that men had angels' wings, but he thought they should at least try to fly. ''Let us recognize that the true use of philosophy is to help us to live,'' he wrote, ''and having recognized that, let us pour into it all that we know and can learn of what we ourselves are and what the world is like in which we move.''[18]

A careful and inventive stylist, he was able to break away from the stultified vocabulary that made most political writing ponderous and impenetrable. How was it possible, he asked one sultry week in August 1915 when he took over the ''Books and Things'' column from Philip Littell, ''to write or think about the modern world with a set of words which were inchoate lumps when Edmund Burke used them?'' Political writing, he complained, was ''asphyxiated by the staleness of its language.'' How could one write about politics with only ''a few polysyllables of Greek and Latin origin,'' how could one leave out Bryan and Hearst and Billy Sunday, or even Champ Clark? It was not the political writers but the novelists, he insisted, who could convey the ''curiosity and formlessness of modern life,'' who realized that ''the true speech of man is idiomatic, if not of the earth and sky, then at least of the saloon and the bleachers.''

He had a sure sense for that idiom. This is what made him so valuable an asset to the NR. Yet at times he tired of turning out columns of carefully reasoned copy week after week. ''Each of us, I suppose, experiences at some time the nausea of ideas,'' he noted offhandedly in a book review one week. ''The language of thought goes stale in us, the fabric of theories and impression seems overworn and musty.'' He fought against that nausea, as he fought against the caution that went with writing responsible advice for practical people:

That is what kills political writing, this absurd pretense that you are delivering a great utterance. You never do. You are just a puzzled man making notes about what you think. You are not building the Pantheon, then why act like a graven image? You are drawing sketches in the sand which the sea will wash away. What more is your book but your infinitesimal scratching, and who the devil are you to be grandiloquent and impersonal?

The truth is you're afraid to be wrong. And so you put on these airs and use these established phrases, knowing that they will sound familiar and will be respected. But this fear of being wrong is a disease. You cover and qualify and elucidate, you speak vaguely, you mumble because you are afraid of the sound of your own voice. And then you apologize for your timidity by frowning learnedly on anyone who honestly regards thought as an adventure, who strikes ahead and takes his chances.

You are like a man trying to be happy, like a man trying too hard to make a good mashie shot in golf. It can't be done by trying so hard to do it. Whatever truth you contribute to the world will be one lucky shot in a thousand misses. You cannot be right by holding your breath and taking precautions.

At twenty-five Lippmann was still feeling his way. He had not fully cast off his youthful iconoclasm or totally embraced the "practicality" of the lawyers and financiers around him. Skeptical of the radicals and the utopians, he had not yet made his final break. In his confusion about the war and his uncertainty about politics lay room for experimentation. "All but an infinitesimal portion of the stuff I have written rests on guesses and hopes, which in quiet moments I pray the gods will furnish some evidence and reason to justify," he wrote Justice Holmes late in 1915. "I don't love any idea sufficiently to worry ten minutes if some one compelled me to abandon it. But isn't it true that we cannot start life with all our convictions reasoned out? Would we ever start if we had to wait?"[19]

For a moment Lippmann could have gone either way: toward the romantic idealism that drew him to writers like H. G. Wells and infused his early essays, or toward a more abstract intellectualism. Events were crowding him. The sense of freedom, the joy in experimentation that marked his first few years out of college had given way to uncertainty. The outbreak of the war in Europe had shattered the easy optimism of a generation that believed life could be made anew and that man's potential for good was unlimited. The war, and the choices it entailed, had become inescapable.

◄ 8 ►

"Hypocritical Neutrality"

> Nothing is so bad for the soul as feeling that it is dis-
> pensed on nothing. . . . We are choked by feelings
> unexpressed and movements arrested in mid-air.
>
> — "Uneasy America," December 25, 1915

UNTIL August 1914 Lippmann had hardly given a thought to foreign affairs. He had, as he later said of himself, grown up believing that "money spent on battleships would be better spent on school-houses, and that war was an affair that 'militarists' talked about and not something that seriously-minded progressive democrats paid any attention to." When Graham Wallas warned him, as he was leaving Harvard in 1910, that a great war might soon break out and would smolder on for thirty years, he had "no notion that it would ever touch me or jeopardize interests of the country."[1]

The other editors at the *New Republic* were as ill-equipped as he to cope with the issues of the war. They thought of themselves as domestic reformers and the magazine as an instrument to "brighten the coinage of American opinion," in Croly's words. "We started out on the assumption that we were enlisted as loyal, though we hoped, critical members of the Progressive movement," Lippmann later wrote of himself and his colleagues. "We thought that Roosevelt would continue to lead it. We never dreamed that there would be a world war before our first issue was printed."[2]

Lippmann found himself writing about the war with a set of second-hand ideas. Initially he drew on what he had been taught: that war stemmed from colonialism and imperialism, that America must not become enmeshed in Europe's quarrels, that evil or stupid rulers led the people into war. Despite an effort to appear unbiased, his sympathies were with Britain and France, and for reasons that had little to do with the balance of power. His grandparents had come to America as liberals fleeing Prussian authoritarianism. He had literally learned a distaste for things Prussian at his grandfather's knee. Although he had traveled in Germany and admired Nietzsche and Goethe, his intellectual heroes were English: Ruskin and Swinburne, Shaw and Wells, Wallas and the Fabians. He could hardly be neutral in thought, even though he felt that the Allies might be as much to blame for the war as the Germans.

Periodically he and the *NR*'s other editors fulminated against the way the British fleet prevented Americans from trading with the Central Powers, and advised their readers not to become partisans of either side. But as Lippmann told Robert Dell, the *NR*'s Paris correspondent, "Our sympathies here are with the Allies, although we do not accept the British case at its face value, or hold the Allies entirely guiltless." Those sympathies were so obvious that after a strongly pro-Allies editorial in an early issue, the British government, working through one of its publishing agents, offered to buy fifty thousand copies a week for the duration of the war if the *NR* continued to take a similar line. The editors were shocked at being offered a bribe for saying what they so earnestly believed.[3]

President Wilson had declared that America must be neutral "in thought and in deed." But by respecting Britain's blockade of German ports, its seizure of cargoes bound for the Central Powers, its mining of the North Sea to prevent neutral trade, and its blacklisting of American firms doing business with Germany and Austria-Hungary, Wilson was clearly favoring the Allies. The German effort to break the blockade with the dreaded U-boats endangered this policy. In February 1915 Berlin announced that all ships entering the war zone around the British Isles would be sunk without warning. Pacifists in Congress moved to avoid incidents by preventing Americans from traveling on Allied ships. Wilson refused to accept this infringement of America's "neutral rights." On May 7, 1915, the British liner *Lusitania* was sunk by a German submarine, with the loss of 1,100 civilians, among them 128 Americans.

Shunning emotion, Lippmann pointed out to the *NR*'s readers that the *Lusitania* incident dramatized that the United States did not have the naval power to enforce its rights of neutrality. American trade was carried in British bottoms, Americans crossed the Atlantic on British ships, even the Monroe Doctrine depended on British sea power for enforcement. The United States had to either cooperate with Britain or build a fleet rivaling the Royal Navy. For Lippmann the choice was obvious: the *Lusitania*, having "united Englishmen and Americans in a common grief and a common indignation," might ultimately "unite them in a common war and conceivably a common destiny."

These were hardly the words of a neutral or a pacifist, but then Lippmann was neither. He and the other editors of the *NR* urged Americans to avoid entanglement in the European war. But in doing so they labored to distinguish between a supine "passivism" that abdicated American "responsibility," and their own brand of "aggressive pacifism," which involved "taking up arms against the malefactor" and forming a coalition of neutral nations. To play that role America would have to build up its military strength. "We may not be in the slightest danger of invasion," Lippmann explained early in 1915, "but if in an armed world we disarm, we shall count less and less in the councils of nations."[4]

While the *Lusitania* incident agitated the public, there was still little enthusiasm, at least beyond the Anglophile eastern seaboard, for entering the war. "The feeling against war in this country is a great deal deeper than you would imagine by reading editorials," Lippmann wrote the British socialist Alfred Zimmern. Part of that feeling was due to the horror of war, part to fear that American nationalism would be gravely strained by fighting a country to which so many German-Americans felt an attachment, and part to "general international irresponsibility and shallowness of feeling."

The equation of neutrality with "irresponsibility" was one that Lippmann was to make increasingly as the war dragged on. Even though he wanted the United States to assume its undefined international "responsibilities," he opposed the entry of America into the war as a full belligerent. Though most of the press was biased against Germany, he wrote Robert Dell, "we here and a great mass of the people besides want to avoid getting into the struggle, if it is at all possible. We have everything to lose and nothing to gain by taking part in it. It would only mean that the last great power was engulfed in the unreasonableness of it all, and that American lives, far from being safer, would be a great deal more in danger. . . . We have got to stay out if there is any way of doing so."[5]

In contrast to the pro-Allies press, the *New Republic* seemed almost a model of impartiality. For the first six months of the war it warned its readers against choosing sides, took a skeptical attitude toward tales of German atrocities in Belgium, and questioned the logic of all-out "preparedness" zealots like Theodore Roosevelt. Even after the sinking of the *Lusitania* and the magazine's drift toward what it called "differential neutrality" — that is, open sympathy for Britain and France — the editors stopped short of blaming Germany for the war. Eminent Anglophiles like Ralph Barton Perry accused them of being "pro-German," and even Santayana, living in Oxford, joined in. The attack was hardly fair, since the magazine had taken the Allies' side on nearly every crucial issue. In an editorial response to the *NR*'s critics, Lippmann reminded them that America had a higher obligation. "We should be standing against the uselessness of hate, against the insanity which proposes to atone for a crime by more crimes. Then we should be in a position to serve Europe. Then we should be able to contribute to the terms of peace."

His pose of neutrality pleased no one. "It seems that I commit all the outrages and Herbert [Croly] suffers all the trouble," Lippmann complained to Frankfurter. "The British ambassador thinks that because I took tea with him I ought not to have said that he lost his temper. George [Rublee] thinks that Herbert is pro-German. And I have had three letters in the past two days telling me that I am becoming a pro-British maniac."[6]

In his editorials for the *NR* Lippmann oscillated between an aversion to war and a feeling that America could not indefinitely sit on the sidelines. To get his own thoughts in order he decided to write a small book on foreign affairs. In June 1915 he once again gathered Kuttner in tow and rented a small house — this time in the village of Bellport on the south shore of Long Island. By the end of the summer — despite constant trips into the city to edit the *NR* — he had finished a sophisticated treatment of nationalism and imperialism. The book was both an analytical study and a reflection of the anxieties of a young man whose faith in human reason had been shaken. The striking self-assurance of Lippmann's first two books was replaced by a somber acknowledgment that things had gotten out of hand. "Like sheep in a shower we huddle about the leader," he wrote of the conformity induced by the war. "The old shibboleths are uttered without a blush, for all old things are congenial to us now . . . and though the assurance they offer is disheartening, it is assurance, and panic is in the air."

The Stakes of Diplomacy, as he called the book, combined an analysis of power rivalries and imperialism with a foray into the psychological aspects of nationalism. Lippmann maintained that the war had not been caused by the collapse of the power balance in Europe, but rather by the struggle for influence in the "backward" areas of the Balkans, China, and Africa. Nationalism, he argued, intensified competition by touching something elemental in human nature. "It is the primitive stuff of which we are made, our first loyalties, our first aggressions, the type and image of our souls. . . . They are our nationality, that essence of our being which defines us against the background of the world." Modern man values himself by the standing of his nation: if it is honored and admired he is proud, if it is defeated or despised he is humiliated and thirsts for revenge. "Just as strong men will weep because the second baseman fumbles at the crucial moment, so they will go into tantrums of rage because corporations of their own nationality are thwarted in a commercial ambition."

Lippmann's discussion showed a remarkable sensitivity to the emotional origins of nationalism. "What is called pride of race is the sense that our origins are worthy of respect," he wrote in words that touched chords of his own being.

. . . Man must be at peace with the sources of his life. If he is ashamed of them, if he is at war with them, they will haunt him forever. They will rob him of the basis of assurance, will leave him an interloper in the world.

When we speak of thwarted nationality like that of the Irish, the Jews, the Poles, the Negroes, we mean something more intimate than political subjection. We mean a kind of homelessness upon the planet, a homelessness which houses of brick can obscure but never remedy. We mean that the origins upon which strength feeds and from which loyalty rises — that the origins of these denationalized people have been hurt.

Later generations can find something strikingly contemporary in the study of nationalism Lippmann wrote in 1915, long before the rise to political consciousness of the Third World.

On a practical level Lippmann suggested that friction between imperial powers could be lessened by separating commercial interests from national ones. Corporations operating in the "backward" areas should be forced to work through international commissions rather than through their own governments, thus preventing them from unfurling the flag whenever they felt their privileges threatened. This plan for quarantining the underdeveloped areas anticipated the principle of the trusteeship system set up after the First World War to administer Germany's colonies.

The United States had to involve itself in the "stabilizing of mankind." Investing in backward countries would, he suggested, "give our diplomacy a leverage in events." This is precisely what Wall Street and enlightened financiers such as Willard Straight had been arguing. Like them, Lippmann was convinced that America had a great world role to fill. "We have all of us been educated to isolation, and we love the irresponsibility of it," he lamented. "But that isolation must be abandoned if we are to do anything effective for internationalism. . . . The supreme task of world politics is not the prevention of war," he added pointedly, "but a satisfactory organization of mankind."

When he came back to the office in the fall of 1915, after his productive sojourn in Bellport, he began in earnest trying to push Croly and Weyl away from "differential neutrality" and toward open help for the Allies. He got strong support from Norman Angell, the prominent British anti-imperialist, who had come to New York that spring under the sponsorship of the Carnegie Endowment for International Peace and had soon become an unofficial member of the *NR*'s editorial board. Under Angell's guidance the magazine promoted a "new kind of war." By this it meant economic assistance to the Allies in the service of a just peace without indemnities or territorial aggrandizements. In this way it could avoid aiding British imperialism, eliminate Prussian authoritarianism, and help bring about a better world.[7]

While the men at the NR did not yet think the United States should enter the war as a full belligerent, they were anxious about being left out of the settlement. They berated Wilson for his caution and yearned for a "great genius among statesmen" — an obvious allusion to Roosevelt. Even more than the others, Lippmann was getting nervous sitting on his hands. "Nothing is so bad for the soul as feeling that it is dispensed on nothing," he complained in the Christmas issue of 1915. "We Americans have been witnessing supreme drama, clenching our fists, talking, yet unable to fasten any reaction to realities. We have nothing to exercise our emotions upon, and we are choked by feelings unexpressed and movements arrested in mid-air."[8]

While many of the NR's readers were perfectly content to have the United States sit out Europe's war, others shared Lippmann's sense of being left out. "What you say is exactly right," Dwight Morrow, one of Straight's partners at J. P. Morgan, wrote him. "It will do much good." The Morgan firm, which served as Britain's banker and purchasing agent in the United States, had reason to feel tender toward the Allied cause. To those who objected to Britain's flagrant violation of America's right to trade with Germany, Lippmann argued that the question was not the legal one of neutral rights. Rather, American foreign policy would face a "crowning disaster" unless it were governed by "a vision of the Anglo-American future."[9] Here for the first time he laid down his thesis that the fate of America and that of Britain were inextricably linked — a theme he was to strike so many times in the decades that followed.

Wilson at last seemed to be moving in the same direction. In February 1916 the President gave his conditional approval to a secret agreement between his chief confidant, Colonel Edward M. House, and the British foreign secretary, Sir Edward Grey. The United States would offer to mediate a peace along lines acceptable to the Allies, and if the Germans refused, America would probably enter the war on the side of Britain and France. The "probably" offered Wilson a way out, but it was too big a hole for the Allies to accept, and nothing came of the venture.

While House was in London negotiating with Grey, Lippmann wrote Graham Wallas that anti-interventionist feeling in America was running high. "If Germany ever backed down completely on the submarine issue — disavowed the past and started no new entanglements — then the anti-British sentiment in Congress would become formidable." Nonetheless, he pointed out, Wilson and Secretary of State Robert Lansing were "unalterably opposed" to any embargo against Britain, "so you have nothing to fear except their irritability and tendency to say nasty things." One possible wedge for American involvement lay in public sentiment for protection of neutral nations like Belgium. For the United States to sign the peace treaty as a guarantor of Belgian independence, Lippmann wrote Wallas, would be a "very valuable experience in world responsibility, and an inspiring way of emerging from our isolation." It could also serve, he added, as the basis for a naval agreement with Britain that would be the "sine qua non of cooperation in the future."[10]

Support for the Allies got a new boost a few weeks later, in April 1916, when the Germans torpedoed the French paquebot *Sussex* in the Channel, causing the death of several Americans. Wilson threatened to break off relations with Germany unless it suspended unrestricted submarine warfare. Berlin reluctantly agreed to do so, unwilling for the moment to bring America into the war. Yet Wilson had tied his own hands. If the Germans went back on their pledge, he would be virtually obliged to break off relations. Lippmann, who was in Washington at the time of the *Sussex* incident, had talked with four members of the cabinet and complained to Wallas that "there wasn't one of them who had looked beyond the possibility of a rupture with Germany and had tried to think out policy in case things became still more acute. That's why we are so utterly discouraged about Wilson." What the *NR* now hoped to do, he confided, was "to invent some kind of coercive policy which would have an actual relation to the submarine issue."[11]

That very week Lippmann revealed what he had in mind. In an editorial dramatically entitled "An Appeal to the President," he explained how the United States could use its power for moral ends. "If we declare war, join the Allies, sign their pact, we shall have begun for the purpose of vindicating our right to travel at sea, but we shall end by fighting to change the political control of the Near East," he admitted. Yet simply to stand aside was unthinkable to the men at the *New Republic*. The answer lay in "differential neutrality" against Germany. "We no longer intend to be neutral between the violator and his victim," Lippmann proclaimed. The United States must be ready to use "its moral power, its economic resources, and in some cases its military power against the aggressor." It was time, he told the President, to "make this crisis count." That same month, April 1916, Lippmann told a gathering of academics and businessmen that America's own safety and the triumph of liberal principles throughout the world lay in the "unity and supremacy of sea power" in Anglo-American hands.[12]

But the moment was not yet ripe to dispense totally with what he had contemptuously labeled "hypocritical neutrality." Isolationist sentiment was still too powerful and public suspicion of Allied imperialism too great. A British Empire that kept India in bondage and had brutally repressed the Easter uprising in Ireland did not seem, to many Americans, worth preserving. "An arrangement with Tories and chauvinists and imperialists is unthinkable," Lippmann admitted. But there was an alternative. The neutrals could unite and impose a just peace. "Only the intervention of the neutral world can give power to the liberals in all countries and make a just peace desirable and durable."[13]

Lippmann's radical friends, having long ago decided that the war was basically an imperialist squabble, were distressed by his growing enthusiasm for intervention. John Reed, after fleeing the embraces of Mabel Dodge, discovering comradeship and revolution in Mexico, and going to Europe to report on the carnage, was convinced that, as he wrote in the *Masses,* "this is not our war." The fiery Reed was so disgusted by Lippmann's attacks on the pacifists and on American isolationism that in February 1916 he accused his friend of playing the game of Wall Street financiers and warmongers like Roosevelt. His language was harsh, his tone cruel. Lippmann, stung by Reed's accusation, struck back angrily.

"I do not suppose that I was entitled to expect any kind of patient fairness from you, even though I have tried to be patient and fair with you for a good many years," he wrote his former comrade-in-arms. "I continued to believe in you even though many times I have felt that you had acted like a fool or a cad. I would have supposed that the least you would have done after you had come to your weighty conclusion about me was to talk to me about it instead of writing me a hysterical letter." Declaring Reed to be "totally and ridiculously mistaken" about what he really believed, Lippmann gave him no quarter.

You are hardly the person to set yourself up as a judge of other people's radicalism. You may be able to create a reputation for yourself along that line with some people, but I have known you too long and I know too much about you. I watched you at college when a few of us were taking our chances. I saw you trying to climb into clubs and hang on to a position by your eyelids, and to tell you the truth, I have never taken your radicalism the least bit seriously. You are no more dangerous to the capitalist class in this country than a romantic guerrilla fighter. You will prick them at one point perhaps once in a while; but for any persistent attack — for anything which really matters, any changing fundamental conditions — it is not your line. You have developed an attitude which is amusing and dramatic. But do not get the idea that you are one of those great strong men whom the vested interests of this country fear.

"And I will make one little prophecy, which may sound to you like a boast," he added, giving one last twist to his rapier. "I got into this fight long before you knew it existed, and you will find that I am in it long after you quit."

Reed, delighted to have driven Lippmann to such fury, framed the letter on his wall. For a few weeks the two friends studiously ignored each other. Then Lippmann extended the olive branch. "You and I haven't any business quarreling," he wrote Reed. "You wrote hastily and hurt me. I answered hastily and hurt you. But it's all damned foolishness. Let's have lunch together some day this week."[14] A few months later, when Reed was hospitalized in Baltimore for a kidney operation, Lippmann went to visit him, taking along the tempestuous Louise Bryant — then Reed's fiancée, later Eugene O'Neill's mistress, and ultimately William Bullitt's wife.

But the reconciliation was only temporary. By early 1916 Lippmann had made his break with his old radical friends. He had never been fully comfortable with them. Their passions had always seemed excessive, their politics self-promoting, their living habits unduly messy. He was more at home among the "realistic" liberals at the NR, among progressives like Judge Hand and skeptics like Justice Holmes, among forward-looking financiers like Willard Straight and Dwight Morrow, among those who saw the war as an opportunity to assert America's international "responsibilities."

His rejection of political radicalism spilled over into the arts, where he now saw artistic experimentation tinged with self-indulgence. "Painters, poets, novelists are happiest when they live in a moral tradition," he charged in a rambling attack on the modernists in the spring of 1916, shortly after his quarrel with Reed. If art was made to "increase life," then clearly "art cannot do its work if it remains incommunicable." The artist should respond to "moral conflicts" in direct ways that the layman could understand. Artists had turned away from "significant themes" because the themes were too hard to grasp, he contended. "They have transformed an evasion, a necessary and perhaps inevitable evasion, into a virtue." Lippmann was not so much a social realist or a philistine as he sounded. When he complained about those who considered themselves to be modernists "by taking a beam or two from Bergson, a wheel from Freud, some gearing from William James and the discards of alchemists, Hegelians and mental healers," he was complaining about those who refused to be practical and to come to terms, as he did, with the compromises of the real world.[15]

Lippmann was impatient with the radicals and scornful of the pacifists. When in the spring of 1916 Wilson finally endorsed American participation in the League to Enforce Peace — a forerunner of the League of Nations — Lippmann described the event as a "decisive turning point in the history of the modern world. . . . There is," he told the readers of the NR, "something intensely inspiring to Americans in the thought that when they surrender their isolation they do it not to engage in diplomatic intrigue but to internationalize world politics." To Senator Henry Hollis, who he knew would relay his words to Wilson, he declared that the President's endorsement of the peace league was "one of the greatest utterances since the Monroe Doctrine . . . easily the most important diplomatic event that our generation has known."[16]

While in the *NR* he argued that American support for the league would purify world politics, to his friends he confided that it would help bring America into the war. "You know that I have not too much faith in the whole of it," he wrote British diplomat Eustace Percy regarding the peace league "arrangement," but it offered the "only one in which average American opinion could be induced to break with a tradition of isolation." Admitting that the *NR*'s "preaching of Anglo-American agreement can reach only a minority," he predicted that the public would eventually accept the league, and that its core would be an alliance of British, French and American sea power. Here Lippmann echoed the geopolitics of Admiral Alfred Thayer Mahan, the apostle of sea power and of Atlantic unity, and whose views had so influenced *The Stakes of Diplomacy*. But even the promise of the league was not enough to overcome American neutrality. Participation, Lippmann told Wallas in August 1916, depended on three things: "a just and moderate peace . . . the control of England by liberal-minded people . . . the re-election of President Wilson."[17]

Lippmann's conversion to the reelection of Woodrow Wilson had come slowly and with a good deal of soul-searching. Ever since the previous fall he had been trying to decide whether he could support Roosevelt in a return bid for the presidency. "It's the most difficult political decision I ever had to make," he wrote Wallas. "Wilson is impossible. He has no sense of organization and no interest in the responsibilities of the socialized state. He has no grasp of international affairs, and his pacifism is of precious little help to the peace of the world." But the Republican party without Roosevelt meant "capitalism unashamed." The Progressives had disintegrated as a political force, and the Socialists had become "purely negative and orthodox." "Roosevelt alone of men who are possible has any vision of an integrated community," Lippmann told Wallas. "He is always better in action than in his talk. He is the only President in fifty years who gave social invention an impetus. And I am not sure but he is a more realistic pacifist than most. His talk has often been sickening," he admitted, "but we think we know him well enough to understand that in the opposition he spends his energy in violent utterance, whereas in power that energy goes more largely into constructive effort." It was "the Devil's Own Choice," but the magazine could not much longer defer taking a position.

A few weeks later Lippmann went to the Middle West to talk to Progressive leaders. "The most important thing I did was to think over the question of TR," he wrote Frankfurter shortly after his return in January 1916. "I had long talks with all sorts of people out there, ranging from Miss Addams to the Roosevelt-at-any-price people, and I am pretty well convinced that T.R. will not do. . . . The kind of people who are turning out to support him are a crowd that I do not want to see in power in the United States. . . . After all, you and I have been banking on a theoretical Roosevelt, a potential Roosevelt, but not a Roosevelt who at this moment is actually at work." To Eustace Percy he complained: "TR gets on my nerves so much these days that I shall become a typical anti-Roosevelt maniac if I do not look out."[18]

Lippmann was feeling leaderless and a bit bereft. In a rambling essay he took out his dissatisfaction, not on TR, but on the public — on the "vices of the American character, its trust in the magic of words, its collective irresponsibility, its shirking of facts and the harder realities of life." The nation needed a sense of purpose, he complained. TR's prescription was military service for all able-bodied males. But Lippmann had a different answer to what he called the "general slouchiness of distraction of the public morale." He would nationalize the railroads and set up a national system of health, accident, maternity, old age and employment insurance to achieve a truly "integrated America." What he had done, of course, was simply to fall back on the old Progressive formula of using economic means to transform culture — exactly what he had argued in *Drift and Mastery*. But it was a weak reed to lean on, as he himself realized. By the end of the article he was calling for a national "vision" and suggesting that only TR had the capacity to grasp it. "That is why he survives every defeat. . . . That is why we cannot stop talking about him," Lippmann wrote with mingled admiration and exasperation. "He is forever tantalizing us with the hope that we have in him a leader equal to our needs."[19]

Even Lippmann's patience, however, wore thin when TR began courting Republican conservatives like Elihu Root and accused Wilson of cowardice for not having protested Germany's invasion of Belgium a year and a half earlier. This was a bit much, since the great Bull Moose had not himself uttered a word of protest when the invasion occurred. Lippmann decided that TR had hit below the belt. But he also felt somewhat sheepish about the part he himself had played at the time. In the fall of 1914 Lippmann had scored Wilson for "timidity" in the face of the German invasion, and bumptiously declared that had TR been in the White House "ruthlessness would have received the severest jolt it ever imagined." Now it was time to eat a little crow. The *New Republic* publicly apologized to Wilson for having used the Belgian issue against him.[20]

Although Lippmann had decided that TR "will not do," Willard Straight was still loyal and Croly on the fence. Lippmann decided to push them. In April, while Straight was in Europe and Croly in New Hampshire, he wrote a barbed editorial berating Roosevelt for cuddling up to the GOP conservatives, and accused him of being "an extremely impressionable man altogether too likely to take his color from the people he is most intimately associated with." If the progressives were serious about TR, Lippmann advised, they would have to wrest him from the conservatives and "fight for the possession of his soul."

Croly was distressed when he read the editorial printed in his absence. "We are making an impression of unfriendliness. We use fair words and then apply the whip," he wrote Lippmann, reminding him that Straight had been promised before going to Europe that "whatever else we did we would not nag Roosevelt. We have not done that, but in his state of mind he will think we have done it." Straight did indeed think they were nagging TR, and sent a sharp cable of complaint. An explanation was in order.

"You know that I started out with an immense prejudice in his favor," Lippmann replied to the *NR*'s publisher. "From the very first we have leaned over backwards in his favor, and if my conscience troubled me about our attitude towards him, it would be that we have not been as candid about Roosevelt as we have been about Wilson." The classic example, he continued, was the Belgium issue, where the *NR* had made such a gaffe. Having complained ever since November 1914 that TR would have acted differently from Wilson, "it was clearly our duty to eat our words and if possible make Roosevelt eat his." There were "few things in Roosevelt's career that have shocked me as much as this revelation of how his mind works." Roosevelt was "not one man but many men." The role of the *NR*, Lippmann advised, was not to back Roosevelt all the way, but to nudge him where they thought he should go: "If he talks on foreign policy, we are going to have to push him towards the Anglo-American alliance and show that the logic of his position drives him in that direction."[21]

While ostensibly still a "friend" of Roosevelt, Lippmann was setting out his lines to the Wilson administration. Since the fall of 1915 he had been traveling regularly to the capital to gather material for his *NR* column, "Washington Notes." Through Croly and Straight he had met a good many important government people, including Wilson's political adviser and alter ego, Colonel Edward House. These men were quite aware of the *New Republic*'s influence on Progressives. And he was intent on making the most of that awareness.

"The paper is beginning to count here, more than we hoped," Lippmann had told Wallas. "It has some influence in Washington, and a very good deal among the younger intelligentsia." Relations with the President had become "very cordial." Wilson "really is a very considerable man, and so is Colonel House," Lippmann reported. "They both have imagination and the courage of it, which is a good deal at this time." Extending his highest praise, he described Wilson's as the ·

"most freely speculative mind we've had in Washington, and as disinterested as a man could wish. If only so many people didn't make it their chief business to distort his phrases."[22]

Having become disenchanted with TR, Lippmann had glimpsed another leader worthy of his admiration.

◄ 9 ►

Electing a War President

What we're electing is a war President — not the man
who kept us out of war.

— To Herbert Croly, September 1916

LIPPMANN'S move into Wilson's camp was greatly eased by the President's decision to embrace such Progressive legislation as farm credits, a child labor law, and an eight-hour day for railroad workers. Wilson knew he needed the Progressive vote to win in 1916 and he was willing to bid high for it. In a gesture particularly pleasing to the men at the *NR* he nominated their friend George Rublee to the Federal Trade Commission and the controversial Boston lawyer Louis D. Brandeis to the Supreme Court.

The decision to appoint Brandeis, notorious for his attacks on big business and his support of organized labor, shocked conventional opinion. The fact that he was also a Jew, the first to be nominated to the high Court, did not help his chances. Former President William Howard Taft, convinced that the Court seat should be his, led the attack from his perch at Yale Law School. Harvard president A. Lawrence Lowell sent the White House an anti-Brandeis petition signed by fifty-one prominent Bostonians. The *New York Times* spoke for its conservative readers in dismissing Brandeis as "essentially a contender, a striver after changes and reforms." Support for the controversial Bostonian was restricted mostly to populist papers in the West and a few liberal magazines.

Although the men at the *NR* had often criticized Brandeis's antitrust stand as sentimental Jeffersonianism — preferring instead to control big business through government agencies — they could not let the conservative attack go unchallenged. "*The New Republic* must get into the Brandeis fight with its heaviest guns," Lippmann wrote Frankfurter. He also approached Brandeis directly, assuring him that "all of us here look upon the fight as the most important one now taking place in

Washington," and pointing out that "the thing at stake is much greater than our personal affection for you." [1]

Lippmann plunged into the Brandeis fight as though it were a crusade. He wrote impassioned editorials denouncing the Brahmins and reactionaries who feared Brandeis, spent weeks in Washington trying to convert congressmen, and conspired with his *NR* colleagues — especially Frankfurter, who provided the legal arguments — to get the nomination through the Senate. Conservatives distrusted Brandeis, Lippmann charged during the confirmation fight in the winter and spring of 1916, because he was a "rebellious and troublesome member of the most homogenous, self-centered and self-complacent community in the United States." To Boston Brahmins the lawyer was anathema because "an attack made by him seemed to come from an enemy within the gates." [2]

Although grateful for the *NR*'s crusade on his behalf, Brandeis took a sublimely detached approach to the confirmation battle. He "treated the whole fight as if it were happening on the planet Mars," Lippmann reported incredulously to Frankfurter. "I had to rub my eyes every once in a while to remind myself that the whole row was about him." [3] Finally, after months of argument and Senate hearings, the issue came to a vote in June 1916. Wilson, with the support of liberals, won his fight. The Senate confirmed Brandeis, bringing to the Supreme Court its first Jew, and paving the way for Felix Frankfurter himself twenty-three years later.

The confirmation fight, combined with the approaching presidential elections, gave Lippmann his long-sought opportunity for a private interview with Wilson — one set up by the *NR*'s contact man, George Rublee. Lippmann prepared a sheaf of questions, intending to use the meeting profitably. Wilson never gave him a chance. "So you've come to look me over," the President said, rising from his desk to greet the young journalist who had been ushered into the Oval Office. Rather than letting his visitor ask questions, Wilson seized the initiative. "Let me show you the inside of my mind," he suggested, as he launched into a dazzling monologue covering virtually every major issue, from the Mexican imbroglio to German designs on Brazil, from TR's ambitions to dilemmas of neutrality.

Lippmann, who had had considerable experience with politicians, had gone to the White House a skeptic. He emerged from his interview with Wilson a virtual convert. The change had been as sweeping as it was abrupt. Only a year earlier Lippmann had written a devastating portrait of Wilson as a man too self-righteous for this world, "one of those people who shuffle off their mortal coil as soon as they take pen in hand." Wilson's rhetoric, he had charged, was "always cleaner, more sterilized, than life itself'' — and a good deal too noble. "When you have purged and bleached your morality into a collection of abstract nouns, you have something which is clean and white, but what else have you?'' he asked.[4]

But after his interview he felt there was a good deal else. By the time he went to Chicago in June 1916 to cover the Republican convention, Lippmann had decided that Wilson, "bleached morality'' notwithstanding, might be the best choice. Nothing happened at Chicago to make him change his mind. Roosevelt did not have a chance. The Old Guard took its revenge on the man who had bolted the party in 1912. Contemptuously ignoring TR, the party bosses gave the nomination to Charles Evans Hughes, a Supreme Court justice and former governor of New York. "The sense of brute power was overwhelming, like that of a great monster with little brain which plodded forward and could not be stopped,'' Lippmann wrote of the way the Old Guard had crushed TR.

Everything about the convention appalled him. It was, he reported from Chicago, chaotic, banal and sordid, "the quintessence of all that is commonplace, machine-made, complacent and arbitrary in American life. To look at it and think of what needs to be done to civilize this nation was to be chilled with despair.'' Some would have been amused by the spectacle; he was filled with disgust — at the party bosses, at the people for whom this charade was being played, at a travesty of democracy that he considered an affront to a serious man's intelligence. "I shall not soon forget the nine and a half hours I sat wedged in, listening to the nominating speeches and subsisting on apple pie and loganberry juice — hours of bellow and rant punctuated by screeches and roars,'' he wrote in a spleen-filled passage.

I think there were fifteen nominations plus the seconding orations. It was a nightmare, a witches' dance of idiocy and adult hypocrisy. DuPont, for instance, and his wonderful grandfather, and the grand old state of Ohio, and the golden state of Iowa, and the flag, red, white and blue, all its stripes, all its stars, and the flag again a thousand times over, and Americanism till your ears ached, and the slaves and the tariff, and Abraham Lincoln, mauled and dragged about and his name taken in vain and his spirit degraded, prostituted to every insincerity and used as window-dressing for every cheap politician. The incredible sordidness of that convention passes all description. It was a gathering of insanitary callous men who blasphemed patriotism, made a mockery of Republican government and filled the air with sodden and scheming stupidity.

After the Old Guard handed its crown to Hughes, the once-proud Bull Moose Progressives slunk off to a nether part of Chicago to hold their own convention and beseeched Roosevelt to be their standard-bearer. But TR had had enough. Rejecting those who in 1912 had followed him to Armageddon, he suggested with studied contempt that they give their nomination to the conservative Henry Cabot Lodge. In a dying gesture they struck back by nominating him anyway. Thus did the Bull Moose party lumber to oblivion. A few shed tears. Lippmann was not among them. He had only disdain for the faithful who had followed TR to this final resting place. "They clung to him as a woman without occupation or external interests will cling to her husband," he wrote pitilessly. "They clung so hard that they embarrassed him with their infatuation. They loved too much. They loved without self-respect and without privacy. They adored him as no man in a democracy deserves to be adored." [5]

Lippmann had stopped loving. No longer could he reconcile the opportunist who consorted with Republican conservatives and rattled sabers over Mexico and Germany with the knight-errant to whom he had given his heart at Madison Square Garden and at Oyster Bay. His friends within the Progressive party still clung to the Roosevelt ideal and were uncertain of which way to turn, but Lippmann had made his decision. The Bull Moose carcass would have to be buried. "I do not a bit agree with you about TR," he wrote Frankfurter shortly after the convention. "Your attempt to read into his words all the glowing aspirations of your heart simply will not work. He does not understand industrial preparedness; he does not know what he means by social justice. He has no vision of the class struggle and you cannot jolly him into an understanding." [6]

Lippmann may have made his decision, but the other editors at the *New Republic* were in disarray over the events at Chicago, and Croly was inclined to stick with the Republicans. Hughes was a progressive, after all, and the GOP seemed more likely than the Democrats to use government as an instrument of social reform. But Lippmann was determined to bring Croly around, and worked on him all through the summer. The important thing to remember, he insisted, was that Hughes would probably be dominated by the party's Old Guard. The return of the Republicans to power would mean a return to the "most evil-smelling plutocracy that this country has," he wrote the *NR*'s London correspondent, S. K. Ratcliffe. Even though Hughes was able and respected, the Old Guard ran the Republican party. "There is this much to be said for Wilson," Lippmann explained: "that he has learned a lot, has admitted most of his errors, and has begun to surround himself with a new and rather more hopeful crowd of men." [7] "I do not think it is possible to overstate the irrelevance of this election to the issues in Europe," Lippmann reported to his London friend Eustace Percy. Both parties intended to be neutral, neither intended to fight Britain's blockade of German ports, and the voters saw no great contest over issues — only politicians on the outside wanting to get in.

The prevailing tone of the Hughes supporters is protectionist. Protectionist as regards tariff, as regards large industry, and as regards military affairs. The ideal they preach is that of a self-sufficing, rather aggressive, and somewhat bad-tempered nationalism. Their impulse is to defy everybody, and politically this works out as a defiance of the Allies.

You will understand how this comes about. If you preach absolute independence and sovereignty and destiny hard enough, you are bound sooner or later to align yourself against British sea power and against the internationalizing tendencies of the Entente. I think if the thing had to be phrased, you might say: the Democrats consist of people who are by tradition isolated, led by a group which in a somewhat naive way hopes to join a European cooperative arrangement; whereas the Republicans consist of people who on the whole believe in aggressive isolation and lean heavily towards imperial expansion in Latin America and the Pacific.[8]

Although Lippmann expected Wilson to pick up support as the campaign moved along, he realized the fight would be a close one. Hughes, despite a bad platform technique, was a formidable opponent, and Wilson needed the support of the Republican progressives who had voted for Roosevelt in 1912. The *New Republic* spoke for those progressives, and thus the *NR* had to be won over.

Norman Hapgood, magazine editor and the man Wilson counted on to win the Bull Moose vote, advised the President that "Lippmann is the ablest of *The New Republic* editors, and the one who is working to swing the paper openly to you." Wilson followed through by inviting Lippmann to spend an afternoon in late August at his summer home, Shadow Lawn, in New Jersey. For nearly two hours the President outlined to his young guest his commitment to social reform at home and a "benevolent neutrality" toward the Allies. "I remember sitting on the upstairs veranda with Wilson and talking about the campaign," Lippmann later recalled. "We were beginning to get ready to support him, and I was asking questions to reassure ourselves on various issues — mostly domestic." Then the discussion turned to the war. Wilson knew what Lippmann wanted to hear. Neutrality, "benevolent" or otherwise, Wilson said, was becoming more difficult. "Let me show you what I mean," he added, and dramatically pulled out a cable from the embassy in Berlin predicting that the Germans would resume unrestricted submarine warfare after the American elections in November. "It's a terrible thing to carry around with me." The implication was clear. When the Germans sank the *Sussex* five months earlier Wilson had said that he would break relations if they resumed unrestricted submarine warfare. Now he had to either back down or go to war. He showed no indication of backing down.

Lippmann hurried back to New York to meet with Croly and Straight.

"Now we'll have to face it," Lippmann told them. "What we're electing is a war President — not the man who kept us out of war. And we've got to make up our minds whether we want to go through the war with Hughes or with Wilson." For his own part Lippmann had no doubts. "I have come around completely to Wilson," he wrote Wallas. The Republicans were "disorganized, inarticulate, commercially imperialist and conventional-minded"; only Wilson had the "imagination and the will to make a radical move in the organization of peace." Hughes had proved to be a "great disappointment," and because of his opposition to intervention, was "far worse than Wilson at his worst." Wilson had over the past few months "developed a power of decision unlike anything he has shown before. . . . It would be a sheer calamity to throw him out."⁹

Above all, Wilson was willing to cast aside "hypocritical neutrality" and take an active involvement in European politics, even if it meant entering the war. "Barring catastrophe, I'm for him, though he's no saint, by God," Lippmann told Learned Hand. "Hughes is incredible, and I don't see how any good, unneutral pro-Ally can vote for him without hating himself. Wilson's brand of neutrality . . . is about 90 percent better than we had reason to expect." To his British friends he was even more explicit. "Wilson is frankly unneutral in his purposes," he assured H. G. Wells. "He will resist any pressure to break your illegal blockade of Germany, while Hughes goes up and down the country declaring for an impartial neutrality in the orthodox pro-German sense. He promises to uphold our 'rights' against you, and he's just pigheaded enough to try it."¹⁰

At first Croly resisted, but gradually he gave way under Lippmann's pressure and the ineptitude of Hughes's campaign. "It was a great struggle," Lippmann later explained. "Croly didn't want to do it. Straight didn't want to do it. I did. Finally, by September I persuaded them that Hughes was taking a pro-German line with a feeling toward the pro-German vote, and that Wilson was the man for us." In mid-October, six weeks after the visit to Shadow Lawn, Lippmann was at last able to make it official. "I shall not vote for the Wilson who has uttered a few too many noble sentiments," he told puzzled readers who for two years had been regaled with the *NR*'s accounts of Wilson's incompetence, "but for the Wilson who is evolving under experience and is remaking his philosophy in the light of it." Wilson had grown from a laissez-faire Democrat into a "constructive nationalist," and transformed the Democrats into the only party "national in scope, liberal in purpose, and effective in action." Wilson was not at all neutral, he maintained, but "consistently and courageously benevolent to the Allies"; he understood that the "cause of the western Allies is in a measure our cause."

By early fall virtually the entire contingent of Bull Moose Progressives had swung behind Wilson, including John Dewey, Jane Addams, Amos Pinchot, Frederick C. Howe, Lincoln Steffens and William English Walling. Pacifists like Randolph Bourne and anti-British Irishmen like the *NR*'s Francis Hackett came out for the President. Even Max Eastman and John Reed swallowed their socialist scruples and voted for him. Their reasons were as varied as their politics. For Lippmann and Croly, Wilson was the man who would end America's "pernicious neutrality." For Bourne and the socialists at the *Masses*, he would resist the warmongers. Each saw in Wilson what he wanted to see. But for Lippmann, Wilson's purposes were clear. "We never believed Wilson when he said he would keep us out of war," he later said. "We were convinced we were going to get into the war." [11]

Not only did Lippmann help swing the *NR* behind Wilson, he wrote speeches for the President and even delivered campaign talks in upstate New York from the back of a trailer truck. Reiterating his promise to pursue domestic reform, the President squeezed by with a margin of twenty-three electoral votes. The support of the Progressives had been crucial. Wilson remembered who had helped swing the Progressives behind him. Hardly had the ballot boxes been put away when Lippmann received an engraved invitation in the mail:

The President and Mrs. Wilson
request the pleasure of the company of
Mr. Lippmann
at dinner on Tuesday evening
December the twelfth at eight o'clock
1916

Arriving early at Pennsylvania Station, Lippmann waited patiently at the gate where the Washington train was scheduled to depart. Soon his traveling companion arrived, a slight, well-dressed man in black overcoat and homburg, a briefcase in his hand and a look of bemused detachment on his face. Lippmann hailed the older man and greeted him warmly. They immediately fell into animated conversation as they made their way to a private drawing room for the trip to Washington and the President's gala dinner.

Edward Mandell House — Colonel House, as he preferred to be known by his honorary Texas title — although not a cabinet official, judge or congressman, was among the most influential men in the nation. A Western progressive who had engineered the successful gubernatorial campaign of the Texas reformer James Hogg, he had expanded his talents to a national stage. In 1912 he helped Wilson capture the

Democratic nomination by winning over the die-hard followers of William Jennings Bryan. House offered his services to Wilson, who desperately needed a go-between adept at political bargaining, and gave a progressive tone to the first Wilson administration. House, like many good progressives, wanted government *for* the people, but was rather dubious about government *by* the people. The best form of government, he indicated in his anonymous novel *Philip Dru, Administrator,* was one where a benevolent autocrat ruled in the people's best interest.

Wilson could hardly have survived without House, and soon became dependent on the ingratiating, English-educated Texan who was so expert in dealing with politicians. A tight bond linked the two men. House became Wilson's most trusted adviser, his ambassador to the lower world of politics. "He was able to serve Wilson because he was in almost every respect the complement of Wilson," Lippmann later wrote.

The things which Colonel House did best, meeting men face to face and listening to them patiently and persuading them gradually, Woodrow Wilson could hardly bear to do at all. The President was an intellectual, accustomed to acquiring knowledge by reading and to imparting it by lecturing and by writing books. Wilson was annoyed, quickly bored, and soon exhausted by the incoherence, the verbosity, and the fumbling of most talk, especially the talk of practical men of affairs. . . . Colonel House, on the contrary, was as nearly proof against boredom as anyone imaginable. Lacking all intellectual pride, having no such intellectual cultivation as Woodrow Wilson, he educated himself in the problems of the day by inducing men of affairs to confide in him.[12]

As part of his effort to mediate the European conflict, Wilson had, in the fall of 1916, instructed House and Secretary of State Lansing to draw up a peace plan. They had hardly begun when the Germans made a stunning proposal to the Allies to discuss a compromise peace. The offer reached Washington on the very night of Wilson's gala reelection dinner, December 12, and left the President's embryonic peace initiative in a shambles. At the White House that night Lippmann moved deftly among the congressmen, diplomats and cabinet officials. Then he went over to the President and posed the question directly: would the United States support the German peace bid? Wilson looked pained. The Allies would undoubtedly reject Berlin's offer, he replied, for a negotiated peace would leave Germany the dominant power on the Continent. Berlin would then resume unrestricted submarine warfare. America could not stand by. "If they don't let me mediate, we'll be drawn into the war," he said mournfully. "We've got to stop it before we're pulled in."

Excited by the rush of events, Lippmann returned to New York to confer with his colleagues at the *NR*. "I went to Washington, attended and enjoyed a State Dinner at the White House, and was sucked deep into the excitement over Germany's master stroke,'' he reported to Mabel Dodge. ''It really is the most brilliant political coup imaginable, and whether it brings actual peace or more war, Germany is certain to gain. What it really amounts to, I think, is a deep and successful thrust into the morale of the Allies, plus a new spiritual unification of Germany.''

The *New Republic* faced an editorial crisis. Should it endorse or reject the German peace bid? Lippmann insisted that the German offer was simply a ploy to consolidate territorial gains on the eastern front. If accepted, it would amount to a "peace without victory" that would humiliate the democracies and leave Prussian militarists in control of Central Europe. Finally persuading Croly and the others that Berlin's offer had to be turned down, Lippmann laid out his argument in the lead editorial. Its title, "Peace without Victory," was splashed across the cover of the magazine.[13]

No reader of the *NR* that Christmas week of 1916 was more attentive than the President himself. Outmaneuvered by the Germans and hamstrung by the refusal of the Allies to attend a peace conference under his mediation, he felt that he had no alternative but to push ahead with his own plan. A few weeks later, at the end of January 1917, he went before the Senate and declared that the war must be brought to a negotiated end, that the only solution was a compromise peace, a "peace without victory."

The press immediately picked up the phrase and linked it to the *NR* editorial — even though Wilson had used it in a very different way. The assumption was that Lippmann had inspired the speech, and had even had a hand in Wilson's abortive December peace offer. The supposed link between the White House and the *NR* — strengthened by the fact that Croly and Lippmann were known to visit Colonel House every week at his New York apartment — did nothing to harm the *NR*'s reputation as the insider's journal. Readers eagerly snapped up each issue in the belief that they were getting a preview of administration policy. Speculators bribed news dealers for advance copies to find clues for playing the stock market. Circulation shot up to over twenty thousand. The claim that Lippmann was the author of the President's ill-fated December peace plan, though untrue, inflated his reputation even further. C. P. Scott, editor of the *Manchester Guardian,* asked him to contribute to the paper, observing that it was "quite recognized here that you are in intimate connection with the President, and anything which you may send is pretty certain to receive the attention of the Cabinet.''

When he wrote of these events years later, Lippmann claimed it was all exaggerated — that House never told them anything the President was going to do and never asked him and Croly to publish or not publish anything. ''In our own minds we followed the logic of the situation as we saw it," he explained. "Partly by coincidence, partly by a certain parallelism of reasoning, certainly by no direct inspiration either from the President or Colonel House, *The New Republic* often advocated policies which Wilson pursued." While this is probably the way Lippmann saw it and particularly the way he remembered it, others had some reason to assume that more than a "certain parallelism of reasoning" accounted for the *NR*'s privileged position.[14]

By the end of 1916 Lippmann had become House's partner in the effort to persuade Wilson, and the nation, that the United States must come into the war on the side of the Allies. America had a great role to perform, Lippmann told the *NR*'s readers in January 1917: it would be "something to boast of that we have lived in a time when the world called us into partnership." He did not have long to wait. When the Allies turned down Berlin's peace bid, the Germans resumed unrestricted submarine warfare. They hoped, by cutting off Britain's supply of food and arms, to squeeze the country quickly into submission before American troop strength could be felt on the western front. Germany's announcement came as the *New Republic* was going to press. In a hurried postscript to the February 3 issue, Lippmann called for an immediate break in diplomatic relations, the seizure of German ships in American ports, mobilization, and full assistance to the Allies. The United States, he elaborated a week later, must join Britain and France — even though they too had violated the law of the sea — because "they were fighting in the main for the kind of world in which we wished to live."[15]

His call to battle was clear enough. But although Wilson broke diplomatic relations the first week in February, he delayed calling for a declaration of war, and the Germans did not provide him with a convenient pretext. "When the break came the administration absolutely expected a sensational outrage within a few days and had set its mind in preparation for war on the strength of it," Lippmann explained to Frankfurter in late February 1917. Wilson "could have carried the country with him had the facts gone as he supposed they would go. The failure of the facts to act up to expectation has put him in a hole; whereas if he acts aggressively and seems to declare war he will lose the very public opinion which he needs most. The reason he broke off so triumphantly was that all aggressions had come from Germany. If he acts now, the aggression will seem to come from Washington."

The interventionists were in a bind. To win over the *NR*'s pacifist-minded readers, Lippmann enlisted the help of Norman Angell, the British internationalist who had worked with the editors during his visit to the United States two years earlier. "Ever since the Germans proclaimed their new submarine warfare, we have had an exceedingly hard time in this country dealing with the pacifists who simply want to avoid trouble," Lippmann told Angell. "An article from you justifying America's entry into the war on liberal and international grounds would be of immense help to us." As a well-known anti-imperialist, Angell was just the man to sway skeptical American internationalists. The opportunity, Lippmann underlined, was "decisive in the history of the world, because there is a chance by America's entry into the war to crystallize and make real the whole league of peace propaganda."[16]

The "whole league of peace propaganda" was dear to Angell's heart, for he saw the war as an opportunity to achieve world government. But for Lippmann the justification was less utopian. His argument for American entry into the war rested, not on visions of an international community, but on the struggle for mastery of the seas. "Our own existence and the world's order depend on the defeat of that anarchy which the Germans misname the 'freedom of the seas,' " he wrote in February 1917. "We shall uphold the dominion of the ocean highway as men upheld the Union in 1861, not because the power exercised by Great Britain is perfect, but because the alternative is intolerable."

A week later he spelled out his argument in one of the most important editorials he ever wrote, one that governed his approach to foreign policy for the rest of his life. America, he argued, was an integral part of the community of nations bordering the Atlantic. An attack on that community was a threat to America's own security. Germany's war against Britain and France was a war "against the civilization of which we are a part." By cutting the "vital highways of our world" through submarine warfare, Germany threatened the existence of what he called — coining a phrase that was to stick — the "Atlantic community."

The United States, he admitted, could remain neutral by embargoing arms to the Allies and forbidding Americans to travel on British ships. But the real issue went beyond rights of neutrality; it meant ensuring that "the world's highway shall not be closed to the western Allies if America has the power to prevent it." The message was clear, the conclusion unmistakable. If the German fleet threatened to gain command of the seas, America should come in on Britain's side. "The safety of the Atlantic highway is something for which America should fight."[17]

Lippmann was ready, Wilson was not. The period of "watchful waiting" went on through February and into March. The Germans still hoped to avoid war with the United States. Chancellor Theobald von Bethmann-Hollweg blamed Wilson for provoking the crisis by acquiescing in the British blockade of Germany and turning America into an Allied war arsenal. The accusation was true, Lippmann admitted to House, after visiting the colonel at his apartment, and was making an impact on public opinion. "But where we differ profoundly from Bethmann-Hollweg is in our belief that this differential neutrality has been for the interests of this nation and for the world.'' After a visit from Lippmann and Croly, House noted in his diary that he was ''finding it difficult to keep them in line because of the President's slowness of action.''

A few days later Lippmann went to Washington to present a memorandum to Wilson on the war issue. At the library of the Cosmos Club he drafted a note stressing that Germany's accusation of discrimination had to be countered, and pacifists shown the ''correlation between the peace program and the warlike measures which may be necessary.'' The President's task, he stressed, was to persuade Americans that the confrontation with Germany was rooted in America's ''vital interest in a just and lasting peace.'' Eschewing realpolitik, he appealed to the President's idealism: Germany was ''fighting for a victory subversive of the world system in which America lives. The only victory in this war that could compensate mankind for its horrors is the victory of international order over national aggression.''[18] Wilson read the memo, but declined to see Lippmann. He was not yet ready to make the fateful move.

Then a startling event occurred. Riots broke out in Petrograd, capital of imperial Russia. Troops joined the demonstrators, a provisional government took power, and on March 15 Tsar Nicholas II was forced to abdicate. No longer did a tyrannical Russian dictatorship taint the Allied cause. Liberal resistance to American participation in the war began to weaken. The Germans clumsily antagonized American opinion when they sank three unarmed United States merchantmen in late March, and then compounded their diplomatic ineptitude by promising Mexico — as revealed in the intercepted ''Zimmermann telegram'' — large chunks of Texas, Arizona and New Mexico if it would enter the war against the United States. With American patriotism outraged, the stage was now set for Wilson to make his move.

Persuading himself that he could ''do no other,'' the President went before a joint session of Congress on the evening of April 2, 1917. ''It is a fearful thing to lead this great peaceful people into war,'' he told the hushed assembly. ''But the right is more precious than peace.'' The United States, with no selfish interest, would enter the war ''for democracy, for the right of those who submit to authority to have a voice in their own government, for the rights and liberties of small nations . . . and to make the world itself at last free.'' His ambition, designed to inspire American idealism as well as to still the qualms of his own conscience, was no less grandiose than his rhetoric: ''The world must be made safe for democracy.'' Congress cheered, and four days later, with only six senators and fifty representatives opposed, voted Wilson's declaration of war.

If Wilson spoke with a heavy, or at least divided, heart, Lippmann was ecstatic. ''The President's address is magnificent,'' he wrote Colonel House. "It puts the whole thing exactly where it needed to be put and does it with real nobility of feeling. We are delighted with it here down to the last comma." Lippmann could hardly contain his excitement and relief. "Other men have led nations to war to increase their glory, their wealth, their prestige," he proclaimed in the *NR* that week. "No other statesman has ever so clearly identified the glory of his country with the peace and liberty of the world." To make sure that the President did not miss his bouquet, Lippmann sent Wilson a personal letter of congratulations, repeating the flowery phrases he had used in the magazine. "Our debt and the world's debt to Woodrow Wilson is immeasurable. Any mediocre politician might have gone to war futilely for rights that in themselves cannot be defended by war. Only a statesman who will be called great could have made American intervention mean so much to the generous forces of the world, could have lifted the inevitable horror of war into a deed so full of meaning."[19]

His doubts swept away, Lippmann set aside his own strategic arguments about sea-lanes and the Atlantic community and became infected by the same passion for action he had once so decried. The man who in 1915 wrote that "because a whole people clamors for a war, and gets it, there is no ground for calling the war democratic," now declared that the cause of the Allies was "unmistakably the cause of liberalism and the hope of an enduring peace." The overthrow of the tsar and the entry of America into the conflict made it "as certain as anything human can be that the war which started as a clash of empires in the Balkans will dissolve into democratic revolution the world over."[20]

A week later, at the end of April 1917, Lippmann went to Philadelphia to give the keynote address at a meeting of the American Academy of Political and Social Science. A singular honor for a man only twenty-seven, the invitation reflected the influence he was believed to wield as shadow adviser to Wilson and Colonel House. Looking young but immensely self-assured, Lippmann drew an inspiring picture of the "spiritual force" unleashed by democracy in Russia and an aroused internationalism in America. The stakes of diplomacy had changed. No longer were they a struggle for markets and influence in backward areas. These had now become "entirely secondary," as an imperial squabble had given way to a "people's war." Its objective, he told his listeners, was nothing less than "a union of liberal peoples pledged to cooperate in the settlement of all outstanding questions, sworn to turn against the agressor, determined to erect a larger and more modern system of international law upon a federation of the world." The war "is dissolving into a stupendous revolution. The whole perspective is changed today by the revolution in Russia and the intervention of America. The scale of values is transformed, for the democracies are unloosed."[21]

Whether or not the "scale of values" was transformed, Lippmann was. Everything he had written about the irrationality of nationalism and the imperial origins of the war now went by the board. He had glimpsed a transcendent value in the war, one that went beyond his own more mundane arguments about the "Atlantic highway." Like Wilson he found a way to persuade himself that the war could be redeemed by the better world that would follow. By elevating the decision to fight to the higher plane of political morality he could quiet the fear, as he himself had earlier expressed it, that by joining the Allies in a righteous cause the United States would "end by fighting to change the political control of the Near East."[22] But in 1917 he was sure the United States would hold the upper hand after the war, that it could prevent the Allies from imposing Draconian peace terms. He could not easily have anticipated what later happened at the Paris peace conference.

Lippmann was not alone in rallying to the colors. Most of the leading progressives, including John Dewey and Charles Beard, supported the war. They too had become frustrated sitting on the sidelines, "choked by feelings unexpressed and movements arrested in mid-air," as Lippmann had so tellingly written. Infused with optimism and driven toward action, they came to believe that only through participation could they steer the world in a liberal direction. Suspending the powers of critical analysis on which they prided themselves, they became tacticians of a war they had once said America must never be drawn into. With mixed relief and excitement they "scurried to Washington," in John Dos Passos's phrase.

These war liberals were seized, as the lonely pacifist Randolph Bourne wrote at the time, by "an unanalyzable feeling that this was a war in which we had to be." What he called the "war intellectuals" justified themselves by saying that "only on the craft, in the stream," was there any chance of "controlling the current forces for liberal purposes." But Bourne was pitiless in pointing out — in an obvious allusion to Lippmann — "how soon their 'mastery' becomes 'drift,' tangled in the fatal drive toward victory as its own end, how soon they become mere agents and expositors of forces as they are."[23]

Lippmann was unmoved by such complaints. He did not want to be an outsider in the great moral adventure. "Only saints, heroes and specialists in virtue feel remorse because they have done what everyone was doing and agreed with what everybody was thinking," he had written a few years earlier. He had persuaded himself that the war was a step toward a noble end, and predicted that the old nationalism would be replaced by a new internationalism. "We are living and shall live all our lives now in a revolutionary world," he wrote the week after America went to war. There would be a "transvaluation of values as radical as anything in the history of intellect." Concepts like liberty, equality and democracy would have to be reexamined "as fearlessly as religious dogmas were in the nineteenth century.'' There would be a new fertility of invention. ''This war and the peace which will follow are the stimulus and the justification.''[24]

He wanted to believe it; to justify his own ardor he had to believe it.

To the Colors

> I'd literally rather be connected with you in this work
> in no matter what capacity than do anything else there
> is to do in the world.
>
> — To Colonel Edward M. House, September 24, 1917

THE war demanded an army, and the army a draft. Even before the
United States entered the war Lippmann had warned Wilson that an
all-volunteer army was too risky: it would unleash jingoism, hatred for
the "Hun," and stir up a "newspaper campaign of manufactured
hatred." Wilson agreed, and his selective service bill, covering all men
from eighteen to forty-five, cleared the Congress in May.

Lippmann, only twenty-seven and in fine health, was eminently eligible for the draft, but felt there were better ways to use his talents. "I'll
be pretty well occupied in New York for the summer unless I'm con-
scripted, and I don't in the least think I ought to be just now," he wrote
Felix Frankfurter, himself then thirty-four and recently recruited to serve
as troubleshooter for Secretary of War Newton D. Baker. "What I want
to do is to devote all my time to studying and speculating on the approaches to peace and the reaction from the peace. Do you think you
can get me an exemption on such high-falutin' grounds? . . . The
things that need to be thought out," he explained, "are so big that there
must be no personal element mixed up with this."[1]

Frankfurter put in a word with Baker, and then Lippmann followed
through. "I have consulted all the people whose advice I value and they
urge me to apply for exemption," he wrote the secretary of war. "You
can well understand that that is not a pleasant thing to do, and yet, after
searching my soul as candidly as I know how, I am convinced that I can
serve my bit much more effectively than as a private in the new armies." Although reluctant to ask a favor, he added pointedly that the
matter was "complicated for me by the fact that my father is dying and

my mother is absolutely alone in the world. She does not know what his condition is, and I cannot tell anyone for fear it would become known."[2]

As it turned out, his father was not to die for another ten years, but the appeal struck a sympathetic ear. Baker was eager to add Lippmann to a cluster of bright young assistants that included, in addition to Frankfurter, Eugene Meyer, later publisher of the *Washington Post;* Frederick Kappel, future head of the Carnegie Corporation; Stanley King, later president of Amherst College; and his own aide from Cleveland, Ralph Hayes. All were progressives, infatuated with proximity to power, and eager to help in the war for democracy. Baker told Lippmann to come and be his special assistant.

This was just where Lippmann wanted to be. Once-sleepy Washington had become the nerve center of the nation, the logical place for those who craved influence. "It's a job at which I would work with all my heart," he wrote Baker with a blend of flattery and charm that had become second nature, "because I'd rather be under a man in whose whole view of life there is just the quality which alone can justify this high experience. I needn't tell you that I want nothing but the chance to serve, that salaries, titles, ambitions play no part whatsoever," he added. "Problems of organization, the creation of agencies for hearing and seeing, for simplifying, are things which have always fascinated me."[3]

As soon as he landed the job as Baker's assistant, Lippmann broke the news to Croly. The editor did not receive it in a patriotic spirit. He told Lippmann that he could do far more to promote liberal values through his editorials at the *NR* than by working in a government office. Lippmann was unmoved. The charms of West 21st Street palled beside the excitement of wartime Washington. Croly even pleaded with Colonel House, insisting that the magazine could not get along without Lippmann. The colonel promised that if things got really bad he would ask Baker to release Lippmann. Grudgingly Croly accepted the inevitable. Early in June readers found a small notice in the magazine:

> Mr. Walter Lippmann has temporarily severed
> his connection with the editorial board of
> THE NEW REPUBLIC to enter the service of
> the War Department.

Set free from the *New Republic*, Lippmann still had one tie linking him to New York. The cerebral political analyst was — quite unknown to his friends — courting a young lady. For more than a year he had been seeing Faye Albertson, the daughter of the Boston socialist parson who had been his first employer. After the *Boston Common* folded and the Boston — 1915 movement fizzled out, Ralph Albertson had moved to New York. Faye, now quite grown up and restless living at the Farm with Hazel and the younger children, had followed her father. During his years at Harvard Lippmann had scarcely noticed Faye. She was just a chubby child. Now she had become a beautiful young woman with a striking figure and long ash-blond hair. When their paths crossed in New York, Faye was working as a dance teacher and recuperating from a broken heart. Walter was a sympathetic listener as she told him of an unhappy love affair with a man in Boston. Although Faye was no intellectual, she was high-spirited and radiated a vitality he admired. He began to take an interest in her quite apart from his friendship with her father. He invited her to the theater, took her for rides on the Staten Island ferry, walked with her through Central Park in the snow. Gradually she realized that he looked on her as more than her father's daughter. At first she was surprised. Then she came to accept his interest as she had always accepted the attention of men.

Faye and Walter were a curious combination. She cared no more for politics than he did for the tango. She enjoyed people, loved to dance and go to parties; he was preoccupied with reforming the world. They had hardly any interests in common. Their differences alone drew them together. She was impressed by his intelligence, his growing renown, his circle of influential friends; he, by her beauty and infectious gaiety. It was enough for an enjoyable affair, though perhaps not for the "wise and kindly marriage" Graham Wallas had earlier counseled. But Lippmann was not the kind to dabble at affairs. He was wrapped up in his work, and ever since he left Harvard had been churning out books and articles at such a rate that there was little time for idle flirtations.

For several months he kept his involvement with Faye a secret from his friends. Mabel Dodge was one of the few who knew about it. Although she may not have been successful in her own love life, having gone through two husbands and innumerable lovers before she settled in Taos with a Navajo Indian, she was a shrewd judge of others. As a friend of Hazel Albertson she had known Faye for several years. She did not much like what she saw. "I feel queer things over them," she wrote Hazel after the young couple had come to visit her one Sunday in November 1916 at her farm at Croton-on-Hudson.

I felt him preoccupied with her every minute, and I felt her at very low ebb as far as he is concerned. Indifferent. She has to make an effort. Frankly, he bores her when he comes to her level, where he is not at his best. People are only really amusing and at their best when in their highest levels — but Faye probably would never "get" Walter on his. It's missed, it seems to me. I wonder what will come of it. I am not very hopeful at too much effort on Faye's part because she can't keep it up. She will have to go back to being herself and natural —

which she can't be much with him and which she could be with some dancing playmate.[4]

What was obvious to Mabel was not to Lippmann. On alien ground where the emotions were concerned, he was not a good judge of other people. He saw no warning signs. Through the fall of 1916 and the winter of 1917, between his weekly trips to Washington, he spent most of his evenings with Faye. He always had, as Mabel once observed, a "predilection for Nordic blondes," and Faye was as engaging as she was beautiful. She listened attentively when he spoke of politics, and even made a stab at political involvement by marching in suffragette parades.

While ostensibly a political radical, Lippmann had always been a conventional young man. He dressed with care for the proprieties, wore his rubbers when it rained, and rarely missed a good night's sleep. Though women invariably found him attractive — he was solidly built, well groomed, with an open, intelligent face and, as Mabel had once said, "a fine poise, a cool understanding, and with all the high humor in the world shining in his intelligent eyes" — there was nothing of the dashing bachelor about him.[5] Serious about everything he did, he cherished stability and took for granted a well-run, comfortable home where dinner was always served on time.

At twenty-seven he thought it was time to get away from his parents' home and set up on his own. The outbreak of war had turned the minds of many young men to marriage. In late April 1917, as he was negotiating his draft exemption, he made his decision. Faye said yes, and now he broke the news to his friends. "It's an old love and a very happy one, and it's been the only one," he wrote to Felix Frankfurter. "Faye knows all about you, what friends we are, and we'll make it a three-some." To Graham Wallas he explained, with some exaggeration: "We've been sweethearts for many years, ever since I was a freshman at Harvard. So far as a man can be happy with the world as it is, I am happy."[6]

He no doubt meant it. Lippmann had an awesome ability to find compelling reasons to do what he wanted, and to persuade himself that whatever he believed now was what he had always believed. A quality of his work, it was equally true of his life. With absolute sincerity he could tell Learned Hand that his love "has always been one of those things that were sure and splendid." Hand responded with his usual banter:

I didn't guess, and it is a surprise, and yet, and yet. Tho I am no reader of women's minds, some things get even to me. Last winter on Fifth Avenue east side about 33rd St. I did pass you in a big ulster and the woman was nestled under your arm in a way! I said, *tiens, tiens, ce Walter,* he is like the rest of us after all. But you aren't, you are a good deal like yourself and rather more than usually so to find your balance in your freshman year, even if it was only yesterday.

I thought that notwithstanding the under-my-wing effect that evening, that all your evenings were being spent with E. M. House or Newton Baker or other guys like that; I suspected you not — being a judge and a guileless fellow. It all seemed to me further corroboration of what a hell of an important young thing you were. And I was right, you were important, only I didn't know just where it was. I don't know yet, but I am going to learn as soon as you will let me.

"I always feel envious of people who are just in love — who aren't just, but never mind," Hand added in a guarded allusion to the tribulations of his own marriage to a difficult woman. "I took mine neurotically, as I have taken most else, and it seemed to me fiercely serious. I couldn't have said like you, 'sure and splendid,' they are good words and I believe them quite literally. They are particularly good words for you because, my hearty, they hit you off pretty well yourself."

Lippmann was euphoric. With the war, his new job and his impending marriage, he was beginning a different life. "Your letter moves me profoundly," he replied to Frankfurter's congratulations. "That I should find you, that I should find Faye — that such things happen in this turbulent world is all the sanction I ask to go on. You and I, to a common hope. Faye and I from such different beginnings. Think of it, Felix. She rode over the mountains as a baby in a prairie schooner and lived part of her childhood in a Georgia community devoted to the Brotherhood of Man!"[7]

The decision made, the deed was quickly done. Walter and Faye were married on May 24, 1917, by a city magistrate at his parents' home on East 80th Street. Ralph Albertson and Jacob Lippmann served as witnesses. The bride was twenty-four and a nominal Congregationalist, the groom twenty-seven and a nonpracticing Jew. Ralph Albertson, always in awe of Lippmann, beamed with pleasure at this unexpected and remarkable addition to his family. Jacob smiled benignly, assuming, as he always had, that Walter knew what was best. Daisy accepted with ill-concealed disapproval her son's choice of a woman who was not rich, socially prominent, artistically accomplished, or Jewish. Faye seemed a peculiar choice, and Daisy was not happy with it.

Lippmann wanted to take Faye to California for their honeymoon, but had to report to Washington immediately. A few days after the ceremony they boarded the train to the capital and moved into a red brick house at 1727 Nineteenth Street. Owned by Robert C. Valentine, a friend of the *NR* and a sometime poet who had been commissioner of

Indian affairs in the Taft administration, the house served as a kind of commune for young men in the government. The half-dozen resident bachelors hired a housekeeper, gave continual parties, and invited everyone who was famous, important or interesting. They argued about politics and took themselves so seriously that Justice Holmes, a frequent visitor, dubbed the place the "House of Truth."

During his frequent trips to Washington for the *NR* Lippmann had often stopped by the House of Truth for a meal and a rundown of current politics. When he took the job as Baker's assistant it seemed natural that he should live there. The only problem was Faye. No woman had ever lived in the house, although many had graced its dinner table. But Frankfurter, then in residence, assured Lippmann that the place could use a woman's touch. A little bedroom on the second floor was set aside for the newlyweds. The situation was an odd one for Faye but she handled it well, bringing some order into the household accounts and providing a welcome adornment at dinner. The men teased and doted on her, and it was a tribute to her easygoing nature that she could get on so well with such ambitious and independent-minded intellectuals. One of her greatest admirers was Justice Holmes, who used to come from the Court chambers in the late afternoons to play double solitaire with her. Once during a game she gently pointed out to him that he was cheating. "But it's such a small thing, my dear," he sighed through his great drooping mustache, "and no one will suffer from it but me."

A place of honor was always reserved for Holmes. Irreverent, cynical, sharp-tongued, he attracted a devoted band of admirers as much by his celebrated wit as by his judicial learning. "Life is an end in itself," he said in one of the many aphorisms for which he was renowned, "and the only question as to whether it is worth living is whether you have had enough of it." Part of his appeal to young people was his disrespect for tradition. "The Constitution is an experiment, as all life is an experiment," he argued from the bench. "Congress certainly cannot forbid all effort to change the mind of the country." Although a social and economic conservative, he strongly believed in judicial restraint. The criterion of constitutionality, he argued, was not whether a law seemed to be in the public good, but whether the legislature had the right to enact it — a position that had a profound influence on such disciples as Felix Frankfurter.

Reveling in the play of ideas, Holmes found the bright young men at the House of Truth to be "the fastest talkers, the quickest thinkers" in Washington. He was particularly fond of Lippmann, whom he had met through the *New Republic,* and who was, as he said, "one of the young men I delight in." On his visits to Washington Lippmann had often visited Holmes at his home at 1720 Eye Street. Although an early supporter of the magazine, Holmes treated it and its earnest writers with a certain levity. "That part of the NR that shapes our destinies I generally skip," he told Harold Laski in a gentle swipe at the magazine's Olympian posture. Yet "God knows," he added, "I have as deep a respect as anybody for the ability of Croly and Lippmann."[8] "I don't want any of this onward-and-upward stuff," he once told Lippmann. "You young men seem to think that if you sit on the world long enough you will hatch something out. But you're wrong."

Lippmann, won over by Holmes's irony and wit, his graceful manners and irreverent tongue, took a special pleasure in being one of the young men the justice delighted in. In March 1916, when Holmes celebrated his seventy-fifth birthday, Lippmann wrote an adoring tribute in the NR:

He has lost nothing that young men can have, and he has gained what a fine palate can take from the world. If it is true that one generation after another has depended upon its young to equip it with gaiety and enthusiasm, it is no less true that each generation of young depends upon those who have lived to illustrate what can be done with experience. They need to know that not all life withers in bad air. That is why young men feel themselves very close to Justice Holmes. He never fails to tell them what they want to hear, or to show them what they would wish men to be.

Sixteen years later, when Holmes retired from the Supreme Court, Lippmann wrote another tribute that was even more touching, and a good deal more personal:

There are few who, reading Judge Holmes' letter of resignation, will not feel that they touch a life done in the great style. This, they will say, is how to live, and this is how to stop, with every power used to the full, like an army resting, its powder gone but with all its flags flying. Here is the heroic life complete, in which nothing has been shirked and nothing denied — not battle or death, or the unfathomable mystery of the universe, or the loneliness of thought, or the humors and the beauties of the human heritage. This is the whole of it. He has had what existence has to offer: all that is real, everything of experience, of friendship and of love, and the highest company of the mind, and honor, and the profoundest influence — everything is his that remains when illusion falls away and leaves neither fear nor disappointment in its wake.[9]

Graced by Holmes's irony and embellished by a bounteous table, the House of Truth became an unofficial social center for ambitious young men who flocked to wartime Washington. Among those who joined Frankfurter and the Lippmanns were Eustace Percy, now returned to Washington as right-hand man to the British ambassador, and Philip Kerr, who twenty years later, as Lord Lothian, became Britain's envoy to the United States. Nearly every night the large downstairs dining room at the House of Truth rocked with argument and wild gesticulation. A favored guest was the organizer of Belgian relief, Herbert Hoover, who impressed Lippmann with his sharp mind and gift for exposition. Lippmann found him "an entrancing talker," and later said he had "never met a more interesting man, anyone who knew so much of the world and could expound so clearly what to almost all Americans in 1917 were the inscrutable mysteries of European politics."[10] Hoover also impressed Faye, but for a different reason. One night at dinner she watched in fascinated horror as, absorbed in an argument taking place at the table, he slowly chewed his way through an unlit cigar.

The day after moving into the House of Truth Lippmann reported to Baker at his office in the State, War, Navy Department Building down the street from the White House. Baker set Lippmann up in a little anteroom outside his own office and gave him the title of "confidential clerk to the secretary of war" with a salary of fifteen hundred dollars a year — less than half what he had been making at the *NR*. While the title sounded impressive, the job consisted mostly of being on hand whenever Baker felt like unwinding. In the evenings, after the secretaries and aides had gone home, Baker would call Lippmann into his office, put his feet up on the desk, and muse about the ironies that had made a pacifist like him the secretary of war.

Part of Lippmann's job was to serve as one of the three government representatives on the Cantonment Adjustment Board, designed to deal with labor grievances arising from the construction of some thirty military training camps. His most important task, however, was to hold the hand of Samuel Gompers, the vain and cantankerous head of the American Federation of Labor. This task was complicated by the fact that the conservative Gompers was convinced that Lippmann — because of his association with the *New Republic* — was a dangerous radical. After a few months with Gompers, Lippmann was promoted to serve as War Department representative on an interagency committee dealing with wages at arsenals and navy yards.[11] There he first met his Navy Department counterpart, a debonair New York lawyer only a few years older than he, Franklin Delano Roosevelt.

The excitement of wartime Washington, his close relationship with Baker, and the spirited evenings at the House of Truth — all this was a good deal more heady than anything the *NR* could provide. "I should not want office work for life," Lippmann wrote journalist Norman Hapgood, "but at the present time under war conditions I had rather be doing it than attempting to write." Whatever its daily frustrations it was, after all, in a noble cause. "There is an immense amount of good work being done here," he wrote the British socialist Alfred Zimmern. "The temper of those in charge is about as good a combination of liberal feeling and willingness to act drastically as I have ever seen in American politics."[12]

While those in charge had no qualms about acting drastically, their liberal feeling was open to question. No sooner had he declared war than Wilson moved to smother dissent by appointing journalist George Creel to head a new government propaganda agency euphemistically called the Committee on Public Information. The Creel committee, as it soon was known, promoted the war with a barrage of newspaper ads, leaflets, newsreels, public speakers and publicity stunts. Congress did its bit to legislate conformity by imposing espionage and sedition acts so sweeping that people were prosecuted for obstructing the sale of government bonds, discouraging recruitment, or uttering abusive words about the government or military uniforms. Hundreds were sent to prison for questioning the war, including perennial Socialist candidate for President, Eugene V. Debs. There he languished until 1921, when Harding pardoned him. The government set up a nationwide spy system, infiltrated supposedly "dangerous" organizations, incited them to illegal acts, raided their premises without warrants, and destroyed their property. Wilson himself became a prisoner of the war fever. "Force, Force to the utmost, Force without stint or limit," he cried in a Flag Day address, "the righteous and triumphant Force which shall make Right the law of the world, and cast every self dominion down in the dust."

As war hysteria gathered momentum, the repression increased: 1918 was marked by a mass indictment of Wobbly leaders, the banning of the *Masses* from the mails and the indictment of its editors, the harassment of Villard's pacifist *Nation,* and the denial of mailing privileges to "suspect" journals. Even the *New Republic* was thought to be insufficiently militant about the war. The Espionage Act, which made it a crime to suggest that Germany was within its rights in attacking merchant ships, or that a referendum should have preceded a declaration of war, was upheld by the Supreme Court. Holmes wrote the majority opinion, establishing conditions — in this case opposition to the draft — under which free speech could be restricted on grounds of "clear and present danger." "You can't even collect your thoughts without getting arrested for unlawful assemblage," Max Eastman told an audience in July 1917. "They give you ninety days for quoting the Declaration of Independence, six months for quoting the Bible, and pretty soon somebody is going to get a life sentence for quoting Woodrow Wilson in the wrong connection."

In grotesque imitation of the federal government, states and cities launched their own spy hunts, firing radical teachers, harassing people of German heritage, forbidding German music to be played or the language to be taught, even renaming sauerkraut "liberty cabbage." Americans, John Reed said in the fall of 1917, had "acquiesced in a regime of judicial tyranny, bureaucratic suppression and industrial barbarism." Reform was dead, and liberalism itself was suspect. "One has a sense of having come to a sudden, short stop at the end of an intellectual era,'' Randolph Bourne mourned.[13]

Many had seen it coming. Even Lippmann, for all his enthusiasm about the great crusade, had urged Wilson to put censorship in the hands of those with ''real insight and democratic sympathy.'' The greatest danger, he wrote the President shortly before war was declared, would come not from the ''conventionally unpatriotic'' but from those who ''persecute and harass and cause divisions among the people.'' It would be more important to control untruth than to suppress the truth, he stressed, and the ''protection of a healthy public opinion'' was of ''the first importance.'' In urging Colonel House to set up an official news bureau, he underlined the need to avoid arbitrary censorship. ''We are fighting not so much to beat an enemy,'' he reminded the colonel, ''as to make a world that is safe for democracy.''[14]

When the government tried to ban the socialist *Call* and the *Jewish Daily Forward* from the mails on the vague grounds that they were impeding the war effort, even pro-war liberals like John Dewey reacted sharply. At the urging of Sydney Hillman — president of the radical Amalgamated Clothing Workers and later founder of the Congress of Industrial Organizations — Lippmann approached Louis D. Brandeis with an appeal to use his influence on Wilson. The suppression of socialist journals, Lippmann told the justice, would not only anger Jewish socialists, but ''give the Russian extremists every cause for insisting that American reactionaries were completely in the saddle.''[15]

By October 1917 the situation had grown so serious that Lippmann decided to take it up with Colonel House. Although the colonel was not particularly sensitive to the civil liberties issue, he agreed with Lippmann that attempts to muzzle the press were undermining national morale and rebounding against the President. He asked Lippmann to draw up a memorandum for Wilson. Radicals and liberals were in a ''sullen mood'' over censorship of the socialist press, Lippmann noted in his memo. The best course for the administration was to be ''contemptuously disinterested'' in socialist diatribes against the war, while respecting the right to free speech. Censorship should ''never be entrusted to anyone who is not himself tolerant, nor to anyone who is unacquainted with the long record of folly which is the history of suppression.'' While he refrained from underlining the obvious, Lippmann clearly had Creel in mind as one to whom such delicate tasks should not be entrusted.

He was also careful to retain his own credibility and not be considered a sentimental liberal. ''So far as I am concerned, I have no doctrinaire belief in free speech,'' he told House. ''In the interest of the war it is necessary to sacrifice some of it. But the point is that the method now being pursued is breaking down the liberal support of the war and is tending to divide the country's articulate opinion into fanatical jingoism and fanatical pacifism."[16] This was "realistic" language that politicians could understand.

It also expressed Lippmann's own feelings. When Croly complained about the government's suppression of dissent, Lippmann showed little patience and even less understanding. "I told him," he noted in his diary, "he couldn't afford to . . . simply express his vexation every week because the war is a brutal and unreasonable thing, that if he wanted to count in favor of a discriminating diplomacy he would have to make the paper sound as if it really believed in a vigorous fighting policy while the war lasted." Concerned with being effective, Lippmann told Croly that the NR now "sounded as if it were bored with the war and was ready to snatch at any straw, no matter how thin, which pointed toward peace."[17]

Repression had not silenced the accusation that America had been dragged into an imperial war. Rumors spread that the Allies were bound by secret pledges to carve up Central Europe and take over Germany's colonies. Finally the Roman Catholic Church — responding to a growing war-weariness in Europe and a fear that the Bolsheviks might topple the tottering Kerensky regime in Russia — broke its long silence. On August 1, 1917, Pope Benedict XV called for a peace based on disarmament, arbitration, freedom of the seas, renunciation of indemnities, evacuation of occupied territory, conciliation of grievances, and no territorial aggrandizements. Berlin responded favorably, although avoiding any promise to withdraw. London and Paris, however, were not interested in such a compromise — particularly now that America had entered the war.

The pope had waited too long. Not even Wilson any longer sought a "peace without victory." He wanted victory first, then a peace he would negotiate. He could not, however, reject the Vatican's plea out of hand. Once again he turned to Lippmann for a reply that would assuage the liberals without irritating the Allies. Lippmann went to work, and in the draft he submitted to the President, declared that a mere cease-fire would leave the German ruling class in power. Only by breaking the grip of the military and the Prussian autocrats could Germany be made democratic. "If the German people are to be weaned from this governing class, they must be made to believe that they can be safe, prosperous and respected without dependence upon their government as it exists," he explained. It was essential to focus on the "*method* of peace rather than the terms of peace, because such a reply really represents our stake in the war, keeps us clear of entanglements, justifies a continuation of the war if it is rejected, and yet leaves the door sufficiently ajar so that the President cannot be accused either by Germany or by the American people of prolonging the war."

This was what Wilson wanted to hear. It allowed him to pursue the war for the most idealistic motives. "Lippmann is not only thoughtful," he told Baker, "but just and suggestive." A few days later he sent his official reply to the pope. "The object of the war," Wilson told the pontiff, stressing Lippmann's distinction between the German people and their leaders, was "to deliver the fine peoples of the world from the menace and the actual power of a vast military establishment controlled by an irresponsible government. . . . This power is not the German people but the masters of the German people."[18] The message was clear: continuation of the war would redeem Germany for democracy.

Having rejected the pope's peace offer, Wilson now felt obliged to come up with something of his own. Early in September he instructed Colonel House to assemble some experts to draw up material for the eventual peace conference. The group would be entirely independent of the State Department and under no obligation to the Allies. To ensure secrecy it would be based in New York rather than Washington, and be financed out of the President's special fund. House, operating without any specific instructions, moved to set up a staff. A prime consideration was that the directors be unquestionably loyal to him personally. He thought immediately of Lippmann.

At the end of September 1917, Baker called Lippmann into his office and said that Colonel House was in Washington and wanted to talk to him about a secret matter. Lippmann hurried downstairs to meet the colonel, who suggested they go for a little walk. As they strolled around the White House fence, past Pennsylvania Avenue and down Seventeenth Street toward the Potomac, the colonel outlined Wilson's instructions, and the secret nature of the plan. Lippmann was gripped by a mounting excitement. Here was the chance to become directly involved in policy to "speculate on the approaches to the peace." "Nothing has ever pleased me more or come as a greater surprise," he wrote House after the colonel's return to New York. "The work outlined is exactly that which I have dreamed of since the very beginning of the war, but dreamed of as something beyond reach. I'd literally rather be connected with you in this work in no matter what capacity than do anything else there is to do in the world."[19]

Lippmann cleared up his desk at the War Department and bid goodbye to Baker. Early in October 1917 he and Faye packed their bags, had a farewell dinner with the somewhat perplexed band at the House of Truth, and took the train to New York. They had been in Washington for five months.

The next morning Lippmann began work on a project so secret it did not have a name.

◄ 11 ►

The Inquiry

Sometimes I fairly itch to be back in journalism so that
I might tell a few of the things I know . . .

— To Ralph Hayes, December 14, 1917

ON their return to New York in early October, Walter and Faye
found an apartment at 21 East 57th Street, just off Fifth Avenue.
The location was ideal: a few blocks from Colonel House's quarters and
within easy walking distance of the intelligence unit's makeshift offices
at the New York Public Library on 42nd Street.

The project's very existence, let alone its purpose, was shrouded in
mystery. Even the head librarian was pledged to secrecy. To keep the
project under his personal control, House picked as director his brother-
in-law, Sidney Mezes, a fellow Texan who was then president of City
College. A philosopher of religion, Mezes knew little about foreign affairs, but had the supreme virtue of unquestioned loyalty to House. Administrative and legal matters fell under David Hunter Miller, a law
partner of House's son-in-law, Gordon Auchincloss. To complete the
directorate House added historian James T. Shotwell of Columbia University and geographer Isaiah Bowman, director of the American Geographical Society. Lippmann, by far the youngest of the group, served
as general secretary. In House's view he was the perfect middle man —
still trailing vestigial ties to the left liberals, yet "realistic" in accommodating his idealism to political necessity.

For the first few weeks the group had no staff, no offices except a few
rooms in the bowels of the library, and no clear idea of what it was supposed to do. It did not even have a name. At first they called it the
"War Data Investigation Bureau," but then decided that was too obvious. Searching for something vague, they finally settled on "the Inquiry," a name that would be, as Shotwell explained, a "blind to the
general public, but would serve to identify it among the initiated."

The Inquiry's mandate was as broad as it was vague, consisting, as

House told Lippmann, "not only of a study of the facts, but of quiet negotiation, especially with the neutrals, so that America could enter the peace conference as the leader of a great coalition of forces." In fact, the Inquiry would be drawing up the embryonic outlines of the postwar world. The group began by collecting data on virtually everything likely to come up at the peace conference. Lippmann's job was to coordinate the work of the specialists, put their data into readable reports for House and Wilson, and give an overall political direction to the project. His salary of five hundred dollars a month was second only to that of Mezes.

Despite the attempt at secrecy, the Inquiry was soon flooded with letters from scholars offering their services. Judge Learned Hand asked Lippmann if he should leave the bench to work on the peace project. John Dewey, tempted by Lippmann's suggestion that he head an Inquiry branch in Moscow, also volunteered — although nothing ever came of the plan. What the Inquiry needed was specialists, not stars. "On many of the problems of first-rate importance there is a real famine of men, and we have been compelled practically to train and create our own experts," Lippmann wrote Newton Baker. "What we are on the lookout for is genius — sheer, startling genius, and nothing else will do because the real application of the President's idea to those countries requires inventiveness and resourcefulness, which is scarcer than anything."[1]

Within a year the five-man directorate burgeoned to a staff of 126 geographers, historians, political scientists, economists, psychologists, and even archaeologists — among them such scholars as Archibald Cary Coolidge, Robert Lord, Charles Seymour, Vladimir Simkhovitch, Samuel Eliot Morison, Wolcott Pitkin, George Louis Beer and Stanley Hornbeck. Cramped for space, the group in November 1917 moved uptown to the American Geographical Society's offices at 155th Street and Broadway. There it had not only privacy and space, but access to the society's library and maps — crucial to those redrawing the frontiers of Europe.

Among those lured by the glamour of the Inquiry was Felix Frankfurter. But Lippmann, at House's instruction, gently tried to put him off. "Strictly between ourselves the job goes well, but it has not reached a point where you can be drafted into it with any fairness to the work you are now doing," he wrote Frankfurter. "The Colonel has been exceedingly busy on other work and has not been able to give much time to this, so we have been going along on our own. . . . We have made only a beginning, but it is a beginning, I think. The discretion required in carrying out this work is huge, superabundant and overflowing."[2]

The reference to discretion was not accidental. Rumors about the Inquiry's existence and mission had been leaking out ever since late September when journalist Lincoln Colcord blew the cover in a Philadelphia newspaper. A furious Wilson suspected Frankfurter, who was a friend of Colcord and who had access to secret information through his job as Newton Baker's assistant. Lippmann tried to draw the scent away from Frankfurter, but Colonel House was not dissuaded. "The Jews from every tribe have descended in force, they seem determined to break in with a jimmy if they are not let in," House complained to the President. But he exempted his protégé. "The objection to Lippmann is that he is a Jew, but unlike other Jews he is a silent one."³

House had reason to protect Lippmann. He was invaluable both as a link to the liberals — there was "none who had so much influence and was at the same time so easy to get along with as Lippmann," House had told Isaiah Bowman — and as an idea man. Lippmann bombarded House, Baker and Wilson with suggestions on arms control, demobilization, economic reconstruction, and postwar international cooperation. "Unity of purpose and control" among the Allies was essential, Lippmann told the President, "to that general purification of aims which must precede a fine peace." The "spiritual reaction" from such a movement would "put new heart into the humble if they saw through the war the rise of an international structure," and give vitality to a league of nations.

Disgruntlement among the "humble" was very much a problem, for middle western farmers, as William Allen White had reported to Lippmann, "don't seem to get the war." But Lippmann remained convinced that the cause was noble even if the means were sometimes harsh. "It is an everlasting comfort to think of you in Washington doing what you are," he wrote Baker a few weeks after joining the Inquiry in New York. "For it means, doesn't it, the largest assembly of force for an entirely disinterested purpose ever known to history? The weapon is drawn by men who cannot worship it. That is what I cling to in this agony."⁴

That fall Lippmann frequently went to Washington to confer with officials. On one trip he stopped by the State Department to see the people in the Near Eastern division. The division turned out to be one man, who had never been to the area, and a small filing cabinet. Lippmann then went upstairs to talk to the secretary of state. He explained to Robert Lansing what the Inquiry was doing and how it had to deal with the problems of the Balkans, such as the borders of Yugoslavia and the Macedonian issue. "Let me just show you on the map," Lippmann suggested to the secretary, pulling down one of the big roller maps attached to the wall. The map was fifty years old, showing the frontiers that existed before the first Balkan wars.

The War Department seemed a model of efficiency by comparison. One October afternoon Newton Baker, the secretary of war, startled Lippmann by showing him a sheaf of top-secret documents — the treaties the Allies had secretly signed with one another to divvy up the spoils of war. Although rumors of the "secret treaties" had been floating around for months — always vociferously denied by the Allied governments — details were known only to a few key officials. The treaties spelled out how the Allies — Britain, France, Italy, Russia, Japan — planned to reward themselves after the war at the expense of the Central Powers — Germany, Austria-Hungary and the Ottoman Empire. A war fought for indemnities and territory hardly squared with the noble ideals Wilson had been proclaiming, nor was it likely to persuade the German people to turn against their government.

Wilson insisted that the United States would not be bound by the secret accords, and in October 1917 sent Colonel House to Paris to persuade the Allies to repudiate the treaties. He was eager, not only to orchestrate a more equitable peace in line with his ideals, but also to save the shaky parliamentary government of Alexander Kerensky. The moderate, pro-Allies Kerensky was under mounting attack from Russian radicals, particularly the well-organized Bolshevik faction, who wanted to negotiate an armistice, with or without the Allies.

Wilson's efforts were futile. The Allies, feeling that only the promise of spoils could justify the sacrifices of the war to their own people, refused to moderate their demands. In Petrograd the inept parliamentary government stumbled toward oblivion. In early November, as House was in Paris meeting with the Allies, the Bolsheviks overthrew Kerensky and called for peace negotiations based on self-determination and a German withdrawal from occupied territories — in effect, a "peace without victory."

When the Allies rebuffed this appeal, the Bolsheviks decided to act on their own. The very survival of their revolution was at stake. Under assault from counterrevolutionary White armies, backed by foreign arms and money, they tried to save themselves by opening negotiations with Berlin for a separate peace. They justified this bid by making public the secret treaties the tsar had signed with the Allies. These treaties, mostly negotiated during the first two years of the war, had been designed to win over such neutrals as Italy and Rumania, and to provide security and reparations for the victors. France would at last recover Alsace and Lorraine, lost in the war of 1870, and gain parts of the Saar; Britain would take over Germany's African colonies; Italy would gain the Austrian-held territories of Istria and Dalmatia; Japan would acquire the Shantung Peninsula of China.

The Bolsheviks published the treaties for both strategic and ideological reasons. They hoped this action would force Britain and France to revise their war aims, thereby persuading Germany to accept a negotiated peace. As Marxists they also wanted to unmask capitalist duplicity and reveal the so-called war for democracy as a scramble for spoils. Once the Allied peoples understood how they had been deceived, the

Bolsheviks reasoned, they would turn against their imperialistic governments.

The revelation of the secret treaties was an embarrassment to the Allies and a calamity for Wilson. Binding the Allied cause in an unholy web of bribes and rewards, the accords mocked both Wilson's rhetoric and his intentions. Although he denied any "official" knowledge of them, he certainly had known of them unofficially. Both House and the American ambassador to England, Walter Hines Page, had got wind of the treaties as early as 1916; and in April 1917, shortly after America entered the war, British Foreign Secretary Arthur Balfour outlined the treaties to both Colonel House and Secretary Lansing. Wilson did not intend to be bound by the treaties, and had his own plan for putting pressure on the Allies. "When the war is over we can bring them around to our way of thinking," he told Colonel House, "because then, among other things, they will be dependent on us financially."[5] If this was to be Wilson's trump card, he never knew how to play it. The secret treaties sat as a grotesque centerpiece at the Paris peace conference, defeating Wilson's ambition to forge an equitable peace.

Divulgence of the secret treaties came at a moment when Allied morale had fallen to new depths. The French army was rocked by mutinies, while in Britain demands mounted for a cease-fire. American radicals declared that the secret treaties proved the culpability of the capitalist war-makers. Fearful of their effect on public opinion, the administration had tried to prevent the treaties from being published in America, but pacifist Oswald Garrison Villard printed the complete text in his paper, the *New York Evening Post*. Only nine other papers, however, published even short excerpts. The pro-war *New York Times* spoke for most of the American press, and for the administration, in denouncing the Bolsheviks' revelation as "beyond the pale . . . an act of dishonor."

Wilson, his goals now compromised, had to nullify the impact of the treaties and explain why he would not accept the "peace without victory" the Bolsheviks had called for. He found his answer in the memo Lippmann had written four months earlier in reply to the pope: there could be no lasting peace until German militarism was crushed. In early December 1917 the President tried to assuage antiwar sentiment by intimating that he would not be bound by the secret treaties. "The opinion of the world is everywhere wide awake and fully comprehends the issues involved," he told Congress. There must be no "covenants of selfishness and compromise."

Pacifists jeered and cynics shook their heads, but the *New Republic* spoke for liberals in calling the President's address "a political offensive of the first order" that would speed a German surrender and persuade Russia to stay in the war. Lippmann offered his usual bouquet.

"The whole world seems better because of the message," he wrote Baker, declaring that it had the "simplicity and directness of an epic, and a kind of unfrightened candor which will cheer people everywhere." Only a "catholic idea" would sustain popular support; the people "won't fight much longer to establish anybody's imperial influence or round out somebody's notion of destiny." Wilson had raised the struggle to a higher level. "I should have dreaded the future of our cause had we not found at this time just such leadership as the President has given," Lippmann added. "Without him there would have been, I think, a kind of creeping paralysis moving from East to West . . . consent was fading in the last four months for lack of a catholic idea. For purely military reasons the President's message is a stroke of genius." Wilson saw no reason to disagree. "Lippmann's letters all make one like him," he told Baker on reading the accolade.[6]

However inspiring Wilson's speech, the British and French were unmoved. The terrible toll of the war had made them even more determined to destroy German power and seek spoils. Now Wilson had to extract himself from the machinations of the Allies and set forth a peace plan of his own, one that would satisfy the legitimate aspirations of the Allies, but not their more cynical ambitions. Wilson agreed that the peace terms must not only "purge and pacify" the Allied cause, but must be so tempting to the German people that they would turn against their military leaders. He told House to put the Inquiry team to work.[7]

In the second week of December 1917 House called Lippmann to his 57th Street apartment and repeated the President's instructions. He had no suggestions to make about form and content, other than that the plan must provide the outlines of a durable peace and, most urgently, counter the adverse effect of the secret treaties. Lippmann was entirely on his own. At this point the Inquiry was only two months old. With a still rudimentary staff the job was awesome: to draw up frontiers for postwar Europe that would be either the basis for a lasting peace or cause for another war.

While it was possible to devise frontiers on logical geographic or economic grounds — along rivers and natural barriers, or according to access to raw materials and ports — the problem was infinitely compounded by the demands of various national groups. Some, like the Czechs, Slovaks and Serbs, demanded new states of their own. Others, like the Poles, sought to have ancient kingdoms restored. To complicate matters further, many European nationalists, having found asylum in the United States, exerted political pressure on the administration. Lippmann had dealt with some, including Czechs Eduard Beneš and Thomas Masaryk, and the Polish pianist-patriot, Ignace Paderewski.

The Inquiry, working from maps and piles of statistics, attacked the question of frontiers by drawing up charts showing the concentration of national groups within Europe. Lippmann then coordinated these charts and lists with national political movements to determine how these ethnic entities could be granted self-determination without triggering new European rivalries. Then he correlated this blueprint with the secret treaties — deciding which territorial changes were acceptable and which defied justice and logic. Once the Inquiry team — Lippmann, Bowman, Miller and Mezes — had matched the aspirations of the ethnic groups with the geography and economics of each region, Lippmann organized the conclusions into a series of points corresponding to provisions of the secret treaties.[8]

For three weeks they worked night and day, sometimes not even going home to sleep. On December 22, 1917, an exhausted Lippmann presented Colonel House with a document entitled "The War Aims and Peace Terms It Suggests." The memo delineated the new European frontiers, explained how each decision was made, and illustrated the points with maps. On Christmas Day House went over the memo with the President, and returned from Washington with instructions for clarification. For another week the Inquiry team worked virtually nonstop. On January 2, 1918, Lippmann gave House a revised memorandum, and two days later House went over it point by point with the President. Wilson made some changes, but accepted most of the Inquiry's recommendations. He then added six general principles of his own to the territorial points. On January 8 he assembled Congress in joint session and presented the results in his historic Fourteen Points address. This was the basis of his "New Diplomacy," designed to reach the European peoples over the heads of their governments. On the basis of the Fourteen Points the Germans, ten months later, asked for the armistice that ended the war.

Lippmann was exultant over Wilson's speech. Many of the phrases had come almost intact from the memorandum he had produced from the Inquiry data. He felt a sense of paternity toward the Fourteen Points, just as he had toward the "peace without victory" address a year earlier. Not yet thirty, he was a trusted presidential counselor and the author, in part at least, of the document that was to serve as foundation for the peace settlement. "This is the second time that I have put words into the mouth of the President!" he boasted to Isaiah Bowman.[9] The geographer, jealous of Lippmann's influence and resentful of his lack of deference, did not share his pleasure.

The Fourteen Points had to reconcile complex and even contradictory goals: to meet the national aspirations of each ethnic group, yet keep them limited; to satisfy governments, yet avoid erosion of public morale; to outline a possible peace, yet preserve Allied unity. Through his initiative Wilson hoped to push the Allies toward more liberal peace terms, drive the German people away from their own government, and establish an entente among the Allies, the German people, and the national groups that formed the Austro-Hungarian Empire.

The first five points and the fourteenth, all added by Wilson, dealt with general principles: open diplomacy, freedom of the seas, lower tariffs, disarmament, respect for colonial peoples, and a league of nations. These were the points that captured the public's enthusiasm. But the territorial provisions in the other eight points were the crucial ones to the warring governments.

Point Six, the first of the territorial provisions, affirmed the Inquiry's recommendations for a liberal policy toward revolutionary Russia. In calling for a settlement that would grant Russia the "independent determination of her own political development and national policy and assure her of a sincere welcome into the society of free nations under institutions of her own choosing," Wilson deliberately repudiated British and French efforts to overthrow the Bolshevik government by aiding the counterrevolutionary White armies. Point Six, as Lippmann later explained, was "intended as a reply to Russian suspicion of the Allies, and the eloquence of its promises was attuned to the drama of Brest-Litovsk," where the Bolsheviks were negotiating a separate peace with Germany.[10]

Point Seven called for the evacuation and restoration of Belgium. Point Eight concerned the touchy problem of Alsace-Lorraine. The French were determined to annex the entire area — not only the part that had been taken from them in the Franco-Prussian War of 1870 — and even laid claim to portions of the Rhineland. The Inquiry recognized that if a plebiscite were held, most people in the Saar, and many in Alsace, would prefer to unite with Germany rather than with France. Lippmann labored hard over the wording, trying to satisfy the French while not yielding to their more extreme demands. Finally he worked out a definition that ruled out annexation of the Saar basin without explicitly saying so.[11]

In Point Nine, Wilson skirted the imbroglio over Italy's claims to parts of Austria, Trieste, and the Dalmatian coast — claims that the Inquiry looked upon with disfavor — by stating simply that Italian frontiers should be fixed "along clearly recognizable national lines." This merely postponed the problem, for the Italian claims rested specifically on the secret treaties: the territories were the bribe the Allies gave to bring the Italians into the war. This pledge returned to haunt Wilson at the peace conference.

Point Ten focused on the critical problem of Austria-Hungary. Here Wilson accepted the Inquiry's argument that Central Europe not be "balkanized" into a congeries of weak nation-states. Instead, Point Ten supported internal autonomy within the empire for nationalist groups like the Serbs and Czechs. Agitation of the various nationalities should be encouraged, but Vienna given "assurances that no dismemberment of the Empire is intended." Wilson was driven from that position at Paris by pressure from emigré groups and from the British. Ultimately he agreed to dissolve the empire, a concession Lippmann later described as having destroyed the political balance in Central Europe and opened the way to Hitler.[12]

On Point Eleven, concerning the Balkans, Wilson was far more vague than the Inquiry, which had made specific recommendations about the boundaries of Serbia and Bulgaria, and had concluded that an independent Albania was "an undesirable political entity." Wilson, however, merely urged that Serbia be given access to the sea, and affirmed that its frontiers should rest on national, economic and historic rights. Regarding the Ottoman Empire (Point Twelve), Wilson accepted the Inquiry's recommendation that Turkey be guaranteed security and its subject peoples granted autonomy.

Point Thirteen dealt with the eternal Polish question. The Poles were as insatiable as they were unrealistic — demanding the return of kingdoms long since gone, if not forgotten. After endless hours of study and debate the Inquiry decided it would be best to have Poland attached as an autonomous state to a democratic Russia or a liberal Austria-Hungary. Wilson, however, preferred independence, declaring that the new Poland should include territories inhabited by "indisputably Polish populations" — a phrase deliberately meant to exclude what Lippmann later called those "geographical fantasies" that reached into Lithuania and the Ukraine.[13] But Wilson also insisted that Poland have "free and secure access" to the sea. This posed an insoluble problem, for if the new Polish state were confined to lands predominantly inhabited by Poles, it would have no ocean frontier. To gain a port on the Baltic it would have to include lands predominantly German — thereby violating the rule of ethnic self-determination. Wilson dealt with the conflict between ethnic and economic boundaries by pretending it did not exist.

The Fourteen Points were greeted with cheers by the people and an ominous silence by the Allied governments. At first this puzzled Lippmann, for he had assumed that Wilson had coordinated his plan with the Allies before making it public. He had not, and for a good reason: he knew they would turn it down. Defeated in his efforts to persuade the Allies to repudiate the secret treaties, he had tried to induce the peoples of Europe to put pressure on their own governments. The tactic failed, and as a result the Fourteen Points were simply a unilateral American pronouncement rather than a declaration of Allied policy. At the Paris peace conference Wilson learned how little binding power they had on the Allies.

The one area not covered by the Fourteen Points was fast becoming the most critical of all. In Russia, racked by revolution and a mounting civil war, the Bolsheviks were negotiating with the Germans for a separate peace. The Allies, in turn, sought to overthrow Lenin by aiding the counterrevolutionary White armies. Lippmann felt it was possible to work with the Bolsheviks and disastrous to join the Allied intervention. "We must beyond question maintain as friendly as possible an attitude towards the Russian revolution," he told Newton Baker. "We should not scold the Russians, no matter what peace they make. We ought to make it as clear as possible to them that we have not lost faith in the revolution, even though it is costing us much." Rather, the United States should speak to the Russians "with charity and understanding," make no reproaches, let them know that "we view the revolution as one of the real victories of the war" and that Russia's interests would be safeguarded at the peace conference.[14]

At the time Lippmann wrote Baker it still looked as though the Russians might be persuaded to stay in the war. The truce they had arranged with Germany in December had broken down a few weeks later when Berlin demanded Poland and huge chunks of the Ukraine. To force the battered Bolsheviks to agree to their terms, the Germans launched a new offensive in mid-February that took them to the gates of Petrograd. At that crucial moment Lippmann, using Baker as an intermediary, tried to dissuade Wilson from joining the anti-Bolshevik intervention organized by the Allies. Baker agreed, and told George Creel of the Committee on Public Information that "our only chance in Russia is to reestablish, as quickly as possible, confidence in our absolute honesty and disinterestedness."[15]

As the debate raged within the administration, Lippmann had a long conference with Lincoln Steffens. Shortly after the overthrow of the tsar a year earlier, Steffens had gone to Russia. One of his fellow travelers on the ship from New York was Leon Trotsky, homeward bound after years of exile to become Lenin's deputy. The sight of revolutionary Russia, the crowds, the excitement, the joy, had stirred Steffens to a rapture from which he never quite recovered. The Bolshevik revolution in November only increased his admiration, as well as his conviction that he had a special link to the radical leaders of Russia. When it became clear that the British and French were conspiring to overthrow the Bolshevik government, Steffens got in touch with Lippmann and urged that some way be found to persuade the Soviet leaders that Wilson's Fourteen Points were not merely imperialist propaganda. After meeting with his old mentor, Lippmann reported to House that Steffens believed, "quite shrewdly, I think, that . . . if somebody who is a friend of Trotsky could say to him that the President means what he says, it would make a great difference in Trotsky's behavior."[16]

Steffens volunteered to return to Moscow with a message from the President and suggested that Raymond Robins, director of the American

Red Cross Commission to Russia and a partisan of the revolution, be used as middle man between Wilson and Trotsky. He also proposed that John Reed, en route to the United States after having thrilled to the event he was to celebrate in his *Ten Days That Shook the World*, be enlisted in the cause. "It would be very simple for Steffens to convince Reed and use him as an intermediary," Lippmann explained to House. "I know Reed well, as we were classmates at Harvard, and could help if it were considered wise." House thought it worth a try, and encouraged Steffens to cable Reed, who at that time was being detained in Christiania (now Oslo). But Reed, by then a dedicated convert to the revolution, thought Steffens was behaving like a sentimental liberal. The overture fell flat.[17]

Indicted under the Espionage Act with the other editors of the *Masses* for opposing the war, Reed decided to return home to face trial and vindicate himself. Before his departure, Trotsky, in a fanciful gesture, had appointed him Soviet consul general to the United States. Raphael Zon, one of Reed's friends connected with the Inquiry, pointed out to Lippmann that it might have a bad effect on Russian opinion if an official representative of the Soviet government were arrested as he got off the boat in New York harbor. Zon urged Lippmann to use his influence to get the State Department to respect Reed's diplomatic immunity. But when Reed's ship docked in April 1918, government agents searched his luggage for revolutionary propaganda and confiscated his notes for *Ten Days That Shook the World*. When Steffens suggested that he enlist Lippmann to get the notes returned, an unforgiving Reed replied bitterly, "I wouldn't ask Walter L for anything for the whole world."[18]

Acquitted in two successive trials, Reed was arrested several times for making "incendiary" speeches. After being expelled from the Socialist party for excessively radical views, he formed the Communist Labor party. During the "Red Scare" following the war he was indicted for sedition, and in 1920 fled the country on a false passport, returning to Russia. There, in October, at the age of thirty-three, he died of typhus and was buried within the Kremlin walls.

The Russian revolution went on without Reed, and so did the attempt to strangle it. By the spring of 1918, following Lenin's acceptance of German peace terms at Brest Litovsk, Wilson had turned away from House's policy of accommodation with the Bolsheviks and acquiesced to a Japanese landing at Vladivostok. Three months later seven thousand American troops were put ashore in Siberia, ostensibly to protect two divisions of Czech soldiers who had been trapped in Russia and were on their way to the western front by a most circuitous route.

Lippmann's opposition to the intervention against the Bolsheviks had little, if any, effect on Wilson. His influence on this issue, as on others, worked only when his thinking reinforced administration policy, not when it ran counter to it. Yet if his influence was not as great as he might have liked, he had come very far in a very short time. Only a year earlier he had been writing editorials for the few thousand readers of a liberal weekly. Now he was at the vertex of high politics. His close association with Colonel House and his work at the Inquiry put him in touch with the highest administration officials. He was, as Randolph Bourne had written critically of such war intellectuals, "on the craft, in the stream." He loved every minute of it: the meetings with House, the late-night sessions at the Inquiry, the trips to Washington, the deference from those less well placed, the gratification of being at the center of action.

His new life seemed to suit him well. He doted on Faye, was delighted by her ability to get on well with his parents and friends, and approved her involvement with the suffragettes in their protests for the right to vote. Nearly every day he would meet her for lunch at a restaurant. He wanted so much to please her, even though he found it hard to show his affection. "I got home very late and found Faye pretending that she missed me, which pleased and flattered me, and which I never would let her know," he wrote in his diary that fall. Harold Laski, who dined with the Lippmanns at the end of December 1917 found Walter "vastly improved by homely pleasures," and told Justice Holmes that "the wife is as sensible in friendship as she is wealthy in looks. *Quid magis?*"[19]

Long since cut loose from the radicals, and cut off by them, Lippmann had a new circle of friends, young men like himself, ambitious and practical minded, who had found in the war a new outlet for their reformist zeal — men like Frankfurter, Fred Keppel, Stanley King and Ralph Hayes. With them he was at ease, and they responded with affection. "We miss you Walter — not only the intellect, for which all of us had an unholy admiration, but the grinning countenance for which we had a big love," Hayes wrote him from Washington. "Somebody said a few days ago that you kept more under cover than any person he knew. I agreed. Ain't it the truth?"[20]

What he kept under cover was his natural warmth. Only his friends saw it. Others saw his impatience with dullness and sloth. Some were irritated, others were envious of a man so evidently well placed, so clearly ambitious, and so aware of his privileged position. This made for bad feelings at the Inquiry. James T. Shotwell resented that Lippmann had taken over his job as editor, and complained that he "regarded his own place in the Inquiry as more important than that of any other."

Isaiah Bowman, the ambitious director of the American Geographical Society, resented him most of all and set about undermining him. He told Colonel House that under Lippmann's direction the map program had become "completely disorganized and demoralized," and that Lippmann was a "bad influence" because he would "disorganize whatever work was started by anyone else, taking men off work for his own special purposes." Such rivalry is endemic to bureaucracies, but in this case it was compounded by the fact that Bowman — who considered Mezes a "stooge for Colonel House" and of a "stupidity nothing short of colossal" — had relegated the director to a largely symbolic role and wanted to take over the Inquiry himself. To counter some of the antagonism Lippmann offered to take a 50 percent cut in salary to three thousand dollars a year. But the grievance was about power, not money. Bowman, who later accused Lippmann of being "selfish, superior, accepting but not giving information or favors, treacherous, and ambitious to an inordinate degree," was not going to let the younger man stand in his way of his becoming director.[21]

By the spring of 1918 Lippmann's relations with Bowman, Miller and Shotwell had become distinctly unpleasant. He also found the work less challenging than it had been. The exciting part — drawing up the frontiers of the postwar world, elaborating the Fourteen Points — had been mostly done. What remained was the framework for the projected League of Nations. This was a technical task for lawyers, but of little interest to one whose talents lay in coordinating and synthesizing ideas.

At this moment — with Bowman plotting to take over the Inquiry, Miller sulking in resentment, and Mezes blocking projects Lippmann considered essential — fate intervened. One morning in the middle of June 1918, an engaging fellow wearing the bars of a captain in military intelligence came up to 155th Street and approached Lippmann with a most novel proposition.

12

Captain Lippmann, Propagandist

I am glad of the whole experience, and I am glad it is over.

— To Newton D. Baker, February 7, 1919

LIPPMANN's visitor that morning, Captain Heber Blankenhorn, was a young journalist with some ideas about propaganda. A stint with Creel's information bureau had persuaded him that the army should have its own organization to get America's message across to the other side, rather than relying on the British and the French. Blankenhorn made his pitch as Wilson — in the wake of the secret treaties — was trying to distinguish America's war aims from those of the Allies. His plan fell on receptive ears in the War Department, but was opposed by Creel, who was wildly jealous of rivals. Blankenhorn decided to put together a small team capable of doing propaganda work, and then go straight to Secretary of War Newton Baker for permission to set up an army intelligence unit independent of the Committee on Public Information.

By the time he walked into Lippmann's office, Blankenhorn was ready to sign up several recruits, including Charles Merz, Washington correspondent of the *New Republic,* and Edgar Montillion Woolley, a teacher at Yale Drama School who later incarnated the "Man Who Came to Dinner." To fill out his team Blankenhorn needed someone who understood the politics of Germany and Austria-Hungary and could explain Wilson's diplomacy to the Europeans. Having heard about the Inquiry and Lippmann's involvement in it, Blankenhorn decided to play a long shot and approach the young editorialist directly.

"Do you not think that the time has come for active cooperation between us?" he had written Lippmann in early June 1918. "Writing unofficially I know that the Military Intelligence Branch needs you; I believe that you need the MIB." Blankenhorn sagely phrased his plan in a way that would appeal to Lippmann's idealism. "Our conceptions of 'propaganda' are the ideas of civilians, writers and students thinly veneered with khaki, who see in President Wilson their model of a propagandist and who conceive their job to be the organization of machinery for carrying into practice America's war of ideas,'' he explained. "If the Inquiry is laying the thoughtful foundations of a democratic peace . . . is it not your business to help guide the building of that peace by bringing your ideas early to the German mind? Can a democratic peace be made in a cloister?'' Now, after a few minutes of polite preliminaries in Lippmann's office, Blankenhorn made his bid. How would Lippmann like to be appointed American representative to the Inter-Allied Propaganda Board in London for several months? Blankenhorn moved boldly, knowing that if he landed Lippmann he would have a good chance of winning the secretary of war's blessings.

Lippmann was intrigued. He had long been fascinated by propaganda and public opinion. He and Blankenhorn discussed how the Inquiry's work could be dovetailed with the propaganda effort. How could the Fourteen Points be publicized where it counted most? What was the good of noble war aims if the German people did not know about them? Would not the promise of a just peace persuade the Germans to turn against their autocratic rulers? Blankenhorn drew a flattering picture of how America needed Lippmann to spread Wilson's ideals. He had no reason to think the bait would work. But to his surprise Lippmann mused a moment and then said: "I think I might like to do that.''[1]

That night he talked it over with Faye, and the next morning broached it to Colonel House. "I would want to do this work only in a way which the President and you would approve,'' he explained of Blankenhorn's plan to use the Inquiry in his propaganda work. There would be nothing crude about it; rather, it would be "getting away from propaganda in the sinister sense, and substituting for it a frank campaign of education addressed to the German and Austrian troops, explaining as simply and persuasively as possible the unselfish character of the war, the generosity of our aims, and the great hope of mankind which we are trying to realize.''[2]

House was delighted by the idea. It would solve the nasty situation at the Inquiry by shunting Lippmann off to Europe and allowing Bowman more leeway; it would give him a trusted man in Europe to deal with the British counterpart of the Inquiry; and it would remove the sting from Creel's crude propaganda efforts. He gave his enthusiastic approval, telling Lippmann there was "no one who could serve the government so well in such a capacity.'' That took care of it. "So far as I'm concerned, this settles the matter,'' Lippmann told Blankenhorn, "and I'm ready to pitch in if the MIB wishes it.'' Blankenhorn was amazed at how easy it had been to pry Lippmann loose, and concluded that he must have had a quarrel with House. He guessed wrong on the reason, but was dead right in his judgment that Lippmann was "mighty restive where he was" and eager to get off to Europe.[3]

While Blankenhorn went to Washington to get War Department approval, Lippmann outlined to Baker the advantages the scheme offered. The Inquiry's work would be "enormously strengthened" by direct access to current intelligence work in Europe and an American-controlled propaganda program could get the President's views across to the Germans. "The moral basis of our part in the war is a startling and perplexing novelty" in European affairs and a source of great strength, he noted in an appeal to Baker's idealism. The Americans should not be mere "mechanical transmitters of propaganda" written by the Allies. Propaganda should have a "distinctly American flavor" and use the President's speeches as a text. "We should avoid all the tricky and sinister aspects of what is usually called propaganda, and should aim to create the impression that here is something new and infinitely hopeful in the affairs of mankind."[4]

Baker gave his approval, but warned that "this education over the lines must be absolutely honest." With good reason Baker wanted to keep the leaflet program out of Creel's hands, for as tsar of American propaganda, the zealous Creel wanted to limit the army to distributing material prepared by the CPI. Any independent American propaganda unit would have displeased him — and particularly one including Lippmann. Creel had not forgiven Lippmann for having taken him to task three years earlier in the *New Republic* over a civil liberties issue in Colorado, where Creel had worked as a journalist. At that time Lippmann, in an unsigned editorial, had questioned Creel's honesty and called him a "reckless and incompetent person who . . . has shown himself incapable of judging evidence and determined to make a noise no matter what canons of truthfulness he violates." Creel had replied in kind, and the affair still rankled.[5]

As soon as Blankenhorn received Baker's go-ahead he wired Lippmann in New York: PLAN APPROVED. CAN YOU COME HERE AT ONCE. THE IRON IS HOT. A few hours later he followed it up with a second telegram: CAN YOU BE HERE IN TIME FOR DINNER AT SEVEN WITH US AND MASARYK. BRING MRS LIPPMANN.[6] Blankenhorn had been conferring with Thomas Masaryk, who was in Washington to promote the creation of an independent Czech-Slovak nation. Masaryk was all for the propaganda program. Get through to the captive peoples of the Dual Monarchy, he told the Americans, and the empire would be so weakened it would have to drop out of the war.

Within four days of Blankenhorn's first visit to the Inquiry, the War Department approved his plan. A week later Lippmann received his commission as captain in the United States Army, "appointed for serving on Intelligence solely and will not be assigned to any other duty or to the command of troops under this appointment,'' according to the War Department order. Lippmann now wore two hats: one as propagandist, the other as House's personal representative to the Allied intelligence offices to coordinate their work with that of the Inquiry. Along with his army orders he carried a letter signed by Lansing designating him as envoy of the State Department with instructions to make "special studies in economic and political matters" by methods "entirely at your discretion."[7] Word went out to the American ambassadors in London, Paris and Rome to cooperate with the young emissary.

Conferring one last time with Colonel House, Lippmann set off for Europe in his uniform. With his letters of introduction in hand, and captain's bars on his shoulders, he kissed Faye and his parents good-bye, and took the ferry to Hoboken, where he joined Blankenhorn, the five other members of the propaganda team, and several hundred draftees on the *Northern Pacific*. The next morning, July 14, 1918, Bastille Day, they set out, zigzagging across the Atlantic to avoid submarines. Arriving in Brest on the twenty-second, they marched through the town to the cheers of the inhabitants, and then took the train to American Expeditionary Force headquarters at Chaumont, a provincial town 150 miles east of Paris. No sooner did they lay down their packs than Lippmann and Blankenhorn set off for London to attend the inter-Allied conference on propaganda.

There they received a rude shock. James Keeley, a former Chicago publisher who directed the CPI office in Europe, told them that while they were crossing the Atlantic the initial agreement on lines of responsibility had been changed. Now, instead of the army's MIB being in charge of both preparation and delivery of propaganda across enemy lines, it would be confined merely to distributing propaganda material at the front. Creel's CPI would handle everything else. This would undercut the army unit's position. Quickly adapting to the ways of bureaucracy, Lippmann and Blankenhorn decided that since they had not been officially notified of the change, they would ignore it.

At the inter-Allied conference they sat in on planning sessions and savored a dizzying round of luncheons and dinners. The conference, directed by the press boss Lord Northcliffe, included such people as Lord Reading, the lord chief justice; Lippmann's old friend Eustace Percy from the Foreign Office; Wickham Steed of *The Times;* and R. W. Seton-Watson. "We are quite blasé from meeting bigwigs," the slightly dazed Blankenhorn reported to his wife. "The information we've wanted we've gotten freely from the founts at the top of Parnassus. Much business here is transacted at dinners and luncheons. We're going at it like those to the manor born. State secrets between glasses of Graves, that's the method."[8]

While the conference went well, Lippmann was disturbed by Keeley's news about the arrangement between the MIB and Creel's unit. From London he wrote House of the "somewhat confused" relations between the government units, and of the "need to create a real center of political information" in Europe to coordinate American propaganda. People in the Foreign Office and propagandists on Northcliffe's staff had told him that the CPI's work in Europe was "very bad." Turnover was constant and Creel's people knew nothing about British journalism or European politics. "Their reputation among the English is very low," Lippmann reported of the CPI. Creel's man Keeley complained of having no support from Washington, and even admitted his own inability to handle the job: "He feels completely lost when he has to sit down and discuss the complicated problems of Central Europe with the very expert staff that Lord Northcliffe has collected around him." Lippmann urged House to set up a propaganda unit independent of Creel and appoint as director Hugh Gibson, a foreign service officer who had worked with Herbert Hoover on Belgian relief and with General Pershing on intelligence.[9]

Propaganda was not Lippmann's only job in London. As official emissary from the Inquiry, and the unofficial representative of Colonel House, he conferred with Sir William Tyrell, director of what the Americans called the "British Inquiry." Tyrell did not quite know what to make of Lippmann or how much authority he had, and decided to check with his New York agent. The young baronet Sir William Wiseman had established a warm rapport with Colonel House and was well placed to answer Tyrell's query. "I would not say that Lippmann is very closely in House's confidence," Wiseman wired London. Rather, he was employed by House because he was "undoubtedly a very able young man and represents a certain section of the more intelligent radicals" in America. "House, however, has not very much confidence in his judgments and would certainly not think of letting him organize a political intelligence department on your side."[10] It was natural that British officials would be confused about Lippmann. His reputation both as a radical and as confidant to House had preceded him — two roles they did not find easy to reconcile. Yet he spoke with such self-confidence that it was generally assumed he must be a person whom it would be unwise to take lightly.

Lippmann reported back to House that both Tyrell and Eustace Percy had urged that the League of Nations be set up immediately to quiet the pacifists and prevent the Allied governments from backing down on their pledges. Talks with journalists such as C. P. Scott of the *Guardian* had also persuaded him of a "growing feeling that the old liberal leadership of the President has not been exercised sufficiently." Wilson, he advised, should reiterate his faith in the league, support the liberation of the east European nationality groups, and repeat "America's refusal to enter any selfish economic league against a reformed Germany."[11]

Lippmann's comments on Creel's propaganda unit and on British attitudes toward the league soon reached the White House. Wilson was not pleased. The President had a personal interest in the propaganda program and shared his friend Creel's concern that the army was taking over the CPI's activities in Europe. He was also irritated at Lippmann for the *New Republic*'s criticism of his administration's suppression of dissent. As far as he was concerned, Lippmann was still part of the *NR* crowd. Thus, when House passed on Lippmann's letter, Wilson viewed it as a personal criticism. "I am very much puzzled as to who sent Lippmann over to inquire into matters of propaganda," he replied testily to House. "I have found his judgment most unsound, and therefore entirely unserviceable in matters of that sort because he, in common with the men of *The New Republic*, has ideas about the war and its purposes which are highly unorthodox from my own point of view." He also was suspicious of those Lippmann quoted with such approval. "What he says about his interviews with Sir William Tyrell interests me very much, but if he thinks that Lord Eustace Percy is equally trustworthy, he is vastly mistaken. He is one of the most slippery and untrustworthy of the men we have had to deal with here." Colonel House, in an effort to mollify Wilson, explained that Lippmann had been sent over by the War Department to deal with propaganda, and added: "I do not know how recently you have been in touch with Lippmann, but my impression is that he is not now in sympathy with the men who govern policy of *The New Republic*. . . . He was always the ablest of that group and he is young enough to be weaned away from them and be broadened."[12]

At the very moment that House was trying to appease Wilson, Lippmann, having left the conference and sent Blankenhorn back to Chaumont, was in Paris meeting with diplomat Hugh Gibson and Arthur Frazier, number two man at the American embassy and House's contact man there. They shared Lippmann's contempt for Creel and encouraged him to complain to House over State Department lines. In a blistering critique of the Creel operation, Lippmann cabled House that the CPI failed to understand that propaganda was a means, not just of winning the war, but of laying the groundwork for a just peace. "In every European country propaganda against the enemy is treated as an instrument of diplomacy and the men who direct it are high in the council of government." Why did the American war effort have to suffer such incompetence?[13]

If Lippmann's complaint was well taken, his timing could hardly have been worse. Wilson had barely cooled down after Lippmann's letter from London when this new cable from Paris crossed his desk. Creel demanded that Lippmann be recalled immediately. Wilson agreed to muzzle Blankenhorn's unit and put all propaganda under the CPI. "I have a high opinion of Lippmann, but I am very jealous in the matter of propaganda," he told Lansing, ". . . [and] want to keep the matter of publicity in my own hands."

House warned Lippmann that his complaints were causing "friction" and that he should avoid "talking or cabling anything of a critical character." Stung by the colonel's rebuke, Lippmann explained lamely that he was merely trying to help unsnarl "one of those unfortunate affairs where men are trying to take each other's jobs away. You know, of course, that I am a thousand times more interested in the Inquiry than in propaganda, and that I only went into it because I was told I was needed."[14]

Lines of authority continued to be blurred for the remaining months of the war, but Creel kept the upper hand. Lippmann did not openly challenge him again, but when it was all over summed up his feelings in a bitter article for the *NR*. "One of the genuine calamities of our part in the war was the character of American propaganda in Europe," he wrote. "It was run as if an imp had devised it to thwart every purpose Mr. Wilson was supposed to entertain. The general tone of it was one of unmitigated brag accompanied by unmitigated gullibility. . . . The outfit which was abroad 'selling the war to Europe' (the phrase is not my own) gave shell-shocked Europe to understand that a rich bumpkin had come to town with his pockets bulging and no desire except to please."[15]

By the end of August the dispute between Creel and the MIB had been resolved, and the little band of propagandists had moved into their headquarters at Chaumont: half a room in a casern built during the Napoleonic wars. The door of their makeshift nerve center bore the imposing title "Inter-Allied Propaganda Commission." To give the office the proper tone, and to hide the cracks in the plaster, they pasted propaganda leaflets, maps and charts on the four-foot-thick walls. Office furniture consisted of a few rickety tables piled high with handbills, old newspapers, and copies of Wilson's speeches.

As ranking literary member of the team, Lippmann's job was to write the propaganda leaflets to be dropped behind enemy lines. But since there was no place in Chaumont to print them, he had to go to Paris to use the presses of the French propaganda bureau. He could hardly conceal his delight at escaping the barracks. "God how he hated the army!" Blankenhorn recalled.[16]

The first leaflets rolled off the presses early in September. Designed to encourage desertion, they stressed the good treatment prisoners of war would receive. "Do not worry about me," read one of Lippmann's efforts. "I am out of the war. I am well fed. The American army gives its prisoners the same rations it gives its own soldiers: beef, white bread, potatoes, prunes, coffee, milk, butter . . .'' Ultimately they ran off over a million copies of this leaflet — the most effective of all American propaganda material and the one found most frequently on captured German soldiers. During September and October 1918 Lippmann's minuscule subunit in Paris produced more than five million copies of eighteen different leaflets. The first batch was spread by patrols penetrating enemy lines and by unmanned balloons. Later the propagandists shifted to delivery by airplane. Pilots in open cockpits stuffed the leaflets between their legs and threw them out over the German lines.

Lippmann's work kept him moving. "The job of getting propaganda started now that the Germans are beginning to move backward has kept me constantly on the jump around France, and even up to the front," he reported to Bowman, in an effort to establish better relations. "I haven't got the heart to go there to exhibit what nerve I may possess, but to go because the job requires it occasionally is peculiarly satisfactory. . . . The Inquiry,'' he continued in an inspirational vein, "has a tremendous part to play, for America has an influence over here on men's minds and hearts beyond anything one can imagine. We shan't fail, I am certain, for lack of good will. We dare not fail for lack of understanding.''

To Mezes, who remained as titular head of the Inquiry, though his power had been sapped by Bowman, Lippmann wrote that there were "just four Americans who exist in the consciousness of people over here.'' The first was the President, "a figure of mystical proportions, of really incredible power but altogether out of reach of direct contact. . . . You always take a kind of immunity bath by prefacing your remarks with a pledge of undying devotion to the principles laid down by President Wilson.'' The second was Colonel House, "the human Intercessor, the Comforter, the Virgin Mary . . . his advice is sought because it is believed to be a little nearer this world than the President's.'' Third was Herbert Hoover, "who incarnates all that is at once effective and idealistic in the picture of America"; and fourth, General Pershing, "about whom there is heartfelt enthusiasm among the troops.''[17]

Lippmann's own contact with the troops was exceedingly limited. Not until late September 1918, after the battle of the Argonne, was the propaganda unit moved up toward the front. There, in General Pershing's office, Lippmann had a reunion with Newton Baker; Ralph Hayes, Baker's private secretary; and Willard Straight, then serving as an aide to Pershing. Baker, who was being squired around the front by a bevy of generals, asked Lippmann to come along on the tour through the camps and bombed-out villages. The Germans, having exhausted themselves two months earlier in the second battle of the Marne, were now in retreat. The war was nearly over. Baker, the ruminative pacifist, had organized the machine that had brought more than a million American soldiers to France and had transformed an impasse into an Allied victory. "What a country we are," he said to Lippmann. "Do you know that I have a petition about a mile long asking me not to move supplies on Sunday!"

Lippmann stayed on at the front for several weeks, interrogating prisoners. During this time one of Pershing's aides discovered that he and Charles Merz had worked for a magazine of "pronounced Bolshevist trends," and demanded that the two covert revolutionaries be sent packing. Blankenhorn saved them by bringing in Major Willard Straight, who explained that he was a partner in J. P. Morgan and Company, and that his magazine, the *New Republic,* had supported the reelection of Wilson in 1916.[18]

With the success of the Allied offensive and the surrender of Bulgaria in late September 1918, the collapse of the Central Powers was at hand. On October 3 the Germans appealed to Wilson for an armistice based on the Fourteen Points. Now the Allies balked. They had never officially accepted the Fourteen Points — which were purely a unilateral American declaration — and with victory at hand they wanted the spoils of war. An irritated Wilson dispatched House to Europe with instructions to get the Allies to agree to Germany's surrender on the basis of the Fourteen Points.

The colonel arrived in Paris on October 25, set up headquarters on the Left Bank at 74, rue de l'Université, and immediately had Lippmann transferred to his staff. House realized that he could get nowhere with the Allies until he had a detailed explanation of exactly what the Fourteen Points meant. Meanwhile, the fighting continued as the Allies haggled over terms. "We can dally no longer over this armistice," he told Lippmann. The Germans had accepted the President's conditions, and now there had to be a formula to end the fighting. He was meeting the Allied leaders and would lay the Fourteen Points on the table. He had to explain exactly what Wilson meant by such terms as "open diplomacy" and "freedom of the seas," and where the new boundaries would be drawn. "You helped write these points," he told Lippmann. "Now you must give me a precise definition of each one. I shall need it by tomorrow morning at ten o'clock."

Lippmann left House's office slightly dazed. He had less than twenty-four hours to elaborate in detail the terms of Wilson's peace plan. He did not have a single document with him; everything was at the Inquiry's headquarters in New York. No one in France had ever worked on the material. He did not even have a copy of the points. Nor did the American embassy. Finally he tracked one down at the Paris *Herald.* Racing back to his desk, he sat down and one by one began to write out precise explanations of the Fourteen Points. During the night Frank Cobb, editorial-page director of the New York *World,* dropped by to elaborate the point concerning the League of Nations. Working nonstop, Lippmann finished at three in the morning and rushed the memoranda to the coding room to be cabled to Wilson for approval. The President's acceptance came back just in time for House's meeting with the Allies.[19]

For a week House argued with the British, French and Italians over the terms of the settlement. At one point he even threatened to sign a separate peace. Finally, on November 4 they agreed to accept a German surrender loosely linked to the Fourteen Points. The fight had been bitter. The British reserved the right to interpret "freedom of the seas" to mean supremacy of the Royal Navy; the French insisted that the Germans pay for damage done to civilian property. But agreement had been reached, and on November 11 the Germans signed the armistice. To Lippmann it seemed a heroic beginning. "I must write you this morning because I couldn't possibly tell you to your face how great a thing you have achieved," he wrote House with an appreciation no less real for being effusively flattering. "Frankly I did not believe it was humanly possible under conditions as they seemed to be in Europe to win so glorious a victory. This is the climax of a course that has been as wise as it was brilliant, and as shrewd as it was prophetic. The President and you have more than justified the faith of those who insisted that your leadership was a turning point in modern history. No one can ever thank you adequately."[20]

House, having pushed through the armistice, moved to begin preparations for a peace settlement. He set up headquarters for the Commission to Negotiate Peace at the Hotel Crillon, transferred Lippmann and Willard Straight to the commission staff, and prepared to add his son-in-law, Gordon Auchincloss, as secretary-general and Frank Cobb as chief of the press bureau. But Wilson had other plans. Not wanting to share the glory of his triumph, not fully trusting House or anyone else to bring about the just peace he so desired, Wilson decided to head the peace delegation himself, using Lansing as a deputy. The secretary of state, eager to bring his department back into the negotiations, named his own men to the American delegation, appointing Joseph Grew to head the staff and George Creel to direct the press bureau. The little band in Paris was shocked when they heard the news. House, instead of running the show, would be only an adviser. The commission staff would be downgraded, perhaps ignored.[21]

House had incurred Wilson's displeasure by urging him not to conduct the negotiations himself, warning that it would be dangerous to invest his personal prestige at a time when he should be at home shaping American public opinion for the final settlement. But Wilson was convinced that only he could achieve an equitable peace, and jealously suspected House of wanting to cheat him of his triumph. House, his work in Paris completed, returned to the United States to prepare Wilson for the delicate negotiations that were to follow. From mid-November, when House left, until mid-December, when Wilson and the negotiating team arrived in Paris, Lippmann had little to do but wait for the colonel's return and grow increasingly disheartened by the hardening of the Allies' positions.

At the end of November both Lippmann and Willard Straight came down with influenza, victims of the epidemic that ultimately took some twenty million lives. After a few bad days Lippmann recovered. But Straight grew steadily worse, racked by fever and terrible pain. Lippmann sat by his bedside as he fought for life, and together with Wilson's personal physician, Dr. Grayson, and Mrs. Borden Harriman, was with him when he died on December 1. "In the last eight weeks I was closer to Willard than ever before," Lippmann wrote Dorothy Straight. "Up at the First Army we talked far into the night, hoping, planning, sometimes doubting, but in the end renewed. In that personal loneliness which is the background of so many of us here, there was mixed also a fear that what we had meant, and what alone could justify it all, was not the meaning and the justification of those who will decide."[22]

He did not have to wait long for his fears to be realized. Two weeks later, on Friday, December 13, Wilson's ship, the *George Washington,* arrived in Brest, bringing a delegation of thirteen hundred Americans. A century earlier Britain had sent exactly fourteen diplomats to the Congress of Vienna to end the Napoleonic wars. Among this enormous throng was a twenty-three-man contingent from the Inquiry — including Mezes, Bowman, Shotwell, and Charles Seymour. They had not the slightest idea of what they were supposed to do, had never met with the President, and had been confined to the most cramped and dingy part of the vessel. Their inauspicious entry accurately indicated the part they would play in Paris. Wilson was intent on running his own show. The Inquiry group was absorbed into the State Department assemblage under the direction of Lansing.

On December 14 Lippmann stood on the balcony of the Hotel Crillon, alongside his friend Ralph Hayes, and watched the President make his triumphant entry into Paris. Across the Seine the multitudes around the Chamber of Deputies began to sway, and then a great roar erupted as the procession surged across the bridge into the place de la Concorde. Wilson had come as a messiah, and for the next four weeks — until the peace conference opened on January 12 — he was greeted with veneration as he traveled through France, Britain and Italy, the symbol of the principles that would transform the world.

Wilson thrilled to the applause, confirmed in his belief that the peoples of Europe stood at his side. But beneath the euphoria political lines were hardening. Wilson had his vision, the Allies had their demands. "I have yet to find one person who is optimistic as to the sort of peace that can be secured,'' Ralph Hayes told Newton Baker a few days after the President's arrival. House was unable to gain control over the American Commission to Negotiate Peace; and the American team was staffed with incompetents. Lippmann was "greatly discouraged,'' and blamed the American diplomats for not "wanting anything but eyewash'' out of the settlement, Hayes said.[23]

Ten thousand people converged on Paris that winter, all claiming to have some crucial connection with the peace conference. Five hundred reporters grasped at scraps of news and fed one another with rumors that were then pumped into front-page dispatches. Even practiced journalists seemed lost in the labyrinth of rumors, lies, leaks and innuendos. Censorship and propaganda made it impossible to distinguish reality from rumor. "At Paris men looked out upon two continents in revolt, upon conflicts and aspirations more intricate and more obscure than any they had ever been called to resolve,'' Lippmann wrote of the scene a few months later.

The pathetically limited education of officials trained to inert and pleasant ways of life prevented them from seeing or understanding the strange world that lay before them. All they knew and cared for, all that life meant to them, seemed to be slipping away to red ruin, and so in panic they ceased to be reporters and began bombarding the chancelleries at home with gossip and frantic exclamation. The clamor converged on Paris, and all the winds of doctrine were set whirling around the conferees. Every dinner table, every lobby, almost every special interview, every subordinate delegate, every expert adviser was a focus of intrigue and bluster and manufactured rumor. The hotels were choked with delegations representing, and pretending to represent, and hoping to represent every group of people in the world. The newspaper correspondents, struggling with this elusive and all-pervading chaos, were squeezed between the appetite of their readers for news and the desire of the men with whom the decisions rested not to throw the unconcluded negotiations into this cyclone of distortion.[24]

From those discouraging weeks came, four years later, Lippmann's great work on public opinion and his inquiry into the effect of propaganda on democracy itself.

Sitting in his little office in the Hotel Crillon, Lippmann had long, dispiriting talks with the journalists: Frank Cobb, Herbert Bayard Swope, Ray Stannard Baker, William Allen White and Lincoln Steffens; with young members of the American delegation: Adolf Berle, William Bullitt, John Foster and Allen Dulles, and Samuel Eliot Morison; with Felix Frankfurter, who had come to Paris representing the Zionist movement; with a cynical English economist on his country's Treasury team, John Maynard Keynes; and with an entertaining art historian whose passion for politics and influential connections had enabled him to wangle the job of "interpreter first class," Bernard Berenson.

The bedlam at Paris would have been tolerable to Lippmann had he enjoyed a major role on the negotiating team. But Colonel House was no longer in full control, and without a powerful protector Lippmann was vulnerable. Bowman was director of the Inquiry team, and was not eager to find a place for a man whose talent he envied and whose ambition he resented. "Lippmann has been much troubled for many weeks," Ralph Hayes wrote Newton Baker. "Walter's liberalism is the source of much whispering about him whenever he gets close to a throne. So he has been puttering about here on a multitude of jobs without being given any definite and sizeable job."[25]

After waiting for weeks to be given an assignment, Lippmann approached Bowman directly to ask for a place on the Inquiry. Bowman was unsympathetic and complained about his attitude in New York, and how he had ousted Shotwell from his job as editor. As he left Bowman's office Lippmann realized how much the director resented him and that he would never get back on the Inquiry. Nor, having annoyed Wilson with his criticism of Creel's propaganda work, and being considered one of House's men, would he be able to work on the peace commission. Convinced that he could no longer play any effective role at the peace conference, he turned down an offer to go on a diplomatic mission to Berlin and asked to return to the United States.[26]

On December 28, two days after his orders came through, he wrote Dorothy Straight that he had wanted to leave Paris ever since the end of November, but that Colonel House had talked him out of it. "He wisely urged me to stay, help in the preliminaries, learn the situation better before returning. But he did agree that what America thought counted most, and that anything which could be done to explain matters at home would be most worthwhile." Since Willard Straight's death, he told her, he had spent "weeks of wandering in the labyrinth of indecision, and the case is typical. I am very anxious to get back into fresh air."[27]

As the delegates gathered in Paris for the peace conference, Lippmann said good-bye to his friends, wished Colonel House good luck, and took the train to Brest. There, on January 23, 1919, he boarded the S.S. *Cedric* for New York. For weeks he had been under great strain. Now he was drained, swept by the melancholy that occasionally seized him. "The general depression which I've been fighting off for about three months nearly got me in Brest," he confided to Bernard Berenson, to whom he had drawn close in Paris, "but with a little [luck] I came aboard, and with a decent rest I shall probably be all right soon. Taking a rest now is rather a nuisance — a little like losing your wind in the last quarter of a mile."

At the end of January he landed at Hoboken — a little more than six months after he had first optimistically set sail for Europe. Faye and his parents were there to hail their war hero and escort him back to East 80th Street. Returning to his wife, to the *New Republic,* to an America transformed by the war, to an uncertain peace, he painfully began to rebuild his old life. A letter from Harold Laski was waiting for him. "You must not let these glimpses of the underworld disturb you," the British socialist wrote. "I doubt whether you realized against what traditions you were fighting on the Commission, how fiercely you were resented, how eagerly intrigue against you was fanned into a vivid flame. The real thing is that amidst it all you did not lose your hold on liberalism and that you have come home to fight for it. It never needed your aid so badly as now."

What had begun as a crusade had ended in confusion and disillusion. "I am glad of the whole experience," Lippmann wrote Newton Baker a few days after his return to New York, "and I am glad it is over."[28]

13

"This Is Not Peace"

Sometimes I think we are a damned generation.
— To Bernard Berenson, July 16, 1919

DON'T hesitate, whatever the difficulties, to go back to the paper,"
Harold Laski counseled Lippmann on his return to New York.
"It wants your style, your sense of the right path, your eager alertness
to the perspective of events. It is a great platform and the kind of organ
worthy of you." Laski was not an idle flatterer. He knew that the *New
Republic* needed Lippmann. "Only you can do the great human service
of bringing to maturity the ideas and hopes which struggle for expression in Herbert's mind. Please remember that for a year while you were
on it, it made history week by week."

Lippmann returned to the *NR,* saw his old friends, took on an assignment as correspondent for the *Manchester Guardian,* and tried to pick
up where he had left off. But his old optimism was gone. "The whole
process of statesmanship has left him with the conviction that the real
truths are in the great books of the world," Laski reported to Justice
Holmes. "I am eager for you to see him again — he is more critical,
less facile, and, to say the same thing differently, with a deeper sense
that you don't find truth by skimming milk." [1]

Reports from Paris provided little ground for enthusiasm. The French,
seeking security in Germany's weakness, wanted to detach the left bank
of the Rhine and set up puppet states. The Poles, citing boundaries of
long-forgotten kingdoms, demanded territories inhabited mostly by Germans, including East Prussia. The Italians, invoking the secret treaty of
1915, made claim to the German-speaking South Tyrol, the coast of
Dalmatia, and the Slavic city of Fiume (later Rijeka). Wilson, it was
rumored, was caving in to Clemenceau and Lloyd George. No one knew
what he was giving away from pressure, or weariness, or failure to understand.

By mid-March 1919 an apprehensive Lippmann wrote Colonel House of the "resentment" caused by the President's failure to explain what he was doing. "The temper of the country is noticeably cooler, and it would be a great mistake if the Americans in Paris compromised too much with the Jingoes who are trying to terrorize public opinion," he warned House. Wilson need only "explain clearly and definitely why each move he makes is related to a program of permanent peace in order to win over all the opposition that counts."

But to Bernard Berenson, with whom he had struck up an instant friendship during those weeks in Paris, Lippmann was less circumspect. "Parsifal's visit to this country did not help much," he wrote caustically of Wilson's brief return to America, "and he left a lot of people with the impression that he was not quite sure what his own product meant." The superpatriots had "turned into a band of 'little Americans' shouting that by no means must America be contaminated by Europeans," and a wave of anticommunist hysteria had seized the country. "The people are shivering in their boots over Bolshevism, and they are far more afraid of Lenin than they ever were of the Kaiser. We seem to be the most frightened lot of victors that the world ever saw."[2]

While America was going through the first stages of the Red Scare — with the jailing and deportation of suspected "radicals" and aliens — Britain and France moved to prevent the Bolshevik revolution from spreading westward. Frightened by uprisings that for a time put communists in control of Berlin, Munich and Budapest, they sent troops to seize Russia's Arctic ports, aided the counterrevolutionary White armies, imposed a blockade of food shipments to Russia, and moved to set up an anticommunist buffer zone in eastern Europe.

Wilson's initial refusal to join the intervention encouraged the young diplomat William C. Bullitt to go to Moscow — with Colonel House's blessing — to see what terms he could work out with Lenin. Lincoln Steffens went along for company, and when they returned three weeks later Steffens was so overwhelmed by what he had seen that he proclaimed, in a phrase forever linked to his name, "I have been over into the future and it works!" Bullitt returned with something more tangible: a promise from Lenin to pay Russia's war debts and to offer economic concessions to the West in exchange for diplomatic recognition of the Bolshevik regime. Colonel House saw possibilities of a deal. But Wilson, whose relations with House had cooled and whose antipathy toward the Bolsheviks made such an arrangement unpalatable, vetoed Bullitt's initiative. He then succumbed to Allied pressure by joining the Anglo-French intervention against the Bolsheviks and sending American troops to Soviet ports in the Arctic. An embittered Bullitt angrily resigned from the diplomatic service. Wilson would soon feel his ire.[3]

From his friends in Paris — Keynes, Berenson, and Philip Kerr —

Lippmann received disquieting reports of Wilson's compromises. By the middle of March he could contain his anxiety no longer. In a long speculative essay that marked his official return to the *New Republic*, he gave voice to the doubts he had been nurturing since he left Europe. The peace outlined by the Fourteen Points was no longer possible, he argued. The old order had been shattered by the Bolshevik revolution, the destruction of German power, and the disintegration of the Austro-Hungarian Empire. Reactionaries were trying to prevent reform by raising the Bolshevik bogey. Clemenceau and Lloyd George wanted to turn eastern Europe into a "cordon sanitaire" against the spread of radical ideas. It could not work, he warned. "Unless the bridges to moderate radicalism are maintained, anarchy will follow." If the Europeans botched the peace, Americans would not bail them out. "We shall stay with you and share the decisions of the future if you will make the peace we are asked to share, a peace that Europe will endure," Lippmann wrote. "But if you make it a peace that can be maintained only by the bayonet, we shall leave you to the consequences and find our own security in this hemisphere. It will have to be a very bad peace indeed to justify any such action on our part, and nothing less than that would ever justify it."

"The Political Scene," as he called the essay when it was published in the *NR* that March and later in book form, made a powerful impression. "He has a mind like a knife and will be a great power one day," Laski wrote Justice Holmes. Learned Hand told Lippmann that his essay showed a "breadth and certainty of treatment, a kind of depth in foundation, which makes what you say massive and correspondingly impressive." Even though he disagreed with some of the conclusions, Hand hailed Lippmann's return to the *New Republic* as a "thing of genuine public interest. . . . If you can sustain such power and scope you will make yourself a noticeable force in American political ideas," he predicted. "The war was a bad enough thing, but it certainly has been a blessing for you."[4]

Lippmann had said that only a "very bad peace indeed" might force America to repudiate the settlement. The following weeks made such a peace all too likely. "I expect a compromise all along the line," he wrote Berenson early in May. "Life will have considerably stained the radiance of the Fourteen Points." Yet there seemed to be no alternative to the treaty. "We here shall grumble and accept the results for two reasons — no peace means Bolshevism everywhere in Europe, and we don't want that; and the League is enough to build on if the parties get in control in France and Britain that wish to use it."[5]

A few days later the treaty was published, confirming Lippmann's worst fears. Germany not only lost Alsace-Lorraine, which was expected, but was stripped of its colonies in Africa and the Pacific, forced to admit that it alone was responsible for the war, burdened with a fifteen-billion-dollar indemnity plus reparations still undetermined, disarmed, and placed under Allied economic control. With the creation of an independent Poland, two million Germans fell under Warsaw's rule. East Prussia was severed from the rest of Germany by the Polish Corridor. The new state of Czechoslovakia included German-inhabited Sudetenland. Austria became a separate state, forbidden to join the new German republic. The Italians, though denied Fiume, won the Austrian South Tyrol. Even Japan came away with booty, taking over Germany's economic control of the Chinese province of Shantung, and gaining a league mandate over German-owned Pacific islands. Bad as it was, the treaty might have been even worse. Wilson prevented France from annexing the Saar and setting up puppet republics in the Rhineland, denied Italy the coast of Yugoslavia, and resisted Polish demands to annex East Prussia.

For Lippmann and his colleagues at the *NR*, the treaty was a terrible betrayal. Not only did it "balkanize" Central Europe by breaking up Austria-Hungary, but it imposed a reparations burden that threatened to overwhelm the fledgling German republic and breed a spirit of revanche. "Looked at from above, below, and from every side I can't see anything in this treaty but endless trouble for Europe, and I'm exceedingly doubtful in my own mind as to whether we can afford to guarantee so impossible a peace," Lippmann wrote a friend in mid-May. "I am very deeply discouraged about the whole business." To Wilson's press secretary he was equally direct. "For the life of me I can't see peace in this document," he told Ray Stannard Baker, "and as the President has so frequently said, statesmen who cannot hear the voice of mankind are sure to be broken."[6]

The men at the *New Republic* had prided themselves on their pragmatic adjustment to political "realities" and had even boasted of helping to bring America into the war. But they were not prepared for this treaty. At an editorial conference Croly argued vehemently that such a cynical settlement would forever taint the league. Lippmann, who had been inclined to support the treaty to save the league, was persuaded, and by unanimous vote the editors decided to oppose the treaty. "It is a bitter decision to make," Croly wrote Justice Brandeis, "because it is practically a confession of failure, so far as our work during the last few years is concerned," but there was no doubt that "the League is not powerful enough to redeem the Treaty."

In the May 17 issue the editors unleashed their attack. IS IT PEACE? they asked in words emblazoned across the cover. "Looked at from the purely American point of view, on a cold calculation of probabilities, we do not see how this treaty is anything but the prelude to quarrels in a deeply divided and hideously embittered Europe," Lippmann wrote in the lead editorial. "The immediate task for Americans is to decide coolly just how they will limit their obligations under the Covenant. That they must be limited seems to us an inescapable condition."[7]

The following week the *NR* answered its own question. THIS IS NOT PEACE the editors declared in another bold pronunciamento. "Americans would be fools if they permitted themselves now to be embroiled in a system of European alliances. . . . The peace cannot last. America should withdraw from all commitments which would impair her freedom of action." Article Ten obliged the United States to defend an unjust territorial settlement. America could not play that game. "It would be the height of folly to commit a great people as the guarantor of a condition which is morbidly sick with conflict and trouble." Once the decision was made, Lippmann was unflinching. "It will require at least a generation of force to secure the execution of this treaty," he told some five hundred distressed Unitarians in Boston who had assembled to lend support to the league. "What confronts us is one of the greatest schisms of society."[8]

He felt he owed his friends an explanation, and above all Newton Baker. "For several weeks I've wanted to write to you and always I've hesitated because I could not quite find the words to express my disappointment at the outcome in Paris," he wrote his former chief. Looked at either from the moral point of view and the pledges given by Wilson, or coldly from the viewpoint of its workableness, the treaty was a disaster. "I know that to you the promises made by the President were the major reality which underlay the whole conflict. How in our consciences are we to square the results with the promises?" Rather than restoring the French boundaries of 1871, the treaty gave France control of the Saar and set up a "humanly intolerable" regime over the ethnic Germans there. Such a transfer of territory was expressly excluded under the armistice agreement, and it was precisely to block such expansionist French ambitions, Lippmann reminded Baker, that in drafting the memoranda on which the Fourteen Points were based he had used the formula "the wrong done to France in 1871" rather than citing French claims dating back to earlier wars.

Nor was France alone in its aggrandizement. After saying he would give Poland territory inhabited by "indisputably" Polish populations, Wilson acquiesced in putting two million Germans under Polish rule, along with the indisputably German city of Danzig. In Schleswig-Holstein the victors had detached so much territory from Germany that the Danes refused to accept it. They prohibited Austria from voluntarily choosing to unite with Germany, and in Bohemia and the Tyrol put more ethnic Germans under alien rule. "All of this we have done at the conclusion of a war which had its origin at least partially in the violation of national principles," Lippmann charged. "We have done this after the most solemn kind of assurances that we would not do it. We have made a League of Nations and from it we have excluded the German Republic though we have disarmed it and left it without any means of defense." And by fixing reparations without specifying an amount, and by permitting the "most drastic kind of interference" to ensure payment, Britain and France were allowed to gain the "ultimate control of all phases of German life."

"I presume that you hardly believe that this is either a just or a workable peace," he continued, "and I suppose that you keep your faith in the future by hoping that the League of Nations can modify the terms and work out a genuine settlement. I can't share that belief. . . . It seems to me to stand the world on its head to assume that a timid legal document can master and control the appetites and the national wills before which this Treaty puts such immense prizes."

Responsibility for the disastrous treaty lay with Wilson. "I can find no excuses in the fact that he had a difficult task in Paris. No one supposed that he would have an easy one." He should have demanded that the Allies abrogate the secret treaties and accept his program before the war was over. Part of the trouble lay in his failure to use men to whom he could delegate such tasks, part in his "curious irresponsibility in the use of language which leads him to make promises without any clear idea as to how they are to be fulfilled." And part lay in the lack of public support, which itself was traceable to the "intolerance and suppression of criticism in which he so weakly acquiesced. It is a very dark moment," Lippmann concluded in his plaint to the secretary of war, "and the prospect of war and revolution throughout Europe is appalling. The responsibility resting upon the men who commit the American people to detail participation is simply enormous."[9]

A few weeks later in a letter to Norman Hapgood, the journalist who served as Wilson's unofficial liaison with the press, Lippmann explained that Wilson's greatest mistake was his failure to see that he did not have to compromise his principles in order to win Allied support for the league. Instead of assuming he had to buy their assent to the league by "accepting the program of imperialism," he should have insisted that America would not join unless the Allies accepted the principles of the Fourteen Points. As it was, the league was a "fundamentally diseased" effort to uphold an "impossible settlement." Later, in an obituary of the settlement, Lippmann explained why the Americans, "starting with all the aces in the pack," were unable to play their cards. Failing to see that American participation in the League of Nations was far more important to Britain and France than to the United States, and that they should have purchased a generous settlement with Germany in return for continued American participation in European affairs, they instead "consented to a wretched peace, having fallen into the illusion that this was the price they had to pay for European willingness to create a League! They bought the League from France and Britain with a bad peace instead of selling it to France and Britain for a good peace."[10]

For liberals like Lippmann the hardest part of the treaty to swallow was Article Ten, which obliged members of the League of Nations to uphold one another's "territorial integrity." When he wrote Newton Baker in June, Lippmann said he would be willing to support the league if all guarantees were removed from the covenant "which in any way bind us in advance to support the status quo" and encouraged France in its "old dream of Louis XIV and Napoleon." But by the end of the summer he had even given up that hope. "You ask how can the League humanize the Treaty," he wrote Raymond Fosdick, an aide to General Pershing who later served the league. "A month ago I was still trying to believe that it might. I don't think I believe it any longer. So far as the League is concerned, on the Continent it is today a bureau of the French foreign office, acting as a somewhat vague alliance of the Great Powers against the influence and the liberty of the people who live between the Rhine and the Pacific Ocean."[11]

Lippmann also owed someone else an explanation. "I had hoped to the very last for a Treaty which would in a measure redeem our promises to the world, for a Treaty that would not open the suspicion that the Covenant is a new Holy Alliance," he wrote Colonel House. The least that Wilson could do was to admit he had failed. "The world can endure honest disappointment . . . but I see nothing but pain and disorder and confusion if this first act of honesty is not performed." While Lippmann's wish was earnest, it is hard to know what such a confession on Wilson's part would have accomplished, especially since the President thought that, all things considered, he had won a great victory at Paris. Perhaps it would have unburdened Lippmann of a sense of involvement in an undertaking that now seemed tainted. If the President admitted he had failed, then at least the effort, and Lippmann's part in it, would have been vindicated.

Reluctant to admit that the failure to foresee an unjust peace might have been as much his fault as Wilson's, he preferred to see it as an administrative problem. "The bottom fact of the whole failure was a failure of technique," he wrote Frankfurter. "The intentions were good enough. What Paris has demonstrated is that you cannot in ignorance improvise a structure of good will." Wilson should have demanded agreement on war aims before the United States entered the conflict. "This omission vitiated everything else, but it was compounded by the fact that we had no diplomatic service capable of diagnosing Europe, that we had never negotiated but simply enunciated, that what diplomatic service we had was insulated from the President, who worked by intimation from Colonel House, who had his own irresponsible diplomatic service."[12]

All this was true. But in the months just before American entry Lippmann had issued no warning to secure an accord on war aims, made no complaints about the President's "insulation" from the diplomatic service and the "irresponsibility" of House's staff. Instead, he had extolled the "Atlantic highway" and his vision of a worldwide "democratic revolution." The failure went beyond technique, beyond the embassies staffed with what he contemptuously referred to as "well-to-do young gentlemen with good manners" who merely "retailed the gossip of the capital." Going even beyond Wilson, it involved all the war liberals who, like Lippmann, thought they could tame the tiger by riding it. Wilson's failure was also their failure.

Despite the *NR*'s denunciative editorials, many readers saw the editors' opposition to the treaty as an example more of crankiness than of principle. The magazine lost some ten thousand subscribers. "We are reactionary, of course, and the so-called liberals have most of them entered a monastery where they contemplate ecstatically the beatitudes of the League of Nations," Lippmann wrote sarcastically to Frankfurter. To a British colleague puzzled by the *NR*'s attitude, he said he thought it "amazing that we should be the only country in the world in which some kind of democratic action on the treaty is taking place." Defeat of the treaty might result, he admitted, in "emasculating the League, though as a matter of fact I think on the whole we are improving it, but even its emasculation is preferable to death by inanition."[13]

While disappointment with the treaty would have been natural, Lippmann felt something more: a sense of personal betrayal. In 1917 he had argued that American entry would transform an imperialist war into a democratic crusade. Two years later pacifists like Bourne and Villard seemed to have been right — although he would never admit it. "I was the typical fool determined to hope till the bitter end," he wrote Berenson that summer of 1919 from a country house he and Faye had rented at Whitestone, Long Island. "Well, it's bitter, and we've had the pleasure of fighting the treaty here practically single-handed."

The country was in the grip of the Red Scare, "the blackest reaction our generation has known," Lippmann reported. "My crowd is distinctly unpopular — parlor 'Bolsheviks' etc. But it's a good fight, and if I didn't long for quiet and a chance to do my book, I'd be blissfully content to enjoy the attack on us. Popularity would be a little bit discreditable when the world is so mad." The summer house at least offered a retreat from the furor. "Living in the country redeems much," he mused. "One gets a good sense of the things that do not matter, and a decent relief from the feverish factionalism of the city. But I'm afraid it's a long pull before any considerable number of us can cultivate our gardens. Sometimes I think we are a damned generation. I suppose we are in comparison with the late Victorians."[14]

Despite the curious alliance of isolationists and disillusioned liberals, public support for the treaty remained high. Senate ratification seemed assured — if only Wilson would accept some relatively minor reservations to ease fears aroused by Article Ten. But Wilson would not permit the slightest revision of what he had negotiated at Paris. His intransigence played into the hands of the moderate reservationists gathered around Senator Henry Cabot Lodge, Republican chairman of the Foreign Relations Committee, and the fourteen "Irreconcilables" led by the Idaho populist William E. Borah.

Unable to defeat the treaty outright, these opponents delayed ratification through endless amendments and hearings. Lippmann proved extremely useful in this delaying process. He provided committee members Borah and Senator Hiram Johnson of California with information he had gained at the Inquiry and on House's staff — particularly the connection between the secret treaties and the Fourteen Points. With his questions in hand they asked Wilson, when he appeared before the committee, why he had not forced the Allies to repudiate the secret treaties before taking America into the war. The President replied that he had not been informed of the treaties until he reached Paris in December 1918. Lippmann was incredulous. "I was staggered by the President's statement," he told Johnson, and in the *NR* accused the President of duplicity. "Only a dunce could have been ignorant of the secret treaties," he charged in a slashing editorial, recounting the "almost miraculous coincidence" of the Fourteen Points with the treaties.[15]

Declining Johnson's invitation to testify before the committee, Lippmann suggested an alternate: William Bullitt. There could not have been a more willing witness. Furious at his treatment by Wilson after his return from Moscow, Bullitt was eager to tell all, including behind-the-scenes stories of the negotiations at Paris. With unconcealed glee he revealed that Secretary of State Lansing had told him the treaty was a disaster and the league useless. The administration cried foul, but Lippmann was exultant. "Wilson has begun to wander," he reported to Berenson after Bullitt's devastating testimony. "The initial lie has taken the decency out of him. He is as unscrupulous today as LG [Lloyd George] and a great deal less attractive. Billy Bullitt blurted out everything to the scandal of the Tories and delight of the Republicans. When there is an almost universal conspiracy to lie and smother the truth, I suppose someone has to violate the decencies."[16]

Wilson had incurred Lippmann's displeasure, not only because of the tainted treaty he had presented to the Senate, but also because of his decision to intervene against the Bolsheviks by sending American troops to Soviet Arctic ports and to join the Japanese invasion of Siberia. "Our behavior at Archangel and in Siberia is one of the least gratifying episodes in our history," Lippmann wrote Newton Baker that summer of 1919. "We've got no business taking part in unauthorized civil war in Russia. We've got no business either in law or morals or humanity trying to starve European Russia in the interests of Kolchak, Denikin and the White Finns." To make matters worse, the government was censoring and deliberately distorting information about the intervention. "I can understand these things happening in a reactionary administration," he complained. "I can't understand them happening where Woodrow Wilson is President. Sometime surely the limit of acquiescence must be reached." Later, when Alexander Kerensky, the hapless provisional leader deposed by Lenin, came to the United States to stir up support for intervention against the Bolsheviks, Lippmann had no sympathy. "The tragedy in Russia today is too grim for courtesies to men who have spent three years trying to incite foreign armies to invade their country," he wrote Berenson. "The only thing in Russia the outer world can fight is the famine. Anti-Bolshevism is the task of men in Russia, not of disappointed politicians in foreign capitals." [17]

Intervention against the Bolsheviks, however strongly desired by conservatives, was a sideshow compared to the Senate battle over ratification of the treaty. As that battle was coming to a climax in the fall of 1919, Lippmann found new ammunition for his attack. From friends in London he had heard that the English economist he had met in Paris had written a savage critique of the treaty, demonstrating that the reparations imposed on Germany were unworkable and dangerous. Lippmann had been impressed by John Maynard Keynes, a tall, slightly stooped, clever man a few years older than he, with a passionate interest in ballet and painting, and a taste for the pleasures of life. As Treasury representative at the peace conference he had witnessed the machinations firsthand and had resigned in disgust. To a handful of young Americans and Englishmen he had fulminated in the bar of the Crillon against the stupidity of the Allied statesmen. His scorn was biting, his wit cutting. Lippmann urged Keynes to let the *New Republic* publish parts of his book in serial form.

At Christmas 1919 the first of three installments of *The Economic Consequences of the Peace* appeared in the *NR* with devastating impact. Beneath a bland title Keynes tore to pieces the Paris settlement and the men who made it. His portrait of Wilson was cruel: a "blind and deaf Don Quixote" who had been "bamboozled" by the canny Europeans. Wilson's naiveté and self-righteousness had allowed the British and French to impose a treaty of "senseless greed overreaching itself." Keynes's malicious descriptions of the peacemakers were quoted everywhere, his arguments used in the Senate debate, his reputation made as a polemicist.

The Senate voted twice on the treaty: in November 1919 and March 1920. Both times Wilson refused to consider any changes and forbade Democrats to support the minor reservations that would have won the support of Republican moderates. Unamended, the treaty failed to win the necessary two-thirds margin and went down to defeat, taking with it American participation in the league. The *NR* hailed the results as "desirable and wholesome." [18]

American intellectuals began their long postmortem. One of the first was Harold Stearns, with whom Lippmann had made his ill-fated crossing to Belgium in August 1914. In his book *Liberalism in America,* Stearns charged that his fellow liberals had been no less guilty than Wilson. They had been seduced by the lure of power and had suspended their critical judgment. By stripping away the moral foundations of action, they had reduced pragmatism to a device of expediency. The substitution of method for moral values, Stearns maintained in a phrase that has long outlived his book, was the "technique of liberal failure — the method of compromise . . . whereby one hopes to control events by abandoning oneself to them."

Stung by Stearns's accusations, Lippmann decided to review the book himself. Never one for *mea culpas,* he defended American intervention as necessary to prevent German control of the "Atlantic highway." The fault of the liberals, Lippmann responded, was not in supporting the war, but in failing to build the league on a democratic foundation. The betrayal at Paris, he charged, came from what he called the "defect of the liberal mind . . . its apathy about administration, its boredom at the problems of organization." Liberals were guilty of "shrinking from intellectual effort" because the "urban temper and tolerance of liberalism easily confuses itself with something very close to indolence." He even found a good deal to admire about the other side. "At Paris the conservatives had a better grip on their case than did the liberals," he complained. "They had worked harder. They had planned more thoroughly. They had manipulated better. . . . They knew how to go past the fragile reason of men to their passions. They made liberalism in the person of its official representative seem incredibly naive. They knew how to do everything but make the peace."

However just Lippmann's accusation might have been, it was mixed with a good deal of self-justification. He found it easier to blame Wilson than to accept his own complicity in believing that an imperialist war could be transformed into a democratic crusade. "How did you and I ever have any faith in the Wilson administration?" he asked William Bullitt. "I mean any faith?" [19] But it was not Wilson who led Lippmann into war. Rather, it was Lippmann who found, first in morals, then in strategy, the arguments to persuade Wilson that American entry was necessary. In blaming the "liberals" when it all went sour, and even praising the conservatives, he tried to exonerate himself.

Several years later, after passions had cooled, Lippmann looked back with more perspective, and also more charity toward Wilson, describing the President as a man whose sympathy toward the Allies was "chastened by a certain irony about their moral pretensions, a suspicion of their motives, and a conviction that unfortunately they too were mad." Wilson, he claimed, "never accepted the official propaganda even when it blew the hottest . . . and could hardly bear to listen to it"; what he wanted "above all things was to keep out of the hideous mess." Colonel House became the "honest broker" between Wilson, "who longed for peace without entanglement," and those who sought to draw America into the war. It was House who persuaded Wilson that by entering the conflict he could prevent future wars; House who supplied the President "with the rationalizations by means of which Wilson was able to bow to a destiny that was overbearing him, and even ultimately to sow the seed of a triumph that may make him immortal."

But it was not House alone who supplied Wilson with the rationalization he both sought and dreaded. It was Lippmann who had argued that only through participation could America ensure a just peace and bring democracy to Central Europe. In explaining Wilson's defeated idealism, Lippmann ultimately had to come to terms with his own. Later he came to regret his opposition to the treaty. The decision was basically Croly's, he claimed; "I followed him, though I was not then, and am not now, convinced that it was the wise thing to do. If I had it to do all over again, I would take the other side; we supplied the Battalion of Death with too much ammunition."[20]

At the time, however, he was in the front ranks, leading the charge.

As the war had wrecked the domestic reform movement, so the defeat of the treaty marked the eclipse of Wilsonian idealism. By 1920 Americans had had enough of noble ideals. The radical reformer was silent, zealots searched for "Reds," and the Ku Klux Klan was on the rise. Wilson, felled by a stroke, lay paralyzed in the White House, his peace plan in a shambles, his league repudiated, his programs scuttled by a Congress preoccupied with outlawing Demon Rum. "What a Goddamned world this is!" exclaimed the Kansas newspaper sage William Allen White. "If anyone had told me two years ago that our country would be what it is today . . . I should have questioned his reason."[21]

Anti-Bolshevik hysteria and superpatriotism spurred the most severe repression since the Alien and Sedition Acts. Wilson's attorney general, A. Mitchell Palmer, orchestrated an "anti-Red" dragnet in which more than four thousand people were arrested in a single night in January 1920 on suspicion of being "communists." In a paroxysm of zeal the New York State Assembly expelled five legally elected members of the Socialist party. "The events of the last few months are too disturbing and the behavior of the administration too revolutionary not to put a severe strain upon men's patience," a distressed Lippmann wrote Newton Baker that January. "You know what hopes were put in this administration, how loudly and insistently it proclaimed its loyalty to the cause of freedom. Well, it was possible to fail in those hopes. It was credible that the wisdom and the strength to realize them would be lacking. But it is forever incredible that an administration announcing the most spacious ideals in our history should have done more to endanger fundamental American liberties than any group of men for a hundred years." Not since the time of John Adams, he charged, had officeholders made "so determined and so dangerous an attack" upon constitutional liberties. The "hysterical" deportation without trial of aliens, the "ferocious" sentences for political offenses, censorship and repression of speech had all instituted a "reign of terror in which honest thought is impossible, in which moderation is discountenanced, in which panic supplants reason." Instead of moderating the panic, the administration had "done everything humanly possible to add fresh excitement to an overexcited community." Eventually there would be a "reaction against this reaction," he predicted. "I fear it will not be moderate if this madness continues much longer. I am not speaking of revolution. The soil of revolution does not exist in America today. What I am speaking of is a hurricane of demagogy out of a people finally awakened to the meaning of what is now occurring."[22]

The fear — amounting to a virtual panic — of Reds and anarchists had been stimulated by the Bolshevik revolution and brought to a high pitch by labor agitation and anarchist violence within the United States. This provided a fertile climate for demagogues on the far Right and for men on horseback, such as General Leonard Wood, governor-general of the Philippines and former army chief of staff. Wood, seeking to capture Theodore Roosevelt's still faithful public, and sharing TR's belligerence, though not his concern for social reform, was the favorite of right-wing Republicans for the 1920 presidential nomination. To head off Wood, whom he denounced as having the "prejudices of the Junker" and the "mood, if not the courage, of the coup d'etat," Lippmann scoured the pack for a moderate and eligible Republican. His eye settled on Herbert Hoover.

Later maligned and ridiculed for his inept handling of the depression, Hoover at the time was a national hero, the man who organized Belgian relief and fed starving Europe, "the only man who emerged from the ordeal of Paris with an enhanced reputation," in Keynes's words.[23]

Ever since Lippmann first met Hoover at the House of Truth in 1917 he had been impressed by the millionaire engineer's wide-ranging mind and firm grasp of public issues. Although few knew what political party Hoover belonged to, in the political climate of 1920 it hardly mattered. Both Republicans and Democrats were eager to recruit him to their ranks. Deftly avoiding labels, Hoover defined himself as late as March 1920 as "an independent progressive" who objected as much to the "reactionary group in the Republican party as I do to the radical group in the Democratic party."

This perfectly expressed Lippmann's own politics, and thus it was hardly surprising that he would consider Hoover the ideal candidate. That winter he launched Hoover's trial balloon in the *New Republic*. While Hoover was glad for the boost, he was reluctant to climb down from the fence. He feared, with some reason, that if he came out openly as a progressive he would lose the conservatives who dominated the Republican party. Lippmann tried to push him into taking a stand, but got no results. "Yesterday I had a telephone call from Hoover to come and see him," he wrote Felix Frankfurter early in April. "I found him in a bewildered state of mind at the political snarl in which he finds himself. He really wants to take a liberal line, but he does not know how to take hold. He knows that the liberal people and the Progressives generally are slipping away from him."[24]

Lippmann, after touching base with Colonel House, went to see Hoover and suggested that he threaten to abandon the Republican party if the Old Guard nominated a reactionary. The fear that he might run on a third-party ticket, or even join the Democrats, Lippmann explained, would give him a trump card at the convention. But Hoover was too cautious for such a ploy. Instead of remaining aloof, he declared that he was a faithful Republican. Now the Old Guard, having nothing to fear, could nominate one of its own. The party pros retired to the famous smoke-filled room and emerged bearing an amiable nonentity from Ohio, Senator Warren G. Harding. His job was cut out for him. "He was put there by the Senators for the sole purpose of abdicating in their favor," Lippmann wrote contemptuously. "The Grand Dukes have chosen their weak Tsar in order to increase the power of the Grand Dukes." Harding's election would mean the "substitution of government by a clique for the lonely majesty of the President."[25]

But the full measure of his scorn was reserved, not for the conservatives who triumphed, but for the progressives who lost. From Chicago, where he had witnessed the proceedings, Lippmann blamed the liberal Republicans for their own defeat. "What reason was there for listening to the independents who can unite on no platform, on no strategy, and on no man?" he asked. "The progressives do not know what they want. They just want to be a little nobler and a little cleaner, provided they do not have to stay out in the wilderness too long." The argument was familiar. He had used it against the socialists at Schenectady, the Bull Moose faction at Chicago, and the liberals at Paris. Taking them to task for trying to be a "little nobler and a little cleaner," he objected to their ineffectuality as much as to their compromises. Lippmann was not a man who admired dreamers and amateurs in politics.

Not that the Democrats offered any serious alternative. Three weeks later at San Francisco the party was confronted with the choice between Mitchell Palmer, the Red-baiting attorney general, and William G. McAdoo, Wilson's son-in-law and former secretary of the treasury. Of the two McAdoo was unqualifiedly better: a free-trade, antitrust progressive with a populist strain. He also enjoyed the backing of the nation's most unscrupulous and politically ambitious press lord, William Randolph Hearst. While recognizing McAdoo's abilities, Lippmann distrusted him and described the candidate in the *NR* as a "statesman grafted upon a promoter," a man with few principles but a "remarkable sense of what a governing majority of voters wants and will receive." McAdoo, he told C. P. Scott, editor of the *Manchester Guardian,* for which Lippmann worked as a stringer, was "brilliant in genius, liberal but without a sound intellectual equipment, and with a slight untrustworthiness . . . by all odds the keenest politician in America today."[26]

But McAdoo, although strong, fell short of the then needed two-thirds margin. The convention went into deadlock. Finally on the forty-fourth ballot, the weary delegates turned from both McAdoo and Palmer to a compromise candidate. Governor James G. Cox did not have a chance, but he offended no one. History remembers him only for having chosen as his running mate the popular assistant secretary of the navy, Franklin Delano Roosevelt of New York. Lippmann, who had got to know FDR a bit during his War Department days, thought it a hopeful sign. "When cynics ask what is the use," he said in a congratulatory telegram to FDR, "we can answer that when parties can pick a man like Frank Roosevelt there is a decent future in politics."

As far as Lippmann was concerned, it was still a dismal choice. "I can remember no time when the level of political discussion was so low," he wrote Graham Wallas after the conventions. "If it is possible to speak of 'the mind of the people,' then it is fair to say that the American mind has temporarily lost all interest in public questions." The choice, he told S. K. Ratcliffe, lay between "two provincial, ignorant politicians entirely surrounded by special interests, operating in a political vacuum. Nobody believes in anything. Nobody wants anything very badly that he thinks he can get out of politics . . . nobody will be enthusiastic about anything until a generation grows up that has forgotten how violent we were and how unreasonable."[27]

Election day offered no surprises, even though women voted for the first time. Harding walked away with sixteen million votes to Cox's pathetic nine million. The victor, with a better feeling for public sentiment than for grammar, called for a politics of "normalcy." His huge plurality reflected not so much a vote of confidence as a desire to be rid of Wilson, the war, and the league. "Harding is elected not because anybody likes him or because the Republican party is particularly powerful," Lippmann told Wallas, "but because the Democrats are inconceivably unpopular." The women's vote did not affect the result, but only emphasized it. "Unless one is prepared to regard the election as the final twitch of the war mind (that is the way I regard it)," he added, "there would be cause for profound discouragement with universal suffrage."

Four months later, as Harding and his gashouse gang entered the White House, Lippmann tried to take the long view. "There's no use pretending that the atmosphere is cheerful here," he wrote Wallas a few weeks after the inauguration. "It is not. The hysteria has turned to apathy and disillusionment in the general public, and cynicism in most of my friends. I feel that we shall not have much immediate influence in America for perhaps a decade, but I'm not discouraged because we can use that time well to reexamine our ideas."[28]

Among the ideas he wanted to reexamine was the notion that the average man could form an accurate picture of the world beyond his immediate knowledge.

◂ 14 ▸

Pictures in Their Heads

> . . . the common interests very largely elude public
> opinion entirely and can be managed only by a special-
> ized class.
>
> — *Public Opinion*, 1922

YEARS earlier Graham Wallas had made Lippmann wary of a traditional political science that talked of institutions while ignoring
people. The war and his propaganda work had shown him how easily
public opinion could be molded. Most political theory assumed that the
average man could, if presented with the facts, make reasonable decisions. But what if access to the facts was blocked by propaganda, ignorance and willful distortion? How would this affect the assumption that
the average man could make intelligent decisions about public issues?

"I have started to write a longish article around the general idea that
freedom of thought and speech present themselves in a new light and
raise new problems because of the discovery that opinion can be manufactured," Lippmann wrote Ellery Sedgwick, editor of the *Atlantic*, in
the spring of 1920. "The idea has come to me gradually as a result of
certain experiences with the official propaganda machine, and my hope
is to attempt a restatement of the problem of freedom of thought as it
presents itself in modern society under modern conditions of government and with a modern knowledge of how to manipulate the human
mind." Sedgwick, eager to lure Lippmann away from Croly, urged him
to speculate as much as he liked. By the fall Lippmann had completed
two articles, which Sedgwick ran in the magazine, and which, together
with a third essay, were published in book form a few months later as
Liberty and the News.[1]

In this now-forgotten little volume Lippmann staked out new ground
by arguing that traditional theories of government were outmoded because they failed to take into account the power of public opinion.
"Decisions in a modern state tend to be made by the interaction, not of

Congress and the executive, but of public opinion and the executive,''
he argued. Government operated by the ''impact of controlled opinion''
upon administration. This shift in the locus of sovereignty placed a
''premium upon the manufacture of what is called consent.'' If sovereignty had shifted from the legislature to public opinion, then clearly the
public had to be assured of accurate, reliable information. The protection of the sources of its opinion had become ''the basic problem of
democracy.''

In an earlier era men like John Milton and John Stuart Mill had
argued that liberty depended on a press free from censorship and intimi-
dation. They were concerned primarily with freedom of belief and expression. But in modern democracies the problem was different. The
press could be ''free'' and still fail to do its job. Without accurate and
unbiased information the public could not form intelligent decisions.
Democracy would be either a failure or a sham. The modern state,
therefore, had a critical interest in keeping pure the ''streams of fact
which feed the rivers of opinion.'' Liberty had become not so much permission as the ''construction of a system of information increasingly independent of opinion.''

The press was, in this sense, literally the ''bible of democracy, the
book out of which a people determines its conduct.''[2] But was the press
providing the reliable information the public needed? Lippmann's propaganda work had made him realize how easily public opinion could be
manipulated, and how often the press distorted the news. To test his
theory that the public was being denied access to the facts, he decided to
conduct an experiment. Enlisting his friend Charles Merz, he examined
press coverage of a crucial and controversial event, the Bolshevik revolution, for a three-year period beginning with the overthrow of the tsar
in February 1917. They used the *New York Times* as their source because of its reputation for accurate reporting.

Their study, which they called ''A Test of the News,'' came out as a
forty-two-page supplement to the *New Republic* in August 1920 and
demonstrated that the *Times*'s coverage was neither unbiased nor accurate. The paper's news stories, they concluded, were not based on facts,
but were ''dominated by the hopes of the men who composed the news
organization.'' The paper cited events that did not happen, atrocities
that never took place, and reported no fewer than ninety-one times that
the Bolshevik regime was on the verge of collapse. ''The news about
Russia is a case of seeing not what was, but what men wished to see,''
Lippmann and Merz charged. ''The chief censor and the chief propagandist were hope and fear in the minds of reporters and editors.''
The reporters, in other words, relied on hearsay and their imagination;
the editors allowed their prejudices to infect the news columns. Even
though few newsmen had deliberately tried to suppress the truth, most

were guilty of a "boundless credulity, an untiring readiness to be gulled, and on many occasions a downright lack of common sense." Their contribution to public knowledge at a time of supreme crisis was "about as useful as that of an astrologer or an alchemist."³

When he first began writing on sloppy reporting, censorship and propaganda, Lippmann thought that stricter and more professional standards might resolve the problem, that "trustworthy news, unadulterated data, fair reporting, disinterested fact" could give the public the information it needed to make intelligent judgments on public issues. But the more he thought about it, the less sure he was. *Liberty and the News* had delineated the failures of the press and suggested some paths of reform. But what if the problem lay, not merely in reporting and government interference, but in the very nature of the way the public formed its opinions?

The previous year, in reviewing a new book by Harold Laski, Lippmann had criticized those who talked about political institutions without regard to the psychological forces that animated them. "To discuss simply overt acts and the political theories which have surrounded them is, it seems to me, to circulate in a logic doomed forever to deal with accident," he wrote of Laski's book. "The hidden motives travel to the overt act not by a straight and narrow path but through a maze of junctions and crossroads, along which they are baffled or seduced. A political science which deals merely with the terminals can never hope to control seriously the direction of human affairs." Laski did not share Lippmann's fascination with hidden motives. "I wish Walter Lippmann would forget Freud for a little, just a little," the political scientist had complained to Justice Holmes a couple of years earlier.⁴ But Lippmann was intent on examining what he called that maze of junctions and crossroads.

To give himself more time he decided to let S. K. Ratcliffe take over his seventy-five-dollar-a-week job as stringer for the *Manchester Guardian*. Then he told Alfred Harcourt that he wanted to discuss a book he was thinking of writing. Harcourt, who had set up his own publishing house with Donald Brace, was eager to sign up Lippmann as one of his authors. When Lippmann outlined his idea for a book analyzing public opinion, an excited Harcourt offered a contract on the spot. But Lippmann shied away from a written agreement. He did not need the small monetary advance Harcourt could offer and he did not want to be pressured by a contract in case he ran into trouble in writing the book. Instead, they made a gentleman's agreement: Harcourt would have the first view with an option to publish.

Lippmann had been working with Harcourt, Brace for some time. The firm had published *Liberty and the News,* and for several months he had been advising the editors on manuscripts, suggesting ideas for books, and helping them find new authors. His twenty-five-hundred-dollar-a-year retainer turned out to be the best investment Harcourt, Brace ever made. One of the first authors Lippmann brought them was John Maynard Keynes, whose *Economic Consequences of the Peace* proved a great critical success. Keynes in turn introduced them to his friend Lytton Strachey, whose *Queen Victoria* and *Eminent Victorians* became phenomenal best-sellers. Through Strachey the firm corraled most of the Bloomsbury group, including Virginia Woolf, whose novels enriched it for decades.

In 1920, at about the same time he took on the job with Harcourt, Lippmann began writing a regular column for *Vanity Fair,* a slick monthly of the arts. Cynical, sophisticated, stylish, the magazine appealed to well-educated and well-heeled people who wanted to feel they were in the know. The articles were easy enough to do — they rarely took more than a day or two — and brought him four to five hundred dollars a month. *Vanity Fair* put him in touch with a different kind of audience: middlebrow readers with an interest in public affairs, a passion for culture, and an abhorrence of boredom. Instead of heavy thinkers like John Dewey and Charles Beard, his editorial companions were now iconoclasts like H. L. Mencken, and gadflies like Broadway critic George Jean Nathan.

Lippmann enjoyed writing for *Vanity Fair* and stayed with it until 1934. Rather than diluting his style, the magazine brought out a side of his character — irony, a gift for character analysis, intellectual playfulness, and even a romantic idealism — that had been dampened at the ponderous *New Republic.* He did some of his freest and most engaging writing for *Vanity Fair,* and in 1927 put together a selection of his favorite pieces, mostly portraits, in a book he called *Men of Destiny.* Among the least known of Lippmann's books, it contains some of his sharpest insights and offers a revealing glimpse of the social conflict and political turmoil of the misnamed Jazz Age.

In these articles Lippmann enjoyed himself, and in them one can see his gift for making abstract ideas come alive and for pulling readers into subjects that might normally make them yawn. "Not long ago I was at work in my study writing when, as was her custom, the lady across the way burst into song," he began a serious article on censorship. "There was something about that lady's voice which prevented the use of human intelligence, and I called upon the janitor to give her my compliments and then silence her. She replied with a good deal of conviction that this was a free country and she would sing when the spirit moved her; if I did not like it, I could retire to the great open spaces." In an analysis of the Republicans' 1920 candidate for President, he began: "If an optimist is a man who makes lemonade out of all the lemons that are handed to him, then Senator Harding is the greatest of all optimists."

Lippmann's "writing is flypaper to me," Justice Holmes told a friend on reading the book; "if I touch it, I am stuck till I finish it."[5]

Lippmann had taken on the *Vanity Fair* column not only for the exposure and the pay, but because it offered an escape from the hothouse atmosphere of the *New Republic*. The excitement of the early years had long since given way to a dull and predictable earnestness. The *NR* no longer had privileged access to the White House; its progressive-minded readers had drifted off to Europe, to speakeasies, or to get-rich-quick schemes; and its calls for reform fell mostly on deaf ears. "Where Are the Pre-War Radicals?" a symposium of the time plaintively asked, with the answer that most had gone out to lunch. Even the staff of the *NR* had changed. Walter Weyl had died of cancer in 1919, Charles Merz had gone over to the New York *World,* and Herbert Croly was drifting slowly off into the ether of mysticism. Lippmann kept away from the office both from boredom and from a desire to avoid Francis Hackett, the literary editor. Hackett, a fanatical Irish nationalist, had been hostile ever since 1916 because he thought Lippmann too soft on Britain for its suppression of the Easter uprising in Ireland.[6]

Eager to get away from the *NR* and to have more time for his own work, Lippmann persuaded Croly to let him hire as managing editor a talented young man he had found at *Vanity Fair*. The twenty-five-year-old Edmund Wilson needed a job that would pay his bills, but not take much time. The *New Republic* seemed tailor-made. "When you become a regular editor at the NR, you draw a large salary and never go near the office, but stay home and write books," Wilson wrote his friend Stanley Dell.

The magazine has become so dull that the editors themselves say they are unable to read it, and the subscribers are dying off like flies. The editors, who started out as gay young free thinkers, have become respectable to the point of stodginess. Lippmann is the liveliest of the lot. They are also very much at odds with each other. Each one has taken me aside and told me confidentially that the rest of the staff were timid old maids.

Although Lippmann may have been the "liveliest of the lot," this was relative as far as Wilson was concerned. "Nothing more correct could be imagined than the home life of the Lippmanns," he told Dell, following a dinner at their Madison Avenue apartment, where he had been "so depressed by the extreme conventionality of these eminent intellectuals" that he fled to a party in Greenwich Village.[7]

With Wilson in charge of editorial chores, Lippmann in April 1921 took a six-month leave of absence from the *NR* to work on his public-opinion book. He and Faye moved out to Wading River, a village on the north shore of Long Island, where a year earlier they had bought a ramshackle old house. Rustic and rambling, the house was near the beach, had two beautiful elms in the front yard, was only a few hours from New York and cheap enough at sixty-five hundred dollars for Walter to manage. He borrowed money from friends and closed the deal. Ever since returning from the war he had been on his own financially. He had urged his father either to sell or fix up the tenements he owned on the Lower East Side, and when Jacob did neither, Walter decided he would accept no more money from his parents. He could get by on what he earned, so long as he and Faye lived frugally.

Life was simple at Wading River. Walter wrote most of the day, while Faye cooked and typed his manuscript. Her father, Ralph Albertson, once again footloose, helped around the house with a paintbrush and hammer. Friends came out from the city for visits, like Harold Laski, who wrote Justice Holmes of the "grand weekend" he had spent at Wading River, where he and Walter had "talked the universe over and he made me very happy by his patience and wisdom and insight." Laski also passed on Walter's discontent at the *NR*. "Croly has the religious bug very badly, and Hackett is simply Sinn Fein, with which Walter doesn't sympathize." [8]

Although Lippmann was supposed to return to the *NR* in the fall, the nearer the time came, the less appealing it seemed. Late one afternoon, as he was musing over his future, a chauffeured limousine pulled into the driveway bearing Herbert Bayard Swope. Already a legendary figure, the fast-talking, high-living Swope had recently become editor of New York's most influential liberal paper, the *World*. "Walter," he said, dispensing with the amenities, "You're too good a writer to stay buried on the *New Republic*. You need a wider forum, some place where your ideas can have a real impact. Ralph Pulitzer and I have decided that you're just the man we need at the *World*. How would you like to come over as Frank Cobb's deputy and write editorials for us? Just think of the audience," Swope said, drawing a picture of impressionable millions waiting to be instructed in the intricacies of politics. "You'll be reaching ten times as many people — and you can write on anything you like. And we can pay you a lot more than you're getting over there."

Lippmann was tempted, but had a few misgivings about the *World*. Its crusading liberalism tended a bit toward the bleeding heart, and its news pages had long rivaled Hearst's for yellow journalism. But Joseph Pulitzer's eldest son, Ralph, who had taken over the paper on his father's retirement, was trying to lead it away from the yellow toward greater respectability. Also, the paper had some of the best columnists in journalism in what was the nation's first "op ed" page. Lippmann admired Swope's professionalism and had great respect for Frank Cobb. Under Cobb's direction the *World*'s editorial page had won a deserved reputation for courage and integrity. Liberal papers all over the country took their lead from the *World* — and often their editorials as well. The easygoing Cobb was a sweet-natured and likable person whom Lippmann had come to know in Paris that feverish night in December 1918 when they put together the official commentary on the Fourteen Points.

Swope's offer was attractive: assistant director of the editorial page, $12,500 a year plus two weeks' vacation and two weeks' leave of absence, and above all a chance to break into a wider world.[9] Lippmann had been with the *NR* for seven years. There was nothing more he could learn there, the magazine's influence was declining, and life with Croly was getting uncomfortable. After a long talk with publisher Ralph Pulitzer, he agreed to take the job, starting January 1, 1922.

Now he had to explain the move to his friends. "I see now that my effective influence on the NR is over," he wrote Frankfurter in June, shortly after he and Pulitzer had agreed on terms. "Herbert and I no longer learn from each other, and for two years our intellectual relationship has been a good-natured accommodation rather than an interesting adventure." The *NR* was "not the paper I want to make it," he explained. "My influence is positive only in my articles, entirely negative otherwise. And in the book department I'm afraid that the mere thought of me is an incitement to violence." By this time Lippmann and the temperamental Irish-American book editor, Francis Hackett, were not even on speaking terms. "Among the sub-reasons for going is, of course, FH," he admitted. "He has made the intellectual tone steadily more uncharitable, more querulous, more rasping. He has taken the department which deals with the freer life of the mind and made it more factious than the political part."[10]

The feud between Hackett and Lippmann had disrupted life at the *NR* for several years. The gentle Croly was caught in the middle, desperately needing Lippmann, but tolerant of Hackett's Anglophobia and his congenital inability to work in a group. He wanted them both to stay, and was unhappy over Lippmann's defection, even though he understood the lure of more money and a wider audience. When he later spoke of Lippmann's departure, "a look of pain passed over his face," Edmund Wilson recalled. Harold Laski, too, regretted Lippmann's shift to the *World*. "I don't know why, and I am sorry," he wrote his faithful correspondent, Justice Holmes. "Daily journalism corrodes the soul; and I think he'll take from the NR a vividness of quality that they can't replace in their circle. . . . I presume he has good reasons, for he is capable of infinite deliberation, and his wife's head is as wise as charming. But Croly will have a bad time." Philip Littell, the *NR*'s gentle arts editor, was more sympathetic. "Not only do I advise you, feeling as you do, to go: I think I understand how you feel," he wrote Lippmann. "If I were your age, had your mind, your talents, all your different futures to choose from, I shouldn't think of staying on the NR. Herbert's mind is growing more and more incapable of even trying to profit by criticism of its deeper assumptions, and he is therefore a less and less interesting person to work with. Particularly for you, who are more and more critical of everybody's assumptions, your own included.''[11]

The deal with the *World* quickly settled, Lippmann returned to his manuscript. By the end of August he had completed a book far longer and more ambitious than anything he had ever attempted before. He turned it over to Alfred Harcourt, who was delighted with the results and gave him a five-hundred-dollar advance against royalties, promising to bring the book out early in 1922. Lippmann was now free until January, when he would begin his job at the *World*. Ralph Pulitzer, as a lure to his new editorial writer, had invited Walter and Faye on a combination holiday and fact-finding tour of Europe. The trip would also be the couple's long-deferred European honeymoon. Two and a half years had passed since a disillusioned Lippmann had boarded a troopship at Brest to return to America. Now he was less disillusioned, less idealistic, and a good deal more comfortable. Instead of a troopship and barracks it was first-class hotels, chauffeured limousines, and all the luxuries to which the Pulitzers were accustomed. Lippmann served as companion and guide for the publisher, squiring Pulitzer through the foreign ministries and newspaper offices of Paris, Berlin, Warsaw and Vienna, before leaving Pulitzer with his widowed mother at her villa in Antibes and continuing on to Italy with Faye.

With a little trepidation Lippmann approached I Tatti, the palatial villa in the hills outside Florence where Bernard Berenson had set himself up in the trappings of a Renaissance prince. The two men had not met since the Paris peace conference, where they had established an instant liking for one another, and a common disillusion with the peace that compromised their ideals. "Do you happen to recall how I came to see you in your office in the corner of the rue Royale during the peace conference,'' Berenson later wrote Lippmann of those days. "You were still in uniform at your desk. I came to ask you whether you were aware that we Americans were being betrayed, that no attention was being paid to our aims in the war, and that a most disastrous peace treaty was being forged. You said nothing, but your eyes filled with tears. I have loved you since.''[12]

The disillusioning days in Paris were enough, at least, for an affectionate recollection. Yet much else bound together these two very different, but in many ways similar, men. The difference in age — Berenson was twenty-four years older than Lippmann — gave a father-son tone to the relationship, a kind that Lippmann had often sought. The difference in profession was of little importance. Although Lippmann, despite his youthful notion to become an art historian, knew very little about art and cared even less, Berenson was fascinated with power and those who wielded it. He yearned to know the inside story of great events. This was the public side of his well-developed taste for gossip and intrigue. Judging from those who graced his table at I Tatti, he was as interested in politicians, diplomats and millionaires as in artists. With his nimble mind and irresistible charm, he could have been a remarkable statesman.

Brought to Boston from Lithuania by his parents when he was ten, Berenson astounded his teachers, charmed his betters, and made such an impression on Isabella Stewart Gardner that she helped pay his way through Harvard, and then to Oxford and Berlin for further study. Drawn to Italy, which he adored and where he was to spend the rest of his life, he began his career as assistant to a Catholic prelate. In the Italian churches, with their rich collections of paintings, frescoes and drawings, he gained the knowledge that was to serve him so well in his career as authenticator and art historian. He polished his eye, sharpened his taste, and became an authority on Italian Renaissance art. From the commissions he earned on the paintings he bought for Mrs. Gardner, he expanded his repertoire, becoming an authenticator of Italian paintings for wealthy collectors and beneficiary of a profitable business arrangement with Joseph Duveen, the art dealer. His impeccable taste, quick mind, brilliant conversation, aristocratic manner and sharp business sense brought him great fame and equally great comfort. At I Tatti, where he lived with his ailing American wife, Mary, and his German-Italian mistress, Nicky Mariano, he received admirers from near and far, basking in their tributes and handing down, for their edification and admiration, pronunciamentos on art, literature and politics.

Berenson, with his sharp eye for talent, found in young Walter Lippmann a man rather like himself, one who loved being among movers and shakers, one who had an ability to cut through cant and an instinctive feel for politics. Lippmann was the kind of son the childless Berenson would have liked to have had, perhaps even the kind of man he might have been had he taken a different turning a quarter-century earlier. Lippmann, for his part, saw in Berenson a princely version of the father he was always looking for. For four decades he exchanged with Berenson letters of remarkable frankness. To BB, as Berenson was called by his friends, Lippmann confided not only what he really thought about politicians and events, but — in a rare gesture of intimacy — his personal troubles. Their friendship endured until Berenson died in 1959 at the age of ninety-four.

After savoring Berenson's hospitality and receiving his benediction, Walter and Faye continued slowly through the churches and museums of Tuscany and Umbria, breaking the bucolic spell with their arrival in

Rome. The capital was shaken by disorder and cynicism. The Italians, reeling from a war that had taken more than 600,000 lives, resentful at the refusal of their allies to grant the Dalmatian lands they had been promised by treaty, suffering inflation and unemployment, were turning for solutions to radicals on the Left and the Right. Communists and fascists battled daily on the streets and the republic was on the verge of collapse. Lippmann had seen the same thing in Germany a few weeks earlier. "You feel a fundamental instability in Europe that makes all current prophecies, and all the timid maneuvers for peace the merest guesswork and groping," he wrote his father from I Tatti. The Europeans "live for the moment, they live by expedients . . . and if they have any faith about the future, it is that by some tour de force they will be extricated."[13] The extrication came less than a year later when Mussolini's Blackshirts marched on Rome and seized the government.

The breakdown of parliamentary government in Italy confirmed Lippmann's suspicions of the liberal assumption that the best government was the one most responsive to the popular will. In Europe parliaments were responsive, and the results were often chaos or paralysis. Part of the problem lay in special-interest groups that used bribery and pressure. But part, Lippmann was convinced, lay in the very nature of the public opinion that legislators were presumably representing. Classical theory assumed that the people understood crucial issues and could make rational judgments about them. But what if, through no fault of their own, the people could not make such judgments? What if the problem went far beyond that of accurate reporting to the very nature of how opinions were formed? This was the problem Lippmann was grappling with in the book he turned in to Alfred Harcourt just before sailing to Europe.

In the decades since its appearance in 1922, *Public Opinion* and the concepts it advanced have become part of the modern vocabulary. Appearing at a time when social psychology was still in its infancy, it pushed beyond the sterile doctrines of a traditional political science and helped spawn whole schools of inquiry: public-opinion polls, academic courses, scholarly journals, even graduate degrees. Lippmann called the book his first "really serious" one; it is probably his most enduring.

Its bland title concealed explosive concepts. Political science focused on how decisions were made — by political parties, voting, the branches of government. In *Public Opinion* Lippmann went behind such mechanics to scrutinize the centerpiece of democratic theory: the "omnicompetent citizen." That theory assumed that the average citizen, being rational, could make intelligent judgments on public issues if presented with the facts. The job of the press was to present those facts objectively. This is what Lippmann himself had written in *Liberty and the News* only two years earlier.

Now, however, he had had to abandon that faith. Having learned from his wartime propaganda work how the facts could be distorted and suppressed, he realized that distortion was also embedded in the very workings of the human mind. The image most people have of the world is reflected through the prism of their emotions, habits and prejudices. One man can look in a Venetian canal and see rainbows, another only garbage. People see what they are looking for and what their education and experience have trained them to see. "We do not first see, and then define, we define first and then see," Lippmann wrote. Since no man can see everything, each creates for himself a reality that fits his experience, in effect a "pseudo environment" that helps impose order on an otherwise chaotic world.

We define, not at random, but according to "stereotypes" demanded by our culture. The stereotypes, while limiting, are essential. Man could not live without them. They provide security in a confusing world. They serve as the "guarantee of our self-respect . . . the projection upon the world of our own sense of our own value." But if stereotypes determine not only how we see but what we see, clearly our opinions are only partial truths. What we assume to be "facts" are often really judgments. "While men are willing to admit that there are two sides to a 'question,' " Lippmann noted in one of his more disturbing assertions, "they do not believe that there are two sides to what they regard as a 'fact.' "

Using the analogy of Plato's cave, where people who have been chained all their lives imagine that the shadows they see are real figures, he argued that the average citizen's contact with the world was second-hand. For most people the world had become literally "out of reach, out of sight, out of mind." This posed no serious problem in a small community where the decisions each citizen had to make rarely went beyond what he could directly experience. This was the world that the eighteenth-century fathers of democratic theory had written about. But modern man did not live in that world. He was being asked to make judgments about issues he could not possibly experience firsthand: the tariff, the military budget, questions of war and peace. What was reasonable in a Greek city-state was impossible in a modern technological society. The outside world had grown too big for the "self-centered man" to grasp. This posed a political dilemma, for classic democracy "never seriously faced the problem which arises because the pictures inside people's heads do not automatically correspond with the world outside." They did not correspond for a number of reasons — stereotyping, prejudice, propaganda. The result was to erode the whole foundation of popular government. It was no longer possible, Lippmann asserted, to believe in the "original dogma of democracy: that the knowledge needed for the management of human affairs comes up spontaneously from the human heart."

The malady was fundamental, and the press could not provide the answer. The defects of democracy could not be cured, as he had earlier believed, by better reporting, "trustworthy news, unadulterated data." This was asking too much of the press and too much of the public. The press could not carry the burden of institutions; it could not supply the truth democrats believed was inborn. At best it could draw attention to an event. It could not provide the "truth," because truth and news were not the same thing. "The function of news is to signalize an event, the function of truth is to bring to light the hidden facts," he underlined in a crucial distinction. The press, if it did its job well, could elucidate the news. It was, he observed in a striking metaphor, "like the beam of a searchlight that moves restlessly about, bringing one episode and then another out of the darkness into vision." This was a worthwhile task but a limited one. The press could not correct the flaws of democratic theory; men "cannot govern society by episodes, incidents, and eruptions."

Even if the press were capable of providing an accurate picture of the world, the average man had neither the time nor the ability to deal with a perplexing barrage of information. The Enlightenment conception of democracy — based on the assumption that every man had direct experience and understanding of the world around him — was totally inadequate to a mass society where men had contact with only a tiny part of the world on which they were being asked to make decisions. What was possible in an eighteenth-century rural community was unworkable in great cities.

This ruthless analysis left Lippmann with the conclusion that democracy could work only if men escaped from the "intolerable and unworkable fiction that each of us must acquire a competent opinion about public affairs." The task of acquiring such competent opinions had to be left to those specially trained, who had access to accurate information, whose minds were unclouded by prejudice and stereotypes. These people would examine information, not through murky press reporting, but as it came from specially organized "intelligence bureaus" untainted by prejudice or distortion. With their advice the legislature and the executive would be able to make intelligent judgments to submit to the citizens for approval or rejection. The average man, the "outsider," in one of Lippmann's most telling phrases, could ask the expert whether the relevant facts were duly considered, but could not for himself decide what was relevant or even what due consideration was.

This was a sweeping rejection of traditional theories of democracy and the role of the press. Where once Lippmann had thought that intellectuals could be philosopher-kings, now he saw them as mere technicians furnishing information to "insiders." Disillusioned with mass democracy and wary of propaganda and an unreliable press, he could see no alternative: "The common interests very largely elude public opinion entirely, and can be managed only by a specialized class."[14]

The analysis was provocative, the prescription unsettling. With some reason John Dewey called *Public Opinion* "perhaps the most effective indictment of democracy as currently conceived ever penned." Decades later the book continues to stir controversy. The strength of Lippmann's analysis lies in a lucidly conceived and relentlessly argued thesis; the weakness, in a conclusion that looks to a "specialized class" for salvation. Even if the average "self-centered" man is a victim of his own stereotypes, one must ask, do not the "experts," like all human beings, have their own stereotypes? Do they too not have "pictures in their heads"? And if they provide information for a specialized class, in what sense could it be said that the people rule? Lippmann was not quite ready to face this dilemma. He still wanted to find a way of reconciling a lingering faith in human goodness with the gloomy conclusion of his argument. Not until three years later, with the publication of *The Phantom Public,* would he face the full implications of his own analysis.

The critics were impressed, but not quite sure what to make of the book. Most hailed *Public Opinion* as a major breakthrough, revealing problems that few political scientists even knew existed. While conservatives liked its pessimism about the wisdom of the "people," liberals were troubled for the same reason. Harold Laski spoke for many in describing it as "brilliantly written," with a "spare, nervous strength in his style that obviously reflects great mental power." Yet "what does it say at the end," he asked Justice Holmes. "The truth will be easier to obtain if we have objective measurement of facts." The equivocal conclusion did not bother Holmes, who found the book "really extraordinary. . . . Perhaps he doesn't get anywhere in particular," the justice told his English friend Sir Frederick Pollack, "but there are few living, I think, who so discern and articulate the nuances of the human mind."[15]

Judge Learned Hand, while admiring the analysis, was nonetheless troubled by the conclusion. "I want not to have to deal with *homo sapiens* at all in the bulk," he wrote Lippmann. "I want someone with power who will select you and me to rule. That you admit is insoluble." Hand wondered about the "hopeless proclivity of us all to enjoy getting discharged emotionally, the glorious reality of a welter of the good old reliable manly reflexes. . . . How in hell are we ever going to get rid of the delights of these?" Lippmann recognized the delights of the "good old reliable manly reflexes," but hoped that a way could be devised to insulate them from politics. "Have we the right to believe that human reason can uncover the mechanism of unreason, and so in the end master it?" he replied to Hand.

In a sealed and more or less enclosed community, such as the Greeks took for their premise, I should not find it difficult to maintain such a faith. Science is power if you can fence off the area in which it operates long enough. But as I said in the last chapter, the rate at which science expands is much slower than the pace of politics. If there is no way of slowing up the invasion (by birth and by immigration) I think the Hearsts will overwhelm us before they are tamed.

But where do such ideas lead us? Golly, did you ever read Santayana on Walt Whitman? I never recovered from that essay. But one thing I'm sure of. . . . We can't beat the Hearsts by using their methods, as Mencken, for example, thinks. We'd merely be Hearsts in the end. We have to do the other thing, even if we get licked.[16]

What Santayana had said about Whitman was that the poet of the Open Road had a corrupt desire to be primitive. Lippmann had never been in danger — at least not since his undergraduate days — of sentimentalizing the common man. But neither would he write him off, like the vitriolic Mencken, as part of the mindless "booboisie." He was a rationalist, an idealist, and an optimist. He had an abiding faith in American democracy, even though he was skeptical about the men and women who comprised it.

Nowhere did this faith come through more dramatically, and more incongruously, than in the final paragraphs of *Public Opinion*. There, after having undercut democratic theory by questioning the capacity of the average man to make informed judgments, he concluded his pessimistic analysis with an expression of hope. "It is necessary to live as if good will would work," he insisted. "It is not foolish for men to believe . . . that intelligence, courage and effort cannot ever contrive a good life for all men." Even in the horror of war some men had shown they were incorruptible. "You cannot despair of the possibilities that could exist by virtue of any human quality which a human being has exhibited," he protested. "And if amidst all the evils of this decade, you have not seen men and women, known moments that you would like to multiply, the Lord himself cannot help you."

What a remarkable ending to a book designed to explain why democracy had to be protected from the incapacities of the common man! It was as if Lippmann were trying to reassure his readers, reassure himself, that he was one with the man at the clambake and in the bleachers. During those first few years after the war Lippmann wavered between a lingering romantic idealism and a growing intellectual detachment. The former offered the human warmth he sought, the latter the emotional protection he needed. By the mid-1920s he would resolve that conflict. He would choose a self-protective intellectualism. But for a few years he shared with his readers, far more than he intended, his vulnerability and his romanticism.

Part of what he called each man's "conflict with life" can be found in his writings, and nowhere more powerfully than in an essay he wrote in the fall of 1920 on H. G. Wells's *Outline of History*. "A race of men will inhabit this earth to whom our triumphs and our defeats will seem a dim antiquity," he wrote as though from some long-repressed emotion.

They will not remember who strutted the best, or shouted the loudest, or was so magnificent as to put out your eye.

Is that not the beginning of wisdom? And does it not lead, as no other possession leads, to the happiness that only those achieve who in some way are permitted to carry the torch of life? The happiness of creating, and of enhancing, of inventing, of exploring, of making — and finally, of drawing together the broken, suspicious, frightened, bewildered and huddling masses of men. To be excluded from that happiness is tragic as no suffering and no calamity are tragic. To exclude oneself because of embarrassment and timidity is pitiable forever. It is to have turned away from the light of what Wells calls "that silent unavoidable challenge . . . which . . . is in all our minds like dawn breaking slowly, shining between the shutters of a disordered room."

It is to stumble through life without sharing in the beginning of the knowledge that man can, if he wills it, become the master of his fate, and lift himself out of misery and confusion and strife. He need not forever drift helplessly. He can, if he will dedicate himself to the task in an inquiring and tolerable and reasonable spirit, go a very great way towards closing the gap between his experience and his ideals. For history, although almost every page is stained with blood and folly, is a record also, not perhaps of ideals realized, but of opportunities explored and conquered, by which ideals can ultimately be realized.[17]

This was the voice of Lippmann the romantic, before that voice was muted by caution, eminence and skepticism, the voice of a man whose anxieties, like his dreams, were very near the surface. What might he have been had he given full play to that romanticism? Perhaps not the man he became: sober, sound, rational — the fascinated spectator of the human drama. Perhaps a man who would have taken more chances, who might have failed. But then maybe not; perhaps he became, like most of us, the man he had to be.

◄ 15 ►

A Conspicuous Race

Because the Jew is conspicuous, he is under all the
greater obligations not to practice the vices of our civilization.

— "Public Opinion and the American Jew," 1922

BENEATH the poise and self-assurance the world saw in Walter Lippmann, there was another man who suffered anxieties and felt hos-
tilities. Some of these, far more than he would admit, were connected
with being Jewish. Although he had grown up in a Jewish world, he
resisted confining himself to it, or even identifying with it. He dealt
with his Jewish identity largely by choosing to ignore it. Only briefly,
during the period between his return from the war and his move to the
World, did he address the issue directly. The results were such that he
never tried again.

In choosing to ignore classification as a Jew, Lippmann was hardly
unique among people of his class and generation. He had grown up at a
time, and in a social milieu, when "cosmopolitanism" — the rejection
of a specifically Jewish orientation — was considered to be a mark of
cultural liberation. Wealthy second-generation families like the Lippmanns considered themselves more German than Jewish, and more
American than either.

However distinct they might have felt from the white Protestant majority, they felt even more so from the recently arrived Jewish immigrants. These immigrants, having fled persecution in Russia and Poland, spoke broken English and clung to their ghettos for security. The
older immigrants from Germany looked upon the new arrivals with
apprehension and even distaste. Considering themselves the bearers of a
higher culture, and having won acceptance into American life, they did
not want to be identified with the Yiddish-speaking immigrants on the
Lower East Side. They referred to the Russian and Polish immigrants as

"Orientals," and to Yiddish — a German dialect they understood perfectly — as a "piggish" jargon.

But even the assimilated German Jews could not seal themselves off from the tide of anti-Semitism that swept America near the end of the nineteenth century. Not only the immigrants but the older generation of cultured and thoroughly "Americanized" German Jews were excluded from fashionable clubs, resorts, and college fraternities and sororities. In response the wealthy German Jews retreated to their own privileged redoubts, separating themselves from the Gentiles who discriminated against them and from the eastern European immigrants they found so distasteful.

Anti-Semitism made it impossible for them to retain this detachment. Since Gentiles insisted on lumping all Jews together, the assimilated Jews would raise the immigrants to what they considered a higher cultural level. Millionaires like Jacob Schiff launched philanthropic programs to uplift the eastern European Jews. However generous the effort, it was not entirely altruistic. "All of us should be sensible of what we owe not only to these . . . co-religionists," observed the *American Hebrew*, "but to ourselves who will be looked upon by our Gentile neighbors as the natural sponsors for these, our brethren."[1] Since the Lower East Side could not be ignored, it would be elevated.

During the time Walter was in school and college, the Zionist movement was still in its infancy among American Jews, and particularly among Jewish progressives, who denounced it as a product of the ghetto and incompatible with their loyalty as Americans. "We have fought our way through to liberty, equality and fraternity," declared the financier-diplomat Henry Morgenthau, Sr. "No one shall rob us of these gains. . . . We Jews of America have found America to be our Zion. Therefore I refuse to allow myself to be called a Zionist. I am an American." One of the most striking examples of the assimilated Jew was Louis D. Brandeis, who never joined a synagogue or fraternal order, and who as late as 1910 condemned those who favored "habits of living or of thought which tend to keep alive differences of origin or classify men according to their religious beliefs." Such attitudes, he declared, were "inconsistent with the American ideal of brotherhood and are disloyal."[2]

But within two years, under the impact of anti-Semitism and his own indignation at the plight of the immigrant Jews, Brandeis converted to Zionism. He was the first wealthy, prominent, non-Russian Jew to do so, and his conversion was a public event. Zionism, he declared, was not only compatible with Americanism, but was the expression of its highest ideals. "To be good Americans, we must be better Jews, and to be better Jews, we must become Zionists." Drawn by his example, a number of distinguished Jews joined the movement. A good many Jewish intellectuals, however, continued to view Zionism as another form of parochialism. They preferred a "cosmopolitanism" that blurred ethnic differences and disavowed all narrow class or religious loyalties.

The Zionist issue concerned Gentile intellectuals as well as Jews. Thorstein Veblen hoped that Jews would not form a nationalist movement of their own, and argued that only by escaping from his cultural environment could the gifted Jew — "a naturalized, though hyphenate, citizen in the Gentile republic of learning" — come into his own as a creative leader. "It is by loss of allegiance, or at the best by force of a divided allegiance to the people of his origin that he finds himself in the vanguard of modern inquiry."[3]

Other Gentiles, like Randolph Bourne, saw Zionism as a positive force that would enrich the cultural diversity of America. Applauding the failure of the melting pot to turn all immigrants into imitation Anglo-Saxons, Bourne held out the promise of a "trans-national America" that would be the "first international nation," a place where men from many cultures could retain their distinctiveness against a common American background. Bourne praised Zionism as offering an "inspiring" path to transnationalism, and hailed the contributions to American life of such younger Jewish intellectuals as Lippmann, Frankfurter, Horace Kallen and Morris Cohen.[4]

Lippmann, however, was not particularly flattered by Bourne's praise, nor impressed by his theory of dual allegiance. "I am considerably puzzled over the whole matter of dual allegiance, and have been for some time," he wrote Henry Hurwitz, editor of the *Menorah Journal*, the liberal Jewish magazine in which Bourne's article had appeared. Hurwitz had asked Lippmann to write a critical reply. But the moment, December 1916, was not conducive to such speculation. The Germans had just made their surprise peace bid, and Lippmann, pulled into the great events by Wilson and Colonel House, was writing the "Peace without Victory" editorial. "I'm so busy with the other questions through which I must find my way first, that I don't want yet to write anything about Jewish questions," he told Hurwitz.

I will say that Bourne raises issues which go to the roots of political science, and it is a trifle hard for me to see just whence he derives his faith. Frankfurter, Kallen and I are slender reeds on which to lean, and Bourne's estimate of transnational Belgium is at least rosy, and just what Bourne and the rest of you mean by culture I can't make out.

If you get rid of the theory and the biological mysticism and treat the literature as secular, just what elements of a living culture are left? Of a culture that is distinct and especially worth cultivating?[5]

Lippmann's lack of enthusiasm for Zionism was no surprise to Hurwitz, who had unsuccessfully tried to enroll him in the Menorah Society when they were both at Harvard, and later to write for the *Menorah Journal* after its founding in January 1915. Hurwitz had been distressed by Lippmann's critical attitude toward the Jews, and especially by an article in the *New Republic* excerpted from *The Stakes of Diplomacy.* There Lippmann had written, in a discussion of patriotic nationalism, that just as "Jew-baiting produced the ghetto and is compelling Zionism, the bad economic habits of the Jew, his exploiting of simple people, has caused his victims to assert their own nationality."

Hurwitz was not happy with the suggestion that Jews were responsible for anti-Semitism. He told Lippmann that he was amazed at such a "sweeping indictment . . . against my own people by a member of the same blood. . . . Here is a Jew who unqualifiedly repeats the false allegations of anti-Semitism." Lippmann offered no apologies. "Your letter is an example of the morbid sensitiveness which constitutes one of the chief factors of the Jewish problem," he told Hurwitz. "Nothing is more disheartening to me than the kind of tribal loyalty which you ask of me. You need not expect it from me. You need not expect me to subscribe to the myth of an innocent Jewish people unreasonably persecuted the world over. The guilt is not as one-sided as most Jews would like to believe." Chastising Hurwitz for his "hideous complacency" in glossing over Jewish flaws, and for turning his magazine into a "prospectus of our virtues and an anthology of our woes," he asserted that the Jews could well stand criticism from their fellows. "My personal attitude is to be far severer upon the faults of Jews than upon those of other people."[6]

The faults Lippmann saw — "bad economic habits," ostentatious dress, gaudy manners — were those of any *nouveaux riches,* just as the celebrated Jewish "clannishness" was that of any oppressed group. Instead of demonstrating the irrational basis of anti-Semitism — how the Jews, like other minority groups, were used as scapegoats — Lippmann accepted its premise by blaming the Jews for fulfilling the role imposed upon them by Gentile society. He criticized the Jews for being "different," rather than the Gentiles for emphasizing and punishing those differences. Unlike such philo-Semites as Bourne, Lippmann thought the Jewish cultural heritage should be diluted rather than embraced.

Bourne's vision of a transnational America transcending ethnic parochialism was not only appealing to many Jewish intellectuals, but seemed on the verge of realization. The war shattered that vision. In its wake came the Red Scare, the Ku Klux Klan, anti-Negro urban riots, and suspicion of anyone "different." Cosmopolitanism was on the defensive as Henry Ford financed an attack against the "world Jewish conspiracy" and the Klan fomented hatred of the Jews.

Some Jews reacted by turning their backs on cosmopolitanism and embracing Zionism. One of these was Leon Simon, whose book *Studies in Jewish Nationalism* urged all Jews to become Zionists and help build a Jewish state in Palestine. Hurwitz thought that Lippmann would be the perfect person to review Simon's book for the *Menorah Journal*. Lippmann decided to give it a try.

In January 1921 he sent his review to Hurwitz, accompanied by an unusual request that the editor not show it to anyone else. A few days later, having had second thoughts, he insisted that the review be returned. An astounded Hurwitz asked him to reconsider, but Lippmann was adamant. Before sending it back, Hurwitz had a copy made for his files. It is the only existing record. "I am obviously one of the large number of Jews whom Mr. Simon deplores, regrets, shakes his head at, and regards as 'The Problem,' " Lippmann wrote in his unpublished draft — "one of those assimilated creatures to whom the Jewish past has no very peculiar intimate appeal, who find their cultural roots where they can, have no sense of belonging to the Chosen People, and tremble at the suggestion that God has imprudently put all his best eggs in one tribal basket." So much for the Chosen People. So much, too, for Zion. Simon's contention that Jews could maintain their ties with Palestine by speaking Hebrew at home was, Lippmann charged, a "telepathetic miracle." The Zionist call for a dual allegiance was "other-worldliness of a peculiarly dangerous sort," based on the assumption that "while the Palestinian Jew is to integrate body and soul, his politics and his culture, the extra-Palestinian Jew is to keep his body in one place and to attach his mind somewhere else."

If younger Jews seemed less "Jewish" than their elders, this was, he explained, because "they have opened their eyes to a whole new order of problems for which orthodoxy is simply no guide." What would be so tragic if Western Jews dissolved completely into their communities, he asked. "What after all can we do better in our little lives than to build them into the Englishmen or Americans of tomorrow? . . . It is a splendid thing to build Zion in Palestine, but it is no less splendid to fulfill the American dream." He would not, he declared, "worry about my identification then or now, knowing full well that what is genuinely distinct and individual will persist, while unreal distinctions are not worth cultivating. People who are tremendously concerned about their identification, their individuality, their self-expression, or their sense of humor always seem to be missing the very things they pursue."[7]

What Lippmann objected to was not Simon's contention that Jews should have a homeland, but that all American Jews were supposed to feel allegiance to such a Jewish state. To an assimilated cosmopolitan like Lippmann — typical of many Jews of his class and time — this was a regression to the "tribalism" internationalists had been deploring for decades. In *The Stakes of Diplomacy* he had shown how sensitive he was to the power of nationalism and the "thwarted nationality" of oppressed minorities. "What is called pride of race is the sense that our origins are worthy of respect," he had written in 1915. "Man must be at peace with the sources of his life. If he is ashamed of them, if he is at war with them, they will haunt him forever. They will rob him of assurance, leave him an interloper in the world."

Four years later, in an introduction to Carl Sandburg's book on the Chicago race riots of 1919, he drew an interesting relationship between the oppressor and the victim. The "parvenue, the snob, the coward who is forever proclaiming his superiority" stimulated his victims to imitate those very attitudes. The result was, Lippmann suggested in a perception that writers on colonialism were to explore decades later, the "peculiar oppressiveness of recently oppressed peoples," among them "the Negro who desires to be an imitation white man," dreaming of a "white heaven and of bleached angels." [8] If Lippmann tried to surmount the confines of his Jewish identity, the discrimination he had encountered — at Harvard, in New York clubs he could not join, in resort hotels catering to a "restricted clientele" — gave him an acute sensitivity to the anguish of others.

Only a year after withdrawing his manuscript from Hurwitz, Lippmann accepted an invitation in the spring of 1922 to contribute, along with a number of prominent Jews and Gentiles, to a special issue of the *American Hebrew* devoted to "The Better Understanding Between Jew and Non-Jew in America." His topic, "Public Opinion and the American Jew," was right in line with the book he had just completed. But what he produced was hardly an academic, or even a dispassionate, treatment of the subject.

The real cause of anti-Semitism, he declared, lay neither in the racist propaganda disseminated by those like Henry Ford, nor in the fevered visions of a world Zionist conspiracy held by unsophisticated people. Rather, anti-Semitism was rooted in the fact that Jews are different. "The Jews are fairly distinct in their physical appearance and in the spelling of their names from the run of the American people," he pointed out. "They are, therefore, conspicuous." Whether or not Jews were really more vulgar than others, the fact remained that "sharp trading and blatant vulgarity are more conspicuous in the Jew because he himself is more conspicuous." Given this fact, the proper course for the Jew, according to Lippmann, was to make himself less noticeable. "Because the Jew is more conspicuous he is under all the greater obligation not to practice the vices of our civilization." He should be temperate, for he cannot "get away unscathed with what less distinguishable men can."

The idea that the good Jew should lie low, dress and behave unobtrusively, and be as indistinguishable as possible from the crowd was hardly unusual at the time. Minority groups, as Lippmann recognized, often suffered for being perceived as "different" from the majority. Assimilated Jews had long since learned that the price of toleration in hostile societies was to maintain a low profile and to play down their differences. Thus they resented the "conspicuousness" of the eastern European Jews as well as the vulgarity of the *nouveaux riches,* who drew attention to themselves and by extension to all Jews. "The rich and vulgar and pretentious Jews of our big American cities are perhaps the greatest misfortune that has ever befallen the Jewish people," Lippmann complained in the easily recognized voice of the wealthy German Jew. "They are the real fountain of anti-Semitism. When they rush about in super-automobiles, bejeweled and furred and painted and over-barbered, when they build themselves French châteaux and Italian palazzi, they stir up the latent hatred against crude wealth in the hands of shallow people; and that hatred diffuses itself." The so-called "Jewish smart set in New York and the Jewish would-be smart set," Lippmann charged,

can in a minute unmake more respect and decent human kindliness than Einstein and Brandeis and Mack and Paul Warburg can build up in a year.

I worry about upper Broadway on a Sunday afternoon where everything that is feverish and unventilated in the congestion of a city rises up as a warning that you cannot build up a decent civilization among people who, when they are at last, after centuries of denial, free to go to the land and cleanse their bodies, now huddle together in a steam-heated slum.[9]

The crudeness, even the cruelty, of Lippmann's attack on his fellow Jews was in dramatic contrast to the sensitivity he had shown to other minority groups and to individuals suffering discrimination or poverty. It was inconceivable that he would have written anything comparable about, for example, the Irish, the Italians or the blacks, all of whom had their parvenus. What seemed to bother Lippmann most was not that certain rich Jews spent their money unwisely — hardly unique to the Jews — but that by being ostentatious they drew attention to themselves. They were, in his word, conspicuous. That newly rich Gentiles might be equally conspicuous was irrelevant, for they were judged by different standards. Above all else the assimilated Jew wanted to be like everyone else — perhaps a little better and a little richer, but not too much so lest others take notice and become resentful. The fear of being noticeably different was what bothered Lippmann: the fear of inciting envy was only one step removed from that of inciting hatred. This is the typical response of the assimilationist who seeks acceptance through submergence rather than through affirmation, who has failed to come to terms with his origins and seeks to escape his identity through anonymity. Identification with the larger cultural group, even acceptance of its prejudices, is a common response to discrimination. It may also be a form of self-rejection.[10]

In rejecting his Jewish identity Lippmann echoed the sentiments of many third-generation American Jews. "Your point of view in emphasizing the fact that the Jew lays himself open to prejudice by the mere fact that he is conspicuous strikes us as not only admirably presented but valid," the editors told him when he submitted the article. Rather than outraging the assimilationist readers of the *American Hebrew*, Lippmann reflected their prejudices and their ambivalence toward their Judaism. A special 1924 issue on "Who's Who in American Jewry" hailed Lippmann as one whose "ultimate aspiration" was for truth, and who furnished the ideal example of "a whole man and a perfect critic."[11]

The fear of being conspicuous — the conviction that Jews must not be thought "pushy" lest they antagonize others and thus trigger resentment and prejudice — was especially evident in the attitude of Jews like Lippmann to educational and professional advancement. While they wanted their fellow Jews to gain access to such restricted areas as medicine, finance and university teaching, they also feared that too great an influx of Jews into the elite universities might rebound against them. It was the old problem of conspicuousness: by being too numerous, and therefore too noticeable, Jews would invite prejudice against themselves. Rather than directly confront, or even seriously question, a system that produced such prejudices as anti-Semitism, many Jews preferred to keep their place and maintain the precarious advantages they had. Lippmann avoided the perils of "conspicuousness" by the fact that he did not "look Jewish," and by immersing himself — through his marriage, his social life, his professional contacts — into the dominant white Protestant culture.

While Lippmann was urging Jews not to be ostentatious, the revival of anti-Semitism in the early 1920s had so infected public life that private universities began to restrict admission of Jewish students. Harvard was not immune to this pressure, and efforts to impose a quota on Jews were temporarily staved off in 1922 only after a bitter faculty debate. But the Brahmin president of Harvard, A. Lawrence Lowell, insisted that something had to be done about the "excessive" number of Jews at the university and appointed a committee to review the decision. One committee member, Arthur Holcombe of the government department, asked Lippmann for his opinion, and the response he got was a masterpiece of equivocation. Although it would be "an abandonment of its best tradition" for Harvard to adopt a quota policy, Lippmann replied, nondiscrimination was not an absolute but a matter of degree. It would be "bad for the immigrant Jews as well as for Harvard if there were too great a concentration.'' One solution to the problem of so many qualified Jewish applicants for admission might be, he suggested, for Massachusetts to set up a state university under Jewish leadership ''to persuade Jewish boys to scatter.'' This would take the pressure off Harvard.[12]

Later that fall of 1922 Lippmann outlined his views at greater length to a member of Lowell's committee. ''I am fully prepared to accept the judgment of the Harvard authorities that a concentration of Jews in excess of fifteen per cent will produce a segregation of cultures rather than a fusion,'' he stated in the first draft of his reply. ''I do not regard the Jews as innocent victims. They hand on unconsciously and un-critically from one generation to another many distressing personal and social habits, which were selected by a bitter history and intensified by a pharisaical theology.''

When a large number of Jews are concentrated in a university like Harvard, he continued, two groups confront each other, neither having a deep attachment to the ideals it professes — Jews being cut off from their ancestral traditions, Gentiles with their traditions in flux. In the clash between cultures, ''my sympathies are with the non-Jew,'' he confessed. ''His personal manners and physical habits are, I believe, dis-tinctly superior to the prevailing manners and habits of the Jews.'' But as the exclusiveness of the Jews broke down, he predicted, Jews would adopt Gentile habits and lose their racial identity. Even Zionism could not prevent this. Indeed, the Zionist movement was

a romantic lost cause, a good deal like Jacobinism in England or Orleanism in France. The racial identity of the Jews in America is rapidly ceasing to have any meaning, because neither Jewish history nor Jewish theology can offer a culture that is sufficiently interesting to bind the Jews together into a spiritual community. They will not go to the rabbis for their beliefs, and therefore, in the long run they will not go to the Jewish elders for their marriage certificates.

Having established his desire that Jews be fused into a wider — and, by his own avowal, superior — non-Jewish culture, Lippmann re-iterated that he was ''heartily in accord with the premise of those at Har-vard who desire to effect a more even dispersion of the Jews, and of any other minority that brings with it some striking cultural peculiarity.'' He drew the line, however, at setting up a specific quota for Jews. There must be ''no test of admission based on race, creed, color, class or sec-tion.'' As a way out he proposed that Harvard raise its admission scores and select its students from a wider geographical area. This, he thought, might dilute applications from New York and Boston, where many of the Jewish immigrants were concentrated, with those from predomi-nantly Protestant areas. Thus did Lippmann try to find a formula to reduce the number of Jews at Harvard to a "manageable" level without accepting a quota.

Despite the spirited intercession of former president Charles W. Eliot, then in his eighty-ninth year, Harvard did impose an informal quota on Jews. Lippmann publicly disavowed the quota, and in an unusually harsh attack on Lowell in the *World* charged that at Harvard there had been "a change of soul at the top. . . . In the place of Eliot, who embodied the stern but liberal virtues of New England, there sits a man who has lost his grip on the great tradition which made Harvard one of the true spiritual centers of American life. Harvard, with the prejudices of a summer hotel; Harvard, with the standards of a country club, is not the Harvard of her greatest sons."[13]

Though Lippmann was offended by the quota system, he accepted the mentality behind it: that Jews were conspicuously different from the white Gentile majority and should be treated differently. Once these differences were eliminated, he believed, there would no longer be grounds for rejection. The assimilated Jew could be granted a passport for full acceptance into American life. He himself, after all, had made the leap. Not completely, of course. There were still clubs he could not join, homes in which he would not be welcome. But for the most part Lippmann had crossed the Great Divide; others had only to do as he had done for the Jewish "problem" to be resolved.

Some of his friends had crossed that divide, but perhaps not so successfully as he. Once, in the late 1930s in a letter to his wife, he referred to his friend Carl Binger as having that "rather common Jewish feeling of not belonging to the world he belongs to." Lippmann said he understood that feeling, although he personally had "never been oppressed by it" and could not discover in himself "any feeling of being disqualified for anything I cared about," nor any response to a "specific Jewish ethos" in religion or culture. Rather, he insisted that he always felt more at home in the "classical and Christian heritage" despite the "biological superstition" of racial theories. How regrettable, he said in reference to Binger, that a mature man should mind that Jews were not admitted to certain social clubs or summer resorts, or not given "perfect justice" in jobs. "To be oppressed by that sort of thing is a sign of not having learned to care about those things which anyone can have if he is able to care about them," he maintained. Lippmann dealt with the Jewish issue, in other words, by insisting it did not touch him.

While he did not conceal being a Jew, neither did he ever talk about it. He refused to join Jewish organizations, to speak before Jewish groups, even to accept an award from the Jewish Academy of Arts and Sciences.[14] He became one of the very few Jews invited to join such social clubs as the River in New York and the Metropolitan in Washington. There were also clubs that would not have him, such as the Links and the Knickerbocker in New York. He simply never let such prejudices touch his life — or at least never gave any sign that they did. Unless others raised the issue, and they rarely did, the fact of his being a Jew never arose. Some of his friends did not even know he was Jewish until they heard it from others — a fact that may say as much about the intensity of his friendships as about his own self-protectiveness. Those who knew realized his sensitivity about it and avoided ever talking about Jews — no easy feat. One friend confessed that she avoided even using "Jew" in the word game Scrabble for fear it might upset him. No matter how little he thought about it, or how little he claimed it meant to him, Lippmann could not avoid the "Jewish problem." It is the anti-Semite, as Jean-Paul Sartre once wrote, who defines the Jew. The Jew then has no alternative but to define himself.

In rejecting, or at least circumnavigating, his Jewishness, Lippmann had to deny a part of himself. He became more cautious, more guarded. Having cast off the burdens of Judaism, he also lost the advantage it offered of being a fully accepted member of a larger group. No one could protect him but himself. Just as the war had undermined his idealism, so his personal vulnerability eroded his romanticism. He had gone as far as he could on the road he had followed since joining the *NR* eight years earlier. Without "an entirely different pattern," as he had written so revealingly of himself in *Public Opinion,* "the end of the war is to you what it was to so many people, an anti-climax in a dreary and savorless world."[15]

When he came back from Europe with Faye in December 1921 he had found a "different pattern" that would shield him from his vulnerability as a self-protective person and as a Jew, from the threatening unpredictability of the masses on whom he had displaced so many of his own anxieties, from the idealism that had not been vindicated, from a marriage that had not worked out as he had hoped, from a job that had grown routine. His perch high in the tower of the *World* building on Park Row offered both the distance and the change he sought.

Walter about to embark on a ride in Central Park, 1893

The seniors at Sachs Collegiate Institute, 1906. Lippmann seated seco. from right; his friend Carl Binger standing third from left

Lippmann (above) and John Reed,
editors of the Harvard Monthly, *1910*
(Photo Harvard Crimson)

Lippmann in 1914
(Pirie MacDonald)

*Lippmann and Alfred Booth Kuttner,
Bellport, Long Island,
the summer of 1915*

*Lippmann, Franklin D. Roosevelt
and Frank Alpine, a labor official,
at a labor relations board session
in Washington, D.C., 1917*

Mabel Dodge at the
Villa Curonia, Florence
(The Bettmann Archive)

In regard to the restoration of French territory it might well be argued that the invasion of Northern France, being the result of the illegal act as regards Belgium, was in itself illegal. But the case is not perfect. As the world stood in 1914, war between France and Germany was not in itself a violation of international law, and great insistence should be put upon repairs the Belgian case "distinct and symbolic. Thus Belgium might will a claim reimbursement not only for destruction but for the costs of carrying on the war. France could not claim payment, it would seem, for more than the damage done to her north eastern departments.

The status of Alsace-Lorraine was settled by the official statement issued a few days ago. It is to be restored completely to French sovereignty.

Attention is called to the strong current of French opinion which claims the boundaries of 1814 rather than of 1871. The territory claimed is the Valley of the Saar with its coal field. No claim on grounds of nationality can be established, but the argument turns upon the possibility of taking this territory in lieu of indemnity. It would seem to be a clear violation of the President's proposal.

Attention is called also to the fact that no reference is made to the status

ne Mather, the Lippmanns' ward, at sixteen
(Photo taken by Walter Lippmann)

Walter and Faye on the top deck of
the Leviathan, *bound for England, 1926*
(Photo by Jane Mather Wilmerding)

w York World *editorial staff. Seated, left to right: Charles Merz, Walter Lippmann, John L. aton. Standing: William O. Scroggs, James M. Cain, Allan Nevins, Rollin Kirby, L. R. E. Paulin*

Lippmann challenging champion golfer Bobby Jones, Atlanta, 1920s

Lippmann and Ambassador Dwight Morrow on the steps of the American embassy,
Mexico City, February 1928 (Photo courtesy of Jane Wilmerding)

◄ 16 ►

Lord of the Tower

God damn it, I'm not going to spend my life writing
bugle-calls!

— To James M. Cain, 1930

Iꜰ Lippmann was looking for an "entirely different pattern," the *World* was the place to find it. The fourteen-story *World* building in lower Manhattan, with its grinding presses, clamorous city room, and circulation-obsessed business office, was a far cry from the cloistered gentility of the *New Republic*. The *World* was built on exposé and nourished by orgies of yellow journalism. Under the iron hand of the legendary Joseph Pulitzer — patron of the Columbia School of Journalism, benefactor of the prizes that bear his name, cosponsor with William Randolph Hearst of the "splendid little war" with Spain — the *World* had become one of the most powerful papers in America.

Jingoist and sensation-mongering under old JP, it was also professedly populist. Every day on its masthead it declared its dedication to truth, justice, and a square deal for the common man. The *World,* JP had proclaimed, would "always fight for progress and reform, never tolerate injustice and corruption, always fight demagogues of all parties, never lack sympathy for the poor," and so on. In addition to its noble struggles it had grown fat on such circulation-bloating gimmicks as bringing the Statue of Liberty to New York harbor, sending Nellie Bly around the world in seventy-two days, exposing French graft in the Panama Canal deal, sponsoring the first flight from Albany to New York City, forcing the dismissal of a prison warden for cruelty, and sending a Santa Claus ship to the warring countries of Europe.

It was that kind of paper, especially in its heyday. But after JP died in 1911 and his eldest son, Ralph, took over as editor, the *World* began moving toward respectability. Ralph, a man of good intentions and liberal instincts, wanted to put out a great paper. He believed in all the noble causes, but he wanted to leave yellow journalism to the tabloids, while strengthening the *World*'s news and editorial sections. To help him run the paper he leaned heavily on Frank Cobb, the inspired director of the editorial page, and Herbert Bayard Swope, a great reporter and a bigger-than-life character.

Swope was the kind of journalist that newspaper dramas are written about: a flamboyant, self-publicizing, high-living promoter with a keen instinct for the news. Swope was by instinct and experience, his city editor James P. Barrett wrote, "a gate crasher; a beater-down of obstacles and opposition; a dominator; a skillful opportunist; a showman and a salesman; a quick, sharp thinker, but not a logician; an eager grasper of highlights and display points, but not a searcher for deep things."[1] He had a special affinity for the rich and the fashionable.

Starting out as a reporter, Swope won the first Pulitzer Prize awarded for journalism; created the public images of several statesmen, particularly Bernard Baruch; worked out a front-page style that was the envy of every paper in town and a model for *Time;* invented the opposite editorial, or "op ed," page; consorted with millionaires and lived like one; and attracted some of the best journalists in town to the *World,* including Marc Connelly, E. B. White, Edna Ferber, George S. Kaufman, Ring Lardner, Franklin P. Adams and Heywood Broun. The secret of his success, he once said, was to "take one story each day and bang the hell out of it." His formula for running a paper was equally simple: "What I try to do in my paper is to give the public part of what it wants to have and part of what it ought to have whether it wants it or not."

The part the public wanted was the gossip columns and the exposés; the part it was supposed to have was usually supplied by Frank Cobb's editorials. Cobb was the opposite of Swope: gentle, modest, soft-spoken. He wore his heart on his sleeve, and his editorials wrapped around it. Whenever he spied an injustice on the horizon, the kindly Cobb was there with cannons blazing. If Swope was addicted to race-horses, actresses and millionaires, Cobb worried over the fate of abandoned mothers and exploited garment workers. Cobb had put together a fine editorial team, including such younger writers as Maxwell Anderson, Lawrence Stallings, Arthur Krock, Charles Merz, and W. O. Scroggs, along with two survivors from JP's days, L. R. E. Paulin and John L. Heaton. His one gap — a first-class writer on foreign affairs — was neatly filled by Lippmann's arrival.

Lippmann soon became one of the stars of Pulitzer's firmament, but it took the staff a while to get used to him. With his elegant pin-striped suits, his bowler hat, and his walking stick — then *de rigueur* among well-dressed gentlemen — he seemed more like a corporate director than a journalist. When he first descended from his tower office to the city room, editor James Barrett — a reporter of the shirt-sleeves, ink-stain school — found him so distinguished that he assumed he must be one of the unemployed gentlemen the paper used as messengers. "Sit down and wait," Barrett shouted at the impeccably dressed man who appeared at his desk one morning in January 1922. "I'll have the package ready for you in a minute." The man looked at Barrett quizzically, his large hazel eyes bulging slightly more than usual. "Excuse me," he said, "I'm Walter Lippmann. I wanted to ask you about the housing story."[2]

Although Lippmann soon became better known at the paper, his influence was felt more than seen. Along with Pulitzer's and the other executives', his office was high up in the tower, just under the celebrated golden dome, above the clamor of the city room and the presses. There he sat down every morning with Cobb to go over the news and hand out the day's assignments. Lippmann usually took the foreign-affairs piece, Cobb the lead domestic story. Although Ralph Pulitzer often sat in on editorial board meetings, he never dictated policy and rarely interfered with a decision made by his editors.

During his nine years on the *World* Lippmann wrote some twelve hundred editorials, about a third of them on foreign affairs — a high proportion at a time when Americans were presumably not interested in what went on across the seas. His very first piece for the *World,* an analysis of France's harsh policy toward Germany, took up an entire page of the paper. "The effect of the reparations clauses," he began an article that showed his ability to pull the reader into a complex discussion, "was as if you locked a bankrupt in jail, put a pistol to his head, made him sign a promise to pay $10,000,000 in ten years, and then added that he must spend the next ten years in which he was earning this money as a model prisoner on a stone pile."[3] That rare knack for synthesizing complicated material and putting it into language the average reader could understand made him an invaluable asset.

It was an agreeable life. Lippmann wrote fast, respected Cobb, liked being part of an editorial team, and enjoyed the freedom that writing unsigned editorials gave him. "So far I've seen nothing to make me question the fundamental goodwill of the people in charge of the *World,*" he wrote Frankfurter a few weeks after starting his new job in January 1922. "And I have a great deal of affection and admiration for Frank Cobb. He's a sort of humorous Yankee titan, 100% American as William Allen White is and as none of the 100% professionals are."[4] His new authority, the satisfaction of working on a team, the chance to write anonymously on a wide range of issues and to meet people in the wider world of finance, industry and show business offered Lippmann just what he wanted.

The *World* was, by tradition and sentiment, a Democratic paper — given to sighing indulgently over the antics of Mayor Jimmy Walker, finding hidden virtue in Tammany Hall, and applauding Governor Al

Smith. Lippmann had no problem with this, for it allowed him to take potshots at the corruption-ridden Harding administration and the inept diplomacy of Secretary of State Charles Evans Hughes. "I find the *World* job easy to do," he wrote Berenson after a year on the job. "It takes my whole time and it is very exhilarating to know that the writing is effective. . . . Our criticism of Harding and Hughes has been persistent and cruel, and has given the lead and most of the arguments to the provincial newspapers. . . . We have had some fun."[5]

The easy pace at the *World* continued until the summer of 1923, when Frank Cobb was stricken with cancer. Lippmann became acting director, with a salary boost to fifteen thousand dollars a year. When Cobb died at the end of the year he took the title of editor, with another raise to twenty thousand dollars, including a guarantee of three months off every year to travel and to write books and articles. Along with his new responsibilities Lippmann gained a seat on the *World*'s policy-making body, the Council, where he joined Pulitzer, Swope, business manager Florence White, and Arthur Krock. Council meetings tended to be contentious, with Lippmann complaining that the news pages were so thin that he had to rely on the *Times* to know what was going on, while Swope countered that the editorials were wishy-washy.

While Lippmann admired Swope as a reporter, he was critical of what he believed to be Swope's lax journalistic morals. At the *World* and for years afterward Swope enjoyed a cozy relationship with the Wall Street financier and self-styled "adviser to Presidents," Bernard Baruch. Swope worked as Baruch's public-relations adviser, promoting him in the paper as a financial wizard, and in return getting insider's stock-market tips. The tips must have been good, for within a few years Swope, who came from a family of relatively modest means, was trading hundreds of thousands of dollars a day. "I thought he made a fortune out of his position as a newspaperman through Baruch," Lippmann later said privately of Swope. "Having started as an ordinary newspaperman with an ordinary salary, he ended up with about twelve million dollars." Baruch's other friend at the *World,* Arthur Krock, apparently had a similar arrangement, one that continued long after he switched over to the *New York Times.* "Arthur used to quote Baruch once a week in his column as if he were the wisest man in America," Lippmann said. "Actually Baruch was not very wise. In fact, he was rather uneducated. He was a character manufactured by public relations."[6]

Krock, in addition to alerting the public to Baruch's financial genius, also enjoyed a moonlighting job with the banking firm of Dillon, Read — one that he himself delicately referred to as that of "private counsel on a matter of public relations." This arrangement got him into considerable trouble when one day at the office Lippmann overheard him on the phone talking with a Dillon, Read agent about an upcoming editorial likely to affect the price of certain stocks. Lippmann accused Krock of giving the Wall Street firm advance information on the editorial. Krock denied the charge, but the incident caused bad feeling between the two men for years. Lippmann banished Krock from the editorial page, where he had been a part-time contributor. Not long after, Krock left the paper for the *Times*, where he became Washington editor and later a columnist.[7]

While Lippmann's promotion to director of the editorial page gave him more money and prestige, it also involved more work, including editing the copy of his staff. Even the best needed editing, although few readers would have noticed their slips, and most other editors would have let them pass. But Lippmann was a stickler for grammar, as his writers soon found out. One day Lippmann, who had been out of town on vacation, returned to the office in an irritable mood. He focused on James M. Cain, who wrote the "human interest" editorials and later became a successful novelist. "You of all men!" he said, brandishing an editorial Cain had written in his absence. "All right, I'm guilty," Cain replied, "but tell me what I did." "Look at the way you've ended this sentence," Lippmann said, shoving the paper at him. "You've written 'not as easy as it looks.' " Cain was puzzled. "Don't you know," Lippmann said wearily, "that after the negative the proper word is 'so,' not 'as'?" When he later wrote about the incident Cain explained that he was actually pleased, for it showed that Lippmann took his work seriously. He was, he said, proud to work for "one man in the newspaper business to whom such things mattered." That such a fine stylist as Lippmann "would respect my style, and the pains I took to achieve it, was a big thing in my life."[8]

Lippmann was finicky about style, not as a grammarian, but as one who cared about language and the precision with which words were used. "Experience that can't be described and communicated in words cannot long be vividly remembered," he wrote an administrator who sought his advice on teaching English in public schools. "When you have looked at the stars once and remarked that they are grand, and then again only in order to say that the heavens are swell, why not look at the Wrigley chewing gum sign on Broadway which is equally grand and swell? Without words to give precision to ideas the ideas themselves soon become indistinguishable." He was always careful to keep each editorial focused on a single idea. "You tried to cover too much of the subject instead of remembering that in journalism, at least, you can't count on any reader going back over an article to seize the connections," he told a young woman who asked his opinion on an article she had written. Keeping the subject matter uncomplicated was not a vice of journalism but a merit, he insisted, "for it means that the writer has to conceal a lot of the machinery by which he reaches his effect . . . he must have mastered the subject so completely that it becomes very simple in the statement.''

Cain had particular reason to be grateful for Lippmann's concern with style, for it helped him land his job on the *World*. Arriving in New York in 1924 with only a cardboard suitcase and a letter of introduction from H. L. Mencken to Arthur Krock, Cain timorously dropped by the *World*. Krock led him straightaway into Lippmann's office, leaving Cain speechless before a man whose writing he had much admired. Lippmann asked to see some samples of his work, and a few days later, to Cain's astonishment, offered him a job. As it turned out, Cain had come along at just the right moment. Maxwell Anderson had hit the Broadway jackpot with *What Price Glory?* and had resigned the week before. Lippmann needed a human-interest writer, and as he later told Cain of their first meeting, ''when my ear caught the participles that didn't dangle, the infinitives well buttoned in, the pronouns all with antecedents, it occurred to me that you could take Anderson's place.''

In fleshing out the staff of the editorial page — he soon added historian Allan Nevins — Lippmann sought men who could write and think clearly, not flashy stylists. ''I don't set much store by capacity to write brilliantly,'' he told Frankfurter in seeking his help in finding a writer on legal matters. ''I do set store on lucidity, brevity and what I think Holmes called the instinct for the jugular.''[9] The tough and graceful prose of the editorial team, together with the cartoons of Rollin Kirby, gave the *World* the best-written and most influential editorial page in the nation.

Although Cain and a good many others held their boss in awe — the reporters in the city room referred to him as the ''lord of the tower'' — Lippmann was barely thirty-four when he inherited the editorial page. Exuding self-confidence and never revealing the slightest doubt of his ability — if indeed he felt any — he ruled his domain with a firm grip. A hard driver of his staff, he was no less hard on himself. During his nine years on the *World* he wrote the lead editorial nearly every day, except during his frequent periods of vacation and travel, when he turned the page over to his deputy, Charles Merz. While lacking Cobb's old-shoe informality, he won the respect of his staff by the care he took with their copy, his support of their interests, his tenacity, his refusal to succumb to outside pressure, and his personal concern about those in need.

When the Pulitzers tried to slash costs by firing older writers, Lippmann fought to keep them. When William Bolitho, the gifted young correspondent in Rome, got in trouble with Mussolini for critical reporting, Lippmann backed him to the hilt. When Cain had to go to a sanatorium for tuberculosis, Lippmann kept him on the payroll and gave him free-lance assignments. He even helped give Cain his first break as a novelist by persuading Alfred Knopf to publish the predecessor to Cain's *Post-*

man Always Rings Twice after two other publishers had turned it down, then driving a hard bargain with Knopf on Cain's behalf.

Lippmann, in his own quiet way, "fought harder for more justice for more people on the *World* than anyone else, and for more of them than most of them knew, or ever will know," wrote Franklin P. Adams, the "FPA" of the popular op-ed column "The Conning Tower." Cain, though often critical of Lippmann, agreed. Lippmann had a "courtesy far finer than is commonly encountered in newspapers," Cain later wrote. "If you didn't believe in the idea, he didn't want you to write it." He treated his staff as colleagues rather than employees. He was, in Cain's words, "pleasant, courteous, and . . . waived rank in favor of gracious informality, which, of course, made him quite likeable." Very little of this gentle charm came through in his writing, and was perhaps what most surprised those who saw his popular television broadcasts in the early 1960s.

Many, too, were surprised at his physical appearance. Lippmann did not correspond to the popular image of a frail intellectual or litterateur. He was big-boned, muscular and vigorous, with a heavy chest, a small waist, and strong hands. His 190 pounds lent a sense of power to his five-foot ten-inch frame. Cain had reason to be grateful for Lippmann's physical strength. Once when they were coming back from lunch Cain carelessly stepped off the curb just as a taxi was speeding around the corner. At that moment, he recalled, an "iron hand caught my arm, to pull me, almost lift me, back to the curb. . . . It yanked me back, make no mistake about that. It would. It was that kind of hand and he was that kind of man."

Sensitive, even a bit vain, about his appearance, Lippmann had long since lost his chubbiness. No one now would think of likening him to Buddha. He was solid and strong, but he still fretted about his weight and exercised regularly at a gym. His squash and tennis partners were often surprised at the ferocity he brought to the game. His determination to win belied his normally placid manner. His bearing was sure, his hazel eyes expressive and sensitive. He was a handsome man, with the kind of presence that women were drawn to and men found impressive. Only the voice seemed out of key, a bit high-pitched for one built like a grand-opera baritone. Fastidious about his dress, Lippmann was conservative, given to dark, expensively tailored suits and gray fedoras. Always conscious of how others were dressed, he took great care with his own wardrobe. Once when he and Cain were talking about Jimmy Walker, the Tammany playboy mayor of New York who was invariably described as "well dressed," Lippmann said: "I think he's horribly dressed; he looks like a vaudeville entertainer."[10]

Lippmann's position on the *World*, and the growing reputation he gained from his books, made him a prominent figure in New York and for the first time gave him a national influence. Politicians like Al Smith and financiers like Thomas Lamont courted him, hostesses sought him out for their dinner tables, universities began awarding him honorary degrees. An engrossing and entertaining speaker, he became a popular figure on the lecture circuit. He liked to travel; it got him out of the office and allowed him to meet kinds of people he never saw in New York. He often took the train to the West Coast, and several times a year to the Middle West and the South. He played an active part in the newly formed Council on Foreign Relations — an internationalist-minded group of businessmen, journalists, and academics — and wrote frequently for its quarterly journal, *Foreign Affairs,* whose editor, Hamilton Fish Armstrong, became one of his closest friends.

Despite the fact that he ran a Democratic paper, he had a high reputation in Washington during the Republican years. Calvin Coolidge, after becoming President on Harding's death in 1923, summoned him to the White House for lunch. "Silent Cal" was, despite his sobriquet, quite garrulous, and given to interminable monologues on such burning issues as thrift, sobriety and the pan-American highway. Lippmann found the President "very loquacious," if not particularly stimulating, and gave him high points for never once indicating, during the many times they met at the White House, that he had ever read any of Lippmann's editorials denouncing his administration. Coolidge held no grudge against his journalist critics, or even paid much attention to them. After years of scorning Coolidge for a "genius for inactivity," Lippmann decided that he was admired for what he symbolized rather than for what he did, that among Americans he "called forth an ancient piety toward the origins of their life." [11]

Lippmann, now a journalistic celebrity, savored his new fame — enjoyed knowing the rich and the mighty, being invited to fashionable parties, being recognized on the street by strangers, and being among those whose opinion mattered. In 1923 he and Faye moved out of their apartment at 785 Madison Avenue and rented a small carriage house at 50 Washington Mews on the northern fringe of Greenwich Village. After three years there they were able, with the larger salary he was drawing, to move to a grander apartment across the street at 39 Fifth Avenue. There they led an elegant and active life, going out to dinner or the theater nearly every evening. The weekends, at least from May to October, were reserved for Wading River. The sleepy country village, though unprepossessing, had its own local gentry and even a Saturday afternoon polo team. Lippmann, mounted on his white pony, often served as referee.

There was nothing particularly grand or socially pretentious about Wading River. The houses were mostly run-down and the farmers lived on the potatoes they grew. But there was a small community of weekenders, including Edward Kempf, a well-known psychiatrist, and Walter Binger, a childhood friend of Lippmann who had become an architectural engineer and had bought an old house down the road. Often friends would come out from the city for the weekend. The eclectic group included Harold Laski, Alexander Woollcott, Edna Ferber, George Kaufman, Franklin P. Adams, Jim Cain, Allan Nevins, Bobby Jones, Dwight Morrow, Learned Hand and Felix Frankfurter. There were also Faye's friends, Broadway personalities like the Martin Becks, or local polo players like Jesse Heatley. Walter was often bored by Faye's crowd, but never made a fuss. He hated any kind of quarrel, and preferred merely to go along with whatever Faye had organized. Also, he liked having people around. It was his way of relaxing. Their lively social life helped fill some of the dead space that had developed between them.

One way to have dealt with that deadness would have been to have had a child. They both wanted one, or thought they did, and Faye even went to a doctor to find out why she had been unable to conceive. She never got a satisfactory answer, and gradually just came to accept that they would probably never have a child. Instead they found one on the beach: a red-haired and mischievous ten-year-old girl who lived with her family in a weather-beaten old house nearby. Jane Mather was a tomboy, high-spirited and a little wild, but a wonderful pet around the house. Both Walter and Faye were enchanted by her, and she often stayed with them when her parents — itinerant Shakespearean actors — went on the road.

When Jane's father died in 1925 and her mother was unable to keep the family together, Walter and Faye made Jane their ward. She became the child they never had. Walter, always so careful to conceal his emotions, to evidence no sign of parental longings, became devoted to Jane. In many ways she was his opposite — nonintellectual, spontaneous, athletic — and he loved her for those qualities. His relationship with Jane — he was part parent, part comrade, part frustrated lover — was an enduring and rewarding one that continued for the rest of his life.

At Wading River and on the *World* Lippmann came into contact with a diverse and unlikely group of people; perhaps none was more unlikely than the master escape artist, Harry Houdini. Lippmann had been fascinated by mind readers and crystal gazers ever since his college days when psychologist Hugo Münsterberg had first interested him in hoaxes. Houdini shared that interest, and had gone on a one-man crusade to debunk the claims of spiritualists — then enjoying a great vogue. Lippmann heard about Houdini's work and hailed the escape artist in the editorial columns of the *World*.

Houdini, naturally pleased by Lippmann's support, invited him to a demonstration at the swimming pool of the Shelton Hotel. There Houdini was put in a sealed coffin and immersed for fifty minutes at the bottom of the pool, emerging no worse for wear. Lippmann congratulated his host on his skillful performance and took Houdini off to the hotel bar. Over a drink he suggested to Houdini that he might put on a demonstration that would undermine the current faith in spiritualism. Credulity had reached such lengths that even eminent English writers like Gilbert Murray and Sir Arthur Conan Doyle claimed to have communicated with the dead. The cult was moving dangerously close to home, for only a few days earlier Ralph Pulitzer had announced to Lippmann that there might be something in this thought-transferral business. Lippmann decided that something drastic had to be done, and that Houdini was just the man to do it. The two concocted a plan.

On a Sunday afternoon in May 1924 a specially invited group gathered at Houdini's brownstone on West 113th Street. In addition to Walter and Faye, the group included Pulitzer and his wife, Peggy Leech; Dr. Edward Kempf; Arthur Train; Herbert Bayard Swope and his wife, Margaret; Bernard Baruch; and Houdini's own wife and brother. The experiment began when Houdini instructed his guests to lock him up in a room on the third floor. Meanwhile, in the parlor below, each guest wrote out a thought on a piece of paper and then whispered it to his neighbor three times. Dr. Kempf thought of Buffalo Bill's monument in Wyoming; Baruch, of the phrase "Don't give up the ship." Lippmann, true to form, contemplated matters of state: Lord Curzon in the Foreign Office. After the thoughts were whispered around, Houdini was allowed to return downstairs. Pressing his fingers to his temples, he told Kempf he saw "a man killing buffalo," and Baruch an image of "heaving water and a ship." Lord Curzon, however, elicited a blank. For the second part of the experiment, Houdini went back upstairs, where he took off all his clothes and climbed into a casket hoisted on two chairs. With Lippmann and Pulitzer standing guard over the casket, the others downstairs all focused on a single thought: a portrait of Mrs. John Barrymore. Liberated from the casket, Houdini uttered the single word "Barrymore." Properly impressed, the guests congratulated Houdini. The whole point of the experiment, he explained to them, was to show that any talented magician could perform "mind-reading" feats. There was nothing supernatural in what he had done. But despite the insistence of Pulitzer, who would not easily relinquish his faith in spiritualism, Houdini would not reveal how he had performed his trick.[12]

Spiritualism was hardly the gravest problem facing America in the 1920s, but Lippmann took a lively interest in it, just as he did in scores of other issues far removed from foreign policy and high politics. When he heard that several women were dying from radium poisoning as a result of painting watch dials, and that the watch company refused to pay them compensation, he launched a veritable crusade on the editorial page. It was, he charged, "an outrage that the company should attempt to keep these women from suing," and that they were "allowed to die with justice denied them because the courts and lawyers in New Jersey are too busy and too little interested to give them their day in court." When a bob-haired bandit named Cecilia Cooney, whose exploits of armed robbery had tantalized readers of the *World*'s news pages for months, was finally arrested, Lippmann's sentimental side was touched. Instead of a romantic stickup artist he saw "a pitiable girl; instead of an amusing tale, a dark and mean tragedy . . . a product of this city, of its neglect and its carelessness, of its indifference and its undercurrents of misery." When the State Department banned the Countess Karolyi, a Hungarian exile, from entering the United States for a lecture tour — on grounds that she harbored dangerously leftist ideas — Lippmann organized a spirited, though ultimately ineffective, campaign to reverse the ban. He even tried, at the urging of Mabel Dodge, to help D. H. Lawrence enter the United States, despite the government's fear that the author of *Lady Chatterley's Lover* would be a bad moral influence on Americans.[13]

Even while turning out the lead editorial nearly every day and editing his staff's copy, he somehow found the time to do his monthly column for *Vanity Fair,* write frequent articles for other magazines, publish no fewer than four books, and give a considerable number of public addresses. During his first year on the *World* he did an important series of six articles for the *New Republic* on intelligence testing. The recently developed Stanford-Binet tests were being touted at that time as a foolproof method for measuring the innate intelligence of any child, regardless of family background or education. Skeptical of such sweeping claims, Lippmann became persuaded that the tests had been oversold, misinterpreted, and even deliberately used to justify a system of social stratification.

The IQ tests, he charged, did not measure intelligence, but simply classified people by their ability to do arbitrarily selected puzzles. "The claim that we have learned to *measure hereditary intelligence* has no scientific foundation. We cannot measure intelligence when we have never defined it, and we cannot speak of its hereditary basis after it has been indistinguishably fused with a thousand educational and environmental influences from the time of conception to the school age." Intelligence was based on an "unanalyzable mixture of native capacity, acquired habits and stored-up knowledge, and no tester knows at any moment what he is testing." Refuting the claim by scientists that they could measure a capacity to learn fixed by heredity, Lippmann charged that intelligence testing "in the hands of men who hold this dogma could not but lead to an intellectual caste system in which the task of education had given way to the doctrine of predestination and infant damnation.'' Lippmann's articles set off a controversy that raged for months in the pages of the *NR*, and were being cited decades later in an unending argument over acquired and innate intelligence.[14]

As an editor Lippmann was particularly concerned by infringements upon press freedom, as well as abuses by the press of its privileges. Some of his toughest editorials were directed against his colleagues. ''The combination between the courts and the tabloids has produced a situation for which there is really no precedent,'' he wrote of the collusion between lawyers, judges and reporters in some of the sensational divorce and murder trials of the 1920s. ''If you take the succession of cases — Arbuckle, Rhinelander, Hall-Mills, Browning and Chaplin — and consider how they are worked up by officers of the law, by lawyers and journalists . . . how they are exploited for profit, it is evident that what we have here is a series of national spectacles put on for the amusement of the crowd. . . . The whole atmosphere of them is fraudulent. They are produced by swindlers for suckers.'' Later, during the 1930s, he would score the legal system of New Jersey for the ''intolerable abuses of publicity'' committed during the trial of Bruno Hauptmann for the kidnap-murder of the Lindbergh baby, and the press itself for its ''cruel curiosity'' that forced the Lindberghs to flee to England. The Lindberghs, he wrote, were ''refugees from the tyranny of yellow journalism . . . denied their human, their inalienable right to privacy.''[15]

If journalists were under pressure from editors to write stories that went against their consciences, they should, he suggested, change jobs. ''A journalist who can do something else, if only drive a taxicab or make shoes, is a free man if he wants to be. No man ought to go seriously into journalism who is absolutely and solely dependent upon what he can earn by it.''[16]

As editor he had to cope with the problem of censorship as well as that of privacy. The Jazz Age had its Victorian underside. The flapper rebellion of the 1920s triggered a spate of Broadway shows featuring chorus lines, scanty costumes and dirty jokes — scandalous stuff for the times. Did this fall under the First Amendment guarantee of free speech? Lippmann thought not. When the New York police, in an election year show of concern for public morals, raided the popular girlie revue Earl Carroll's *Vanities,* Lippmann gave a nod of approval. The show was guilty of a ''deliberate and commercial'' obscenity, he charged, and ''aimed to provide the maximum erotic excitement the law will permit.'' Punishing Earl Carroll through his pocketbook would ''discourage the too-rapid advance of competitive smut.''[17]

While this sounded a bit priggish, Lippmann felt he was on solid ground. The line between pornography and art was difficult to draw, he admitted. But it had to be drawn by somebody, and if not by ''somebody with taste and intelligence and a sense of the value of a free and searching theatre the line will most certainly sooner or later be drawn by fools and philistines.'' Obscenity depended upon the context. ''Tear a picture out of a medical treatise and hang it in the parlor — it will seem obscene. . . . Play 'Red Hot Mama' on the organ at a church wedding — it will sound filthy.'' Spectacles like Carroll's *Vanities* were, he maintained, a ''wholly different kind of thing from the frank animalism which in the Bible and Homer, through Chaucer and Shakespeare to the great modern novelists, has been a permanent strain in human nature. These modern spectacles are not ribald. They are not gay. They are not searching. They are not profound. They are a lazy and solitary and safe indulgence in the vices of others.'' Dirty magazines presented no problem at all. They should be ''driven off the newsstands and put out of sight. . . . There is no more reason why these things should be displayed on the streets than that the garbage should be dumped in City Hall Park.'' But Lippmann drew the line at the classics. When Arthur Krock thought that a production of *Love for Love* should be shut down as being too racy for a popular audience, Lippmann wrote his colleague: ''I will not personally be a party to a suppression of a Congreve play, even supposing that it were all you say it is. I should oppose the suppression of *Love for Love* as I should oppose the suppression of nude statuary at the Museum, of Boccaccio, or of the *Arabian Nights,* or Rabelais.''[18]

His attitude toward censorship was clearly not absolutist. It depended on the context and the kind of censorship involved. When Congress passed a tariff bill with a provision for censorship of imported books and films, he saw no constitutional issue at stake. ''It cannot properly be called censorship, for the essence of censorship is prohibition by administrative act,'' he argued in drawing a distinction between prior restraint and punishment after publication or performance. ''Prosecution by trial and jury is a wholly different kind of procedure.'' To those who sought the elimination of all obscenity laws he maintained that it would be ''impossible today to persuade the overwhelming mass of Americans that there should be no law to deal with commercialized pornography.''[19] This may have been true, but Lippmann also did not feel that the issue was important enough to persuade the ''overwhelming mass'' to change its mind.

While he could be roused by social injustice, Lippmann was not by nature a crusader. Readers used to Cobb's thundering denunciations complained that the *World* tended to straddle issues rather than to come down squarely on one side. Lippmann, unlike Cobb, did not see the world in black and white, but rather in various shades of gray. Under his direction the paper's editorial tone became less strident, more intellectual and attuned to nuance. While this more subtle approach pleased many, it rankled others used to the old days. "Cobb was always hot in the wake of the *World* news," wrote city editor James Barrett. "Lippmann liked to think things over first and also see what the *Times* and the *Herald-Tribune* had to say about it before sounding any bugle calls. As a matter of fact, he sounded no bugle calls."

When the paper got into financial trouble in the late 1920s many blamed its inadequate news coverage and its failure to choose between a blue-collar and a white-collar audience. Some critics focused on the editorial page. In a dissection of the *World* for his magazine, the *Nation*, Oswald Garrison Villard charged that the editorial page was far weaker under Lippmann than under Cobb. Where Cobb drove home an issue with the tenacity of a bullterrier and the staccato thuds of a jackhammer, Lippmann wrote with elegance and dialectical subtlety. His editorials, Villard charged, "were extraordinarily learned, very well written, but so clever as to be Machiavellian in their finesse. One feels that there is something metaphysical about it all; that there is a special pleader weaving his web with singular skill, but enticing nobody." Cobb's one-note thumping did not accord with Lippmann's way of seeing three or four sides to an issue. For Villard the *World*'s editorial page was marked by an "inability to take a position and hold it through to its logical end. Too often it charges right up to the breastworks and then slowly retreats or even yields its arms and its entire position."

Stung by Villard's accusation, Lippmann took Cain out to lunch one day at his club to talk it over. For all his admiration of Lippmann's talents, Cain considered his boss more a "poet of ideas" than a newspaper editor. Lippmann was "always trying to get away from the plain banalities of polemic and find the grain of ultimate truth." The problem, he told Lippmann at lunch that day, was that he was trying to make an editorial more than it could be, and often achieving less than it ought to be.

"If you ask me," Cain explained, "the most that any newspaper should try to do is choose sides in a fight, and then fight as hard as it can, even when it secretly wishes the fight were going a little differently. But you are always trying to dredge up basic principles. In a newspaper it won't work. For example, turn to music. A piano has eight octaves, a violin three, a cornet two, and a bugle has only four notes. Now if what you've got to blow is a bugle, there isn't any sense in camping yourself down in front of piano music."

"You may be right," Lippmann retorted. "But God damn it, I'm not going to spend my life writing bugle-calls!"[20]

Not only was he not writing that kind of music, he was not writing for that kind of public.

◄ 17 ►

Tyranny of the Masses

My own mind has been getting steadily anti-democratic.

— To Learned Hand, June 1925

THE qualities that made Lippmann's editorials so impressive — their elegance, subtlety, and emphasis on underlying principles — also made them seem remote to the *World*'s blue-collar readers. The paper had made its reputation as the voice of the "little man," flagellating injustice, calling public officials to task, extolling the virtues — as well as pandering to the more lurid tastes — of the masses. This was still Swope's formula for the news pages. The old hands at the *World*, and many of its readers, saw Virtue marching out every day in unending combat with Privilege and Corruption. Lippmann could never see it that way. He was becoming convinced that democracy had to be protected from the masses.

Public Opinion, with its evocation of an unseen environment and of citizens with "pictures in their heads," had asked whether the average man could make intelligent decisions about public issues. While raising the question, Lippmann had not come fully to terms with the implications of his own analysis. He had never been satisfied with the equivocal conclusion of *Public Opinion*, with its touching, though not quite convincing, declaration of faith in the "possibilities that could exist by virtue of any human quality which a human being has exhibited." In truth, he was unwilling to confront his own pessimism. "I have written and then thrown away several endings to this book," he confessed to his readers in the final chapter.

But the enthusiastic reception of the book emboldened him to push his analysis all the way. Early in June 1923 he and Faye shut down their New York apartment and moved out to Wading River for the summer. There Walter worked almost full time on a sequel to *Public Opinion*. Chained to a grueling schedule, he would get up at six, have breakfast and a quick swim, write his daily editorial for the *World* — which he would telephone in to Charles Merz, who was tending shop during his absence — and spend the rest of the day on the book. Weekend guests were gently discouraged, except for Graham Wallas, who came for a long stay and served as a sounding board for some of the ideas Lippmann was testing in the book.

Writing fast, and with his usual discipline, Lippmann managed to turn out a long manuscript of some hundred thousand words by the end of the summer. He was pleased with what he had done, though uncertain of how it would be received. One of the persons whose opinion mattered most was Learned Hand, to whom he dedicated the book when, pruned and sharpened, it was published in 1925. "I've tried to say what public opinion can do, and how it can do that more effectively, assuming no intellectual or spiritual improvement in its quality," he wrote the jurist. But the book's thesis was so pessimistic, he told Arthur Holcombe, a professor of government at Harvard, that he was likely to be "put on trial for heresy by my old friends on *The New Republic*."[1]

Those old friends on the *NR* would indeed find a good deal to discourage them. In *The Phantom Public,* as he called this sequel to *Public Opinion,* Lippmann scuttled some of the equivocations that had marked the earlier work. He now declared it a "false ideal" to imagine that the voters were even "inherently competent" to direct public affairs. "I cannot find time to do what is expected of me in the theory of democracy; that is, to know what is going on and to have an opinion worth expressing on every question which confronts a self-governing community," he declared modestly. The implication was, of course, that if he could not, who could?

The problem, rooted in the very nature of democracy, could hardly, as many reformers imagined, be corrected by more democracy — that is, by extending the suffrage or getting out the vote: "If the voter cannot grasp the details of the problems of the day because he has not the time, the interest or the knowledge, he will not have a better public opinion because he is asked to express his opinion more often." It was not fair to expect too much of the average man. As Lippmann explained in one of his clever analogies, "The public will arrive in the middle of the third act and will leave before the last curtain, having stayed just long enough perhaps to decide who is the hero and who the villain of the piece." Advanced societies could not be governed so casually.

The only hope lay in taking the weight off the public's shoulders, in frankly recognizing that the average citizen had neither the capacity nor the interest to direct society. Thus the accepted theory of popular government, resting on the belief that there is a public that directs the course of events, was simply wrong. Such a public was a "mere phantom," an abstraction. In actuality the public was not, Lippmann explained, a fixed body of individuals, but "merely those persons who are interested in an affair." The only way this public could affect decisions was by supporting or opposing those with the power and the knowledge to act. Its job was to identify those capable of making decisions, to align itself for or against a proposal, and to choose between the contending parties by electing the Outs when it had lost faith in the Ins. This was the limit of its competence: "With the substance of the problem it can do nothing but meddle ignorantly or tyrannically."

The crucial distinction, he underlined, was not between specialists and amateurs, but between insiders and outsiders — between those who had the necessary information to act and those who did not. This was no new distinction. Lippmann had first drawn it a decade earlier when, lamenting the voters' rejection of a new state constitution for New York, he complained that insiders had reason for their "subtle distrust for popular action," their "feeling that the people do not choose the better part." Now the intimation had become an assertion. "Only the insider can make the decisions, not because he is inherently a better man, but because he is so placed that he can understand and can act."[2]

While democratic theory decreed that the people were sovereign, in practice that sovereignty meant mostly the power to say yes or no, to throw the old rascals out and bring new rascals in. The public should have the power of veto, but not be asked to make day-to-day decisions. This would allow the "insiders" to do their work and free the public from choices it was incompetent to make. "The public must be put in its place so that it may exercise its powers," Lippmann wrote with little attempt to be politic, "but no less and perhaps even more, so that each of us may live free of the trampling and the roar of a bewildered herd."

The language was a bit brutal, but the outline of the argument had been laid down three years earlier in *Public Opinion*. "The democratic fallacy," he had written there,

has been its preoccupation with the origin of government rather than with the processes and results. The democrat has always assumed that if political power could be derived in the right way, it would be beneficent. His whole attention has been on the source of power, since he is hypnotized by the belief that the great thing is to express the will of the people, first because expression is the highest interest of man, and second because the will is instinctively good. But no amount of regulation at the source of a river will completely control its behavior, and while democrats have been absorbed in trying to find a good mechanism for originating social power, that is to say, a good mechanism of voting and representation, they neglected almost every other interest of man. For no matter how power originates, the crucial interest is in how power is exercised. What determines the quality of civilization is the use made of power. And that use cannot be controlled at the source.

The Phantom Public merely took that argument to its logical conclusion. That argument, for all its bleakness, deserved a better hearing than it got. Those who had hailed *Public Opinion* were distressed and even bewildered by its successor. Although a few managed to see a ray of hope in what John Dewey called its "reasonable conception" of how democracy could be made to work "under an exaggerated and undisciplined notion of the public and its powers," most reviewers were disheartened by its seeming pessimism. *The Phantom Public* soon went out of print, and in the years since has been virtually forgotten. This neglect is unfortunate, for it is one of Lippmann's most powerfully argued and revealing books. In it he came fully to terms with the inadequacy of traditional democratic theory.

There, too, he revealed a good many of his personal anxieties and the loss of his prewar idealism. The book was, as Arthur Schlesinger, Jr., has written, a "brilliant exercise in skepticism" in which "every universal pattern, every central perspective seemed to have washed out from under him." First went socialism, then his faith in science, then his belief that the majority was fit to rule. Last to go, but go it did, was his trust in experts. No longer did he assume they knew best; only that they might know better than the common folk. "The problems that vex democracy," Lippmann wrote ruefully, "seem to be unmanageable by democratic methods."[3]

In a review of the book, H. L. Mencken described Lippmann as one who "started out life with high hopes for democracy and an almost mystical belief in the congenital wisdom of the masses," and had come around to the conclusion that the masses were "ignorant and unteachable." Mencken exaggerated, as always, but was not totally off the mark. He had misjudged only the beginning. As early as 1911 Lippmann, still in his socialist phase, had urged liberals to accept "once and for all the limitations of democracy," and to "recognize clearly that the voting population is made up of people, pretty busy with their affairs." Such people would no more become political specialists than professors of theology, he explained. "They haven't a lifetime to devote to the study of the complicated machinery of government. What they have time for, what they must find time for if they haven't, is the making of judgments as to the direction which the machine shall take." But the details, he underlined, should be left to "specially trained men" who should be judged by their "human result" rather than their "professional technique."[4]

These words, written when Lippmann was only twenty-two, a full eight years before his disillusionment with the propaganda machine and the lost peace, suggested where he was heading. That road, one critic wrote in response to *The Phantom Public,* led toward H. G. Wells's " 'new order of samurai' — an aristocracy of mind and character whose members are dedicated to making democracy work for the best, whether the populace wants it or not."[5]

While unquestionably an attack on traditional democratic theory, *The Phantom Public* can also be seen as a study in class conflict and resolution. Lippmann seemed to be arguing that decisions, however arrived at, have no moral value. They are bad, not because they may be unjust, but only if they cause social conflict. The main criterion is not justice, but tranquillity. Thus what Hobbes saw as justification for the Leviathan (each man surrendered his individual power to the absolute monarch because even tyranny was better than an anarchical war of all against all), Lippmann saw as the virtue of democracy — a mechanism for resolving conflict peacefully. "The justification for majority rule in politics is not to be found in its ethical superiority," he wrote. "It is to be found in the sheer necessity of finding a place in civilized society for the force which resides in the weight of numbers . . . an election based on the principle of majority rule is historically and practically a sublimated and denatured civil war."

Even some of Lippmann's staunchest admirers were unhappy with the logic of *The Phantom Public*. It was not enough merely to undermine complacency about the workings of democracy, Graham Wallas wrote his former pupil. "You are also writing for the young Alexander Hamilton, or Jeremy Bentham, or Walter Lippmann . . . and you don't indicate to him how to make his brains and energy and love and pity for his fellows most effective, through many different kinds of services and experiences, for the good of mankind. Your clear-cut distinction between 'inside' and 'outside' will only baffle and confuse him."

But Lippmann no longer was, or was writing for, the kind of young man Wallas had met at Harvard in 1910. He had grown disillusioned in his ideals, tired in his enthusiasms. "For when the private man has lived through the romantic age in politics and is no longer moved by the stale echoes of its hot cries," he wrote in one of the strikingly personal passages that mark this powerfully argued book, "when he is sober and unimpressed, his own part in public affairs appears to him a pretentious thing. . . . He is a man back from a crusade to make the world something or other it did not become: he has been tantalized too often by the foam of events, has seen the gas go out of it."[6]

Lippmann's disillusion reflected that of his age. The old Progressive movement was played out, a victim of the great crusade that had been botched. Its enthusiasts had become, in Walter Weyl's derisive phrase, "tired radicals." The prewar intellectuals turned away from politics. Some, like Herbert Croly, moved from a search for social progress to one for moral regeneration. Others, like the "lost generation" of painters and writers, went off to Paris, where they could live well on a little money and forget about the problems of America.

Lippmann never ran away from politics, never lost his conviction that the examined, committed life was the only one worth leading. But he, too, needed an explanation for the collapse of his own prewar ideals. What some found in the corruption of politics itself, and a few in the inadequacy of their own assumptions, he discerned in the incapacity of the average man to rule. In *The Phantom Public* lay the rationale for the "new order of samurai," and, between the lines, the disillusion of a man "tantalized too often by the foam of events."

Just about the time that Lippmann sent the manuscript of *The Phantom Public* off to the publishers, an event in the mountain town of Dayton, Tennessee, confirmed all of his suspicions about the prejudices of the masses. There, in the spring of 1925, a young schoolteacher named John Scopes was indicted for teaching Darwin's theory of evolution in defiance of state law. A minor incident in the Bible Belt became a national controversy when William Jennings Bryan joined the prosecution and the famed criminal lawyer Clarence Darrow took over the defense. The trial, deliberately set up by civil libertarians to test the constitutionality of the Tennessee statute, offered Lippmann an ideal chance to examine what he called the "dogma of majority rule."

Lippmann was unable to attend the trial because he was stuck in Baltimore, where Faye was having a major operation for removal of her spleen. But he churned out a stream of impassioned editorials, comparing Scopes's trial to that of Galileo, accusing the legislature of establishing a state religion, and declaring that the efforts of popular majorities to rule over individual consciences was the "chief tyranny of democracy." Yet for all his indignation over the trial, he recognized that the weight of the law rested on Bryan's side: the legislature clearly had the legal right to decide what should be taught in the public schools.

"This is a difficult principle to controvert," Lippmann admitted to Graham Wallas. "Personally, I am pretty well persuaded that it's necessary to controvert it. But in doing so it will be necessary to invent some sort of constitutional theory under which public education is rendered rather more independent of the legislature than it is at present." The power of legislatures was "far more harassing and dangerous to freedom of thought" than that of rich donors on private universities, he argued. Democracy did not have to mean majority tyranny. "It seems to me that majority rule is after all only a limited political device, and that where some great interest like education comes into conflict with it, we are justified in trying to set up defenses against the majority."[7]

One obvious defense against majorities was the courts — even though liberals were generally opposed to court vetoes over popularly elected legislatures. This path appeared closed, however, since the statute in question seemed clearly constitutional. "Now I know this is progressive dogma as we all accepted it in the days when the courts were knocking out the laws we wanted,'' Lippmann wrote Learned Hand. "But I wonder whether we don't have to develop some new doctrine to protect education from majorities.'' Hand, who was usually willing to give legislatures *carte blanche*, even when he did not like what they voted, offered little encouragement. But Lippmann was undeterred. "My own mind has been getting steadily anti-democratic,'' he told the judge. "The size of the electorate, the impossibility of educating it sufficiently, the fierce ignorance of these millions of semi-literate, priest-ridden and parson-ridden people have gotten me to the point where I want to confine the actions of majorities.''[8]

The legal case was clear-cut. Scopes had violated a law that the legislature had had the power to enact. The trial might have ended there had the defense not called Bryan to the stand to explain his view of how the study of evolution conflicted with the teachings of the Bible. The "boy orator of the Platte'' might have been spurned three times by the voters, but he had lost none of his gift for rhetoric. Soaring to awesome heights of hyperbole, Bryan declared that yes, indeed, the Bible must be taken literally: Jonah had certainly been swallowed by the Whale, Eve had been fashioned from Adam's rib, and Joshua had made the sun stand still. Bryan had fallen into Darrow's trap, and under the lawyer's merciless ridicule was laughed off the stand by a hooting audience. A few days later, humiliated and morose at this absurd end to a remarkable career, he suddenly died of a heart attack.

While the newspapers focused on the drama of the case — Darrow against Bryan, science against faith, hicks against city sophisticates — Lippmann probed deeper into the underlying issues. For him the Scopes trial was important, not because it dramatized the naive faith of Tennessee mountaineers, but because it raised the question of the limits of majority rule. Should a numerical majority be sovereign in all areas? Does the legislature have the power to declare what and how people shall learn?

Bryan, Lippmann pointed out, had been logically consistent in arguing for a majority veto on the teaching of evolution. The Great Commoner believed literally in the biblical text and had always insisted that the people should rule — without ever saying how or what they should rule. Given Bryan's two premises — that the Bible was literally the word of God, and that majority rule was an absolute principle — there could be no logical objection to a law imposed by Tennessee fundamentalists.

Laying aside the religious argument and concentrating on the premise that the majority should be sovereign in all things, Lippmann charged that Bryan had "reduced to absurdity a dogma which had been held carelessly but almost universally.'' The people of Tennessee had used their power to prevent their own children from learning, "not merely the doctrine of evolution, but the spirit and method by which learning is possible.'' In so doing they had revealed the "deep and destructive confusion" that lay within the dogma of majority rule.

The confusion, he explained, lay in assuming that the spiritual doctrine of the equality of human souls meant that all men were equally good biologists. The spiritual realm had to be separated from the practical realm. Majority rule was not a moral principle resting on the equality of all human beings. It was merely a political device, a "pacific substitute for civil war in which the opposing armies are counted and the victory is awarded to the larger before any blood is spilled.'' It could not be said that fifty-one Tennesseans were better than forty-nine, only that there were more of them, and "in a world ruled by force it may be necessary to defer to the force they exercise.'' The minority might have to yield temporarily, but should not accept the results as morally valid. Guidance for the school system could come only from educators. "The votes of a majority do not settle anything here and they are entitled to no respect whatever.''[9]

The Scopes trial confirmed the gloomy view of democracy Lippmann had laid out that same year in *The Phantom Public*. The news clips that crossed his desk provided fresh material for his skepticism. When the headline-hunting mayor of Chicago, "Big Bill" Thompson — who had promised to "tweak King George's nose" if the British monarch ever set foot in the Windy City — ordered the suppression of all favorable references to Britain in public-school textbooks, Lippmann made no attempt to conceal his disgust and pessimism. The "naive assumption" of nineteenth-century liberals that any people could govern itself through the ballot had been "rudely challenged" in the last generation, he told the *World*'s readers. "The plain fact is that democracy has had more failures than successes.'' Chicago posed the example of a demagogue rising to power by appealing to the "very lowest prejudices" of the people. "How long can popular government endure on a foundation of this kind?''[10]

Lippmann was coming to look upon the public as a Great Beast to be tamed rather than as a force that could be educated. The lurid treatment given by the press to the juicy divorce and murder cases of the 1920s persuaded him that most people had no serious interest in public affairs. Whether one was to regard this as a good thing or a bad depended, he wrote, on how desirable one thought it was to have the people take a direct part in government. For himself, he questioned whether "in view of the technical complexity of almost all great public questions, it is really possible any longer for the mass of voters to form significant public opinions.'' The issues were too complicated, the rhetoric too stale, the competition from the "big spectacles" of murder, love and death too overwhelming. "The management of affairs tends, therefore,'' he concluded, "once again to rest in a governing class, a class which is not hereditary, which is without titles, but is none the less obeyed and followed."

To escape what he considered the tyranny of popular majorities, Lippmann began looking beyond legislatures, courts, and even constitutions. In a series of lectures at the University of Virginia in the spring of 1928, later published under the title *American Inquisitors*, he examined the Scopes case as a conflict between scientific method and religious belief. "In our age the power of majorities tends to become arbitrary and absolute," he concluded glumly. "And therefore it may well be that to limit the power of majorities, to dispute their moral authority, to deflect their impact, to dissolve their force, is now the most important task of those who care for liberty." [11]

This suspicion of mass wisdom and mass enthusiasms, this search for restraints upon the authority of the public, inevitably colored the editorials Lippmann wrote for the *World*, and noticeably muted the crusading tone that had been the paper's hallmark. Not everyone was pleased with the change.

◄ 18 ►

A Muted Trumpet

> You must not complicate your government beyond the
> capacity of its electorate to understand it. If you do
> . . . in the end it will let loose all the submerged an-
> tagonisms within the state.
>
> — "The Setting for John W. Davis," 1924

LIPPMANN'S suspicion of the masses, his growing caution, his rejection
of the old Progressive creeds, and his high regard for the opinions
of Wall Street troubled a good many of his old friends. None was more
outspoken than Felix Frankfurter. Their friendship, never calm or easy,
dated back to the early days of the *New Republic* and was rooted in a
shared attachment to the Bull Moose brand of progressivism: a belief in
strong leaders and in government as an agent of reform. Intellectually
they often stood together, but temperamentally they could hardly have
been more different.

Short, intense, aggressive, with an indefatigable energy that overwhelmed his listeners, Frankfurter could not resist organizing for whatever cause captured his attention. Bellicose by nature, this Napoleonic
figure liked nothing better than a good argument, no holds barred and all
guns blazing. What was the elixir of life to an aggressive person like
Frankfurter was to Lippmann a threatening assault. Brought up in a genteel household where disagreement was smothered, a show of defiance
considered bad manners, and disobedience a cause for cold withdrawal,
Lippmann looked on verbal boxing not as an intellectual game but as a
deadly contest. Even though he could dish out biting invective on paper,
he abhorred confrontation, and could not easily endure personal criticism from his friends.

Frankfurter was a man of many passions, including Zionism, which
he embraced, like his idol Brandeis, at a mature age. Hardly a public
issue escaped his interest. Through his contacts in government, academia and politics — his "two hundred best friends," as his wife called

them — the Harvard law professor spread his net wide across the country, placing his top students in important government posts and carrying on a voluminous correspondence with scores of influential people. A man of such intensity also provoked intense reactions, ranging from adoration to contempt. His admirers, particularly among lawyers, have been vocal and legion. There were others, such as John Kenneth Galbraith, who thought him "poisoned by the need for identification with the great and for applause," and Cain, who called him "the most offensive, disagreeable human being I ever had contact with." [1]

When Lippmann went to the *World* Frankfurter was delighted to have what he considered a privileged forum for his views. From his post in Cambridge he bombarded his friend with letters, sometimes several a week, expostulating his views on virtually every subject in the news. Where others suggested gently, Frankfurter instructed. With a dogmatism reinforced by years of lecturing students, he had not the slightest hesitation in presenting his opinions as dicta. His handwritten letters to Lippmann flowed on inexorably: five, six, seven pages of relentless logic in heavy, humorless prose. They were not so much letters as legal briefs, imploring, cajoling, directing.

Not long after Lippmann took over the *World*'s editorial page from the dying Frank Cobb in the summer of 1923, Frankfurter first made his distress felt. The cause of his displeasure was an article Lippmann had written on the dismissal of Alexander Meiklejohn as president of Amherst College. Normally such an issue would not have been expected to excite the subway-strap readers of the *World*. But Meiklejohn had become a national figure through his fight with the trustees and the old-guard faculty over his efforts to reform the college. Two of those trustees — Stanley King and Dwight Morrow — were friends of Lippmann, and King was a friend of Frankfurter from War Department days.

Lippmann's sin, so far as Frankfurter was concerned, was in being impartial about an inflammatory issue. In his full-page article for the *World*, Lippmann had managed to come down somewhere in the middle. He admired Meiklejohn, but condoned the action of the trustees. The controversial president was a "fine educator and a great spiritual leader of youth," but an "unsuccessful leader of men." He had done "magnificently" with the students, but failed with the grownups. "He could inspire but he could not manage." The trustees had reason to fire him, but his departure would be a great loss. [2] This argument was certainly balanced, but understandably irritated partisans on both sides. Frankfurter, for one, did not find it good enough and, typically, did not hesitate to say so. "The piece you did left me quite dissatisfied, and you will want to know that others whose opinions you highly value felt, quite independently, as I did," Frankfurter wrote Lippmann. "The source of the difficulty, to my mind, is of course not in your intentions. You are not a reporter — and you did a reporter's job. From you we want not 'the facts' but a critique of the facts."

Such criticism, with its innuendo about others "whose opinions you highly value," rankled Lippmann. He took it as an attack on his integrity, not to mention his reportorial skill, and for five weeks maintained an ominous silence. Whenever he was angry, he once told his friend Gilbert Harrison, he sat on his anger until it passed. This time he refused to budge. "Now that I've cooled off I can write you again," he finally told Frankfurter. "But please, the next time we disagree, don't adopt quite the same tone and don't misread what we are supposed to be talking about." His talks with Meiklejohn's own friends had convinced him, he told the law professor, that his article was "sufficiently objective to satisfy the best informed people on both sides," and that the struggle was one in which the "rights and wrongs are confused, and judgment very difficult to deliver. . . . But for the love of Mike," he concluded conciliatorily, "let's adjourn this. Harding is dead and Coolidge is President of the United States. That's woe enough for the gloomiest." [3]

Frankfurter, who had just returned from a social visit to trustee Stanley King on Martha's Vineyard, agreed to drop the subject. But intent, as usual, on having the last word, he also felt obliged to tell Lippmann a few things he did not want to hear.

. . . You hate discomfort, and our correspondence has been uncomfortable to you. I know also that it came at a bad time. You were tired, your mind was on other things, it was hot, etc, etc. I know. And so you allowed yourself to get hot, and to find comfort in the approval of your article by others, instead of trying to get what it is that so aroused me.

For you know that I'm neither a fool nor a crank, and not apt to have decided views without reason. I care little for the views of the "best informed people on both sides," just because they are entangled in the "facts." You and I have the great advantage of being on the outside. But if the opinions of others mattered, I could show you those of people who, I venture to believe, you care a good deal more about than those to whom you refer.

All this is beside the point that ought to concern you. In view of our relations, my friendship for you, the kind of person you know me to be, I should think that you would be most anxious to face what I'm talking about. Even if I temporarily irritate you, surely you must realize that what I have written you in our recent correspondence, I have written not only because I care greatly about the issues in the Meiklejohn case, but also because I deeply care about you. From that angle, I hope you will reconsider our letters. From that angle, I hope you will want to resume the adjourned discussion. [4]

Though self-righteous in tone, the judgment was not unfair. But Lippmann was not in a mood to receive lectures on his character. Frankfurter seemed to assume that "anyone who wasn't for Meiklejohn was morally defective," he complained to Learned Hand. "What in Sam Hill has got into Felix to make him so suspicious, so querulous, and so argumentative? Enough. I quit writing to Felix in order not to quarrel with him. After I'd quit he wrote and told me I hated inconvenience and that was why I'd quit."[5] Lippmann had a reasonable grievance, but Frankfurter had a point.

Relations were suspended for several months. But even after their anger blew over, periodic discord and hurt feelings punctuated their friendship. A few years later, for example, they disagreed over a case where the Supreme Court had ruled that pacifists could be denied naturalized citizenship. Lippmann thought the Court's judgment constitutional, if harsh; Frankfurter considered it outrageous and proceeded to lecture his friend. Feeling besieged, Lippmann complained to Frankfurter that his hectoring tone was "intolerable" and that he was being "made to feel that honestly to see difficulties is discreditable." Stung by this reproach, Frankfurter replied:

For years it has puzzled me and troubled me that we should have such a happy and hearty feeling of community when I express agreement with you, and yet almost inevitably that I should evoke irritation in you when I express disagreement. Now the fellow who from time to time writes you letters of admiration and appreciation is precisely the same friend who expresses occasional disagreement and dissent. Maybe I'm doctrinaire and foolish in thinking that the quality of our friendship would be falsified if I suppressed disagreement. Being the kind of critter I am, such a practice of suppression would gradually lead to an evaporation of feeling.

Lippmann assured the law professor of his undiminished affection, but added that he often felt in Frankfurter's argument "an unconscious dogmatism which gives me a sense of being rushed and pushed, not unlike that of being physically jolted."[6] Many others felt similarly about Frankfurter, but for Lippmann such dogmatism was particularly hard to bear. Sharp criticism from friends seemed a form of rejection, and his instinctive reaction was to draw away. It was indicative of Frankfurter's egotism that he was too self-absorbed to realize this.

Scarcely was the Meiklejohn episode over and the two friends reconciled, than they were at it again. "A full and frank talk between us is long overdue for the sake of candid friendship," Frankfurter wrote in the summer of 1924. "The quality of our friendship — certainly its integrity and depth — are involved in being conscious of where we are and whither we are going." This time they were quarreling over which candidate the *World* should support for the Democratic presidential nomination.

The Democrats, still reeling from the 1920 debacle, when Harding had plowed under the hapless James Cox, were divided between northern liberals and southern fundamentalists, western radicals and eastern conservatives. The main issues — now that membership in the League of Nations had been relegated to the ash bin — were prohibition and the Ku Klux Klan. The two leading candidates reflected the divisions within the party. William G. McAdoo, in a second shot at the nomination, appealed to many progressives, but was tainted by his connection to the Teapot Dome scandal as lawyer for the indicted oil tycoon Edward Doheny. McAdoo, though he had little sympathy for the Klan, refused to condemn it because he wanted votes from the South and Midwest, where the Klan was strong. In opposition stood Al Smith, governor of New York, speaking for the anti-Klan, antiprohibition forces, for urban America and the big-city ethnic minorities.

Meeting in New York in the sweltering heat of late June, the delegates were evenly divided between the two candidates. They argued for seven days before deciding not to condemn the Klan in the platform, then went into deadlock for another nine days over the nomination. "This thing has got to come to an end," humorist Will Rogers said. "New York invited you people here as guests, not to live." While the balloting dragged on, Lippmann unleashed a salvo of editorials warning that McAdoo was a "menace to the party and the nation," and extolling Smith. The New York governor was, Lippmann declared, the authentic voice of the "millions of half-enfranchised Americans . . . making their first bid for power."[7]

The struggle between the urban Northeast and the rural South and West was so evenly balanced that the Smith-McAdoo deadlock could not be broken. After the ninety-fifth ballot delegates started drifting away from both candidates in search of a compromise. Finally they settled on the silver-haired Wall Street lawyer and former ambassador to Great Britain, John W. Davis. Lippmann took special pleasure in McAdoo's defeat. "The *World* led the fight against him, and it was the hardest, bitterest, most successful battle I've ever been [in]," he wrote Berenson. "We exposed his record, rallied the whole bloc of northern and eastern delegates against him, and after 103 ballots he broke down entirely." Nor was Lippmann displeased with the compromise choice. Davis, he reported, had "far more sheer ability than Wilson, a much richer experience in both industrial and diplomatic affairs, and is a man of finer grain."[8]

Not everyone agreed. During the deadlock, when Lippmann began hinting that Davis might be a suitable candidate for liberals to rally around, Frankfurter had dashed off an impassioned letter to Lippmann, accusing Davis of having been a "silent ally" of bigotry during the Red Scare. Other Democrats, put off by Davis's Wall Street connections, flocked to the third-party candidacy of Robert M. La Follette. Running on a revived Progressive party ticket, the Wisconsin senator damned monopoly, urged government ownership of railroads and water power, and favored allowing Congress to override the Supreme Court. Though his chances were slim, La Follette attracted most progressives, including such luminaries of the American reform movement as John Dewey, Amos Pinchot, Ernest Gruening, Fiorello La Guardia, Helen Keller, Harold Ickes, Jane Addams, and Oswald Garrison Villard.

Lippmann's name was noticeably absent from the list. Even had he approved of La Follette's politics, he would not have supported a maverick whose candidacy was sure to drain off votes from Davis. He worked for a Democratic paper and he was going to support the Democratic candidate. Praising the party's choice, he described Davis as a "liberal." This was too much for Frankfurter, who sent Lippmann a sharp missive reminding him that only three months earlier, before the convention, the *World* had run an editorial saying that the Democrats should turn to Davis only if they were "looking for a conservative." Now they had one. "Coolidge and Davis have nothing to offer . . . except things substantially as is," Frankfurter complained to Lippmann. "The forces that are struggling and groping behind La Follette are, at least, struggling and groping for a dream."[9]

Frankfurter should have known better than to think he could get the editorial director of a Democratic paper to dump the party candidate in favor of a renegade third-party progressive. Nonetheless he kept trying, and for weeks bombarded the paper with letters attacking Davis. Lippmann patiently printed several of these and then decided that Frankfurter had spoken his piece. "I am exercising an editorial right to close a correspondence in which the correspondent has no further claim upon our space," he told the law professor. "Your letter has been published. The *World* has made its reply. We do not wish to conduct an argument with you."

Frankfurter was flabbergasted. He was not used to being shut off, and saw no reason why he could not continue to use the pages of the *World* to point out the paper's inconsistency. "Put out of reach, for a short time, the power of authority which you can so easily exercise against me and any other correspondent," he implored Lippmann, urging him to take counsel "from the quiet recesses of your reason, with which your mind has been so richly endowed."[10] Lippmann resisted the advice, and Frankfurter disappeared, momentarily at least, from the letters column of the *World*.

Lippmann had an uphill battle promoting Davis. The public knew little about him, and the Republicans did not even deign to notice his presence. Instead they trained their artillery on La Follette, virtually accusing the Wisconsin Progressive of being a Soviet stooge. The real issue, Calvin Coolidge declared, was "whether America will allow itself to be degraded into a communistic or socialistic state or whether it will remain American." Fiery words, but hardly applicable to La Follette. Rather than a cry of revolution, the Wisconsin senator's campaign was an echo of the past. His demand for the breakup of the trusts evoked the prairie populism of Bryan — a position Lippmann had ridiculed a dozen years earlier in *Drift and Mastery.*

Yet however dated parts of the Progressive platform were, and however ill-organized was a campaign that ran no candidates on the state or city level, La Follette was nonetheless cutting into Davis's support — particularly in the far West and the industrialized areas of the East. The Democrats' only chance lay in rallying the entire anti-Coolidge vote. This meant smashing La Follette. "The all-important thing is the defeat of La Follette," James Cox, the party's standard-bearer in 1920, wrote Lippmann. "La Follette is to be defeated by the election of either Coolidge or Davis, and votes should be cast for the man who stands the best chance."[11]

Lippmann adopted the anti–La Follette strategy as the only hope for electing Davis. "A vote for La Follette is a vote for Coolidge," he charged in the *World.* "A vote to disrupt the Democratic party is a vote to make the reaction supreme." As far as Lippmann was concerned, La Follette was a spoiler, not a serious alternative to Coolidge. He had "united the conservatives and divided the progressives . . . paralyzed the liberals and revivified the reactionaries . . . muddled every issue, dragged a red herring across every trail, and done his complete and most effective best to insure the re-election of Coolidge." In La Follette's candidacy Lippmann saw no crusade, but simply more liberal factionalism. "As long as the liberal forces exhibit an incapacity to unite and govern themselves," he wrote, ". . . they will not win and they do not deserve to win."[12]

Denying that La Follette was a true progressive, Lippmann described his program as "violently nationalistic and centralizing," his antitrust policy as an "illogical mixture of the individualism of 1890 as expressed in the Sherman Act and pre-war Socialism," his foreign policy as irresponsible and isolationist. "I feel that if I am to cast my vote for a candidate who cannot be elected, and by that vote to help elect the man I think ought not to be elected," he explained, "then at least I ought to be able to vote for a man who is bravely and lucidly expounding what seems to me a liberal program. Mr. La Follette does not offer me that compensation."[13]

Lippmann also saw something else at work: a dangerous tendency toward unrestrained majoritarianism and collectivism. La Follette, he warned, stood for the principle of the "unlimited right of the majority to rule . . . and in government the enlargement of the federal power as against the power of the states." Lippmann's turnaround was now complete. A decade earlier he had argued for Hamiltonian centralization as against Jeffersonian states' rights. Now he was declaring that Davis's "strong Jeffersonian bias against the concentration and exaggeration of government is more genuinely liberal than much that goes by the name of liberalism." Whereas La Follette inveighed against monopoly profits, Lippmann now declared that the "decentralization of the federal political power and the reduction of government at Washington is the paramount political issue of our time."[14]

In arguing for decentralization, Lippmann was not indulging in the standard conservative diatribe against big government. His concern was not economic, but political; not protecting the privileges of the rich, but the rights of the minority. "Ten years ago we should have said that democracies are educated," he wrote in explanation of his vote for Davis.

Today with our experience of how the mind of the mass of men can be moved, with our enormously increased electorate and our greatly complicated life, we should be less certain that we wish to accentuate the struggle for power. . . . You must not complicate your government beyond the capacity of its electorate to understand it. If you do, it will escape all control, turn corrupt and tyrannical, lose the popular confidence, offer real security to no man, and in the end it will let loose all the submerged antagonisms within the state.

Lippmann's growing suspicion of the masses, worked out analytically in *Public Opinion* and *The Phantom Public*, could now be justified as a defense of democracy. In supporting Davis, even more in coming out so forcefully against La Follette, he showed his fear of unleashing those "submerged antagonisms" within the state.

He need not have worried. Coolidge, riding the crest of the economic boom, racked up fifteen million votes, compared to a pitiful eight for Davis. La Follette took nearly five million and outpolled Davis in seventeen western states. The *World*, Democratic though its label might have been, did not seem upset by the results. "If to know exactly what you want and where you are going is the prime virtue in politics," Lippmann wrote in the lead editorial the following morning, "then Coolidge and Dawes deserved to win. The *World* salutes the victors!"[15]

Coolidge prosperity was not matched by Coolidge tranquillity. If "submerged antagonisms" were kept within bounds, they nonetheless erupted in ways that forced even political moderates to take sides. The social disruption that had given rise to the Red Scare, labor strife and the Klan seemed to reach its peak in the Sacco-Vanzetti case — a case that posed a particular dilemma for Lippmann by forcing him to confront head-on an issue he would have preferred to straddle.

The trial and execution of two Italian-born anarchists, Nicola Sacco and Bartolomeo Vanzetti, for robbery and murder, polarized Right and Left, divided families, destroyed friendships, and convinced radicals that the existing social order was inequitable beyond redemption. From the beginning, when the two men were picked up in 1920 for distributing anarchist literature and accused of murdering a payroll clerk, the case was played out against a background of prejudice and anti-Red hysteria. Barely able to speak English and committed to the overthrow of capitalism, they became the symbol of everything that seemed terrifying and alien to many Americans. The jury, intimidated by a trial judge who privately vowed to get "those anarchist bastards," convicted them of a murder they denied.

For years they languished in prison as appeals unsuccessfully went through the courts. Then in March 1927 Felix Frankfurter published a controversial magazine article on the case. Suddenly Sacco and Vanzetti became an international issue, with radicals ennobling the condemned men and conservatives insisting upon their guilt. The fact that a professor at the Harvard Law School had attacked Massachusetts justice in the respected Boston-based *Atlantic* gave new authority to those who charged that the men had been unfairly condemned.

Frankfurter's argument — that the evidence was largely circumstantial, that the trial judge, Webster Thayer, had connived with the district attorney to inflame the jury, that the trial was conducted in an atmosphere of hysteria — was reinforced when a convicted criminal in a Providence jail confessed to the murder. But Judge Thayer refused to permit a new trial, the Supreme Court of Massachusetts was not empowered to demand a retrial under a different judge, the U.S. Supreme Court declined to intervene, and Governor Alvin Fuller would not commute the sentence. As criticism mounted, however, Fuller agreed to appoint an impartial commission to review the case and decide whether a new trial was necessary.

The three-man panel was dominated by its chairman, the patrician Bostonian president of Harvard, A. Lawrence Lowell. Partisans of the condemned men took heart. Harold Laski, whom many Harvard alumni considered dangerously leftist, told Holmes he expected Lowell would be fair. He had indeed been fair to Laski, having defended the socialist professor against demands that he be fired from Harvard for supporting the Boston police strike in 1919. John F. Moors, a member of the Harvard Corporation, spoke for many in saying: "Now we can sleep nights, in the thought that a president of Harvard is on the committee."

Lippmann, like many others sympathetic to Sacco and Vanzetti, assumed that the three-man board would raise enough doubts about the conduct of the trial to allow Governor Fuller to commute the death sentence. This turned out to be wishful thinking. After weeks of deliberation the Lowell committee confirmed the jury's verdict of guilty and refused to recommend a new trial. Defenders of the condemned men were stunned, and accused Lowell of class bias. Lowell, John F. Moors now declared, "was incapable of seeing that two wops could be right and the Yankee judiciary could be wrong." Laski told Holmes that Lowell's "loyalty to his class has transcended his ideas of logic and justice."

Naturally it was assumed that the *World,* having proclaimed the bias of the judge and the need for a new trial, would condemn the Lowell report. It did not. Writing the lead editorial himself, Lippmann described the report as marked by "fairness, consideration, shrewdness and coolness," and declared that the case against Sacco and Vanzetti had been "plausibly and comprehensively stated." Since there were no grounds for a new trial, the only thing left, he concluded, was for the governor to commute the sentence to life imprisonment.[16]

Lippmann's logic may have been impeccable. But when Felix Frankfurter read his endorsement of the Lowell report, he exploded. Having managed to secure one of the three existing copies of the report, he took the first train to New York and marched into Lippmann's office with the offending document in hand. Together they went over the report point by point, with Frankfurter demonstrating that the Lowell committee could not possibly have read the trial testimony. The *World* must condemn the report. At first Lippmann resisted, arguing that the governor had committed himself to the report and that the only hope for saving the men lay in an appeal for mercy. Finally, however, he backed down under the combined weight of Frankfurter's aggressiveness, the evidence, and the misgivings of his own editorial team. Four days after endorsing the Lowell report, the *World* reversed itself. "Because the whole testimony before the committee was not public," Lippmann wrote, "the chain of reasoning which led to the committee's conclusion was not perfectly evident . . . multitudes of open-minded men remain unconvinced." Without disputing the integrity of the committee, Lippmann demanded that it show why the judge's prejudice should not require a new trial.[17]

In an effort to explain his initial resistance, Lippmann told Franklin P. Adams that he had no grounds for challenging either the fairness or the intelligence of the committee's verdict.

We assumed, therefore, that it was better to make a simple plea for mercy and to argue for commutation of sentence on the ground that it was bad public policy to execute two men about whose guilt a large part of the public had such serious doubts. We recognized that this policy would seem tepid to a great many people whose feelings were very strong, but I myself believed that their feelings were of no importance and that what counted was the impression we might be able to make upon the moderate conservative opinion in newspaper offices in Massachusetts.

He may have made an impression on "moderate conservative" newspaper editors, but not on the governor. Fuller refused clemency. On August 19, with the scheduled execution only a few days off, Lippmann made a dramatic break with precedent and agreed, under strong prodding from the staff, to turn over the entire editorial page to the case. One of Rollin Kirby's most powerful cartoons filled the upper righthand corner of the page, flanked on the left by three editorials in which Merz ripped apart the Lowell report, Cain dramatized the injustice of executing men whose guilt was uncertain, and Lippmann urged commutation. "Everywhere there is doubt so deep, so pervasive, so unsettling that it cannot be ignored," Lippmann wrote in words directed to the governor. "The honor of the American Commonwealth is in your hands."[18]

While Lippmann was appealing to reason and compassion, columnist Heywood Broun was spitting fire on the op-ed page. The normally lazy and easygoing Broun had been roused to a rare display of energy by the Lowell report. A member, like Lippmann, of the Harvard class of 1910, he bore a grudge against his alma mater for having denied him a place on the *Crimson*. Unlike Lippmann he felt no loyalty or attachment to his old school. "It is not every prisoner who has a president of Harvard University throw the switch for him," he wrote in his column. The condemned men should "take unction to their souls that they will die at the hands of men in dinner coats or academic gowns." The next day he came through with an even fouler blow: "Shall the institution of learning at Cambridge which we once called Harvard be known as Hangman's House?"

Many readers were delighted. This was the old *World* — outrageous, irreverent, iconoclastic. Circulation soared. So did indignant letters to the editor. Harvard alumni expressed their distress. Pulitzer's friends told him his paper had gone off the deep end. Advertisers threatened to cancel their contracts. The business office demanded that Broun be silenced. Pulitzer, a decent but timorous man, sympathized with Sacco and Vanzetti, but feared the wrath of conventional opinion even more. He told Lippmann to order Broun to stop writing about the case. Broun protested that he could hardly write about anything else but the "legalized murder conducted under academic auspices and prestige." Having latched onto a lively issue, he continued churning out columns in the same vein. Finally, with Lippmann's tacit support, Pulitzer told Broun he would not print any more of his columns on Sacco and Vanzetti.

Broun retaliated by going on strike. He came back to the *World* a few months later, but in 1928 he left for good.

Broun's strike won him considerable sympathy as a champion of the oppressed. But some of his colleagues, like city editor Barrett, thought he was merely grandstanding. Lippmann, for his part, was convinced he had done the right thing in helping to gag Broun. The *World*'s editorial line, he told Franklin P. Adams, "has been very much more effective because we have not been drowned out by Heywood's soprano. There are a few times when a crisis is so great that a paper, if it's to be any use at all, must speak with one voice," he emphasized.

. . . The question has been whether Heywood or the editorial page was to be the voice of the New York *World* in Massachusetts.

It's idle to pretend that the public, way up there, would separate Heywood from the paper, as a small minority here in New York who knew the inside and make the necessary discount.

But the great mass of boobs who are milling around have no such inside knowledge, and when they hear Heywood say that Governor Fuller never intended to do justice, they conclude simply that we're an organ of one of the propaganda committees and that nothing we say need be listened to.

Neither Broun's soprano nor Lippmann's carefully modulated appeals to compassion moved the governor. On August 23, 1927, four days after the *World*'s full-page salvo, Sacco and Vanzetti went to the electric chair. To many their execution seemed an effort by the ruling class to assert its authority, rather than an act of justice. "It forced me to accept a doctrine which I had always repudiated as partisan tactics — the class war," said Robert Morss Lovett. The execution of a "good shoemaker and a poor fish peddler" reverberated around the world: French workers rioted in Lyons, Britons marched on the American embassy, in America demonstrations erupted in a score of cities.

The following day readers of the *World* opened their papers to find a short editorial entitled "Patriotic Service." Without a shred of irony it congratulated Lowell and his associates for suffering a "disagreeable duty bravely" and for being "willing to stake their reputations, to sacrifice their comfort, to face danger, in an effort to get at the truth." In the same dispassionate tone it praised Frankfurter and the defense committee for their readiness to "uphold the rights of the humblest and most despised."[19] With perfect evenhandedness Lippmann was congratulating both sides for an onerous job well done.

While many were soothed by this balm, others were puzzled and some openly contemptuous. Cain felt that his boss was engaging in "logic-chopping" and had approached the whole Sacco-Vanzetti affair as "an intellectual exercise, nothing more." Amos Pinchot, in a biting attack on Lippmann in the *Nation* a few years later, accused him of trying to allay the consciences of Back Bay conservatives, and said the offending editorial demonstrated his belief that "the important thing is that the contending factions should be united by a common appreciation of Walter Lippmann's fairness." A resentful Heywood Broun described Lippmann as being the "greatest carrier of water on both shoulders since Rebecca at the well."[20]

If such reactions were overheated, they were not entirely off the mark. While Lippmann did want to save the condemned men, the issue was not an emotional one for him. He cared with his head rather than his heart. He did not want his editorial page to be considered an "organ of the propaganda committees," as he had told FPA, for it would not be listened to. And being listened to was what mattered. He was writing for thoughtful, even-tempered readers, not for the "great mass of boobs." Unlike Broun he was not emotional or consumed by an overriding personal need to identify with the downtrodden. He respected authority and wanted to be respected by it. In the Sacco-Vanzetti case the august imprimatur of Harvard made it virtually impossible for him to conceive that the Lowell report might have been inadequate, let alone biased.

For the most part he was supported by those whose opinion he most cared about. "Everybody up here was with you," Learned Hand wrote of his Cornish, New Hampshire, summer neighbors — Herbert Croly, Philip Littell, architect Charles Platt, novelist Winston Churchill, sculptor Augustus Saint-Gaudens — ". . . except Felix, to whom it was monstrous because even hypothetically it assumed that the report could be treated as emanating from human beings at all." Yet even Hand assumed that "probably the men were not fairly convicted, and that the case remains a miscarriage of justice." Graham Wallas, writing from England, felt there was insufficient evidence to convict the anarchists. "I am sorry for Lowell, whom I believe I know rather well. He is public-spirited, with a vast amount of administrative drive, but if one goes for a long walk with him one finds him a little stupid. He will suffer horribly over the Sacco-Vanzetti business."[21] Wallas's prediction was right; controversy over the case hounded Lowell for the rest of his days.

Although Lippmann always felt the sentence was too severe, and even questioned whether the evidence warranted conviction, he never doubted the sincerity of the Lowell committee, nor seriously contemplated the possibility that class bias might have been involved. Yet he was less reconciled to the outcome, and to his own part in the controversy, than he ever indicated in print. "I have not been so troubled about anything since 1919," he confessed to Learned Hand a few weeks after the execution, when against what I really believe was my own deepest and best feeling, I let irritation against Wilson's stupidity push me into intransigent opposition to the Treaty.

The Sacco case was particularly difficult because I had so confidently assumed that the Lowell report would in no event mean the death penalty. The briefness of the time allowed for reaching an opinion, the atmosphere of horror and the very real danger of Red violence followed by White violence, made me feel as if we were being rushed into the gravest kind of decision without freedom of mind to consider it.

You know that I was never convinced that they were innocent. At the end my feeling was a) that Sacco might be guilty and Vanzetti less probably, b) that the evidence against both was insufficient, c) that the trial was almost certainly conducted in a prejudiced atmosphere, d) that the Governor, though probably sincere within his lights, was infected with the psychology of class conflict which the case had provoked, e) that a commutation was the wiser course even though one could sympathize with the Governor's difficulty in yielding after the threats had been made.

These were strong words: the trial conducted in a "prejudiced atmosphere," the governor infected with the "psychology of class conflict." But they were not the words Lippmann used in his editorials. Instead he muted his attacks, not wanting to be dismissed as partisan, fearing to encourage class struggle, leftist violence and rightist repression, reluctant to cut himself off from respectable, and respected, opinion. With his long-standing fear of mass passions, he overestimated the dangers of violence. "The event has shown that stability of this society is beyond anything we had imagined," he told Hand, "for it was subjected to a strain which I thought ominous. One of the real issues of the affair, if our conservative classes had insight, is that they are so strongly entrenched they could abandon their panicky state of mind and rule the country with some flexibility and ease. They sit upon the rock of Gibraltar and behave as if they were upon a raft at sea."

Two years later he publicly questioned whether either of the executed anarchists was guilty. "If Sacco and Vanzetti were professional bandits," he wrote in a promotion blurb for Frankfurter's book on the case, "then historians and biographers who attempt to deduce character from personal documents might as well shut up shop. By every test that I know of for judging character, these are the letters of innocent men."

Lippmann's emotionally-restrained approach to the Sacco-Vanzetti affair found an echo two years later in the case of Rosika Schwimmer, a Hungarian pacifist denied U.S. citizenship by the Supreme Court because her refusal to bear arms ostensibly showed insufficient attachment to the Constitution. Although Lippmann ridiculed the Court's decision, he did so not on the free speech grounds asserted by Justice Holmes in his ringing dissent ("if there is any principle of the Constitution that more imperatively calls for attachment than any other it is the principle of free thought—not free thought for those that agree with us, but freedom for the thought that we hate"), but rather because Schwimmer was being treated differently than a native pacifist. He avoided taking a stand on the issue of conscientious objection, telling Frankfurter that it was "one on which frankly I haven't been able to form an opinion," and wrote in the *World* that since conscription was not currently the law of the land, "it would seem to be going pretty far for judges to deal with applicants for citizenship as if conscription was our permanent policy."[22]

The case of Sacco-Vanzetti, and in a different way that of Schwimmer, revealed the emphasis on order and authority that ran through Lippmann's brand of liberalism. He cared about justice, but it was not an emotional issue for him. He also cared about his influence as a public person. His respect for authority, his fear of being cut off from centers of power, his distaste for too close an association with radicals often muted his voice. Agitation was not his style, not only because he disliked hyperbole, but also because he did not want to be relegated to the fringe. To be effective meant to have the ear of those who made the decisions.

Beyond that, and more important, was his preoccupation with social stability. Government, to his mind, was a delicate set of controls; democracy, a way of sublimating the tyranny of popular majorities. He felt so strongly the "trampling and the roar of a bewildered herd," as he had phrased it so tellingly in *The Phantom Public*, that he ignored voices he might otherwise have listened to.

◄ 19 ►

The Mexican Connection

The greatest difference between European and American imperialism is that Europeans are used to imperialism and that Americans are rather new at it.

— Editorial, New York *World*, December 29, 1926

IN that sweltering August of 1927, as the Sacco-Vanzetti affair was reaching its denouement, Jacob Lippmann died of cancer after a long and painful illness. Walter felt more relief than sorrow. He and his father, as he had told Learned Hand, were "never very intimate, but affectionately friendly." Daisy went into mourning, took a trip to Europe, and a few years later married a wealthy man named Isador Stettenheim. Walter continued to visit her ritualistically until her death twenty years later. But he never forgave her for her indifference to him as a child, and their relations remained strained and formal.

By the time of Jacob's death Walter had long since ceased to need any financial help from his family. He and Faye lived quite comfortably on his salary from the *World,* and the paper also paid for his annual trips to Europe. In the summer of 1927 they decided to move uptown, leaving their apartment on lower Fifth Avenue for an imposing brick town house at 158 East 63rd Street. The rent was a steep $415 a month, but well within Walter's salary. In addition to a lush garden with sculptured nymphs and satyrs, and a bar worthy of a small cocktail lounge, the house — which was owned by New York's most fashionable show girl, Peggy Hopkins Joyce — featured beaded curtains, a bed large enough for several people, and a mirrored-ceiling bedroom. Several gentlemen had keys to the outer gate and, not having been apprised of the owner's absence, would occasionally appear at odd hours.

As befitted people of their means, the Lippmanns had a maid, a cook, a Chevrolet for weekend trips to Wading River, and a demanding social life. The rigorous entertainment schedule was part of Walter's job, but he also liked it — liked clever conversation and gossip, the attention of attractive women and of intelligent men, knowing people whose opinion mattered, and being a celebrity. Though a shy man, he savored the spotlight.

He had become a public personality: a commentator on issues of the day for the *World,* an observer of the human scene in *Vanity Fair,* a foreign-policy expert at the Council on Foreign Relations, a counselor to politicians seeking office or editorial favor, an editorialist whose "pool of silence" was balanced by the pleasure of working with others on a great newspaper. "I loved working on a daily paper, being part of a team, and above all the anonymity of editorial writing," he said later of his decade on the *World.* "It gave me a freedom unlike anything I've ever known since." [1]

Lippmann — although he tried to take a detached view of the issues that other men spilled blood over — was never a mere bystander at the political carnival. From his dome above the *World* building he not only analyzed events but actively tried to influence them. Unknown to many of his readers he plotted strategy with politicians, drafted programs for secretaries of state, advised senators, promoted friends for public office, launched presidential booms, wrote speeches for candidates, and even helped negotiate a secret agreement that averted an American invasion of Mexico.

The Mexican episode, a remarkable story he never fully revealed, began when his friend Dwight Morrow became ambassador to Mexico in the fall of 1927 at a time when American oil companies and Catholic militants were urging Coolidge to overthrow the Mexican government. Their ire had been raised by two events: first, the decision of President Plutarco Calles to nationalize the vast land holdings of the Catholic Church, break its hold on Mexican education, and expel foreign-born priests; and second, his move to gain control for Mexico of the oil and mineral rights held by foreign owners.

The oil companies feared expropriation, while the Knights of Columbus sensed godless atheism afoot. Together they joined in urging Coolidge to send in the United States Army and replace the stubborn Calles with a more "cooperative" regime. There was nothing unusual in this request. For decades Washington had been dispatching troops to Central America and the Caribbean to "keep order" and promote a "healthy climate" for U.S. private investment. When Harding became President in 1921 U.S. naval officers were running Haiti and Santo Domingo, and U.S. troops were suppressing a liberal uprising in Nicaragua. Harding's secretary of state, the old-line progressive Charles Evans Hughes, managed to pull the marines out of Nicaragua. But when Coolidge succeeded Harding he sent the marines right back. The Latins were getting out of line.

This reversion to dollar diplomacy inspired Lippmann to a biting editorial. Washington's actions made it clear that Nicaragua was "not an independent republic, that its government is the creature of the State Department, that management of its finances and the direction of its domestic and foreign affairs are determined not in Nicaragua but in Wall Street." Nicaragua had been an "American protectorate" since 1910, and as much a part of an "American empire" as ever Egypt was of the British Empire. "The greatest difference between European and American imperialism is that Europeans are used to imperialism and that Americans are rather new at it," Lippmann pointed out. "We continue to think of ourselves as a kind of great, peaceable Switzerland, whereas we are in fact a great, expanding world power. . . . Our imperialism is more or less unconscious." This provided an excuse for behavior, particularly in Central America, either "disgraceful" or injurious to American prestige.[2] The accusation was hard for most Americans to accept, for it went against the image of the United States as a revolutionary power and the scourge of imperialistic tyrants.

But that image was very different from the one held abroad, and especially south of the Rio Grande. The Mexicans had had a long experience with American imperialism, unconscious and otherwise, dating back to the early days of the republic. They had never forgiven the United States for seizing their northern territories, including Texas and California, and deeply resented interference in their internal affairs. Yet Americans took that interference for granted. Even Woodrow Wilson had landed troops to teach them to "elect good men."

Relations between the two countries had calmed down under the diplomatic direction of Charles Evans Hughes. But when Calles became president in 1924 and, spurred by radical nationalists, demanded that American oil companies exchange their titles for fifty-year leases, the Coolidge administration reacted indignantly. Secretary of State Frank Kellogg, a longtime friend of the petroleum industry, accused the Mexican government of breaking a solemn "contract" with the American oil companies. President Calles, he told a Senate committee, was secretly conspiring with Nicaraguan revolutionaries and Soviet agents to impose a "Mexican-fostered Bolshevik hegemony" in Central America.

Lippmann, long contemptuous of Kellogg, sought to put the issue in a wider context. In a long article for *Foreign Affairs* he examined what he called "the conflict between the vested rights of Americans in the natural resources of the Caribbean countries and the rising nationalism of their peoples." Such nationalism, he pointed out, had nothing to do with bolshevism, as Kellogg imagined, but stemmed from the "desire to assert the national independence and the dignity of an inferior race." To maintain, as Kellogg had done in his relations with the Mexicans, that American investments abroad were under the ultimate jurisdiction of the United States, and not of the countries in which they were located, would inevitably mean an "irreconcilable collision" between the United States and its neighbors. The safety of American overseas investments had to rest on the faith of the borrowing nations, Lippmann argued. "They must believe that American capital profits them, and is consistent with their own national interest." Nothing would so arouse ill will among the Latins, and with that ill will a danger to American security, as the "realization in Latin America that the United States had adopted a policy, conceived in the spirit of Metternich, which would attempt to guarantee vested rights against social progress as the Latin peoples conceive it."

There was nothing particularly "leftist" about Lippmann's argument. He merely wanted to take account of an aroused Latin nationalism. He was not concerned so much with the economic exploitation that put the Latin nations into economic subservience to the United States as with revising the terms in a way that would assuage Latin sensibilities. As he wrote an American businessman who had complained of the "pro-revolutionary" tone of his editorials: "I wonder if you wouldn't gain more by attempting to work with this growing nationalist movement, by winning the confidence of its leaders, and by striving to persuade them that you are not their enemies." The root of the trouble, he suggested, was a "group of men so firmly convinced that they are in the right that they cannot adjust their minds to a new phenomenon and a new situation."[3]

The American business community was divided on the Mexican issue. While the oil companies wanted the marines to overthrow Calles, the banks favored a peaceful settlement that would protect their bondholders. Enlightened financiers — among them Lippmann's friends at the house of Morgan, Thomas Lamont, Russell Leffingwell, and Dwight Morrow — felt that more could be won by the carrot than the stick. Caring less about ideology than about profits, stability and the safety of their investments, they were quite willing to make a reasonable accommodation to Latin American nationalism.

Lippmann's job, as he saw it, was to persuade responsible businessmen that a military intervention would be self-defeating. Only this, he was convinced, could deflect Coolidge and Kellogg from the invasion they were planning. His scheme was two-pronged. First, he had to discredit the idea that the Mexican revolution was part of a communist plot to bolshevize Latin America. This he did in a barrage of editorials stressing that "the thing which the ignoramuses call bolshevism in these countries is in essence nationalism, and the whole world is in ferment with it." Second, he had to come up with a workable alternative. "I feel I know pretty well how to carry on an agitation against the use of violent methods," he wrote lawyer George Rublee, "but this agitation will come to nothing in the end unless the people who are opposed to them can work out a program. . . . Out job, as I see it — by that I mean all the people who are opposed to a break in diplomatic relations — is to show how a possible settlement could be made." In this effort Lippmann had to overcome the skepticism of Ralph Pulitzer, who was being urged by his business friends to support intervention. One of these oil men charged into Lippmann's office, shook his fist, and accused Lippmann of being a Bolshevik.[4]

The problem of an ignorant secretary of state and a President who had declared that "the business of America is business" was compounded by an ambassador in Mexico City who considered Calles a communist agent and an embassy staff composed largely of what Lippmann sarcastically described as "swell young gentlemen" who spent their time at teas and cocktail parties, yearning for the day when they would be transferred to Paris or London. Not a single official in Washington dealing with the Mexican imbroglio had ever served in Mexico. To have expected them to show an independence of mind, let alone a sensitivity to Latin nationalism, would have been asking more than most were capable of.[5]

The steady anti-intervention barrage from the *World* and other journals so irritated Coolidge that he demanded that reporters clear their stories on Mexico with the government before printing them. This did not go down well with the press. Lippmann, setting the tone for the smaller papers, gave the President a lecture. "It has not been the custom in America to let government officials edit newspapers. It is not going to be the custom," he wrote in a classic statement of press freedom.

There is a name for the kind of press Mr. Coolidge seems to desire. It is called a reptile press. This is a press which takes its inspiration from government officials and from great business interests. It prints what those in power wish to have printed. It suppresses what they wish to have suppressed. It puts out as news those facts which help its masters to accomplish what they are after. Its comments on affairs consist in putting a good face on whatever the interests which control it are doing. It makes no independent investigation of the facts. It takes what is handed to it and it does what it is told to do.[6]

Finally Coolidge, under pressure from the press, congressional leaders and Wall Street, laid aside the big stick. In the spring of 1927 he appointed Henry Stimson to mediate the troubles in Nicaragua, and in the fall replaced the war-happy American ambassador in Mexico City with his Amherst classmate Dwight Morrow. This was, as Lippmann pointed out, "no routine diplomatic appointment," but a signal that the administration was willing to compromise. Lippmann hailed the choice as the "most extraordinary appointment made in recent years."

Morrow, an old friend of Ralph Pulitzer, had become a friend of Lippmann as well. They lunched together at the financier's downtown club, met at the Council on Foreign Relations and at dinner parties, and played tennis on weekends at Morrow's home in Englewood, New Jersey. A successful lawyer with a sense of public service and a personal attractiveness that won him friends beyond Wall Street, Morrow seemed groomed for high office. The combination of ambition and asceticism made him a compelling figure. After Morrow's early death Harold Nicolson wrote a laundered biography that only hinted at Morrow's complexity, but noted in his private diaries that Morrow "had the mind of a super-criminal and the character of a saint . . . he was a very great man."[7]

Pleased with Morrow's appointment, Lippmann helped steer it through the Senate by writing flattering editorials and buttering up Senator William E. Borah, whose Foreign Relations Committee had to approve the nominee. Some committee members suspected that Morrow was being sent to make sure that the Mexicans paid off J. P. Morgan's bondholders. In Mexico the current gibe was "first Morrow, then the marines." The J. P. Morgan connection did not auger well for a disinterested approach to Mexico's nationalization program. "I saw today a copy of young Bob La Follette's editorial in which he has nothing to say against you personally," Lippmann wrote Morrow as the Senate moved toward a confirmation vote, "but argues that the Morgan interest in Mexico is a bond-holder interest, that it is a mere accident that the bond-holder interest is for stability and is opposed to the oil interest, which is for intervention, and that no one could tell when the bond-holder interest might coincide with the oil interest. If you believe the materialist interpretation of history in its most rigid and orthodox form, and if you disregard all the actual facts, young Bob's formula is fairly effective."[8]

Morrow, impatient to begin, set off for Mexico in October 1927 without even waiting for the Senate vote. In sharp contrast to his predecessor he moved freely among the Mexicans, greeted President Calles with the customary Latin hug and two kisses, and — picking up on a suggestion from Lippmann — invited the hero of the hour, Charles Lindbergh, to fly from New York to Mexico City as a goodwill gesture. Having won the cheers of the Mexicans, Lindbergh met and soon married the Morrows' daughter, Anne.

Morrow's task was to find a compromise that would assuage the American oil companies while satisfying Mexico's demands for ownership of its natural resources. Beyond that he also sought a resolution to the church-state dispute that would be acceptable to Mexican anticlericalists on the one side, and to Mexican bishops, the Vatican, and militant American Catholics on the other.

Tackling the oil issue first, Morrow worked out a deal with Calles that allowed the oil companies to keep pre-1917 concessions in return for accepting the principle that all mineral rights theoretically belonged to Mexico. This posed a slight problem for Calles, who could not cancel the popular expropriation decrees without considerable loss of face. He ingeniously surmounted this by instructing the Mexican Supreme Court to do it for him. The court obligingly declared unconstitutional those provisions of the petroleum law that limited pre-1917 concessions to fifty years. The accord, worked out in less than two months, was a personal triumph for Morrow. Lippmann hailed his performance as "one of the most brilliant exploits in American diplomacy."[9]

An even more difficult problem lay ahead. The dispute between the Mexican government and the Catholic Church had inflamed American Catholics, many of whom felt that their coreligionists were being persecuted by a godless regime. The Church saw its vast landholdings and its control over education as a way of protecting the faith. Mexican revolutionaries considered the Church — which often found common cause with the great landowners — a barrier to social equality and political justice. The crux of the conflict, as Lippmann later wrote, "was not really the status of the Church as the guardian of souls, but the position of prelates and clergy on the burning question of whether the revolution was to survive."[10]

When Morrow arrived in Mexico in the fall of 1927, civil war had been in progress for more than a year, with atrocities being committed by both sides. In an effort to mediate the conflict, Morrow sought to win the confidence of both the government and the clerics. This delicate maneuver was greatly aided by Lippmann, who was brought into the operation as an unofficial link between American Catholics and Morrow's embassy in Mexico. Through two prominent Catholics — James Byrne, the wealthy General Electric lawyer, and Michael Williams, editor of the liberal Catholic weekly, *Commonweal* — Lippmann conferred with Father John Burke, general secretary of the Catholic Welfare Conference. Burke told him that the critical issue was the question of controlling foreign priests through a registration system. If the Mexicans would allow the Church to decide which particular priests could be registered, the Church would accept the principle of government registration, Burke said.

Armed with this new negotiating position, Lippmann sailed for Havana on February 11, 1928, joined by Faye and their eighteen-year-old ward, Jane Mather. Ostensibly he was going to cover the Sixth International Conference of American States — attended by an all-star delegation including Coolidge, Kellogg and Hughes — for the *World*. He was also on a secret diplomatic mission. Morrow had come over from Mexico City for the conference, and while the delegates argued over trade and Yankee intervention, Lippmann and the ambassador met secretly with a group of Mexican bishops who had come to Cuba to confer with them. At the end of the ten-day conference, Morrow and the Lippmann party sailed for Mexico with an outline of a compromise in hand. President Calles eagerly awaited their arrival. When their ship pulled into Veracruz harbor, frigates fired off a salvo of greetings, a marching band played, and Calles escorted them to Mexico City on his presidential train.

On their arrival in the capital the Lippmanns and Jane moved into the ambassador's residence so that the two men could work together without being observed. Every morning they met in Morrow's study to map out strategy, and every evening to discuss the day's events. For the next three weeks Lippmann, officially "on vacation," met continuously with government officials, bishops, journalists and businessmen to probe terms of a compromise. Since neither side would speak directly to the other, Lippmann and Morrow served as intermediaries. They drafted letters in the name of the president to be sent to the archbishop, and of the archbishop to be sent to the president. Each letter brought the two sides nearer an agreement until finally they reached a compromise on the key issue of registering priests.

At the end of March 1928, after nearly a month in Mexico, Lippmann, together with Faye and Jane, took the train to Washington. There he met with Father Burke and, over a long lunch at the Carlton Hotel, explained the compromise he and Morrow had tentatively worked out. Calles had agreed to cease interference in internal Church affairs in return for the right to register priests. Burke was so encouraged by the suggested settlement that he decided to go to Mexico to confer secretly with Calles over details. Lippmann promised to enlist Morrow as intermediary for their secret encounter. Before they parted, he and Burke together drafted a memo of the proposed accord to send to the Vatican and the Mexican bishops. After leaving the priest Lippmann went over to the State Department to explain the plan to Under Secretary Robert Olds, and then took the train back to New York. "Our friend . . . is in a difficult position," he wrote Morrow of his meeting with Burke.

He has authority of a limited kind. He can speak for his superiors, but his superiors do not know whether they have any authority to compel their subordinates who are scattered around to accept what is arranged. In fact they have been told that some of them won't accept, and they are afraid to exercise their full disciplinary powers. It is a case where Mr. Coolidge is in the right frame of mind, but his Borahs are on the loose, and if he is too rough with them he does not know what will happen.[11]

Burke was momentarily blocked from going to Mexico when the *Herald Tribune* got wind of his trip, forcing both sides to issue indignant denials of any such meeting. By late April publicity had died down enough for him to travel clandestinely to Veracruz, where he met Calles in an abandoned fortress. There they drew up an accord, along lines worked out by Lippmann and Morrow, under the terms of which the priests would call off their religious strike in return for government assurances that it had no intent to "destroy the identity of the Church." The accord in his pocket, Burke set off for Rome to get Vatican approval. After a year of seesaw negotiations an agreement was reached in June 1929 to reopen the churches and end the civil war.

Although Lippmann's part in the settlement was considerable, he gave Morrow the entire credit. "I have always regarded my own knowledge of the Church situation as so wholly confidential that I had no right to share it with anyone, and to use it only to inform my own comment on matters which became public in the natural course of events," he told Reuben Clark, Morrow's legal aid in Mexico. "For that reason the news staff of the *World* . . . has never known any more about the matter than is common knowledge, or than that which they could deduce."[12]

The Mexican settlement launched a minor Morrow boom. Lippmann urged him to seek the 1928 Republican nomination for President. Morrow declined, realizing that he had no chance against front-running Herbert Hoover. The next year, however, he entered the U.S. Senate when the governor of New Jersey appointed him to fill a vacant seat. Writing in the *World,* Lippmann told the citizens of New Jersey that they were blessed to be represented by "one of the best equipped men in public life today, a man almost unique in the degree to which he has the confidence of progressives and conservatives alike." A few months later Lippmann cautiously launched a trial balloon. "It is certainly premature to talk about a Presidential boom," he wrote editorially, "but it is not premature to remark that it is some time since an American public man has aroused the same intensity of belief in his ability, his character and his purposes."[13]

Morrow seemed on his way. In a special election early in 1931 he ran for a full Senate term, calling for the repeal of Prohibition — a position not unpopular in New Jersey. Lippmann hailed him as a bold and imaginative political leader, and the voters seemed to agree, sweeping him into office by a huge majority. Lippmann congratulated them on their good sense and rejoiced editorially that a man of Morrow's quality could "emerge triumphant from the test of a popular election."[14] Morrow had entered the Senate in March 1931, with predictions that the White House would be his next home. Six months later he was dead of a cerebral hemorrhage.

"It would require more composure than I can muster in the first shock of the news of Dwight Morrow's death to attempt an estimate of the man or a just tribute to his qualities," Lippmann wrote only a few hours after hearing the news. "It is too sad a day for such things." In Morrow he found a "statesman who, by the integrity of his spirit, the wisdom of his judgment, and the sympathy of his mind, was destined, but for this irrevocable decree of fate, to play a central role in the life of his people." Morrow was a man who, as Lippmann wrote in a more composed eulogy the following day, lived "at a pitch of mental activity many stages above that of the normal active-minded man . . . everlastingly purposeful, endlessly raising questions, forever finding explanations and solutions."[15]

Morrow for him was not a mere politician but the kind of natural leader whom Wells would have welcomed into his "new order of samurai" — the leader Lippmann was forever seeking and was so rarely able to find.

◄ 20 ►

Men of Destiny

Statesmanship . . . consists in giving the people not
what they want but what they will learn to want.

— *A Preface to Morals*, 1929

WHEN Lippmann returned from Mexico in March 1928, a plan for
resolving the church-state dispute under his arm, maneuvering
had already begun for the Democratic presidential nomination. The
World was not coy about its candidate. The paper was pledged, in the
words of James Barrett, "hook, line and sinker" to Al Smith. Swope,
Pulitzer and Lippmann formed part of Smith's brain trust and the
World's night city editor was drafted as publicity adviser for the campaign.

The Mexican situation, with the fears it had aroused of Vatican interference in politics, had done Smith no good. Pressure for military intervention from Catholic militants like the Knights of Columbus only
made things worse. The Knights, Lippmann wrote Swope at the
height of the crisis, had done more "to make moderate, tolerant and liberal people worry about the effect of making Al Smith president than all
the propaganda for years in the past." If war with Mexico broke out,
"Smith's chances are absolutely finished."[1] Fortunately for Smith the
war scare blew over before he had to confront the issue.

To moderates like Lippmann, Smith seemed an impressive candidate.
Born in 1873 of Irish immigrant parents on the Lower East Side of
Manhattan, he quit school at fifteen to work at the Fulton Fish Market,
joined his fortunes to Tammany Hall, ultimately went to the state legislature, where he racked up an imposing record, and in 1918 was elected
governor — a post to which he was reelected three times. At Albany he
pushed through a sweeping program of social legislation and, despite his
Tammany background, ran an honest and efficient administration. With
his Irish enthusiasm for talk, his politician's love of a crowd, and his al-

derman's ability to bring government down to the ward level, he may well have been, as Lippmann described him, "the foremost master in our time of the art of popular government."[2]

The qualities that made Smith unique also worked against him. Religious bigots, fanned by the Klan, disliked his Catholicism. Small-town fundamentalists resented his opposition to Prohibition. Provincials feared that his election would mean the triumph of the great cities, with their immigrants and alien ways. Smith did not have the proper "feel" of a President. People who were comfortable with amiable bumblers like Harding, or dour Yankees like Coolidge, did not know what to make of a former ward heeler who went to Mass, spoke through his nose in a New York accent, owed his job to Tammany Hall, and probably drank bootleg gin.

For all his big-city background and appeal to urban immigrants, Smith was a perfectly conventional politician, "what a conservative ought to be always if he knew his business," as Lippmann pointed out. The real opposition to Smith lay not in his politics but in his image. He represented virtually everything that rural America found alien and frightening. Smith was the "first man of the new immigration wave" in whose candidacy "millions of half-enfranchised Americans are making their first bid for power," Lippmann wrote; one who represented the new urban society against that "older American civilization of town and country which dreads and will resist him." In Lippmann's view he was a "man of destiny" who exemplified the contest between the "new people, clamoring to be admitted to America, and . . . the older people defending their household gods." His opponents were inspired, not only by a fear of Tammany, but "by the feeling that the clamorous life of the city should not be acknowledged as the American ideal."[3]

Diligently Lippmann worked behind the scenes to reassure voters about Smith's Tammany background. "The corruption issue is one which has to be handled with great intelligence and shrewdness," he wrote Frankfurter just before the Democratic convention in July 1928. Rather than trying to detach Smith from Tammany — which would have been like removing the smile from the Mona Lisa — Lippmann laundered Tammany. He discovered what he called a "new Tammany," one that would "bear comparison as to its honesty, its public spirit, and its efficiency with any other political organization which operates successfully anywhere in the country."

Even the Tammany issue was a trifle compared to Prohibition. Smith, like most big-city politicians, was a "wet." He had opposed the Eighteenth Amendment, which in 1920 made the sale of alcoholic drinks illegal, and the Volstead Act, designed to enforce it. Although the law was openly flouted in cities like New York, where even upright citizens had their bootleggers and speakeasies, hypocrisy could not easily be scuttled. No Democrat could condemn Prohibition and hope to carry the Bible Belt; without the "solid South" no Democrat could win election. That was Smith's dilemma. "Wetness," Lippmann ruefully admitted, "is the one unmistakable national cause with which the Governor is clearly identified."[4]

Lippmann told Smith he had to take a definite stand on the issue. As the Democrats were meeting at Houston to choose their candidate, Lippmann drafted a telegram for Smith to send to the delegates urging repeal of the Volstead Act. This may have been forthright, but Smith's staff thought it would be political suicide, and with the help of Herbert Bayard Swope suppressed the telegram until after Smith was safely nominated. Then the delegates received the telegram expressing Smith's belief that Prohibition was "entirely unsatisfactory to the great mass of our people." The southern "drys" were furious. "It was the *World* which literally drove Al Smith into sending that fool telegram after the Houston convention telling how wet he was," Franklin D. Roosevelt complained to a friend. "Al had every wet vote in the country, but he needed a good many million of the middle-of-the-road votes to elect him President. . . . If Walter would stick to the fundamentals, fewer people would feel that the *World* first blows hot and then blows cold."[5]

But Lippmann was not blowing cold on Smith. He plunged headlong into the campaign, traveled to Albany on the governor's private railway car for strategy sessions, helped to draft his formal acceptance speech, briefed him on foreign-policy issues, and plotted with Belle Moscowitz, Smith's political adviser and alter ego. "It's necessary to remember that in creating a public picture of the governor we are not attempting to depict a man who sprang into the world full armed and perfect," he wrote Moscowitz during the campaign, "but rather a picture of a man who started under every kind of handicap and gradually became what he is. That's the truth, and it's also a very appealing truth."[6]

Smith had a good deal to learn, and not only about foreign policy. "I urged him and begged him, and even shouted at him as much as a year and a half ago that he must seriously begin to form convictions about national questions and express them," Lippmann dejectedly wrote Newton Baker during the campaign. "The plain truth is that he did practically nothing, except on prohibition, and in a somewhat amateurish way on farm relief until he'd been nominated. His heart is all right, his character is all right, his head is all right, but his equipment is deplorable."[7]

One of Smith's many equipment problems concerned immigration. Congress, with prodding from organized labor and small-town Protestants, had levied strict quotas on the entry of aliens, particularly from eastern and southern Europe. These restrictions, designed to preserve a nineteenth-century racial "balance," fell most heavily on Catholics and Jews. Lippmann had supported the original 1924 bill on grounds that the public schools could not hope to "assimilate successfully a great mass of children with very different social backgrounds from those of the mass of the American people," and that northern European immigrants could be more easily absorbed "because their habits and family traditions are so much more nearly like the American," as he delicately phrased it in the *World*.

By 1928 pressure had mounted for even more stringent restrictions. Lippmann told Smith he would have to take a stand on the issue. "I could see at once that he really didn't know what was meant by the 1890 census, the national origins provisions, etc.," Lippmann recounted to a friend. "He said to me: 'I have lived among these people all my life. I can't shut the door in their faces.' His position was purely sentimental. I pointed out to him that whether he liked it or not, his party had shut the door, and that restricted immigration was now the settled policy of the country and that it was no business of his to try to change that policy."[8] Nor was Lippmann going to try to persuade him to challenge that policy.

Despite his dismay over Smith's deficiencies, Lippmann eloquently defended him in the *World* against accusations of drunkenness, allegiance to the Vatican, and subservience to Tammany. He even persuaded William Allen White to withdraw his charges that Smith had vetoed bills to curb saloons, gambling and prostitution because of Tammany pressure. Lippmann thought the crusading Kansas newspaper editor should have known better. "White surely is about the best thing that the Middle West and the small town in the Buick–radio age has produced," Lippmann complained to Herbert Croly during a trip through the Western states.

And judged by any standard of civilized liberalism, it's a pretty weedy flower. He made me feel as if defeating Al Smith had in it an enterprise about equivalent to heaving a stray cat out of the parlor. Intellectually he's able to comprehend, of course, that Smith is a real person, representing real things, but emotionally he's no more able to comprehend the kind of things you and I feel than he would be if we suddenly announced that we'd embraced Buddhism.[9]

White, a longtime progressive who had made a national reputation by his bold fight against the Klan, understood very well what the issues were, and that Smith, despite his support for social welfare, was no less conservative than Hoover on most economic issues. Given the choice, he preferred a candidate free from the Tammany taint. So did many others. Newton D. Baker, whom Lippmann had unsuccessfully pushed for the vice-presidential slot, said he would vote for Smith only to help "kill religious prejudice," not because he considered Smith a liberal. A Smith victory might be costly, he told Lippmann, "if it means that some of the Governor's spokesmen at Houston are to be his trusted advisers."[10]

Baker's fears turned out to be well founded. No sooner was Smith nominated than he named John J. Raskob, a Republican businessman with links to Du Pont and General Motors, as his campaign manager, and four other millionaires to the campaign committee. Rather than reassuring conservatives — who in any case would vote for the Republican nominee, Herbert Hoover — Smith alienated liberals. A good many abandoned him to cast a protest vote for the Socialist candidate, Norman Thomas.

Although Lippman pushed Smith energetically, he also admired Herbert Hoover, whom he had, it will be recalled, promoted for President eight years earlier. In fact, shortly after Smith and Hoover were nominated by their respective parties, he assured the readers of the *World* that whoever won in November, the next President would be a "distinguished and trustworthy person." At the time he seemed to have some trouble telling the candidates apart: "If Mr. Hoover and Mr. Smith met in a room to discuss any concrete national question purely on its merits," he wrote in *Vanity Fair,* "they would be so close together at the end you could not tell the difference between them."[11] He meant it as a compliment. Others found it a reason for sitting out the election or voting for Thomas.

Two virtually identical candidates was Lippmann's idea of a perfect election. He never accepted the argument that the parties ought to stand on firm ideological principles. The American people could be split into liberal and conservative camps only if there were some paramount issue on which they divided evenly, he argued. But in America the real alignments were local, and the national alignments "mere coalitions which create, not parties of principle, but governing majorities." The parties served to unite factions which might otherwise be irreconcilable. Thus it was, he maintained, that the "very absence of consistent national principle in either party . . . is fundamental to the domestic peace of the United States."[12] What some saw as a failing of the American party system, Lippmann considered its redeeming grace.

While Lippmann may have thought Hoover would make a "distinguished and trustworthy" President, this was not winning any votes for Smith. And the *World,* after all, was supposed to be a Democratic paper. The party faithful were upset about such evenhandedness. Reluctantly, Lippmann took off his gloves a few days before the election and blasted Hoover as a "partisan reactionary." It was too late to make any difference. A combination of Coolidge prosperity, Prohibition fervor, religious bigotry, and fear of the urban ethnics overwhelmed Smith. Although he won more votes than any Democrat ever had, and united the big-city ethnic minorities into a cohesive political force, he lost the electoral college by a five-to-one margin and carried only two states outside the South: Massachusetts and Rhode Island. The Republicans took both houses of Congress and most of the state capitals.

To show there were no hard feelings, Lippmann wrote an editorial congratulating Hoover, and then set off on a speaking tour of the Middle West. On his return a few weeks later he checked in briefly at the paper, where Merz was handling his editorial chores, and then set off with Faye for a winter holiday at Yeamans Hall in South Carolina, traveling with their new friends, Thomas and Florence Lamont, in an opulently appointed private railway car thoughtfully provided by Lamont's firm, the house of Morgan. They got back to New York a few days after Christmas, 1928, just in time to attend a farewell dinner for Swope, who had astonished everyone a few weeks earlier by resigning. He gave no good reason, but his departure was viewed as an ominous sign. Things were not going well at the *World*. Circulation was slipping, ad linage was down, and it was even rumored, though firmly denied by the Pulitzers, that the paper might be up for sale. Swope seemed to be getting out before the water hit the gunwales.

Part of the problem at the *World* was the penny pinching and capriciousness of the Pulitzers. They wanted a serious paper to rival the *Times,* but were unwilling to pay for it. Lippmann shared some of Swope's frustration, and told him, in a flattering farewell latter, that he thought his decision to leave "a wise one," since the Pulitzers would not give him freer rein. "I have never seen so clear a case, as it finally developed, of an irreconcilable conflict between a powerful temperament and a settled tradition," he told Swope. "The *World* did you no injustice, though your own vitality was too much for it."[13] For all his mixed feelings about his colleague, Lippmann could not help admiring him. "Herbert," he said at Swope's farewell dinner, "you are a lucky, fascinating devil!"

The paper got on without Swope, but lost a good deal of its old energy. In February 1929 Lippmann once again turned the editorial page over to Merz and set off on his annual tour of Europe. These excursions had become a ritual, with London, Paris, Geneva, Berlin and Rome as regular stops, and interviews with the prime minister and foreign secretary of each major country a matter of course. This time he and Faye crossed on the *Aquitania* with the Lamonts, and dined in the first class salon with John Foster Dulles, the Wall Street lawyer; Owen Young, chairman of General Electric; and David Sarnoff, head of the Radio Corporation of America.

The long transatlantic crossing gave Thomas Lamont a good deal of time to discuss the European political and economic situation with Lippmann. A former newspaperman and publisher — he once owned the

New York Evening Post and for years supported its literary offspring, the *Saturday Review* — Lamont considered press relations his bailiwick at the house of Morgan. His charm and familiarity with the trade enabled him to persuade many journalists to look upon the activities of the Morgan firm no more critically than he did himself. Naturally he considered Lippmann one of his more important contacts. Walter and Faye were frequent guests at the Lamonts' Rockland estate or their summer home at North Haven, Maine. Thomas Lamont was a great admirer of Walter, and in quite a different way of Faye.

Lamont was particularly interested in the fact that Lippmann had scheduled an interview with Mussolini. This touched Lamont's pocketbook as well as his political sense, for the Morgan firm was financing the Italian economy through American loans. Lamont did not particularly admire the Duce; he neither approved nor disapproved. What mattered was the regime's solvency, not its politics. With equal vigor, and with no sense of contradiction, he also urged that the United States establish formal diplomatic ties with the Soviet Union and extend trade agreements and credits. Unhappy with the *World*'s ferociously anti-Mussolini editorials, Lamont urged Lippmann to take a less hostile attitude, and warned him against a "relapse into anti-fascism." Shortly before sailing Lamont had alerted the Italian ambassador that he was eager to have Lippmann gain "as accurate an impression as possible of present-day Italy."[14]

Mussolini's corporate state had impressed a good many others besides Lamont. Bernard Shaw considered the Duce a superman, and Lincoln Steffens, soon to embrace Stalin, thought him the leader of the future. British politicians like Austen Chamberlain and Ramsay MacDonald expressed unstinted admiration, and Oswald Mosley, organizer of the British fascists, draped his own followers in black shirts. Even Herbert Croly saw Italian fascism as offering a spiritual reconstruction of society through leadership and purposeful activity. For a time Mussolini enjoyed the virtually unanimous support of the American press, with the popular *Saturday Evening Post* leading the way. Henry Luce's *Fortune* devoted an entire issue to a favorable analysis of the "Corporate State." Among the major magazines, *Harper's* and the *Atlantic* stood in lonely opposition.[15]

The *World*, as one of the few daily newspapers to take a critical attitude toward Italian fascism, was continually under attack by the regime for Lippmann's editorials and the scathing dispatches of its Rome correspondent, William Bolitho. "We do not trust Mussolini because we regard his regime as the supreme menace to the peace of Europe," Lippmann wrote in 1925, as dissenters were being murdered or imprisoned. "The fascist regime in Italy is a dictatorship which has had to become more dictatorial the longer it has held power." Lippmann's editorials, combined with his support for Gaetano Salvemini when the anti-fascist scholar sought refuge in the United States, marked him as one of the early American opponents of Mussolini. When a former Italian diplomat, Luigi Sturzo, wrote a book attacking the fascist regime, Lippmann praised it in the liberal Catholic weekly, the *Commonweal*, and warned American Catholics — to whom Mussolini had a considerable appeal — that they should follow Aquinas in holding natural law above the demands of the state.[16]

Lippmann arrived in Rome at the end of March 1929, after having enrolled Jane Mather as a special student at Oxford. The meeting with Mussolini, his second in five years, was carefully prepared by the Duce, who greeted him warmly at the doorway of his vast marble office. Mussolini had just returned from swimming at Ostia, where he had got sunburned and cut his nose. "Do you think I am as handsome as ever?" he asked. Their talk ranged over the usual issues: disarmament, the suppression of Italian political parties, Mussolini's designs in Europe and Africa. The dictator was affable but evasive. Lippmann came away no more impressed that he had arrived.

His visit to Italy had reinforced his doubts about a centralized state. "I want to clarify my mind on the difficult question of the necessity of it," he wrote Berenson from the ship back to New York a few weeks later. "Centralization, as such, even with the Rights of Man in operation at the capital, is, I think, incompatible with effective self-government. The failure to feel this made me wonder if Italian liberals really understood self-government." This fear of a centralized society had been growing for some time. A few years earlier, in *The Phantom Public,* Lippmann had written that men must "contrive somehow to frustrate the declared purpose of that central power which pretends it is the purpose of all." The fear of the "Servile State," which he had first raised fifteen years earlier in *Drift and Mastery,* was now becoming a preoccupation.[17]

The growing disorder he had seen in Europe, the rise of fascist parties in France and Germany, the fragility of the economic structure confirmed his conviction that the United States had to play a more central part in the European balance. Having repented his opposition to the Versailles treaty, he argued all through the 1920s for stronger American links to Europe. Although the league issue was, as Harding said in his first message to Congress, as "dead as slavery," Lippmann worked actively to involve the United States in the league's peacekeeping efforts. Like many others he believed that military power led to war, and he looked to disarmament as the most effective restraint on international violence. Thus he endorsed the five-power naval moratorium signed in Washington in 1922.[18] Along with other internationalists he supported

American participation in the World Court, urged that Washington reduce or cancel Allied war debts, supported the Dawes Plan for stabilizing the German mark through American loans and the Young Plan to reduce Germany's war reparations, and criticized the high tariff policies of the Republican administrations.

These efforts continually involved him, as either ally or opponent, with the powerful chairman of the Senate Foreign Relations Committee. The maverick Idaho Republican William E. Borah was a mass of contradictions: an isolationist who favored cutting Allied war debts, a conservative who urged diplomatic recognition of the Soviet Union, a populist who opposed an amendment restricting child labor. Often voting against his own party, Borah was, as Lippmann wrote in exasperation, a "host in himself," an "instinctive conscientious objector" who avoided becoming an outcast by making common cause at one time or another with virtually everyone.[19]

The isolationist Borah and the internationalist Lippmann nonetheless became bedfellows on a number of issues. Their curious collaboration began in 1919, when Lippmann furnished Borah and the other Irreconcilables with damning evidence against the Paris peace accords. It continued through the 1920s, with the two men cooperating to cut Allied war debts, spur naval disarmament, oppose U.S. military intervention in Latin America, and extend diplomatic recognition to the Soviet Union. They often worked together behind the scenes, with Lippmann suggesting positions for Borah to pursue, and Borah coordinating his speeches with the *World*. Borah had helped Lippmann gain refuge for Salvemini in the United States and, with less success, seek a visa for the Countess Karolyi.[20]

Borah was a man of consuming vanity, and Lippmann's long experience with politicians had taught him how to massage it. When the senator ran for reelection in 1924 the *World* hailed him as "the most useful and most inspiring figure in the national life of this country" — no mean encomium for an isolationist Republican from a Democratic paper. Detesting "entangling alliances," Borah defeated a plan favored by Lippmann and other internationalists to bring the United States into the World Court. Then, true to his record for unpredictability, he turned around and supported an international agreement to "outlaw" war.[21]

A plan to declare war "illegal" had been suggested years earlier by Chicago lawyer Salmon Levinson. Lippmann had thought it ridiculous at the time, and no less so in its updated version. "It did not seem possible that the State Department could have been spending its efforts on a project so obviously absurd as this one seemed to be," he told the *World*'s readers when Secretary Kellogg revived the scheme in 1927. The notion that "Europe should scrap its whole system of security based on the enforcement of peace and accept in its place a pious, self-denying ordinance that no nation will disturb the peace" seemed ludicrous. Particularly jarring was the "extraordinary spectacle" of a campaign to outlaw war led by those, like Borah, who thought it intolerably binding for the United States to join the World Court, let alone the League of Nations.[22]

The Pact of Paris, or the Kellogg-Briand Pact, as the plan was popularly known, offered every nation a chance to endorse peace and brotherhood without the slightest inconvenience. While outlawing war, it proposed no method to decide who was an aggressor, nor any enforcement mechanism. If any nation resorted to war, the others were free to act as they wished. The French insisted that the pact must not prevent them from acting in self-defense against Germany, the British that it not preclude war in defense of their empire, and the United States that it not contravene the Monroe Doctrine — meaning that Washington could continue to intervene at will in Latin America. Stripped of all enforcement provisions and qualified into insignificance, the Kellogg-Briand Pact was, in the words of Senator James Reed, "an international kiss."

The Senate promptly ratified the treaty to "renounce war as an instrument of national policy" and to resolve all disputes by "pacific means" by a resounding margin of 85 to 1. Sixty-two nations ultimately signed the pact. It is formally in effect to this day. A skeptical Lippmann reminded his readers that under the treaty "nations renounce war as an instrument of national policy only where no national interest is at stake," and observed that in the absence of any enforcement mechanism, "the renunciation of war and treaties of arbitration are . . . excellent devices for stopping wars that nobody intends to wage."[23]

With little faith in such treaties, he suggested that the only realistic hope was to find what he called — turning a phrase of William James — a "political equivalent of war" based on some form of world government. He did not find the prospect entirely inspiring. "I can sympathize with those who prefer the liberty of our present international anarchy to the responsibilities of an international society," he wrote. "I am inclined to think that a stable international order would be oppressive and unpleasant in many ways, and I am not wholly sure that I am prepared to pay the price which the establishment of peace on earth would cost." Nations as favorably placed as the United States enjoyed considerable advantages. If Americans wanted to retain their freedom of action, they should not deceive themselves with the notion that they were trying to abolish war. "For war will not be abolished between the nations until its political equivalent has been created, until there is an international government strong enough to preserve order, and wise enough to welcome changes in that order," Lippmann counseled. "We may never live to see that. We may not wish to see it. But that, and nothing less, is what international peace will cost.''[24]

One of the many anomalies of the plan to outlaw war was that it excluded, so far as the United States was concerned, Europe's most populous nation. This "queer arrangement," as Lippmann phrased it, led him to renew his campaign for diplomatic recognition of the Soviet Union. The outbreak of fighting in Manchuria between Russia and Chinese nationalists in 1929 provided a perfect hinge. A settlement of the Sino-Soviet dispute, Lippmann wrote Borah, "might be the moment to launch a campaign, for then we should have a demonstrated case of American reliance upon the good faith of Russia's word. . . . If a newspaper campaign, and a campaign in the Senate led by you were perfectly timed, we might get somewhere." Borah heartily approved, and the campaign got under way.[25] It soon ran into a veto from President Hoover, who feared that it would alienate conservatives. Not until four years later, under Franklin D. Roosevelt, did Washington finally exchange ambassadors with Moscow.

Despite his skepticism of schemes to outlaw war, Lippmann continued to see hope in naval disarmament as a way of preventing aggression. In the fall of 1929 he met with British Prime Minister Ramsay MacDonald, who had come to the United States to lay the groundwork for a new naval conference, and when that conference opened in London in January 1930, Lippmann hailed it as a "stupendous vindication . . . of the idealism of 1919." In place of a world of self-centered nation-states he saw "in actual being a world in which no government any longer dares to deny its responsibility to the community of states. In any long view of events this is the deepest revolution in political affairs since the rise of national states broke up the unity of Christendom in Europe."

So it seemed to many at the time. Yet a dozen years later, during the war against Germany and Japan, Lippmann publicly apologized for having been "too weak-minded to take a stand against the exorbitant folly" of naval disarmament and for having "celebrated the disaster as a triumph and denounced the admirals who dared to protest."[26] Here, too, he exaggerated. The disaster was not in the disarmament pacts themselves — which prevented a nonsensical arms race between the United States and Great Britain and reduced tensions with Japan in the Pacific — but in the failure to enforce the pacts and the unwillingness of the United States to build up its fleet even to full treaty strength.

During the 1920s, and much of the 1930s as well, Lippmann was neither consistent nor persuasive in his prescriptions for preventing war. Simultaneously espousing disarmament and American naval strength, international cooperation and an Anglo-American domination of the seas,

American freedom of action and a "political equivalent of war," he reflected the confusions of the age. Like the broad-minded financiers who were his friends, he wanted stability within the framework of an international system that, far more than he realized, was already breaking down.

◄ 21 ►

The Disinterested Man

> The adult has to break this attachment to persons and things. . . . He can no longer count on possessing whatever he may happen to want. And therefore he must learn to want what he can possess.
>
> — *A Preface to Morals,* 1929

THE 1920s were frenetic and confusing years for most Americans, but for Lippmann a time of consolidation and achievement. He had put his iconoclasm, along with his brief experiment in political radicalism, behind him. He had become an influential person. Success had not so much changed him as it had brought out his innate conservatism. He had never been much of a rebel, and his socialist interlude had been little more than modish Progressivism. Even at the high point of his political iconoclasm as a young man he had been impatient with rebels, had deplored their romantic impracticality and dogmatism.

At the beginning of the 1920s he was thundering against the betrayal of the wartime crusade and blaming the censor and the propagandist for misleading the people. By the end of the decade he was worried about the excesses of democracy and declaring that "to limit the power of majorities, to dispute their moral authority, to deflect their impact, to dissolve their force is now the most important task of those who care for liberty." His inquiries into propaganda and the effect of the mass media on public opinion had left him with a deep and abiding skepticism about mass democracy. "The herd instinct . . . has surreptitiously acquired the sanction of conscience in democracy," he wrote in deploring what he called the "cult of the second best."[1]

Lippmann was not alone in his skepticism. After a decade of prosperity the Progressive movement had shrunk to a few fringe journals like the *Nation* and the *New Republic,* and to voices in the wilderness like that of Robert M. La Follette, Sr. "The opportunities to make money were so ample that it was a waste of time to think about politics," Lippmann wrote in 1927 of the general public lethargy. Expanding on a note he had sounded more than a dozen years earlier, he declared that the "more or less unconscious and unplanned activities of businessmen are for once more novel, more daring, and in a sense more revolutionary than the theories of the progressives." This was hardly a new tack for Lippmann — he had been saying it ever since *Drift and Mastery*. But it expressed the mood of an era when many intellectuals considered a concern with politics to be a sign of bad taste. "The old reformer has become the Tired Radical, and his sons and daughters drink at the fountain of the *American Mercury*," sighed Norman Thomas. "They have no illusions but one, and that is that they can live like Babbitt and think like Mencken." [2]

The cult of experience, which Lippmann himself had helped promote before the war, now seemed elusive and inadequate. "As I recall my own state of mind when we stood at Armageddon with TR, the day of victory seemed ever so far ahead," he wrote of those dimly glimpsed years.

Insofar as we imagined what it would be like, we had vague notions that mankind, liberated from want and drudgery, would spend its energies writing poetry, painting pictures, exploring the stellar spaces, singing folk songs, dancing with Isadora Duncan in the public square, and producing Ibsen in little theatres.

We seem completely to have overlooked the appetite of mankind for the automobile, the moving picture, the radio, bridge parties, tabloids and the stock market. Those were the days when we believed in Man and forgot there were only men and women, when we believed that all you had to do to save the world was to rearrange the environment; when expectant mothers read Emerson and H. G. Wells to improve the minds and character of their offspring. [3]

Many intellectuals, particularly artists, revolted against not only Progressivism but all forms of politics. "It was characteristic of the Jazz Age," Scott Fitzgerald said, "that it had no interest in politics at all." Writers and painters became absorbed in craftsmanship and style rather than content, and extolled self-expression as an end in itself. The passive nihilism of T. S. Eliot's *Waste Land*, the anarchic individualism of Hemingway's war-weary hero who declared his private *Farewell to Arms*, the bitterness of Pound, who saw a generation sent to die "For an old bitch gone in the teeth / for a botched civilization," the renunciation of industrial society in the search for the Noble Savage, the fascination with primitivism in the "discovery" of African sculpture and of jazz — this was the mood of an age that declared that nothing was worth doing, and yet set off an explosion of artistic creativity.

Unlike many men of his generation — Eliot, Pound, Fitzgerald — Lippmann never turned his back on politics. Nor did he have much patience with those who did. When George Jean Nathan declared that he had "too humorous a disesteem for the democratic form of government" to concern himself with anything so low as politics, Lippmann responded tartly. "A man who can endure all that Broadway has to offer," he said of the popular drama critic, "who can make a life work talking about the Broadway theatre, is neither so humorous nor so delicately attuned, but that he could endure the grossness and stupidity of politics under the democratic form of government." Nathan's lack of interest in politics was not due to his superior taste, Lippmann suggested, but to "an inferior education, to a somewhat lazy incomprehension of what politics deal with, and to an imagination which is defective in dealing with realities that are complex, invisible and elusive."[4]

While Nathan was too shallow to merit more than passing ridicule, Lippmann took the critic's coeditor on the *American Mercury,* the bilious H. L. Mencken, a good deal more seriously. Mencken was a complex figure, at once a serious scholar and grotesque lampoonist of democracy. Famous for his attacks on "homo boobus," as he called the average man, and as a debunker of sacred cows, he also promoted such writers as Theodore Dreiser and Sherwood Anderson, helped find an American audience for Nietzsche and James Joyce, and wrote an important scholarly study of the American language. Mencken's popular fame rested on his iconoclasm. Deriding not only the "booboisie" but the democratic system that produced a hick culture, he defined the statesman as a "glorified smeller and snooper," the congressman as a "knavish and preposterous nonentity," and the civil service as a "mere refuge for prehensile morons." In denigrating the values of small-town America — prohibition and religious fundamentalism, puritanism and boosterism, whether backed by the "swinish rich" or the "anthropoid rabble" — Mencken spoke for those who considered themselves members of what he termed the "enormously civilized minority."

Lippmann, while he would not use Mencken's vocabulary, could not help sympathizing with it. What Mencken had done, he pointed out in an appreciative essay for *Vanity Fair,* was to "destroy, by rendering it ridiculous and unfashionable, the democratic tradition of the American pioneers."[5] For all Mencken's outrageous hyperbole, Lippmann found a kindred spirit in the great debunker of mass democracy. What Mencken saw as a joke, Lippmann viewed as a dilemma. Both questioned the premise of majority rule and wrote for an audience that considered itself above the plebeian mob.

Above all Lippmann admired Mencken's toughness, his abhorrence of cant, sentimentality and self-pity. What drew him to Mencken was exactly what turned him against the other great critic of American mores: Sinclair Lewis. With no effort to conceal his contempt, Lippmann wrote a long, biting attack on America's most popular novelist, pronouncing Lewis's books to be overrated, his style imitative, his perceptions puerile, and his international fame unmerited. In the celebrated author of such works as *Babbitt* and *Main Street* he found, not a serious social critic, but a "revolted provincial" and an inventor of facile stereotypes. Lewis's Babbitt, he charged, was not a man, but a prejudice, and the author's works nothing but a collection of prejudices and rubber stamps. "Had his gift been in a different medium," Lippmann wrote disdainfully, "he could have manufactured wax flowers that would make a man with hay fever sneeze."

The trouble with Lewis was that he had no perspective. To have become the creator of the American comedy of manners instead of the "mere inventor of new prejudices . . . he would have had to care more about human beings than about his own attitude toward them." This Lewis was incapable of; he did not understand that "a more conscious life is one in which a man is conscious not only of what he sees, but of the prejudices with which he sees it." Lewis's terrible judgments about the provincial civilization of America flowed from the "bitterness of a revolted provincial . . . too much a part of the revolt he describes ever for long to understand it." In the just-published *Elmer Gantry*, Lippmann charged, the "revolted Puritan" had become fanatical. "The hatreds are turned inward, as if the effort to escape had failed and become morbid." Lippmann was so offended by Harcourt, Brace's massive publicity campaign on behalf of *Elmer Gantry* that he severed his own relations with the firm, telling Alfred Harcourt that it did "not provide any longer the right medium for such books as I write." [6]

Lippmann's scornful portrait of Lewis was discerning and clever. He had not lost his instinct for the jugular. He saw the shallowness and self-loathing in Lewis's novels at a time when most critics were hailing his genius and even awarding him a Nobel Prize. But the vehemence of his attack went beyond literary criticism. Lewis seemed to have touched a raw nerve. Lippmann's attack raised a good deal of comment. One critic observed that Lewis saw Babbitt with the "half-crazed introspective clarity of a bitter consciousness of kind, as an anti-Semitic Jew sees his fellow Jews." [7] The parallel was carefully chosen.

In a sense Lewis was a rebel, the kind of person who — as Lippmann had written in another context a few months earlier — "feels his rebellion not as a plea for this or that reform, but as an unbearable tension in his viscera." Such a rebel had to "break down the cause of his frustration or jump out of his skin." A conservative, by contrast, was wedded to the structures of his life: family, church, nation. "His institution is to him a mainstay of his being; it exists not as an idea but in the very nature of his character, and the threat to destroy it fills him with anxiety and with fury." Such matters as censorship, Lippmann concluded, were not questions of principle so much as "organic conflicts between the adjusted and the unadjusted. In conflicts between the two, the "neutrally-minded person with a somewhat liberal disposition" was often left out; the passions of the issue did not "really touch him." Lippmann was the "neutrally-minded person," Lewis the rebel jumping out of his skin.[8]

Ironically, Lewis was trying to deal, in his own crude and often inadequate way, with the same upheaval in values that Lippmann himself had been troubled by — what Lippmann had called the "vast dissolution of ancient habits." The growing secularization of American life, the loosening of the family, the decline of traditional authority had not resulted in liberation — as the early rebels had thought — so much as in a pervasive malaise that left people adrift and in search of a moral rudder.

Lippmann sensed this malaise strongly. The same qualities that had prevented him, unlike so many of his contemporaries, from either leaving the country or rejecting politics made him acutely aware of the anxiety that lay behind the easy money and the easy virtue of the Jazz Age. As was often the case, his way of working out a problem was to write a book about it. He had begun drafting the book in 1925, just after *The Phantom Public* came out, and by the summer of 1927 it had virtually taken over his life. Often rising at five in the morning, he would work on the book before breakfast, write his editorial for the *World,* and go to the office for a day's work of editing and meetings. Late in the afternoon he would hurry home, take a bath, have a quick dinner, and work on the book until midnight.

It was a terrible summer. His father lay dying, Sacco and Vanzetti were facing execution, the Mexican crisis was coming to a head. Yet somehow he managed to juggle his work, his private life and the book. On weekends he fled to Wading River, and was able to spend a few weeks there in September. "I have been writing so much this summer that I have almost had a revulsion against using a pen," he wrote Learned Hand from the country.

I am approaching the end of the book, not in final form for publication by any means, but at least in a form where I think the argument and the sequences hold together. I shall finish, I think, before we come back to town the last week in September.

I shall feel as if I had been freed, having an unwritten book on one's mind is a form of tyranny which never lets me alone. I really don't enjoy anything or really want to do anything until it's done. Sometimes I think it must be a kind of compulsion neurosis.[9]

He finished the draft by the end of the summer and worked on revisions during the fall and the following winter and spring. Finally he sent the manuscript off to his new publishers, Macmillan, in the summer of 1928, having endured one of the most sustained and intellectually draining experiences of his life.

He came back from his winter tour of Europe, where he had interviewed Mussolini and spent several weeks with Berenson, at the end of April 1929, just in time for the publication of *A Preface to Morals*. The book illuminated the quandary of a generation that had passed, as he had himself, from the reformist optimism of Progressivism to the cynicism of the twenties, one which, "having ceased to believe without ceasing to be credulous, hangs, as it were, between heaven and earth and is at rest nowhere." What he called the "acids of modernity" had corroded religious faith, science had demolished belief, and Freud had violated the sanctity of the human soul. Where men had once lived in an ordered tradition, there were now "brave and brilliant atheists who have defied the Methodist God and have become very nervous," women who had "emancipated themselves from the tyranny of fathers, husbands and homes, and with the intermittent but expensive help of a psychoanalyst, are now enduring liberty as interior decorators." It had become "impossible to reconstruct an enduring orthodoxy, and impossible to live well without the satisfaction which an orthodoxy would provide." The distinguishing mark of the rebels was not their audacity but their disillusion with their own rebellion.

Lippmann was not suggesting a return to the church, nor a submersion into the authority of the secular state. Both had lost their authority. Since modern man could not find security in institutions, he would have to look to himself — to adapt to the world as it was, and find in his own resources the means for dealing with it. He would have to stand back emotionally from it, become "disinterested." The new system of morals would be built, not on revelation or on science — both of which had been tried and found wanting — but on humanism and emotional restraint. "When men can no longer be theists, they must, if they are civilized, become humanists."

Lippmann had been impressed by Woodrow Wilson's observation that speculations on political philosophy were colored by whatever happened to be the prevailing view of the physical universe. Newtonian mechanics inspired political imagery until the middle of the nineteenth century, when it was replaced by Darwinian biological equivalents. By the 1920s Darwinism had become outdated, its place usurped by the relativity theory of Einstein. But the new physics could not be translated into political terms. The result, Lippmann told Newton Baker, was that "our political thinking today has no intellectual foundations." Analogies to the physical sciences no longer applied. "We know that human beings do not really behave either like wild animals in a jungle or like a collection of molecules. The foundations for us must lie, really not in nature, as our immediate forefathers believed, nor in super-nature as their forefathers believed, but in human nature. That is to say, in an objective understanding of what we really are."[10]

The humanism Lippmann proposed was not so much a philosophy as a mode of conduct. It rested on detachment — a detachment that, however appealing in theory, was most difficult to practice. His mature man would, apparently, be above emotion. He would not despair at failure, Lippmann explained, for "the aspect of life which implicated his soul would be his understanding of life, and, to the understanding, defeat is no less interesting than victory." A man possessed of such stoical detachment

would face pain with fortitude, for he would have put it away from the inner chambers of his soul. Fear would not haunt him, for he would be without compulsion to seize anything and without anxiety as to his fate.

. . . Since nothing gnawed at his vitals, neither doubt nor ambition, nor frustration nor fear, he would move easily through life. And so whether he saw the thing as comedy, or high tragedy, or plain farce, he would affirm that it is what it is, and that the wise man can enjoy it.

Despite its ascetic outlook — perhaps because of it — *A Preface to Morals* was an instant success. His first book to be chosen by the Book-of-the-Month Club, it became a popular sensation and an immediate best-seller. By the end of the year it had gone through six editions. Eventually it was translated into a dozen languages. It spoke to its audience in the language people wanted to hear. "A serious book, but beautifully written and simply written," William Allen White said in recommending it to his fellow judges at the book club. "There isn't a paragraph in it that the average intelligent American cannot understand, and to me that is everything about a book."[11]

The book was perfectly attuned to its times, codifying the anxieties of a generation that had grown tired of its binge and was ready for a little renunciation. Not everyone, of course, had the capacity to become the model of Lippmann's "disinterested" person. But the very act of reading the book seemed to give one access to the sanctum of the elect. Lippmann had put his finger on the problem of the moment, laid it out in terms simple to grasp, phrased it in a vocabulary that flattered the reader's intelligence, and proposed a self-sacrificing but noble way out of the maze.

Readers embraced the book's stoicism, its bleak humanism, and its rewarding conclusion that he who had lost his religious faith could find salvation in a secular humanism that only innately superior sensibilities could glimpse. Critics praised its eloquence, profundity and courage. Justice Holmes congratulated Lippmann on "a noble performance," Berenson expressed his surprise "that you should have obtained so early in life what it took me twenty years to get to,'' and Laski called it ''simply masterful.''¹² Lippmann's second wife later confessed that she first fell in love with him on reading the book.

There were also dissenters. Many who admired Lippmann's diagnosis of the modern malaise were not content with his prescription. The critic for the *Saturday Review* pointed out that Lippmann's ''disinterestedness is only a fine name for disillusionment, and the detachment is that of an indifferent, because purely rational, observer.'' The Catholic *Commonweal* saw in the book the ''spiritual dissatisfaction of the modern Jew who has been severed from his religious community,'' and commented, with perhaps greater accuracy than the critic realized, that the Jew ''who seeks to live as an individual in our at least nominally Christian world, who finds the way back into the temple obscured, inevitably surrenders that sense of 'being together with others' so essential in all Hebraic history.'' This was a point that troubled some Jewish readers. ''Since Mr. Lippmann's deepest interest is, after all, in the good life, with morality,'' complained the *Menorah Journal,* ''he might have saved some of that concern he lavishes on the decline of the supernatural Christianity of the Middle Ages for the fate of a tradition that more nearly shared his own moral interest, namely Judaism.''¹³

Lippmann's ''high religion'' of detachment and acceptance bore elements of Spinoza and of Santayana's ''religion of disillusion.'' But where Santayana embraced the variety of natural passions and insisted on the moral relativity of all philosophies, Lippmann seemed to offer only a rationalization for disillusion. His vaunted disinterestedness was not so much a philosophy as a moral attitude. His observations were trenchant, his understanding of the current discontent profound. Yet in the end he offered less a ''high religion'' than an intellectual justification for rolling with the punches. He was trying to spin a philosophy from what was at best an acceptance of disappointment. The book, as Edmund Wilson wrote in an otherwise laudatory review, was marked by a ''certain unreality'' that made it difficult for readers to have contact with the things Lippmann was writing about: ''We are not so ardently responsive as we should like to be because the point of view which Lippmann commends seems to exclude intense feelings of any kind, and even to err on the side of complacency.''

Santayana touched on this quality in his own review of Lippmann's book. Writing from his retreat in Rome, he praised *A Preface to Morals* as an ''admirable book'' by a ''brave philosopher . . . who confidently believes that mankind can endure the truth.'' Yet he questioned a ''high religion'' defined as ''pure science,'' and feared that Lippmann's preface to morals was really ''an epilogue to all possible moralities and all possible religions.'' In such detached contemplation ''the pure intellect is divorced as far as possible from the service of the will — divorced, therefore, from affairs and from morality; and love is divorced as far as possible from human objects, and becomes an impersonal and universalized delight in being," he wrote. Far from guiding human morality, such "ultimate insights" were in danger of subverting it.[14]

If *A Preface to Morals* concentrated on the higher planes of life, it did not leave the lower ones totally unnoticed. An entire chapter dealt with "Love in the Great Society," although its remedy for the troublesome Eros was to transmute it into the more manageable Agape. Commenting on the revolution in mores caused by scientific methods of birth control, Lippmann maintained that marriage could not long survive as an institution if based purely on physical attraction and sexual gratification. "Love and nothing else very soon is nothing else," he wrote in an oft-quoted passage. "The emotion of love, in spite of the romantics, is not self-sustaining; it endures only when the lovers love many things together, and not merely each other."

As an unsentimental institution, marriage had to rest on unsentimental premises: shared interests, mutual respect, compatibility. "Given an initial attraction, a common social background, common responsibilities, and the conviction that the relationship is permanent, compatibility in marriage can normally be achieved," he declared in the tones of a marriage counselor. The problem with a marriage based on love alone, he wrote, was that when love faded there would be little to hold the partners together. "There is nothing left then but to grin and bear a miserably dull and nagging fate, or to break off and try again."

The analysis was not abstract. For years it had been obvious that he and Faye had little in common. He could not talk to her about politics and the things that mattered to him, and he was not very successful when he tried to operate at her level. He wanted a woman whose intelligence he could respect, she wanted a "dancing playmate," as Mabel Dodge had sagely pointed out before their marriage. They stayed together, going through the motions, because neither had the courage or the willpower to break it off. Rather than deciding that he had made a mistake in 1917 and trying to start over, Lippmann elevated his unhappiness to a moral principle. He gave it a stoic veneer by calling it "disinterestedness."

Between the lines of the book one can read the rationalization of his own relationship to Faye. "My marriage was a failure from the very start," he confessed a decade later to his second wife, ". . . and it was in that time that I made the adjustment which is *The Preface to Morals*." By the time he wrote the book he had come to view marriage as a necessary affliction, urging couples "who propose to see it through . . . to transcend naive desire and to reach out towards a mature and disinterested partnership with their world." He had reduced his own expectations of what life could offer until they matched what he had. Having thus been able to transcend "naive desire," he brought his life into a joyless balance.[15]

To outsiders he seemed to have everything: a prestigious job, a beautiful wife, a national reputation, entrée into the highest levels of American political and social life, good health, and a quiet handsomeness that attracted women without threatening men. In the summer of 1929, with the success of the new book assured and another salary increase that came with Swope's retirement and his promotion to executive editor, he bought a $51,000 town house at 245 East 61st Street. There he installed a soundproof study on the top floor, and made sure that his desk was so placed that he could not look out the window while working. What he had called his "pool of silence" would be unrippled. He and Faye inaugurated the new house in September with a large wedding reception for Jane Mather. While studying at Oxford, where she had enrolled as a special student earlier that year, she had fallen in love with a young and very rich American economist, Lucius Wilmerding.

Although Jane seemed happy, Walter had mixed feelings about the impending marriage. She had become an important part of his life and he did not want to let her go. As his relations with Faye had become strained, he had grown more dependent on Jane for affection and companionship. He regretted her leaving him. Indeed, he vaguely resented it. Yet he could not confess this, nor even reveal it by innuendo. Never did he tell Jane of his sorrow at that moment when she left his household to form one of her own. Only years later, when he told his second wife of his unhappiness during this period, did he also speak of his feelings toward Jane:

You know that my marriage was a failure from the very start in many senses, that it left me without any human thing to whom I could give anything. For about five years Jane partially filled that emptiness, and it was in that time that I made the adjustment which is *The Preface to Morals*. But as Jane grew older I realized that if I did not do something there would grow up between us an attachment which would falsify her life. I had enough knowledge of life to know that no one can become integrally a man or a woman who is not in adolescence fully weaned from those who are his parents or stand in loco parentis. I had become, emotionally and spiritually, Jane's father.

I realize that there was the possibility of a further compensation from her side because I did not seem very old to her, and because I was in most things . . . like a contemporary. I mean in sports, amusements, etc. So I decided not only to send her away to school, but to send her so far away that she would feel herself truly separated, and so I arranged about her going to Oxford.

It cost me a lot. I remember the rainy evening driving back to London, after I had left her at Oxford, and the dreary emptiness of my feeling that I had given her up, and that it was over. And I remember how, during that winter, I would be wracked by her increasingly occasional and distant letters, wracked by the conflict between that side of me which had willed her detachment which was obviously succeeding, and the other side of me which hated to see it happen, and then towards spring I had her letter saying she had fallen in love with Lou, and then she came back and I met Lou, and I did not like him much, and yet I was afraid I did not like him mainly because I was losing Jane, yet all the time the better part of me wanted to lose Jane until such time as she would be an adult and we could come to an adult relationship.

As he approached his fortieth birthday that September of 1929, Lippmann had come to an emotional dead end. Jane was building a life of her own, his marriage with Faye had settled into a dull routine. Yet there seemed to be no alternative. He would find his satisfactions in his work and make the best of it. Instead of trying to overcome his detachment from an emotionally arid life, he would transform it into a virtue. His life had become a process of filtration and exclusion. "You are such a strange creature," his second wife wrote him a decade later during their dramatic courtship. "It seems to me as if you had been born expecting very little, whereas most people expect the sun to stand still for them and have to learn very painfully that it doesn't. Then instead of being angry, proud or envious, you seem to have merely withdrawn. . . . But," she added more gently, "in your withdrawal you have found a calm strength and wisdom."[16]

Lippmann carried his personal stoicism into politics. Whereas he had once urged intellectuals to become men of action, he now preached the virtues of "a quiet indifference to the immediate and a serene attachment to the processes of inquiry and understanding." A few months after the publication of *A Preface to Morals* the stock market collapsed. The boom was over, and as the prosperity of the twenties turned into the depression of the early thirties, Lippmann urged scholars to detach themselves from a world they could not correct. "What is most wrong with the world is that the democracy, which at last is actually in power, is a creature of the immediate moment," he told the graduates of Columbia University as they set out in search of jobs they were unlikely to find. "With no authority above it, without religious, political or moral convictions which control its opinions, it is without coherence or purpose. Democracy of this kind cannot last long; it must, and inevitably it will, give way to some more settled social order."

Until there was such a settled order, the true scholar, he counseled, would "build a wall against chaos, and behind that wall, as in other bleak ages in the history of man, he will give his true allegiance, not to the immediate world, but to the invisible empire of reason." This was not the last crisis in human affairs, he told the students. "The world will go on somehow, and more crises will follow. It will go on best, however, if among us there are men who have stood apart, who refused to be anxious or too much concerned, who were cool and inquiring, and had their eyes on a longer past and a longer future."[17]

Lippmann would be one of those who, from temperament as much as from conviction, stood apart.

◄ 22 ►

The End of the *World*

Don't let the Bankers get you.
— From William Allen White, April 19, 1932

Bᴼ the late 1920s the *World* was in trouble. Readership was down, advertising revenues had failed to keep pace with rising costs, and the paper had shrunk to half the size of the rival *Times*. Instead of trying to cover all the news, it focused on exposés and spot coverage. Partly an effort to save money, this also reflected the preference of the news editors. In answer to the *Times*'s famous slogan, the editors retorted, "The *World* does not believe that all the news that is fit to print is worth reading." But much that was worth reading never got printed, and what was printed was not always worth reading.

The problem with the paper, James M. Cain later wrote, was that it had "an editorial page addressed to intellectuals, a sporting section addressed to the fancy, a Sunday magazine addressed to morons, and twenty other things that don't seem to be addressed to anybody."[1] Even before Swope's departure in 1928 the paper had lost much of its drive. The business department was badly run, and to make up for falling ad revenues the Pulitzers had raised the price of the paper to three cents in 1925, thinking the *Times* and the *Herald Tribune* would go along. They did not. Circulation plummeted from 400,000 to 285,000. By 1927 the paper was running a deficit. The price went back to two cents, but the *World* never won back all its lost readers.

Lippmann continually complained to Swope about the thinness of the news coverage and the obvious bias of the reporting. "The intelligent public thinks we are crusading most of the time," he told the news editor in one of his many memos from the tower. "It is our business to report objectively." That was not the tradition Swope had grown up on, nor the kind of paper JP had founded. "I never found myself in conflict with the old *World* traditions in the sense of public policy," Lippmann later said. The problem was that the tabloids had taken over the field of yellow journalism in which the *World* had made its reputation. Lippmann thought the paper should not stay stuck in that field, but move on to something better. "I felt that what we ought to do was to make a paper which took away the cream of the potential circulation of the *Times*, and for doing that we must have a better editorial page than they did — which I think we did have," he explained. The *World* fell down on the news. It "tried to be all things to all men . . . as yellow as Hearst, as accurate as the *Times*, and as intellectual as the old *Evening Post*." [2] It suffered the fate of those that cannot make up their minds.

By late 1929 the financial situation had become so bad — the paper was reportedly losing a million dollars a year — that Herbert Pulitzer, JP's youngest and favorite son, returned from his ten-year sojourn in the watering spots of Europe and took control of the paper from Ralph. To the reporters in the city room Herbert was an exotic figure, with his London-tailored suits, soft collars, long hair and perfumed cigarettes. They referred to him as the "young Marster." But there was nothing soft in his determination to stop the *World*'s drain on his income. In a ruthless effort to cut costs he fired eighteen veteran reporters and made radical cuts down the line. Lippmann pleaded that men who had served the paper for many years could not be fired summarily. Despite his intercession the cuts continued, and it was clear that the good old days were over. Rumors circulated that the *World* might be up for sale.

This seemed unlikely. In his will JP had explicitly forbidden his heirs to sell the paper. On his death JP left his papers — the *World* and the *Evening World*, and the *St. Louis Post-Dispatch* — in trust with Charles Evans Hughes as trustee. Allowing his three sons only a portion of the income, he named his grandchildren as beneficiaries of the twenty-million-dollar estate. The division reflected JP's dislike for his eldest son, Ralph; his indifference to his second son, Joseph, Jr.; and his partiality to his youngest son, Herbert, who took 60 percent of the estate's income. Although all three sons received large incomes, they had no access to capital. The papers also had no capital, and were prohibited by the will from borrowing.

Through a series of dubious maneuvers by their lawyers, the sons managed to gain control of the trusteeship. Joseph took over the *St. Louis Post-Dispatch*, and Ralph the New York *World*. With a good business head, and with his paper enjoying an entrenched position in a large territory, Joseph prospered. Ralph, who was, as Lippmann confided to Berenson, "lazy, well-meaning, incompetent, neurotic and a selfish spender," had a harder time in New York, where competition was severe. The sons took profits and huge salaries out of the *World*, and starved the paper for capital improvements. Adolph Ochs, by contrast, plowed the *Times*'s earnings back into his paper. Yet the *World* had the city's most faithful readers.

"The *World* held and still holds a tremendous circulation based upon an extraordinary popular faith in its independence and its courage," Lippmann wrote Berenson in June 1930. But he could see that the situation was growing critical. "I have a thousand assurances that I am indispensable, etc, etc. I feel certain very strong personal and public obligations to members of my staff not to leave them at this critical time. I do know, however, that my resignation is only a question of time, and I know also that I have no particular desire to take executive responsibility in another commercial newspaper. I would rather write, or if I edited, I would prefer not to work for a daily newspaper but to deal at a somewhat more leisurely pace and more reflectively with events."

For the time being he let things ride, continuing to nourish the idea that he really wanted to leave newspapers and write only books and essays. "At the end I want to cut loose entirely from journalism for as long as my savings will hold out," he told Berenson, "then to get along with a book which I have under way. I do not find that journalism interferes, but I do find that administrative worry does. . . . Don't take this all too seriously," he concluded. "I have never taken newspaper work very seriously. It is to me a livelihood, a means of practical influence, and a laboratory for testing theories. I am not at all worried about myself. I should like to wind up my term on the *World* in a pleasant way and see that my own staff was provided for. I have enough in cash savings and somewhat depressed securities to live for a while either here in the country or abroad."[3]

Lippmann told Herbert Pulitzer that he wanted to be relieved as editor when his contract expired in September 1930. There were a good many alternatives. Harvard had offered him a chair in government, and the University of North Carolina its presidency. "The mere suggestion is shameless flattery," he told the officials at Chapel Hill. "But I am not qualified by training, experience or inclination for the House of Lords." The *Yale Review*, for which he wrote regularly, sent out feelers. The Council on Foreign Relations, where his friend Hamilton Fish Armstrong worked as editor of *Foreign Affairs*, thought he would make a fine director of studies.

One tempting possibility was to become editor of a new weekly magazine that Thomas Lamont, owner of the *New York Evening Post* and the *Saturday Review*, was contemplating. "If such a project were adequately financed, and if it had the business management which Tom could find for it," Lippmann told Berenson, "if in other words I had no financial responsibilities or worries and could go into the open market for the first-raters among writers, I think a weekly could be made which might have real interest and usefulness."[4] Lamont never followed through.

As the months went by, the situation at the *World* became more omi-

nous. Lippmann still made no decision. "I could not leave in these critical times," he wrote Berenson on Christmas Eve, 1930,

without bringing personal disaster to a large number of men with whom I have
worked for years, and I have been pressed from many outside quarters to
remain because it is said that with the latent panic among small people in NY
any drastic change in a newspaper which they look upon as one of the Gibral-
tars would be dangerous. I don't know. In any event, I have held on, trying to
keep speaking sanely amid the hysteria. . . .
    I have learned that the sense of calamity is relative. I see people every day
who are in deep gloom because they have to give up a limousine. Their world
is tottering and they have it harder than the poor devils who are selling apples
on the street corners.[5]

The ax fell in early February 1931. Herbert Pulitzer called Lippmann
into his office and, pledging him to secrecy, revealed that he was going
to sell the paper to the Scripps-Howard chain. The price, it soon leaked
out, was five million dollars. Lippmann was not consulted, he was informed. He told Pulitzer that the half million dollars earmarked for
workers' severance pay was not enough. The publisher had his mind on
other matters.
    Before the sale could be completed, JP's will — which forbade sale
of the paper — had to be broken. As a battery of Pulitzer lawyers
argued before the surrogate court, various groups frantically tried to
block the sale. William Randolph Hearst wanted to merge the *World*
with his flagship paper, the *American*, and put Swope at the helm.
Swope also had another iron in the fire as front man for a group of financiers headed by Bernard Baruch and backed by the North American
Newspaper Alliance. Ogden Reid, publisher of the *Herald Tribune*,
then entered the field. Adolph Ochs, fearing that a *Trib-World* merger
would have a disastrous effect on the *Times*, offered to put up money
for the *World*'s employees who were trying to buy the paper themselves.
    The Pulitzers were not interested. They were determined to sell to
Scripps-Howard. Within hours after the surrogate judge broke JP's will
they signed the sale papers and sent out dismissal notices. The *World*'s
presses rolled for the last time on February 27, 1931. Lippmann greeted
the decision with mixed relief and regret. "There were no bidders in the
field except groups of rich men who were not interested in publishing an
independent newspaper, but in acquiring an instrument of power," he
wrote Newton Baker. "I much prefer to have the *World* die a clean
death than to have it become a newspaper kept by ambitious politicians
and financiers." Above all he did not want to see Bernard Baruch take
control. Roy Howard was at least a crusader in the old spirit of the
World.[6]

If Lippmann thought the paper had been cynically axed by the Pulitzers, his final editorial showed no trace of resentment. He praised the new owners for their "courage, sincerity, independence and sympathy," and declared that in the circumstances the merger with the Scripps-Howard *Telegram* seemed "logical and appropriate." Extending his usual handshakes all around, he paid homage to the paper, to those who made it and those who read it, and ended his valedictory with a quote from Mr. Valiant-for-Truth in *Pilgrim's Progress:* "Though with great difficulty I am got thither, yet now I do not repent me of all the trouble I had been at to arrive where I am. My sword I give to him that shall succeed me in my pilgrimage, and my courage and skill to him that can get it."

The *World* did not have to die. At its sale it had a circulation of 320,000 daily, 500,000 Sunday, and 285,000 evening. Though it had been milked for years by the Pulitzer brothers, it could have been salvaged. "There is absolutely no doubt that if Herbert had shown some courage and thrown his private resources behind the paper, he could have carried it through the depression," Lippmann later said. "Every paper was in the red — the *Times* too — but it was a matter of having reserves. If the paper had been kept going for another year and a half to two years, when the tide turned in 1933, it would have pulled out and would undoubtedly have been a prosperous paper."[7]

The death of the *World* was a sad day for American journalism, yet the paper had ceased to be its old self long before 1931. Some blamed Swope for carelessness and the Pulitzers for stinginess, others Lippmann for lack of conviction. Cain, although often critical of Lippmann as editor, rejected the allegation. Lippmann was not fainthearted, he insisted in his postmortem. "Nobody who ever tried to buck him on any issue whatever could have any doubts about his spirit. He will not back down, and he will not compromise, whether his personal fortunes are involved or not." Yet neither did Cain think him a diligent editor: "Nobody who watched his boredom with the job of getting out his page, his impulse to wish all the chores off on Merz, his frequent betrayals that he had not even read the letters in his own forum, could have supposed he was an editor," Cain charged. "He had no interest in editing, and it is not surprising that his page often showed it." Instead, Cain considered him a "poet of ideas," given to spinning elaborate theories, as in the Scopes case, rather than sounding clear bugle notes. A poet jarred by banalities, "he never let himself lose his perspective through the emotions of combat," Cain wrote. "Indeed, when he was aware of the combat, he was always trying to bring it to a gentlemanly level; he seemed to regard it as a sort of amateurs' tennis tournament, as indicated by his invariable desire to shake hands afterward."[8] To Cain a postgame handshake was a way of saying that the contest did not matter. To Lippmann it meant that even adversaries had to live in the same world and communicate with each other.

About the time the *World* was collapsing Lippmann gave a speech positing a kind of reverse Gresham's law for journalism: that the good papers would ultimately drive out the bad. Reviewing the history of the press, he pointed out how newspapers had freed themselves from government control by finding commercial sponsors and catering to mass tastes. But eventually readers tired of a diet of sensationalism, he maintained. As they matured they desired papers "more and more sober, less and less sensational, increasingly reliable and comprehensive." A paper that continued to repeat the original formula would gradually fail. To succeed it would have to become "less Napoleonic at the top and less bohemian at the bottom." His observations seem borne out. The old tabloids either evolved into respectable newspapers or succumbed to new and more sensational rivals. Lippmann was trying to turn the *World* into a more comprehensive paper, and might have succeeded had the Pulitzers not abandoned it when times got hard.[9]

Once the paper was sold, it sank without trace into the *World-Telegram*, which three decades later was absorbed into the *Herald Tribune* before they all disappeared in the New York newspaper bankruptcies of the mid-1960s. The stars did all right, the others as best they could. Swope, having left early, found a comfortable niche in corporate boardrooms. Allan Nevins went to Columbia University to teach history. Charles Merz joined the *Times* and eventually became director of its editorial page. Cain wrote the big best-seller he had always dreamed of and went to Hollywood to write for the movies. Heywood Broun continued doing his column for the Scripps-Howard papers and in 1934 formed the American Newspaper Guild, the first journalists' union.

Even before Roy Howard bought the paper he asked Lippmann to join the new *World-Telegram* as editorial director. Hearst tried to snag him for the *American* and offered him fifty thousand dollars a year to write a signed column. The most intriguing offer came from the conservative *Herald Tribune*. On the morning that the surrogate announced that the paper could be sold, Lippmann received a phone call from Helen Reid, wife of publisher Ogden Reid and the power behind the throne. "Walter," she said, "we have something we would very much like to talk to you about. Could you meet Ogden at the Century for lunch?" The two men met at the midtown sanctuary for gentlemen of the arts and letters, and as Lippmann nursed his vodka on ice, Reid came to the point. "The *World* is doomed, but something can still be done to save its editorial page," he said. "The standards you set must be salvaged. So," Reid continued with a slight pause, "Helen and I had this idea — that you come over to the *Tribune* and write signed editorials for us."

This was an astonishing suggestion. As the *World* was supposed to have been the voice of the masses, so the *Herald Tribune* made its pitch to Republican businessmen. Although Lippmann was no radical, or even a progressive, the *Tribune*'s readers on Park Avenue and in Oyster Bay still considered him suspiciously leftist. This did not bother the Reids. "It doesn't matter that you've been running a Democratic paper, and we're a Republican one," the publisher told him. "We want the Democratic circulation of the *World*. Come and write Democratic editorials for us and sign them. Take any position you wish. We would never try to restrict you."[10]

Lippmann said he would think it over. A few days later he and Faye took the train to Florida. For several winters they had been going to Anna Maria Island, on the Gulf Coast near Sarasota, and in 1934 built a small home there. On the beach at Anna Maria, Lippmann mulled over his future. For all his scholarly interests, he was not an academic. He cared too much about being connected to events and people who made the news. Neither teaching nor writing books could provide this access, or the money to live in the style to which he was accustomed. "If I'm going to have any hand in public affairs as a journalist," he had confided to Berenson a few weeks before the Reids' offer, "I must continue living in New York, and to live in New York and write books also means living in a house, and that means more money than quarterlies can afford." The more he thought about writing for the *Tribune,* the more tempting he found it. "I would not only be free to differ with the policy of the paper," he explained to Newton Baker, "but expected to differ, and this attracts me a great deal."[11]

As he pondered the Reids' proposal, he received a phone call from Adolph Ochs. The *Times* publisher did not say exactly what he had in mind, but implored Lippmann to see him before making any decision. Word of Ochs's interest quickly got back to the Reids, who enlisted Thomas Lamont to nudge Lippmann in their direction. With his well-practiced finesse Lamont assured Lippmann that though Ochs was "quite a wonderful man," a syndicated column for the *Tribune* would spread his ideas across the country and "serve to enhance your already excellent reputation and wide influence. . . . If any objection might exist to the *Times*' connection for a man of your calibre," he advised, it was that "you would probably have to conform to the *Times*' mold, whereas at the *Herald Tribune* you would make your own mold."

On his return to New York at the end of March, a tanned and relaxed Lippmann went to see Ochs. He assumed that the *Times* wanted him to direct its editorial page. He was wrong. "I very much want you on the paper," Ochs told him, "but not to run the editorial page. Our views don't coincide enough for that. What I had in mind was for you to go to Washington to run our office there. You could be a kind of 'high commissioner of events' on political affairs." Taken aback, Lippmann said he would think it over. The prospect of living in Washington, then still a provincial town, did not appeal to him.[12]

The following day Lippmann had lunch with both the Reids. He now had four firm offers: to run the editorial page of the *World-Telegram,* to do a column for Hearst, to go to Washington for the *Times,* or to join the *Herald Tribune.* Of the four the *Trib* offered the most possibilities. A step into the unknown, it also provided, as Lamont had pointed out, the freedom to make his own mold. Going over the proposal once more with the Reids, making sure there would be no attempt to censor him no matter how much he might disagree with the paper's editorial policy, he agreed to come on at the *Trib.* He would begin his column early in September.

Under the terms of the contract Lippmann agreed to write four times a week, the length and subject matter to be at his discretion. The *Tribune* guaranteed a base that would assure him a minimum salary of at least twenty-five thousand dollars a year. In addition it would offer the column to other papers on a syndicated basis, taking the first fifteen thousand dollars itself, and splitting the remainder evenly with him. Lippmann would retain control over reprint rights, and would have the freedom to write books and magazine articles on the side. The paper would provide a secretary, travel expenses for fact-gathering trips, and two paid vacations a year: two weeks in winter and six in summer.

While he was conducting his negotiations with the Reids, Lippmann was guest of honor at a mammoth dinner given at the Hotel Astor on March 25, 1931, by the Academy of Political Science. If his plans were still a mystery, his prominence — confirmed by a cover story in *Time* that very week — was unquestioned. The ever-thoughtful Thomas Lamont had organized the tribute and had assembled, among the five hundred guests, such eminent personages as Learned Hand, Colonel House, Paul Warburg and Owen D. Young. Lamont, leading a standing ovation, called on the academy to pass a resolution of gratitude to Lippmann for his services to American journalism. Acknowledging the applause, Lippmann rose to his feet, calm and self-assured, a slight smile of pleasure crossing his lips, looking healthy and youthful at forty-one, and hailed by his colleagues and peers, in the words of *Time,* as "their Moses, their prophet of Liberalism."

His subject was "Journalism and the Liberal Spirit," and as he expounded his definition of liberalism it became clear why he was held in such esteem by the distinguished gentlemen before him. "The fighting faiths of the reformer of twenty years ago no longer arouse the generation to which we belong," he told the assembled businessmen, lawyers and jurists. "Who but a political hack can believe today, as our forefathers once sincerely believed, that the fate of the nation hangs upon the victory of either political party? . . . Who can believe . . . that the cure for the corruption of popular government [is] to multiply the number of elections? Who can believe that an orderly, secure and just economic order can be attained by the simple process of arousing the people against the corporations?''

This was an old refrain for Lippmann, but now he seemed to be going out of his way to show that liberalism and big business could go hand in hand. "The progressives of the last generation were attempting to police what seemed to them an alien intruder upon their normal existence,'' he explained. "For us the problem is to civilize and rationalize these corporate organizations. . . . The simple opposition between the people and big business has disappeared because the people themselves have become so deeply involved in big business." At a time when millions were out of work and wages were being slashed, the kind of involvement most people had with big business was not that which Lippmann's speech suggested. "It is vain to suppose that our problems can be dealt with by rallying the people to some crusade that can be expressed in a symbol, a phrase, a set of principles or a program,'' he assured the dignitaries. "If that is what progressives are looking for today, they will look in vain. For the objectives to which a nation like this could be aroused in something like unanimity are limited to a war or to some kind of futile or destructive fanaticism." The true liberalism, he maintained, lay in the "right of men to differ in their opinions and to be different in their conduct."[13]

This was classic liberalism of the Alexander Hamilton variety, an affirmation that led *Time* to tell its readers that Lippmann had arrived at "a state of mind where he believes, in effect, that a class of wholly 'disinterested' men should govern with the consent of the People, if not with their advice. What would save such a brainpower oligarchy from becoming tyrannous would be public education and the Liberal Spirit." *Time* was not alone in questioning Lippmann's brand of liberalism. Harold Laski, who saw Lippmann the day he returned from Florida, expressed his misgivings to Justice Holmes: "I think wealth has done two things to him. A good deal of his sensitiveness is gone. He is interested in external things, queer little worthless comforts, e.g. a bad display of temper because the servant forgot a cup of coffee he ordered. And he has arrived at the stage where he is not eager to take intellectual risks. . . . I found that he had ceased to read much outside modernities and he lacked a sense of perspective. He lives in the immediate moment and is not poised about it."[14]

Two days after his speech, Lippmann and Faye boarded the Italian liner *Saturnia* and settled into a spacious first-class cabin for their transatlantic crossing. Their traveling companions — Thomas and Florence Lamont, the Norman Davises, Thomas Cochrane, and the younger

Henry James — would not have distressed readers of the *Herald Tribune*. Every night it was black tie and champagne at the captain's table, every day a leisurely game of shuffleboard after perusing the news and stock-market ticker. This was not another pulse-taking trip to the European capitals, but the beginning of an excursion through the isles of Greece. The Lamonts had organized a trip for their friends that was designed to be as instructive as it was luxurious.

When the *Saturnia* docked at Patras, Lamont and his party were ceremoniously greeted by the governor of the province, the harbor master in full gold braid, a representative of the Greek cabinet, and the American consul. Such was the excitement — with the bands playing and officials rushing by tender from the ship to the town — that the Lippmanns' luggage never made it ashore. Minus their two trunks, but their arrival properly hailed, Walter and Faye joined the others, on a yacht provided by Lamont, for a two-week cruise of the Peloponnesus and the Aegean islands. To evoke historic allusions, Lamont had arranged for the services of the Oxford classicist Gilbert Murray, who gave a little lecture at each archaeological site. After stops at Olympia and Mycenae, they arrived at Piraeus and set out in a fleet of hired limousines over unpaved roads to Delphi. There, at the citadel of the gods, they had lunch on a damask cloth under the cypresses and read aloud poems about Greece from a little book, *The Englishman in Greece*, that Walter had given Florence Lamont.

"I felt horribly unconnected in Greece," Lippmann confessed to Learned Hand after the trip.

But somehow hundreds of odd bits of half-forgotten and half-learned lore — mythology, history, and so on, seemed to put themselves in order by looking at concrete things. The country seemed to me the most beautiful I had ever seen, but how much of its beauty is the sea, mountains and wildflowers and the light, how much association, I could not say — that is, I wouldn't know whether the same landscape would seem as utterly beautiful if it was, say in Alaska, or some place with no human part.

I can say that after two or three visits I honestly felt the Parthenon was the greatest structure I have ever seen, and though I distrusted myself, I really got to believe it was somehow absolutely perfect. One visit would have done that for me, but going to it eight or ten times and loafing on the Acropolis, I felt it.

We had a gorgeous trip to Delphi, where Gilbert Murray was at his best . . . but though I would not dare to utter the sentiment out loud, I thought he had a pronounced tendency to make very humane Englishmen out of the ancient Greeks. He would have none of what seemed to me the obvious brutality of their policy in wiping out rivals, nor of infanticide and slavery, nor of what seemed to my corrupt eye evidence of phallic worship at some of the more primitive shrines.

Hand's reaction was typical. "Oh, my God," he replied to Lippmann's account of Gilbert Murray rhapsodizing at Delphi. "Those Englishmen and their God-damned Greeks!" [15]

After journeying with the Lamonts to London, Walter and Faye went to Provence for a few weeks, and then to Florence to see Berenson. The leisurely sojourn at I Tatti ended in mid-June when they boarded the train for Berlin. The Weimar Republic was clearly tottering as the Nazis — who had emerged as the major party in the previous year's elections — and the communists battled daily in the streets. Lippmann set off on his usual round of interviews with government officials and journalists. He was much impressed by Chancellor Heinrich Brüning, who he told Berenson had the "face and bearing of a priest" and a "kind of imperturbable conviction of his own mission — not a man people would love, but something strong and erect to hold on to in a hurricane." [16] A year later Brüning, who had governed by emergency decree, resigned. Six months after that Adolf Hitler became chancellor. The spectacle of a democracy on the brink of disintegration reinforced Lippmann's belief in the need for a strong executive capable of making unpopular decisions.

Walter and Faye returned to New York in early July, drove up to Maine for a few days in August to visit the Lamonts at North Haven, and then over to the Adirondacks to see the Reids at the palatial "camp" they called Wild Air. Between rounds of golf, tennis and croquet, they managed to iron out the few remaining details of Lippmann's column for the *Herald Tribune*. The title was a problem. Lippmann wanted to call it "Notes and Comments." The Reids thought that hopelessly dull. Finally they settled, despite some misgivings on Lippmann's part, on "Today and Tomorrow" — a title Lippmann had used in 1914 for his *Metropolitan* magazine series. The name took, and for the next thirty-six years, T&T, as it was known in the trade, was his rubric.

On August 25 Walter and Faye were back in their house on East 61st Street. Three days later Walter went up to his attic study and started to sketch out his first column. On September 8 it appeared, warning the *Trib*'s Republican readers that the current crisis was not just a trade depression, but "one of the great upheavals of modern history." The Reids tried to prepare their readers for the arrival of their prize acquisition. "We expect Mr. Lippmann to be no more neutral in his articles than in his editorial columns," they noted in an explanation accompanying his debut. "He is to write freely upon such topics as he selects, expressing whatever opinion he holds. We are confident that whether our readers happen to agree or disagree with his views, they will take only benefit from his expression of them."

The appearance of New York's leading liberal editorialist in the city's most respectable Republican newspaper brought predictable responses. Some were enthusiastic, others sarcastic. "Walter Lippmann's bugle call crashing through the columns of the most important Republican right-wing newspaper in America will rally free-thinking, forward-walking men all over America," his friend William Allen White wrote approvingly. The rival *Times,* perhaps tasting sour grapes, was more caustic, declaring that the ability to express his contrary views in the *Trib* "must seem to Mr. Lippmann to be in accord with his own favorite doctrine of the liberal mind." Lincoln Steffens thought the move logical. "I see that Walter Lippmann is back from his travels with Tom Lamont and is to have a column in the *Herald Tribune,*" he wrote his future wife, Ella Winter. "It will express Wall Street, I predict. And Wall Street needs a voice, and a mind."

Some of his old friends were not pleased. Although Ralph Hayes had said that Lippmann's move was "a fortunate one, for him and for the paper, and for liberalism," Felix Frankfurter was not so sure. "Undoubtedly Walter brings an independent mind to the *Tribune* and will continue to speak it freely," he told Hayes.

But so far as essential outlook goes, there is no incongruity in Walter's association with the *Tribune.* For he has steadily moved to the right, and the logic of psychological forces will continue that process. . . .

Of course I know that you believe that Walter will tincture the *Tribune* and its readers with liberalism rather than strengthen the conservative forces. I think I know the argument and understand it, but am wholly unpersuaded by it. This doesn't mean that Walter won't from time to time and perhaps even frequently write articles which I shall read both with stimulus and with gratitude. But it does mean that the acquisition of Walter by the *Tribune* is not an occasion for jubilation by me.[17]

Whatever his friends' caveats, the column was an overnight sensation. Orders flooded into the *Tribune* from papers all over America; editors fought over exclusive rights to carry the column within their geographical area. Within a year "Today and Tomorrow" was being syndicated to 100 papers with a combined circulation of ten million; by 1937 it was going to 155 dailies, and ultimately to more than 200. After a year Macmillan brought out a selection of his columns, *Interpretations, 1931–1932,* edited by Allan Nevins, and three years later a second volume covering the years 1933 to 1935.

He had become a public personality. "To read, if not to comprehend, Lippmann was suddenly the thing to do," Arthur Krock wrote churlishly in *Vogue.* One writer admiringly dubbed him the "man with the flashlight mind." James Truslow Adams wrote in the *Saturday Review* that he was the "only national leader who has appeared in these post-war years," and predicted that "what happens to Lippmann in the next decade may be of greater interest than what happens to any other single figure now on the American scene." Magazines ran cartoons about him. The *New Yorker* showed two dowager ladies in a railroad dining car, one with a newspaper in her hand saying to the other: "Of course, I only take a cup of coffee in the morning. A cup of coffee and Walter Lippmann is all I need." Lippmann liked this cartoon so much that he asked the artist, Perry Barlow, for the original and hung it in his study. Even songwriters brought him into their lyrics. In the musical comedy *Pal Joey* a stripper disrobed ,under colored lights to the lines: "Zip, Walter Lippmann wasn't brilliant today . . ."[18]

Lippmann's leap to popular fame had several causes. His was the first political column devoted entirely to opinion. Columnists who began somewhat earlier — David Lawrence, Mark Sullivan, Frank Kent — were reporters and inside dopesters rather than analysts. The personal editorializing of "Today and Tomorrow" rested on a frank recognition that, as Lippmann had argued in *Public Opinion,* most journalism was not about facts, but about interpretations of what seemed to be "facts." Lippmann attributed his success, and that of other columnists who followed his example, to the growing complexities of public life and the need of newspaper editors for someone with New York and Washington connections who could put the news into perspective. Most could not afford correspondents of their own. With the New Deal and the expansion and centralization of the federal bureaucracy, the effective capital of the United States moved from New York to Washington, and the Washington journalist insider came into his own. "But for that historic change the profession of the syndicated columnist would not, I believe, have developed," Lippmann later said.[19]

Because of the phenomenal success of Lippmann's column, the admiring James Truslow Adams was not alone in thinking that Lippmann might be drawn into a more active political role. But political office — the Senate, the State Department, let alone the White House — had no allure for Lippmann. He was too thin-skinned to stand the personality conflicts and power maneuvers of politics. A brilliant critic and analyst of politics, he could never be a prime mover. In thanking Adams for his effusive profile Lippmann admitted that he had given some thought to what he would do "after this present boom subsides," and was sure it would not be politics.

I am too old a hand in these matters to have the slightest illusion about the maintenance of an influence like that of these syndicated articles in a country as easily bored as the United States.

I don't think, however, that when the boom is over, I shall feel like an old actor who can't live without his audiences. For, as a matter of deep personal choice, I should not want to do this kind of thing all my life, nor even for a great many years. I should like to keep it up, perhaps, until the present crisis is weathered and a period of comparative calm sets in. But then after that I should be very happy to live more quietly and to work on books and more careful and more considered kinds of writing.[20]

The period of "comparative calm" never did set in. For the next thirty-six years, through one "present crisis" and another, he continued to write his column. In December 1934 he cut back from four to three times a week in order to have a day for research between columns, and in April 1955, when he was sixty-five, to twice a week.

Fame came quickly, perhaps too quickly, to him. "You are a vogue. Your leadership is unquestioned among the people who think," William Allen White wrote him when the column was barely six months old. White recognized the dangers — not only the obvious ones of egotism that go with sudden fame, but the more subtle ones of seduction by the rich and the powerful. An old-fashioned prairie Progressive, White felt there was some cause for concern. " 'Beware when all men speak well of you,' " he warned Lippmann. "I want you to know how proud I am of you, and to caution you to watch your step. Don't let the Bankers get you."

This was no idle advice. Lippmann was finding more in common with the enlightened financiers of Wall Street than with crusading progressives. He lunched, played golf and tennis, spent his weekends with them. Shortly after he joined the *Herald Tribune* his friends Lamont and Russell Leffingwell cleared his way into New York's fashionable River Club, making him one of the few token Jews to be granted membership. Lippmann's journey from youthful socialism to mature respectability had been long, but not particularly arduous. Still a youth fresh out of college he had written of a new business world producing a "new kind of business man" with professional standards. Even then it was expertise more than ideology that he valued. In 1927 he had declared that the "more or less unconscious activities of business men are for once more novel, more daring, and in a sense more revolutionary, than the theories of the progressives." Even earlier, in 1922 when *Public Opinion* came out, Learned Hand had gently chided him for having "become so respectable a person as somewhat to disconcert the WL of ten years past. You have secured an authority with the more amenable of the conservatives which I like and yet I don't like."[21]

The switch from the *World* to the *Herald Tribune* was quite in key with his growing conservatism. Felix Frankfurter had some reason to find his appearance in the flagship paper of Wall Street Republicanism "not an occasion for jubilation."

Part Two

1931–1974

◄ 23 ►

An "Amiable Boy Scout"

Even assuming that Roosevelt isn't any better than
Hoover, a new man for a little while will be better than
a man who's worn out and used up.

— To William E. Borah, November 3, 1932

"IT is a marvel, looking back on it now," Lippmann wrote in his first
column for the *Tribune* on September 8, 1931, "that we could ever
have so completely thought that a boom under such treacherous conditions was permanent." Industrial production had fallen by nearly 50
percent from predepression levels, seven million Americans were unemployed, a million jobless roamed the country in search of work, "Hoo-
verville" shacks sprang up on empty lots. The market crash — which
wiped out forty billion dollars in stock prices during the last four months
of 1929 — weakened financial institutions and undermined the
confidence of Americans in the businessmen who had so recently been
their heroes. Hunger marches and riots erupted in the cities. Farmers
banded together with rifles to prevent banks from foreclosing their
mortgages. "In other periods of depression it has always been possible
to see some things which were solid and upon which you could base
hope," Calvin Coolidge said just a few days before his death in January
1933. "But as I look about, I now see nothing to give ground for hope,
nothing of man."

Such pessimism would have been inconceivable only a few years earlier. When Herbert Hoover took office as President in March 1929 it
seemed as though the key to peace and prosperity had at last been
found. The boom rolled on, world trade was at an all-time high, the war
debts–reparations snarl had been largely resolved, moderates ruled in
Tokyo and democrats in Weimar, and war had been outlawed. Within
six months it all came apart. The frenzy of stock-market speculation
exploded into the great crash of October 1929. Businesses faltered,
banks closed, and American loans to Europe were recalled. Foreign

trade plummeted as each nation sought salvation by beggaring its neighbor, dumping its surpluses abroad, and manipulating its currency for temporary trade advantage. In 1930 Congress passed the Hawley-Smoot tariff, setting the highest rates in American history. Europeans retaliated by raising their tariffs against American goods, and the downward spiral intensified. Unable to clear American tariff hurdles, the Europeans were forced to repudiate some twelve billion dollars in war debts, thereby feeding American isolationist sentiment.

Economic failure undermined the middle class, taking away its jobs, savings, and self-assurance. Desperate men turned to demagogues who promised them work and an explanation — foreigners, capitalists, Jews, the Versailles treaty — for their ordeals. Communists and fascists gained a wide audience, even in the United States. In Europe and Japan the fascist brand of totalitarianism triumphed, linking nationalism with militarism and monopoly capitalism.

"Today we know that we have not yet made peace and that nothing is really got for nothing," Lippmann wrote on New Year's Day, 1931. "We begin to know that we do not know. We begin to see that we are not guaranteed an unending good fortune. . . . There are no phrases to save us. There are no miracles. There is only the courage to be intelligent and sober." [1]

Hoover, the great engineer, the organizing genius of Belgian relief and European postwar reconstruction, seemed incapable of coming to grips with the emergency. Although a man of decent instincts and great administrative talents, he could not modify the faith in self-reliance and voluntary cooperation he had inherited from more tranquil times. Yet he was not a reactionary. He used the powers of government to an unprecedented degree to compensate for the failure of local and private initiative. He authorized public works projects, set up a system of home-loan banks, encouraged farm cooperatives, created the Reconstruction Finance Corporation to lend money to ailing businesses and banks, and made the federal government ultimately responsible for relief when local sources proved inadequate. In an unplanned manner he adopted most of the principles that were later implemented in the early years of the New Deal. His "historic position as a radical innovator has been greatly underestimated and . . . Mr. Roosevelt's pioneering has been greatly exaggerated," Lippmann later wrote. "It was Mr. Hoover who abandoned the principles of laissez faire in relation to the business cycle, established the conviction that prosperity and depression can be publicly controlled by political action, and drove out of the public consciousness the old idea that depressions must be overcome by private adjustment."

Hoover's foreign-policy record — so overwhelmed by the domestic crisis that defeated him — seemed a model of enlightened restraint. He opposed Wilson's intervention against the Bolsheviks, worked for Russian relief, sought international arms agreements, withdrew the marines from Nicaragua, tried to ban foreign loans to Latin America for military purposes, and opposed economic warfare against Japan during the Manchurian crisis. Hoover, Lippmann wrote appreciatively three decades later during the Vietnam War, "never believed in America as a global power with military and political commitments in every continent. He was an isolationist and, insofar as his beliefs could be reconciled with his duties as president and commander in chief, he was a conscientious objector."[2]

Hoover's faults were in part a magnification of his virtues. Believing in individual initiative, he stubbornly clung to the idea that federal relief to the jobless and the hungry would undermine national character. Aid, he believed, should come from local and private sources. Not without human charity, he lacked political instinct. When a band of unemployed veterans came to Washington to plead unsuccessfully for early payment of their bonuses, he sent the army to disband them. The spectacle of Army Chief of Staff Douglas MacArthur leading cavalry and tanks to rout impoverished veterans and their families did little to improve Hoover's appeal. With his dour personality and his homilies about prosperity being just around the corner, he won a deserved reputation for political rigidity.

The defeatism that marked the last two years of his term could not have been foreseen at the time of his election, when the nation was still riding high with the Coolidge boom. Lippmann was not alone in feeling that Hoover, as he wrote just before the 1928 election, was a "reformer who is probably more vividly conscious of the defects of American capitalism than any man in public life today." If Hoover had his way, Lippmann predicted, he would "purify capitalism of its predatoriness, its commercialism, its waste, and its squalor, and infuse it with a very large measure of democratic consent under highly trained professional leadership."[3]

Within six months of his inauguration the crash — itself the inevitable result of the frenzied speculation that marked the Coolidge boom — plunged the nation into a collapse for which no one had a remedy. Lippmann, who had kept up his ties with Hoover, saw a good deal of him during this time and was sympathetic to his troubles. "Hoover's had a wretched first year," he wrote Herbert Croly in March 1930, after lunching with the President. "Everything he touches seems to sour on him. And yet I cannot quite bring myself to condemn him completely. For underneath all his failures, there is a disposition in this administration to rely on intelligence to a greater degree than at any time, I suppose, since Roosevelt. Hoover seems to be the victim partly of bad

luck, partly of a temperamental weakness in dealing with irrational political matters, and partly of bad advice in matters where he has no personal experience.''

What particularly troubled Lippmann was Hoover's failure to stand
up to special-interest groups, and his capitulation to the lobbyists who
pushed through Congress the trade-crippling Hawley-Smoot tariff of
1930. "For some reason, which is beyond the scope of ordinary explaining, he surrendered everything for nothing," Lippmann complained in the World. "He gave up the leadership of his party. He let his
personal authority be flouted. He accepted a wretched and mischievous
product of stupidity and greed.'' Hoover's "peculiar weakness," he
told the readers of Harper's, was a fear of controversy, a reluctance to
intervene in the "hurly-burly of conflicting wills. . . . In the realm of
reason he is an unusually bold man; in the realm of unreason he is, for a
statesman, an exceptionally thin-skinned and easily bewildered man.''

Lippmann's disenchantment mounted over the summer, and in the fall
of 1930 he told Frankfurter that Hoover had a "bad temperament" for
public office. "Ambition and anxiety both gnaw at him constantly. He
has no resiliency. And if things continue to break badly for him, I think
the chances are against his being able to avoid a breakdown," he predicted. "When men of his temperament get to his age without ever having had real opposition, and then meet it in its most dramatic form, it's
quite dangerous."[4]

Hoover made a modest stab at federal intervention by creating the
Reconstruction Finance Corporation and proposing that it be empowered
to lend $1.5 billion to ailing banks, railroads and financial institutions.
Lippmann was not impressed. "The needs of the country at this time
cannot be met by voting large sums of money," he told his readers. He
felt, as he told Frankfurter, "rather doubtful as to any positive good"
coming from such lavish federal spending. Yet he had no plan of his
own. "If the only remedy is deflation to the bitter end, it will come in
spite of this Corporation, though I admit it will be delayed and the
agony prolonged. If, on the other hand, it is true that a certain amount
of artificial credit can arrest an unnecessary amount of deflation, then
perhaps we may tide ourselves over unnecessary disasters. Surely here
is a case where all our choices are second bests."[5]

Like Hoover, and indeed like Franklin Roosevelt at the time, Lippmann believed that the budget must be balanced and that deficit financing would set a bad example to the people. The government should have
the courage to raise taxes to cover its deficits, he told Newton Baker,
and it should begin with the rich. Not because taxing the rich would
yield much revenue, he explained, "but because it's morally necessary
to begin with the rich.'' He also agreed with Hoover that federal relief
to the unemployed would "corrupt" the recipients. Since private

sources of relief had dried up, and many cities were too impoverished to provide assistance to the hungry and jobless, he suggested that the government siphon money through the states as the "least demoralizing" way of aiding the indigent. Sharing the conservative hostility to government intervention, he had opposed the child-labor amendment, a federal guarantee of civil rights, and early payment of veterans' bonuses. When a bill came up to provide pensions for widows and orphans of veterans he declared that such special-interest groups posed a "menace not only to the budget but to popular government itself." [6]

Instead of recognizing that the crisis demanded extraordinary measures, Lippmann stressed the need for thrift. The American people had no "firm and convincing standards by which to control the growth of their appetites for material things," he complained in the *Woman's Home Companion*. The ability "to stop, to look around, and to do something else is the ultimate liberty that men surrender when they imprudently acquire appetites they cannot easily and permanently afford to gratify." He seemed to ignore that for many those appetites were as simple as a job, a roof, and a meal.

In preaching thrift and self-reliance he was expressing, not only the conventional wisdom, but the views of such Wall Street friends as Thomas Lamont and Russell Leffingwell of J. P. Morgan. By Wall Street standards these men were liberals, and indeed later even supported the New Deal. Lippmann relied on them — particularly Leffingwell — for advice on the technicalities of finance. At that time most financial experts were on Wall Street, not in Washington. Although he had a good feeling for economics, Lippmann needed help on financial questions and would often test an idea on Leffingwell before presenting it in his column. Lippmann had considerable respect for his friends at the house of Morgan. "The most exhilarating thing I have seen is the courage and quiet unselfishness of some of the big bankers who have really done extraordinary things," he wrote Berenson at Christmas 1930 of the efforts of Morgan and other banks to maintain stock prices by heavy purchases. "The burden which Tom Lamont, for example, has carried has been immense, not of course personal to himself or his firm, but for the banking community."

Later a congressional investigation, conducted by scrappy young lawyer Ferdinand Pecora, revealed that J. P. Morgan and his nineteen partners had paid no federal income taxes for 1931 and 1932 and that they kept a list of favored outsiders — including William G. McAdoo, General John Pershing, Owen Young, Charles Lindbergh, John W. Davis, Calvin Coolidge and Newton D. Baker — who were allowed to buy stocks under the market price. Lippmann was shocked by the disclosure and, having praised the bankers, suddenly reversed himself and told his readers that no set of men, "however honorable they may be, and however good their traditions, can be trusted with so much private power."[7]

The economic crisis seemed to threaten the survival of popular government itself. Lippmann's trip to Europe in the winter of 1932 convinced him that without strong presidential leadership, as he wrote on his return, "the course of events here may not be unlike that in other lands." The refusal of Congress to pass a sales tax revealed the power of political pressure groups on the legislature. When Frankfurter pointed out to him that a sales tax weighed unfairly on the poor, Lippmann agreed that it was a "wretched tax" that could not be justified except by the inability to raise money another way. Assuring Frankfurter that he regarded the distribution of income in the United States as "wholly undesirable," he pointed out that the rich could easily escape the full impact of the income tax. Only an inheritance tax could touch the sanctuary of the tax exempts. In the meantime a sales tax was unavoidable. "My observations in Europe convinced me profoundly," he emphasized, "that the balancing of the budget was an extremely urgent necessity."[8]

Lippmann's faith in a balanced budget showed he was no more economically sophisticated than most. What he wanted was for someone to take hold. After a luncheon meeting with Hoover in April 1932 he was convinced that the President had lost control. On his return to New York he published one of his gloomiest columns, evoking the "dark forebodings" and "despairing impotence" that had seized the nation. "A demoralized people is one in which the individual has become isolated and is the prey of his own suspicions," he wrote. "He trusts nobody and nothing, not even himself. He believes nothing, except the worst of everybody and everything. He sees only confusion in himself and conspiracies in other men. That is panic. That is disintegration. That is what comes when in some sudden emergency of their lives men find themselves unsupported by clear convictions that transcend their immediate and personal desires.

Offering no practical alternatives, he decried the "moral apathy of those in high places" and approached the problem as one of ethics more than of economics. "For if you teach a people for ten years that the character of its government is not greatly important, that political success is for those who equivocate and evade, and if you tell them that acquisitiveness is the ideal, that things are what matter, that Mammon is God, then you must not be astonished at the confusion in Washington. . . . You cannot set up false gods to confuse the people and not pay the penalty."[9] When Lippmann had finished chasing the money changers from the temple, however, he was not sure what came next.

One obvious answer was a new man in the White House. With Hoover sure of renomination, the only hope lay with the Democrats.

The clear front-runner and favorite of the progressives was Franklin D. Roosevelt. Ever since his landslide reelection as governor of New York in 1930, FDR had been rounding up delegates and establishing himself as natural leader of the party. Lippmann had known Roosevelt since their work together in Washington, and in 1928 he had urged him to run for governor on the assumption that it would help Al Smith carry New York State in his presidential race. That spring he had made several visits to Roosevelt's home at Hyde Park to help overcome FDR's hesitations and the opposition of his strong-willed mother. FDR, with support from Eleanor and pressure from the party pros, did of course make the race and won a smashing victory that carried him to Albany. But Al Smith did not even carry his home state; he never forgave FDR his victory.

Although subjected to massive doses of FDR's celebrated charm, Lippmann remained unimpressed. "I am now satisfied," he wrote Newton Baker in November 1931 of FDR's record at Albany, ". . . that he just doesn't happen to have a very good mind, that he never really comes to grips with a problem which has any large dimensions, and that above all the controlling element in almost every case is political advantage." Roosevelt coddled Tammany and showed petty jealousy toward Al Smith, Lippmann charged. "He has never thought much, or understood much, about the great subjects which must concern the next President," and was really little more than a "kind of amiable boy scout." [10]

Lippmann was not alone in his harsh judgment. Elmer Davis called FDR "a man who thinks that the shortest distance between two points is not a straight line but a corkscrew," the Scripps-Howard papers dismissed him as "another Hoover," and Oswald Garrison Villard said he would lose the nomination if it were awarded "on the grounds of great intellectual capacity, or proved boldness in grasping issues and problems, or courage and originality in finding solutions." That they all lived to eat their words made them no less sure of their judgment at the time.

By January 1932 FDR was such a heavy favorite that Lippmann decided drastic measures were necessary. Early that month he made a biting attack on Roosevelt — one long remembered by both FDR and Lippmann's detractors. "Sooner or later some of Governor Roosevelt's supporters are going to feel badly let down, for it is impossible that he can continue to be such different things to such different men," he wrote in his column, noting that FDR was the favorite of both left-wing progressives like Senator Burton Wheeler, and the conservative *New York Times*. Rhetorically asking which of the two guessed right, Lippmann pointed out that "the art of carrying water on both shoulders is highly developed in American politics." Charming but slippery, Roosevelt was "a highly impressionable person without a firm grasp of public affairs and without very strong convictions. . . . He is an amiable man with many philanthropic impulses, but he is not the dangerous enemy of anything." Too eager to please and too cautious to take political risks, FDR was, Lippmann concluded, merely "a pleasant man who, without any important qualifications for the office, would very much like to be President."

Lippmann's critics never let him forget that phrase, later citing it as evidence of his bad judgment. Yet at the time it was not so far off base. FDR had a spotty record, tried to be all things to all men, and was blatantly playing for the support of the isolationists and of William Randolph Hearst. Of his famous column Lippmann later said: "That I will maintain to my dying day was true of the Franklin Roosevelt of 1932."[11] Even many of FDR's admirers were forced to agree. Lippmann recognized that FDR was a pragmatist and an experimenter, a man without any theoretical guideposts. What he failed to notice was the tenacious will.

Among his complaints Lippmann cited Roosevelt's equivocal attitude toward the corruption-ridden Tammany organization. This was ironic coming from one who four years earlier had, in promoting Al Smith's 1928 campaign, discovered a "new Tammany" with uptown standards. But Lippmann was less interested in consistency than in stopping FDR. In this effort he had a powerful ally in Smith. The former "man of destiny" was envious of Roosevelt for having replaced him at Albany and angry at his failure to show the proper deference in the interval. Smith's personal pique was reinforced by an ideological aversion to FDR's patrician populism. When in the spring of 1932 FDR evoked the plight of the "forgotten man at the bottom of the economic pyramid," Smith angrily retorted, "This is no time for demagogues." Smith knew that he could never win the nomination himself, yet he had a good chance of blocking FDR and swinging it to someone else. The two most likely alternatives were John Nance Garner of Texas, Speaker of the House, and Newton D. Baker.

Baker, the indefatigable voice of Wilsonian idealism, had a sizable following. Many remembered his impressive record as Wilson's secretary of war, his eloquent espousal of the League of Nations, his background as a crusading progressive. Those with shorter memories knew him as a well-paid lawyer for the electric utility companies and counsel for the powerful Van Sweringen interests in Cleveland. Lippmann, as ever, thought he would make a fine President. "The feeling for you has . . . passed the phase of individual admiration and assumed the proportions of what politicians call groundswell," he wrote Baker in the fall of 1931. "By native equipment, experience and tested purposes, you're the man the country needs." Baker agreed, and to soften resistance among isolationists abandoned the cause he had championed for years:

American entry into the league. "Nothing is to be gained by an exaggerated interest in the machinery of peace," he declared in a statement Lippmann had written for him.[12] The disavowal seemed to help, and as the convention approached, his prospects improved.

Lippmann, who had gone to Chicago the second week in June to watch the Republicans glumly renominate Hoover, went back east to pick up an honorary degree at Dartmouth, and then returned to Chicago on the twenty-fourth for the Democrats' show. His companions on the observation car of the Twentieth Century were a lively lot of prima donnas — Swope, Baruch, Krock, Frank Kent and Clare Boothe Brokaw (later Luce) — all united by a single desire: to block Roosevelt. Swope was officially pledged to Al Smith, but was working behind the scenes for his brother's colleague at General Electric, Owen D. Young. Brokaw had ambitions of starting a new political party dominated by women. "If Roosevelt gets the nomination," Lippmann told her as they got off the train at La Salle Street Station, "you can put me down as a member of your new party." He then took a taxi over to the Ambassador East Hotel, where the Democratic moguls were quartered, and went into conference with the stop-Roosevelt diehards: Al Smith, Carter Glass and Judge Samuel Seabury.

Roosevelt took a commanding lead on the convention floor, but after three ballots was unable to marshal the necessary two-thirds margin. The challengers pressed forward: Baker, Smith, Garner, Governor Albert Richie of Maryland. Even Lippmann's hat found its way into the ring, lobbed by Heywood Broun of all people. Lippmann was a "more profound student of national and international affairs than any of the Democrats for whom delegates have been instructed," Broun wrote in his syndicated column for the Scripps-Howard papers.[13]

The delegates, to avoid a repeat of the 103-ballot disaster of 1924, began searching for a compromise candidate. House Speaker Garner, with the powerful backing of McAdoo and Hearst, started to gain ground. Baker moved up fast. Only the iron grip of Huey Long on the southern delegations prevented a flight from FDR. Lippmann did his part by undermining FDR and promoting Baker. Shortly before the convention opened he had told his readers that "the trouble with Franklin D. Roosevelt is that his mind is not very clear, his purposes are not simple, and his methods are not direct." Now, coordinating with Ralph Hayes, Baker's deputy, he moved to push his candidate into the foreground. As the balloting moved into the third day he wrote an impassioned column urging the delegates to unite around Baker. The Cleveland lawyer was, he maintained, "the real first choice of more respectable Democrats than any other man, and . . . an acceptable second choice to almost everyone," the Democrats' "most experienced, their most eloquent, their most widely trusted man."[14] The next morning Baker's aide Ralph Hayes made sure that copies of the paper containing Lippmann's article got into the hands of every delegate before breakfast.

Sensing a panic, Roosevelt's supporters moved quickly to prevent a deadlock. Joseph Kennedy, the millionaire real-estate speculator and a key FDR backer, warned William Randolph Hearst that Garner did not have a chance, and that if FDR did not get the nomination soon, the convention would turn to Baker. The publisher detested Baker for his pro-league sentiments, and whipped the California delegation into line for FDR. William G. McAdoo, another Californian, whose own presidential prospects had been doused in 1924 by Al Smith, now saw his chance to even the score by supporting the person whom Smith most detested. With a self-pleased smile he stepped to the podium and announced that California would switch to Roosevelt. Suddenly it was all over. The other delegations fell over one another to follow suit and make FDR's nomination unanimous. Roosevelt, in a striking break with tradition, flew to Chicago to accept the nomination.

If the Democrats had closed ranks, Lippmann had not. A contest between Roosevelt, Hoover, and Socialist Norman Thomas was not his idea of a choice. "Those who can find in any one of these men or in any of these parties the ideal of their heart's desire are fortunate indeed," he declared glumly. "The rest of us will, I imagine, spend the next months realizing that John Morley was right when he said that politics was the science of the second best."[15]

Others shared his discouragement. The *New Republic,* after listening a few weeks to Hoover and Roosevelt proclaim the sanctity of a balanced budget, labeled the campaign an "obscene spectacle." Professor Paul Douglas of the University of Chicago, later a Democratic senator from Illinois, declared that the destruction of the Democratic party would be "one of the best things that could happen in our political life." John Dewey said it would be "suicidal" for progressives to back Roosevelt. Henry Hazlitt, Elmer Davis and Reinhold Niebuhr vowed they would vote for Norman Thomas. Lewis Mumford took the logic a step further: "If I vote at all it will be for the communists, in order to express as emphatically as possible the belief that our present crisis calls for a complete and drastic reorientation."

With the campaign in abeyance until the fall, Lippmann began his annual six-week summer vacation at the end of July. Setting off in their Chevrolet, he and Faye visited his mother at Saranac Lake in the Adirondacks, and then continued north to spend a week with Hamilton Fish Armstrong and his wife, Helen, in the woods of Quebec. Over the past decade the two men had developed a close friendship. Lippmann wrote frequently for Armstrong's magazine, *Foreign Affairs,* published by the Council on Foreign Relations, and in 1931 and 1932 edited the council's review of events, *The United States in World Affairs*. Lippmann was attracted to Armstrong's easygoing charm and ardent internationalism, and to Helen Armstrong's high spirits, ready wit and quick intelligence.

Over the campfire he and Armstrong weighed Hoover's known record against FDR's optimism and seeming willingness to experiment. Even though Roosevelt might not be up to the job, he at least offered a hope for change. By the time Lippmann got back to New York early in September, he was taking a far more positive approach than he had only three months earlier, when he gave his gloomy "wall against chaos" speech at Columbia. In fact, even before he left on vacation he had written a guardedly upbeat column declaring that no problem was beyond resolution, or at least improvement. "It is a cruel and bitter time for those who are the present victims of disorder," he wrote that summer of 1932.

But for the young and for those who are free in spirit it is a time of liberation and of opportunity. For them there remains, come what may, their own energy, and the richness of the earth, the heritage of invention and skill and the corpus of human wisdom. They need no more. Their paths will be more open, and what in one light is a vast breakdown of hopes is in another light the clearing away of debts and rigidities and pre-emptions that would choke them on their way.

Although by the end of the summer Lippmann had decided that even FDR was better than Hoover, he was not happy with the choice. "The two things about him that worry me," he told Frankfurter, "are that he plays politics well and likes the game for its own sake and is likely to be ultra-political almost to show his own virtuosity. The other fear I have is that he is such an amiable and impressionable man, so eager to please, and, I think, so little grounded in his own convictions that almost everything depends on the character of his own advisers."[16]

Certainly there was nothing in FDR's platform to inspire the bold or frighten the fainthearted. Pledging to balance the budget, lower tariffs, relieve the needy, restore purchasing power, and alleviate unemployment, FDR seemed a model of financial orthodoxy. Yet as the campaign progressed some of his speeches took on a flavor that presaged the New Deal. Even though no one knew exactly where he stood, his jaunty spirit, irrepressible optimism, and taste for experimentation were a welcome change from the dour and discredited Hoover.

In early October Lippmann finally swallowed his doubts and announced to his readers that "having become convinced that the Governor's abilities have either been underrated or, as is more likely, that he has been young enough to develop and mature impressively," he would ". . . vote cheerfully for Governor Roosevelt." Noting that FDR's campaign speeches had "done much to allay my fears," he argued that the election of Roosevelt "will not only facilitate many readjustments which it is imperative to make, but will insure the cooperation and the patient responsibility of a multitude of men who would otherwise be merely embittered and reckless." The more enlightened men on Wall Street also fell into line. Russell Leffingwell wrote Lippmann that FDR's "smile and cheerful friendliness and willingness to hope for the best and try to please everybody will have a sedative effect upon men's minds and souls. . . . The hungry and the unemployed," he reminded the columnist, "might be hard to handle this winter if we were in for four more years of the same policies and the same President."[17]

Although Lippmann may have been ready to vote "cheerfully" for FDR, the readers of the *Herald Tribune* were not. Outraged at such heresies in a newspaper that was supposed to be the quintessence of Republicanism, they deluged the editors with complaints. On October 10, three days after the endorsement appeared, Ogden Reid suggested to Lippmann that he take a more neutral stand. Lippmann ignored the suggestion and continued to strike at Hoover's record. On November 3, just five days before the election, Lippmann turned in a column accusing Hoover of having used emergency federal relief funds to bolster his political image. The Reids were unhappy and told Lippmann to cut the part of the column that attacked Hoover's integrity. Lippmann, whose mild social manner concealed a fierce temper when aroused, stormed out of the office telling the Reids they could "go to hell." In a hot fury he picked up Faye at the house and headed for Wading River. During the long drive out to the country his temper cooled. When they got to Wading River he called the Reids to say that he would go along with the cuts. By that time the column, as he wrote it, had already gone over the wire to other papers of the syndicate, and appeared in the first edition of the *Boston Globe* before it could be killed.

By agreeing to cut a five-paragraph section attacking Hoover, Lippmann felt he had been more than obliging. But when he picked up the *Tribune* the next morning he found, not only the truncated column he expected, but under the column an editor's note quoting — in order to "keep the record straight" — the parts of Hoover's speech that Lippmann had criticized in his column. This was a slap in the face. "I was amazed at the substance and the manner of your editorial note attached to my article this morning," he wrote Ogden Reid in a fit of anger, "and I have spent most of the day defending you against the consequences of it. I never dreamed you would put an editorial note inside the space reserved for me. That is a humiliating procedure which has the appearance of a public reprimand." Declaring that he considered this "unwarranted and misleading" editorial note to be a "matter of first importance" in their future relations, Lippmann nonetheless covered up for his employers, and publicly denied that the Reids had ever asked him to make any cuts. Some people remained skeptical. In passing on Lippmann's explanation to Felix Frankfurter, Lawrence Winship, editor of the *Boston Globe,* noted that "somebody isn't telling the truth."[18]

The incident was soon forgotten and the *Trib*'s readers steeled themselves for the prospect of a Roosevelt victory. FDR's lead in the polls was so commanding that the results seemed a foregone conclusion. Lippmann approached the balloting with guarded optimism. "It will be a great relief to have the election over," he wrote Senator Borah on the eve of the vote, "and to me at least, though I have the deepest reservations about Franklin Roosevelt, a relief to be rid of the present administration. It is so utterly discredited that it no longer has any usefulness as an instrument of government. And even assuming that Roosevelt isn't any better than Hoover, a new man for a little while will be better than a man who's worn out and used up."[19]

The country shared Lippmann's feeling. FDR captured 472 of a total 531 electoral votes and every state but six. The popular mandate for a new policy was overwhelming. But no one knew what Roosevelt would do — not even the President-elect himself.

For the moment there was nothing to do but wait. A few days after the election Lippmann went to Amherst to attend the festivities for the inauguration of his old friend Stanley King as president of the college. On his return to New York he dined with Joseph Kennedy, who told him of Bernard Baruch's manipulations to become FDR's secretary of state. Lippmann winced at the thought that a man for whom he felt such contempt might even have a chance for so critical a post. In early December he went to Yeamans Hall, a golf resort in South Carolina much favored by Thomas Lamont and his other Wall Street friends, and returned to New York shortly after Christmas, just in time to attend the gala opening of Radio City Music Hall with the Herbert Bayard Swopes, Al Smith, Rose Kennedy, and the Gerard Swopes. Lippmann was not greatly impressed by what the Rockefellers had wrought. Radio City, he wrote in his column, was "a monument to a culture in which material power and technical skill have been divorced from human values and the control of reason."[20]

Lippmann waited for FDR's inauguration with mixed apprehension and optimism. For years he had been arguing that the purpose of government was, as he had written in *A Preface to Morals,* "not to direct the affairs of the community, but to harmonize the direction which the community gives its affairs." Now he was no longer sure that government could take such a passive role. There was a time for restraint and a time for action. He had said so himself a decade earlier when, writing of the Harding administration, he had looked back nostalgically on the days when government was inconspicuous and incidental. "There is no surer test of reason in politics than to be able to remember that politics and government are secondary and subsidiary, not goods and ends in themselves,'' he had written. Yet abdicating power was not the same as abolishing it. "Government is not automatic, but an affair of pushing and pulling among interests . . . when the chief abdicates, the petty chieftains take charge.'' Therefore, he continued,

after a very brief experience of an abdicating President who believes in separated powers, the mass of voters turn again to the search for a man who will unify power, and wield it, as a big stick, upon the pushing and pulling minorities. When they find the man who can do that, they are better pleased, even though the powerful Presidents have their decided drawbacks. For while they may accomplish the immediate object of bringing order and coherent purpose into government, the disposition to over-govern is more than flesh can resist. It is so hard to govern well and at the same time remember what government is for. It is so hard, and yet so necessary, to combine the method of the active presidency with the ideal of the passive presidency.[21]

Lippmann wanted an active President. In FDR he found one — and rather more than he had bargained for.

A Reluctant Convert

The danger we have to fear is not that Congress will
give Franklin D. Roosevelt too much power, but that
it will deny him the powers he needs.

— "Today and Tomorrow," February 17, 1933

DURING the four months between Roosevelt's election and his inauguration in March 1933 the depression, which seemed to have abated during the fall, resumed with fierce intensity. Industrial production foundered, unemployment mounted to thirteen million, farmers could not pay their mortgages, state treasuries were unable to meet relief payments, and thousands of banks closed their doors. Some people were drawn to authoritarian solutions. "A mild species of dictatorship will help us over the roughest spots in the road ahead," suggested the business weekly *Barron's*. The American Legion passed a resolution declaring that the crisis could not be "promptly and efficiently met by existing political methods." The venerable Nicholas Murray Butler complained to the freshman class at Columbia that totalitarian societies seemed to bring forward "men of far greater intelligence, far stronger character and far more courage than the system of elections."

For four months the nation waited, looking to Roosevelt for an answer, uncertain of what he would do, as he was uncertain himself. On inauguration day, March 4, 1933, banks in thirty-eight states closed their doors. Eleanor Roosevelt recalled the inauguration ceremony as being "very, very solemn and a little terrifying . . . because when Franklin got to that part of his speech when he said it might be necessary for him to assume powers extraordinarily granted to a President in war time, he received the biggest demonstration."[1]

Lippmann saw FDR twice between the election and the inauguration. In mid-January they met in New York at a testimonial dinner for A. Lawrence Lowell, who was retiring as president of Harvard. They chatted briefly and FDR suggested that Lippmann, who was planning to spend February in Florida, stop off to see him at Warm Springs, Georgia, where he took treatments for his paralysis. Lippmann arrived at the resort on February 1, just in time to sit in on a mammoth press conference that Roosevelt orchestrated with his usual aplomb.

The two men then went back to FDR's cottage, where, over lunch, Lippmann tried to sound out the President-elect on the program he would follow. The result was frustrating. Roosevelt, amiable as always, would provide no specifics because he had none. Lippmann, who feared that without strong presidential leadership the people would grow desperate, would not accept such nonchalance. He reminded FDR of what had happened just two days earlier in Nazi Germany, where Hitler had come to power over a moribund executive and a deadlocked parliament. "The situation is critical, Franklin," he said. "You may have no alternative but to assume dictatorial powers."

The starkness of the phrase, particularly from Lippmann, took Roosevelt aback. Yet it was not inconsistent with Lippmann's view of the crisis. "The effort to calculate exactly what the voters want at each particular moment leaves out of account the fact that when they are troubled the thing the voters most want is to be told what to want," he had written just a year earlier, during the darkest days of the Hoover administration. "The enduring popularity of public men does not come from trying to guess what the people will applaud but from conveying to them the feeling that they can rely on the superior judgment of that man when they need him. It is no comfort whatever to know that he is a good judge of public opinion; they will really trust him only if they have some evidence that he is a good judge of the public interest." The thing that had always bothered Lippmann about FDR was his desire to be popular and not to offend. But the times had grown so desperate that democracy itself was in danger. "Popular government is unworkable except under the leadership and discipline of a strong national executive," Lippmann had told his readers only two weeks earlier. "Any group of 500 men, whether they are called Congressmen or anything else, is an unruly mob unless it comes under the strict control of a single will."[2]

After leaving Warm Springs he urged in his column that Congress not be allowed "to obstruct, to delay, to mutilate, and to confuse." It should give the President a free hand by suspending debate and amendment for a year. Laying the groundwork for what he had said to FDR in private, he insisted that the use of " 'dictatorial powers,' if that is the name for it — is essential. . . . The danger we have to fear is not that Congress will give Franklin D. Roosevelt too much power, but that it will deny him the powers he needs." With the Weimar Republic clearly in mind, he warned: "A democracy which fails to concentrate authority in an emergency inevitably falls into such confusion that the ground is prepared for the rise of a dictator."[3]

From the day he took office and told an apprehensive nation that the "only thing we have to fear is fear itself," Roosevelt captured the public imagination. Though he had no answers, he conveyed boundless energy, optimism, and an eagerness to experiment. On March 5 he decreed a bank holiday, and four days later sent to Congress an emergency banking act for reopening the banks and increasing the powers of the Treasury. He then sliced half a billion dollars from paychecks of veterans and government employees in a short-lived effort to balance the budget and, fulfilling a campaign promise, called for the repeal of Prohibition.

Lippmann was exaggerating only slightly when he told his readers, scarcely a week after FDR's inauguration, that the nation had "regained confidence in itself." Comparing Roosevelt's performance to the second battle of the Marne, he brushed away fears of a presidential abuse of power: "The wise thing is to give the Administration ample power, more power than it may need, and to let the use of that power be determined by the judgment of circumstances as they develop." Lippmann had now reversed himself. The man whom he had described only a year earlier as having no particular qualifications for the office had become, by force of circumstance and his own energetic performance, an inspirational leader. "By the greatest good fortune which has befallen this country in many a day," Lippmann wrote, "a kindly and intelligent man has the wit to realize that a great crisis is a great opportunity."[4]

As much as FDR welcomed Lippmann's support, he understood the danger of agitating Congress unnecessarily with talk of dictatorial powers. He asked Felix Frankfurter — who had installed himself as unofficial White House adviser and talent scout — to calm Lippmann down. "This constant harping on the inadequacies and obstructions of Congress fits in with the miseducation on that subject for the last ten years and gives impulse to . . . the fascist forces," the law professor told the columnist. Lippmann was not moved. "My plea for concentration of authority for Roosevelt was not made until I had been satisfied as to the essential wisdom with which he would use such authority," he replied.[5]

"There are," he told Frankfurter, in a clear statement of his view of popular democracy, "elements of corruption down deep in the electorate which . . . are part of the old Adam in every man. . . . It seems to me that you seem to imply that the wickedness and selfishness that pervade society come entirely through bad example from the top. I do not subscribe to that doctrine one hundred per cent. The evil works down from the top, but it also works up from the bottom."[6]

At the moment Lippmann was interested in action, not theory, and accused Frankfurter of being "a little bit hesitant about breaking the eggs to make the omelet. . . . Do you really think, for example, that I should have urged Congress to consider carefully and attempt to understand thoroughly the provisions of the banking bill before passing it," he asked of the emergency banking bill that FDR had sent to Capitol Hill and Congress had whooped through in a record eight hours, "or was it right to call upon Congress to take the thing on faith, suspending debate, suspending the process of education, suspending the deliberative method? I faced that choice honestly in my own mind, and I am prepared to risk the potential dangers which you point out for the sake of averting the much more actual dangers which were right upon us." For Lippmann, the problem of educating the public was abstract. There was not time. "The matters are too intricate, prejudices are too deep and complex, the necessary technical knowledge is too lacking." In his long-standing suspicion of public opinion he found the justification for granting powers far in excess of anything Roosevelt sought. When Frankfurter showed FDR the columnist's letters, Roosevelt correctly predicted that before long Lippmann's view of government would drive him into opposition.[7]

Improvising all the way, FDR propelled through an action-hungry Congress a dizzying succession of measures to restore economic stability. In March he reorganized the banks and set up the Civilian Conservation Corps; in April he took the nation off the gold standard; in May he made relief a federal responsibility, provided mortgage aid for farmers, set up the Agricultural Adjustment Administration to support farm prices, realized Senator George Norris's dream of a Tennessee Valley Authority, and instituted an agency to protect investors from stock-market frauds; in June he sent to Capitol Hill a farm credit bill, a federal insurance bill for bank deposits, a homeowners' loan bill, and the National Industrial Recovery Act, which suspended antitrust laws to encourage industry-wide planning. When Congress adjourned on June 16, exactly one hundred days after the session began, it had passed the most sweeping economic program in American history.

Lippmann backed the entire package, swallowing every one of his earlier strictures about government intervention in the economy. He even backed the National Recovery Administration, with its corporate state "codes" governing wages, hours, working conditions and prices. "If the economic system is to be organized and planned and managed, it follows inevitably that the system must be protected against external forces that cannot be controlled," he told the graduates of Union College in Schenectady in June 1933. "This means economic nationalism, for international planning, management and control are hardly as yet within the realm of practical possibilities."[8]

Economic nationalism meant control over domestic prices and wages. Yet so long as the dollar was pegged to the international price of gold, this was impossible. FDR's bright young advisers — the "brain trust" that followed him to Washington — urged him to cut loose from gold. Sophisticated voices on Wall Street quietly agreed. The choice FDR faced in early March was between remaining on the gold standard and watching farm prices and wages sink even further, or abandoning gold in an effort to stabilize domestic prices. FDR took the first step toward a controlled currency on March 6 when he froze the export of gold and prohibited Americans from redeeming paper dollars for gold.

To abandon gold completely, however, was a more drastic step. Lippmann was convinced that FDR had to take it. In early April, shortly after Lippmann got back from California, where he had received an honorary doctorate at Berkeley to add to his growing collection, he went down to 23 Wall Street to lunch with his friends Lamont and Leffingwell at J. P. Morgan. The two bankers agreed that the steady erosion of commodity prices, which was causing open revolt on the farms, could not be halted unless the administration gained full control over the currency. It was simply no longer possible, as in previous depressions, to let farm prices collapse. Anarchy was stalking the countryside. The political stability of the nation was at stake. "Walter," Leffingwell told Lippmann as their lunch drew to a close, "you've got to explain to the people why we can no longer afford to chain ourselves to the gold standard. Then maybe Roosevelt, who I am sure agrees, will be able to act." [9]

Lippmann went out to Wading River that night, and the next morning retreated to his office in the garage. Two hours later he finished one of his most influential columns. Every nation had been forced to decide whether to defend the gold standard or its internal price level, he had written. No nation could do both. "A choice has to be made between keeping up prices at home and keeping up the gold value of the currency abroad." Germany tried to hold the line on gold; the result was depression, unemployment and the Nazis. Britain took the other course and sacrificed gold to price stability. America was at a crossroads. To stick to gold meant to abandon credit expansion, relief and public works. The evidence was conclusive: "a decision to maintain the gold parity of currency condemns the nation which makes that decision to the intolerable strain of falling prices."

As soon as he finished writing the article, Lippmann called Leffingwell, read it aloud, and went over details to make sure his argument was tight. Then he dictated the article to his secretary at the *Herald Tribune*. The next morning, April 18, millions of Americans found Lippmann calling for an abandonment of the gold standard. This was not advice they had expected from a man who only a few months earlier had inveighed against government centralization, veterans' bonuses, and federal relief for the poor. Admitting that many might find his current advice "gravely heretical," he explained that these were "times when men must be willing to accept the conclusions of the evidence as they see it, and be ready to take the risks of stating their conclusions."[10] Wall Street did not take long to react. Cutting the dollar loose from the international gold rate meant the government would have more flexibility in reflating prices. This seemed good for business recovery, and thus for the market. The *Herald Tribune* with Lippmann's article had barely hit the street when the stock exchange was off and running in a day of frantic trading. His column, to be sure, was only a straw in the wind, but Wall Street considered him an insider and was ready to pounce on any rumor that presaged a halt to skidding prices.

The same evening in Washington FDR met with a group of advisers, ostensibly to discuss the forthcoming International Monetary and Economic Conference, scheduled to open in London in June. FDR was not at all enthusiastic about the conference, which he had inherited from Hoover and which was designed to stabilize the world's leading currencies. He had not yet decided how to approach that problem, but he had made a decision about the convertibility of dollars into gold. It would cease. The nation, he told his assembled advisers, was going "off gold." Then he asked for their congratulations. A shocked silence settled over the room. Budget director Lewis Douglas warned that the action would lead to inflation and economic chaos. For hours the advisers argued among themselves, while an amused FDR remained firm. When the meeting broke up, Douglas turned to James P. Warburg and said, "This is the end of Western civilization."

The prediction was premature. Wall Street was ecstatic as buyers rushed to accumulate stocks. J. P. Morgan hailed FDR's move, and Leffingwell told the President he had "saved the country from collapse." Conventional opinion was predictably outraged. Bernard Baruch complained that abandoning gold meant the triumph of "mob rule" and would benefit only one-fifth of the population, the "unemployed, debtor classes — incompetent, unwise people."

The move had given the United States greater control over the dollar, but had plunged the world financial markets into confusion. Would the United States still accept an international stabilization agreement on currencies? As delegates from sixty nations gathered in London in June for the world economic conference, no one knew the answer, not even Roosevelt's closest advisers. The American delegation — a strange hodgepodge of politicians and businessmen, some protectionists, others free traders, one a silver fanatic and another an isolationist — had received no instructions from the White House. Their confusion was compounded when FDR sent over economist Raymond Moley, chief of his brain trust, as an unofficial observer.

Lippmann, having decided to cover the conference, arrived in England on June 23 on the *Ile de France*. The next day he lunched with

Keynes. This was a chance, not only to renew an old friendship that meant a great deal to him, but also to brief himself on the issues. Keynes agreed that slavish adherence to the gold standard was intensifying the crisis. The industrialized countries should float free from gold and devalue their currencies by as much as one-third, he said. This would allow commodity prices to rise and stimulate savings and investment. A managed currency was the first step toward recovery. Impressed by Keynes's argument, Lippmann made it the focal point of his column on June 29.''

Over their long lunch at his London club, Keynes also explained to Lippmann the new theory on which he was working — one that would soon revolutionize thinking about economics. A few years earlier, in his *Treatise on Money,* Keynes had shown that business cycles were not a mysterious aberration of the capitalist economic system, but part of its nature. So long as demand was stagnant, business would not increase investment — regardless of the level of savings. To increase employment, Keynes reasoned, the government would have to spur demand through public works and other programs. The way out of the depression, in other words, lay not in a balanced budget, but in debt. To even out the business cycle the government should spend in bad times and tax in good times.

Lippmann listened with rapt attention as Keynes outlined the argument he would elaborate three years later in his most important work, *The General Theory of Employment, Interest, and Money.* With Keynes's guidance Lippmann grasped fully what he and many others had been groping for instinctively. For the first time he understood why a balanced budget not only was unnecessary, but might actually stand in the way of recovery. By trying to bring accounts into balance, conservatives were only further constricting demand — thereby intensifying the depression they sought to alleviate.

Keynes's prescription for countercyclical spending seemed to provide a compromise between laissez-faire capitalism and Marxist socialism. It removed the sense of helplessness in dealing with the depression and offered a middle way for those, like Lippmann, who wanted to use the power of the state to achieve economic stability without allowing the state to become, as it had in Germany and Russia, all-powerful.

Although Keynes revolutionized thinking about economics, his formal academic training was in mathematics. This interest, combined with his taste for gambling, allowed him to make, lose, and make again a small fortune in the stock market. Keynes embodied everything that Lippmann admired: intelligence, wit, urbanity, fame, wealth, influence, participation in the highest levels of his country's literary, political and social life. His beautiful wife, Lydia Lupokova, was a Russian ballerina who had been a star of the Diaghilev company. During Lippmann's visit to London he went with Keynes to Covent Garden to watch her dance the title role in *Coppelia*. "My friendship with Keynes," he later said, "was one of the happiest of my life."[12]

More than Lippmann realized, Keynes was a man of many parts: charming, cunning, versatile, with tastes that ran the gamut from mountain climbing to practical jokes, from the collection of abstract paintings to that of His Majesty's Guardsmen. Lippmann knew almost nothing of Keynes's private life until he read, many years later, a biography of Keynes's intimate friend, Lytton Strachey. Although he had met most of Keynes's Bloomsbury friends — Strachey, Clive Bell, Roger Fry, Virginia and Leonard Woolf — he found them rather mad and perverse, given to wearing strange costumes, practicing elaborate jokes, and speaking in riddles. He never knew quite what to make of them, or how to connect the Bloomsbury Keynes with the government adviser and economic theorist.

Keynes not only approved the American decision to go off the gold standard, as Britain earlier had done, but was skeptical of the whole concept of stabilizing international exchange rates. Since this would oblige governments to deflate their currencies to maintain parity, he feared that such an agreement would merely intensify the world depression. So did FDR. While cruising off the New England coast and safely beyond the reach of his diplomatic advisers, the President had decided that the time had come to make a clean break. On July 3, as the conference delegates were inching toward agreement on a stabilization pact, Roosevelt sent a message denouncing, in no subtle terms, the "old fetishes of so-called international bankers." Currency stabilization, he declared, was nothing but a "specious fallacy." He would have none of it. The United States would control its own prices. It would not link the dollar to gold or to any other currency.

FDR's message fell like a bombshell on the conference. The French, who had remained on the gold standard, were apoplectic. Prime Minister Ramsay MacDonald, the embarrassed host of the conference, called Lippmann to 10 Downing Street and beseeched him to use his influence on FDR to accept some compromise. Most of the delegates were furious and started packing to go home. The liberal *Manchester Guardian* called FDR's message a "manifesto of anarchy." Some, however, stayed to applaud. Keynes wrote an article declaring Roosevelt to be "magnificently right," and back-bencher Winston Churchill echoed his approval. Russell Leffingwell sent FDR his congratulations, and Lippmann told his readers that the President had "wisely rejected" proposals that would interfere with his effort to raise commodity prices.[13]

In a desperate effort to salvage the conference, Moley tried to find a compromise position that the delegates could agree on. Working against the clock before the conference collapsed, he summoned Lippmann,

Keynes, and Herbert Bayard Swope to the American embassy on the night of July Fourth. Over sandwiches and a bottle of whiskey they hammered out a draft that an embarrassed Secretary of State Cordell Hull could present to the angry delegates. As they emerged into the sleeping city at four in the morning, the code clerks were sending off their efforts over the embassy cables to Washington.

For all practical purposes the conference was over. There was nothing it could do in the face of American opposition. As the delegates desultorily adjourned, Lippmann took the Golden Arrow boat train to Paris for a meeting with Socialist leader Léon Blum. After four days in the French capital he boarded the *Majestic* at Cherbourg. Whiling away the crossing by playing Ping-Pong with film star Norma Shearer and Hollywood boy wonder Irving Thalberg, he arrived back in New York on July 18. Faye and Jane were waiting at the dock.

Lippmann had returned from London, and his talks with Keynes, convinced that Roosevelt was on the right track. At Amherst, where he spoke that fall at the inauguration of Stanley King as president, he defended FDR's course as guided "not by abstract theory produced by the brains trust, but [by] the concrete necessities and the brute facts he inherited from the post-war period." To those who saw the lineaments of socialism in the New Deal he counseled calm: "What we are witnessing is not the birth by revolution of a new society under the influence of doctrinaires, but the reconstruction of the old American society under the influence of experience and the compulsion of necessity."

Yet even in this flush of enthusiasm for the New Deal he warned that such "experiments in central control" were potentially dangerous. "These experiments have their roots in the desire for recovery rather than in a popular enthusiasm for the ideal of an authoritarian state and a planned economy. They are, therefore, practical expedients rather than revolutionary processes." The danger, he warned, was that the expedients might give way to more drastic ones, and thereby "themselves deepen the dislocation by inhibiting the free enterprise upon which an essential part of recovery depends."[14]

Thus, in January 1934, less than ten months into FDR's first term, Lippmann drew a clear line between recovery and reform, between government action necessary to end the depression and that designed to make fundamental changes in American society. Once the panic had been stemmed by Roosevelt's decisiveness and the innovations of the first hundred days, Lippmann ceased talking of "dictatorial powers." What he would grant in an emergency, he would take away once the emergency had passed.

Like Keynes, and Roosevelt himself, he recognized that the liberal capitalist state could be saved only by abandoning orthodox formulas. "Policies and programs are only instruments for dealing with particular circumstances," he told an audience in Cambridge, where in the spring of 1934 he delivered the Godkin Lectures at Harvard. "He who would be loyal to the end must in changing circumstances be prepared to alter the means." If democracy were to survive in a world rife with totalitarianism, it had to provide the security that people had come to demand as their birthright: jobs, health and retirement insurance, social welfare. "Laissez-faire is dead and the modern state has become responsible for the modern economy as a whole," he told his listeners. "The task of insuring the continuity of the standard of life for its people is now as much the fundamental duty of the state as the preservation of national independence."

Government intervention was unavoidable; the question was its degree. Totalitarian states practiced what he called "absolute collectivism" in "directed" economies. The democratic alternative was "free collectivism" through a "compensated" economy where the government would balance the vagaries of private spending and investment. What the authoritarian state would do by compulsion, the democratic state would achieve by spending, taxation, and interest rates. It would, he explained in his lectures, "counteract the mass errors of the individualist crowd by doing the opposite of what the crowd is doing; it saves when the crowd is spending too much; it economizes when the crowd is extravagant, and it spends when the crowd is afraid to spend . . . it becomes an employer when there is no private employment, and it shuts down when there is work for all."

This formula, based on the theory that Keynes had explained to Lippmann a year earlier, seemed quite logical. Yet how could the people be persuaded that interest rates should go up when they most wanted credit, or that the government should increase spending when its books were already out of balance? Would a democracy authorize the government, its creature, to do the opposite of what the majority wanted? Admitting that this was unlikely, Lippmann took the next step and suggested that democratic government itself be restructured. Officials would have to be made "reasonably independent of transient opinion and organized pressure." The White House should have full control over taxes and spending, with Congress limited to imposing ceilings. Congressional interference in economic decision-making was the "root of the perversion and corruption of representative democracy and of the weakness of democratic government."

No one would have had trouble finding the old Lippmann in this recent convert to Keynesian economics. Where he had once placed his faith in enlightened executives who would conduct their business as a science, he now turned to government officials. He still believed that democracy could be saved from its own excesses only by a disinterested elite immune to public pressure and follies. Under his new Keynesian cloak Lippmann remained the eternal Platonist, "still hunting for the philosopher-king, the samurai, the uniquely qualified governing class," John Chamberlain caustically wrote in reviewing the lectures when they came out in book form as *The Method of Freedom.*[15]

If Lippmann's argument for a guiding elite had some pragmatic basis, his equation of political freedom with capitalism was questionable. Also, his explanation of the difference between the "compensated" and the "directed" economy was arbitrary and fuzzy. It rested largely on the assertion that the "compensators" could be recalled by popular vote, but the "planners" could not be. This he stated rather than demonstrated. Disliking a planned society, Lippmann was convinced that it could not be compatible with political freedom. Certainly Soviet Russia provided graphic evidence of how a perverted collectivism could be linked to political tyranny. But Nazi Germany and fascist Italy were equally good examples of how businessmen could find common cause with dictators. The connection Lippmann tried to draw between capitalism and democracy on the one hand, and socialism and authoritarianism on the other, was more labored than convincing.

His reasoning persuaded neither radicals nor conservatives. Lewis Gannett in the *Herald Tribune* complained that the paper's prize columnist had set up a "straw man of 'absolute collectivism' going far beyond what either Hitler or Stalin attempts to practice, and demolishes it with unfair ease. Then, occupying a middle ground felicitously named that of 'free collectivism,' he evades the duties of precise definition." If freedom really rested on an economically secure middle class, and if "compensators" free from public control could really ensure the "method of freedom," why was it, Clifton Fadiman pointedly asked in the *New Yorker,* that "over in England, where according to Mr. Lippmann, they use only the *very best* compensation, Sir Oswald Mosley's army of discontent traitorously gives the lie to Mr. Lippmann's large and comfortable words?"[16]

Events abroad were already crowding Lippmann's efforts to find a middle way. But he believed that in America, at least, that way had been found — so long as the New Deal did not get out of hand.

◄ 25 ►

Times out of Joint

When the times are out of joint some storm the barricades and others retire into a monastery.

— *The Good Society*, 1937

FOR two years Lippmann remained a staunch, though not uncritical, supporter of the New Deal. He was one of FDR's most important journalistic assets, a crucial link between government administrators and the business community. For the moment he was pleased. "The present policy of Roosevelt gives me great satisfaction," he wrote Berenson in January 1935. "It's just about what I have been hoping for a year. . . . The vogue of planning, regimenting and regulating and being generally bureaucratic and officious has passed in Washington and is passing all over the country. There is really from my point of view an amazing intellectual and moral recovery in this country, by which I mean a sloughing off of ideas that characterize extreme deflation and political instability."[1]

With business slowly recovering, conservatives had regained their lost confidence and began resenting the government initiatives they had welcomed during the panic. Hoover toured the country warning that the Constitution was being undermined by a federal erosion of states' rights. Businessmen, demoted from the pantheon of heroes by professors and planners, muttered that FDR harbored dictatorial ambitions. Right-wing Democrats, led by such former party standard-bearers as Al Smith and John W. Davis, and backed by Du Pont money, in 1934 organized the American Liberty League to replace the New Deal with an administration devoted to "free enterprise."

Lippmann thought they were crying wolf too soon. "Business is very much better than the state of mind of the businessman," he wrote Berenson in March 1935 from Florida, where he and Faye were spending the winter at Anna Maria, "and it would be ludicrous if it weren't so sad, to read the financial pages and see production increasing and profits rising while businessmen declare the end of the world is at hand.'' Roosevelt, he reported, ''is amazingly confident, and his political insight has so far proved to be uncanny.''

Through that spring Lippmann continued to take a hopeful attitude toward the New Deal, which he described to his readers as ''a system of free enterprise compensated by government action.'' Speaking to the Boston Chamber of Commerce in May, he urged businessmen not to go into ''irreconcilable opposition all along the line,'' nor to allow ''private prejudices and particular dislikes to carry us to a point where the nation is so torn by factionalism that coherent government becomes impossible.'' At Harvard he denigrated laissez-faire as a doctrine ''preached by men who wish other men to practice it,'' and insisted that ''if we are to have economic liberty we must accept the ancient truth that liberty is not the natural state of man, but the achievement of an organized society.''[2]

His support for the New Deal put Lippmann at odds with a good many of his old friends. John W. Davis, one of the pillars of the Liberty League, told him that FDR was leading the country down the road to communism. ''I am perfectly persuaded that, whether we like it or not,'' Lippmann replied to the man whom he had backed for President in 1924,

responsibility for the successful operation of a nation's economy is now just as much a function of government as is the national defense. Personally I wish it were not the case, for I can see the enormous and perhaps insuperable difficulties, but the tendency seems to me world-wide, cumulative, and irresistible. . . . I should much prefer a world in which governments did not have to attempt so tremendous a task. But I don't think we live in that kind of world any longer.''[3]

When the Supreme Court in May 1935 struck down the NRA as an unconstitutional delegation of power to the President, Lippmann — although he himself had criticized the agency — sent Roosevelt a friendly letter urging him to reexamine other New Deal measures that might suffer a similar fate. A series of votes affirming the major New Deal policies ''would completely answer the people who are saying that the whole New Deal has been shattered, would put an end to all the talk that you are trying to upset the Constitution by indirection, and would put the reactionary Republicans and reactionary Democrats clearly on record once again as to where they stand on the agricultural bill, the securities act, etc, etc,'' he counseled. ''It would be equivalent to asking and obtaining a new vote of confidence from Congress.''[4]

As far as Lippmann was concerned, the NRA's sudden death was a boon in disguise. ''My own view,'' he wrote Hamilton Armstrong, ''is that not only intrinsically but politically the destruction of NRA was

Roosevelt's greatest stroke of luck since 1933'' — one that relieved him of the "embarrassment of trying to enforce codes that were breaking down of their own inherent foolishness."

But instead of reexamining his programs to accommodate the Court's objections, as Lippmann had suggested, FDR boldly moved to extend the New Deal. In the summer of 1935 he sent Congress the Wagner Act, establishing a labor relations board to enforce collective bargaining with unions; the Guffey Act, to set up "little NRA" codes in the coal industry; an extension of the Federal Reserve Act; authority to regulate the utility holding companies; the landmark Social Security Act, to provide old-age assistance; and a sweeping "wealth tax" setting higher brackets and inheritance levies on the rich.

The Hearst press branded the program, particularly the wealth tax, as "essentially communistic," and the Liberty League declared that the President had gone amok. Lippmann, for his part, saw it for what it was — a clever ploy by which FDR hoped to recoup his NRA defeat and outflank critics like Huey Long who were accusing him of ignoring the voiceless poor. The Republicans had so overplayed their hand that Roosevelt "drifted easily into the position of champion of the common man against unreconstructed and unregenerated wealth," Lippmann explained to Armstrong.

Unless another fit of mid-summer madness strikes him, and I don't guarantee that it won't, he is now in the incredibly strong position where in about a month he will have completed the most comprehensive program of reform ever achieved in this country in any administration, and at the same time he is well set for a very substantial business recovery. If he wants to play the cards that are now in his hand, I believe that he can come to the election next autumn with reform and recovery both achieved, with the currency stabilization well in sight.

What the Republicans would have left to complain about under these conditions I can't imagine. The thing that will prevent Roosevelt from achieving that result, I think, is that he is restless and would get bored with his job if he didn't have something big under way, and the idea merely of administering what he has achieved doesn't appeal to him. So instead of digging in for a year, which would be the sensible thing to do, he will probably start a new putsch just when the Republicans badly need an issue.[5]

FDR had good reason to strike out boldly. He was under attack, not only from the Liberty League on his right, but from a hodgepodge of communists, fascists, populists, single-taxers, evangelists, hate-peddlers and aspiring demagogues. At one extreme stood an incipient American fascist party, led by former Wall Street banker and Harvard graduate Lawrence Dennis, and a variety of other fascist groups that promised to save white Protestant America from blacks, communists and Jews.

Among the hate-peddlers none was more virulent than Father Charles Coughlin, the radio priest whose weekly program enraptured forty million Americans. An early supporter of FDR, Coughlin by 1935 was labeling the President an "anti-God" and his program the "Jew Deal." His racist campaign did not disturb the Hearst press, which observed: "Whenever you hear a prominent American called a 'Fascist,' you can usually make up your mind that the man is simply a Loyal Citizen Who Stands Up For Americanism." At the other extreme stood the minuscule American Communist party, its ranks expanded not only by FBI informers but also by those who feared the growing power of Nazism, and who, persuaded by Stalin's 1934 decision to support alliances with liberals and socialists, believed they could be both good Americans and good communists.

Between these two authoritarian groups were a variety of native American causes and crackpot schemes. An elderly California doctor named Francis Townsend, appalled that thrifty retired people like him could lose their homes and savings through no fault of their own, announced his plan to end the depression. He would have the government give everyone over age sixty a pension of $200 a month, with the proviso that he must spend it. Lippmann ridiculed the idea — although it was probably not so absurd as it sounded, for it would have increased demand, thereby stimulating investment and production. The good doctor shrugged off the complaint by noting that his plan was "too simple to be comprehended by great minds like Mr. Lippmann's." Ridiculous or not, the plan attracted five million followers who, in Townsend's words, "believe in the Bible, believe in God, cheer when the flag passes by."

If the elderly saw hope in Townsend, millions of other Californians were rallying to the muckraker-novelist Upton Sinclair. With his program for a statewide net of socialist communes and for the return of idle farmlands and factories to the unemployed, Sinclair had swept the gubernatorial primaries with more votes than his eight Democratic rivals combined. He won the endorsement of such people as Theodore Dreiser, Archibald MacLeish, Morris Ernst and Clarence Darrow. He also evoked panic among conservatives. The major Los Angeles papers refused to print a word of his EPIC (End Poverty in California) program. The Democratic machine disavowed him, MGM produced a fake newsreel showing an Okie invasion if he were elected, Republicans forged documents to prove him a communist, and a corporate-financed public-relations campaign overwhelmed him with lies and innuendos.

Far more serious than any fringe group, crackpot or romantic idealist was the challenge posed to FDR by the Louisiana Kingfish, Huey Long. A backwoods prodigy born in a shack, Long finished Tulane Law School in eight months, and was elected governor of Louisiana in 1928 at age thirty-five. Defying the oil monopoly and the big property owners, he exempted the poor from general property taxes, abolished the poll tax, built twenty-five hundred miles of paved roads in a state that had had only thirty, provided free textbooks and school buses for children, and treated blacks as equals. While pushing through his populist program he intimidated the legislature and the courts, and turned the entire state into his personal fiefdom. In 1930 he had himself elected to the Senate. Although an early supporter of FDR, he soon turned against the President, taunted him for refusing to nationalize the banks and expropriate large fortunes, and, as part of his own presidential campaign, launched his "Share Our Wealth" program designed to make "every man a king." A seductive demagogue, Long struck a powerful response from the poor. A secret White House poll in 1935 showed that a third-party ticket headed by Long could siphon off four million votes from the Democrats and throw the 1936 election into the House.

Lippmann had met the Kingfish only once, when in the spring of 1933 he wandered unannounced one afternoon into Lippmann's office at the *Herald Tribune*. "I was just passing through and wanted to see what you looked like," he explained. His curiosity assuaged, the senator and his bodyguards went on their way down the hall.

In Huey Long's demagoguery Lippmann saw the outlines of an incipient American fascism. Long's appeal to the voters led Lippmann — his mind fixed on what had already happened in Italy and Germany — to question publicly "whether men must acquiesce in the overthrow of democracy if the dictator can obtain the support of the majority of the voters." Soviet Russia, fascist Italy, and Nazi Germany had shown the fragility of democratic institutions. Many were saying "it can't happen here" less frequently and with less conviction. "Free institutions," Lippmann wrote in an ardent appeal for restraints on majoritarianism and, *in extremis,* on free speech,

are not the property of any majority. They do not confer upon majorities unlimited powers. The rights of the majority are limited rights. They are limited not only by the Constitutional guarantees but by the moral principle implied in those guarantees. That principle is that men may not use the facilities of liberty to impair them. No man may invoke a right in order to destroy it.

The right of free speech belongs to those who are willing to preserve it. The right to elect belongs to those who mean to transmit that right to their successors. The rule of the majority is morally justified only if another majority is free to reverse that rule. To hold any other view than this is to believe that democracy alone, of all forms of government, is prohibited by its own principles from insuring its own preservation.[6]

Never an absolutist on free speech, Lippmann was deeply concerned about the appeal of totalitarian movements abroad and at home. Like his idol Holmes, he took the "clear and present danger" yardstick for measuring a tolerable level of unpopular or inflammatory speech. During the twenties he had defended the right of anarchists, communists and the Ku Klux Klan to demonstrate. "It is the minority which needs protection, even though that minority may consist of persons who, if they had the power, would destroy the liberty which as a minority they invoke," he had written in 1928. "We are prepared to defend the legal right of anyone to say anything he chooses short of actual incitement to a breach of law." But in the mid-thirties, he took a considerably more restricted view. A free nation could tolerate feeble communist and fascist societies "as long as it is certain that they have no hope of success," he now wrote. "But once they cease to be debating societies . . . they present a challenge which it is suicidal to ignore. . . . It is a betrayal of liberty not to defend it with all the power that free men possess."[7]

By this time he was willing to restrict speech on even narrower grounds than "clear and present danger." When the U.S. government in 1935 deported John Strachey, a British Marxist, for giving lectures in which he equated capitalism with fascism, Lippmann had no objections. Since fascists and communists do not preserve civil liberties for their opponents, he wrote, "their advocates cannot ask for the use of the facilities of liberty as a matter of right." When a reader complained that free speech should be protected because truth conquers falsehood, he replied that history usually showed the opposite. "I am perfectly willing to let Mr. Strachey argue about the evils of free speech, but I am not willing to let him organize a movement using physical force to prevent me from arguing back," Lippmann wrote. "Free speech in actual life depends upon certain rules of the game, and the most important of them is a willingness to continue free speech. When men appear who say that they will argue with you once, and then never permit you to argue with them again, they render the rules of the game unworkable and their force has to be met with equivalent force."[8]

The fear of European totalitarianism and domestic extremism that led him to take a restricted view of free speech also began to color his view of the New Deal. He stressed the distinction between recovery from the depression and reform of the social structure. In early July 1935, with the launching of the reform programs of the Second New Deal, he began complaining that "an overpowering desire for the improvement of society leads to policies which put too great a strain on institutions." Ten days later, when FDR tried to push through the "wealth tax" without congressional hearings or debate, he suggested that the President was becoming the "victim of tempting delusions that invariably beset men who have played a great role on the world's stage." By late August he was asking whether FDR was substituting "some kind of planned collectivism'' for a free economy and declared that "blanket powers and blank checks are an abdication by Congress, a usurpation by the Executive.'' Would the President return to the people "the extraordinary powers they granted him in a moment of grave danger for the single purpose of achieving recovery,'' or would they have to take those powers from him? For Lippmann the issue was clear: "The people gave Mr. Roosevelt a sword to lead them in a particular battle. That battle is over, and that sword should now be returned to its scabbard.''

Despite his qualms over FDR's intentions, Lippmann had not yet cut his ties with the White House. "I am deeply troubled about Roosevelt personally,'' he wrote his friend Edward Sheldon in early September 1935.

He has a good heart, though not a great one. And he certainly hasn't a great mind. And his best virtues — which are sensitiveness and zeal and courage — are not qualities with which to withstand the corroding effect of authority.

I don't know what to think of him, whether to believe that he is a man of the moment and that he has served his purpose and cannot adjust himself to new circumstances. I am afraid that he is not thoroughly matured and that he is more suited to a crisis than to longer efforts.

I think all this will be disclosed in the next four or five months before Congress convenes, and for me the test will be whether he recognizes that the particular crisis that made him great is no longer with us.[9]

Several days later Lippmann went to Hyde Park to have lunch with Roosevelt. The President took him on a tour of the estate in a specially built Ford he could operate entirely with his hands. After a visit with the formidable Sarah Roosevelt they went to FDR's quarters. As they talked about the tax bill and the extension of the New Deal into a full-scale reform program, the President seemed on edge. When his wife came in and interjected her own comments — which were quite irrelevant in the context — he barked at her: "Oh, Eleanor, shut up. You never understand these things anyway.''

At the time Lippmann shared FDR's irritation with Eleanor, but later changed his opinion considerably. "My feeling about Eleanor Roosevelt has grown from thinking that she was rather a silly woman to thinking she's one of the great people of our time,'' he later told an interviewer. "But in the first days she was something of a goose about public affairs. . . . The way Eleanor buzzed around sort of like a fly annoying you was fairly characteristic of her then.''

When Lippmann left Hyde Park late that afternoon of September 16, he felt that he and FDR had had a meeting of minds, that, as he recorded in his engagement book, the President was ready to take a "breathing space'' on the New Deal. "He does seem to have made up his mind that he has gone as far as he should go with the reforms that require important mental adjustments by the people,'' he reported to Sheldon. Then he added, in a curious repetition of the remark he had made about Hoover several years earlier, that he thought the President was "dangerously tired, and that if he were confronted with very difficult decisions at this moment his judgment couldn't be depended upon and that it might lead to a severe nervous breakdown. . . . He will be put to a very severe test in the next few months because the attack on him will be relentless, and I don't know whether his inner resources are sufficient to meet it.''[10]

FDR's inner resources proved more than sufficient, but Lippmann's patience did not. From his uneasy perch on the fence he clambered over into the opposition. By the end of the year, convinced that FDR was intent on pushing through his reform package, he began contemplating ways of dumping the President. "Since last spring I have begun to feel that a situation might develop . . . where it would be absolutely necessary not to re-elect Mr. Roosevelt,'' he told Newton Baker. FDR's problem, he elaborated in the same vein to Harvard professor Arthur Holcombe, was that he had decided to "burn his bridges so far as the conservative Democrats go and to stake his chances for re-election on an appeal to sectional and class feeling.'' As a result an opposition group was forming that was "entirely inchoate, without principle, and without common conviction.'' Such a coalition of reactionaries and extremists would "appeal to passion and primitive emotions, and if they win, which I think not at all unlikely, we may very well face a period of severe reaction.'' What, he asked, was a "sober and critical friend of the New Deal'' to do?

Sober and critical, yes. A friend, hardly. In a fanciful effort to block FDR's renomination he found common cause with such anti–New Deal Democrats as Lewis Douglas and Dean Acheson. "It looks more and more like the real fight will have to be made within the Democratic party,'' he told Douglas, who had resigned as budget director over the gold-standard issue, "though I haven't closed my mind to the possibility of crossing the line.'' Not that the Republicans held much appeal. "There is very little over there to invite men who think as we do, and there are really more people who take our view of things still in the Democratic party than elsewhere.'' The problem, he told the mining magnate, was that "we are in danger of getting into a situation where no effective opposition to the collectivist side of the New Deal will be made,'' and that the country, "for lack of an effective opposition, won't be made to see the things that are really bad.''[11]

While Lippmann hoped he would not have to switch over to the Republicans, he was drawing a fine line with men like Douglas, who were not easily distinguishable from their Republican colleagues on Wall Street. A "wealth tax,'' let alone a reshuffling of the economic deck, seemed unsound and even immoral to such men. Thus when the Republicans nominated Governor Alf Landon of Kansas, a former Bull Mooser, many had no trouble switching their party allegiance.

Lippmann, too, easily swallowed his misgivings, although he would have no part of the Roosevelt-hating Liberty League. "I am pretty clear in my mind that I am going where you're going," he told Douglas in late July 1936. This was not based on any enthusiasm for the Kansas governor, whom he had met a few times. Landon, he later admitted privately, "was a dull and uninspired fellow, an ignorant man. He was of no account; it was a protest vote from my point of view." To his readers he justified his choice by claiming that Landon would unite all Republicans and most Democrats, while FDR's election would mean one-man rule.

Even so, he was not happy about his decision. "For me the choice of this campaign is a choice of evils," he wrote a friend in late September, "although not of intolerable evils, because I do not regard Landon and Roosevelt as sufficiently far apart to make the choice between them catastrophic." By supporting the Republicans, he reasoned, "I can do more to check Roosevelt at the points where I think he needs to be pushed than by getting on the band wagon." [12]

Despite the virtually unanimous opposition of business leaders and the nation's press, and the pollsters' predictions of a Landon triumph, FDR was unbeatable. Huey Long's assassination in the fall of 1935 had removed his most serious challenger. The Townsend movement, which controlled the legislatures of seven western states, fell apart in the summer of 1936 when its manager was charged with embezzlement of members' contributions. Father Coughlin had frightened a good many sympathizers by his hate-filled diatribes and his fascistic armed brigade. Roosevelt forged a powerful coalition of western farmers, urban workers, the Solid South, and the old progressives. He even retained the support of such financiers as Russell Leffingwell, A. P. Giannini of the Bank of America, and Thomas Watson of IBM.

Although Lippmann realized that Roosevelt was unbeatable, he urged his readers to vote against him since "nothing could be worse for Mr. Roosevelt, or for the Democratic party, or for the country, than another Democratic landslide." On election day he dutifully marked his ballot for Landon. "I too voted with a sick heart," he wrote Learned Hand, "feeling very much like the boy who tried to stop the tides by sticking his finger in the dike. Only, as I remember it, he did stop the tides." That tide triumphantly rolled FDR back into office. He swept every state but Vermont and Maine and brought with him an even greater Democratic majority into Congress. Lippmann consoled himself with the conviction, as he told Grenville Clark, that "the truth behind the nonsense which the Republicans talked is a seed planted in the public mind which will grow into something capable of checking Roosevelt."[13]

FDR, however, was already being checked, not by the public, but by the Supreme Court. After grudgingly going along with Roosevelt's emergency measures, a conservative majority on the Court had by 1935 dug in its heels against any effort at reform. With numbing regularity it struck down every congressional attempt to regulate agriculture, mining, manufacturing, and labor conditions, then, to drive home the point, denied the same powers to the states. The Court, as Al Smith crowed triumphantly at a Liberty League dinner, was "throwing out the alphabet three letters at a time." Given the Court's mood and record, the newly passed Wagner labor act and the Social Security Act seemed sure to be invalidated.

Viewing his landslide victory as a popular mandate, FDR moved to defy the obstructive power of the Court. In early February 1937, just two weeks after his second inaugural, he tackled the holiest of American political institutions by asking Congress, as part of a judicial reform bill, to allow him to expand the Court by adding one new judge, up to a maximum of six, for every current judge over the age of seventy. This transparent scheme to ensure a pro–New Deal majority touched off a furor far greater than anything FDR had contemplated. Conservatives denounced him for trying to destroy the Constitution and set up a personal dictatorship. Even many Democrats abandoned him. Congress balked at the plan, and conservatives at last had a real issue with which to bludgeon the President. They made the most of it.

Lippmann led the pack. In uncharacteristically intemperate language he accused the President of being "drunk with power" and of plotting nothing less than a "bloodless coup d'etat which strikes a deadly blow at the vital center of constitutional democracy." The Court plan, combined with the hostility Lippmann felt toward a powerful central government, triggered a reaction totally out of proportion to anything FDR had proposed or contemplated. Starting in February 1937, and for the next five months, Lippmann devoted thirty-seven columns — half those he wrote during the entire period — to denunciations of FDR's Court plan. He even warned that if the bill passed Congress an emboldened Roosevelt would next try to muzzle the press. The administration, he charged, was "proposing to create the necessary precedent, to establish the political framework for, and to destroy the safeguards against, a dictator."[14]

Yet Lippmann was also eager to demonstrate that it was the threat to the Court's integrity he opposed, not FDR's economic reform program. He admitted that the Court was unduly rigid in its approach to economic problems, and even suggested amending the commerce clause of the Constitution. That clause, interpreted in ways that its original authors had never intended, was the instrument by which the conservative Court had struck down New Deal social legislation.[15] In the fight over the Court bill Lippmann was able to move back into the liberal mainstream. Even many who counted themselves New Dealers were appalled by what they considered an assault on the system of checks and balances. Oswald Garrison Villard told a Senate committee that FDR's scheme "opens the way for dictatorship."

Interestingly, one of those who did not speak out against the Court bill was Felix Frankfurter. Only three years earlier the Harvard law professor had written that "to enlarge the size of the Court would be self-defeating." But when FDR actually made the move, Frankfurter kept a discreet silence, and even privately urged him not to compromise. William O. Douglas, then on the Securities and Exchange Commission, and not one of Frankfurter's admirers, called his silence "duplicitous." Even an admiring biographer admitted that Frankfurter's loyalty to FDR "exacted a price in distortion of judgment and of the scholar's role."[16] That loyalty did not go unrecognized. A year and a half later FDR appointed the helpful Frankfurter to the Supreme Court.

Lippmann was not surprised by the professor's silence. He had often enough seen the less admirable side of Frankfurter's character: his blatant flattery of Roosevelt, his attraction to those who could be useful to him and his indifference to those who could not. Ever since FDR took office Frankfurter had bombarded the President with letters of advice and cloying encomiums. A periodic visitor to the White House, where he indulged FDR's high opinion of himself, he served as an unofficial employment bureau for the New Deal, staffing the agencies with his brightest and most loyal law students.

By the time the Supreme Court issue erupted, Lippmann and Frankfurter had for four years been on very bad terms — for reasons to be discussed later. "I found it impossible to be an independent journalist and a good friend of Frankfurter's at the same time," Lippmann later said. "He was too demanding. If you gave him a chance, you'd get such a deluge of letters, and the passion would be so heavy, and the intimation was always that if you didn't agree with him there was some moral turpitude about it."

Their relations were not improved when in June 1936 Lippmann gave a speech in which he made a pointed reference to the corrupting effects of government on intellectuals. "Members of the university faculties have a particular obligation not to tie themselves to, nor to involve themselves in, the ambitions and pursuits of the politicians," he declared. "Once they engage themselves that way, they cease to be disinterested men, being committed by their ambitions and their sympathies. They cease to be scholars because they are no longer disinterested, and having lost their own independence, they impair the independence of the university to which they belong.'' It was, he added, "impossible to mix the pursuit of knowledge and the exercise of political power, and those who have tried it turn out to be very bad politicians or they cease to be scholars. . . . If the professors try to run the government, we shall end by having the government run the professors.''

Lippmann mentioned no names, nor needed to. His speech "set me thinking," Learned Hand wrote Lessing Rosenthal. "I rather think that he had in mind among others, Felix, and whether it was or not, it will not improve relations between the two distinguished gentlemen.'' Relations, in fact, remained cold long after the passing of the Roosevelt administration, and did not improve greatly until the 1950s when Washington art collectors Marjorie and Duncan Phillips, at the urging of critic Kenneth Clark, brought them together at a dinner party.[17]

Although FDR's assault on the Court had set off more of a furor than he had counted on, it also had a desirable effect on the honorable justices. Within six weeks after Roosevelt unveiled his plan, Justice Owen Roberts abandoned the reactionary "Four Horsemen" and joined the three progressives — Brandeis, Stone and Cardozo — and the moderate chief justice, Charles Evans Hughes, to form a new majority. In an abrupt about-face the Court upheld the Wagner Act, which had seemed doomed to invalidation, and a Washington state-minimum-wage law virtually identical to the one it had earlier struck down in New York. The Court had got the message, and the signal was clear that New Deal legislation would receive a more favorable hearing. FDR discreetly withdrew his bill. Having lost the battle, he won the war. Within three years, as a result of retirement, he was able to name five of his own men to the bench: Hugo Black, Stanley Reed, William O. Douglas, Frank Murphy and Frankfurter. The Republican Court became a New Deal Court.

The fight, however, marked Lippmann as an implacable reactionary in the eyes of New Deal loyalists. He was attacked in the left-wing press as an economic royalist and a mouthpiece for Wall Street. So bitter were the attacks that during the height of the Court battle he felt obliged to defend himself. "I have supported almost every New Deal measure, some with misgivings, some with qualifications, but none the less almost all of them," he reminded his readers. He had supported emergency powers in 1933, the gold policy, the Agricultural Adjustment Administration as a two-year experiment, the NRA as an emergency measure, the reciprocal tariff act, the securities and stock exchange acts, the TVA, the soil conservation act, Social Security, and collective bargaining with independent unions. What made him turn against the New Deal in 1935, he explained, was FDR's desire to make the NRA permanent, and his attempt to shove the tax bill through Congress without hearing or debate. Rather than criticize the reform measures themselves, he focused his attack on what he called "personal government by devious methods." Denying that he considered FDR a potential dictator, he instead predicted that as a result of his methods there would be a "fierce reaction against Mr. Roosevelt and the whole liberal and progressive movement."

While technically his self-defense was well taken, his qualifications about some measures and his later repudiation of others were such that no New Dealer could have considered him a true believer. Yet his fears that a cavalier attitude toward the law might play into the hands of an indigenous American fascism were deeply felt and not without some chilly European examples. Unlike many liberals, who were willing to swallow some very questionable means to achieve morally desirable ends, he abhorred dictatorship and demagoguery so much that he was less sensitive than he might have been to economic injustice and inequality. He saw the New Deal, not as a touch-and-go process of experimentation, but as a step toward authoritarianism. "The road of progress toward the collectivist state I distrust and dislike with all my heart," he wrote his friend Lucie Rosen as the Court fight was coming to a head. "The people are selling their liberties, which they have taken for granted, and of course they never earned them." [18]

His concern over the spread of totalitarianism and his exaggerated view of the New Deal were cogently laid out in the book he had been working on for several years and published in the fall of 1937. *The Good Society*, as he explained to his editor, Ellery Sedgwick, was really two books in one: the first "a sustained indictment of all the implications of the authoritarian and collectivist state," the second "a vindication and a reconstruction of liberalism." [19] A book that tried to do too many things, it suffered from a split personality.

In the first part of the book Lippmann looked at European totalitarianism and concluded that its guiding principle was collectivism — itself a disorder of nineteenth-century liberalism. All collectivism — communism, fascism, even the New Deal — was rooted in the concept of economic planning, and therefore dangerous. Gone was the distinction he had made only three years earlier in the Godkin Lectures between "free" and "absolute" collectivism. Now they were indistinguishable. Both leftist and rightist totalitarians shared the pernicious notion that an economy could be consciously planned. Planning, Lippmann charged, was incompatible with human freedom; it could not be achieved without regimentation. Thus it was contradictory to speak of a planned democratic society: if it were democratic, the plan would ultimately break down; if the plan were to work, democracy would have to be replaced by coercion. "To the liberal mind the notion that men can authoritatively plan and impose a good life upon a great society is ignorant, impertinent and pretentious."

Having equated all forms of planning with collectivism, and having then obliterated distinctions between forms and degrees of collectivism, he could lump together the New Deal with fascist Italy, Nazi Germany, and communist Russia. Fortunately, according to his analysis, they were all doomed to an early demise, since collectivism was the mark of a primitive society. Modern industrial nations required a division of labor and a market economy, neither of which was possible under regimentation. Totalitarian societies, demanding absolute obedience of their citizens, would never be able to elicit the support of resourceful men. Such states were doomed to atrophy and failure.

This was a curious argument; in effect, a kind of distorted Marxism, as historian John Diggins has pointed out. It rested on the assumption that the economic aspect of collectivism induced totalitarianism, that totalitarianism was inextricably linked to war, and that such regimes, whether communist or fascist, would be destroyed by their own inner contradictions. His analysis assumed that economic collectivism produced totalitarianism, when, in fact, it was the other way around. Both German and Italian fascism and Soviet communism imposed corporatism and collectivism; they did not emerge from it.[20]

Lippmann got his sequence backward because, like the Austrian economist Friedrich von Hayek — to whom he gave a sweeping bow in the text — he wanted to believe that political and economic liberalism went hand in hand. Eight years earlier, in *A Preface to Morals*, he had argued that fascism and Bolshevism resulted from the "breakdown of a somewhat primitive form of capitalism"; they could take root in Russia or Italy, he argued in 1929, but not in industrially advanced countries like Germany, Austria or Japan.[21] By 1937, in the face of what had happened in Germany, he had modified his argument to put the blame for totalitarianism on collectivism rather than on industrial backwardness. But he still sought the cause in economics. Not understanding the emotional appeal of either fascism or communism, he argued, almost as though trying to persuade himself, that these doctrines were based on a false conception of human nature. In truth the appeal of authoritarianism reflected a side of human nature he was loath to recognize.

The second half of *The Good Society*, what he called an "Agenda of Liberalism," was designed to show that opposition to collectivism did not make him an enemy of social progress. There he drew up a blueprint — including public works, social insurance, income equalization through taxation, countercyclical spending, and the abolition of monopolies — that was not very different from what FDR had been trying to achieve with the New Deal. The result was perplexing. The book seemed intellectually split down the middle: half classic laissez-faire, half welfare-state liberalism.

Later Lippmann explained that *The Good Society* was intended as a plea for social reform through a system of law rather than by administrative fiat. "There are two ways of doing this thing. One leads to a centralized state administered by government office holders, and the other leads to a system of law in which corporations and everything else are accountable and can be sued, and the judiciary decides the issues. It is the second which I proposed as the change by which liberalism could disembarrass itself of *laissez faire* and still remain liberal." The theory depended on the judiciary, "but I didn't want and do not much care for an elected judiciary," he explained. "If you can't elect good enough men to be trusted with the appointment of judges, then you're not going to elect good enough men to govern the country anyway."²²

This was a good explanation, but not a satisfying one. In arguing against economic planning Lippmann was not only contradicting the argument he had made many years earlier in *Drift and Mastery,* but, more important, ignoring the central question of economic power. To have basic economic decisions made by private corporations rather than by public authorities does not mean the society will be more free — let alone more just. It merely ensures that the maximization of profits will be the primary criterion in allocating and distributing resources. Not wanting to be considered an economic royalist, or even a laissez-faire liberal, Lippmann tacked on an "agenda of liberalism" that contradicted the intellectual argument he had made in the first half of the book.

In effect *The Good Society* reveals not so much Lippmann's conservatism as his confusion. Distrusting the collectivist state with all his heart, as he said, and frightened by what was happening in Europe, he found a theory that seemed to link the two, and made that borrowed theory the central thesis of his argument. The trouble was that the theory could not stand the weight he put on it — the weight of his own doubts about the kind of laissez-faire that Hayek preached. Lippmann's great talent lay in analysis and explanation, not in theorizing. When he went wrong, it was in trying to impose an intellectual grid — especially, as in this case, a borrowed one — on situations about which he had conflicting feelings.

While Lippmann's fears of totalitarianism were certainly understandable at a time when European democracy was under assault from fascism and communism, they led him to see diabolical method in the New Deal where there was only haphazard experiment. He seriously misread the New Deal, viewing it as revolutionary rather than reformist, and its halfhearted efforts at planning as a giant step toward what he called, in G. K. Chesterton's phrase, the Servile State. There was much to criticize in the New Deal, with its backhanded corporatism, as exemplified by the NRA, and its piecemeal reformism. In retrospect its programs seem hardly earthshaking and its recovery measures ineffective. The United States didn't fully emerge from the depression until

World War II. Among its partisans the New Deal raised hopes it never fulfilled, and among its adversaries, fears that never materialized. Lippmann's criticisms of the New Deal seem, decades later, not reactionary so much as overwrought.

The critical response to *The Good Society* reflected the political passions of the day. "Those who regard Mr. Lippmann as a renegade are ready with their jeers before his book has left the press," wrote Ralph Barton Perry. "Those who approve him as one who, having sowed his wild oats in youth has in his mature years become a reliable defender of the existing order, are prepared in advance to cheer him." Anti–New Dealers found him admirably sound. Catholic writers were particularly pleased by his discovery of the "higher law" — a fact that led gossip columnist Walter Winchell to predict, erroneously, to "Mr. and Mrs. America" that Lippmann was about to enter the Church.

Those who came to jeer had a field day. Corliss Lamont, Thomas's dissident son who had been to Russia and liked what he saw, labeled his father's friend "the intellectual hope of American finance capitalism." John Dewey thought the book gave "encouragement and practical support to reactionaries" and described it as "liberalism in a vacuum." Lewis Mumford, referring to Lippmann's comments about the inflexibility of economic planning, declared that his "confusions and contradictions are so massive as to be intellectually discreditable in a man of his attainments." Edmund Wilson, who still looked on Stalin's regime as one "designed to make exploitation impossible," found ample confirmation for his view that Lippmann was little more than the tool of Wall Street.[23]

Yet Lippmann had a far better sense than his left-wing critics of the realities of Soviet-style communism — as many of them later came to realize. When John Dewey, appalled by Stalin's purge trials of the late 1930s, charged that Leon Trotsky was the victim of a conspiracy organized by those who had betrayed the principles of Lenin's revolution, Lippmann retorted that Trotsky was in truth the victim of the principles he had helped impose on Russia. The shocking purge trials could help emancipate Western liberals "from the dominion that Russian communism has exercised over their minds in the past twenty years," he wrote. "To have realized that the present Russian government repudiates the principles of truth and justice must, I think, eventually lead to the realization that this is not a corruption of, but the inevitable consequences of, the ideals of communism."[24] To describe Lippmann as an economic conservative is to miss the point. He was a liberal deeply repelled by all forms of totalitarianism, whether of the Right or of the Left.

In retrospect *The Good Society* can be seen as more than simply an attack on the New Deal. Even though Lippmann at times seemed to forget the distinction he had drawn only three years earlier between "free" and "absolute" collectivism, he nonetheless accepted the public need for economic security. "Liberal remedies require the liquidation of some, and the modification of many, vested rights," he wrote. "The status quo cannot be reformed and yet preserved as it is." He was willing to liquidate a good many of those vested rights. Where he went wrong was in trying to find an economic basis for the spread of totalitarianism. He focused on "collectivism" because the only alternative would have been to look to human nature. He was, with his Enlightenment faith in human reason, so wedded to the belief that man had an unquenchable will to be free that he could never admit the emotional appeal of mass movements with their mass loyalties and mass enthusiasms. *The Good Society* was, as Henry Steele Commager later wrote, "an effort to find not so much a compromise as an escape, and the escape was into that eighteenth century past which had laid so firmly, as Lippmann felt, the foundations of true liberalism." [25]

The theory he applied in *The Good Society* turned out to be faulty, and later he would discard it. But the very contradictions of the book — its fear of centralization, along with its acceptance of the welfare state — are, in a sense, a mark of its honesty. It would have been easy for Lippmann to have become either an ardent partisan of the New Deal, with the contempt many New Dealers felt toward constitutional restraints on their power, or else an inflexible right-wing obstructionist. Instead, he sought a middle way, however untidy and even confused it sometimes seemed.

Like most compromises, his was full of inconsistencies and loopholes. Yet it was an honest effort at a time when some men were joining communist cell groups, others were donning black shirts, and some of his own friends were hissing Roosevelt at Liberty League gatherings. "In epochs like our own, when society is at odds with the conditions of its existence, discontent drives some to active violence and some to asceticism and other-worldliness," Lippmann wrote of this period that left him so agitated and perplexed. "When the times are out of joint some storm the barricades and others retire into a monastery. Thus it is that the greater part of the literature of our time is in one mood a literature of revolution and in another, often completely fused with it, a literature of escape."

If Lippmann was not the kind of man to revolt, neither would he try to escape into a monastery. He worked diligently at his trade, often, as he confessed in his introduction to *The Good Society,* "writing about critical events with no better guide than the hastily improvised generalizations of a rather bewildered man." [26] The troubling pace of events abroad intensified that bewilderment.

◄ 26 ►

Treading Water

As long as Europe prepares for war, America must
prepare for neutrality.

— "Today and Tomorrow," May 17, 1934

A^T a time when most Americans looked inward, Lippmann kept one
eye abroad. For all his disillusion with Wilson, he remained an ardent internationalist. All during the twenties he had earnestly supported
naval disarmament, cooperation with the World Court and the League of
Nations, reduction of European war debts and German reparations, and
a league-centered force to keep the peace. "The effort to abolish war
can come to nothing," he had written in 1929 of the Kellogg-Briand
Pact, "unless there are created international institutions, an international
public opinion, an international conscience which will play the part
which war has always played in human affairs." The world needed a
"political equivalent of war" so that necessary changes in the status quo
could be achieved peacefully. The key was arms reduction and international arbitration of disputes. An agreement by the great powers to trim
their navies, he wrote on the opening of the London disarmament conference in 1930, would be a "stupendous vindication" of Woodrow
Wilson's dream.[1]

But by the mid-1930s he had lost his faith in disarmament and the
league. The rise of Hitler, the growing militancy of Japan, and the failure of the league to deal with aggressive fascism shattered his Wilsonian
idealism. American security, he became convinced, lay in a strong navy
and a hands-off policy toward both Europe and Asia. No longer believing that it was possible to avoid war by arousing what he had called an
"international conscience," he urged the United States to stay neutral
and pursue an "effective pacifism" based on military strength.

Like virtually everyone else, he overestimated the will of France, the
strength of Britain, the willingness of Mussolini to defy Hitler. Above
all, he would not go against the powerful tide of American isolationism.

This lent a strange inconsistency to his arguments. He wanted cooperation with the European democracies, yet shied away from alliance. He stressed the importance of European stability, but would not support any commitment to sustain it. Despite his low esteem for the public's wisdom, he was no less confused than the average man. Rather than taking a consistent attitude toward neutrality, he approached and withdrew in response to events.

At the beginning of the thirties he still believed in "collective security" based on the peacekeeping powers of the league. He thought it would be an "absolute disaster," he told Russell Leffingwell in October 1931, if the league failed to impose sanctions on Japan for invading Manchuria. Although the Chinese may have been "morally guilty of the original provocation" by defying Japan's treaty rights in the territory, he explained, cooperation with the league was the least dangerous way of dealing with the situation — "that is to say, least dangerous from the point of view of drawing Japanese fire upon ourselves." The Manchurian incident was not just an Asian problem, but a test case in Europe of whether or not there was organized security in the world. "I'd be willing to take enormous risks to meet that test successfully," he declared.[2]

The European members of the league were not so willing. They wanted to hold Japan to the Nine Power Treaty of 1922, which guaranteed the territorial integrity of China; yet they feared provoking Tokyo. In a diplomacy of infinite subtlety that satisfied their consciences without threatening their interests, they solemnly invoked the Kellogg-Briand Pact and called for Japan to withdraw from Manchuria, but refused to impose the economic sanctions that might have forced such a withdrawal. They had made their gesture to "collective security"; they would do no more.

The league's failure to take effective action put the pressure on Washington. Secretary of State Henry Stimson, an old Asia hand, former governor-general of the Philippines, and a firm believer in an Open Door for American economic and political interests in China, wanted the United States to impose its own sanctions upon Japan. President Hoover, realizing there was no public support for such action and seeing no vital American interest in Manchuria, said no. Lippmann, who knew that the European members of the league were not going to inconvenience themselves seriously over events in Asia, saw another way of putting pressure on Tokyo. Since the league would not impose economic sanctions, why not at least refuse to recognize the fruits of Japan's aggression in Manchuria pending a settlement? He decided to test his idea. "Japan seeks a recognition of her treaty claims in Manchuria," he wrote in his column in late November 1931, keeping his Washington audience very much in mind. "She cannot get it from puppet governments. She can get it only by an internationally recognized legal procedure."[3]

He waited a few days for the suggestion to sink in, then went to Washington to talk over the idea with Hoover and Stimson. They seemed amenable, and so he pressed home the plan. It would be wrong "even to consider the coercion of Japan," he told his readers on his return from the capital. A settlement lay in giving Japan "her full rights, but no new advantages as a result of the adventure." With the public alerted, Lippmann again approached Stimson. If the United States could persuade the Europeans to withhold recognition of Japan's claims in Manchuria, "we could then afford to sit and wait, leaving Japan indicted and on the defensive." Such an action, he added optimistically, might even encourage Japanese democrats to subdue the militarists who had gained the upper hand after the intervention. "Since all resort to force is barred to us," such halfway measures as withdrawing ambassadors should be avoided, he wrote the secretary, "for gestures of that kind are effective only if the nation making them is prepared to go to the limit if necessary."[4]

Here lay the origins of the "nonrecognition" policy, or Stimson Doctrine, as it was called a few weeks later when the secretary of state formally embraced it. Early in January 1932 Stimson told China and Japan that the United States would not recognize any agreement that impaired American rights under the Open Door policy or that violated the Kellogg-Briand Pact. Thus Hoover's caution, Lippmann's suggestions, and the precedent set by William Jennings Bryan in 1915 in refusing to recognize Japan's draconian Twenty-one Demands on China overcame Stimson's desire for a confrontation with Tokyo.

Indifferent to either moral pressure or nonrecognition, the Japanese generals proceeded with their mopping-up operations, and within a few weeks controlled Manchuria. Lippmann bowed to the inevitable. "I believe it's too late now to stop Japan," he wrote Learned Hand in February 1932, while reposing in Berenson's villa outside Florence after a disheartening round of interviews in London, Paris and Geneva. With the prestige of the Japanese military caste at stake, sanctions would merely prod the generals into a desperate gamble. "There are many belligerent pacifists at Geneva wanting another war to end war and another war to make Asia safe for democracy," he reported of his visit to the league's headquarters. "I don't believe in them, and much as I hate to see the impotence of the League demonstrated so spectacularly, I can see no other course which doesn't involve terrific bloodshed and economic exhaustion." He underlined this point to his readers. It would be "sheer folly" to provoke the Japanese into a war, he insisted in the column he wrote that morning at I Tatti, and foolish for the United States even to withdraw its ambassador from Tokyo or to impose a "one-sided embargo" on arms.[5]

Lippmann's hands-off policy in Asia applied to Europe as well. The stunning rise of Hitler frightened him, but did not change his conviction that Nazi Germany was primarily a European problem. Before Hitler's attainment of power in January 1933, Lippmann had shared the widespread belief that the Germans had been badly treated at Versailles when they were saddled with ruinous reparations and stripped of their colonies. He had urged that reparations be pruned, and that the Polish Corridor and some African colonies be returned to Germany. Yet once Hitler became chancellor Lippmann opposed any territorial concessions to the Nazis. "There can be no revision of frontiers except by force, and therefore, the cause of peace is now identical with the maintenance of the status quo," he wrote in April 1933, only three months after Hitler came to power. "The only kind of peace now possible in Europe is one which freezes the existing frontiers." It was too late "to suggest that the cause of peace can be advanced by placing another human being under the heel of the Nazis."[6]

Lippmann had no illusions about Hitler's territorial ambitions or his ruthlessness. Yet he showed a surprising insensitivity to the human dimension of the Nazi threat, especially as it concerned the Jews. Not only did Lippmann go to great lengths to avoid any hint of partiality, as did many other Jews in public life, he ignored Jewish concerns altogether. He approached the Nazi phenomenon as a foreign-policy analyst, not as a Jew. That was his job and he performed it with scrupulous objectivity. But in this case he carried his celebrated "disinterestedness" rather far.[7]

Shortly after the infamous night in May 1933 when the Nazis made funeral pyres of books written by Jews and "liberals," Lippmann warned in his column that Hitler was preparing for war. Only two things held the Nazis in check: the French army and the persecution of the Jews. Repression of the Jews, he explained, "by satisfying the lust of the Nazis who feel they must conquer somebody and the cupidity of those Nazis who want jobs, is a kind of lightning rod which protects Europe." While the analysis was not illogical, the idea that a pogrom against the Jews offered protection to Europe was, to say the least, peculiar coming from a Jewish writer.

Just in case he was unaware of what he was saying, Frankfurter sent him a sharp note of distress over the "implications of attitude and feeling behind that piece." This note followed on the heels of a complaint Frankfurter had made two weeks earlier when he heard — mistakenly, as it turned out — that Lippmann was to speak at a dinner honoring A. Lawrence Lowell on his retirement. Frankfurter told Lippmann that Harvard's president, with whom he had tangled over the "Jewish quota" issue, was little more than a "refined Adolf Hitler."[8] Lippmann, thinking that Frankfurter had gone a bit overboard, tried to mollify his friend. A week later Lippmann again wrote about the Nazis. This time he analyzed a seemingly conciliatory speech in which Hitler claimed that Germany would not try to press its claims by force. Eager to believe that the dictator was now willing to moderate his revolutionary nationalism, to temper what Lippmann called the "ruthless injustice of the treatment meted out to the German Jews" and the barbarism of the bookburning orgy, he described the speech as a "genuinely statesmanlike address" that offered "evidence of good faith." Then he continued in phrases as remarkable in retrospect as they must have seemed at the time: "We have heard once more, through the fog and the din, the hysteria and the animal passions of a great revolution, the authentic voice of a genuinely civilized people." By this he meant that the Germans should not be judged simply by Nazi rantings or treated as permanent outcasts. Urging his readers to recognize the "dual nature of man," he maintained that "to deny today that Germany can speak as a civilized power because uncivilized things are being done in Germany is in itself a deep form of intolerance." People were capable of both good and evil. Would it be fair, he asked, to judge the French by the Terror, Protestantism by the Ku Klux Klan, the Catholic Church by the Inquisition? Or for that matter, "the Jews by their parvenus?"[9]

Read as a whole the column was less shocking than some of its parts. The Nazis had been in power less than three months and no one could have been certain that Hitler's reassurances were totally insincere. Rearmament, aggression and genocide still lay down the road. Lippmann was not alone in fearing that Hitler would only increase his strident demands if the German people were made pariahs. What Lippmann himself was later to call the "ice-cold evil" of the Nazis was far less apparent than their hysterical nationalism.

Yet there was something deeply offensive about the column. To draw attention to Germany's grievances against the Versailles treaty did not require him to describe Hitler's speech as "statesmanlike" and the "authentic voice of a genuinely civilized people." Nor did his homily about the dual nature of man require him to link the French Terror, Ku Klux Klan lynchings, and Nazi brutality with the flashiness of Jewish "parvenus." This was to suggest that Hitler was guilty of little more than bad manners. It even implied that perhaps the Jews had brought their persecution on themselves — just as a dozen years earlier Lippmann had suggested that Jews were to blame for anti-Semitism. Such analogies, however careless, are deeply revealing. In his tortured analysis Lippmann went beyond his celebrated disinterestedness to an invidious comparison that shocked a good many readers.

No one was more disturbed than Frankfurter. Rather than dashing off an aggrieved letter, his usual practice, he kept an ominous silence. For more than three and a half years he maintained that silence. Never once during that time did he write or phone Lippmann. Nor did Lippmann, if he was puzzled by his friend's silence, try to find out the reasons for it. Not until the fall of 1936 did Frankfurter finally write to Lippmann.

Only recently I learned that you expressed regret that I should have "dropped" you because we happened to differ politically. Since to no friendship have I ever given more concern than to my relations with you, it is perhaps just as well — if you are correctly reported — that I ought not to leave you under a misapprehension.

Surely identity of views has not been the basis of my friendships, and disagreement in opinion has for me never been a barrier to intimacy. I should like to remind you that in the early days of this Administration we had an extended correspondence, in which our disagreement touched not your hostility to the New Deal but your complete acceptance of it. Your later questionings of the New Deal no more affected my feelings than did your earlier unquestioning support of it.

But when, in your column of May 19, 1933, you described Hitler as "the authentic voice of a genuinely civilized people" — I'm not unaware of the context — and likened the Reich's cold pogroms and the expulsion of some of its greatest minds and finest spirits, merely because their grandmothers or their wives happened to be Jewesses, to the fact that "Jews have their *parvenus*," then something inside of me snapped.

Rather than being apologetic, Lippmann reacted indignantly. "I was away when your letter reached me and I was so astounded by its contents that I have refrained from answering it till I had returned and could re-read my article," he replied.

I was prepared to believe that I might unintentionally have laid myself open to the interpretation you put upon it. But on re-reading it I am satisfied that the manner in which you have torn phrases from their context and ignored the historical circumstances in which the article was written, is inexcusable. It betrays a lack of personal good will which is emphasized by the fact that instead of trying to clear up the misunderstanding at the time, you have waited nearly four years to raise the question. It is now too late to raise it.[10]

Lippmann may have been sincere in believing that only a "lack of personal good will" could have led Frankfurter to interpret the column as he did. The "cold pogroms," after all, had not yet begun in 1933, and the Nuremberg Laws, which reduced Jews to second-class citizens, were not issued until September 1935. Yet the Nazis had practiced discrimination against the Jews from the moment they took power, and anyone who had looked at *Mein Kampf* could hardly have had any illusions about Hitler's attitude toward the Jews. Lippmann was obviously embarrassed by the column, for he kept it out of the collection of his pieces published two years later. Even after persecution of the Jews became severe, he counseled against an official American protest, which would merely, he reasoned, "undermine fatally the position of the liberal opposition in the persecuting countries." Instead, he favored an unofficial complaint "made with dignity and restraint."[11]

Lippmann's argument at least had the virtue of consistency. Since the United States was not going to join the European democracies in restraining Hitler, since it would not come to the aid of Czechoslovakia or Poland, or even France, if they were attacked, Americans could try to avoid hypocrisy. "Not only have we no right to intervene even by exerting moral pressure," Lippmann wrote in December 1933, "but it is against our best interest to do so." When the U.S. Senate a few months later set up a committee under isolationist Gerald P. Nye to investigate the munitions industry and determine whether it helped instigate wars, Lippmann made no attempt to go against the prevailing neutralist sentiment. "As long as Europe prepares for war," he advised in May 1934, "America must prepare for neutrality."[12]

A trip to Europe with Faye and the Armstrongs in the fall of 1934, punctuated by a month's sightseeing in Egypt and a long visit with Berenson at I Tatti, reinforced his pessimism. Hitler had ruthlessly eliminated all opposition and was blatantly rearming. Paris had been shaken by fascist-led riots, and King Alexander of Yugoslavia, who had come to France to negotiate an alliance against Hitler, had been assassinated in Marseilles. The growing militancy of the Fascist parties in Britain and France, the incapacity of parliaments to deal with social unrest, the failure of the European democracies to unite against Nazism reinforced Lippmann's conviction that Europe was headed for war. Yet he still did not urge an American alliance with the democracies. Public opinion was not ready for such a move, and he was not yet certain that it was absolutely necessary.

His old Wilsonianism, which he seemed to doff and don over the years according to his mood, once again lost its appeal. When the U.S. Senate early in 1935 turned down American participation in the World Court he treated it as a matter of little consequence. The people had spoken, he said, and "those who believe in democratic government must, of course, abide by the results." Not always had he accepted the judgment of the people with such equanimity. Having long preached internationalism, he had now lost his enthusiasm. "I am not an isolationist and never have been one," he explained to the editor of the *Texas Weekly* when the Senate voted down participation. "But I have always recognized that there are times when political cooperation with Europe is possible and there are times when it is not. The present moment is one when it is not, in my opinion. But the judgment of what is possible and what is not possible should not be identified with the feeling of what one might like to see."[13]

Nonetheless, Lippmann felt he owed his readers an explanation of his stand. A few days after the Senate vote he wrote a reflective column recounting how his wartime idealism had turned to disillusion, how in the twenties he had thought that peace could be ensured by joining the court and cooperating with the league, and how the refusal of the Europeans to impose sanctions on Japan after Manchuria persuaded him that the league was "a European institution and not a world institution, and that it must stand or fall on its power to contrive a peace in Europe." The United States should not contribute to that pacification effort. "My sympathies are with the powers aligned with the status quo," he explained,

not because they are for the status quo, but because they are free nations and are resisting the spread of tyrannical government. But sympathies do not make a national policy, and a cold appraisal of the American interest, which is, I take it, to protect our own development as a free nation, seems to me to lead to the conclusion that we can contribute nothing substantially to the pacification of Europe today, that vague commitments would only mislead Europe and mask the realities. For the time being, therefore, our best course is to stand apart from European policies.[14]

Since the United States was not willing to confront the menace of an aggressive Germany in Europe, where its own primary interests were threatened, any involvement in the Far East was foolishly gratuitous. Japan's seizure of Manchuria and Outer Mongolia was not primarily an American problem. "In the whole great region in which Japan claims predominance we have no particular political interests of our own to protect," Lippmann wrote in the spring of 1934. "If there is to be any concerted action, let the policy emanate from the governments which have a definite stake in the area." By this he meant Russia, China and the European powers. The United States should stay in the background, avoid political intervention, and defend only its minimal rights. "This is not a policy of scuttle," he reiterated nine months later. "It is a policy of realism in which the United States would decline to take the sole responsibility and bear the whole onus of dealing with Japanese expansion."[15]

That expansion was taking the Japanese army into northern China, but in Europe the situation was even more alarming. In March 1935 Hitler denounced the provisions of the Versailles treaty forbidding rearmament and began conscripting an army. Rather than challenge Hitler's defiance, Britain, France, and Italy contented themselves with verbal protests. At the same time Mussolini, dreaming of an African empire, prepared to invade Ethiopia from Italian-controlled Eritrea and Somaliland. The Russians, fearing a Hitler-Mussolini alliance and another German aggression, called on Britain and France to join them in an antifascist coalition. The democracies, governed by conservatives who feared communism as much as they did fascism, thought they could buy off Hitler with concessions. They spurned the Soviet approach.

Lippmann was convinced that any effective European alliance had to include Russia. Having for years urged American recognition of the Soviet government — which FDR finally achieved in 1933, with a helping hand from Wall Street — he now wanted to use Russian strength to contain Hitler. This meant a settlement of the border dispute with Japan over Manchuria, which was tying down Russian troops in Asia. To bring Japan "into the circle of more or less contented powers" would be worth a "very large price," Lippmann told Newton Baker in April 1935. "Every step that is taken to improve the relations between Russia and Japan is a step towards the strengthening of the forces of peace in Europe." That same day he wrote Cordell Hull, urging the secretary of state to consider "with the utmost seriousness" conversations with Japan to achieve a "full settlement of the outstanding issues." Such an effort, he suggested, might turn Japan from being an "agitator in the family of nations to a defender of the existing international order."

The developing crisis in Europe made an accommodation with Japan a matter of urgency. Lippmann was now willing to bury the nonrecognition doctrine he had helped formulate. "It would be a mistake to proceed on the assumptions of the Wilson era at a time when those assumptions have no reality," he wrote Hugh Wilson, American envoy to Switzerland. "We have got to swallow the Stimson doctrine. We have got to give up the idea that we're the guardians of China, and I think that we have got to limit and redefine the area of our interests in the Pacific."

Lippmann had given up all hope of collective security and placed his faith in armed neutrality. As Mussolini's legions massed for their assault on Ethiopia he rejected an appeal to the Kellogg-Briand Pact, noting that the treaty was "merely a pious resolution that each signer may interpret as he sees fit." Since the United States had never joined the league, it had no right to judge the Ethiopian dispute. The European victors were to blame for the breakdown of the postwar system, he charged. Instead of defending their spoils, or else establishing a more equitable system, they merely proclaimed the sanctity of the Versailles settlement. They had "neither the will to defend it with force nor the wisdom to save it by concessions. In a world of rebellious great powers they have tried to combine the advantages of imperialism with the conveniences of pacifism." It was too late for a world community where aggression would be restrained by an international conscience and channeled by international law. All that, he disconsolately declared, was now "a shattered dream."[16]

A few months later, in October 1935, Mussolini launched his long-threatened attack on Ethiopia. Roosevelt, acting under the recently passed Neutrality Act, ordered an embargo on arms to Italy and a moral embargo on raw materials. The league branded Italy the aggressor and voted economic sanctions. But Britain and France, thinking they could use the Duce against Hitler, did not want to antagonize him. Thus they continued to ship Middle East oil to Italy and to allow Italian ships — loaded with troops and weapons — to use the Suez Canal en route to Ethiopia. Lippmann, although critical of Mussolini's aggression, feared that the Neutrality Act and FDR's "moral embargo" might rebound against the British and the French. "The thing that troubles me most is the effort to have us 'cooperate' in the sanctions by preventing or discouraging the sale of raw materials to Italy," he wrote Hamilton Armstrong in November. "Suppose that Britain and France are involved in a really first-class war with Germany. The precedent we now establish would then become a vital handicap to them and would nullify their sea power."

Accepting the prevailing consensus that Americans must stand aloof from European affairs, Lippmann argued only for the freedom to change course at some future time. "The policy of the United States is to remain unentangled and free," he declared in January 1936, in one of his periodic radio broadcasts. "Let us follow that policy. Let us remain unentangled and free. Let us make no alliances. Let us make no commitments. By the same token let us pass no laws which will bind the future, tie the hands of the government, deprive it of its freedom, cause it to be entangled in a statute based on what somebody at this moment thinks the government ought to do in the future."[17] If Lippmann had a clear sense of what should be done, he was not conveying it. If he felt strongly opposed to isolationism, he was unwilling to challenge popular sentiment directly. He went along with the tide, justifying his own lack of firm conviction by the obduracy of the public. He was biding his time, hoping that Japan would show restraint, that the Europeans would contain Hitler, that the United States could sit on the sidelines without fear or danger.

While America burrowed into neutrality, Europe lunged toward war. In March 1936 Hitler denounced the Locarno treaties and sent his troops into the demilitarized Rhineland. Britain and France, paralyzed by timidity and vacillation, refused to challenge him. In October Mussolini confounded his admirers — who thought he could be used as a bulwark against Hitler — by reaching an accord with Germany. In November Japan linked hands with Germany in the so-called Anti-Comintern Pact.

The fascist nations were now joined for an assault on the tenuous balance of power.

Mussolini's Ethiopian adventure was a preview. The European test came in Spain in July 1936 when right-wing army officers rebelled against the legally elected popular-front government. The European powers pledged themselves to nonintervention and imposed a naval blockade of Spain. The British and French refused to sell arms to the Spanish republic, and the United States declared a "moral embargo" even though the Neutrality Act of 1936 did not technically apply to civil wars. Mussolini expressed his gratitude to the democracies for their "impartiality." He then proceeded to send planes and troops to aid the fascist-led rebels under General Francisco Franco. Hitler dispatched the Luftwaffe into action in a test run for the coming battle for Europe. The Spanish government, abandoned by the Western democracies, turned to Russia for help. Despite strong sentiment in the United States for the beleaguered republic, the administration, fearful of alienating the pro-Franco Catholic Church, beat back congressional efforts to lift the arms embargo.

Lippmann urged a hands-off policy. He praised the British and the French for remaining neutral, maintained that neither the legally elected Loyalists nor the Fascists were "able or fit to organize a government," and insisted even after Mussolini's intervention that the Spaniards "must work out their own salvation until a favorable moment presents itself for conciliation." He supported the administration's refusal to lift the arms embargo, and then, as the foundering Spanish republic turned to Moscow for supplies, pointed out that it had "steadily degenerated into a proletarian dictatorship under foreign guidance."

Like FDR and Hull, like the British, like the popular-front government in France, he was less interested in saving Spanish democracy than in quarantining the conflict. "What is going on in Spain is horrible," he wrote as the republic foundered under the assault of Franco's army, Mussolini's legions, and Hitler's air force, "but it is nothing to the horror that will engulf all of Europe if Great Britain and France do not succeed in confining the war to the Spanish peninsula." More from wishful thinking than from evidence he thought London and Paris could arrange a "simple and disinterested" truce that would be "very difficult" for the Fascists to reject.

The civil war in Spain aroused passions, divided families, defined loyalties, and spawned a literature of social protest and engagement. For many it was not a political conflict, but a moral contest between good and evil. Lippmann never saw it that way. When the American Newspaper Guild, which he had joined when Heywood Broun organized it in 1933, endorsed the Loyalist cause — along with FDR's Court plan —

Lippmann told the guild's secretary he would not pay his dues and offered to resign. A professional organization, he wrote, had no right to take political positions on behalf of its members. The complaint, however well taken, showed how detached he was from that particular political cause. "I never took a passionate, partisan interest in the Spanish civil war," he later said privately. "I feared it as a thing which was going to start a European war. . . . My hope was that it could be quieted, pacified, rather than exacerbated. I thought the non-intervention program was critical and futile, but I didn't concern myself with it. My mind works like a spotlight on things, and it wasn't one of the things that I was interested in at that time." [18]

What interested him about Spain was not the struggle of the democratic Left against fascism, which ultimately became one of the communist-led Left against fascism, but rather that it seemed to be a preview of the coming European war. The prospect of such a war — one in which America might not be able to escape involvement — made the continuing quarrel with Japan in the Pacific all the more dangerous a distraction. The "vital interests of Japan and the United States do not conflict," he announced in December 1936. A war between the two countries would be a "monstrous and useless blunder." Since America's primary interests lay in Europe, not Asia, it would be a "very opportune moment for the United States to withdraw gracefully from its Far Eastern entanglements." It could, he counseled, "with a perfectly good conscience" allow the fate of Asia to be worked out among the powers most concerned: China, Russia and Japan. "It would be idiotic to become embroiled in that struggle, and we can well afford to say plainly that the Chinese must defend their own country, and that we have no political interests whatever in Asia." [19] If this meant Japanese hegemony over China, so be it. Unlike those conservatives who were isolationist toward Europe and interventionist in the Pacific, Lippmann wanted to pull out of Asia so that the United States would be free to protect its crucial interests in Europe.

There remained the touchy matter of the Philippines. The United States, in a mood of "manifest destiny" and imperial expansion, had seized the islands from Spain in 1898. Within a year it had demanded an "open door" for American trade and influence in China. With the concurrent acquisition of the Hawaiian Islands, it had, without any serious public or congressional debate ever having taken place, become a Pacific power. Missionaries and traders flooded into China and the Philippines, burdening the United States with a responsibility toward those lands that few had ever even thought of assuming. Under the logic of the Open Door — which declared that Americans should have equal rights in China with all others — the United States acquired an interest in China's territorial integrity.

The time had come, Lippmann argued, to disavow that false and dangerous obligation. The United States was not the protector of China and had no vital interest in the Philippines. "The islands are a strategic trap in which we should be caught and held impotent for years," he maintained. That being the case, the only sensible policy was to withdraw. If the Philippines had to be defended, he argued a bit disingenuously, "they can be defended better from Singapore, Hawaii and Alaska than in Manila."[20] In other words, they were not worth defending at all. So much for the Open Door and Theodore Roosevelt's dream of a Pacific empire. Lippmann's sweeping disavowal of responsibility for the Philippines perfectly reflected his view of the nation's priorities. Europe was a crucial interest, Asia a troublesome involvement. The "blue water" strategy he had learned long ago from Alfred Thayer Mahan left him with a rule he held to all his life: the United States Navy should project American power in the Pacific, but the United States must never be drawn into military conflict on the Asian mainland.

Lippmann's argument for withdrawal from Asia and neutrality toward Europe rested on the assumption that the Atlantic would not fall under control of a hostile power. The British fleet was the guarantor of America's self-imposed isolation from Europe's affairs. Germany's threat to Britain's naval supremacy had inspired his strategic argument for American intervention in the European war in 1917. What he had then called the "defense of the Atlantic world" was the prevention of German mastery of the Continent and of the sea-lanes. Now, twenty years later, that threat had arisen again.

If Britain lost control of Atlantic waters, Lippmann wrote in a somber essay for Hamilton Armstrong's magazine, "all that is familiar and taken for granted, like the air we breathe, would suddenly be drastically altered." The implication was clear: Americans could remain neutral "only so long as we feel that there is no fatal challenge to the central power which makes for order in our world." There was no realistic alternative to alliance with Britain. "In the final test, no matter what we wish now or now believe, though collaboration with Britain and her allies is difficult and often irritating, we shall protect that connection because in no other way can we fulfill our destiny."[21] The argument that Lippmann had invoked twenty years earlier for defending the Atlantic world now became the rationale for reexamining the shibboleth of neutrality.

That summer and fall of 1937 the pace of events quickened dangerously. The French government of Léon Blum collapsed, and with it the popular-front alliance including Socialists and Communists; Japan launched its drive to wrench away China's five northern provinces; Mussolini formally joined the anti-Comintern Pact; the Nazis stepped up their agitation against Czechoslovakia for return of the Sudetenland; Congress expanded the Neutrality Act; and FDR's trial-balloon speech for peace-loving nations to join together to "quarantine the aggressors" was shot down by Congress and the press. Lippmann returned from two months on the Continent heavy with pessimism. "I came away from Europe with the feeling that . . . the Western democracies were amazingly complacent, distracted, easy-going and wishful," he wrote in October 1937. "If the democracies *are* decadent, then the future of the Old World is once more in the hands of the warrior castes, and the civilian era, which began with the Renaissance, is concluded."

Germany and Japan, it was clear, would respect the West "only in the degree to which they are convinced that there are definite points at which the Western powers really mean to stand absolutely and to fight totally." The rush of events that summer and fall dispelled his hopes for a negotiated settlement. Unlike appeasers on both sides of the Channel and the Atlantic, he did not believe that the European crisis was a misunderstanding, or that it could be resolved by succumbing to Hitler's demands. Earlier than most he recognized that Hitler's position depended, "not upon receiving tangible benefits by grace of his opponents, but upon taking things by the exercise of his own power. . . . He cannot be placated by gifts; he must appear to conquer what he seeks."[22]

His analysis was uncompromising. Yet for all its cogency it lacked prescription. He knew what was wrong; he did not know what to do about it. He understood that there could be no peace through concessions, and that the democracies had to be willing to fight in order to avoid war. But he was not willing to go even so far as FDR in cooperating with Britain and France to "quarantine the aggressors." The logic of everything he had written about the European crisis dictated that the United States should abandon neutrality and forge a defense alliance with Britain and France. That alone might have prevented the aggression being planned in Berlin, and might have brought Russia into the balance against Hitler.

However, he was still unwilling to follow through on the implication of his own analysis. "There is no use pretending to deny that the three fascist powers have obtained the initiative in world affairs, and that with great skill and daring they are pressing home the advantage," he wrote in November 1937 in the wake of the Anti-Comintern Pact. "The fascist powers, though potentially weaker than the rest of us, are in fact stronger, because they have the will to fight for what they want and we do not have it." Yet he shrank from the logical conclusion. "This is not said in order to suggest even indirectly and by implication that there should be a military alliance to oppose this world-wide aggression," he underlined. "As things stand now, I do not see how anyone can responsibly favor so desperately dangerous a remedy." Nor did he have an alternative. "For my own part I honestly do not know what I think should be done," he confessed. "I know only that there is accumulating evidence to show that, as the liberal powers retreat, the aggression becomes more intense and that there is increasing reason to fear that if the liberal powers do not stand together they will fall separately."[23]

The truth was not that Lippmann, as he confessed, did not honestly know what he thought should be done. He knew very well. Everything he wrote over the preceding months revealed that he knew. But he was not yet willing to say it, not willing to race too far ahead of the pack. He would have had to launch a major campaign to educate his public, perhaps even face ostracism and rejection as an extremist. There were times when he might have risked that, times in the future when he would risk it. But that summer and fall of 1937 was not a period when he could devote his full attention to the political crisis in Europe. He was facing a crisis of his own.

◂ 27 ▸

A Gate Unlocked

I am like a man who has seen in his mind's eye the glories of this existence, but had wandered through endless corridors, looking into empty rooms, till suddenly you unlocked the gate to the real world.

— To Helen Byrne Armstrong, May 29, 1937

DESPITE the great success of his column, and the handsome income of some sixty thousand dollars a year it provided, Lippmann had grown a bit bored with it. Ever since he started "Today and Tomorrow" he had been besieged by other offers: in 1931 to do a column for *Harper's* or be editor of the *Washington Post;* in 1933 to take over the *American Mercury;* in 1934 to be a professor at Columbia, Amherst or Harvard, or to become a salaried columnist for the *Atlantic.* He was often tempted, but he never acted. Despite his complaints about the tyranny of newspaper work, he could never quite bring himself to break with the column. In the spring of 1936 he told Ellery Sedgwick, editor of the *Atlantic,* that he would "certainly stop" his newspaper column by the fall and accept the magazine's offer to do ten long articles a year for a thousand dollars each. But there was always a good reason to delay a little longer: a European trip to make, a political crisis to contend with. The column was demanding, but it offered him an influence and a position of power he could never have enjoyed as a magazine writer or professor.[1]

Still, he was restless. Dissatisfaction with the column was part of a larger disaffection in his life. He had written *A Preface to Morals,* with its prescription of "disinterestedness," partly as an effort to deal with that disaffection. On an intellectual level it had worked, yet the formula left him with an anxiety he could not clearly identify or remedy. Much of the problem was his marriage. He and Faye had never had much in common, and when the romance cooled after a few years there was little left but habit and convenience. Many people like him had discovered, as he wrote more revealingly than he intended in *A Preface to Morals,* that "as the glow of passion cools, it is discovered that no instinctive and preordained affinity is present." His solution there was to call it quits or to make the best of it. Hating confrontation, not sure that anything else would be better, he chose the latter.

For the most part he and Faye had a perfectly acceptable marriage — no worse, it seemed, than those of many people they knew. And there were compensations: for her, the winters at the beach house in Florida, the summers at Wading River, the comfortable town house on East 61st Street, the Broadway first nights, the fashionable restaurants, the famous people Walter attracted and was attracted by; for him, the work he enjoyed, the encounters with the movers and shakers of the world, the yearly trips to Europe, the recognition and the applause. Their life was not a bad one, as such things went. There seemed no pressing reason to change it.

Many people, in a marriage gone stale, cast their eye around for an easy dalliance. Certainly enough of their friends had — often with one another. Faye, still attractive and ready for that "dancing playmate" Mabel Dodge years earlier had wished she would have chosen instead of Walter, did not seem unattainable. Walter was. He had never been the kind of person to enter lightly into affairs — or enter into them at all. Though he had many opportunities, even guarded invitations from mutual friends, he had resolutely turned them aside. Infidelity was not part of his moral code. Children might have drawn them together, but they never had any of their own. Walter, at the beginning, had expressed anxieties about the problems facing offspring of a "mixed" marriage.[2] And when Jane Mather entered their lives she became the child they did not, and need not, have.

Not strongly absorbed in his marriage, Walter found comfort in his work and his friends. Of all the people in his social world, none did he enjoy so much as Hamilton Fish Armstrong and his wife, Helen. They had been good friends since the late 1920s. They dined together in the city, visited each other's country homes, and even toured Egypt and the Mediterranean in 1934. Walter and Hamilton sat together at meetings of the Council on Foreign Relations, lunched once or twice a week at the Century Club, spoke on the phone nearly every day. Their friends referred to them as Damon and Pythias. Armstrong was a most engaging man, with a charm and a personal warmth that Lippmann found highly appealing. He also basked in the admiration Armstrong showered upon him. Isaiah Bowman, who had resented Lippmann ever since their days together at the Inquiry, described Armstrong's attitude as "adulatory." "I have never seen anyone so crazy over another individual, so reliant upon another's judgment, and so foolish in his admiration," said the geographer.[3]

Lippmann enjoyed the company of both Armstrongs. Often he would drop by their house on East 81st Street after dinner — especially when Faye was away at Wading River or in Florida. He had developed a particular attraction to Helen. She had a shrewd intelligence, a sharp tongue and a quick wit. Unlike Faye, she was interested in politics, and asked questions that engaged his mind and activated his talent for exposition. Neither blond nor buxom like Faye, she was slight and well proportioned in the way, as Lippmann once told her, of an adolescent boy. She had short brown hair, darting eyes, a quick temper, and an inquisitive mind that ranged voraciously over politics, literature and the arts.

From her Catholic father and her early training in a convent she had developed an intolerance of priests and religion, and, having left the Church early, never returned. Her education had been expensive and protective, first at a Catholic convent in Belgium, then at the austerely Episcopal and eminently proper Miss Chapin's school in Manhattan. Like most women of her generation and social class, she did not go to college. Nor did it occur to her to have a career. In 1918, after finishing school, she went to Paris as a nurse's aide with the Red Cross. There she was placed under the watchful supervision of her family's friend Edith Wharton. Following the armistice she married Hamilton Armstrong, a young journalist from a distinguished New York family, in the Church of St. Roch in Paris.

Helen was brought up with a taste for comfort and a sense of public service. Her father, James Byrne, had become very wealthy as legal counsel for General Motors, and provided his family with a life appropriate to their station: a town house in Manhattan, an estate on Long Island, and a spacious summer "camp" at Bar Harbor, Maine. Each child received a sizable trust fund and could live very comfortably from the income. A public-spirited man, James Byrne served as president of the New York Bar Association, and was the first Catholic elected to the Harvard Board of Overseers. Loyal to the university, he endowed the chair in administrative law that for many years was held, coincidentally, by Felix Frankfurter.

Helen was her father's daughter in many ways: she had the Irish temper, the charm, the gift for talk, the high-strung sensibility. She also knew how to listen, which made it easy for essentially shy men like Walter to talk to her. At a dinner party in January 1937 — having known each other for more than a dozen years — they fell into a conversation, quite without his knowing how, about love and marriage. Nothing personal was said. But as they separated, Helen touched his hand lightly and looked into his eyes — a gesture he did not find easy to forget. A few days later he went to Florida to put the finishing touches on *The Good Society*. Though he did not return to New York until April, he spent a good deal of time thinking about Helen.

As soon as he got back to New York — Faye had decided to stay on at Anna Maria for a few weeks — he dropped by to see the Armstrongs and to show them the just-completed draft of his book. During the next two weeks he dined with them several times, and lunched separately with Hamilton at the Century Club. One afternoon in May Hamilton called to say he had to attend a meeting that night at the council. He hated to leave Helen alone; would Walter mind taking her somewhere to dinner? This seemed natural among old friends. But Walter was uncharacteristically nervous as he picked up the phone and asked Helen to dine with him that evening. Wanting the occasion to be festive, he suggested the Rainbow Room, the fashionable skyscraper restaurant in the newly constructed tower of Rockefeller Center.

Helen welcomed the chance to see Walter alone. She found him attractive, as many women did. With his solid build kept in good shape by regular workouts at the gym, abundant dark hair, violet-flecked hazel eyes, and prominent cheekbones, he was a most desirable companion. His international fame added to that desirability. Though Helen, like many women, had long found Walter attractive, she had always thought him too serious for dalliance. Yet since reading *A Preface to Morals* she had realized that he was far more complex than the high-minded and slightly aloof man who wrote earnestly of political affairs. The book spoke powerfully of love and marriage and fortitude. When he wrote that "love endures only when the lovers love many things together, and not merely each other," he seemed to be speaking an undeniable truth. And his plea for a mature disinterestedness seemed to illuminate a path for surmounting life's tribulations.

Helen had always assumed that Walter was the supremely adjusted man he described in his book. But as they sat together on that warm spring night early in May, the lights of the city forming a jeweled backdrop through the wall of windows, the orchestra playing melodies from the new Fred Astaire–Ginger Rogers film, *Shall We Dance?*, she found a different man from the one she had known. The music, the lights, the dancing couples floating past their table, the metallic brilliance of the art deco furnishings lent a strange excitement to the evening. Helen, for once, seemed oddly subdued. Each seemed to be waiting for the other to take the lead.

Finally Walter took the initiative. Seized by an overwhelming compulsion he began to talk of his feelings, and in a way he had never spoken to anyone. He began by telling her of his doubts about the value of the column and his temptation to quit daily journalism to write articles and books, and perhaps to teach. Feeling that she understood what he was trying to say, he lowered the barriers he had so carefully erected over the years. He spoke of the space he felt between himself and other people and how — although he had never had any desire to be psycho-analyzed — this probably came from a childhood in which he felt un-loved. For the first time in his life he revealed his loneliness in growing up in a household of uncaring servants and of parents too preoccupied with themselves to give him much attention. He told her how neglected he felt and unloved by his mother, and of how this feeling had put a "chill" on his emotions and made him afraid of getting really close to anyone.

He also talked about his life with Faye: how their marriage had become a habit, devoid of passion or even of real affection; how lonely he had felt with Faye, even lonelier than being by himself; and how this made him pull back yet further into himself. His prescription for "disin-terestedness" in *A Preface to Morals* was, he revealed, in part a way of dealing with that unhappiness. When he had written that "lovers who have nothing to do but love each other are not really to be envied; love and nothing else very soon is nothing else," he had been referring to his own marriage.

Helen was not obtuse. For years she had sensed the tension between Walter and Faye, wondered what it was that had brought them together. Of course she had never said anything. Now she realized that he had torn down a barrier in speaking to her this way; he was treating her not as a confidante but as a woman. He was bringing her into his life. A sense of complicity had grown between them. He had allowed her into an inner sanctum where no one had ever before penetrated. He wanted something from her without quite knowing what it was. She did know. She listened gravely, asked questions delicately, softly laid her hand on his. They drank more wine than they were used to. They danced on the crowded floor, holding each other closer than they ever had before. By the time they left the Rainbow Room and he hailed a cab on Fifth Ave-nue to take her home, they both knew that something irrevocable had happened.[4]

The next day he called her. They arranged to have dinner again on a night when Hamilton would be away — this time not in a fashionable spot where he was easily recognized, but in a quiet neighborhood res-taurant. The relationship had changed. Their meeting had an air of con-spiracy. During the twenty years of his marriage nothing like this had ever happened. Now for the first time in his life the rules seemed sus-pended. They held hands during dinner and spoke wonderingly of the strange thing happening to them. When they left the restaurant they went to a hotel.

They met again the next day, and the next. With their affair fully launched, Helen decided they should have a place to meet freely whenever they could get away. She rented a small furnished apartment on East 95th Street, in the block between Park and Madison. They met there nearly every afternoon. The location was hardly prudent for a tryst. Many of their friends lived nearby. They could easily have been recognized. One evening at a dinner party, having come straight from a rendezvous with Walter at the flat, Helen was astounded when Learned Hand, who was seated next to her, turned and said, "How well do you know Walter Lippmann?" Taken aback, she mumbled a noncommittal, "Why, you know we've been friends with the Lippmanns for years." "Well, my dear," Hand said, his bushy black eyebrows setting off his piercing glance, "I'm sure then you realize that despite his impassive front he is really a highly sensitive person. Don't do anything to hurt him." Her face flushing, Helen protested she was hardly in a position to hurt him. The judge smiled and changed the subject.

Their secret posed enormous complications for their public lives. After a late afternoon rendezvous Helen and Walter would often find themselves, with their respective spouses, at the same gathering in the evening, trying to strike the right tone of casualness, to remember how they had spoken before everything had changed. Dissembling was not easy for him. But he learned. He even learned how to put on a front with Hamilton, whom he continued to see nearly as often as he saw Helen. It pained him to have to deceive his friend, but he was too caught up in the excitement of the liaison to brood about it.

Time seemed very short. Helen was leaving for Europe at the end of May with Hamilton and their thirteen-year-old daughter, Gregor. The Armstrongs were to spend June in Dubrovnik, July in Slovenia and the Austrian Alps. Hamilton would return to New York at the end of July, Helen and Gregor would stay on another month with friends in the south of France. The prospect of a three-month separation seemed intolerable to Walter. Their furtive love affair had begun only a few weeks earlier.

Helen was not a woman to be defeated by geography or inconvenience. Why not meet in Europe in August, she suggested. She could leave Gregor with friends and join him at some discreet place. He could arrange to come on a short fact-gathering trip without Faye. Caught up in the excitement of a clandestine meeting, made bold and a bit reckless by his happiness, he eagerly assented. Helen consulted her well-thumbed Guide Bleu and discovered the perfect spot: the cathedral town of Bourges in the Cher, about two hundred kilometers south of Paris. They would meet there on August 17.

Although both had plunged wildly into this affair, they hadn't given any serious thought to dissolving their marriages. Never having known anything like this, Walter was as disturbed as he was excited by their affair. For the first time since he had courted Faye twenty years earlier, he was in love. This was hardly an adolescent infatuation. He was forty-seven, Helen was forty. He brought to her the passions of a man whose emotional life had long been frozen. He gave himself to Helen completely, as he had never given himself to anyone before. The thought of being separated from her, if only for two months, made him fear for the survival of what they had discovered. "It is very quiet here in my study where I have worked for so many years," he wrote Helen on the eve of her departure for Europe.

But all the familiar things are strange. I know what I have always shrunk from knowing, that though I am in these places I am not of them, and that, but for what you and I have found together, all that was left was to learn to be resigned.

One can go a long way in solitude, but alas one can go no further alone. Those things which make us more than animated and quarrelsome vegetables cannot be had by the imagination alone. . . .

As for myself, I think you know that I am like a man who has seen in his mind's eye the glories of this existence, but had wandered through endless corridors, looking into empty rooms, till suddenly you unlocked the gate to the real world.

. . . Oh my dear, I could go on forever saying always the same thing in a thousand different ways. For you bind me and release me both, you bind me with the sweet grace of your love and release me with the sweet grace of your love, and release me like an old bird who has flown wild, been long caged and is once again on the wing.[5]

As the weeks passed and her absence weighed more heavily, his letters became more ardent and concerned about the future. From the pine forests of Mount Desert Island in Maine, where he and Faye had gone to visit their friends Thomas and Gretchen (Gay) Finletter at the end of June, he wrote Helen that they must never again accept "arrangements that separate us so cruelly." "I know that we have only one fear — the fear of hurting others," he added a few days later, "and . . . I know too that somehow we must and shall at last, go openly together hand in hand."[6]

Helen responded in kind to these veiled promises, encouraging his hope that they could build something more permanent. "When I sailed off on the *Normandie*," she wrote him from Dubrovnik, addressing her letters to the Century Club in order to circumvent both Faye and his secretary,

if you had asked me what my idea of my future was, I think I should have answered vaguely that perhaps at the end of three or four years, when Gregor would be going off to college, perhaps then we might begin that painfully complicated breaking of all those ties which had bound us so long.

We had come together so short a time before, we were so happy when we were together. I felt that, while you were very happy, you still needed from me warmth and reassurance rather than the bringing up of problems which you would then have feared from me — that I decided not to waste any of our precious time thinking of such things.

Now she was not so sure she could wait three or four years. She thought it likely that "after a while, try as we may, we shall betray our real feelings for one another and that this may be more painful to those whom we want not to hurt than an open break." For her there were two choices. "I must either act a part, which if one thinks about it, is contemptible as well as difficult and in the end degrading to both sides, or I must change our whole relationship (I mean my relationship with Hamilton, of course), establish it on a cool, impersonal basis which is so unlike me that I don't think it can be done." And even if she could handle her relations with Hamilton, there was their daughter, Gregor, who might "turn from me for a time more than I like." [7] Yet she made it clear that she was willing to take these risks. What she wanted from Walter was some kind of commitment. He did not realize that was what she meant; nor was he yet willing to offer it.

During the weeks of their separation he tried to lead a normal life. He continued to turn out his column three days a week, traveled to Washington for talks with officials, went to the Middle West to deliver a round of speeches, worked out at the gym, and escorted Faye regularly to dinner parties. One would not have guessed from his columns dealing with the Court-packing plan, then at a critical point, that his mind was filled with thoughts of Helen. As if he did not have enough to deal with, there were other complications. While he was in Bar Harbor visiting the Finletters — denouncing FDR, going over the proofs of *The Good Society*, and trying to sort out his emotions — one of his friends decided that she was in love with him. Sensing that he seemed more estranged than usual from Faye, and thus perhaps more available, the woman rushed in with a declaration of her passion.

This was not a passion he could ever have reciprocated or encouraged. When he reminded her that he was a married man, she laughed disdainfully. And when he told her that, however flattered he was by her attention, he could not return it, she called him a "cold fish." Still refusing to take no for an answer, she demanded to know whether he was in love with someone else. The lie came quickly to his lips. "Oh my dear," he wrote Helen in recounting the episode, "will there be no end to the need for not hurting others?"

But at least my wits did not fail me and I do not have to have anything very tragic on my conscience. It is agreed that I am quite "nonhuman" and that's that, and when I was cornered and asked the question point blank, "Are you in love with someone?," I was able to reply, God help me, "Oh no, no," in a most convincing tone. I hated to say that. I would so much have liked to say: "Yes, completely and everlastingly and uniquely."[8]

A new sense of enthusiasm and hope replaced his old stoicism. "I think a little of myself and know, I think, in a detached way, that there is in me some capacity to see the world, and that I must use it, and use it up before I die," he wrote Helen from Maine. "The other night I listened to a hermit thrush singing in the woods, and I too must sing my little song, I suppose. Now I know that I have written a better book," he said of *The Good Society*, "which will throw a bit of light ahead for some lonely fellows somewhere, because you put your hand in mine that evening last January. The consciousness of that unfroze my spirit while I worked in Florida and enabled me to be impervious to all external things."[9]

The optimism that had entered his life spilled over into his writing. Phrases, paragraphs, sometimes whole columns that harked back to an earlier and more idealistic Lippmann relieved the stale negativism of his anti–New Deal diatribes. When Amelia Earhart set out in July on a round-the-world flight — during which she disappeared over New Guinea — he wrote a lyric column that said a good deal more about his own state of mind than about the bravery of the aviatrix. "The world is a better place to live in because it contains human beings who will give up ease and security and stake their own lives in order to do what they themselves think worth doing . . . who are brave without cruelty to others and impassioned with an idea that dignifies all who contemplate it," he wrote, as though idealizing what he was about to do himself.

The best things of mankind are as useless as Amelia Earhart's adventure. . . . In such persons mankind overcomes the inertia which would keep it earthbound forever in its habitual ways. They have in them the free and useless energy with which alone men surpass themselves.

Such energy cannot be planned and managed. . . . It is wild and free. But all the heroes, the saints and the seers, the explorers and the creators, partake of it. They do not know what they discover. They do not know where their impulse is taking them. . . . They have been possessed for a time with an extraordinary passion which is unintelligible in ordinary human terms.

. . . They do the useless, brave, noble, the divinely foolish and the very wisest things that are done by man. And what they prove to themselves and to others is that man is no mere automaton in his routine, no mere cog in the collective machine, but that in the dust of which he is made there is also fire, lighted now and then by great winds from the sky.

Helen, then in Kitzbühel with her husband and daughter, read the column in the Paris *Herald Tribune*. "I seemed to hear in it an echo of our love," she wrote him. "I liked particularly the phrase about being 'brave without cruelty to others,' the 'free and useless energy,' and love to listen to you when your 'free and useless energy' possesses you.''[10] The thought of them both riding high above the confining ties of earthbound mortals, "possessed for a time with an extraordinary passion which is unintelligible in ordinary human terms," was very appealing to her.

Like all lovers, Lippmann went through periods of elation and depression, sometimes glimpsing a new life that would yield the things he had not found in the old, sometimes fearing their love would never survive. He confided in Helen without reserve. "In me at least, and perhaps to some extent in you, too, there have been long periods, or rather many periods, of heavy-heartedness in the past ten years, so many that I am afraid I have acquired a rather gloomy exterior," he confessed. "Finding the things that mattered to me incommunicable, I have sought solitude behind a curtain of depression." Nothing from the outside, he said, had mattered to him since he had grown up — "not reputation, place, money, habitual comforts, or ambition: I have never since I was a boy worried about getting or losing them. And the world's troubles, though I am really concerned about them, and do brood over them, have never given me personal anxiety." Yet he was, he revealed, "sad and sometimes weary at being alone, all the more so, I suppose, because we are so made, I believe, that things too long unspoken cease to be felt. And there are things to be felt that matter much more, not only to you and me, but really to all men if they knew it, than the Supreme Court or the Nazis or the League and the rest."[11]

He wrote her in this vein nearly every day, a torrent of confessions and vows. She responded in kind. Gradually the weeks of their separation passed. On August 2 Hamilton returned to New York on the *Normandie*, having left Helen and Gregor in Kitzbühel. As soon as he got to the office he called Walter and they arranged to meet for lunch at the Century. As he entered the club Walter discreetly drew the porter aside and asked for his mail. He stuffed a letter postmarked Kitzbühel into his pocket, mounted the stairs to the wood-paneled library on the second floor, and hailed his friend.

Armstrong was ebullient at seeing Lippmann and eager to recount details of the trip that had taken him to Vienna, Prague and Paris. Everything he had seen depressed him: Nazi agitation in Austria for *Anschluss*, the Sudeten Germans' demand for separation from Czechoslovakia, pro-Hitler sympathy among French conservatives, the paralysis of will that had seized London and Paris. "The Paris *Trib* is so pro-fascist it would make you sick," he told Lippmann. "You know, it has suppressed columns by you and Dorothy Thompson critical of Hitler and Mussolini. The British and the French are rotten with appeasement, and here we are just sitting on our hands."[12]

Armstrong looked to his companion for assent, but Lippmann's mind was only half on the conversation. Playing a part made him nervous. He wanted to get away. The situation seemed ludicrous and his own position appalling. "I hope Helen and Gregor are enjoying their holiday," he said politely as they parted. "They'll be in Provence for a few weeks, and then in Paris at the end of August," Armstrong replied. "Won't you be in Paris about the same time? You absolutely must look up Helen when you get there. She'd be delighted to see you," he said.

As his sailing date approached, Lippmann was uncharacteristically lighthearted. The prospect of a month free from writing and a week. alone with Helen kindled a buoyancy that infused the column he wrote just before departing. "Once upon a time I should have said that I was going abroad to talk to public officials and journalists and supposedly well-informed citizens and old friends in order to get a better sense of 'the situation,' " he explained. But now he had "learned better than to go abroad for a few weeks and begin cabling back in hot haste the impressions which I have formed after reading a foreign newspaper at breakfast and after having had lunch with an undersecretary." Still, there were benefits to be gained from foreign travel. "There is nothing so good for the human soul as the discovery that there are ancient and flourishing civilized societies which have somehow managed to exist for many centuries and are still in being though they have had no help from the traveler in solving their problems."[13]

On August 11 Lippmann boarded the *Queen Mary*. Faye came to the dock to see him off. Over the past few weeks she had been unusually attentive and eager to please. Although he was sure she suspected nothing about Helen, she seemed to have sensed a change in his attitude. At the ship they exchanged the usual pleasantries that had made their marriage tolerable. As the last warning bell rang for those going ashore, she put her hand on his arm and said, "Walter, don't come back until you really want to."

At that point he was not sure what he wanted. He had made no decision about Faye. His mind was on Helen. All the way across the Atlantic he was in a state of agitation, planning how he would phone Helen from the Ritz as soon as he arrived in Paris on the sixteenth, how he would take the train to Bourges early the following morning, what he would say when they met at the station, how they would spend their week together. At that moment there was no future. There was so much to consider: the hurt to Faye and Hamilton and Gregor if he and Helen tried to build a life together.

This may have been on his mind when, in putting the finishing touches on *The Good Society* a few months earlier, he had illustrated a political point by the example of an affair between married lovers: "While the two lovers may by consulting their own feelings be able to determine what will be the consequences to themselves, they are not likely to know the consequences for the other lives that are intimately affected.''[14] If this was in his subconscious, he put it aside when he left the *Queen Mary* at Cherbourg and boarded the train for Paris. All he could think of was that he would be with Helen the next morning.

While he was on the ship his carefully arranged plan fell to pieces. The one person whom their affair could hurt most and who could make its continuation impossible discovered their secret. Armstrong learned by accident, but by the kind of accident that resulted from their own carelessness, and perhaps by their own unconscious wish to be found out. They were discovered, as most clandestine lovers are eventually, by their own indiscretion.

The instrument was the letters. All summer long Walter had been writing Helen with the feverish imagination of a man who had found something he had forgotten existed. In the middle of July he wrote her four times within a single week. But by the time those four letters reached Kitzbühel, Helen had already left with Gregor to spend a few days with her friends Alma and Tik Morgan at Talloires in the French Alps. The hotel, instead of forwarding Walter's letters to her there, mistakenly sent them to the address her husband had left for his own mail. Thus, instead of reaching Helen in France, as Walter had intended, the four love letters ended up in Hamilton Armstrong's office in New York.

The first one arrived on the morning of August 16, just as Walter's ship was pulling into Cherbourg harbor. Although the letter was clearly addressed to Helen, Armstrong's secretary — not overfond of Helen — recognized Lippmann's handwriting and, suspecting something might be afoot, opened the letter and handed it to Armstrong.

◄ 28 ►

Starting Over

I do not know how to go on without your love . . . my
heart is now so joined to yours I could not staunch the
wounds if I tore them apart.

— To Helen Byrne Armstrong, September 15, 1937

WHEN the phone rang in Helen's room at the Hotel Central et Angleterre in Bourges that evening, she knew it must be Walter calling from Paris. She had arranged everything. They would take long walks in the forest and drive in an open Citroën through the countryside. They would stroll hand in hand through the marketplace and picnic on the banks of the Cher. They would be alone. No one else in the world, except her friend Mima Porter, knew where they were. Excitedly she picked up the phone. "Darling," she said, "at last."

It was Armstrong. He told her about the letter. He demanded an explanation. "Hamilton," she said in a state of shock, "I just can't talk about this now. We'll discuss it when I get back." He told her she must return immediately. "No," she replied weakly, "I can't do that. Not now." He was adamant. Unless she took the next boat back, he told her, he would come and get her. Stunned, guilt-stricken, appalled at the prospect of such a scene, Helen reluctantly agreed to return to New York.

An hour later the phone rang again. This time it was Lippmann from the Ritz. Still in tears, she told him what had happened. There was no point now in his coming to Bourges. Their plans were ruined. She would come to Paris. They would talk about it there. He met her at the Gare d'Austerlitz the next morning. Instead of a tryst they had a wake. The shock of discovery had unnerved them. They did not know what to do. Walter had not thought seriously about divorcing Faye, and was unsure whether Helen was willing to leave Hamilton. Their talk about building a life together was more a wish than a plan. They walked along the Seine morose and confused.

Walter did not know what Helen wanted from him, or what he wanted for himself. Things had happened too fast, before they had had enough time together. Although he knew he loved her, he was not sure that their love could bear the anger of Hamilton, the resentment of Gregor, the ostracism of their friends. He was afraid to force the issue. Rather than telling Helen to break with Armstrong, he felt she must make the decision on her own. She should go back and face her husband with an open mind. That was the honorable thing to do. If, after seeing Armstrong again, she was still willing to face the upheaval of a divorce, they could build a life together. This was the sensible approach, though not what Helen had hoped to hear.

On August 24 she and Gregor took the boat back to New York. Walter roamed Paris disconsolately, avoiding everyone he knew except Mima Porter, Helen's closest friend. He tried to focus his mind on the European crisis for some French journalists who came to interview him, but his thoughts wandered. Finally he made a decision. If Helen should stay with Hamilton, he would not return to America. It would be too painful to be in the same city and not be able to see her. He would abandon his column, retire from journalism, and live in monastic seclusion in one of the little houses on Berenson's estate in Settignano. He would continue to write, but not to publish. And he would divorce Faye.[1]

When Helen boarded the *Normandie* she did not know what to do or what Walter wanted, although she was sure that he needed her. "For him the worst part of all," she wrote Mima Porter from the ship, "is that all his life he has been quite alone in a solitude which is perhaps splendid and has certainly made him what he is and able to write as he does, look at things from a long, not an immediate point of view." But finding someone he could really talk to had, she explained, "unfrozen his spirit and made him happy in a way that I think he had never known before." For this reason he must not think of her as "gone out of his life, as disappeared and as something forever unattainable. . . . To make Walter laugh," she added,

tell him that we are having a terrible time with that huge parcel of sheet proofs of *The Good Society*. We cannot seem to get rid of it! We didn't dare leave it in the hotel for fear it would be snatched up and published somewhere else! We forgot about it on the way down and could never be unobserved enough last night to hurl it into the sea. But G just this minute reports that she has hurled the last sheet out the porthole. It is like trying to dispose of a corpse![2]

Walter, feeling sorry for himself, contemplating retirement and monasticism, dropped by to see Mima a few days after Helen's departure. She showed him the letter Helen had sent just before the ship sailed. Finally he realized that Helen was quite willing to leave her husband, but that he must make the first move by divorcing Faye. He telephoned

Helen on the ship and the next morning wrote her a long letter declaring that he had "come to that clarity, without which I could never be any good, as to what I mean to do, not eventually, not in some dim, distant and horribly postponed future, but just as soon as it is practicable to do it decently, humanely and decisively." He would tell Faye the truth. "I shall not want to do anything to press you, both for Hamilton's sake and Gregor's, and likewise I think you should do nothing overt until we have met and talked and decided it together."

For him to return to Faye without telling the truth would be unthinkable. "That would paralyze me intellectually and emotionally and I should find it intolerable." He was also certain that he and Helen could not drift indefinitely. "A reasonably definite and not too long a time we can wait, but what we tried to believe when we parted would be morally destructive and would break our hearts. You might be able to go through with it, though I think at a terrible cost. But I cannot and could not by sheer will power make my mind and heart turn from their longing for you and devote them to the work I am supposed to do."[3]

Although Helen did not receive this letter until she arrived in New York, the phone conversation with Walter reassured her. Being a shrewd and practical woman who knew what she wanted, she was impatient with his high-mindedness. "I do not want to be given up for *my own good*," she wrote Mima Porter from the ship. "Because I am quite clear in my own mind and know, beyond the shadow of a doubt, that I am prepared at whatever time seems right, to take the final step." But Walter, she feared, being so tenderhearted and idealistic, "cannot bear to hurt people, and this is so true that perhaps he *really* cannot bear it." She was preparing herself for the possibility that "while he may decide in time to leave Faye (and I hope that he does), he may never want to take any further step." If he could go through the publicity and marry her without regrets or inhibitions, he would be happy, she was sure, and their life together "something unusual." But, she added, "if he does not do this quite wholeheartedly we shall not be happy, he will lose his desire and ability to write (for I believe he is one of those who can only write what they believe and feel). And he will be more truly unhappy than if he has given me up and lives all alone with his ideas."[4]

On August 30 Walter went to London, as much to clear his mind as to keep the round of appointments he had scheduled weeks earlier. His depression had lifted. What only two weeks earlier had seemed hopeless now gave the promise of bringing what he desperately wanted. Like Helen he could rationalize the justice and reasonableness of whatever he might want. "Had that letter not gone astray," he wrote her of Armstrong's discovery, "we could have carried on for a year or two for Gregor's sake, and have decided how to do what we want to do with great care and deliberation." But that was no longer possible, and he could not regret it. "At the bottom of my heart I think that what looked like very bad luck was really very good luck." Although he believed that she had done the right thing in returning to New York after receiving her husband's ultimatum, he "hated the decision. . . . I was resentful and rebellious and in despair, and yet determined, except for those few moments when I let go of myself, to do what I could to strengthen you. I can see now, darling Helen, that you were throughout more lucid than I, that you had realized from the first that only the resolution not to separate and not to renounce our love could make the interval tolerable."[5]

On the same day that Lippmann went to London, Helen's ship docked in New York. Armstrong was waiting at the pier. Instead of being angry, he was affectionate and conciliatory. He told her he was willing to forgive all so long as she still loved him. That was not what she wanted to hear. She had made up her mind that if Walter would definitely leave Faye, she would divorce Hamilton. Until she knew what Walter wanted, she could do nothing. She would wait.

The next morning she went to the Colony Club, where Lippmann had been told to write her, and sent him a long letter. Without seeming to pose demands, she made it clear that she found herself in an intolerable situation. "Can I really succeed for a long time in such a state either without Hamilton realizing it, or — I suppose a possibility — my breaking down?" She put him on the defensive. "You are in a strange way," she declared reproachfully, "when you say things like 'go back and give it a chance' you are not exactly disposing of my feelings." He seemed to think she could turn off her feelings like his "disinterested" man, or that they could be altered at will to make the world more manageable. "I feel badly to put all this so brutally and to tell you things and details that I know are undoing any composure you may have acquired," she explained, "but I think I have to because I really, honestly, can't protect you against the truth; you've got to know it, and I believe so much in you that I think in the end you can face it."

Now that he had reached his decision about Faye, her letter told him what he was waiting for. "I spent the morning reading and re-reading your letter, seeking to make perfectly sure that I had the right to send you this letter," he wrote her on his return to Paris. He was ready to tell her what she wanted to hear: "I am going to leave Faye and I want to marry you." And he would not look back. "If you did not exist I might not, through sheer inertia, leave Faye," he confessed, "but I should become progressively more useless to myself, to the world, and even to her. I am not going to be modest: I think the juice of life is in me, and that I have something to say not merely to the minds but to the hearts of a few in this generation and perhaps to more in another. That juice was drying up. You only have known how to tap its sources and make it flow once more." Now they must decide to come openly and permanently together. He would break the news to Faye, and although it would be a "shock and a hurt to her pride," she would be "losing nothing that she ever had."[6]

A few days later, before he had a chance to hear from Helen, he took the train for Florence, where he planned to meet Jane and Lucius Wilmerding and to visit Berenson at I Tatti. On his way he stopped off in Milan to phone Mima Porter for news of Helen, and at a café in the Galleria sat down and wrote her another letter. He tried to explain how unhappy he had been to send her back to New York, but felt that "honor required that you must make your final decision about Hamilton when you are with him, and not with me." That is what he had meant by "giving it a chance." As for himself, he continued, "I do not know how to go on without your love. I cannot lock you in my heart and leave it at that, and then do the work you would wish me to do. I write with my heart, my brain is merely its instrument, and my heart is now so joined to yours I could not staunch the wounds if I tore them apart."

This was what Helen had hoped for. She was not the kind of woman who suffered from uncertainty, nor did she share his concern about what others might consider the "honorable" thing to do. "My mind made up last May," she cabled him on receiving his letter. "Am ready to proceed as fast as you want." The next day she rented what she described to him as a "rather miserable room and bath at 228 West 13th Street where we can meet and I think be more private than in 95th Street!"[7]

The decision was made, but the worst lay ahead. He had to tell Faye, and the prospect paralyzed him. A personal confrontation was out of the question. He could not stand such a scene. Yet to ask on paper for divorce seemed too cold. Finally he hit on the idea of having someone else tell her, someone close to her. Her father seemed the logical choice. Ralph Albertson would understand why Walter had decided he could no longer live with Faye. Albertson was a decent and gentle man. He was also greatly indebted to Walter, not only for kindness, but for a good deal of financial help over the years. The former clergyman obligingly came through. "I truly understand and sympathize," he cabled in reply to Lippmann's request, reporting that he had broken the news to Faye.

With the ground furrowed by his father-in-law, Lippmann then wrote Faye himself. His letter — which she destroyed — was "quiet but absolutely decisive," he told Helen. He insisted that they not meet again, and that he would see only her representative. "I do not know," he recounted in a gem of understatement,

whether this will seem to you an indirect way of dealing with the affair, but the fact is, the fundamental fact in our whole relationship, that Faye and I have never been able to discuss anything. We could only quarrel or ignore matters, and I won't quarrel at this stage of things.

. . . She has had her own way in everything because she has not hesitated to make it either so disagreeable or so plaintive that I submitted. I know that if I did the thing I would like to do, if I went to her and face to face told her the truth, she would dissolve everything in hysteria, real or feigned.

Forgive me if I seem to write bitterly — I shall try never to be bitter about her — but the fact is that she is a coward about life and there is no way in which one can deal in a spirit of human charity with cowards. They have to be "managed" for their own good.[8]

Once the decision was made, he did not want to linger in Europe. Joined by the Wilmerdings, he boarded the *Conte di Savoia* in Naples on September 29 and eight days later was reunited with Helen in New York. They went straight from the pier to the room she had rented in Greenwich Village. Helen told Hamilton she was leaving him and moved out of their 81st Street town house to their country place at Syosset, Long Island. Walter moved his clothes and papers out of his East 61st Street house into a room at the Sherry-Netherland Hotel.

His life took on a new pattern. He lived at the hotel, worked at the office, and met Helen discreetly on West 13th Street. He dealt with Faye through their lawyers. She had decided not to contest the divorce. Her major concern was a good settlement. For advice she turned to her friend Thomas Lamont. On October 19, less than two weeks after Walter's return, she filed for divorce in Bradenton, Florida, near their winter home at Anna Maria. The Associated Press ran a six-paragraph story quoting from her deposition: "Defendant is shrewd and quick in his mental processes, commands a vocabulary virtually unlimited, is a facile veteran in the use of invective and development of criticism, a phase of his equipment that he constantly uses in administering verbal punishment upon complainant."

Faye made an attractive and aggrieved victim and got what she wanted — everything he had. Under Lamont's guidance she asked for a flat settlement rather than alimony, on the assumption that she ought not to be dependent on his future earning power and the vagaries of public taste. She took the two country houses, Wading River and Anna Maria, the proceeds from the sale of the house on 61st Street, and all of his savings, which came to $165,000. These, invested in an annuity, guaranteed her an income of $8,000 a year for life. Lamont insisted that this was not enough, and persuaded Lippmann to give her another $50,000, to be taken from his income over the next five years in installments of $10,000 each. The settlement, as Lippmann told Berenson, was most "quixotic."

He simply gave her what she asked for. She even kept the silver, which had belonged to Walter's mother and grandmother. When it was over the attorney who had shepherded her case through the courts wrote him that "over a period of twenty-one years of practice at the Bar, during which time I have had many occasions to represent people in matrimonial affairs, I have never met anyone who has been as fair, unselfish and generous as you."[9] It was worth it to him to be out of the marriage and to avoid an argument. On December 9 the divorce was approved on the usual grounds of mental cruelty. Not long thereafter Faye married Jesse Heatley, a Wading River polo player, and settled in the village, where she spent the rest of her long, and henceforth uneventful, life. She and Walter never saw one another again.

Helen waited until after Christmas, then went to Reno to put in her six weeks' residency for a Nevada divorce. When she left, Walter went to Washington. New York was becoming uncomfortable for both of them. The affair and the divorce had caused a nasty scandal in the tight social circle of the Armstrongs and the Lippmanns. Not that their friends were prudes; they certainly succumbed often enough to the weaknesses of the flesh, the purse and the bottle. What was not so easily tolerated was an affair followed by a divorce. While adultery was considered to be no one's business but that of the parties concerned, divorce was an affront to the conventions. Society viewed Armstrong, born into an old and prestigious New York family, as the aggrieved husband. Helen had been foolishly indiscreet. Lippmann, it was widely believed, had behaved like a cad. He had been sneaky toward his most intimate friend, and to make matters worse, had been cowardly toward Faye. Instead of telling her he loved another woman and wanted a divorce, he had sent his father-in-law to do it. This was carrying delicacy to the point of dishonor.

Dorothy Thompson, whose foreign-affairs column alternated with Lippmann's at the *Trib* and whose office was just down the hall from his own, even discerned international significance in the divorce. A falling-out between two such ardent and influential internationalists as Lippmann and Armstrong, she feared, might weaken the willingness of Americans to confront the Nazi menace. The reasoning was a bit tortuous, but earnest. Lippmann was more amused than irritated. "Did you ever realize how much Dorothy is like the Statue of Liberty?" he wrote Helen. "Made of brass. Visible at all times to all the world. Holding the light aloft, but always the same light. . . . Capable of being admired, but difficult to love. My sympathies, and this is not pure male prejudice, are with Sinclair Lewis, who took to drink and then to the Riggs sanitarium. You know, when I think of it, being moralized over by a woman who has made a mess of two marriages seems to me the height of impudence. Wouldn't it be fun not to have to be a gentleman all the time?"

Faye's friends — an assortment of Broadway denizens and Wading River gentry — dropped him. So did some of Armstrong's. To avoid embarrassing encounters with Armstrong he resigned his committees at the Council on Foreign Relations, though not his membership, and stopped going to meetings. He no longer lunched at the Century, where he and Armstrong had met so often, and turned down all dinner invitations if he thought they might meet. "I was sure that I have been right and am right to distinguish clearly between taking practical steps to save Hamilton embarrassment (and myself) by taking care not to encounter him, and taking any step which is symbolically a recognition of a sense of guilt," he wrote Helen in Reno. "On that ultimate question I am clear with myself and clear with you, and I will not take any action of my own free will which implies even remotely that we have to hide and be ashamed."

The separation and the divorces had taken on the elements of a public scandal. "Helen and I are now passing through the trials of publicity, gossip, rumor and all the rest," Lippmann wrote Berenson. "But we shall pass through them, accepting as good-humoredly as we can what is coming and is to come by way of public disapproval. We are deeply in love." Although they would lose many of their friends, he admitted, they would not stoop to self-justification. Their friends would have to believe that they knew what they were doing. "The others must just think as they like."[10]

Berenson was, as always, understanding and supportive. So were Helen's friends Mima Porter and Alma and Tik Morgan. Lippmann had few close friends and most accepted his marital rearrangements with equanimity. But Charles Merz, his former assistant at the *World,* dropped out of sight, and so did Learned Hand. Lippmann was particularly hurt by Hand's disloyalty, and although the two men eventually resumed their correspondence after a hiatus of several years, they never recaptured their old intimacy. The break was largely due to Frances Hand, a domineering woman who had no compunctions about a second man in her own life, but who was offended by a scandalous divorce.

The hardest loss for Lippmann was the one that was inevitable. Never again did he have a friend to whom he was as close as he had been to Hamilton Armstrong. Their friendship had rested on mutual trust and affection — and on Armstrong's part, a profound and totally uncritical admiration. Lippmann knew there was nothing he could do to revive that, and that Armstrong would probably never forgive him. Yet he felt he had to make an attempt to explain, to convey that although he had done something beyond forgiveness, he had tried to behave honorably. At the end of November 1937, with his own divorce almost final and Helen preparing to go to Reno, he wrote Armstrong.

"I am writing this letter in the hope that you may be willing to read it," he began tentatively.

I have waited until now only because I could not help but feel that you did not wish to hear from me, and that, however much I might wish to say certain things to you, I had no right to force myself upon your attention.

The thing which I want most of all to say to you is that I would have given anything in the world if only this thing had not happened to you and between us. I know that you will find it hard, probably impossible to believe anything I say, but nevertheless it is the truth that since last spring when I realized the situation, the agony of every doubt has centered on you. For as regards Faye the outcome was long in the making and clearly inevitable, and though every separation is intensely painful, for both Faye and me it had to come, if not now then very soon thereafter.

But about you, and about the destruction of a friendship which has meant so much to me, I have gone through, and still know, unabated suffering deeper than I could attempt to describe. I tell you this now not because I think it could or should soften what you must feel about me. I take that to be impossible. I say it because I have been told that you feel I was somehow happy and unscathed. That you must not believe for it is so terribly untrue.

In an effort to explain why he had not spoken of the affair when they met in August, just before his departure for Europe, he maintained that he and Helen had not yet decided what to do, that in fact he "left with the feeling that we would decide to turn back, that because of you and because of Gregor we must decide to give each other up and to renounce even our old friendship." What happened in Paris only confirmed that assumption: "When I said good-bye to her, I thought I was saying good-bye forever." Only after Helen returned to New York, he continued, did he realize that

nothing we had agreed to do could reestablish the past, that there was no way in which we could make the renunciation we had decided upon in France truly irrevocable. I learned that that was impossible while I lived, that it was not within my power, alive or dead, to restore what you wanted. Knowing that, I can only ask your forgiveness for the sorrow which comes from the facts themselves. I do most sincerely ask your forgiveness for that, though I have no slightest hope that you can ever believe, much less forgive. If you have read this much, I can say only that you will have been more magnanimous than I could have hoped that you would be, though you continue to hate me, I shall think of you always as the friend whom I would wish never to have lost. . . .[11]

Rather than mailing the letter, Walter gave it to Helen's younger brother, James Byrne, to deliver personally. Armstrong refused to read, or even accept, it. So great was his bitterness that during the remaining thirty-five years that he was editor of *Foreign Affairs* he never allowed Lippmann's name to appear in the magazine. All references to him by other authors were carefully excised. Although Armstrong had two other wives after Helen, the second of whom made him very happy, he never forgave Lippmann. Not until the late 1960s, when these two elderly men found themselves standing near each other at a large social gathering, could he at last bring himself to speak to his former friend.

Nor did Hamilton ever make his peace with Helen during his lifetime. Yet in a strange and touching gesture he reached across the grave. On Armstrong's death in April 1973 his wife found, among his papers, a small packet of letters with a note attached: "For Helen, on my death." Christa Armstrong delivered the packet to Helen Lippmann. On opening it Helen found four letters bound by a ribbon, and a note from Armstrong to her saying: "I read only the first three lines of one of these." The letters were those Walter had written to her in Kitzbühel in July 1937. Only one had been opened. Thus in 1973 Helen read for the first time the four lost love letters Walter had written her thirty-six years earlier.

In January 1938 Lippmann moved to Washington and took a small apartment on Q Street, NW, near Dupont Circle. Between writing his column and looking for a house for himself and Helen, he prepared the Walgreen Lectures he was to deliver at the University of Chicago in February. "I worked very hard this morning, about four hours of furious writing, and got through the first draft of the second lecture," he wrote Helen at the end of January. "I get a little panicky when I think that three weeks from tomorrow I must leave for Chicago, and while three weeks is an eternity separated from you, it is no time at all in which to make that sloppy heap of words into something with a vital organization of its own. I really tackled too big a subject, and have plowed up too much new ground for the time and energy at my disposal. Today I wrote myself into a kind of extreme fatigue — a thing I did nearly every day for three months when I was finishing the *Preface to Morals*."[12]

Lippmann went to Chicago in mid-February to deliver three lectures on what he called the "American Destiny," that is, that America must become Britain's heir in regulating the world balance of power. Robert Hutchins, the *Wunderkind* chancellor of the university, tried to tempt him to stay in Chicago with the offer of an endowed chair and a teaching schedule of only a few months a year. Although this meant he could drop the column, the idea of teaching put a chill in his bones. "I haven't really considered it at all, which I take to be a sign that I am not very much interested," he wrote Helen of the offer, "and when I think about it now, many almost insuperable objections come to my mind: a) Chicago, which I do not think we should really enjoy, b) teaching, which would, I think, bore me, c) a definite routine and commitment for nine months each year, which seems like a loss of freedom, d) the pettiness of academic life when you are a part of it." Instead, he decided he would leave the *Tribune* at the end of 1939 and write only long articles and books. "The one thing I would like that academic life has to give — association with people who think rather than push their way through the world," he added — "we can work out for ourselves."[13]

During the long weeks of Helen's residency in Reno he wrote her nearly every day, sometimes twice and three times — of his work, their future, their friends, his emotions, his efforts to lose weight and, as he said, "be more beautiful" for her. In one of these letters he tried to dispel the remaining cloud between them, to explain why in Paris he had insisted that she return to Hamilton to "give it a chance." "I think I shall tell you now what I have never told you," he wrote her from Chicago —

the one thing I have spared you — because now I think it will help you to see the underlying terms on which I am able to be at peace with myself about Hamilton, to have, as you have said, sadness but not remorse. It is this: that when you went back in September the thing above all other things I waited to hear, not to hear but to discern, in your letters was whether there was any possibility of restoring anything that could conceivably last. I had made up my mind before you left that if there was any evidence of such a possibility, I would do nothing to interfere with it. I would not try to win you back, to take you away from Hamilton. That is what I meant by that awful phrase about "giving it a chance."

That much you know. But what you do not know, unless you had guessed it, was what I had made up my mind to do if your letters from New York indicated any possibility of a reestablishment of anything. I had made up my mind that it would be absolutely impossible for me to live in New York, not writing to you, not seeing you alone, perhaps meeting you accidentally, and always within reach of a telephone. I had decided that, however awful that would be for me, for you it would be intolerable. It would make impossible a resumption with Hamilton, yet you would never have been free of the consciousness of me. So if you had not written as you did, angrily at me for thinking you could resume, I knew I could not return to New York. I knew, too, that even if I lived, say in Boston or Washington, it would be the same. You would be reminded of me by the things I did, by the papers, by what people said in conversation. So I knew with absolute lucidity that I could never subject you to such torture, and that the only possible thing was really to disappear out of your life.

That sounds very dramatic, but I had come to a near certainty about it while I was in London, when I determined not to send you the letter I had written till I had heard from you. I had not decided to kill myself, though, since death never frightened me, that would have been the cheapest and easiest solution. But I had decided not to return to America, to resign from the *Herald Tribune,* to retire from journalism, and that I would go to a little villino on Berenson's estate and live in seclusion. I had decided to leave Faye, of course, and all forms of public life, and to write but not to publish for a very long time. That is what I meant by locking you in my heart.

But what I had in mind was to make it possible for you to live. I knew you loved me, and so I knew that nothing less than to disappear could make it faintly possible for you to find contentment again. One person only had some perception of this, Mima, and one day she startled me in Paris by asking me if I had ever thought about suicide. I said no and passed over the question because I did not intend to do that, knowing it would break your heart and ruin your life. But I did mean to disappear because on no other terms could you succeed at all if there was any possibility of impairing your life with Hamilton.

I do not pretend that this was not a hard conclusion to come to, but once I had really faced the facts, it was an utterly inescapable conclusion. And then there were two considerations which helped me to accept it. One was that to disappear that way would also be easier for me, the other that to have seen the truth and flinch from it was to betray what you had given me. I should not have been the person you thought I was, and even in giving you up I could not have endured having you believe that.

It was her independent decision to leave Hamilton, he explained, that made it possible that their "love be free." "So that while I am saddened when I think of Hamilton, I am not wracked by conflict and doubt, and I do not think I took you from him in May or sought to prevent your going back to him in September." He had been ready to make her return possible, if she had wanted to return. "More than that I was not able to do, and to have refused you in October would have been criminally quixotic, and probably at bottom a form of worldly cowardice."[14]

Helen's divorce came through on February 21. She took the first train east and met Walter, coming from Chicago, in Baltimore. A few days later they returned to New York — she to her house on East 81st Street, he to a small apartment he had rented nearby. Having observed the proprieties for a few weeks, they were married on March 26, 1938, in a simple civil ceremony, and drove to White Sulphur Springs for a week's honeymoon in the Blue Ridge Mountains.

On April 2 they went back to Washington, where they had decided they would live in order to avoid the gossip and ill feeling that continued to hound them. They stayed just long enough to move some furniture into a house they had rented on Thirtieth Street in Georgetown, and then at the end of May set off on the *Conte di Savoia* for a honeymoon summer in Europe. After a sojourn in Sorrento and Rome, and a few days at I Tatti with Berenson — who was eager to meet the woman he had heard so much about from Lippmann — they motored through northern Italy and on to Paris, where, at the end of June, they rented an apartment on the Ile St. Louis.

Lippmann had what he wanted. He had won the woman he loved. Faye, and all the depression that went with a bad marriage, was irrevocably behind him. He had lost Hamilton and had caused a good deal of scandal among his friends. But he was too happy to brood over that. "I shall not try to write you about the state of the world," he wrote Berenson from Paris. "The best I can say about it is that I can think about it more calmly and with more courage now that the personal things have worked out so perfectly for Helen and me."[15]

◄ 29 ►

The Phony Peace

When I hear people talk about appeasement, I feel as if
they were talking about a wholly imaginary and wholly
incredible state of affairs.

— To Harold Nicolson, December 6, 1938

THE war seemed far away that summer of 1938. Walter was married
to the woman he loved and freed from one he loved no longer. He
and Helen had emerged from their double divorces with most, though
not all, of their friendships intact. Their financial future was secured,
despite his costly divorce settlement, by the great success of his writing
and Helen's sizable trust fund.

The "personal things," as he had told Berenson, had indeed worked
out well. On their return from Italy at the end of June 1938 they moved
into a spacious apartment at 18, quai d'Orleans, with a view of the
Seine and the Left Bank. They wandered the streets of the Latin Quarter, browsed at bookstalls, savored the delights of a city whose daily life
seemed untouched by the mounting political crisis.

At the end of July Lippmann flew to London for a few days of interviews. There, besides various cabinet ministers and politicians, he saw
Max Ascoli. The Italian journalist had recently fled fascist Italy. Later
he would emigrate to America and found the political biweekly *Reporter*. "I took Ascoli to dinner at an Italian restaurant," Lippmann reported to Helen, "and then to see Bobby Sherwood's 'Idiot's Delight,'
an interesting play, but a complete exposure of pacifist delusions of
three years ago when it was the fashion to think that wars are made by
munitions makers. The villain of the piece is a French munitions
king!"[1]

A few days later he returned to Paris, where he basked in the acclaim
surrounding the publication of the French edition of *The Good Society*,
retitled *La Cité libre*. Its message of democracy challenged by totalitarianism could hardly have been more timely to a nation polarized be-

tween Left and Right, with Nazi sympathizers at one extreme and communists on the other. At the end of August two dozen economists and political commentators — including Friedrich von Hayek, Ludwig von Mises, Raymond Aron, and Jacques Rueff — feted him by gathering in Paris for a five-day "Walter Lippmann Colloquium" to survey the prospects for liberal democracy. The French government capped the accolade by making Lippmann a knight of the Legion of Honor.

The headlines in the press gave little support to the personal happiness he felt that summer. Britain and France were rearming for a war they dreaded and sought to avert at almost any cost. Parliamentary governments were torn by factionalism and seemed incapable of decisive action. On his return from a brief and depressing trip to Prague in July, Lippmann began keeping a notebook of ideas for a book whose theme he had only begun to formulate, "the crisis of democracy."[2] Not for another seventeen years would he finally publish the book whose ideas he was beginning to work out that summer.

The rush of events worked against detached contemplation. Hitler was tightening his squeeze on Czechoslovakia, demanding autonomy for the Sudeten Germans. Prime Minister Neville Chamberlain temporized and urged Prague to make concessions. Most Conservatives were with Chamberlain. Although there were those, like Winston Churchill and Duff Cooper, who felt, as Harold Nicolson wrote Lippmann, that it would be "better to risk war immediately than to betray all those principles which, however intermittently and ineffectively, we have tried to further since the war," the country yearned for peace at almost any price.[3] The Left, scarred by the betrayed idealism of the first war, was deeply pacifist; the Right thought Czechoslovakia expendable if Hitler could be bought off.

The appeasement mood was infectious, and one of those most afflicted by it was the new American ambassador to Britain, Joseph P. Kennedy. FDR had appointed the Irish-American financier to the critical London post to disarm the isolationists, just as he had earlier appointed Kennedy to head the Securities and Exchange Commission to disarm Wall Street. Roosevelt assumed that if an Irishman came out in support of American aid to Britain, he could get the troublesome Neutrality Acts revised. But this time FDR had outfoxed himself. Kennedy, instead of urging all-out American support for Britain against the Nazis, felt that the British ought to work out a deal with Hitler.

Writing Lippmann just a few weeks after taking over his new post, Kennedy related how he had told the British, in a speech shortly after his arrival, that "they must not get into a mess counting on us to bail them out." But at the time, March 1938, the British showed few signs of getting into such a "mess." Only a few days earlier Hitler had sent his troops into Austria and extinguished its independence. Britain and

France mumbled ineffectually. "Nobody is prepared to talk turkey to Messrs. Hitler and Mussolini, and nobody is prepared to face the risk of war by calling their bluffs," Kennedy explained. "The British will not do anything to check either one of them unless they actually fire guns." This being the case, clearly "none of these various moves has any significance for the United States, outside of general interest."[4]

Kennedy was not anti-British. Rather, he shared the assumptions of many British conservatives, such as Prime Minister Neville Chamberlain, that Hitler's demands were not totally unreasonable, that a compromise could be arranged, and that it was certainly not worth going to war over such matters as the *Anschluss*, the Sudetenland, or the persecution of the Jews. "There will be no war if Chamberlain stays in power," Kennedy wrote Lippmann at the end of March regarding the Czech crisis. "Germany will get whatever it wants in Czechoslovakia without sending a single soldier across the border. As long as Great Britain will not give unconditional promises to back them up in a fight, the French will not do anything to stop the German domination of Czechoslovakia, and the Czechs in power know that. The Russians are too disorganized and too far away. So where is your war?"

Kennedy's analysis was shrewd, but his bias evident. Sharing Chamberlain's assumptions, he revealed an uncritical admiration for the prime minister. "Chamberlain's speech last Thursday was a masterpiece," he reported to Lippmann. "I sat spellbound in the diplomatic gallery and heard it all. It impressed me as a combination of high morals and politics such as I had never witnessed."

Lippmann, with a long exposure to British politicians and none of the provincial Anglophilia that afflicted so many Americans, was less impressed. "Don't take it amiss if I say that your letter shows some of the same symptoms which have appeared in every American ambassador that I have known since Walter Hines Page, namely the tendency to be over-enthusiastic about the government of the day," he admonished Kennedy.

When you tell me that Chamberlain's speech impressed you as a combination of high morals and politics such as you had never witnessed, I am frankly a little worried for you. British parliamentary oratory is most seductive to Americans after the awful ranting which they are used to in Congress, and the excellent manners and the impressive literary style of the House of Commons manner can very easily affect our judgment as to the substance.

I happen, for example, to believe that Chamberlain is doing the most sensible thing in a bad situation. But that this policy represents "high morals" I do not for a moment believe. He is yielding to superior force and trying to buy off one, at least, of his potential enemies. This is an expedient thing to do, but it hasn't much to do with morals. . . .[5]

Though not admiring Chamberlain's strategy of appeasement, Lippmann saw its logic. "In dealing with these warrior statesmen," he wrote in February 1938,

the democracies must not delude themselves with the idea that there is any bloodless, inexpensive substitute for the willingness to go to war. Collective security, economic sanctions, moral pressure, can be made effective only by nations known to be willing to go to war if necessary. If that willingness to fight does not exist, then Mr. Chamberlain is right when he concludes that he must try to make tolerable terms with the dictators.

. . . For more than three years Europe has been denouncing aggression and retreating before it, and this disparity between principles and practice is so utterly demoralizing that, if it continues much longer, the contempt of the dictatorships for the democracies will become so great that they will become utterly reckless and their actions without bounds.[6]

Hitler, after joining Austria to the Reich in the *Anschluss*, turned his attention to Czechoslovakia, where local Nazis were demanding autonomy for the Sudetenland. Lippmann had gone to Prague in late July, and had been reassured by President Eduard Beneš that Hitler would back down if opposed by a united front of Britain, France and Russia. Beneš seemed strangely confident that they would not let him down. Lippmann felt that Beneš was right — but only if the Czechs were willing to go to war if attacked. In that case the French and the British, no matter how much they dreaded it, would have to come to Prague's defense. "If they can maintain their authority inside their frontiers and if they are prepared to resist invasion, Hitler will either not attack, or, if he attacks, the British and the French must come to the help of the Czechs," Lippmann wrote Berenson in mid-September, during the mounting crisis over the Sudetenland. "To stand aside *if* the Czechs are fighting is almost inconceivable. To attempt it would be such a humiliation that the governing classes in Britain and France would lose all moral authority vis-a-vis their own people." Despite rumors that Chamberlain's emissary to Berlin, Lord Runciman, was at that moment negotiating the dismemberment of Czechoslovakia, Lippmann refused to believe that British public opinion would tolerate such a surrender.[7]

Persuaded that the Czech crisis would be resolved short of war, he and Helen left Paris on September 18 for the United States. On the same day they boarded the *Champlain* at Le Havre, French Premier Edouard Daladier and his foreign minister, Georges Bonnet, arrived in London to coordinate strategy with Chamberlain. They agreed that the Czechs should pay Hitler's price by surrendering the Sudetenland. The Czechs, confronted with a *fait accompli* by their allies, felt they must either accept or face Hitler's armies alone. They accepted. Chamberlain flew to Germany to present Hitler with his peace offering.

But the triumphant Führer suddenly upped the stakes. Flinging the offering back in Chamberlain's face, he now demanded that the Sudetenland be immediately annexed to the Reich. This meant dismembering Czechoslovakia, and turning over to Nazi Germany the powerful fortifications that protected Bohemia and Slovakia and barred Hitler's way to eastern Europe and Russia. Now Beneš balked. He reminded Paris of its alliance with Prague, and urged Britain and France to stand by him. Even Chamberlain was shocked by Hitler's arrogant demands. Soviet Foreign Minister Maxim Litvinov told Daladier that if France intervened, Russia would come to its aid. But the French would not move without the British, and the British would not move at all. London said no to Paris, Paris said no to Moscow, and everyone said no to Prague.

Had the Czechs been willing to fight alone, perhaps the story would have been different. Perhaps, as Lippmann had predicted, the British and French would have been forced by public opinion to come to their aid. But they escaped that dilemma. The Czechs succumbed to the pressure of their allies. Chamberlain and Daladier, having chosen bribery over resistance, went to Munich on September 29 and turned over to Hitler everything he had asked for. Carving up Czechoslovakia, they handed Nazi Germany the Sudetenland, the frontier defenses, and much of the nation's heavy industry. Czechoslovakia lay defenseless and the road to the East now open. The Russians began to reconsider their hope of containing Hitler through alliance with the West.

Chamberlain flew back to London in the rain, telling cheering crowds that he had won "peace in our time." Lippmann did not join the celebration. The Munich accords, he charged, were "a great defeat . . . the equivalent of a major military disaster." Hitler's bloodless victory silenced the generals who wanted to depose him for recklessness, assured German dominance of central Europe, demonstrated the weakness of the democracies, and persuaded the Russians that the British and French wanted to turn Hitler toward the East. Chamberlain had no more intention of bringing Russia into the Munich settlement than of going to war over the Sudetenland. "His major problem throughout the summer was to avert a situation in which the Czechs resisted and the French were compelled to support them," Lippmann wrote to a colleague. "France and England were bluffing all summer, but their bluff worked only with the Czechs and with opinion in the democratic countries."[8]

A year later in Paris, Foreign Minister Georges Bonnet told Lippmann that the British had made it clear as early as November 1937 that they would never fight for Czechoslovakia. That left France, Bonnet said, with only two choices: break with England, or try to bluff Hitler. In August 1938, he claimed, France tried to persuade Poland to support the Czechs. The Poles not only refused, but said they thought it a good idea to carve up Czechoslovakia, since this would give them a common frontier with Hungary. Although the Russians were eager for an anti-Hitler alliance, the British dreaded joining forces with Moscow, even if it meant abandoning Czechoslovakia to Hitler. Yet, Bonnet claimed, France would have come to Prague's defense had the Czechs decided to fight.

Lippmann distrusted Bonnet's explanation, describing the foreign minister as a "tricky and slimy fellow," but thought there was some truth in it. Looking back on the event a few years later he saw Munich not as an exercise in appeasement but rather as a deliberate decision by Britain and France to turn Hitler toward the East. "In sacrificing Czechoslovakia to Hitler, Britain and France were really sacrificing their alliance with Russia," he wrote. "They sought security by abandoning the Russian connection at Munich, in a last vain hope that Germany and Russia would fight and exhaust one another."9

The humiliation Hitler inflicted on the democracies at Munich emboldened him to make his bid for total domination of Europe and to intensify his persecution of the Jews. Repression had been institutionalized in 1935 with the Nuremberg Laws, which stripped Jews of their civil and political rights. In November 1938, two months after Munich, an orgy of violence erupted across Germany as Nazi gangs destroyed Jewish-owned businesses, burned synagogues, and attacked Jews on the street. Scores of Jews were murdered and thousands sent to concentration camps. The streets were littered with glass, giving the name of *Kristallnacht* to an event that shocked the world. President Roosevelt recalled the American ambassador as a gesture of disapproval. American papers deplored the Nazi violence, though few heeded the suggestion of the *New Republic* that American immigration barriers be lowered so that persecuted Jews could enter the United States.10

The strict immigration laws of the 1920s had overtly discriminated against people from southern and eastern Europe — Jews, along with Italians, Greeks and Slavs. American consular officials in Europe were often unsympathetic to those seeking immigrant visas and demanded that Jews furnish documents that could be obtained only from Nazi officials. Congress supported the quota system, as did organized labor, which claimed that immigrants would take jobs away from native Americans — although from 1933 to 1938 more people actually emigrated from the United States than entered it. Roosevelt, under attack from rightists for his Court plan and from anti-Semites for having too many Jewish advisers, was reluctant to push Congress. When Senator Robert Wagner introduced a bill in early 1939 to allow 200,000 German refugee children to enter above the quota, the administration remained silent and the bill died in committee.

The American government, like most others, expressed sympathy for the persecuted Jews seeking to flee Germany, but wished they would go elsewhere. Suggested spots included such European colonies as Angola, Madagascar, British Guiana and Uganda. Nothing came of these schemes, although for a time they captured public attention. Lippmann was among those who thought that Africa offered a solution. Having written nothing on the persecution of the Jews since his unfortunate columns in 1933, he broke a five-year silence in November 1938 with two articles on what he called Europe's "over-population" problem.

Without ever specifically mentioning the persecution of the Jews, he reasoned that Europe, "even if normal," would have to be "relieved" of a million people each year. Since developed nations would not have them, the only alternative lay in sending them to an "unsettled territory where an organized community life in the modern sense does not yet exist." Africa should be developed for European settlement.[11] As a response to the hypocritical indifference of the world community, this was better than nothing. But it wasn't much. While others urgently pleaded for revision of American immigration laws to admit the refugees, Lippmann suggested that "surplus" Jews go to Africa.

Lippmann did not publicly criticize Roosevelt for his moral indifference to the plight of the Jews or the State Department for rigidly interpreting the immigration laws and for actually tightening visa requirements after the war broke out. He did not write about the pitiful plight of the St. Louis, a refugee ship that in mid-1939 carried 930 Jews from Hamburg to Havana, where they were refused permission to land because of faulty visas, and then, when they tried to dock in Miami, were blocked by the American government and forced to return to Europe. Lippmann did not write about the death camps, even though their existence was widely known as early as 1942, or complain that the State Department actually suppressed information about the Nazi plan to exterminate the Jews.

Although Lippmann was hardly alone in his silence, others did speak out. "We had it in our power to rescue this doomed people and we did not lift a hand to do it," Freda Kirchwey wrote in the Nation in May 1943. As the pace of extermination intensified — Auschwitz, where one million people died, was executing twelve thousand people a day — protests against the government's indifference to the refugees and refusal to bomb rail lines into the camps mounted, even within the administration. Secretary of the Treasury Henry Morgenthau, who criticized Hull and his assistant for refugees, Breckenridge Long, prepared a study for Roosevelt charging that the rescue of the Jews was "a trust too great to remain in the hands of men indifferent, callous and perhaps hostile." Even after the war, when the horror of the death camps was fully revealed, Lippmann never wrote about them. Unquestionably he felt the plight of the Jews, perhaps even identified with it. Yet his silence was striking.[12]

If Lippmann evaded the moral issue of the persecuted Jews, he had no illusions about Hitler's aggressive ambitions. He had long argued against any territorial concessions, and had insisted that the democracies back up their diplomacy with military power. This put him squarely in opposition to American isolationists — both on the Right and on the Left. In the spring of 1938 he had a running argument with Bruce Bliven — who had become editor of the *New Republic* on Croly's death seven years earlier — over the need to confront the aggressors with military power. "Insofar as the fascist states believe that we will use only measures that are 'short of the application of force,' they will be undeterred by our wishes," Lippmann told the editor. "I see no way of putting any stop to their aggrandizement except by convincing them that at some point they will meet overwhelmingly superior force."[13]

Until Munich Lippmann had thought that Britain and France could hold back Hitler and that the United States could remain aloof from the European struggle. Now he was no longer so sure. The British Empire appeared to be "in mortal danger," he wrote Harold Nicolson in the fall of 1938. "We watch with a kind of dread what looks to us like the failure of Great Britain to arouse herself to the danger she is in." Clearly the fascists would no longer be content with the territory of others — Czechoslovakia, the Balkans, Ethiopia, Spain and China — he pointed out to the British diplomat-historian. Soon they would be demanding some of the democracies' colonies in Africa, the Middle East and Asia. "In the next crisis, the one now impending, the actual possessions of France and Great Britain, in one important matter, the United States, will be directly threatened — your position in the Mediterranean and ours in the buffer states around the Panama Canal." This would lead to an even more acute crisis than that at Munich. "For while it was possible to surrender Czech territory, how is it going to be possible to surrender French territory?" he asked. "If it isn't possible to surrender it, isn't it going to be necessary to say no to these people, and at long last with an emphasis that really carries conviction? So it seems to me, and therefore, when I hear people talk about appeasement, I feel as if they were talking about a wholly imaginary and wholly incredible state of affairs."[14]

Appeasement, as he explained to his readers, was a policy of the strong toward the weak, "of the magnanimous victor seeking reconciliation with the vanquished." But when the position was reversed, and the vanquished strong enough to intimidate the former victor, then appeasement was "nothing but a proof of weakness, leading to ever more unappeasable demands." The United States could maintain a hands-off policy toward Europe only so long as it was sure that Britain and France could successfully resist Hitler. But if they should be defeated, America itself would become vulnerable to Nazi power.

"The question is not whether something we care about is destroyed, though that is bad enough, but that a power which was on our side of the scale will be transformed to the other side," Lippmann wrote Thomas Lamont in January 1939. The obvious policy would have been all-out support for Britain and France. But the public was not ready for such a bold move, and he hesitated to propose it. "I do not know what the conclusion to be drawn to this is, given the present state of American public opinion," he told the financier, "but I think it very important that the real choices should become clear to us."[15]

Those choices became clearer two months later when Hitler sent his troops into Prague, extinguished Czech freedom, and set up a puppet state. Poland and Hungary rushed to seize a share of the spoils. Chamberlain, finally realizing the futility of his appeasement policy, signed defense pacts with Poland, Rumania and Greece. Mussolini, believing he now had a clear field, invaded Albania. Franco, his conquest of Spain completed with the fall of Madrid, joined hands with his helpers by signing the Anti-Comintern Pact with Germany, Italy and Japan. In the face of this desperate situation Lippmann urged Congress to amend the Neutrality Acts to allow Britain and France to buy American arms on a cash-and-carry basis.[16]

By early June 1939, when Helen and Walter arrived in England on the first leg of a six-week pulse-taking tour, the British were mobilizing. War seemed unavoidable. Joseph Kennedy was gloomy and defeatist. The British did not have a chance against Hitler, he told Lippmann. The British fleet was worthless, German submarines would cut off supplies from America, France was surrounded. "Five hundred thousand Spaniards can hold two million Frenchmen," the ambassador maintained as Lippmann sat in his office for a dispiriting lecture. "Poland has no munitions, Russia is useless, Rumania can't fight, the Japanese will attack in the East. All Englishmen in their hearts *know* this to be true, but a small group of brilliant people has created a public feeling which makes it impossible for the government to take a sensible course." For Kennedy the "sensible course" was to give Nazi Germany a free hand in eastern Europe. "I am also a bear on democracy," the former financier confided. "It's gone already. In England today they have exchange control."

Kennedy was not alone in counseling appeasement. Charles Lindbergh, having recently been decorated by Hermann Göring, declared the Luftwaffe to be invincible, and urged Americans not to allow Jews to prejudice them against Nazi Germany. Many considered the still-boyish hero a political naïf; Lippmann later privately described him as "a Nazilover." He did not, however, publicly criticize Lindbergh at the time.

Nor did he criticize Joseph Kennedy, although later in conversation he said the ambassador was "more than an appeaser — he was actually pro-Nazi and strongly anti-Semitic."[17]

After his interview with Kennedy, Lippmann left the American embassy in a glum mood. He returned to Claridge's to pick up Helen and dress for dinner with Kenneth and Jane Clark. The art historian, then serving as director of the National Gallery, had also invited the Julian Huxleys, Lady Sybil Colefax, and Harold Nicolson and his wife, Vita Sackville-West. Winston Churchill had been lured from his country home to meet Lippmann. The former lord of the Admiralty was in a dour mood as the evening began. His hopes for supplanting Chamberlain had not yet come to fruition, and war seemed near.

After a few minutes of banter the conversation turned to politics. Lippmann, in an effort to rouse Churchill, described the conversation he had had with Kennedy that afternoon. Churchill rose to the occasion with a magnificent tirade. Sitting there hunched, "waving his whisky and soda to mark his periods, stubbing his cigar with the other hand," in Harold Nicolson's reconstruction of the evening, Churchill told Lippmann that, even though "steel and fire will rain down upon us day and night scattering death and destruction far and wide," the British people would only intensify their will for victory. And even supposing that the ambassador was correct in his "tragic utterance," he said to Lippmann with a beady stare, then it would be up to the Americans to continue the struggle, to "think imperially," and to hold untarnished the "torch of liberty."

Lippmann's version — as written out by Helen just after the party — was more prosaic. Britain's air defense could inflict a 20 percent casualty rate on the Luftwaffe, Churchill maintained.

The submarine menace was much overrated. Britain had a million men under arms. The German army could never pierce the *carapace* of the Maginot Line. Spain was negligible. Better to have the Turks than the Italians: Italy a prey, Turkey a falcon. Cut losses in the Far East and settle with Japan after the war. No use telling the Germans they weren't being encircled. Better to overwhelm them with righteous indignation. The only argument that counts is force. At their first provocative action cut German communications with Europe and defy them to do anything about it. As for a negotiated settlement: "There can never be peace in Europe while eight million Czechs are in bondage."[18]

A few days later, after a dinner at Sybil Colefax's with that "small group of brilliant people" that Kennedy had warned him against — such anti-appeasers as Nicolson, Duff Cooper, and Vansittart — Helen and Walter went off to Paris for a round of interviews. The French seemed strangely optimistic. Premier Daladier expressed his admiration for the argument Lippmann had made in *The Good Society*. "We have learned that it isn't liberalism which failed in Europe," he told Lippmann, "but interventionism which ruined liberalism." With regard to Hitler, Daladier said that France would stand firm on its commitment to Poland. And he revealed that France and the Soviet Union would sign a formal alliance within a few days. Russia had demanded control over the Baltic states. A bit harsh, Foreign Minister Bonnet said, but "entirely justified." [19]

With an alliance presumably in the offing that would link Paris and Moscow with London, Hitler might yet be checked. Lippmann was feeling guardedly optimistic as he and Helen set off for New York on the *Normandie*. On their arrival in early July they decided not to return to Washington, where they had bought a picturesque, if impractical, Georgetown house once owned by Alexander Graham Bell. Instead, they went straight to Maine. Helen had spent most of her childhood summers at her family's Bar Harbor estate, and Walter had grown fond of Mount Desert Island from his visits to the Finletters and other friends. They rented what they euphemistically called a "camp" — several comfortably appointed small cabins grouped around a simple house — that belonged to the Arctic explorer Admiral Richard Byrd. There Walter tried to put into book form some of the ideas he had sketched out the previous summer in Paris, a work he tentatively called "The Image of Man." Sixteen years later it would finally be published, in very different form, as *The Public Philosophy*.

The summer was relaxing and social: writing in the mornings, tennis or hiking in the afternoons, dinner with friends in the evenings. Maine agreed with him; it was a relief from the pressures of Washington, of business lunches and business cocktail parties, a chance to unwind, to go for long walks. A few years later he and Helen bought a hundred acres of pine forest at Indian Head, near Southwest Harbor, where they built their own "camp" along the lines of Admiral Byrd's.

Under his easygoing arrangement with the *Herald Tribune* Lippmann had suspended his column early in June, when he went to Europe, and did not pick it up again until the end of August. Even then he did not resume it with gusto. He was getting bored with the column; so bored, in fact, that he wrote the *Trib*'s editor a three-page letter declaring that "the time has come when I must do something else." He was frustrated by the tyranny of trying to keep up with the news. "I find I am increasingly dissatisfied with myself, increasingly aware that I do not deal thoroughly with issues that are too serious to be dealt with superficially, increasingly oppressed by the idea of expressing an opinion every forty-eight hours, increasingly dissatisfied with the sense that the product is superficial and second-rate." His alternative was to abandon the thrice-weekly column and do a series of articles on a single subject. After eight years T&T had lost its novelty for him. [20]

This was hardly the first time he felt bored with the column. A few years earlier he had "definitely" decided to drop it in favor of a regular series of articles for the *Atlantic*. But by the end of this summer his restlessness passed, just as it had a few years before. He had become so absorbed in the onrushing crisis that he allowed the column to go on a little longer. That little while stretched out another twenty-eight years.

Tried and Found Wanting

With the best of intentions but with a deadly misunderstanding, we all adopted the isolationist view of disarmament and separateness.

— "Today and Tomorrow," February 27, 1941

WHILE Lippmann was in Maine deciding whether or not to go back
to the column, Hitler and Stalin stunned the world by signing a
nonaggression pact. A week later, on September 1, 1939, Hitler invaded
Poland. The British and French, honoring their pact with the Poles,
declared war on Germany. Having refused to come to the aid of a defen-
sible state a year earlier, they now went to war over an indefensible one.
Roosevelt called Congress into special session to repeal the Neutrality
Acts so that London and Paris could buy American arms. Isolationists
warned against taking sides, while America Firsters charged that FDR
was secretly trying to lead the United States into war.

Although Lippmann favored repeal, he also recognized that the public
dreaded involvement in the fighting. Thus he insisted that arms sales
and neutrality were not only compatible, but linked. The best way "to
keep Americans 3,000 miles from the war and keep the war 3,000 miles
from Americans," he argued a bit disingenuously, was to aid London
and Paris.[1] During congressional hearings on the arms embargo he made
a special appeal to Arthur Vandenberg, the most influential of the Senate isolationists. Lifting the embargo on arms, but retaining it on shipping and finance, offered the "one effective way of preventing our being
drawn into the war," he told the senator. The shipping embargo would
prevent the situation that had occurred in the first war, when American
vessels were being sunk by German submarines. But removing the arms
embargo would allow the British to maintain their naval strength in the
Atlantic. And this would help ensure American neutrality.

"I regard it of crucial importance that we should avoid getting into a
situation where intervention in the European war is even to be consid-

ered as a practical possibility," Lippmann insisted. The growing tension with Japan made it essential that the American fleet remain in the Pacific. "Only a lunatic would contemplate military intervention in the Atlantic with no navy to assure the return of American forces," he told Vandenberg. What should the United States do if Britain and France collapsed? Since he was convinced that it "could not, would not, and should not send an army overseas," it must prepare to take "bold measures" to gain Atlantic bases while building a two-ocean navy.[2]

Lippmann's prescription for noninvolvement was meant to keep the isolationists at bay — for he never wavered in his commitment to the preservation of an Atlantic community linking America to western Europe. But his argument grated on the sensibilities of his British friends. "No one expects, or even desires, that you should come in as you did last time," John Maynard Keynes wrote him in some exasperation. "But the idea that there is some sort of moral beauty about neutrality I find extremely distasteful."

Lippmann tried to explain that he was not preaching neutrality, but rather the lifting of the arms embargo. "You cannot pick any bones with me about the American reaction to the war, because I shall be agreeing with you, I am sure," he replied to the economist shortly after Congress finally voted to repeal the embargo. "There were times during that bitter struggle when it seemed to me that almost any kind of self-respect and self-confidence would have been better than none at all. I don't know whether people in England understand how extraordinarily difficult it was to repeal the arms embargo after war started, and what a price had to be paid for it."[3]

In November 1939, while Congress was debating repeal, the Russians demanded that Finland give up bases and territory along their common frontier. The Finns balked. The Soviets moved troops to the border and threatened to seize the bases. Suddenly the spotlight shifted from Hitler to Stalin. Lippmann shared the general sense of outrage. "Here in the making is one of the most dreadful catastrophes which has menaced Western civilization since the armed might of Islam invaded Europe," he exclaimed. If the Finns had to fight they would be "resisting the advance of another Genghis Khan." In a wistful gesture, he urged German conservatives to purge themselves of the Nazis so that Germany could return to its natural role as "defender of the West" against Eastern barbarism.[4]

Lippmann's overwrought analogy prompted historian Hans Kohn to remind him that Stalin's regime was hardly more "Genghis Khan" than Hitler's, and that the most serious menace to European peace was Nazi Germany, not Soviet Russia. Later, in June 1941 — when Hitler broke his pact with Stalin and invaded Russia, and the Finns then signed an alliance with Nazi Germany — Lippmann agreed. Stalin's demands on

Finland, he now decided, were actually "for the purpose of strengthening his defenses." Later he looked back on the episode with embarrassment. "The most foolish thing I can remember in my many human errors is that during World War II I was one of the people who joined the hue and cry for war against the Soviet Union to save Finland," he told an interviewer. "That was the most nonsensical thing that anybody ever proposed, but I can remember doing it."[5]

In early February 1940, as the Finns were retreating before the Russian advance and Hitler's armies were preparing for their blitzkrieg attack in the west, Lippmann and Helen left on their annual European excursion. In France a bevy of colonels took Lippmann on a tour of the Maginot Line. He spent three days along the outer ring of the forts and never heard a shot fired, even though France and Germany had officially been at war for nearly six months. At Strasbourg he stood at the French side of the bridge across the Rhine, looking at the German soldiers on the other side with their fixed bayonets and cannons, waiting for the signal from their Führer. On his return from the front Lippmann asked General Maurice Gamelin, commander of the French army, what would happen in the north, where the Maginot Line ended along the Belgian frontier. "Oh, we've got to have an open side because we need a *champs de bataille*," the general explained. "We're going to attack the German army and destroy it. The Maginot Line will narrow the gap through which they can come, and thus enable us to destroy them more easily."[6]

The test came soon enough. On April 9 the eerie stillness that had hung over the western front all fall and winter was shattered when Hitler's Panzer divisions crossed into defenseless Denmark and Norway. Without warning the Luftwaffe devastated Rotterdam as German troops tore across the flatlands of Holland and Belgium to the Channel ports. Instead of assaulting the Maginot Line they went around it, mauling the badly led and poorly equipped French army. The British Expeditionary Force, driven to the sea at Dunkirk, faced annihilation until a near-impossible evacuation was carried out. On May 10 Chamberlain resigned in disgrace and Churchill took over as prime minister, offering his people only "blood, toil, tears and sweat" and the hope of eventual victory.

The invasion of France finally brought home to Americans the gravity of the Nazi menace. Public opinion, so staunch against any involvement in Europe, began to shift. Roosevelt asked Congress for another billion dollars for defense and declared that the United States would "extend to the opponents of force the material resources of this nation." Lippmann, drawing a somber picture, warned that if France fell America would be left "isolated in a world dominated on both sides of our oceans by the most formidable alliance of victorious conquerors that was ever formed in the whole history of man." Isolationists remained unpersuaded. "Walter Lippmann has got the jitters again," Oswald Garrison Villard chided in the *Nation* as Hitler's divisions swept through northern France.[7]

On June 12, 1940, the victorious German army entered Paris. The demoralized French, unprepared for the blitzkrieg and sapped by a fascist-sympathizing minority that preferred Hitler to a popular front of leftist parties, capitulated. A collaborationist regime took power under the aged war hero Marshal Philippe Pétain. Virtually the entire continent west of Russia lay under Nazi control. Britain stood alone, girding itself for aerial assault and devastation.

France's capitulation stunned Lippmann as much as it did the general public. He had thought that the repeal of the Neutrality Acts would allow the British and French to hold back Hitler. But even while urging American neutrality he had warned that American safety rested on British control of the Atlantic sea-lanes. Should that control be lost, he had warned a year and a half earlier, "we shall have become for the first time in our history insecure and vulnerable."[8] Throughout 1939 and early 1940 he had tried to appease isolationist sentiment by maintaining that the United States could remain neutral. But by May 1940, as the Nazi armies were closing in on Paris, he could offer no such hope.

The shock of Hitler's armored divisions driving through Denmark, Norway, the Low Countries and France swept away Lippmann's equivocations. Now he espoused openly what he had intimated only hesitantly throughout the thirties: that America's security was vitally connected to Britain's independence and Anglo-American control of the Atlantic. The fact that he himself had been remiss in asserting this made him even more biting in his attack on the isolationists. Why had Americans not realized until the collapse of France that they could not allow British sea power to be destroyed or to fall into German hands? The reason, he charged, was that the postwar generation had never understood the reasons why the United States had gone to war against Germany in 1917. They had been "duped by a falsification of history . . . miseducated by a swarm of innocent but ignorant historians, by reckless demagogues, and by foreign interests, into believing that America entered the other war because of British propaganda, the loans of the bankers, the machinations of President Wilson's advisers, and a drummed up patriotic ecstasy." The real reason America had fought, he explained, was that Germany's declaration of unlimited submarine warfare threatened to starve the Allies into submission and destroy British sea power. To demonstrate this, he quoted from the article he himself had written in February 1917 declaring that the "safety of the Atlantic highway is something for which America should fight."[9]

There was never any doubt in Lippmann's mind that the crucial threat to American interests lay in Europe, not in Asia. Japan's aggression against China was troublesome, and ultimately would have to be dealt with. But it should not be allowed to distract American attention from the urgent need to save Britain. "By no stretch of the imagination can our interests in the Far East be considered as anything but secondary to our interests in this hemisphere and the Atlantic," he wrote an American officer in the Pacific command. "Japan cannot threaten the independence of any state in this hemisphere, either politically or economically, whereas a victorious Germany can and will." Washington should work out a deal with Tokyo that would allow the United States to withdraw its fleet from the Pacific in case of war with Germany.

This was not a popular stand among those isolationists willing to let Nazi Germany dominate Europe but ready to go to war over the territorial integrity of China. "I am not afraid of being called pro-Japanese or anything else," Lippmann wrote Whitney Griswold, then a history professor at Yale and later its president, "and I should gladly advocate any policy which would reduce our liabilities in the Far East and yet protect what I regard as really vital interests in the Pacific Ocean." [10] Like Griswold he believed those interests to be the protection of America's Pacific possessions, respect for Europe's Asian colonies, dissuading Japan from an alliance with Germany, and the continuation of good trade relations with Tokyo.

The administration saw it otherwise, and in January 1940 put pressure on Japan by refusing to renew the commercial treaty. Lippmann angrily denounced the action as the "longest step on the road to war" taken by the United States since 1915, when Wilson decided to hold Germany responsible for the loss of American lives in the war zone. Such action would merely provoke Japan to attack the European colonies in Asia, and force the United States to either accept Japanese supremacy or go to war. "The historians of the future will consider it one of the great ironies of history," he predicted, "that on the eve of a great war the United States was precipitated by 'isolationist' leaders into challenging the vital interests of a great power, and then induced by these same leaders to believe that it could safely deal with the consequences in one ocean regardless of what happened in the other." [11] The United States had put itself on a collision course with Japan at a time when Hitler was consolidating his hold over Europe. Rarely had American diplomacy seemed so perverse and self-defeating.

On June 18, 1940, as a collaborationist regime in Paris sued for peace, and an unknown brigadier general fled to London to raise the banner of French resistance, Lippmann stood before his Harvard classmates at their thirtieth reunion dinner in Cambridge and drew a somber picture of the task ahead. "We here in America may soon be the last stronghold of our civilization — the isolated and beleaguered citadel of law and of liberty, of mercy and of charity, of justice among men and of love and of good will," he told the men who had come to celebrate a happier past. "Organized mechanized evil" was loose in the world, its victories made possible by the "lazy, self-indulgent materialism, the amiable, lackadaisical, footless, confused complacency" of the democracies. "We shall turn from the soft vices in which a civilization decays," he said, "we shall return to the stern virtues by which a civilization is made, we shall do this because, at long last, we know that we must, because finally we begin to see that the hard way is the only enduring way."[12]

Disarmament, collective security, armed neutrality — all of Lippmann's formulas had been found wanting. Now nothing was left but armed resistance and preparing a reluctant nation for a war that seemed inevitable.

Only a few days earlier, as the Germans were closing in on Paris and the British feverishly pulling their besieged troops off the beaches at Dunkirk, Lippmann had received a phone call from his old friend Philip Kerr. Now known as Lord Lothian, Kerr had recently been appointed British ambassador to Washington. He asked Lippmann to come over to the embassy on an urgent matter. There Lippmann found the ambassador pacing the floor. Lothian wasted no time with chitchat. The surrender of France could force a British capitulation, he warned. If Britain lost control of the seas Churchill's government could fall and be replaced by a collaborationist regime — one that would make a deal with Hitler and turn the Royal Navy over to the Nazis. To ward off such a tragedy, he maintained, Britain desperately needed arms and ships — especially destroyers to defend the sea-lanes. They could come from only one place: America.

Lothian was preaching to a convert. Lippmann agreed that the United States should furnish Britain with the destroyers it needed, but realized that the isolationists would first have to be outflanked. He and Lothian discussed various possibilities, and then came up with the idea of a *quid pro quo*. Washington would turn over the destroyers in exchange for British bases in the Western Hemisphere. Even though the isolationists did not care about saving Britain, they were interested in defending the United States. Of little strategic importance, the bases nonetheless provided the means by which Britain could obtain the destroyers.

Lippmann's task was now to present the plan to the public. If the British and French fleets fell to Hitler, he warned, the United States would be faced with a threat to its very survival. Britain's resistance could be sustained only by entering into "specific arrangements" with London and Ottawa to decide what kind of assistance the United States should give, and to provide "specific measures of protection" in the

Atlantic. This must not become a partisan issue or enter into the 1940 presidential campaign, he insisted. Leaders of both parties must share responsibility for aid to Britain.[13]

While Lippmann was unveiling the idea to the public — although not yet specifically mentioning destroyers or bases — Lothian moved to sell it to the Century Group. So named because it met at the Century Club, the group was an offshoot of the Committee to Defend America by Aiding the Allies. Drawing on its impressive array of legal talent, the group prepared and presented to FDR a legal brief indicating how he could get around the Neutrality Acts by justifying the destroyer-bases deal as a defense measure.

As the legal technicalities were being ironed out, Lippmann moved to get a stamp of approval from someone of uncontested authority and prestige. One name immediately came to mind: General John Pershing, the hero of World War I. Lippmann, joined by Ernest Lindley of *Newsweek,* paid a call on the general, then in his eightieth year, and told him that Britain's very survival hinged on his endorsement of the destroyer-bases exchange. Pershing, moved by the plea, agreed to do his bit, and delivered a moving speech hailing the deal. "Today may be the last time when by measures short of war we can still prevent war," he declared. The pro-intervention press hailed the address as a profound statement of American responsibility and political maturity. Lippmann particularly liked the speech. He had helped write it.

Pershing's speech made a great impact on public opinion and distressed the anti-interventionists. The *St. Louis Post-Dispatch,* having heard that Lippmann was the author, tracked him down at his summer home in Maine and demanded to know if the rumor was true. When he admitted it was, the reporter threatened to start a congressional investigation of what he called the "plot to get America into the war" and Lippmann's part as a "warmonger." A bit shaken, Lippmann got on the phone to Joseph Pulitzer, his summer neighbor on Mount Desert Island, and told the paper's owner to rein in his staff. Although the paper denounced the destroyer-bases deal editorially, it never launched the threatened investigation.

Even with Pershing's blessing the deal threatened to become a political football, especially since 1940 was an election year. Lippmann had urged William Allen White to use his influence on Wendell Willkie — FDR's opponent in the forthcoming presidential election — to keep the issue out of the campaign. But the isolationists soon got wind of the scheme. Arthur Krock devoted a column to the "plot" in hopes of getting Willkie to disavow it. Willkie held firm and refused to raise the issue, but the isolationists were furious.

FDR, at last feeling that the ground was safely prepared, announced at the end of the summer that he was giving Britain fifty overage destroyers in return for long-term leases on British bases in the Western Hemisphere. While the deal may well have saved Britain from capitulation, it clearly stretched the congressional ban on arms sales. This time Lippmann was not upset by such use of presidential power, and dismissed the isolationists' objections as petty legalism. "Wherever democracy has been overthrown from within or conquered from without, the disaster has been preceded by a period of indecision, weakness, confusion," he retorted. "Control of the seas by the free nations must not be yielded up if freedom itself is to survive." [14] In the crunch he was willing to give the President full powers — as he had been in 1933. This was a crunch.

The isolationists, though weakened by public anxiety over the fall of France and the raging Battle of Britain, were still a powerful force whose ranks stretched across the political board, including such diverse types as pro-Nazis like Father Coughlin and Gerald L. K. Smith; defeatists like Charles and Anne Morrow Lindbergh, who argued that fascism was the "wave of the future"; old-style progressives like Senators Burton Wheeler and Gerald Nye, who saw the war as another chapter in the bloody volume of European rivalry; socialists like Norman Thomas; antiwar liberals like Robert Hutchins, Charles and Mary Beard, and Chester Bowles; and the Roosevelt-hating Hearst papers and the *Chicago Tribune*. Linking most of these disparate types was the America First Committee, formed in the autumn of 1940.

The America Firsters, mostly Republicans, were dismayed by Willkie's capture of the GOP nomination. A utilities executive who had made a fortune on Wall Street, Willkie still kept his Hoosier accent and rumpled suits — "just a simple barefoot boy from Wall Street," in Harold Ickes's acid phrase. Lippmann liked the combination and thought Willkie would do just fine. He enthusiastically offered his services as unofficial adviser, and spent a good part of July and early August on the phone with the GOP candidate.

Starting out in high gear, Willkie's campaign quickly lost speed. He waffled on the issues and seemed loath to offend the isolationists and party conservatives. "The momentum behind you has slowed down since you were nominated because you have not shown the road you intend to take, and your well-wishers have been moving in several directions at once," a distressed Lippmann wrote Willkie in late July. The campaign should not take an anti–New Deal tack, he warned. The country could not go back to the old system of untrammeled private enterprise. Social gains would not be repudiated, total defense required government planning and regimentation, and even if Hitler were defeated, "economic life cannot for years to come be left to the free play of economic forces; it will have to be directed to national ends."

In warning Willkie against friends with a "1936 mentality" who yearned for the old pre–New Deal days, Lippmann urged him to "appear as the organizer of security and not as the champion of laissez-faire." Roosevelt's great strength was his popularity among the poor. For this reason, "bitter anti–New Dealism will help him, and you will be maneuvered into the position of a supposed reactionary. Your opportunity," Lippmann elaborated,

arises out of the fact that people feel insecure and want the assurance of a strong, competent man. Roosevelt is not a strong, competent man, and that is where you can beat him if you take "the hard line" and summon the people rather than vaguely trying to please them all.

You have nothing to lose, in my opinion, by being the Churchill rather than the Chamberlain of the crisis, and by charging Roosevelt with being the Daladier, the weak man who means well feebly and timidly. You must not let him be the Churchill, for he is not a Churchill. But he will try to seem like one, and if you do not seize the initiative, he may succeed.

The advice was not bad, and Lippmann was right in pointing out how FDR's caution had left the nation rudderless in the face of the fascist challenge. A week later Lippmann publicly chided FDR for his timidity and lack of leadership. "There is bewilderment; the people would like a President who is resolute and imperturbable," he charged.

There is suspicion and division; the people would like a President who is boldly magnanimous and chivalrous. There is vast disorder in human affairs and there are tremendous tasks to be done; the people would like a President who will organize their energies and thereby give them that courage and confidence that can be reached these days only as men, ceasing to brood and worry impotently, are put to work doing efficiently some hard job they believe is necessary. . . . For when the leaders are frightened, soft, untruthful, so meanly ambitious that they stoop to conquer, there is no vision and the people perish.[15]

Even by trying to play Churchill, Willkie was no serious match for FDR, and as his campaign foundered he became desperate. In October he began flirting with isolationism and attacked the President as a warmonger. The campaign turned bitter, forcing FDR into extravagant denials that he would ever send "American boys" off to foreign wars. Lippmann began to lose faith in his candidate. "As for Willkie, I feel very badly indeed," he wrote *Time-Life* publisher Henry Luce in late September. "I hoped and believed he would be the man this country needs, but I think he set his campaign on a fundamentally wrong line back in July and has lost ground since."[16] Urging Willkie not to divide the country on the war issue, Lippmann pulled away from his embrace.

By election day he was sitting squarely on the fence. Disgusted by Willkie's flirtation with the isolationists and the Old Guard, but unable to support FDR, he could not bring himself to make a choice. When

Alexander Woollcott asked him how he planned to vote, he took the occasion to elevate his equivocation to a political principle. "Columnists who undertake to interpret events should not regard themselves as public personages with a constituency to which they are responsible," he explained.

It seems to me that once the columnist thinks of himself as a public somebody over and above the intrinsic value and integrity of what is published under his name, he ceases to think as clearly and as disinterestedly as his readers have a right to expect him to think. Like a politician, he acquires a public character, which he comes to admire and to worry about preserving and improving; his personal life, his self-esteem, his allegiances, his interests and ambitions become indistinguishable from his judgment of events.

In thirty years of journalism I think I have learned to know the pitfalls of the profession and, leaving aside the gross forms of corruption, such as profiting by inside knowledge and currying favor with those who have favor to give, and following the fashions, the most insidious of all the temptations is to think of oneself as engaged in a public career on the stage of the world rather than as an observant writer of newspaper articles about some of the things that are happening in the world.

So I take the view that I write of matters about which I think I have something to say, but that as a person I am nobody of any public importance, that I am not an adviser-at-large to mankind or even to those who read occasionally or often what I write. This is the code which I follow. I learned it from Frank Cobb, who practiced it, and adjured me again and again during the long year when he was dying that more newspapermen had been ruined by self-importance than by liquor. You will remember that he had had opportunity to observe the effects of both kinds of intoxication.

The nomination of Willkie had meant that foreign policy could be kept out of the campaign. This being the case, Lippmann concluded, "I decided that if Willkie stood fast on his commitments and convictions, the best thing I could do in this campaign was to stand aside, and to keep reminding people that they were going to have to live after November fifth with the consequences of the stupid things they do before November fifth."

This was a compelling explanation, if not altogether candid, since Lippmann had never shown such scruples before about backing a candidate. This time he simply did not feel strongly one way or the other. But he did owe his readers an explanation, and a few days later he incorporated his letter to Woollcott into his column, adding a notable caveat. "The individual writer is not a public personage, or at least ought not to be," he wrote, "nor is he a public institution, nor is he the repository of 'influence' and 'leadership'; he is a reporter and commentator who lays before his readers his findings on the subjects he has studied and leaves it at that. He cannot cover the universe, and if he begins to imagine that he is called to such a universal mission, he will soon . . . be saying less and less about more and more until at last he is saying nothing about everything."[17]

Even had Lippmann taken sides, it would hardly have made any difference. FDR buried Willkie by a five-million-vote margin and by 449 to 82 in the electoral college. Lippmann sent FDR a telegram of congratulations, and in his column admonished the President not to be a party leader "along lines which divide the people," but to devote himself entirely to the "defense of the peace and the security of the nation" — in other words, to forget about extending New Deal reforms.[18] That was just what FDR intended, counting on rearmament orders to pull the nation out of the continuing depression.

The returns were barely in when Churchill presented FDR with another shopping list of ships, bombers and munitions. This time he wanted to charge it. Although the Neutrality Acts demanded cash payment, Britain was running out of dollars. FDR responded at a press conference by outlining Britain's plight and drawing a homely parable about a man lending his neighbor his garden hose to put out a fire. In a nationally broadcast "fireside chat" at the end of December 1940 he said the United States must become the "great arsenal of democracy." With FDR's garden hose Lend-Lease was born, transforming the United States from a friendly neutral to an active nonbelligerent.

Lippmann heartily approved. With aid to Britain, he wrote, "this country passes from large promises carried out slyly and partially by clever devices to substantial deeds openly and honestly avowed." Although he refrained from mentioning it, the Lend-Lease bill bore the outlines of a plan he had helped draft in the spring of 1940, at the request of Senator Claude Pepper of Florida, along with presidential adviser Benjamin Cohen and Texas publisher Charles Marsh.[19]

While Congress was debating the administration's Lend-Lease bill, Lippmann took another swipe at the isolationists. They had "forced the United States to make a separate peace and to withdraw from all further association with the other democracies to keep the world safe for democracy," and had brought on the depression by high tariffs and by demanding uncollectible reparations and debts. Even he was not without blame. "We all adopted the isolationist view of disarmament and separateness," he confessed.

Having disarmed ourselves and divided the old Allies from each other, we adopted the pious resolutions of the Kellogg Pact, and refused even to participate in the organization of a world court. Then, having obstructed the reconstruction of the world, and having seen the ensuing anarchy produce the revolutionary imperialist dictatorships of Russia, Italy and Germany, we tried to protect the failure of isolation by the policy of insulation — by the neutrality acts which were to keep us safe by renouncing our rights.[20]

In denouncing a generation that had, in his words, been "tried and found wanting," he repudiated the part he himself had played, and now eagerly backed Lend-Lease and the rejection of an outdated neutrality.

In a series of columns early in 1941 he urged FDR to show the people that America's own security was bound up with Britain's survival. Americans did not understand what was at stake, he charged, because Woodrow Wilson had never explained the real reasons why America had entered the First World War. "He talked of American ideals to the exclusion of American interest and thus led the country to regard as a philanthropic crusade what was in fact a defensive intervention for the preservation of American security."[21] Having himself been a Wilsonian idealist during the 1920s and 1930s, seeking peace in disarmament, collective security, and a "political equivalent of war," Lippmann felt some blame for policies that, never having been fully tried, were now found wanting. Never again would he argue for disarmament, armed neutrality, "aggressive pacifism," or a "political equivalent of war." Henceforth he would urge military preparedness and a hardheaded concentration on the "national interest."

Once Congress approved Lend-Lease in March 1941, American neutrality was barely a polite fiction. Over the next few months Roosevelt seized Axis shipping in American ports, took Greenland under protection, and authorized American ships to convoy British cargoes in the war zone. As isolationists railed against FDR, Hitler pulled a stunning about-face. On June 22, 1941, he repudiated his nonaggression pact with the Soviet Union and invaded his former ally. Hitler's Panzer divisions drove to the banks of the Don and the gates of Moscow. If Hitler could defeat Russia quickly, seize its resources, and turn its population into laborers for the Reich, Britain would face the full brunt of the Nazi war machine. Whether it could long survive was questionable.

As the Nazis unleashed unprecedented acts of barbarism upon the peoples under their occupation, it became clear that the ordered, rational world Lippmann had grown up in, the Enlightenment values of individualism and respect for human dignity, could no longer be taken for granted. For the first time in his life he, like all Americans, was confronted with what he called "ice-cold evil." "The modern skeptical world has been taught for some 200 years a conception of human nature in which the reality of evil, so well known to the ages of faith, has been discounted," he wrote in the fall of 1941. "Almost all of us grew up in an environment of such easy optimism that we can scarcely know what is meant, though our ancestors knew it well, by the satanic will. We shall have to recover this forgotten but essential truth — along with so many others that we lost when, thinking we were enlightened and advanced, we were merely shallow and blind."[22]

Germany's invasion of the Soviet Union gave the Japanese a golden opportunity. With the Soviets preoccupied in Europe they could concentrate on Southeast Asia — waiting for Germany to knock off Russia before claiming their share of the spoils. After the fall of France the military regime in Tokyo had signed the Tripartite Pact with Hitler and Mussolini and taken control of the northern part of French Indochina. Washington had retaliated by clamping an embargo on American shipments to Japan of aviation gasoline and scrap metal. Now, in the wake of Germany's invasion of Russia, Japan took over the rest of Indochina. FDR responded by impounding Japanese funds in the United States, closing the Panama Canal to Japanese shipping, and forbidding the export of vital raw materials.

Lippmann, who had earlier called for an accommodation with Japan at almost any price, now rejected his own reasoning. He supported the administration's hard line toward Tokyo and argued that "economic paralysis" was the best hope for checking Japanese imperialism.[23] This put Washington on a collision course with Tokyo. Yet Lippmann remained strangely optimistic. He always assumed that a war with Japan would be fought entirely with ships and planes, not with American soldiers. America's strength lay "on the seas and in the air and in the factory — not on the battlefields of Europe or Asia," he wrote in September 1941. While favoring a bigger navy and an extended draft, he maintained that a 900,000 man army was actually too big: "Our most effective part in this war is now, and for any predictable future, to help hold the seas and to be the arsenal of those fighting aggression."[24] The House of Representatives, sharing his doubts that the United States need ever fight a land war, acted to extend the draft by only a one-vote margin.

The quarrel between the United States and Japan rested on one basic issue: Tokyo wanted control over China, Washington refused to accept that. During the summer and fall of 1941 the Japanese made a series of hesitant overtures to the United States, offering to withdraw from Southeast Asia if allowed a free hand in China. The administration refused such a bargain. Lippmann, despite his own earlier insistence that the United States must not fight Japan over the territorial integrity of China, and in fact should withdraw even from the Philippines, now backed the administration's confrontation diplomacy. Fear that Japan would seize mineral-rich Malaya and the Dutch East Indies persuaded him that its expansion had to be halted. Like Roosevelt and Hull, he assumed the Japanese would back down if the United States stood firm.

But the militarists in Tokyo, rankling from decades of insults and acts of racial prejudice — exemplified by the Oriental Exclusion Acts forbidding Japanese immigration into the United States — were intent on gaining an empire equal to those of the European powers. The United States stood in the way of that ambition. Determined to expel the Europeans from their Asian colonies, to dominate a hapless China, and to achieve a "co-prosperity sphere" stretching across the western Pacific, the Japanese decided that their best hope was to immobilize American power until they could consolidate their hold on Southeast Asia.

In late November 1941, when Roosevelt flatly turned down their offer of a *modus vivendi* based on their suzerainty over China, they put their war plans into operation. On December 4 Lippmann, having picked up signals from the War Department, which suspected a possible attack on the Philippines, declared that the United States was "really on the verge of actual, all-out war."[25] Three days later the Japanese navy, in a brilliantly executed surprise move, struck not at Manila but at Hawaii, decimating the unprepared American fleet. Roosevelt, citing the "date which will live in infamy," called for a declaration of war. On December 11 Germany honored its pact with Japan and declared war on the United States.

Suddenly the great debate about isolation was over.

◄ 31 ►

Panic and Bungling

I cannot pretend to write dispassionately about General de Gaulle.

— "Today and Tomorrow," April 21, 1960

WITH the nation at war the old arguments over intervention became irrelevant. Isolationists were now apostles of total victory. War orders flowed into long-silent factories, the jobless went back to work, and the pessimistic drift of the thirties gave way to a national enthusiasm and sense of purpose.

In early February 1942 Lippmann went to the West Coast to talk to military officials. The shock of Pearl Harbor had given Californians a bad case of jitters. Fantastic rumors of a possible Japanese invasion mingled with a long-held racial prejudice against Orientals to trigger a near-hysteria. Governor Culbert Olson and Attorney General Earl Warren worked with local officials to invoke laws to dismiss Japanese-Americans (both first-generation Issei and second-generation Nisei) from civil service jobs, revoke their licenses to practice law and medicine, and in some towns even forbid them to do business. Fanned by the Hearst press, white Californians refused to employ "the Japs," to serve them at restaurants or gas stations, or to sell them food. Some tried to justify these acts by charging that Japanese-Americans represented a dangerous "fifth column." No similar charges were made, however, against German- or Italian-Americans on the East Coast. Nor was there any panic in Hawaii, far more vulnerable and with a far greater proportion of Japanese-Americans. "A Jap's a Jap," said General John DeWitt, army commander for the area. "It makes no difference whether he's an American or not." A surprising number of eminent people seemed to agree.

In the wake of the anti-Japanese hysteria that swept California, Assistant Secretary of War John J. McCloy, operating under authority of his boss, Henry Stimson, approved a draconian plan to evacuate all

Japanese-Americans from the West Coast and relocate them in remote "resettlement camps" (later dubbed "concentration camps" by FDR himself) under army guard. U.S. Attorney General Francis Biddle expressed qualms about the plan. While the President was deciding, Lippmann went to San Francisco for a look. After a briefing by General DeWitt, he emerged persuaded that the whole Pacific Coast was, as he informed his readers, in "imminent danger of a combined attack from within and from without." The enemy could inflict "irreparable damage" through an attack supported by "organized sabotage." The army and navy were operating with "one hand tied down in Washington."

Declaring that the entire coast must be considered a combat zone under special rules, Lippmann suggested that, as on the deck of a warship, "everyone should be compelled to prove that he has a good reason for being there." Those who had no such reason could legitimately be removed, since "nobody's constitutional rights include the right to do business on a battlefield." By a deft bit of sophistry Lippmann persuaded himself there would be no assault on civil liberties, since "under this system all persons are, in principle, treated alike."[1] He neglected to point out that the only citizens who had to justify their presence on the West Coast "battlefield" were those of Japanese ancestry. In other words he accepted, although refraining from expressing it outright, the argument that all Americans of Japanese ancestry were potential fifth columnists and should be treated as a class apart from other citizens. It was a rationale the Nazis could have used about the Jews.

This argument, coming from such a prestigious and normally calm observer, gave powerful impetus to the demand for relocation, and may even have intensified the panic. Thomas C. Clark, enemy alien control administrator, accused Lippmann of making hysterical statements. Attorney General Biddle, chastising Lippmann for not consulting him first about the situation, showed him a telegram from a southern California newspaper editor stating: "Alien Japanese situation deteriorating rapidly. Lippmann's column and new newspaper attacks have started local citizens organizing some kind of irresponsible drive." Lippmann was unmoved. The administration had only itself to blame for the hysteria, he told Biddle.[2]

Biddle's efforts to calm the situation had little effect. On February 19, 1942, Roosevelt authorized the War Department to set up military zones on the West Coast and remove any person it chose. Secretary of War Henry Stimson, who had said that "their racial characteristics are such that we cannot understand or even trust even the citizen Japanese," carried out the order through McCloy, Interior Under Secretary Abe Fortas, and the War Relocation Authority director, Milton Eisenhower. The army gave people of Japanese descent forty-eight hours to dispose of their homes and businesses (snatched up by speculators for a fraction of their worth), herded them into trucks, and shipped them to federal "relocation centers" in remote areas of the West. Some 120,000 people, the majority of them American citizens, were confined to barracks surrounded by barbed-wire fences with searchlights mounted on watchtowers. Although they were never physically harmed, their only crime, like that of the Jews in the Nazi concentration camps, was their race.

Virtually no one protested. Senator Robert Taft was the only person to speak out in Congress against the action. The Supreme Court — with Roberts, Murphy and Jackson dissenting — declared that California was threatened with invasion, that military authority took precedence over civil rights, and that no racial prejudice was involved. Congress passed a resolution supporting this decision. Most liberal newspapers remained silent in the face of what the American Civil Liberties Union called the "worst single violation of civil rights of American citizens in our history." Those who later regretted the action blamed it on fear, although this defense was ruled out by those who judged the Nazis at Nuremberg.

Some, like Earl Warren, who became chief justice of the U.S. Supreme Court, came to deplore the part they had played. Lippmann never recanted. After the evacuation began he blamed the government for failing to make the people "feel secure," and complained that the problem should have been treated as one of military security and not of citizenship. "The legal fiction, which in a matter of this sort is profoundly important," he wrote lamely at the time, "could have been preserved that we were evacuating individuals and not members of a racial group." The argument was specious, but it showed — as did his refusal to take a broad definition of free speech in the Schwimmer citizenship case and the Strachey case — that public order and national unity were more important to him during times of crisis than civil liberties.

At the time he justified the expulsion on grounds of military security. Later he found a different rationalization. In the early 1970s, when Earl Warren publicly recanted, a frail and failing Lippmann kept returning to the issue in conversation. "You know, I still think it was the right thing to do at the time," he told his friend Gilbert Harrison, editor of the *New Republic*. "Not for security reasons, mind you, but because it was necessary to protect the Japanese-Americans from the hysterical mobs on the West Coast."[3] Although he would not admit he had been wrong, neither could he put the issue out of his mind.

While the Japanese attack brought America into the war, Europe remained the primary theater of operations and the focus of Lippmann's attention. The secret briefings he received at the White House, as part of a small group of privileged journalists, were supplemented by his contacts at State and War, and his friends at the key embassies. His special ties to the British embassy were loosened, however, when Lord Lothian died of uremic poisoning — a death hastened by his refusal, as a devout

Christian Scientist, to see a doctor. Lothian's replacement, Lord Halifax, a Tory imperialist and prewar appeaser, made it clear, to the despair of many American liberals, that his government had no intention of setting free the colonies after the war. Lippmann, no admirer of the new ambassador, complained to Keynes of the "complete intellectual vacuum" at the British embassy. From listening to Halifax many Americans were beginning to believe, he noted, that while the war in Europe was one of liberation, "the war in Asia is for the defense of archaic privilege."[4]

The British government, not wanting to alienate Lippmann, invited him to London in August 1942. He seized the opportunity to see Britain at war, and was accompanied by Helen, who was now director of the Nurse's Aide in America. They started off uneventfully from Washington, but their military plane got lost over Greenland, had to stop several times for fuel, and did not arrive in London until three days later. Somewhat the worse for wear, they checked into Claridge's.

Unpacking quickly, Lippmann hurried over to see his old friend Keynes. He found the Treasury's chief adviser and his ballerina wife living in the kitchen of their home, since bombs had made most of the other rooms uninhabitable. Keynes, oblivious to the discomfort, was in a state of intellectual excitement over a plan he had evolved at the Treasury for a postwar economic "Clearing Union." "This is the finest piece of work I've ever done in my life," he told Lippmann, explaining that through a system of loans and grants it would be possible to avoid the chaos that followed the first war and restore the devastated regions to prosperity. Most officials scoffed at Keynes's thirty-billion-dollar figure as a grossly inflated estimate of Europe's postwar needs, but it turned out to be very close to the target.

While in London Lippmann conferred with Churchill and General Dwight Eisenhower, then planning the invasion of North Africa. And in a dramatic encounter at Grosvenor House he at last met the man about whom he had heard such conflicting and dramatic reports: General Charles de Gaulle. Until June 18, 1940, when the general issued his *appel aux Français* over the BBC and called on Frenchmen to resist the Nazis and the Vichy collaborationists, few outside of France had ever heard of De Gaulle. Within the French military he was known as a troublemaker. This was in part because of a book he had written in 1934 criticizing the French defense system, based on fortifications and infantry, as inadequate for modern warfare. Instead, he proposed swiftly mobile armored units. The French army scoffed, but the Wehrmacht listened, and in 1940 the Germans used De Gaulle's techniques to roll across France's "impregnable" defenses.

Virtually the only French unit to perform well against the Panzer brigades was the one commanded by De Gaulle, whom Premier Paul

Reynaud had raised to the temporary rank of brigadier general in May, after the Germans broke through the French defenses at Sedan. On June 5 Reynaud appointed De Gaulle as his military adviser. By this time the French army was on the verge of total defeat. Reynaud and De Gaulle wanted to carry on the resistance from Britain and from France's empire in Africa. They found little response in a ruling class saturated with defeatism and convinced that a dose of Teutonic discipline would be a healthy antidote to the "democratic excesses" of the Third Republic.

With the collapse of France, General Philippe Pétain, the World War I hero of Verdun, took over the government, formed a cabinet of collaborationists and Nazi sympathizers, and surrendered to the Germans. Hitler marched triumphantly into Paris and occupied most of France, except for the southern and southeastern parts. Pétain and his ministers retreated to the resort city of Vichy, where they set up a puppet regime that ruled over unoccupied France and the French empire at Hitler's sufferance.

De Gaulle, like Reynaud, refused to cooperate with Pétain's regime. Instead, he flew to London, and there issued his call for French resistance. Vichy declared him a traitor and Marcel Peyrouton, a Vichy official later tapped by the Americans to be governor-general of Algeria, signed a warrant ordering his death. De Gaulle's defection and call for French resistance confronted the British and the Americans with a problem. Should they recognize the self-declared rebel, who commanded not a single military unit? Or should they ignore De Gaulle and work with Vichy, in hope of persuading Pétain to keep the French fleet and France's colonies out of German hands? Churchill leaned toward De Gaulle and offered the general a base of operations in Britain. Roosevelt chose to work with Vichy. His political doubts about De Gaulle were reinforced by a profound personal antagonism. FDR thought De Gaulle willful and egotistical, which he was. But Roosevelt failed to understand, as Lippmann later pointed out, that De Gaulle had to be stubborn in defense of French interests in order to refute Vichy's charges that he was a tool of the British and the Americans.

From the beginning Lippmann had defended De Gaulle's resistance movement. Events had shown, he wrote in December 1940, "how thoroughly right were the Frenchmen who wished to retire to northern Africa and continue the war, how grossly mistaken were those Frenchmen who brought about the capitulation of France." Even earlier, in September 1940, he had praised De Gaulle's resistance movement and condemned those Frenchmen who had made "the terrible mistake of thinking that they could ingratiate themselves with the victors by rendering themselves completely helpless."[5]

For the Roosevelt administration, intent on maintaining good relations with Vichy, De Gaulle was a nuisance and was treated with a disdain bordering on contempt. Lippmann was so distressed by this treatment of the Free French that in January 1942 he complained to Norman Davis, FDR's roving ambassador, that there was "no reason in the world" why the Gaullists should be dealt with "so rudely and inhumanely." The matter was so serious, he added, that unless something was done quickly to improve relations with the Free French in Washington and De Gaulle in London, he would raise the question publicly. Nothing was done. In July 1942, shortly before leaving for London, Lippmann took his case to the public. In a sharply worded column he called on Washington to recognize De Gaulle's organization as a "necessary and critical move in the development of a Western front in Europe" and as a way to assure French support when the Allies landed. A few months later he went even further by arguing for the creation in North Africa of a provisional French government "under the leadership of that man of proven faith, General Charles de Gaulle."[6]

By the time he got to London in August 1942, Lippmann was already halfway into De Gaulle's camp. The fifty-one-year-old general, alerted to Lippmann's sympathetic position by his Washington emissary, René Pleven, and well aware of his importance, greeted the columnist as a distinguished guest. For more than an hour the general treated Lippmann to a dazzling monologue, displaying the breadth of historical knowledge and gift for language that were to impress so many who heard him in the years that followed. Lippmann emerged from the experience deeply impressed, convinced that France had found a spokesman worthy of its nobler qualities.

On his return to the United States, Lippmann became a leading spokesman of the Gaullist cause. As featured speaker at the Foch memorial dinner of the French-American Club of New York in October 1942, he described De Gaulle and his French National Committee as the "true leaders of the French nation," and said that the general himself was "as much the acknowledged leader of the French war of independence as General George Washington was the acknowledged leader of the American." The administration would be "guilty of an inconceivable folly if we failed to use the military genius of this extraordinary man," he declared. If American officials found De Gaulle intractable, that was because "some of the people he has had to deal with have been difficult for him to get on with, difficult chiefly, I suggest, not because they had bad will, but because they have lacked the historical imagination to appreciate his position."

He is an officer in the French army. He is charged by his enemies with treason. In his own eyes, and in the eyes of the bravest and the truest of the French, he is charged with the exalted mission of restoring the liberty, the greatness and the honor of France.

. . . He cannot fulfill his mission if he does not insist at all times upon being treated as the representative of a great power with the most scrupulous and, if you like, tiresome, respect for all the rights and interests of France. Can we not understand that in this way only, by being wholly and completely French in the face of all his allies, can he carry the complete conviction of his good faith to the people of France?[7]

The grateful Gaullists were so pleased by Lippmann's speech that they printed thousands of copies of it as propaganda leaflets.

Word quickly got back to De Gaulle of this remarkable tribute from his influential American admirer. Soon a cable arrived at Lippmann's home from the general's headquarters: "In explaining the reality of French resistance and in stressing its unity, you have rendered a service to France that she will never forget." Nor did De Gaulle forget. When he became premier of France after the liberation he elevated Lippmann to the rank of commander of the Legion of Honor. During his brief term as leader of liberated France, through the dozen years of his self-imposed exile, and after his triumphant return to power in 1958, De Gaulle rewarded such loyalty. Lippmann was one of the few journalists to whom he regularly granted interviews, and one of the handful invited to the sanctuary of his home.

Impressed from the beginning, Lippmann found in De Gaulle what he had always sought in a leader: a man of action who was also an intellectual, a political strategist with a sense of history and a vision of the future, one who refused to bow to adversity, a man who incarnated the qualities of his people. "Having been one of his American admirers since June of 1940, when he raised his flag in Britain and summoned the French to go on with the war, I cannot pretend to write dispassionately about General de Gaulle," Lippmann wrote in 1960 in a salute to the general.[8] This tribute was strikingly similar to one he had made a quarter-century earlier, when he had said: "In regard to Theodore Roosevelt, it would be absurd for me to pretend that I can write objectively." Toward both these overpowering figures Lippmann felt an admiration close to hero worship. Although he could be critical of their actions, he could never quite emerge from the long shadows they cast, or feel that other men fully met their measure.

To illustrate how he felt about De Gaulle, Lippmann in conversation told a story about a dinner party after the liberation of North Africa at which the general was seated next to Robert Murphy — the American emissary to Vichy and later Eisenhower's political adviser. Murphy started to lecture De Gaulle about the political sentiments of the French.

"You're not right about that," De Gaulle said. "The French don't feel that way at all. They don't think that."

"But *mon général,* I've spent three years in France," Murphy replied. "I've been there as consul, consul-general, and counsellor of embassy."

"That may be true," De Gaulle responded. "But I've been in France for a thousand years." ·

"That's the kind of man De Gaulle is," Lippmann said admiringly. "There is conceit in a sense, but also a feeling that he incarnates some of France. Men like that have always fascinated me." Theodore Roosevelt had that quality about America; Nehru, about India. "It's as if the country is inside of them, and not they as someone operating within the country."⁹

While De Gaulle may have been the voice of French patriotism, the Vichy regime controlled France's armed forces. In the hope of avoiding a battle on the North African beaches, the Allies searched for a military figure whom French soldiers would obey. Their gaze settled, not on De Gaulle, but on General Henri Giraud, a World War I hero living in retirement in unoccupied France. Although Giraud had no popular following, and no place in the French military hierarchy, Robert Murphy promised Eisenhower that Giraud could neutralize the French army and assure easy success for the Allied invasion of North Africa.

Allied troops hit the beaches of Algeria and Morocco on November 8, 1942, and, to their astonishment, were met with sporadic fierce resistance by the French forces, who refused to accept Giraud's authority. Murphy now told Eisenhower that he would have to strike a deal with a higher military figure, Admiral Jean Darlan. This arrangement may have been practical, and may have saved some lives, but to many liberals it seemed a betrayal of everything the Allies were supposed to be fighting for. Darlan was not only a treacherous opportunist who had sold out first the Third Republic, then Vichy, but a Nazi sympathizer and a vicious anti-Semite linked to the most reactionary elements of the Vichy regime. The public outcry was so great that Chief of Staff George Marshall had to urge American journalists not to criticize the affair.¹⁰

Lippmann, while accepting the military necessity for the deal, bitterly objected to the fact that Murphy gave Darlan political authority over North Africa and thus, in effect, endorsed him as the symbol of French legitimacy. On November 17, six days after Eisenhower took Murphy's advice and switched from Giraud to Darlan, Lippmann wrote a long memo to Secretary Hull and General Marshall. He urged that they not allow Darlan to perpetuate the Vichy regime (which the Germans had eliminated on November 11 when they overran "unoccupied France") in North Africa, and that they "dispel any idea that we shall recognize and uphold quisling governments." Darlan, he pointed out, had joined the Allies only to maintain Vichy's authority in France's overseas territories, as well as to save his own neck. Had Darlan remained in metropolitan France he would have been executed as a traitor by the French resistance forces after the war.

Instead of setting up Darlan with political power over North Africa, American policy should be to "force out of him all the favors he is capable of doing for us," and liquidate any political authority he might claim. "He is in our power and we must firmly insist on not letting him put us in his power," Lippmann maintained. "We are dealing with a man who betrayed the Allies in 1940, and then betrayed the French Republic, and has now betrayed the Germans." In dealing with such a man the essential point was to "keep him within your power until you are able to liquidate his power to blackmail or to betray you." The worst part of all, Lippmann continued, in an obvious gibe against Murphy, was the "miscalculation in the political preparations." Because of bad advice Eisenhower had put his faith in Giraud, a man who had no authority over the French troops, and then had hastily had to improvise the deal with Darlan. "On the critical points of resistance and collaboration in North Africa, General de Gaulle's intelligence service was more accurate than our own, and it will be a grievous error to continue to ignore it," he added pointedly.

Two days later he made the charge public by repeating most of it in his column. While admitting the military usefulness of the Darlan arrangement, he urged the administration to set up a provisional government in North Africa drawn from the various resistance groups. The greatest obstacle to the union of such groups, he charged, was "an unreasoning prejudice against General de Gaulle on the part of certain of our officials" — an obvious reference to Roosevelt and to Hull himself. "This prejudice must be wiped off the slate and the old resentments and suspicions forgotten. For while General de Gaulle has made mistakes, as indeed who has not, he is one of the historic figures of our generation whom it is as stupid as it is mean not to welcome to our cause."[11]

Hull, whose vanity was matched by a ferocious temper, was irritated when he read Lippmann's memo and outraged by the column. In a coldly formal "dear sir" letter, he berated Lippmann for having the gall to "attack" what Hull called the "record of the American government." Lippmann, who did not consider the rotating officials of the State Department to be synonymous with the American government, was unperturbed by Hull's response and followed up his column with an even more pointed assault on Hull's minions for their "propaganda campaign" against those who dared criticize their North Africa policy.

He particularly singled out Robert Murphy. Declaring that the time had come to "carry the case to the public judgment," Lippmann blamed the entire muddle, including the Giraud fiasco, on the bad advice Murphy had given Eisenhower. "It has seemed to me astonishing that so much reliance has been placed on his judgment," Lippmann wrote of

Murphy's key role in the North African imbroglio. "For he is a most agreeable and ingratiating man whose warm heart causes him to form passionate personal and partisan attachments rather than cool and detached judgments." As illustration Lippmann cited how Murphy, who was counselor at the American embassy in Paris during the fateful spring of 1940, had sided with the pro-appeasement Daladier rather than his antifascist successor, Paul Reynaud. When the Germans entered Paris, Murphy followed the regime to Vichy, where he became a staunch advocate of Pétain. "Knowing that he lacked detachment, and how readily he took his political color from those he associated with, it was hard to feel confidence in his ability to guide Africa," Lippmann observed. American policy was "in the hands of naive and gullible men." [12]

To the great relief of FDR, Darlan was assassinated in December 1942, and Giraud brought back as head of the French political authority in North Africa. Fearing that De Gaulle would soon push the hapless Giraud aside — which is precisely what happened — Murphy secretly promised Giraud that Washington would never allow any "outside elements" into the North African forces (an obvious allusion to De Gaulle and his British sponsors) without his permission. Lippmann, furious when he heard of the deal, denounced it in his column. De Gaulle never forgot how FDR and Murphy had treated him. Later he dealt with the diplomat by describing him as one "able and determined, conditioned by years in good society so that he seemed to think that 'France' meant people whom he met at dinner."

The Roosevelt administration's desperate efforts to prevent De Gaulle from gaining control of French forces in Algeria inspired Lippmann to an outspoken defense of the man he called the "greatest living soldier of France" and "acknowledged leader" of most Frenchmen. The administration's prejudice was "rapidly making this man, already the symbol of French national resistance, the symbol also of French, and not only of French but of European, independence," he warned in words that would take on even sharper meaning two decades later.

. . . Let us not overlook now, before it is too late and the matter is irreparable, that we are pursuing a policy which will estrange the French nation from the British and ourselves. Let us not imagine that the rest of Europe, which has always looked at France, is not watching earnestly how we treat France. Let us not imagine that Europe can be resettled and restored without the full participation of France and without the influence which France alone can exert.

If, therefore, we pursue a policy which estranges her and divides her, there will be no great friendly power in the whole of Europe from the Atlantic Ocean to the frontier of Soviet Russia. But there will be a focus of disorder and of antagonism which bodes only ill for our dearest hopes. [13]

Roosevelt's pettiness toward De Gaulle was just a trifle in the great struggle for Europe. But it indicated, in its small way, the problems that were later to erupt as a result of the failure of the Allies to enunciate fully, or even to understand realistically, the nature of their war aims.

Now that the tide was turning against the aggressors, it was no longer possible to delay decisions about building the postwar world. The administration seemed to assume a resuscitated League of Nations that would punish aggressors and assure eternal peace through majority voting. Lippmann was not so sure.

◄ 32 ►

Realpolitik

We must not write into the constitution of the world society a license to universal intervention. For if we license it, we shall invite it. If we invite it, we shall get it.

— *U.S. War Aims*, 1944

THIS was to be, most people assumed, the second chance to make the world safe for democracy. Wilson's vision of an international community resting on collective security and a League of Nations to punish transgressors had become the dictum of the day. Wendell Willkie, on his return from a tour of Russia and China in late 1942, found a "reservoir of good will" that could, as he described it in *One World,* "unify the peoples of the earth in the human quest for freedom and justice." Americans responded to this inspiring vision by buying a million copies of his book — making it a phenomenon in publishing history, if not in political thought. Sumner Welles, Hull's deputy and FDR's trigger man at the State Department, declared that the principles of the Atlantic Charter "must be guaranteed to the world as a whole — in all the oceans and all the continents." By whom and how he did not say. Many believed, as Henry Luce explained, that the United States would "assume the leadership of the world" and inaugurate what he modestly labeled "the American Century." No less expansively, and even more vaguely, Vice-President Henry Wallace foresaw a "people's revolution" culminating in the "century of the common man."[1]

Lippmann, having shed his clinging Wilsonianism after Ethiopia and Munich, did not share the idealists' faith that the great powers would submit to the wishes of a numerical majority. Distressed by one-world euphoria and by FDR's refusal to draw the outlines of a settlement before the end of the war, he decided to write a small book. Cutting back his column from three days a week to two, and working at a furious pace, he put together his thoughts on what the postwar policy of the United States should be. In April 1943, barely four months after he had first discussed the idea with his editor, the first bound volumes of *U.S. Foreign Policy: Shield of the Republic* began rolling off the press.

The prosaic title concealed some explosive ideas. Repudiating much of what he had earlier believed, Lippmann proposed a very un-Wilsonian view of the world. His conclusions, he confessed, had come "slowly over thirty years, and as a result of many false starts, mistaken judgments and serious disappointments. They represent what I now think I have learned, not at all what I always knew." Having completed the book, he wrote, in a rare admission, "I am much better aware than I was before writing it how wide has been the gap between my own insight and my own hindsight."

Deliberately rejecting the idealists' belief in world law and international parliaments, Lippmann grounded his policy in national interest and alliances. "If there is to be peace in our time," he maintained, "it will have to be peace among sovereign national states." That being the case, nations must seek security by forming combinations with other states. The failure of the Europeans to unite against Hitler had nearly led to Nazi domination of the entire continent. The lesson was clear: the wartime Allies — America, Britain, Russia — must remain united after the defeat of Germany and Japan. "The failure to form an alliance of the victors will mean the formation of alliances between the vanquished and some of the victors." This had happened after 1919; it could happen again. Only through alliance could the great powers assure their security. Britain and America must remain linked by the Atlantic connection, while Russia must be brought into what he called the "nuclear alliance."

Without a common enemy the Russian-American alliance would inevitably be subject to strain. How could Russia be prevented from expanding its power westward in a way that would threaten the security of the Atlantic community? The answer, he maintained, lay in a political accord between Russia and the West that did not require an American military intervention to sustain it. Lippmann's analysis rested, not on goodwill or sentimentality, but on self-interest: both Russian and Western security needs would have to be taken into account. It was "inconceivable" that the Red Army would ever again tolerate anti-Russian regimes on the Soviet border. This meant that the West must not try to rebuild the prewar *cordon sanitaire* of anti-Soviet states in Eastern Europe. There simply was no way to carry out such a policy. Eastern Europe would have to be neutral. A viable settlement depended on "whether the border states will adopt a policy of neutralization, and whether Russia will respect and support it."

The message of *U.S. Foreign Policy* was phrased in a language that everyone could understand. The prose was simple, the analogies revealing, the argument direct. The book came out at a time when Americans were looking for a guidepost. The isolationist era was over. The path ahead was uncharted and murky. The thesis that peace rested on great-power cooperation, not on world parliaments and pacts to outlaw war, was straightforward. Lippmann's appeal for a policy of "realism" resting on a hard calculation of the "national interest" and not on an "abstract theory of our rights and duties" seemed direct and practical. And his dictum that a workable foreign policy "consists in bringing into balance, with a comfortable surplus of power in reserve, the nation's commitments and the nation's power" became a classic definition. The argument seemed irrefutable, although it failed to explain whether, if the two factors were out of balance, power should be increased to match the commitments, or commitments reduced to match available power. In essence it seemed to mean simply: don't bite off more than you can chew. Its corollary seemed equally simple: don't chew more than you can swallow.

An instant success, *U.S. Foreign Policy* quickly climbed to the top of best-seller lists and sold nearly half a million copies. The *Reader's Digest* printed a condensation and told its readers that "no more important book has been written for Americans in a generation." The *Ladies' Home Journal* worked a wondrous transformation by reducing the book to seven pages of cartoon strips. The U.S. armed forces distributed a twenty-five-cent paperback edition to the troops. The book appeared around the world in a dozen languages. Lippmann's formula of great-power cooperation seemed a realistic alternative both to bankrupt isolationism and to wishful universalism.

Not everyone was pleased. State Department official Breckenridge Long sent his boss, Cordell Hull, a thirty-page memo challenging Lippmann's argument. Senator Robert Taft told the American Bar Association that "if world federalism was impractical, a postwar military alliance as advocated by Walter Lippmann and others was frightening." Any Anglo-American accord to police the world would create a "profession of militarists" and induce the United States to "occupy all the strategic points in the world and try to maintain a force so preponderant that none shall dare attack us. . . . Potential power over other nations, however benevolent its purpose," Taft warned, "leads inevitably to imperialism." [2]

Lippmann was not oblivious to that danger, but opposed Taft's appeal for a withdrawal to Fortress America. He also resisted Jacques Maritain's preference for the "heroic ideal" of world federalism. "Security against great aggression, and not the promotion of civilization, is the function of the great power alliance," Lippmann told the exiled French philosopher. "Such an alliance would be not only intolerable, but . . .

altogether unworkable if the allied great powers took upon themselves more than the specific and limited function . . . of providing security against world conquerors." Only a diplomacy of self-interest would provide insurance against the "insidious temptation of imperialism," he insisted, while more transcendent goals would lead to a "new version of Kipling and the white man's burden."

While the Wilsonians wanted a new league based on collective security, Lippmann feared, as he wrote professor Quincy Wright, that any organization committed to suppress aggression, "directed against everybody in general and nobody in particular, would quickly develop a pro and anti-Russian alignment," since the first area of contention would be the states along Russia's frontiers. "The great object of international organization in the next generation is to hold together the alliance and to hold it together at almost any cost," he underlined. "I want to find ways of binding together the Allies which are sure to bind them, and I do not believe they will be successfully bound together by any general covenant." His position, reiterated in scores of T&T columns, was classic: security is based on power, not on abstract principles. Alliances and spheres of influence, not majority votes in an international assembly, would govern nations' behavior.

This notion seemed unduly cynical to those brought up on Wilsonian idealism and a conviction that only Europeans had colonies, client states, and spheres of influence. Senator Henry Cabot Lodge, Jr., grandson of the man who had led the fight against the league, spoke for many in proclaiming that America must lead the world because it alone harbored no imperial ambitions. Lippmann felt obliged to give the senator an elementary lesson in international politics. "You say that Britain has a very practical national aim, which is to maintain the Empire, but that we have no such practical aim," he wrote Lodge. "In fact, in this respect we have exactly the same definite practical aim as Britain: we too intend to maintain our pre-war position — in Alaska, Hawaii, the Philippines, in the Caribbean, and in South America. The British aim to hold what she had is so obviously our own aim too that it is universally taken for granted and outside the bounds of discussion."

While most critics saw *U.S. Foreign Policy* as an attack on One Worldism, the book was also a warning against missionary interventionism to set the world right. "I am more and more convinced that it is just as important to define the limit beyond which we will not intervene as it is to convince our people that we cannot find security in an isolationist party," Lippmann wrote Hugh Wilson, former ambassador to Germany, then on duty with the Office of Strategic Services. The "primary aim" of American responsibility was the basin of the Atlantic on both sides, and the Pacific islands — in other words, the Atlantic community plus a "blue-water" strategy of naval bases and roaming fleets. Outside these regions there should be no permanent military or political commitments.[3]

U.S. Foreign Policy posited two main conditions for the postwar world: great-power cooperation in a "nuclear" alliance, and neutrality for Eastern Europe between the Soviet Union and the West. Little noticed at the time was Lippmann's introduction of the still-embryonic concept of "national security." For him it meant simply the protection of the United States and the preservation of its democratic institutions. Later, in the hands of James Forrestal and his successors at the Pentagon and the State Department, it was to become the basis for a doctrine of globalism that Lippmann spent the last years of his life decrying.

By the time *U.S. Foreign Policy* appeared in the spring of 1943, serious tension had developed between Russia on the one hand, and Britain and America on the other. The Allies were at odds over the continued delay of the promised second front — which left the Soviets carrying the brunt of the land war against Germany. They also disagreed over the question of cooperation with the Vichyites in North Africa, over FDR's insistence on including China among the Big Four, and above all over the future of Germany and Eastern Europe. The second-front problem was settled at Tehran in November 1943 when FDR promised that the cross-Channel invasion would take place no later than the spring of 1944. The Vichy problem was resolved when De Gaulle outflanked the hapless Giraud and assumed full control over France's armed forces.

The problem of Eastern Europe, however, moved to center stage. At Tehran Stalin had made it clear that he intended to incorporate the Baltic states into the Soviet Union and ensure that Poland would never again fall into anti-Soviet hands. He wanted, in other words, a Russian sphere of influence. The Americans professed to be shocked by such a cynical notion, conveniently ignoring their own privileged zone in Latin America and the Pacific. But to Lippmann it seemed clear that the Soviets could not be denied dominant influence in an area they deemed vital to their security. The United States might be very powerful, but it simply could not set up governments everywhere in the world corresponding to its notions of propriety.

"We must not make the error of thinking that the alternative to 'isolation' is universal 'intervention,' " he wrote shortly after FDR's return from Tehran. "A diplomacy which pretended that we were interested in every disputed region everywhere would easily disrupt the alliance." In answer to those who saw the proposed United Nations as an instrument for containing Russia, he insisted that peace had to rest on great-power cooperation and respect for spheres of influence. It was "not only unavoidable but eminently proper that each great power does have a sphere in which its influence and responsibility are primary." To deny that reality would be simply to indulge in "the pretense, wholly illusory and dangerously confusing, that every state has an identical influence, interest, power and responsibility everywhere."[4] Events were pushing Lippmann beyond the thesis of *U.S. Foreign Policy,* where he had argued that Eastern Europe should be neutralized. Now he realized that, like it or not, the region would fall under control of the dominant power — and that meant the Soviet Union.

To spur American thinking about the postwar settlement, he decided he must write a sequel to his earlier book. *U.S. War Aims,* as he called the new book, came off the presses in the summer of 1944, as British and American armies were at last on the beaches of France, and the Western assault on the Reich had begun. In *U.S. War Aims* he now accepted a Soviet sphere in Eastern Europe — thus reversing the neutrality he had urged in *U.S. Foreign Policy* — and proposed a series of orbits to prevent Japan and Germany from instigating a new war: an Atlantic orbit, a Soviet orbit, and an eventual Chinese orbit. Together, the great powers could keep the peace; divided, they would be drawn into a third world war. Downgrading ideology, Lippmann maintained that although America and Russia could not have harmonious relations so long as they remained pledged to different value systems, they could at least achieve a *modus vivendi* based on compromise.

Again he stressed that peace lay in great-power cooperation, not in resolutions from international assemblies. "We cannot repeat the error of counting upon a world organization to establish peace," he warned. "The responsibility for order rests upon the victorious governments. They cannot delegate this responsibility to a world society which does not yet exist or has just barely been organized." Peace could be guarded only by those with the power to maintain it. Wilson had got his priorities backward. Dismembering existing states to promote self-determination had led to anarchy and war. The idea that nations should be forbidden to protect their interests and preserve their integrity was a prejudice "formed in the Age of Innocence, in the century of American isolation." Now he saw self-determination as a reactionary doctrine that denied the ideal that diverse peoples could live together in equality, and that "can be and has been used to promote the dismemberment of practically every organized state." The United States could no longer take its safety and its internal order for granted, he underlined. "We have come to the end of our effortless security and of our limitless opportunities."

Having backed and filled on Wilsonianism for a quarter century — rejecting it after Versailles, embracing it in favor of disarmament during the 1920s and most of the 1930s — Lippmann at last found a policy that fit his goals. Instead of responding to events with no guiding principle other than a pragmatic sense of what seemed feasible in each situation, he now had worked out a consistent diplomacy based on military power, alliances, spheres of influence, and a "cold calculation" of national interests. Combining Admiral Mahan's views of sea power with Nicholas Spykman's geopolitics and Clausewitz's conception of war as the military conduct of diplomacy, he became the apostle of a hardheaded realpolitik.

Now rejecting Wilsonian universalism as delusory and dangerous, he eschewed the globalism central to it. The virtue of spheres of influence was that they would give the great powers a sense of security and prevent a scramble for control of fringe areas. The danger of the universalism preached by the One Worlders was that it invited intervention in the name of self-determination. The results of such meddling, however well-intentioned, could be disastrous. "The constitution of the world society should not be based on the assumption that everything is everybody's business," he counseled. "We must not write into the constitution of the world society a license to universal intervention. For if we license it, we shall invite it. If we invite it, we shall get it."

Few listened to the warning. *U.S. War Aims* appeared at a time when Americans wanted to believe that power politics would be no more and that an Assembly of Man would keep the peace. They did not at all like the idea of spheres of influence. Henry Luce, who had greatly admired Lippmann's earlier book, thought he might serialize *U.S. War Aims* in *Life*. When Luce read the pages describing the Soviet Union as a totalitarian state, he decided against the idea. "It's too anti-Russian," he told Lippmann. At the time Luce, like many conservatives, was in a Mother Russia euphoria stage. He had put a flattering portrait of Stalin on the cover of *Time,* and run a special issue of *Life* extolling the Russians as "one hell of a people" who "look like Americans, dress like Americans, and think like Americans." In the same moonstruck vein his writers described the Gestapo-like NKVD as "a national police similar to the FBI," whose job was "tracking down traitors."[5] A few years later he was calling for a holy war on atheistic communism.

The public responded tepidly to *U.S. War Aims*. Although it appeared briefly on the best-seller lists and was condensed in the *Reader's Digest,* it was far less successful than *U.S. Foreign Policy*. Most preferred the inspirational internationalism of Sumner Welles, whose *Time for Decision* heralded a new League of Nations to keep the peace. Critics named Welles's one of the ten outstanding books of the year, while ignoring Lippmann's. In the prevailing enthusiasm for a revived Wilsonianism, Lippmann's plea for alliances and spheres of influence seemed dangerously out-of-date.

"I can't help feeling that Welles' book did enormous damage in diverting the American people from an understanding of the historic realities," he complained to a colleague. "It was, in a sense, bad luck that I published a book at the same moment, for that stopped me from saying what I thought of Welles' book, and I might have accomplished more by a running criticism of him than I did by my own book." The public was being encouraged to have expectations that could never be satisfied, thus making a realistic policy more difficult to achieve. The struggle within the government "to shape the Wilsonian ideology into something that fits the realities" could be won, he said, "if the public, and particularly the idealistic public, were not so stubbornly naive."[6]

Idealists found their hopes at last turned into reality in September 1944 when the Big Three foreign ministers, joined by China as an honorary member, met at Dumbarton Oaks in Washington to draft a blueprint for the United Nations. They soon reached agreement on the structure of the organization — a general assembly, an economic and social council, and a security council with five permanent members — but bogged down over voting procedure. The Russians, fearing they would be outvoted, wanted a veto in the Security Council — as did the Americans. But they also wanted sixteen votes — one for each constituent Soviet republic — in the General Assembly. This, they calculated, would help offset the U.S.-controlled Latin American bloc and the British Commonwealth. London and Washington were adamantly opposed. Lippmann, who had broken short his summer sojourn in Maine to observe the conference, scored the British and the Americans for making an issue out of voting procedure. None of the great powers would submit to a majority vote if it felt a vital issue were at stake. If the great powers could not agree among themselves, then no organization could preserve the peace: "Any attempt to enforce peace against one of them would simply be a polite introduction to another world war."[7]

When Grenville Clark, an ardent world federalist, told him that Dumbarton Oaks showed that the world was now ready for the "more perfect union" the Americans had achieved in 1789, Lippmann demurred. "We must not substitute for the world as it is an imaginary world such as eighteenth century America," he replied. "We must begin with this world, making as just an estimate as we can of the actual and potential connections and conflicts among nations, and then seek the principles of order which apply to it." There had been no voting accord at Dumbarton Oaks, he explained, because the British and the Americans failed to grasp that "pacification must precede the establishment of a reign of law." The quarrel with the Russians over voting stemmed from the "false major premise that the Dumbarton Oaks organization can and should be a universal society to pacify the world. The truth is that only in a reasonably pacified world can there be a universal society."[8]

Despite Lippmann's misgivings, the principle of an international organization to keep the peace had become so sacrosanct that it was not even an issue in the 1944 presidential election campaign. The Republican candidate, Governor Thomas E. Dewey of New York, like his foreign-policy adviser, John Foster Dulles, was an ardent internationalist. Although Lippmann had no enthusiasm for Dewey, he was reluctant to support a weak and exhausted FDR for a fourth term.[9] Like all who had seen the shocking deterioration in the President's health, he was particularly concerned over the choice of vice-president.

Incumbent Henry Wallace had many admirers, but not among party conservatives, who considered him a maverick and a radical. Even some of his admirers wondered whether he was the right man to take over in case, as seemed quite possible, FDR died in office. Lippmann was among the doubters. To nominate a man "who divides the people so deeply and sharply would produce a profound, perhaps an unreasonable, sense of anxiety, and a loss of confidence in the conduct of government," Lippmann wrote on the eve of the convention vote. For all Wallace's abilities and integrity it was clear that his "goodness is unworldly, that his heart is so detached from the realities that he has never learned to measure, as a statesman must, the relation of good and of evil in current affairs."

Lippmann never had any trouble separating his personal affection for a man from the man's qualifications for public office. He was quite ready to admit that sometimes the better man was the lesser candidate — and to act accordingly. He had known Wallace for years and was good friends with his sister Mary, the wife of the Swiss ambassador, Charles Bruggemann. But he had doubts about Wallace's mental stability, and shortly before the convention told FDR's right-hand man, Harry Hopkins, that Wallace had to go. FDR was too weak and too preoccupied to make a fight over the issue, and the party regulars needed no convincing. When organized labor vetoed the most likely candidate, Senator James Byrnes of South Carolina, the party turned to the little-known former haberdasher from Missouri, Senator Harry Truman.

Although Lippmann yearned to vote Republican, Dewey gave him little reason to do so. A few weeks before the election he was, as in 1940, squarely astride the fence. The owners of the *Herald Tribune* thought such neutrality bad for business. One afternoon the demure but iron-willed Helen Reid came into his office and said, "Walter, I don't know exactly how you feel, but I do hope you will take a stand in this election." "Well," he replied, discomforted at being backed into a corner, "if I do it will probably be against you." "That will be quite all right," she sighed with mixed disappointment and relief, "just so long as you take a stand."[10]

Finally, just two weeks before the election he did — against Dewey. The reason was not merely Dewey's intellectual flabbiness, but his injection of the touchy Polish issue into the campaign by his pledge to help the exiled anticommunist Poles gain power in Warsaw. On the surface this seemed little more than a bid for the Polish-American vote. But at that moment delicate negotiations were taking place between the Russians and the centrist Polish leader, Stanislaus Mikolajczyk. Elements in the State Department were pushing the claims of an avowedly anti-Soviet right-wing faction, thus imperiling Mikolajczyk's efforts to work out a compromise and raising Soviet suspicions. In Dewey's bid to the right-wing Poles, Lippmann saw something more sinister than mere campaign hyperbole. "The implied pledge of American support is tremendous backing to those reactionary Poles in refusing to accept the compromise which the moderate and democratic prime minister has been negotiating," he wrote in his column. Such a pledge seemed to him deliberately "pin-pointed at the current negotiations by someone who does not want a compromise to succeed."[11]

John Foster Dulles, Dewey's likely choice for secretary of state, felt — with some reason — that the accusation was directed against him. Defending the pledge to the rightist Poles, he proceeded to give Lippmann one of his famous lectures on morality. "The basic issue between you and the governor," he wrote Lippmann, "is that you do not believe that the United States should have any policies at all except in relation to areas where we can make those policies good through material force. The governor, on the other hand, believes in moral force."

Lippmann did not appreciate being lectured on morality, least of all by one who had been, to put it gently, insensitive to Nazism throughout the thirties, and who, even after the fall of France, favored the appeasement of Hitler. Rejecting Dulles's explanation, Lippmann suggested it would not be profitable "to argue about who is more aware of the moral issues involved in this war, for that would involve examination of the record, whereas I for one prefer to let bygones be bygones." Four months later, when it became clear that the chance for a true coalition government in Poland had been lost, Lippmann argued that the Republicans were much to blame. During the election campaign, he charged, "votes were sought by statements which encouraged the irreconcilable Poles in London to think that they could afford to reject the compromise which Mikolajczyk was offered."[12]

As it turned out, Dewey's milking of the Polish issue did him little good among the voters. His campaign was so listless that even the *New York Times,* which had come out against FDR in 1940, now supported the President, albeit with "deep reluctance and strong misgivings." That, too, was the best Lippmann could muster. As much as he favored a change, he felt he had no choice but to go along with Roosevelt. "I cannot feel that Governor Dewey can be trusted with responsibility in foreign affairs," he told his readers. "He has so much to learn, and there would be no time to learn it, that the risk and cost of a change during this momentous year seems to me too great.'' [13]

The voters thought so too. They reelected FDR by a 3.5-million-vote margin and sent the isolationists back to their law offices, including such prominent America Firsters as Hamilton Fish and Gerald P. Nye. A new crop of internationalists entered the Senate, led by Wayne Morse of Oregon and J. William Fulbright of Arkansas.

Lippmann was not even around for the tally. On November 1, a few days before the election, he had put on the uniform of a war correspondent and sailed for England on the converted *Queen Mary,* along with fourteen thousand GIs. After meeting with Churchill and Anthony Eden, he boarded an air force plane, flew across northern France at treetop level to avoid enemy fire, and spent several days at the front with the American First and Ninth armies.

In Paris Lippmann dined with De Gaulle and his family. The general had made a triumphant entry into the city in August, although Washington grudgingly withheld official recognition of his authority until October. The general complained to his guest that the recently reopened American embassy had been staffed with the same people who had followed Pétain to Vichy in 1940, career diplomats who had no sympathy with the Gaullist movement or its efforts to purge France of defeatism and collaboration. Lippmann listened sympathetically, and when he got back to Washington wrote a sharp column declaring it to be a "capital error not to staff the embassy with men who have no prejudices from the bad past,'' and against whom Frenchmen held no prejudices. It was a good try, but had little effect. [14]

Washington's quarrel with De Gaulle was matched, on a lesser level, by a dispute with Britain over spheres of influence. Just a month earlier, in October 1944, Churchill had gone to Moscow and worked out a deal with Stalin to divvy up Eastern Europe. Russia could control Rumania and Bulgaria, Britain would get Greece, and the two would divide Hungary and Yugoslavia fifty-fifty. It was a quixotic arrangement, and did not even mention Poland, in which both sides had claims. But it was Churchill's attempt to gain what he could while his cards were still strong.

One Worlders — both idealists and those who thought the United States should run the postwar world — were indignant. They charged that the concept of spheres of influence was a betrayal of what America had presumably fought for. Lippmann, fearing that such an attitude would spoil postwar cooperation among the Allies, wrote an angry column in December 1944 deriding those who seemed to believe that American servicemen had died "to have a plebiscite in eastern Galicia or to return Hong Kong to Chiang Kai-shek. . . . I have seen men brought in from the battlefield who were dying and men who were mutilated," he wrote in a slashing attack on those who moaned that the war had been in vain because the Russians demanded a friendly regime in Poland and the British the same thing in Greece. "I must say that it is hard to bear talk here at home which presumes to measure the meaning of their deeds and the value of their sacrifice by whether some commentator . . . thinks that the solution proposed conforms with some abstract principle from the Atlantic Charter." The country would revert to isolationism, he charged, if America's true interests were obscured by a "collection of generalized rules" about how nations ought to behave.[15]

If the public was confused, it had reason to be. Roosevelt, who resisted outlining any settlement until after the war, had his vision: a revived League of Nations that the United States, by virtue of its preponderant economic and military power, would dominate. Others had different ideas. Churchill was determined to retain the empire, restore the monarchies of Italy, Greece and Belgium, and maintain a sphere of influence in southern and eastern Europe, particularly Poland. Stalin sought, at the minimum, dominance over Poland, and reparations to rebuild the devastated Soviet economy and ensure that Germany would never again be able to invade Russia.

Lippmann, despite his admiration for Churchill as a wartime leader, thought the prime minister's plan for a pro-British government in Warsaw entirely fanciful. An independent Poland could survive "only if it is allied with Russia," he wrote as early as January 1944. If the Poles annexed territory that was German, they would need outside help to hold on to that territory. Only Russia could provide that. Therefore, he underlined, Poland had to come to terms with Russia, "to terms which make Russia the principal guarantor of the western boundary." Stalin knew this, the Germans knew it, and so did the moderate Poles. But right-wing Poles, encouraged by sympathizers in London and Washington, thought the Russians could be excluded. To Lippmann this was a fantasy. There could be "no future for a Poland governed, or even influenced, by those Poles who, even before they are liberated from the Nazis, conceive themselves as the spearpoint of a hostile coalition against the Soviet Union."[16]

These conflicting views over the future of Eastern Europe could not much longer remain unresolved. In February 1945, with the defeat of Nazi Germany now imminent, the Big Three met at Yalta on the Black Sea to iron out their differences. Stalin promised that he would declare war on Japan within three months after the end of the war in Europe. He accepted the American plan for a great-power veto in the UN Security Council, in return for the admission of two or three constituent Soviet republics, and agreed to Churchill's request for a French zone of occupation in Germany.

On the critical issue of Poland, the Russians stood fast, demanding return of the areas seized from them at Brest Litovsk in 1918. The Poles would be compensated by German territory in the west. While insisting that the future government in Warsaw must be friendly to Moscow, Stalin agreed that the pro-Soviet provisional government would be "reorganized" to include some of the Poles from London and the underground movement, and that "free and unfettered" elections would be held. At Roosevelt's request he signed a vaguely worded "Declaration on Liberated Europe," which seemed designed mostly to satisfy public opinion in the United States.

Congress and the press were virtually unanimous in hailing Yalta as a great triumph of diplomacy. The great powers had agreed on the United Nations, Germany would be divided into occupation zones and its war potential forever destroyed, an acceptable compromise had been reached on Poland and Eastern Europe. "There has been no more impressive international conference in our time, none in which great power was so clearly hardened to the vital, rather than the secondary, interests of nations," Lippmann wrote in expressing the consensus. Even John Foster Dulles saluted Yalta as opening a "new era" in which the United States "abandoned a form of aloofness which it has been practicing for many years and the Soviet Union permitted joint action on matters that it had the power to settle for itself."

Although the accords soon broke down under the weight of mutual suspicion and distrust, they certified that the political equation in Europe had been forever changed. The British and the Americans could not compel the Russians to withdraw. In fact, they wanted them to keep advancing west against Hitler's armies. The Americans were not yet willing to accept spheres of influence, or "containment," as it was later to be called. "What we were faced with at Yalta was how to make good our principles in territories that Stalin held," Lippmann later wrote. "Stalin had the power to act: we had only the power to argue." The Yalta accords recognized a *fait accompli:* "the West paid the political price for having failed to deter Hitler in the 1930s, for having failed to unite and to rearm against him." [17]

Although Roosevelt had negotiated tenaciously at Yalta, the conference and the long voyage home depleted his waning strength. Reports from Warm Springs, Georgia, where he had gone for a rest, were alarming. Fearing that the President might not live much longer, Lippmann, as a final gesture to the man toward whom he had had such conflicting feelings, decided to write a tribute to FDR — in effect an obituary — while the President was still able to read it. "His estimate of the vital interests of the United States has been accurate and far-sighted," he wrote. "He has served these interests with audacity and patience, shrewdly and with calculation, and he has led this country out of the greatest peril in which it has ever been to the highest point of security, influence, and respect which it has ever attained.''[18] The column appeared on April 7, 1945. Five days later Roosevelt was dead of a cerebral hemorrhage.

Lippmann had, as he later said, an ''in-and-out feeling'' about Roosevelt and the New Deal: hailing the early initiatives to stem the panic, detesting the administrative legerdemain that culminated in the Court-packing plan, and admiring the compensated economy. He was not close to FDR, and although he often saw the President at White House briefings, was never invited there socially. During the war he changed his mind about FDR's qualities as President. The war changed Roosevelt just as it changed Lippmann. It brought out a new vigor and sense of direction in both men. As it allowed FDR to turn away from a stymied New Deal and a depression that would not go away, so it provided Lippmann with an escape from the sterile negativism of his anti–New Deal diatribes and allowed him to concentrate on the great issues of war and peace. If it took the war to make Roosevelt a truly great President, so the same war, and the cold war that followed, made Lippmann the nation's preeminent analyst of foreign affairs.

At Yalta FDR thought he had laid the groundwork for a durable peace. Stalin had agreed to enter the war against Japan, to allow free elections in Eastern Europe, and to accept the American formula for a United Nations resting on a great-power veto and spheres of influence. The United States would stand as mediator between the rival imperialisms of Britain and Russia. With its overwhelming economic strength, its predominance in Latin America, its undisputed naval power in the Pacific, its incomparable industrial and military machine, its control over the world's raw materials, the United States would have nothing to fear from a devastated and war-impoverished Russia. This great scheme would all be codified in May, Roosevelt thought, in San Francisco with the creation of the United Nations.

That, too, like the final victory over the aggressors, FDR did not live to see. And within a year his plan for great-power unity, the foundation on which everything else rested, would founder on the shoals of fear, distrust, and rival ambitions.

◄ 33 ►

Drifting toward Catastrophe

. . . I say the devil with all catastrophic, apocalyptic
visions of inexorable, inevitable doom.

— To Dorothy Thompson, July 22, 1946

Harry Truman had just moved into the White House when delegates and journalists from all over the world began descending on
San Francisco for the official inauguration of the United Nations. Edward R. Stettinius, a white-haired, toothy businessman with an affable
manner and a nodding acquaintance with foreign policy, headed the
American delegation. Tapped by FDR a few months earlier to take over
the State Department from the ailing Cordell Hull, the new secretary
had strong concerns, though not necessarily about diplomacy. When Lippmann came by on a visit, Stettinius earnestly sought his advice on the
new color scheme of his office. He himself had been chosen, like his
decor, not to offend anyone. So had the American delegation to the conference, which included, in addition to the Democratic faithful, such
Republican stalwarts as Arthur Vandenberg, Harold Stassen and Nelson
Rockefeller. The group symbolized the triumph of bipartisanship and a
determination that the Senate fight over the league would not be repeated.

Among the Republican converts to internationalism, none was more
important or more carefully cultivated than Vandenberg. Lippmann was
one of the chief cultivators. As the Senate's leading foreign-policy
spokesman on the Republican side, and as a long-standing isolationist,
Vandenberg was in a position to sabotage the administration's plans for
the United Nations. The best hope lay in winning him over rather than
fighting him. Some men would be susceptible to argument. Vandenberg
was more easily moved by flattery. A man of inexhaustible vanity and
consuming ambition, he responded only to the kind of logic that flattered both. Lippmann supplied it. Playing on the senator's ill-concealed
desire to run for President in 1948, Lippmann — together with his

younger colleague James Reston of the *New York Times* — persuaded Vandenberg that isolationism was hopelessly old-hat. No man aspiring to be President of the United States, they told him, could turn his back on the nation's vast international responsibilities. It would take a man of great vision to lead the nation, and particularly the Republican party, away from the isolationist delusions of the past. Who was better endowed to play that critical role than the senator from Michigan?

Vandenberg agreed. The way now paved, Lippmann and Reston put together a speech, which Vandenberg read on the floor of the Senate in January 1945. The time had come for a change of policy, he declared; world peace demanded that "the basic idea of Dumbarton Oaks succeed." His colleagues were flabbergasted; this was a complete about-face. But the applause of the Senate internationalists was nothing compared to the hosannas from the press. Reston led the way with a big article in the *Times* hailing the speech as "wise" and "statesmanlike." Lippmann echoed his approval. A few hours later, with congratulatory telegrams already rolling in, Vandenberg went to a diplomatic reception at the Mayflower Hotel and strutted around, as Lippmann later recalled, "just like a pouter pigeon all blown up with delight at his new role in the world." Lippmann, adept at buttering up those who needed to be buttered, had from many years of observing politicians learned how to deal with such a "vain and pompous and really quite insincere man."

Vandenberg's sincerity was soon tested. Lippmann had persuaded the senator to put in his speech a statement urging greater understanding of Russia's security interests in Eastern Europe and suggesting that a Soviet sphere of influence in the area was "perfectly understandable." Vandenberg had seen, Lippmann wrote in his congratulatory column the next day, "that what our allies are seeking is first of all security against the revival of German militarism and aggression . . . that the Soviet Union insists upon governments on her western borders which will be unequivocally her allies. . . ." This was a striking statement at a time when the composition of the new Polish government was fast becoming a source of contention between Russia and the West.[1]

But if Vandenberg had in fact seen the need for such understanding, his vision soon clouded over. His Polish-American constituents around Detroit were not at all happy at what he had glimpsed, nor was the powerful anti-Soviet faction in the State Department. The combination quickly sent Vandenberg into retreat. At San Francisco he fell under the influence of Averell Harriman, who was on leave from his post as American ambassador to Russia to serve as policy adviser at the conference. Harriman took a hard line toward the Soviets, suggesting that American economic power be used to force them into line in Eastern Europe, and declaring that Moscow would understand only a policy of force. "Our objectives and the Kremlin's objectives," Harriman told a group of journalists, "are irreconcilable." Lippmann, who had gone to San Francisco to cover the conference, was so shocked by what seemed a deliberate effort to magnify differences with the Russians that he stalked out of the room, joined by newscaster Raymond Gram Swing.[2]

Retiring to the corridors, Lippmann conferred with Vandenberg and John Foster Dulles, who had found a place for himself as adviser to the Republican delegates. They were solidly in Harriman's camp, and their comments made it clear to Lippmann that hard-liners in the State Department were pressing the gullible and inexperienced Stettinius toward a showdown with the Soviets. If they succeeded, he feared, the peace would be lost and the effectiveness of the fledgling United Nations destroyed. Deciding that he had no alternative but to take his case to the public, Lippmann returned to his room at the Palace Hotel and wrote an angry column denouncing those "who, to say it flatly, are thinking of the international organization as a means of policing the Soviet Union." Such an effort would undermine the UN. "We cannot police the Soviet Union and we must not flirt with the idea of attempting it," he warned. If the Soviets suspected American motives, they had some reason: "At the bottom of all Soviet policy, of all Soviet suspicion, there is the determination to counteract the powerful interests in the Western world which, though they do not avow it openly, have this purpose in mind."[3]

At San Francisco the United States had balked at seating the Polish delegation on grounds that the communist government in Warsaw had not been democratically elected. However, it then insisted on granting admission to Argentina, despite Soviet objections that the Perón regime had been sympathetic to the Nazis. The Russians protested, but the Americans had the votes. It was a brutally effective display of power. The United States was using the conference to embarrass and humiliate the Russians, playing a "straight power game" in Latin America "as amoral as Russia's game in eastern Europe," according to *Time* magazine.[4]

For Lippmann the lesson was ominous. "I saw Stettinius and Nelson Rockefeller marshal the twenty Latin American republics in one solid bloc and steamroll that through the United Nations," he recalled. "I remember . . . feeling this was an ominous thing for the future; if we were going to use that kind of a majority to dominate things, we were going to run into iron resistance to anything else from the Russians." The Soviets depended on the Security Council veto, he pointed out, because the United States controlled a majority in the General Assembly. "They had a good case on Argentina and we wouldn't listen to it." From the conference Lippmann warned that the American "steamroller" tactics would make the great powers "more than ever determined to keep the things that really matter most to them away from the organization.'' [5]

While those seeking a showdown with the Soviets were in the ascendancy, some officials still favored FDR's policy of cooperation. One was Secretary of War Henry Stimson; another was James F. Byrnes, the affable South Carolinian — former senator, Supreme Court justice, and wartime economic tsar — who had just been named by Truman to replace the hapless Stettinius at the State Department. The fight over procedural issues had "only provided ammunition for those people who want to bring about suspicion and distrust,'' Byrnes had written Lippmann in response to his columns. "If we expect them to fulfill promises, we must scrupulously fulfill our pledges as well.''

Lippmann, delighted to find such a sympathetic listener, wrote the secretary-designate from San Francisco. "I have been more disturbed about the conduct of our policy than I have thought it expedient during a great conference of this sort to say in print,'' he revealed. The line drawn between the Soviets and the Americans was "not inherent in the nature of things,'' but rather due to "inexperience and emotional instability in our own delegation.'' Although there was a "far deeper conflict of interest'' between the British and the Soviets than between the Americans and the Soviets, "we have allowed ourselves to be placed in the position where, instead of being the moderating power which holds the balance, we have become the chief protagonists of the anti-Soviet position.'' None of this would have happened if Roosevelt were still alive, he lamented, and it was bound to lead to trouble extending far beyond the Polish issue "if we do not recover our own sense of national interest about this fundamental relationship.'' [6]

By the "national interest'' in this "fundamental relationship'' Lippmann meant what he had outlined in his two wartime foreign-policy books: that the alliance between Russia and the West had to be kept intact; that the Soviets considered Eastern Europe no less their sphere of influence than the Americans did the Caribbean; and that if the allies fell to squabbling among themselves they would soon start wooing the Germans in a deadly race for military advantage.

Lippmann put the blame not only on the "inexperience and emotional instability'' within the American delegation, but on the machinations of the British. Despite his admiration for Churchill, he saw a heavy British hand in the State Department's growing pressure for a hard line toward the Soviets, and in the dispute over Eastern Europe. Moscow's insistence on a "friendly'' Poland clashed with the British and American desire for a "democratic'' Poland. The vague formula worked out at Yalta had not clarified that conflict but only postponed it. The British, seeking to reclaim their sphere of influence in Eastern Europe, were demanding that the noncommunist Poles be given a greater voice in the government. Stalin, feeling that Churchill was reneging on the Yalta accords, countered by suggesting that Greek communists be included in the monarchist regime the British had installed in Athens.

The dispute, Lippmann told historian Hans Kohn, was a "British-Russian conflict in which London overruled the British ambassador in Moscow and asked for an interpretation of the Crimean agreement which made the problem insoluble." The United States could not hope to reach a satisfactory understanding with the British and French empires, he added, "if we continue to give the impression that from Malta to Singapore and Hong Kong our partnership with the British means underwriting their actions." Churchill's insistence on supporting "ultraconservative forces" in southern Europe and the Arab world would, Lippmann told professor Ross Hoffman, ultimately play into Russia's hands. "I do not believe that the pre-war rightist elements can continue to govern in Europe. I do not think it is ideology, but realism, to argue that the support of governments somewhat left of center has the greatest promise of accomplishing the end which you set. Moreover, I raise the question whether a direct challenge to the Soviet power, such as Churchill has made and has tried to persuade us to underwrite, is not inexpedient." [7]

Lippmann saw British foreign policy as colonial, imperialistic, and hostile to any form of radicalism. As early as December 1944 he had criticized Churchill for trying to set up a monarchist government in Greece that excluded the communist-led guerrilla forces. Since the guerrillas had carried the brunt of the resistance against the Germans, he argued, they should be treated as "one of the legitimate pillars of the provisional state." Churchill, however, favored the monarchists and even the collaborators. Now, six months later, it was clear that the British were trying to use American power to regain their prewar influence in Eastern Europe and the Middle East. Going along with Britain's ambitions would "make the Big Five an unworkable thing," Lippmann told his fellow columnist George Fielding Eliot. Rather than allowing itself to be used as an instrument of Whitehall, the United States should be a "mediator" among Britain, Russia and China — a role natural to it since there were "no direct conflicts of vital interests" between the United States and the other major powers. [8]

Sympathetic to Lippmann's argument, Byrnes had the idea that he would try to bring the columnist into the government. In August 1945 he called up Lippmann, who was then vacationing in Maine, and asked him if he would like to run the information and propaganda activities that had just been transferred from the Office of War Information to the State Department. Some jobs might have tempted him: secretary of state, or perhaps ambassador to France. But not this one. He demurely declined, but Byrnes insisted that he think it over. Lippmann decided that he would drive over and talk about it with his neighbor Harry Hopkins.

FDR's indispensable troubleshooter and confidant, wisecracking, cynical and totally unpretentious, Hopkins had started out as a social worker in the New York slums and had become the second most important man in the White House, smoothing relations with Congress, untangling bureaucratic snags, and winning over foreign leaders with a combination of empathy and charm. Even Stalin thought he had "soul." Driven into retirement by the cancer that would soon take his life, he had gone to Moscow late that spring, at Truman's request, to mollify Stalin during the mishaps at San Francisco.

Although Hopkins and Lippmann had argued often about the New Deal, they retained their friendship, and since the death of FDR had drawn together under the force of shared anxieties about the mounting hostility between Washington and Moscow. During that summer of 1945 on Mount Desert Island the two men often went on picnics together with their wives and spent afternoons sunbathing on the rocky coast. "When Hopkins was there, decisions went well and toward good results," Lippmann later wrote. "When he was absent, things went all to pieces." Hopkins had the gift of "cutting aside the details and coming to the crux of the matter, of finding swiftly the real issue which had to be decided, the sticking point at which pride, vested interest, timidity, confusion, were causing trouble. He would bring it nakedly into the open, ruthlessly, almost cynically, with no palaver, often with deliberate tactlessness meant to shock men into seeing the reality. These are not the qualities which make a conventionally successful politician. But in the grim business of war, among men who carry the tremendous burden of decision, they were just the qualities which the times called for."[9]

Hopkins agreed that Lippmann ought to turn down Byrnes's offer, but suggested he do it by setting down conditions impossible for Byrnes to grant — like making the job a cabinet post. Lippmann decided to take a more direct approach, and wrote Byrnes a long letter declining the offer. The whole idea was based on the "misconception" that public relations was a "kind of advertising which can be farmed out to specialists in the art of managing public opinion," he said, when it was really "inseparable from leadership, and no qualified public official needs the intervention of a public relations expert between himself and the people." Byrnes was reluctant to let Lippmann get off so easily, and sent an air force plane to bring him back to Washington for a talk. Lippmann went, but resisted the secretary's blandishments, and it was the last time anyone offered him a government job.

Lippmann never did accommodate himself to a government propaganda agency. He did not like the idea of a Voice of America as a State Department organ "heard round the world singing songs, cracking jokes, entertaining the kiddies." If there had to be such an organization it should confine itself to broadcasting the news, not a government line. "This country," he observed with an idealism shared by few officials, "being a truly free country, does not have any such thing as an official ideology, an official doctrine and an official set of opinions." [10]

After his talk with Byrnes, Lippmann returned to Maine, making a brief stop in Pawling, New York, to pick out a companion he and Helen had chosen for their prizewinning dog, Courage. They had become passionately addicted to poodles. Lippmann even wrote a preface for a book called *How to Train Your Dog* because the author had trained his poodle. The puppy they chose was dubbed Brioche by Alexander Woollcott, and when Courage died four years later they replaced him with Panache. Only poodle lovers could fully understand their devotion to these animals, but devotion it was. Every day in Washington they took the dogs for long walks, often along the canal towpath in Georgetown. They fussed over them as though they were delicate and rather temperamental children, as in fact for them the dogs were.

In mid-September they closed up the camp at Southwest Harbor and moved back to Washington. Since the fall of 1938, when they returned from their honeymoon summer in Europe, they had rented an old and not particularly comfortable brick house in Georgetown. Its distinguishing characteristics were an iron scrollwork balcony in New Orleans style and an annex where Alexander Graham Bell had experimented with his telephone. Aside from character, the Bell house had a convent and an institute for the deaf as neighbors — no mean advantage for a man who craved silence. But the rooms were small and the basement leaked. Wanting something more comfortable, Helen found what she was looking for in a sprawling Tudor house on Woodley Road, just across from the Washington Cathedral. The house, which came to them through their friend the bishop, Angus Dun, had once served as deanery for the cathedral. They agreed to give the cathedral first right to rebuy it when they moved out — a right it ultimately exercised twenty-one years later. With its sunken living room, spacious library, and secluded third floor, where Lippmann installed his office and assistants, the deanery was ideal.

By the time the Lippmanns had returned to Washington, the optimism of the spring had given way to open distrust. The unleashing of atomic bombs over Hiroshima and Nagasaki — an event unreported by Lippmann because he was on vacation — had forced the surrender of Japan in August. But the end of the war merely brought to the surface mounting differences between Russia and the West. At the Potsdam conference in July Truman had made only a very guarded reference to Stalin about the atomic bomb. The decision to withhold this information did not augur well for postwar cooperation.[11]

With the atomic bomb came a euphoria of power, a belief that the United States stood supreme in the world, that perhaps it need not have accepted the compromises with Russia that it had sought only a few months earlier at Yalta, that the exhilarating vision of an American Century might now be turned into reality. Lippmann felt qualms about the new muscle-flexing mood he sensed in Washington, qualms he expressed in the form of a warning. "An awareness that the great power we now possess is newly acquired is the best antidote we can carry about with us against our moral and political immaturity," he wrote in response to the grandiose ambitions that loomed so temptingly.

There is no more difficult art than to exercise great power well; all the serious military, diplomatic, and economic decisions we have now to take will depend on how correctly we measure our power, how truly we see its possibilities *within* its limitations. That is what Germany and Japan, which also rose suddenly, did not do; those two mighty empires are in ruins because their leaders and their people misjudged their newly acquired power, and so misused it. . . .

Nothing is easier, too, than to dissipate influence by exerting it for trivial or private ends, or to forget that power is not given once and forever but that it has to be replenished continually by the effort which created it in the first place. The wisdom which may make great powers beneficent can be found only with humility, and also the good manners and courtesy of the soul which alone can make great power acceptable to others.

Great as it is, American power is limited. Within its limits, it will be greater or less depending on the ends for which it is used.[12]

This was not the advice that American policymakers wanted to hear. To their mind a proper world was one open to American economic and political influence. They did not like what was happening in Eastern Europe. Whereas Stalin looked on a communist government in Warsaw as a guarantee of Soviet security, American officials saw it as a betrayal of the Yalta accords. Washington insisted on free elections in Eastern Europe as a test of Soviet intentions. But from Moscow's point of view, as Lippmann wrote that fall, "our interest in free elections appears as a British-American protection and encouragement of those East European and Balkan factions which are hostile to the Soviet Union." The Russians had reason to question, he noted, "whether our political interest in that orbit is what it professes to be, or is the cover for an intervention designed to push them back to where they were in 1939."

At that time the Soviets had not yet imposed communist regimes throughout Eastern Europe. Elections in Hungary and Czechoslovakia had produced noncommunist governments, while those in Bulgaria had satisfied Western observers by their relative fairness. Nonetheless, the Truman administration took an increasingly hard line — abruptly cutting off Lend-Lease, paring down the German reparation figures suggested at Yalta, and most important, ignoring Moscow's request for a reconstruction loan to rebuild Russia's shattered economy. The United States and the Soviet Union were moving from suspicion toward open hostility. "How far this is Russia's fault, Britain's fault or our own, no honest man can say," Lippmann wrote in November 1945. "What matters is that the thing is happening, that we are all being sucked into the conflict, and that we are not now using a fraction of our power and influence to avert it." The country, he added darkly, was "drifting toward a catastrophe." [13]

To avert that catastrophe Byrnes decided to make a direct overture to Stalin. In December 1945 the secretary flew to Moscow, where he offered to recognize the Rumanian and Bulgarian regimes if the Russians would go along with a German peace treaty and a general agreement on Eastern Europe. Stalin seemed amenable, and a triumphant Byrnes returned to declare, in a nationwide radio broadcast, that the Moscow meeting had produced a "better understanding" between Russia and the West. Lippmann hailed the Moscow accords as a realistic basis for an all-German peace treaty.

But hardly had Byrnes returned when he fell under attack from a disparate collection of One Worlders, right-wingers, and the anti-Soviet faction within the State Department. Sumner Welles charged that spheres of influence, like undemocratic governments in Eastern Europe, were immoral; Vandenberg described the conciliatory language of the accords as reminiscent of "Chamberlain and his umbrella appeasement," and Truman's garrulous adviser Admiral William Leahy called the Moscow communiqué "an appeasement document which gives to the Soviets everything they want and preserves to America nothing."

Lippmann rushed to Byrnes's aid. Spheres of influence were a fact of life, he explained. The United States had one of its own — not only in Latin America, where undemocratic regimes thrived, but also in Japan, where it had locked out the Soviets. Anyone believing it immoral for the Soviets to have a sphere of influence would have to be willing to liquidate America's own, he explained: "otherwise he is following a double standard of morality — nationalist, or, if you like, imperialist, where we have power, and universalist where the Russians have it." But Lippmann's argument made no dent on the hard-liners. They were furious at Byrnes, Lippmann later recalled, for having "very nearly pulled off an agreement" in Moscow which they, and particularly the British, "didn't like at all." [14] Byrnes, feeling isolated within the government and without Truman's support, retreated from his conciliatory approach.

By early 1946 battle lines had hardened. The Russians, who had occupied Iran jointly with the British during the war, refused to withdraw until the British gave them a share of their Persian oil monopoly. London balked. Stalin then declared that uneven economic development in the West could cause "violent disturbances" and the splitting of the capitalist world into "two hostile camps and war between them." In preparation the Soviets would speed up industrialization and collectivization. The speech startled, and even frightened, many. Justice William O. Douglas pronounced it to be the "declaration of World War III." Lippmann, too, thought it belligerent. Since there was no ground for supposing that the Soviet Union lacked the means or the will to pursue "military superiority," he told his readers, the West would have to undertake a "new mighty upsurge of national economy to balance it and withstand it."

Business Week, not normally known for its radicalism, thought that Lippmann had "gone berserk and virtually declared war on Russia." The Kremlin thought so, too. *Pravda* denounced Lippmann as a notorious "representative of imperialist ideology" whose call for an American show of strength surpassed "all records of hypocrisy and cynicism." But the Soviet party daily had never been one of Lippmann's admirers. Two years earlier, on the publication of *U.S. War Aims,* it had colorfully described him as an "ink-stained hyena" for having suggested that Russia's sphere of influence be confined to Eastern Europe.[15]

Although he preached negotiation, Lippmann was becoming increasingly susceptible to the argument that the Soviets were intent on military expansion. The Dardanelles crisis reinforced that view. The Soviets — citing an agreement reached at Yalta and Potsdam — put pressure on Turkey for a naval base in the Dardanelles and joint control over the straits. In late February 1946 Lippmann talked the matter over with Navy Secretary Forrestal, with whom he had grown quite friendly, and together they decided that the United States should make a show of force in the Mediterranean to indicate its interest in Turkey. Forrestal came up with the idea of sending the battleship *Missouri* to return the body of the Turkish ambassador, who had just died in Washington. Lippmann hailed the plan in his column and, in a touch of hyperbole, denounced Soviet pressure on the Turks as a "blatantly crude plan to settle the Mediterranean problem by taking possession of the Mediterranean."[16]

Lippmann had no quarrel with the buildup and exercise of American power — only with its indiscriminate dispersal. An unrestricted "get-tough" policy would, he warned, "commit and entangle us in China, in southern Asia, the Middle East, the Balkans, involve us with all manner of reactionary and obsolete forces, and deprive us of any constructive initiative of our own." The real problem was not merely the expansion of Russian power, but the weakness of Britain, Western Europe and China. His implication was that the United States — without directly engaging itself against the Soviet Union — should try to correct that weakness. Even hard-liners could not object to the military buildup he suggested. "I read your piece of this morning with great interest, and, I suppose because it accords so closely with my own views, I approve," Forrestal wrote him. "I hope you will continue to pursue this line of thought — regardless of whether it is translated into policy in near-term action."[17]

Whether Stalin had been speaking defensively or belligerently, he got what he never intended: a very rough Western response in kind. It was not long in coming. And it came from America's favorite Englishman, Winston Churchill. Only a month after Stalin's speech, Churchill came to the small college town of Fulton, Missouri, and gave one of his most celebrated orations. The old warrior might have lost office, but not his rhetorical gift. He realized that Britain, weakened by the war, could exert real influence only through America. Agitated at Russian obduracy in Eastern Europe, and unhappy in his forced retirement by the British voters, Churchill took the opportunity to make a ringing peroration. "From Stettin in the Baltic to Trieste in the Adriatic an iron curtain has descended across the Continent," he proclaimed. The Russians posed a "growing challenge and peril to Christian civilization." Although they did not want to fight, they sought the fruits of war. They could be held in check only by a "fraternal association of English-speaking peoples," fortified by the American nuclear arsenal, which "God has willed." President Truman beamed from the rostrum, seeming by his presence to endorse Churchill's call to arms. The speech created such a furor that Truman was forced to claim he had not read it beforehand. Yet for all its melodramatic phrasing, it expressed a view widely held in his administration.

The night of the speech Helen and Walter happened to be dining at the Georgetown home of Dean Acheson, then under secretary of state. Fulton naturally dominated the conversation. Acheson, articulate and aggressive as always, hailed Churchill's prescription and said it was high time to stand up to the Russians. Australian Minister Richard Casey and the State Department's specialist on the Soviets, Charles Bohlen, agreed. Henry Wallace, however, now secretary of commerce, dissented sharply. Churchill's call for an Anglo-American atomic bludgeon, he charged, would intensify Russian fears of encirclement, stimulate an arms race, and lead to war. The argument raged most of the evening. Lippmann occasionally nodded in Wallace's direction, but took no stance.

After reading the complete speech in the papers the next morning, Lippmann decided that Wallace was probably right. It was a clear repudiation of Byrnes's attempt to work out a deal with the Russians. Churchill was trying to enlist American power to shore up Britain's shrinking sphere of influence in Eastern Europe and the Middle East. A warning was in order. "The line of British imperial interest and the line of American vital interest are not to be regarded as identical," Lippmann told his readers in the column he wrote that morning. They could become so only if Soviet actions made cooperation with Moscow impossible.[18]

Lippmann had no quarrel with Western unity and rearmament. The United States, he wrote in the wake of Churchill's speech, should make loans to Britain and France, enact universal military training, rebuild the Mediterranean and European fleets, and launch an economic development project for the Middle East. "But if we do any of these necessary, desirable, and inherently constructive things inside an alliance which is avowedly anti-Soviet," he warned, "they will surely accentuate the antagonism of Moscow far more than they reinforce our own influence for a peaceable settlement." In private he was a good deal harsher. "I deplored Churchill's speech," he wrote a colleague in Richmond, "because he presented this necessary and desirable objective in the one way most calculated to make it dangerous and impossible to achieve — namely as a combination against the Soviet Union, and . . . accompanied by a direct incitement to a preventive war within the next five years." The Fulton oration was, he maintained, an "almost catastrophic blunder."[19]

Lippmann's attack on Churchill's speech so offended a conservative Arizona publisher that he threatened to stop carrying the T&T column. Even some of Lippmann's friends had trouble going along with his reasoning. "I think the fundamental trouble with our postwar foreign policy," he wrote his friend Alma Morgan after a heated argument, "is that we have got so fascinated by Russia that we are always dealing with Russian issues and neglecting our own much more important issues. We have spent all our energy on the Polish boundary and the Bulgarian elections, etc, etc, at the expense of the revival of France, Italy and western Europe in general. The greatest victory the Russians have won over us is that we always discuss their concerns and never our own."[20]

Stalin's response to Fulton was sharp and predictable: he rejected the terms of a proposed one-billion-dollar American loan, refused participation in the International Monetary Fund, and put the squeeze on Eastern Europe. Byrnes, now listing toward the hard-liners, took the Iranian complaint to the United Nations — even though the Soviets had quietly agreed to withdraw their troops. This was purely a grandstand move. At a Washington dinner party Lippmann got into a heated discussion with Charles Bohlen, maintaining that such a belligerent policy would destroy the effectiveness of the UN and perhaps even lead to war. Bohlen defended his boss, and as the conversation grew heated, Helen — who had been a nurse's aide in the first war and director of the program in the second — interjected: "Well, Chip, all I can say is that in your war I won't be a nurse's aide!"[21]

Two weeks after the Fulton speech the Lippmanns took off for Europe, stopping in Paris, Berlin, Munich, Vienna and Prague, and Nuremberg for the Nazi war criminal trials.[22] After a round of meetings with Italian officials in Rome, including Communist chief Palmiero Togliatti, they arrived in Florence for a long-delayed reunion with Bernard Berenson. Despite the entreaties of his friends, the art historian, then eighty-one, had remained in Italy throughout the war. Lippmann, having failed to persuade Berenson to return to the United States in 1940, interceded with the State Department to gain special status for him from the Italian government as a protected alien. Though vulnerable as a Jew and an outspoken antifascist, Berenson had been left alone by the Italian authorities.

But when the Germans took over Italy following the Allied landings, his days seemed numbered. All Jews were being deported to the death camps. One morning Berenson received a phone call from the local police office. "Dottore," the commissioner said, "the Germans want to come to your villa, but we are not sure exactly where it is. Could you give us instructions for their visit tomorrow morning?" This was the signal to get out fast. Gathering as many of his favorite books and drawings as he could, Berenson got into his ancient Lancia and had his chauffeur drive him across the valley to the villa of his friend the Marchese Serlupi, the ambassador of San Marino to the Holy See. There, under papal protection only a few hundred yards from the German lines, and with artillery shells whizzing overhead, "Barone Bernardino," to use his transparent cover name, sat out the remaining months of war in the basement, writing his memoirs and having Nicky read to him tales from the *Decameron* — an appropriate choice, since Boccaccio's work had been set in the adjacent villa.[23]

After their reunion with Berenson and Nicky Mariano, the Lippmanns went on to Paris. France was in turmoil. General de Gaulle had abruptly resigned as president in January 1946 because of leftist opposition to his economic program. The French Communist party, traditionally obedient to Moscow, controlled the trade unions and could paralyze the country at will. During his twelve days in the French capital Lippmann met with virtually every important political official, including Communists

Maurice Thorez and Jacques Duclos, and capped his visit with a pilgrimage to De Gaulle, then in retreat at his country home in Lorraine.

Lippmann returned to Washington on April 30, deeply unsettled by his five-week trip. What he had seen in Germany, had been told by American and British officials, and had learned in Paris convinced him that the British — pulling the Americans in tow — were intent on a showdown with the Russians. Having divided Prussia between them, London and Moscow were vying for control of all Germany. Lippmann's articles were harsh and accusatory, blaming the British as much as the Russians for the breakdown of the wartime alliance and the danger of a new war.

The British, he charged, were secretly keeping intact Wehrmacht units and treating Nazi officers with "enough chivalry to justify them in feeling that their careers as professional soldiers were not necessarily and finally terminated." To make matters worse, he added, the Americans did not even know what was going on. Having given the British the richest part of the occupation zone, including the industrial Ruhr, half of Prussia, and the port of Hamburg, the State Department was mindlessly following the Foreign Office. Instead of pushing for a federal system of strong states with limited central government, the Americans were going along with a British plan for a powerful centralized Germany — this time to be enlisted as a bulwark against the Russians.[24]

Lippmann's three-part series on Germany created a sensation, and was reprinted in every important paper in the United States and Western Europe. The British reaction was particularly intense. Lord Vansittart angrily accused him in the *Herald Tribune* of trying to "push Mr. Byrnes back into the policy of appeasement."[25] If that had been Lippmann's intention, it would not have been easy. Byrnes, feeling increasingly isolated within the administration, had by this time largely adopted the hard line pressed on him by Acheson, Forrestal and Harriman. The image of an expansionist, aggressive Russia was fast becoming the new orthodoxy.

As rivalry mounted between Russia and the West, Germany's potential power became increasingly alluring. In July 1946 Vyacheslav Molotov, in a transparent bid for the allegiance of German nationalists, declared that Russia would not stand in the way of the "rightful aspirations" of the German people, and denounced the Western plan for German disarmament and for international control of the Ruhr. Lippmann reacted harshly to Molotov's bait. The Soviets, he charged, were trying to freeze the West out of Germany, forge a Russo-German alliance, and "get hold of Germany before anyone else." But he also suggested that the Russians had reason for their fears; they had seen "plenty of signs, not all of them products of their suspicions," that the

British and Americans were "toying with the idea of controlling Germany to use her against Russia."[26]

Lippmann was as troubled by the obdurate British-American line as by Molotov's speech. "I am oppressed with the feeling that our peace-makers are lost in the details and don't have any general conception of what Europe is and is becoming," he wrote Raymond Gram Swing from Maine in August. Although the Italian peace treaty was an "absurdity" because of the unrealistic frontiers drawn with Austria and Yugoslavia, the "real conundrum is why the Soviets impose such harsh terms on the satellites in their orbit. That is not consistent with the thesis that they want a belt of free states between them and Germany. I can take it to mean only a confirmation of the theory that the Russians have decided they can't rely on the security belt and that they have jumped over it with the object of making an agreement with Germany. We all shrink from that theory."[27]

Suddenly the prospect of war seemed real. Lippmann's fellow columnist Dorothy Thompson sent him a gloom-filled letter from her farm in Vermont, predicting that the Russians would woo the Germans with a second *Anschluss,* giving them not only Austria but parts of Czechoslovakia as well. They would then integrate Russian raw materials with German industry in a vast economic cartel. "I do not think any of this can be stopped except by another war, and I do not think that we will wage that war until we are in a dubious position to win it," she concluded grimly. "Spengler will be proved to have been right, a generation ago, in predicting the Decline of the West."

Lippmann was in no mood for such pessimism. The Russians were indeed being difficult, but they had much to fear from a revived and hostile Germany. The United States was ignoring Moscow's legitimate security anxieties, and the Soviets now seemed to feel they could be secure only by dominating Eastern Europe. Yet Lippmann, putting his faith in history and geography rather than in ideology and "national character," remained hopeful. "As for the future from now on — given all our mistakes and failures — I say: the devil with all catastrophic, apocalyptic visions of inexorable, inevitable doom," he wrote Thompson. "We may be able to avert it. Trying to avert it is the good fight — even if we lose it. At least for you and me, we enlisted too long ago to begin wringing our hands now."[28]

Lippmann may have been ready for the "good fight." But the tide was fast shifting against those who thought it possible to work out a settlement with Moscow.

A. TAVOLA. NON. S'INVECCHIA

Captain's dinner on board S.S. Saturnia, March 1931, en route to Greece. Lippmann, second on right; Thomas Lamont, fourth on right; Faye Lippmann, fifth on right; Florence Lamont, fifth on left; Gilbert Murray, fourth on left (Reprinted from THE THOMAS LAMONT FAMILY, edited by Corliss Lamont, copyright 1962, published by Horizon Press, New York)

Walter and Faye at Wading River, mid-1930s

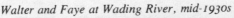

Lippmann in September 1937, following his traumatic flight from Paris, at I Tatti with (left to right) Lucius Wilmerding, Nicky Mariano, Bernard Berenson and Carlo Placci, a friend of BB

Helen Byrne Armstrong 1934
(Photo courtesy of Gregor Gamble)

"Lippmann scares me this morning."

Lippmann and Prime Minister Jawaharlal Nehru, New Delhi, 1949

Helen and Walter, Southwest Harbor, Maine, 1951
(Photo courtesy of Mrs. George Porter)

Walter walking the beach at low tide, Southwest Harbor, Maine, 1955

*Lippmann contemplating the bust of
Lyndon Johnson the night before the
Baltimore speech on Vietnam,
April 1965*

Eric Sevareid interviewing Lippmann for CBS-TV, February 1965 (Photo by Delvecchio)

Walter and Helen on one of their last walks at Mount Desert Island, Maine

34

Swimming up Niagara

It is rather lonely here. I feel a little bit like somebody
trying to swim up Niagara Falls.

— To Raymond Gram Swing, November 13, 1947

THE new mood of suspicion had been evident for some time, but it
had never been laid down in systematic form. That gap was filled
in February 1946 when George Kennan sent an eight-thousand-word
message from the Moscow embassy to his superiors in the State Department. That "long telegram," as it came to be known, summed up everything the administration had already decided about the Soviets.

Russian leaders took a "neurotic view" of the world, Kennan declared, because communist ideology, not security interests, governed
their policy. "Committed fanatically to the belief that with the United
States there can be no permanent modus vivendi," they were determined that the "internal harmony of our society be disrupted, our traditional way of life be destroyed, the international authority of our state be
broken." Obviously there was no point in trying to reach a political settlement with such a state, as those like Lippmann had urged. "Lippmann's appeal for closer 'diplomatic contact,' " Kennan told James
Forrestal, "reflects a serious misunderstanding of Soviet realities." [1]

Kennan's agitated telegram created a sensation in Washington and
neatly buttressed — with its emphasis on communist ideology and Soviet fanaticism — the administration's new line. Lippmann had trouble
with that line. Although he certainly harbored no illusions about Soviet
beneficence, neither did he think the Russians were devils incarnate. He
was more concerned with spheres of influence than with ideology, with
self-enforcing agreements than with vague declarations of policy. He
believed that the Russians had real anxieties about their security, particularly with regard to Germany, and that American policy was intensifying those anxieties.

When the Truman administration in the summer of 1946 proposed a plan for the international control of atomic energy, he tried to explain why the plan harbored a fatal flaw. Under its provisions the United States would release technical information about atomic energy only when an international control and inspection system suiting its taste had been erected. The Soviets would not be allowed to conduct atomic research nor to veto inspections on their territory. The whole veto issue — on which the so-called Baruch Plan rested — was overblown and irrelevant, Lippmann charged. Clearly no nation would use its veto unless it was willing to risk the suspicion that it was preparing for war. If the Russians felt their vital interests were involved they would challenge the accord, veto or not. So would the United States. The administration's plan, Lippmann told one of its drafters, "has not only aroused the Russians, more than is necessary, but . . . has hardened American opinion behind ideas that really, at bottom, make no sense."[2] The hope for international control over the atom was stillborn.

The mutual suspicion that blocked joint control of the atom also infected policy toward Germany. Molotov's July speech dangling the "lost territories" in return for a Berlin-Moscow alliance had triggered a panic in Washington. Fearing another Rapallo accord of the kind that had brought outcast Germany and Russia together in 1922, the administration moved to counter the Russian bid in kind. In September 1946 Byrnes went to Stuttgart and lured the Germans by promising to end production restrictions and restore the Ruhr and the Rhine to a central government. He also suggested that the new boundaries in the east need not be looked upon as permanent. Lippmann, who favored a federal system in Germany based on strong states and a weak central government, unleashed a double salvo against Byrnes's offer. By suggesting the return of the "lost territories" Byrnes was promising something only the Russians had the power to deliver, he pointed out, and by pressing for a strong central government was unwittingly making it easier for Moscow to strike a deal with Berlin.[3]

At the very moment that Byrnes was making his pitch to the Germans, the former vice-president and current secretary of commerce, Henry Wallace, was delivering a startling address in Madison Square Garden that undercut the administration's entire get-tough policy. Truman, who had perfunctorily given his okay to the speech, was embarrassed by Wallace's accusation that the United States was as much to blame as the Russians for the growing confrontation. Byrnes was so angry that he threatened to resign unless Wallace were fired. Truman gave Wallace his walking papers. Lippmann saw the episode as an example of the administration's ineptitude. It showed that Truman had no control over American policy, and that Byrnes, who was spending most of his time flitting from one international conference to another, did not either. While the decision to resist Soviet expansion was unavoidable and right, he wrote, its implementation was "superficial and improvised."

Nor was Lippmann any easier on Wallace. The trouble with the commerce secretary, he continued, was that he was essentially a pacifist who thought that Stalin could be won over by reducing American military power. Lippmann had little patience with pacifists. The true policy, he elaborated, was to "confront power with power at a selected point where a decision is in a military sense possible, and then to use the delicate and unstable equilibrium as an opportunity to be seized for constructive and magnanimous negotiation." Several months later, after Wallace had become the hero of the far Left, Lippmann was even tougher, describing him as a "good and faithful" public servant who lacked both the "intellectual resources to decide the issues and the emotional steadfastness and stability to endure responsibility." A mystic and an idealist, Wallace, he charged, had fled from the "laborious give and take of politics and administration to the comforting applause of coteries, to the development of a cult, and to making himself a sacrificial offering for the sins of the world."[4]

While Wallace occupied, temporarily at least, the pacifist fringe of the Truman administration, the war hawks were well represented by James Forrestal. The former Dillon, Read partner who became secretary of the navy in 1944 moved into the powerful post of secretary of defense in September 1947 when the armed services were unified. To that position he brought the same qualities that had made him rich on Wall Street: aggressiveness, authoritarianism, a work compulsion, a conviction of the moral purity of whatever cause he embraced, and an unquenchable thirst for power. As his responsibilities grew, so did the fears and self-doubts that drove him to paranoia. In March 1949, on the verge of a nervous breakdown, he resigned his office, and two months later, telling his friends that the Russians were coming to get him, jumped to his death from his hospital window.

An early exponent of a global reach for America's military power, Forrestal never doubted that the Soviets were intent on conquering the world. Lippmann, though unpersuaded, nonetheless admired Forrestal for his energy and drive — and he had, as noted earlier, conspired with the navy secretary in March 1946 to send an American battleship to Turkey as a warning signal to the Russians. Lippmann was on good terms with Forrestal, and had no hesitation in doing a little prodding where he thought it might be effective.[5]

One occasion for such prodding occurred in November 1946 when Stalin offered to cut back Soviet ground forces if the United States would scrap the atomic bomb. Lippmann, though he wanted an accord with the Soviets, saw no reason to give up the American atomic monopoly. As soon as word of the Soviet offer came over his private ticker, he

436 PART TWO: 1931–1974

got on the phone to Forrestal. Declaring that the proposal was "one of the most astute and formidable things we've had to deal with yet," he warned that the administration must not "go off half-cocked and not see the real trap in it." The trap, he explained, was that the Russians could remobilize quickly if tensions flared and the deal broke down. "But if you reduce our kind of weapon, which is a complicated thing and takes years to build, you really have disarmed us. What you get is an offer to demobilize in return for an offer to disarm."

"That's correct," replied Forrestal, who had not yet seen the Soviet offer.

"If you first of all eliminate our strongest weapons entirely, and then at the same time reduce the weapons which we have — installations and the process of producing them — they could remobilize in a few weeks, and it would take us years to recreate it," Lippmann elaborated. Should the West agree to the Russian offer, "the balance of power would be decisively in their favor in the coming settlement. That's why we cannot dare get into that trap."

He had no trouble persuading Forrestal, although some of his journalistic colleagues saw the offer differently. "I've already got Raymond Swing and all kinds of people over here, and I've got to spend the day keeping them from jumping at it," Lippmann said. Arms reduction, however admirable in principle, should be only part of a general settlement. Refining the argument, he told his readers that morning that "too much is at stake to justify us in being mealy-mouthed for fear of seeming not to be on the side of the angels, and therefore opposed to immediate disarmament." The United States should hold on to the bomb as the "one most dependable guaranty that atomic weapons will not be used against us."[6]

Burned by his own experience during the 1920s and 1930s, Lippmann could never again see disarmament as a way of preventing war. When the U.S. government a few years later came up with a disarmament plan that would supposedly make war "inherently impossible," Lippmann found it absurd. "To supervise and control these infinitely complicated agreements we have been proposing that all the powers agree to construct a little tin god, to be known as the Authority, with a capital A," he wrote in one of his most sarcastic moods. "And what is the little tin god to do if it finds a violation of the agreement? The little tin god is to report to the Security Council, to the General Assembly, and to all states — all of them 'inherently' incapable of waging war — to permit appropriate action to be taken." With unconcealed contempt for such visions of internationalism — indeed, for schemes that, if put to the test, the U.S. government itself would never accept — he argued that the true goal was to make profitable victory in war improbable, and thereby inhibit the will to start a war.[7] As he often pointed out, it was the nuclear balance of terror, not the UN or any disarmament schemes, that kept America and Russia from war.

The difference between Lippmann and the administration was not over preparedness; he believed in military strength and judicious displays of power, as he showed in the Dardanelles incident. Rather, it was in the nature of the Soviet threat and how to handle it. The administration largely shared Kennan's view of the Soviets as ideological fanatics. Lippmann, on the other hand, saw them as essentially defensive, fearful of a revived Germany, hanging on to Eastern Europe from a sense of insecurity, and distrustful of Western efforts to snatch away their legitimate fruits of victory. Rather than assuaging Russian anxieties, the British and Americans, he charged in a free-swinging article for the *Atlantic* in December 1946, had "furnished the Soviet Union with reasons, with pretexts, for an iron rule behind the iron curtain, and with ground for believing what Russians are conditioned to believe: that a coalition is being organized to destroy them." They had chosen to challenge the Soviets in the one area they considered vital to their security, had narrowed the issue to the "very region where the conflict was sharpest and settlement the most difficult." Everywhere else Britain and America were supreme. They had Japan, the Mediterranean, southern Asia, most of China and Germany, all of Africa, command of the seas and the air, the atomic bomb. "The one thing they did not have was ground armies to match the Red Army in the region which the Red Army had just conquered triumphantly, and at a terrible cost of blood and treasure. Yet that was the region where they elected to put to the test their relations with the Soviet Union and the whole great business of a world settlement. Was it not certain that here they must fail?"[8]

Lippmann continued to believe a settlement was possible, with a few big ifs: if the West would show good faith, if it would accept that Eastern Europe unavoidably lay under Soviet influence, and if the Russians would not try to push their control beyond this area. The administration viewed the conflict in larger terms. The tightening Soviet grip on Poland and Rumania, the Kremlin's new demands for ideological conformity at home and revolutionary fervor abroad, and the electoral successes of communists in France and Italy combined to reinforce fears that a worldwide communist offensive was under way. That fear was also fed by the belief that American prosperity hinged on unimpeded access to world markets, that communism as an ideology posed a threat to American interests, that the entire colonial world was endangered by the communist virus. All this provided a rationale for the new doctrine taking shape in Washington.

Early in 1947 the British informed the United States that they could no longer afford the civil war in Greece. If the Americans wanted the Greek monarchy to put down the communist-led rebellion, they would have to pay for it. The administration did not need to be prodded. Dramatically convening a joint session of Congress, Truman in March asked for an emergency four hundred million dollars to help the Greek government, and the Turkish one as well. And, in a statement little noticed at the time, but which would have sweeping repercussions, he declared that it must be the policy of the United States "to support free peoples who are resisting attempted subjugation by armed minorities or by outside pressures."

Lippmann had no trouble with the aid bill. Although he thought the rightist Greek regime authoritarian, incompetent and unsavory, he did not believe it ought to be overthrown by force of arms. The United States should insist that it broaden its base by setting up a government of national union in which the insurgents could participate. But in the meantime the communists should be kept from taking over completely, and the Russians warned that any attempt by the Greek communists to seize power in Athens would bring "military countermeasures" from the United States. The Turks, for their part, should be given an American guarantee against Soviet pressure in the Dardanelles. And if that pressure intensified, he suggested, the straits should be closed so that Soviet ships could not enter the Mediterranean.[9]

Thus there was nothing "soft," as some critics later charged, in Lippmann's approach to the Greek crisis. He was willing to use the navy for a show of force, issue an ultimatum to the Russians, and forcibly prevent a communist victory in the Greek civil war. What distressed him was the sweeping rhetoric of the President's speech to Congress, which soon came to be known as the Truman Doctrine. It seemed to open the door to unlimited intervention. "Instead of such a large promise followed by a lame anti-climax," he wrote in his column the morning after Truman's promise of American aid to "free peoples everywhere,"

it would be better, much less dangerous, and far more effective to announce, not a global policy but an American Middle Eastern policy. Instead of not naming the Soviet Union, it would be better to address the Soviet Union directly, and to say that in view of the pressure on Greece and Turkey, we are reinforcing them; that our object is to stop the invasion of Greece by bands armed and trained in Yugoslavia, Bulgaria and Albania; to make sure that the settlement between the Soviet Union and Turkey is negotiated and is not imposed by force; that behind the protection of this temporary special guaranty, we are contributing economic and financial assistance in order to strengthen the national life of these two countries.

The advantage of adopting a precise Middle Eastern policy is that it can be controlled for the purpose of maintaining order. A vague global policy, which sounds like the tocsin of an ideological crusade, has no limits. It cannot be controlled. Its effects cannot be predicted. Everyone everywhere will read into it his own fears and hopes, and it could readily act as incitement and inducement to civil strife in countries where the national cooperation is delicate and precarious.[10]

There was a grave danger, Lippmann had warned even before Truman formally enunciated his doctrine, that the administration would dissipate American strength by trying to "reinforce every theater, to fill every vacuum of power and restore at one and the same time the whole shattered economic life of Europe and Asia." Why had Truman and Acheson presented a simple military aid bill as an "ideological crusade"? Because, he charged, they feared they could never sell it to Congress and the public on its own merits. Rather than being honest, they had engaged in a dangerous subterfuge.

To Lippmann it was not an ideological showdown, but a question of balance of power. As he supported the aid bill, so had he approved six months earlier Forrestal's decision to set up American naval bases in the eastern Mediterranean. There was nothing wrong in confronting Russia directly with American power under American command, he maintained. But it was dangerous to confront Russia with "dispersed American power in the service of a heterogeneous collection of unstable governments and of contending parties and factions which happen to be opposed to the Soviet Union."[11] The preservation of primary vital interests was justified and necessary; indiscriminate intervention in support of far-flung and unstable client regimes was wasteful and dangerous. This was an argument he would return to again in the 1950s and 1960s.

The administration was irritated with Lippmann's criticisms, for unlike Henry Wallace he could not be dismissed as a sentimental leftist, or, like Senator Robert Taft, as an isolationist. With the Greek-Turkish aid bill languishing in congressional committee, battered from both left and right, Under Secretary of State Dean Acheson, who rightly looked on the measure as his progeny, was getting edgy. One April night at a Washington dinner party Acheson launched into an impassioned defense of the Truman Doctrine and, carried away by anger and the force of his conviction, accused Lippmann of that ultimate in *lèse majesté,* "sabotaging" American foreign policy. Slow to anger but fierce when aroused, Lippmann hit back. Words flew, fingers were jabbed into chests, faces grew red. Nervously Lippmann lit one cigarette after another. Helen hovered over Walter protectively, like a destroyer escort trying to ward off enemy attacks. The dinner guests looked on with delight at this battle of the titans — a far better show than genteel conversation over brandy. Finally the match ended in a draw as the two distinguished gentlemen stalked off in opposite directions. Lippmann later described it as a "very unpleasant evening." One unexpected benefit, however, was that it induced him to give up smoking. The next morning he woke with such a nicotine hangover that he vowed to give up the weed forever — which, with periodic lapses, he did. The morning after the bout Acheson phoned to apologize for losing his temper. But it would not be long before the two men squared off again.[12]

If the Truman Doctrine — its messianic rhetoric aside — was meant as a signal that Greece and Turkey were squarely within the American sphere of influence, it said nothing about a far graver problem: the European economic crisis. By the winter of 1947 Europe, in the grip of the coldest weather in memory, was suffering a lack of food, fuel, raw materials, and dollars. The Europeans, their old trade patterns disrupted and many of their former markets lost, were unable to pay for the imports they needed. The "dollar shortage" was imperiling European recovery, drying up international trade, and raising the old specter of depression, never fully put to rest by war-induced prosperity. By early 1947 it had become clear that something drastic would have to be done to shore up the European economy and provide a market for American agriculture and industry.

In February 1947, while taking the sun in Arizona with Helen, who was recuperating from an operation, Lippmann wrote several articles on Britain's economic plight. The British were hopelessly overdrawn. Lacking the means to maintain a solvent empire, they had been "driven to expedients, entangling alliances with native oligarchies, and to bringing about a transfusion of American power, based on our fear of Soviet Russia, our quest for oil, and an unconsidered, half-baked form of American imperialism." And yet he shrank from suggesting that the entangling alliances should be scuttled. A "forced and disorderly liquidation" of Britain's imperial holdings might be damaging to Western stability, he warned.[13]

When he returned from Arizona Lippmann met with Acheson, Forrestal and Assistant Secretary of State Will Clayton to discuss ways of staving off the "forced liquidation" and of financing European recovery. They agreed that Britain was only part of the problem, that the European nations needed a massive transfusion of dollars, but that a tight-fisted Congress — taken over by the Republicans during the recent midterm elections — was likely to balk at "handouts." In late March Lippmann kicked off the administration's program by declaring in his column that the United States would have to make a "large capital contribution" to European recovery. And he suggested that the Soviets would be encouraged to allow Eastern Europe to participate in the program if the United States offered them a large reconstruction loan.

Two weeks later he followed up this suggestion with one of his most important columns. Entitling the piece "Cassandra Speaking," a rubric he reserved for particularly solemn occasions, he told his readers that

Europe was on the verge of collapse, and that however dramatic his words might seem, he was saying "only what responsible men say when they do not have to keep up appearances in public." The United States would have to launch political and economic measures "on a scale which no responsible statesman has yet ventured to hint at." He would now go beyond a hint: an American economic aid program equal to that of Lend-Lease, a European economic union stretching across the Continent.

This was exactly what State Department planners had in mind, but were reluctant to propose themselves. Coming from such an independent and authoritative figure as Lippmann, it had an electrifying effect. The unthinkable became respectable. The program Lippmann proposed would achieve what the planners had long sought: European recovery with the economic reconstruction of Germany as its linchpin. The European fear of German resurgence could be mitigated by subsuming Germany, or at least the three-quarters of Germany under Western control, into an all-European union. State Department speech writer Joseph Jones used Lippmann's article in drafting the pathbreaking address Acheson gave in Mississippi in early May 1947 on European recovery.[14]

With the public alerted to what was to come, Lippmann moved to coordinate his program with the administration. At Forrestal's suggestion he met with George Kennan, recently returned from the Moscow embassy to take charge of the State Department's policy planning staff. Over a long lunch at the Army War College, where Kennan was on temporary assignment, the two men discussed the aid program. The problem, they agreed, was a double one: how to sell such a costly program to a suspicious Congress, and how to organize it so that it did not seem either an American ploy to dominate Europe or a blatant anti-Soviet maneuver. These were difficult aims to reconcile. Congress was not going to pour money into Europe without imposing conditions, and was unlikely to approve any plan that put a Soviet hand in the American purse. Nor were the Europeans likely to welcome a program designed to finance American exports and to prevent them from bringing their own economies under greater central direction.

As for the Soviets, Lippmann and Kennan agreed that they should be invited to participate, so long as conditions were favorable to a free-market Europe open to American trade and investment. With regard to Europe, Lippmann had a suggestion: instead of making loans to individual countries, the United States should encourage the Europeans to draw up a plan of their own that would treat the continent as a single economic unit. This would remove the onus of American domination, while encouraging the Europeans to act together. Through economic union it might be possible to resolve the German dilemma and loosen Russia's hold on Eastern Europe. A week later Lippmann laid out to his readers the essence of what became the Marshall Plan. If the Europeans took the initiative by drawing up their own plan, he explained, "our financial intervention in Europe would almost certainly be purged of the suggestion that we were treating Europe as a satellite continent in our contest with the Soviets, and even in Moscow our real intentions would surely become clearer."

There were real advantages to bringing the Soviets in — if they would accept American terms. While "from the point of view of the Senate and American opinion the idea is far more attractive if European union is treated more or less as an anti-Soviet bloc," Lippmann wrote J. W. Fulbright, that would only intensify Russian resistance. "Unless we can push and buy the Russians out of Europe, there is no hope anyway, and I for one don't think it impossible to push and buy them out," he told the Arkansas senator. European union should be promoted as the prize that would follow the evacuation of Europe by the Russians. The only problem was to persuade Moscow that such an evacuation would not threaten its interests.[15]

Stalin was not persuaded. The American aid plan would work against the Soviets by integrating predominantly rural Eastern Europe into industrialized Western Europe. The Soviets would lose both their *cordon sanitaire* and their privileged trading area. For Stalin the Marshall Plan was merely an attempt to achieve by economic means what Truman had failed to win at Potsdam and after: the reversal of the Yalta settlement. The Soviet dictator's suspicions about the intent of the American offer were not entirely unfounded. Russia and the Eastern European states would, as George Kennan later explained, "either exclude themselves by unwillingness to accept the proposed conditions, or agree to abandon the exclusive orientation of their economies." Another Soviet expert, Charles Bohlen, then serving as special assistant to the new secretary of state, General George Marshall, later confirmed that the plan was framed in such a way as to "make it quite impossible for the Soviet Union to accept."[16]

Lippmann, however, continued to believe that the lure of a big American loan might induce the Russians to participate. The problem was to work out a European recovery formula that, "though it could be made to work without eastern Europe and without Soviet collaboration, would work far better if eastern Europe participated and the Soviet Union approved." The basic principle of such a European plan, he explained, would be "not to form a Western bloc which excluded eastern Europe and was defensively and offensively opposed to the Soviets — but to form the nucleus of a European union which is meant to include them, and offers them superior advantages if they collaborate than if they do not."

Although skeptical, the Russians did agree to talk — perhaps in hopes of getting a straight loan with no strings attached. At the end of June 1947 Molotov arrived in Paris for preliminary discussions with eighty advisers and a bevy of Eastern Europeans eager to sign on. The State Department was most unhappy. If the Soviets actually took part in the program, Congress would never provide the money. Soviet participation, Forrestal said, would be a "most disastrous thing."[17] He need not have worried. The Americans turned down flat the Soviet proposal that aid be furnished to nations individually. Molotov stalked out of the conference, dragging the reluctant Eastern Europeans with him. Given the choice between the questionable promise of American dollars and the reality of their hold over the satellites, the Russians chose the latter.

With a sigh of relief the administration then proceeded to sell the aid program as a bulwark against communism. The Russians in turn organized a rival communist trading bloc in Eastern Europe, launched the Cominform (a resuscitated version of the old Comintern) to tighten Soviet direction over the world communist movement, and brought the satellites — then threatened by the Titoist heresy — under more rigid control. Rather than helping to reunite Europe, the Marshall Plan drove one more nail into the wall dividing it.

The administration, having given up hope of detaching Eastern Europe from Soviet control through economic pressure and blandishments, decided to pursue a different tack. The rationale for a new policy was laid out in the summer of 1947 in *Foreign Affairs*. There an author mysteriously identified as "X" — soon revealed to be George Kennan — offered an explanation of Soviet conduct. The Kremlin's diplomacy, he declared in words familiar to those insiders who had seen the "long telegram" more than a year earlier, was not governed by rational considerations of security, but by a messianic ideology and a paranoid sense of insecurity. The men in the Kremlin used "capitalist encirclement" to justify their tyrannical rule to the oppressed Soviet masses, and in their incessant quest for world power would try to fill "every nook and cranny." If the Russians seemed to soften, this was merely a tactic to lull the West; they would move inexorably toward their goal unless countered by "unanswerable force." Soviet expansion could best be "contained by the adroit and vigilant application of counterforce at a series of constantly shifting geographical and political points." Eventually this would lead to "either the break-up or the gradual mellowing of Soviet power."[18]

Lippmann was in Maine when Kennan's article appeared, desultorily picking at one of the several books he never finished. This one, tentatively entitled *Retrospect,* was meant to be a backward glance at some of his earlier predictions and pronunciamentos. Kennan's piece offered him the perfect opportunity to abandon it. Although Lippmann had been impressed by Kennan during their discussions about the Marshall Plan, he was not at all persuaded by the diplomat's analysis of Soviet behavior. Kennan emphasized Marxist dogma at the expense of Russian history — a history marked by invasions from the west, including the Allied interventions of 1919–1920. Lippmann, who always thought geography and history more important than ideology, felt that Kennan ignored the degree to which the men in the Kremlin acted out of insecurity, fear, and their heritage as Russians. The desire to dominate Eastern Europe and win warm-water ports in the Mediterranean was, after all, no Stalinist invention. It had been pursued by the tsars for centuries.

The appearance of Kennan's article in such an influential journal as *Foreign Affairs* was no accident. It was meant as a semiofficial administration pronouncement. Lippmann believed that the whole analysis was wrong in its conception and dangerous in its implications. It would have to be countered. Sitting in his little office in the pine woods at the edge of his Maine "camp," Lippmann outlined a retort to Kennan that was ultimately to run for fourteen successive T&T columns, to be scrutinized in every foreign office and chancery in the world, and to give a new name to the competition between America and Russia.

Addressing the "X" article, Lippmann proceeded to refute its assumptions point by point. First, Kennan's emphasis on Marxist ideology was, he charged, a distortion of Soviet policy. Stalin was merely following in the footsteps of Peter the Great and Ivan the Terrible. The Russians were in Eastern Europe, not because of the demands of a messianic ideology, like Islam in the seventh century, but as a result of World War II. It was Hitler's aggression, not Stalin's, that had brought the Red Army to the Brandenburg Gate. Soviet troops remained there because of Russia's deep-seated and historically conditioned fears for its security — fears that had a rational basis and could not be dealt with as paranoid delusions.

Second, Lippmann attacked Kennan's prescription for dealing with Moscow: the "containment" doctrine. To confront the Soviets at "every point where they show signs of encroaching" was, Lippmann charged, a "strategic monstrosity" doomed to fail. It could be attempted only by "recruiting, subsidizing and supporting a heterogeneous array of satellites, clients, dependents and puppets." Propping up anticommunist regimes around the periphery of the Soviet Union would require unending American intervention. Because many of these regimes were dictatorial, they would be prey to insurrection, which they would beseech the United States to quell in the name of anticommunism. Confronted with such demands the United States would either have to "disown our puppets, which would be tantamount to appeasement and defeat and the loss of face," or else support them "at an incalculable cost on an unintended, unforeseen and perhaps undesirable issue.''

The real quarrel between America and Russia, he insisted, was not in the remote Asian perimeters of the Soviet empire, but in the heart of Europe. Rather than containment on the periphery, Lippmann urged a political settlement in Europe. If the Russians were in Eastern Europe because of fears about their security, the way to get them to leave was to allay those fears. The United States should propose a joint withdrawal of Soviet and American troops. Germany could be reunified under strict guarantees of demilitarization. Were the Soviets really intent on conquest? The answer could not be found in more bickering over the meaning of Yalta. The "acid test" would be for the West to offer realistic terms that would allow the Russians to withdraw from Eastern Europe.

"The history of diplomacy," Lippmann reminded Kennan, the professional diplomat, "is the history of relations among rival powers, which did not enjoy political intimacy, and did not respond to appeals to common purposes. Nevertheless, there have been settlements. Some of them did not last very long. Some of them did. For a diplomat to think that rival and unfriendly powers cannot be brought to a settlement is to forget what diplomacy is all about. There would be little for diplomats to do if the world consisted of partners, enjoying political intimacy, and responding to common appeals."[19]

The first of Lippmann's articles appeared on September 2, 1947, and by the time the final one was printed a month later, they were a topic of discussion wherever people gathered to talk about international politics. A few months afterward they were published in book form, and the title he gave the book, *The Cold War,* became part of the world's political vocabulary. Lippmann is usually given credit for the phrase, although he said he merely picked it up from one used in Europe during the late 1930s to characterize Hitler's war of nerves against the French, sometimes described as *la guèrre blanche* or *la guerre froide*. Herbert Bayard Swope, still doing public relations for Bernard Baruch, claimed that his client was the first to use the phrase.[20]

Interestingly, the father of the containment doctrine eventually came around to accepting Lippmann's critique. Kennan, some years later, after he had left the State Department to become a historian at Princeton, said that the whole disagreement with Lippmann stemmed from a "misunderstanding almost tragic in its dimensions." He never meant that containment be taken primarily in a military sense, he claimed, and he regretted that it had been so understood. At the time, however, when he could have disavowed the military interpretation Lippmann and others had put on his containment article, he did not chose to do so.[21] Despite this episode Kennan and Lippmann remained on close terms, and after Kennan's disenchanted departure from the government in 1953, their views became virtually identical. In the late 1950s Kennan revived and expanded Lippmann's troop withdrawal plan under his own label of "disengagement."

The cold war articles were still coming off the press, raising hackles in the State Department, when the Lippmanns flew to Europe in mid-September on their annual tour. This time Lippmann wanted to test the political temperature behind the Iron Curtain. Their first stop was Poland, where they talked to Communist party chief Wladyslaw Gomulka and visited the Nazi death camp at Auschwitz, where a million people, mostly Jews, had been exterminated. They then went on to Prague, where Foreign Trade Minister Hubert Ripka, a noncommunist member of the coalition government, complained bitterly that the Americans were actually forcing his country into the Soviet camp by refusing to send desperately needed food unless Czechoslovakia openly defied Russia. Did not the Americans understand, Ripka asked dejectedly, that the Czechs could not do such a thing under the circumstances — that the price of their independence was a friendly attitude toward Moscow?

After a quick trip to Berlin for talks with General Lucius Clay, the American proconsul, they continued on to Paris. André Malraux and Gaston Pawlewski, De Gaulle's lieutenants, asked Lippmann if he thought the general — who had resigned from office the previous year and was angling to return to power — could count on American support if he smashed the communist-led trade unions. Lippmann, who was not going to launch any trial balloons on that matter, suggested they ask the American ambassador. The mood in Paris was glum that autumn. Many told him that the communists would come to power through either the ballot box or a coup d'etat in conjunction with general strikes. Columnist Raymond Aron said that war with Russia was inevitable.

But to Lippmann most of these warnings seemed hyperbolic. It was obvious that the Russians could never take over Western Europe except with the Red Army, and their army was checkmated by the threat of American retaliation and the American monopoly on the atomic bomb. If the communists ever tried to seize power from within, he said, there would be a right-wing coup led by De Gaulle in France and the fascists in Italy. His visit to London, where he spent the last ten days of October 1947, reinforced that belief. After meeting with Prime Minister Clement Attlee, Foreign Minister Ernest Bevin, and the new U.S. ambassador, Lewis Douglas, he was convinced that the cold war had entered a more hopeful phase.

Lippmann came back to Washington in an optimistic mood, persuaded that Western Europe had turned the corner toward recovery, that the satellites were restive, and that the Soviets were on the defensive. The communists had been ousted from the governments of France and

Italy. De Gaulle's new anticommunist party had won a stunning victory at the polls. The communists had failed in their efforts to carry through general strikes that fall. The western zones of Germany were on the way to becoming a separate state within an Atlantic bloc. The French had abandoned their attempt to play a neutral role between Russia and the West. And even Secretary Marshall reported that the advance of communism had been stemmed.

To Lippmann the lesson was obvious. The communists, he told his readers, were stalemated in Western Europe, where they could never win more than a third of the vote, and locked out of power. In Eastern Europe the Soviet position had so eroded that Moscow had had to launch violent purges to impose loyalty on the satellites, and to organize the Cominform to keep its empire from falling apart. "My strongest impression," he wrote, ". . . is that the Russians have lost the cold war and they know it." This being the case, the West should be confident and magnanimous rather than frightened. The problem was not how to contain the Soviets, for they were already contained; rather, it was to "push toward a settlement which permits the recovery of Europe and of the world, and to relax the tension, to subdue the anxiety, and to end the panic." [22]

Life pronounced Lippmann naive and devoted an entire page to an editorial informing its readers that the Soviets were intent on bringing about "chaos, the collapse of civilization, and the communization of the Eurasian continent." Later Lippmann said he might have been a bit "reckless" in announcing that the Russians had lost the cold war. People misunderstood the phrase; "it was one of those foolish journalistic statements that had better been said more cautiously, but . . . I think that it was true." There was, he believed, no serious internal communist threat to Western Europe, and the major problem was the presence of Soviet troops in Eastern Europe. "My main preoccupation is to get them out of Europe and back into Russia," Lippmann wrote Berenson in early December 1947. "I don't think any agreements are worth anything while they are there, and it is worth paying a very high price indeed to get them out, and to take big risks to push them out." [23]

But here he was swimming against the current. The administration was less interested in knitting Europe together, or even in getting the Red Army to withdraw, than in building a powerful military phalanx in the West. "Either the Marshall Plan . . . will liquidate the foreign policy of the State Department, or the State Department's policy will destroy the Marshall Plan," Lippmann wrote Raymond Gram Swing shortly after his return from Europe. "The two are so irreconcilable, so incompatible, that at some point there will have to be a showdown or a resolution. Not only the Department as a whole, but the chief individuals in it, and this I am afraid includes George Marshall and runs down through [Robert] Lovett and Bohlen and Kennan and the smaller boys, is suffering from a real case of schizophrenia. When they state the realities they come to one set of conclusions; when they consult their political ideas they come to an opposite set.'' It was "rather lonely" in Washington, he complained; "I feel a little bit like somebody trying to swim up Niagara Falls.''

Lippmann and the administration could not agree because they started from different premises. He saw the Marshall Plan as the prelude to a reunited Europe purged of the cold war and of foreign occupation armies. "The Marshall Plan cannot be made to work unless the cold war diminishes, unless reciprocal trade opens up large holes in the iron curtain, unless economic intercourse between East and West transcends the ideological and political conflict," he wrote.[24] Although Truman and his advisers were not averse to opening "large holes through the iron curtain," they never conceived of the Marshall Plan as a means of reuniting Europe. That might come later, but only after the Soviets were forced to withdraw under the pressure of the West's overwhelming economic and military power. Strength came first; then, at some undefined and distant point, negotiation. And the key to such strength was Germany.

The controversy came to a head in late November 1947 when the Big Four foreign ministers met in London to discuss a German peace treaty. The Western powers had given up hope of a German settlement on any terms they could accept, and were proceeding with plans to set up an independent West German state by fusing the Western occupation zones. The Russians, fearful that such a state would dwarf their predominantly agricultural section of Germany and shatter their lingering hopes for reparations, pressed for a unified Germany.

Shortly before the conference opened Lippmann urgently wrote John Foster Dulles, the Republican lawyer who served as one of the American delegates, that the Germans must not be allowed to take advantage of the dispute between Russia and the West. Above all they must not regain full control of the industrial Ruhr, for they might then make a deal with Moscow at the expense of the West. Rather than turning over the Ruhr to the Germans, the Allies should, Lippmann suggested, establish "some form of ownership designed to be both a form of compulsion and a form of bait" to the Germans. Otherwise they would "be inclined to turn their backs on us once we had made a peace and do all their dealings on the essential subjects with the Soviet Union."

The conference soon bogged down in a spate of mutual recriminations. The two sides sought incompatible objectives. The Russians wanted to treat Germany as a single economic unit so that they could tap the industrial power of the Ruhr for reparations. Britain, France and the United States were intent on building an independent West German state and linking it to Western Europe and to the United States. Yet Lippmann was convinced that creation of such a state would cement the division of Europe. "We must not set up a German government in the two or three western zones, and . . . we must not make a separate peace with it," he told Dulles.

Lippmann was not asking for a meeting of minds, but only a *modus vivendi*. "A settlement with Russia does not depend on a change of heart in Moscow, upon an abandonment of Russian imperialism and a renunciation of the communist ideology," he wrote in his column a few days after the collapse of the foreign ministers' meeting. "It depends upon the restoration of a balance of power. . . . What will matter in the end is not what the Politburo would like to do, but what in fact it knows it cannot do." [25]

His approach was simple: power would be balanced against power to achieve an acceptable accommodation. Ideology played no part in his calculus. The Russians, he told Professor Quincy Wright, "will expand the revolution if the balance of power is such that they can; if it is such that they cannot, they will make the best settlement they can obtain for Russia." Yet he admitted that he would not discuss this openly in his column, for that would merely provoke an argument over Moscow's real intentions, leading to "realms of metaphysics and dialectic where I don't want to go." It is unfortunate that he did not raise that issue publicly, for the question of Russia's intentions lay at the heart of his dispute with the administration.

At the time Soviet intentions seemed, at least to Lippmann, limited enough: the security of the Soviet state, a buffer zone in Eastern Europe, prevention of a unified Germany under Western control. "I do not take a catastrophic view of the proximate future," Lippmann wrote Berenson at Christmas 1947. "There will be peace in Europe and among the great powers — at least no war and no social convulsions. But Asia and Africa will be turbulent for generations, and the feeling of serenity will not exist anywhere for many years to come. That's my general expectation, and so I shall not be too much disappointed." [26]

It turned out not to be a bad prediction. Congress agreed with his assumption that there would be peace in Europe. The legislators languidly rambled through hearings on the Marshall Plan without appropriating a cent of the billions the administration had asked for. The cold war seemed to be dying down.

Then came the coup in Czechoslovakia.

35

War Scare

> The struggle is now a race for military advantage — for
> strategical positions, for allies, and for the development
> of potential into actual military power.
>
> — "Today and Tomorrow," March 15, 1948

At the end of February 1948 the cold war entered a new phase. Following a week of political crisis in Prague, during which communists and anticommunists maneuvered for position, President Eduard Beneš succumbed to Soviet pressure and named a Kremlin puppet as prime minister. Within hours Klement Gottwald moved to smother all opposition. Arrests, purges and executions rocked the capital. Foreign Minister Jan Masaryk, son of the nation's founding president, fell to his death from his office window — probably assassinated. The only democratic government in Eastern Europe was snuffed out. With it went the hopes of many that Soviet communism could be restrained by compromise and negotiation. The Prague coup, in Harry Truman's words, "sent a shock throughout the civilized world."

The Kremlin's brutal action rang alarms in the West that bordered on panic. World War III seemed suddenly close at hand. When word of the coup came through, Lippmann was with Helen in California at the Ojai Valley ranch of Mima Porter. After conferring by telephone with his contacts in Washington, he accepted the administration's interpretation of events. The Prague coup and the recent pressures on Finland, he told his readers, were clearly "strategical actions planned by military men in anticipation of war." A "showdown" was at hand. The contest between Russia and the West had turned into a "race for military advantage — for strategical positions, for allies, and for the development of potential into actual military power." Although the ultimate aim was a negotiated settlement, the United States must in the short run, he argued, go on a war footing with immediate mobilization, the draft, lend-lease, war powers over industry, and the declaration of a national emergency.[1]

During the same week in mid-March that he wrote these agitated columns, he drafted a long letter to his friend Admiral Forrest Sherman, commander of the U.S. Sixth Fleet in the Mediterranean. "We cannot any longer afford to wage a diplomatic and indirect military war against the Soviet empire all over Europe and Asia," he declared in emotion-laden words. Instead of dissipating its strength through global containment, the United States should concentrate on a few critical areas: building up Japan so that the Soviets would have to keep a big army in Siberia, dividing the Arab world in order to maintain Western influence, and preventing a unified China from which only the communists would benefit. If the Soviets reacted violently to the dramatic buildup in American military strength, so be it. Even war was preferable to "being paralyzed all over the world with no prospect of a decision and only the prospect of indefinite and unlimited entanglement." Immediate mobilization was essential for two reasons: "to negotiate, and if we cannot negotiate, to compel the withdrawal of the Red Army to the frontiers of the Soviet Union."

By the time his secretary had transcribed his draft letter from the dictating machine, Lippmann had cooled off. In the letter he actually sent Sherman he allowed that the Russians might have acted defensively. The Marshall Plan's pull on the satellites, and the West's decision to push for an independent West German state, could have led the Russians to believe, he told the admiral, that "time was no longer on their side." One nonetheless had to assume that the Russians, "though not necessarily intending to precipitate war," would take actions they thought necessary "at the risk of war now rather than some years hence."[2]

Returning to Washington at the end of March, he found the capital near hysteria. Pentagon chief James Forrestal — who had long been pushing for a huge increase in the military budget — suggested to Lippmann over lunch that the United States might have to launch a preventive war against the Soviet Union. Air Force Secretary Stuart Symington echoed his boss's sentiments a few days later when he told Lippmann that unless the Russians agreed to pull out of Eastern Europe and open their bases to American inspection, the air force should knock out their key cities with atomic bombs. General Clay had sent an urgent message from Berlin of his "feeling" that war might soon break out "with dramatic suddenness." His feeling soon passed, but the administration wasted no time in taking advantage of the war scare to persuade Congress to provide money for the Marshall Plan and rearmament. That the administration welcomed just such a crisis had been suggested by Lippmann himself only a few months earlier when he wrote of the "notion held by some in Washington that the only way to win the support of Congress for the Marshall Plan is to frighten it."[3]

Even the Prague coup, brutal though it was, hardly demonstrated that the Soviets were planning to march on Western Europe. In fact, the administration had months earlier written off Czechoslovakia as little more than a Soviet satellite. In November 1947 Marshall had told the cabinet that the Russians would probably soon have to consolidate their hold on Eastern Europe by clamping down on Czechoslovakia as a "purely defensive move." George Kennan, who was out of the country at the time the coup took place, cabled the State Department that the Russians seemed to be consolidating their defenses — not preparing for aggression. Few listened. Later Kennan wrote that the Prague coup and the Soviet pressure on Berlin that soon followed were "defensive reactions" to the initial successes of the Marshall Plan and to the Western decision to press for an independent West German state.[4]

Although others in the government shared this view, the spring of 1948 was not a propitious time to express it. The administration desperately needed a crisis to sell the Marshall Plan and the rearmament program the Pentagon had long been pushing. The Prague coup was a gift from Providence. In response to a grim nationwide radio address by Truman on March 17, Congress quickly came up with the long-stalled down payment on the Marshall Plan, restored the draft, and doubled the air-force budget.

Lippmann's panic passed almost as fast as it had erupted. After a few weeks' reflection he decided that the Russians were not looking for a fight after all. "I take a reasonably optimistic view about the avoidance of war," he wrote Berenson. Explaining that the Czech coup had originally made him fear that the Soviets might march west within a year, "the fact that they show no evidence of a military response to our huge military rearmament in this country is a pretty good sign, I think, that they do not intend to march." Six months later Lippmann admitted to his readers that he had probably overreacted, and that the Prague coup was not a preparation for war but a response to the West's plans for a new German state.[5]

The prospect of an independent West Germany containing most of the territory and population of the former Reich, along with the industrial Ruhr, was not a happy one for Moscow. But Washington was determined, and it held the cards. In late March the United States and Britain, soon reluctantly joined by France, announced they were fusing their occupation zones; in late June they made the break final by issuing a new currency in the Western zones, which they then extended to their zones of Berlin. Thus vanished the Soviets' last hope for German reparations and international control of the Ruhr.

Despite Western fears of Soviet aggressiveness, Stalin was far too weak and cautious to prevent this ominous action by force. But there was one point where the West was vulnerable: Berlin. Within days he had shut down surface traffic into the former German capital. Truman responded by launching a round-the-clock airlift to supply food and fuel to the two million people in the Western zones of Berlin. He also made a different kind of gesture by dispatching American bombers equipped with atomic weapons to British bases. Stalin let the supply planes go through to Berlin, but the situation was volatile and tensions high.

Lippmann, though he opposed a West German state, supported the airlift on the grounds that the West should not be forced out of Berlin under duress. He pointed out, however, that the West had weakened its own case for joint control over Berlin by unilaterally ending such control over the rest of Germany. The decision to push for an independent West German state — rather than an all-European union — had triggered the Berlin crisis, he argued, and undermined the legitimacy of the Western military presence in the former all-German capital. "If Berlin ceases to be the capital of Germany, and if 'Germany' is western Germany . . . then we have no more reason to be there than we have to be in Dresden or Leipzig."

In September 1948 Lippmann sent a memo to John Foster Dulles — the likely secretary of state if the Republicans won the November elections — urging a loose German confederation embracing all the occupation zones.[6] The Russians might have been amenable to such an arrangement. They seemed desperate to maintain four-power control over Germany, and had made various feelers for a compromise settlement. But Washington and London were determined to push for a West German state as the linchpin of an Atlantic economic and military community. Lippmann might as well have been baying at the moon.

The airlift was, to everyone's surprise, an enormous success. It eliminated the need for a compromise with the Soviets on the German issue, and it enhanced the claims of the air force for a bigger chunk of the military budget. It also provided a healthy boost for Truman's long-suffering electoral prospects. Facing reelection, Truman tried to deflect public dissatisfaction with his administration by blaming its troubles on the Soviets and the "do-nothing" Eightieth Congress. Picking up support where he could find it, he moved to solidify his links with organized labor and the farmers. And in May 1948 he made a bold bid for the Jewish vote by recognizing the new nation of Israel.

Israel had barely been voted into existence by the United Nations when it was attacked on all sides by Arab armies. Lippmann, like many assimilated American Jews, had never been particularly enthusiastic about the creation of a Zionist state. He opposed the partition of Palestine and thought the only solution lay in an Arab-Jewish confederation. Considering it "preposterous" that London and Washington could not impose peace on the area, he maintained that "among the really difficult problems of the world," the Arab-Israeli conflict was "one of the simplest and most manageable." His sensible formula provided for a peace treaty between Israel and the British client-state of Trans-Jordan, to be followed by the creation of a Palestinian confederation under British and American protection. Such a solution would end the dispute between London and Washington over Zionism and the "scandal of a British satellite army" — Abdullah's Arab League — defying a United Nations resolution. The United States, he told Lewis Douglas — then American ambassador to Britain — should uphold the UN plan for Jewish-Arab confederation by refusing to grant American or World Bank loans to Israel or Jordan alone, but only to an economic union of the two.[7]

Lippmann had his eye on the long haul, Truman on the 1948 elections. The forthcoming elections offered a god-sent opportunity, as far as Lippmann was concerned, to get rid of a public embarrassment. From the beginning Lippmann had considered Truman unfit for the high office he held. "How are the affairs of the country to be conducted by a President who not only has lost the support of his party, but is not in command of his own administration . . . is not performing and gives no evidence of ability to perform, the functions of commander in chief?" he had asked two years earlier, in the fall of 1946, when the Republicans swept the midterm elections and won control of Congress. The best thing Truman could do for his country, he had suggested at that time, was to resign and turn the White House over to the Speaker of the House of Representatives. He even persuaded freshman senator J. W. Fulbright to back this quixotic proposal. "It is a poor conception of the public service which makes it a moral duty for a man to cling to an office, or to be a prisoner in it, if he cannot exercise its functions," Lippmann explained in his column. "The right to resign is one of the cherished privileges of a free man; the willingness to resign, when principle and the public interest are served, is always present in the public-spirited and the self-respecting. They look upon resigning, not as cowardice and quitting and a personal disaster, but as the ultimate guaranty of their useful influence and of their personal dignity." Truman declined the advice.

To Lippmann's mind Truman was an insecure man given to hasty decisions and false bravado to cover his anxieties. "I never thought that his way of shooting from the hip was the way the Presidency should be conducted," he later said on television. He was particularly critical of the decision to use the atomic bomb against Japan. Although he had not written about the devastation of Hiroshima and Nagasaki — being on one of his periodic sabbaticals at the time — he later said that "one of the things I look back on with the greatest regret, as an American, is that we were the ones that first dropped atomic bombs." And, although he himself had supported the doctrine of unconditional surrender during the war, he held Truman accountable for refusing to discuss a negotiated surrender with the Japanese before unleashing the atomic bomb.[8]

By the spring of 1948 Lippmann would have preferred almost anyone to Truman. The field was uninspiring: a coy Eisenhower, an inflexible Taft, a grinning Stassen, a smug Dewey, and a pompous Vandenberg. More from desperation than enthusiasm he settled on Vandenberg as the least of the evils. Swallowing all his scruples about a man he considered a vain and vacuous windbag, he described the Michigan Republican to his readers as the one man "on whom the active candidates could most readily come together." Capable or not, Vandenberg was feasible. And in any case, the country was unlikely to be saddled with him for more than four years.

All that spring Lippmann whispered encouragement and advice in Vandenberg's ear. But the Republican pros had other ideas. They preferred Thomas E. Dewey, the "crime-busting" governor of New York. Lippmann was able to live with the choice, though, as he wrote Lewis Douglas before the convention, he would have preferred Dewey as vice-president on the grounds that Vandenberg was a "little better seasoned." In any case, he added, Vandenberg's health was bad, and Dewey would probably succeed him at the end of the first term, and perhaps before that. The country had been "wanting to have a conservative administration since 1944," and would have "something like a nervous breakdown if it is frustrated much longer."[9]

The possibility that Truman might win never crossed his mind — nor that of most Democrats. The practical question, Lippmann wrote of the Republicans in June, was "not whether they win but how they win." Truman, he charged in a typical comment, "does not know how to be President . . . does not know how to conduct foreign relations or how to be Commander-in-Chief." He was a "weak President and at heart a jingo."[10] Once again Lippmann worked behind the scenes for his candidate. Together with McGeorge Bundy, then serving as a Dewey aide, he drafted a foreign-policy speech for the governor and offered advice. Bundy was at that time on close terms with Lippmann and working with him to update *The Good Society*. Although the project never came off, it helped set the stage for a very different collaboration between the two men a dozen years later during the Kennedy and Johnson administrations.

While Lippmann, along with almost everyone else, thought Dewey an easy victor, he was troubled by the fact that if the Democrats won control of the Senate, Vandenberg would lose his place as head of the Foreign Relations Committee. This would bring about a "nasty mess" in the conduct of diplomacy and pose "endless complications" in Senate confirmation of State Department officials, he wrote his friend David

Wainhouse. One way around this, he had suggested in his column a few days earlier, would be for a few Democratic internationalists like J. W. Fulbright to sit on the sidelines during the vote to organize the Senate so that the Republicans could gain the committee chairmanships "in the public interest." But the suggestion had barely appeared in print when he realized, as he confessed to Wainhouse, that this was "not the way to get things done in this age."[11]

As the campaign entered its final days an overconfident Dewey lost his early lead. To inject some life into his faltering campaign he reverted to some easy demagoguery by accusing the Democrats of "selling out" at Yalta and of harboring nameless "traitors" in the State Department. Lippmann, angered by these devious charges, knew where to assign the blame. It was, he wrote John Foster Dulles, Dewey's foreign-policy adviser, a "perversion of the historical truth" to hold Roosevelt and the Democrats solely responsible for what had been negotiated at Tehran and Yalta. Churchill's responsibility was at least as great, he pointed out, and on the Polish issue the prime minister "was prepared sooner and earlier to concede the Russian demand for a revision of the frontiers than was Roosevelt." Dewey, he advised, should run against Truman, not against the ghost of FDR. If the governor wanted to rake up the past, the Democrats could reply that the relative military weakness of the United States, and its dependence on the Red Army, stemmed from an unpreparedness during the early war years for which the Republicans were largely responsible. "Putting the matter on the lowest ground," he counseled, "there is no important body of votes to be gotten, I think, by the attempt to prove that Dewey would have been a better war President than Roosevelt. It is much easier for him to prove that he will be a better peace President than Truman, and if he sticks to that issue, I am confident he will win without involving himself in controversies that must disturb and may alienate many who are determined to support him."[12]

The Republican strategy backfired. Truman, who had set up a pernicious federal "loyalty" program to deflect Republican accusations, took the offensive. Refusing to let the GOP monopolize the anticommunist issue, he seized it himself. Henry Wallace, who was running for President on a left-wing Progressive party ticket, provided the perfect foil. By denouncing Wallace, Truman could demonstrate his anticommunist credentials. This was not hard, particularly after the Czech coup, which shattered any chance Wallace had of cutting heavily into Truman's constituency. He siphoned off a million votes, mostly in New York, but probably did Truman more good than harm by providing him with an anticommunist plank. Truman made the most of it. Fighting off not only the Wallaceites on the left, but the Dixiecrat, anti–civil rights party on the right, he attacked the "do-nothing" Republican-controlled

Eightieth Congress, outlined a "Fair Deal" social welfare program, and scored the most stunning upset in American political history.

An astonished Lippmann, like most commentators and pollsters, had failed to do his homework. Preoccupied by foreign policy, he neglected to notice that the public's real concerns were jobs, farm price supports, health and housing, and, in the case of blacks, civil rights. Recovering from the shock, Lippmann explained that the election was not so much a vote for Truman as "another Roosevelt mandate." Disappointed at what the electorate had wrought, he and Helen left the next day on a long-scheduled trip to Europe.[13]

Truman stayed on, savoring his victory and the embarrassment of his critics. Few journalists nettled the President so much as Lippmann. The two men rarely met, since Truman never invited Lippmann to the White House, and their correspondence was limited to a few formal notes. Some months after the election, however, Truman — who was notorious for his barnyard language and his inability to suffer his critics (or even critics of his daughter's vocal talents) silently — dashed off an angry three-page letter to Lippmann. Walking into a staff meeting early in June 1949, he handed the letter to Charles Ross, his press secretary, with what Ross described as a "twinkle in his eye." Ross read aloud to the staff Truman's complaint that Lippmann, in a recent column about the administration's foreign policy, was all wrong — just as wrong as he had been when he had predicted Dewey's victory and then had to slink off to Europe. He should have stayed there, Truman said, adding that while he understood the columnist worked in an ivory tower, a latrine would be a better place for him. Ross continued for a few more sentences in the same vein, as the assembled staff members chortled appreciatively. When he finished, Truman, apparently still twinkling, took back the letter and revealed he wasn't really planning to send it. Then he tore it up.[14]

Truman flattered himself if he thought his *bête noire* left town because of the election outcome. The Lippmanns always planned their trips months in advance, down to the last interview and luncheon engagement. This one was part of a now-ritualistic pattern: first to Madrid for an interview with Franco, sightseeing with local nobility, and a midnight dinner in their honor given by the foreign minister; then to Rome for an audience with the pope and meetings with the usual government officials; and then by train to Florence for what Berenson described as a "too, too flying visit" to I Tatti. "Just about thirty years ago that we first met," the octogenarian connoisseur recorded in the diaries he kept so scrupulously until his death a decade later,

both bitter over the way things were preparing to go over the peace treaty with Germany. Since then he has been here a number of times, and more than once we fell out, once over Mussolini, another time over Chamberlain, against both of whom he thought I was too violent. Now I could quarrel with him over his taking far too favorable a view of the near future of Poland, and being far too disposed to agree with France over the settlement of Central Europe. I am no longer as combative as I used to be; besides I feel too strong a current of affection between him and me to waste time, the few hours together, over discussions that can only end in assertions.[15]

Continuing on to Geneva the Lippmanns stopped off to see Gunnar Myrdal. The Swedish economist, then attached to the United Nations, told them that the Americans had themselves to blame for what had happened in Eastern Europe, since Truman's refusal to offer economic assistance had strengthened the communists' hand in Prague and Budapest, and set the stage for the coups and purges that followed. The last straw for the Russians was the West's decision to push for an independent West German state.

When he got to Paris on November 17 Lippmann heard a litany of complaints from French officials, culminating in a diatribe by De Gaulle at his office on the rue Solférino. The general, waiting patiently for the political crisis that would one day bring him back to power, was suspicious of everyone: of the Russians, who wanted a centralized Germany with which they could form an alliance; of the Americans, for being indifferent to France's sensitivities over Germany; of the British, for having "robbed" France of its rightful control over the Ruhr. Lippmann, ever enthralled by the general, if not always in agreement, wrote in his notes that he found De Gaulle somewhat aged and "not inclined to indulge in heroics, mellow, sad, and oppressed with the general weakness of the French position."

The French were particularly upset by Britain's determination to restore the Ruhr to German control. They saw it as an effort to woo the Germans at France's expense, and to ensure West Germany's participation in the projected Atlantic security pact. A minipact, known as the Brussels Treaty, had been formed in March 1948 by Britain, France, Belgium, the Netherlands and Luxembourg. Washington and London now wanted to expand it by bringing in the United States and eventually West Germany, and give it a new title: the North Atlantic Treaty Organization. Senator Vandenberg, primed by Acheson with drafts of flattery that would have made ordinary men reel in embarrassment, had greased the way by gaining advance Senate approval for American participation. The Vandenberg Resolution, as he modestly called it, had put NATO on the drawing boards.

Lippmann wanted it removed. On his return to Washington shortly before Christmas 1948 he ripped into the proposed treaty and those "zealous cold warriors" who thought that every country not occupied by the Red Army should be "drafted" into a Western coalition. If the Soviets had any serious thoughts of marching west, they would be held in check, not by a motley collection of "weak and dubious allies," he told his readers, but by the threat of American atomic retaliation. "The thing has got considerably confused and distorted by the military people who want to establish bases all over the place," he wrote Sumner Welles. They were disrupting Scandinavian regional unity, flirting with fascist Spain, even talking of a guarantee to Greece, Turkey and Iran. "But the most serious complication is the fact, which will of course be denied vehemently, that eventually the North Atlantic Pact is to include western Germany rearmed." Here was the crux of the issue, and one that the administration, for obvious reasons, wanted to sidestep.

Unlike the State Department and Pentagon planners, Lippmann saw no need for a military alliance with Western Europe. "I am convinced that the question of war or peace hangs upon the Soviet willingness to engage in a general war, and not on the strength of the local defenses in any particular part of the world," he wrote Russell Leffingwell. "For that reason I have never believed in the policy of containment as preached by the State Department and as practiced here and there, but not everywhere. Above all, I do not believe in the possibility of creating an army in western Europe capable of fighting the Red Army on equal terms, and I feel sure that the attempt to create it will not only exhaust western Europe and strain us, but probably would throw western Europe into political convulsions."

Lippmann's caveats made little impact on the administration. When the NATO pact was signed in Washington on April 4, 1949, it included not only the United States, Canada, and the Brussels pact countries, but also Denmark, Iceland, Italy, Norway and Portugal. Lippmann's idea of a "little NATO" confined to the Atlantic area became a lost cause in 1952 when Greece and Turkey were allowed to join. "An alliance is like a chain," he wrote in arguing against NATO's expansion. "It is not made stronger by adding weak links to it. A great power like the United States gains no advantage and it loses prestige by offering, indeed peddling, its alliances to all and sundry. An alliance should be hard diplomatic currency, valuable and hard to get, and not inflationary paper from the mimeograph machine in the State Department."[16]

Even as the NATO pact was being signed, some of the reasons for its existence began dissolving. Western Europe was recovering nicely, the French and Italian communists had suffered grave reversals at the polls, the Russians were lifting the Berlin blockade after having failed to win any concessions from the West, and Moscow was calling for a German peace treaty based on neutralization and withdrawal of foreign armies.

The Russian offer changed the whole equation, Lippmann thought, by offering a chance for a negotiated settlement. But the State Department, which was intent on bringing West Germany into an Atlantic coalition, even at the cost of a divided Europe, would have to be prodded. In an effort to get the administration to think seriously about the Russian offer, Lippmann put together a six-page single-spaced memo on the German problem for John Foster Dulles to take to the Paris foreign ministers' meeting in May 1949. In the memo Lippmann urged the demilitarization and neutralization of Germany, along with a withdrawal of all foreign troops. This plan, he argued, would keep German nationalists in check and remove the need for NATO.[17]

The administration was not interested. It dismissed the Soviet proposal as merely a device to block the formation of NATO. This was indeed true. But the more important question was whether NATO was in fact necessary — particularly since it prevented the Soviet withdrawal from central Europe that was presumably a major objective of American diplomacy. When the treaty came up for debate in the Senate it ran into flak on both the Left and the Right. Some critics charged that it would provoke the Russians and drag the United States against its will into a European war, others that it would stimulate an arms race and give the President authoritarian powers untenable in a democracy. Senator Robert Taft, unofficial voice of the Republicans, led the attack, warning that the bill gave the President vast powers to send American troops to Europe without congressional approval. The administration insisted it had no such intention, nor should NATO be considered the precursor of a big arms bill.

Lippmann, although he often disagreed with the Ohio Republican, telephoned to congratulate him, and the next day devoted his column to Taft's criticisms. The senator, he wrote, was right in charging that the administration had secreted an arms bill in the treaty; his objections to the pact were not those of an "irreconcilable isolationist or of an eccentric," but those of a "responsible American legislator." Privately Lippmann told Vandenberg, who was steering the treaty through the Senate, that the only answer to Taft's objections was to insert a proviso in the treaty that the United States had no obligation to furnish arms to its allies. But the administration, even though it insisted no arms aid was implied, vetoed the idea. In late July the NATO treaty sailed through the Senate by an 82 to 13 vote.[18]

On the very day that Truman signed it he presented Congress with a bill for 1.5 billion dollars for military aid for the nation's new partners. To top it off he sought discretionary powers so sweeping that an astonished Vandenberg described the arms bill as "almost unbelievable in its grant of unlimited power to the Chief Executive," one that would make him the "number one war lord of the earth." Lippmann encouraged the senator to fight the bill in committee. "I find it a shocking example of utter disregard for our constitutional traditions and for the very processes of law," he wrote Vandenberg of the "war lord" provisions of the arms bill, adding that Truman's power-grab called for a "stern lecture from you on the need for a return to recognized standards of conduct in dealing with Congress and with the people."

As Vandenberg was giving his stern lecture, Lippmann told his readers that the discretionary powers embedded in the arms bill were nothing less than a "general license to intervene and to commit the United States all over the globe, as, when, and how the President and his appointees decide secretly that they deem it desirable to intervene."[19] The bill, even shorn of its discretionary authority, ran into opposition from cost-cutting congressmen. But the Kremlin came to the administration's rescue. On September 23, 1949, Lippmann's sixtieth birthday, Truman announced that the Soviets had detonated their first atomic device. In fear and trembling at the loss of America's nuclear monopoly, Congress whooped through the arms bill. A few months later, in January 1950, Truman ordered development of the vastly more powerful hydrogen bomb, and the Pentagon polished up secret plans to build a German army as part of a European force.

Unlike the administration, Lippmann was more interested in getting the Russians out of central Europe than in creating a German army to contain them while they were there. He favored a neutralized, unified Germany because he feared that a rump German state would flirt with Moscow for recapture of the lost territories. He was convinced, as he told General Motors executive Charles Gary during the Senate's NATO debate, that the Germans had "always planned to exploit the conflict between East and West in order to recover their position in Europe," and would "never align themselves honestly and reliably with one side or the other." The Germans should be neutralized and threatened with "immediate punishment" if they tried to form an alliance with the Soviets.[20]

But the administration did not want a unified Germany — if the price for such unification were neutrality. Instead, it would settle for the biggest and richest part of Germany and link it to an American-directed Atlantic "community." Each side would have "its" Germany and "its" Europe.

◂ 36 ▸

Room at the Top

This country is going to go either to a frightful crisis at home, or a catastrophe abroad, or both unless somewhere in the system of high command there are changes of men.

— To Daisy Harriman, January 8, 1951

WHILE the Senate was debating the NATO arms bill in the summer of 1949, Lippmann retired to the Maine woods, where he wrote his column — keeping in touch with Washington by telephone — and drew up an outline for a three-volume book on foreign policy covering everything from Bunker Hill to the Marshall Plan. He felt he ought to do a major book on diplomacy, but as he confronted the prospect head-on, decided to postpone it a bit. He never got beyond the outline. During his sojourn in Maine he got word that his mother had died during an emergency operation. Although he had had little love for Daisy, neither had he ever broken with her. They had lunched together occasionally when he was in New York, dutiful, self-conscious affairs that gave neither of them pleasure, and maintained the semblance of familial affection. He helped settle her considerable estate, of which he got a large share.

At the end of September Walter and Helen returned to Washington, driving their Studebaker sedan and sending the poodles and the luggage with a driver in another car. On their first night home, as always, they gave a small dinner so that friends could fill them in on events during their absence — John Miller of *The Times* of London, Marquis Childs, Joseph Harsch, James Reston were among the regulars usually tapped. Then they began preparing for another European excursion.

These annual, sometimes semiannual, pilgrimages had all the casualness and spontaneity of a summit conference. When their detailed schedule had been fixed, it took an act of God to change it. Once, in

1961, Nikita Khrushchev asked Lippmann if he could delay his scheduled visit to Russia for a few days because of an unexpected political crisis. Lippmann said that would be quite impossible. The Soviet leader rearranged his plans. Another time Lippmann and Helen were due to leave France just as rebellious army units were preparing to parachute into Paris and overthrow General de Gaulle. They could have stayed on a few days to see what would happen. But their schedule called for them to leave, and leave they did as soon as the airport reopened.

They carried a red notebook wherever they went, in which Helen listed people to see and places to dine and sleep in every major city. In addition to the usual cabinet ministers and journalists, the book also listed lesser-known people to be consulted if a special need arose: an expert on nuclear energy or the international oil cartel, someone with a line into the Foreign Office or the Finance Ministry.

Helen not only accompanied Lippmann on his trips abroad, but was his assistant, his interpreter, his private secretary, his guardian. She went along on his important interviews, translated where necessary, and took copious notes, which she transcribed as soon as they returned to their hotel. She arranged for the dinner parties, alerting friends like Bernard and Hope Carter of the Morgan Bank in Paris, or Fleur Cowles in London, so that they could invite friends and prominent persons for the Lippmanns to see. These parties were usually small and confined mostly to well-informed people who could fill Walter in on what was happening in each country.

Lippmann saw two kinds of people: those in power at the time, and thus essential to touch base with, and a more permanent group, whose membership changed as a result of death or promotion, of people in or on the fringe of public affairs. They could be journalists, like Janet Flanner, Paris correspondent of the *New Yorker, Le Monde*'s Hubert Beuve-Mery, and Geoffrey Crowther of the *Economist,* or political figures currently out of power, such as Pierre Mendès-France or Anthony Eden.

The fall 1949 trip started out in the usual pattern: meetings in Paris with Jean Monnet, René Pleven, General de Gaulle, and the American ambassador, David Bruce; a quick trip to Germany to see Chancellor Konrad Adenauer and American proconsul John J. McCloy; a weekend in the Swiss Alps and some sightseeing in northern Italy; another flying visit to Berenson; and the customary round of politicians and journalists in Rome. At this point Helen and Walter would normally have returned home after a sojourn in London. But this trip was different; for the first time they were going east of Suez.

From Athens, where Lippmann saw the king, the prime minister, the military strong man (the "usual people," as he noted in his engagement book), they pushed on to Istanbul and Ankara; Damascus, Beirut and the ruins of Palmyra; a leap over Iran and Afghanistan to Karachi; and finally to Delhi for a four-week tour of India. Theirs was not a typical tourist's trip, although they visited most of the obligatory sites, for they were treated as visiting dignitaries, feted with lunches, dinners, tours and an unending procession of Indian officials. Diligently they inspected unnumbered temples, witnessed curious rituals, and talked high politics with the Western-educated elite.

Eternal India, the country outside the drawing rooms and government offices, left Lippmann — as it did most travelers — quite baffled. "The Hindu world is more alien than any I have ever been in," he wrote Berenson. By comparison Islam was "familiar and intelligible." The real Hindu was "more remote from all that we know than any other semi-civilized person." All in all, he recounted, "Calcutta is the most repellent human spectacle I have ever seen. At least a hundred thousand people live on the sidewalks, corpses in the railroad station here and there, extreme luxury and the rest, and in the working class district an intolerable filth and depravity. On a Sunday morning in one district I saw thousands of excited people worshipping Kali and sacrificing black goats." While he liked the Moghul tombs, palaces and paintings, he would "have to be born again to understand and like, however curious and interesting, the Hindu temples and Hindu sculpture." Berenson agreed, replying that after studying Indian art he emerged "with increasing loathing and terror, positive terror that such trains of thought and such feelings should exist."[1]

Lippmann had never been much interested in Asia, except as a geopolitical abstraction, and his trip reinforced his conviction, as he told his readers, that the Asiatic world was "outside the reach of the military power, the economic control, and the ideological influence of the Western world." His two long talks with Prime Minister Jawaharlal Nehru had persuaded him that the Indians could not be enlisted as allies in the cold war with the Soviets. "We have very little power in Asia and we must not think of ourselves as lords of creation who can fix the terms of the bargain on which relations are to be continued," he wrote Russell Leffingwell. Lippmann was sure that Western concepts like democracy and Marxism had a different meaning for Asians. "We must not imagine that the 'police state' as such, or 'free institutions' as such, mean there what they mean in the West," he wrote Berenson from the *Queen Elizabeth* on his return home in late December. "I realized in Turkey what every day I spent in Syria, Pakistan, and India confirmed — that a totalitarian system is normal in Asia, that Western ideas are far more revolutionary than communism, and that it is only against Russian or Chinese imperialism that Asia is likely to resist."[2] Lippmann's calm approach to Asia's convulsions and his belief that nationalism was a more potent ideology than communism or capitalism were not widely shared in the administration.

Helen and Walter returned to Washington on December 27, just in time to organize their New Year's Eve party. Invitations to this ritualistic event — which brought together a carefully chosen collection of ambassadors, senators, government officials, art connoisseurs, and journalists — signaled one's place among the people who mattered. Among the regulars, in a list that changed somewhat from year to year, were Senator Fulbright, *Washington Post* publisher Philip Graham, lawyer Oscar Cox, French ambassador Henri Bonnet, curator John Walker, and art collector Duncan Phillips. The guests customarily gathered at nine in the Lippmanns' elegant sunken living room, had drinks and supper, and at midnight, according to an inflexible rule, joined hands in a circle, sang "Auld Lang Syne," and kissed their neighbor. Not everyone was happy with his place in the circle. Philip Graham complained to his wife, Katharine, that at midnight he always seemed to be holding hands with a bowlegged Indian diplomat.

With the holidays out of the way, Lippmann resumed his habitual rounds, and on January 12, 1950, went with his friend Joseph C. Harsch of NBC News to a National Press Club luncheon to hear Dean Acheson deliver what everyone had been told would be an important address. They were not disappointed. Lippmann, of course, had known Acheson for years, and despite their differences over the Truman Doctrine, the two men had remained on good terms. Patrician, arrogant, unabashedly Anglophile and elitist, Acheson had succeeded General Marshall as secretary of state in January 1949. Lippmann welcomed the appointment, and on the night it was announced happened to run into Acheson at Union Station on his way to New York. He offered his congratulations, and Acheson urged him to come by the State Department for a chat. Lippmann phoned a few times to make an appointment, but Acheson was always busy. Finally he stopped phoning.

Acheson, like Truman, measured his friends by their loyalty. Lippmann, being a journalist, did not think that loyalty was part of his relationship with public officials. He was bound to criticize Acheson, and their first clash came, surprisingly enough, over the China issue. Acheson had hoped to get rid of the China incubus by cutting off American aid to the discredited and corrupt regime of Chiang Kai-shek and accepting the reality of Mao Tse-tung's victory. But right-wing Republicans, backed by the China Lobby — a pro-Chiang pressure group operating on political payoffs — were trying to saddle the Democrats with responsibility for the "loss" of China to the communists. To clear the record, and to gain public support for its effort to block Chiang's siphon into the U.S. Treasury, the State Department in August 1949 released a thousand-page White Paper on American policy toward China. This voluminous document asserted that the administration could not be held to blame for Chiang's defeat, that the "ominous result of the civil war in China was beyond the control" of the American government.

The China Lobby and its key congressional supporters — Walter Judd, William Knowland, Joseph Martin and Kenneth Wherry — predictably cried "whitewash," while most liberals rallied to the administration. But at least one of Chiang's critics thought that Acheson's explanation was not good enough. Lippmann, in three successive columns, tore the White Paper to shreds. If Chiang was as inept and corrupt as the administration said, then why, he asked, had the United States poured three billion dollars into a lost cause? To try to justify American policy on the grounds that the civil war in China was beyond American control, was, he charged, "tantamount to saying that there was no such thing as a sound or an unsound, a right or a wrong, a wise or an unwise policy toward the Chinese civil war." Even though the outcome of the war was beyond American control, America's own actions were not inevitable or outside its control. Why had the United States bet its whole position in China on a government it regarded as "hopelessly incompetent," one that had made "anti-communism and anti-Americanism synonymous in China with its own incompetence, corruption and reaction?" The administration did not have to answer for the "loss" of China, but rather for its own persistence in a policy that it now admitted had been doomed to failure from the start. Lippmann demanded a full-scale inquiry.[3]

His biting words were not inspired by any sympathy for the Kuomintang. He was perfectly willing to let Mao overrun Formosa, to which Chiang fled in December 1949 with his army and China's gold bullion. But he recognized the dangerous ambiguity in Acheson's self-defense. Instead of treating Mao as an independent nationalist, Acheson continued to stress Peking's links with Moscow and imply that China was simply a Soviet satellite. This approach was motivated partly by a desire to appease the administration's right-wing critics, and partly by the anticommunist zeal of such officials as Dean Rusk, assistant secretary of state for the Far East, who dismissed Mao's China as merely a "colonial Russian government, a Slavic Manchukuo on a large scale."

By the end of 1949, however, the administration — despite vicious attacks from the China Lobby and demands that Chiang be granted more weapons and money — seemed to be moving toward an accommodation to Mao's victory. On January 5, 1950, Truman announced he would not "pursue a course which will lead to involvement in the civil conflict in China." And a week later Acheson went before the National Press Club — in the meeting that Lippmann attended — to put sharp limits on the containment doctrine in Asia. He declared that American aid should be extended only where it could be effective and where the government had the support of the people — a clear slap at Chiang. He also announced a new strategic defense line in Asia extending through Japan and the Philippines — a line that seemed to exclude both Formosa and Korea. Acheson told the Chinese communists that Moscow, not Washington, was the greatest threat to China's security, and that the United States would not try to prevent them from assuming China's seat in the United Nations.

Lippmann left the Press Club luncheon heartened, and in his column hailed the speech as one of "great moment throughout Asia." Acheson had spoken with "sagacity and deep penetration." At last the administration seemed ready to break with Chiang. Yet despite the boldness of Acheson's speech, there was no follow-up. The administration, under pressure from the China Lobby, was caught in a bind of its own making. It wanted to avoid further entanglement in Chiang's hopeless fortunes, yet was afraid to antagonize its right-wing critics by abandoning him. It wanted to take advantage of the potential rivalry between China and Russia, but feared that any overture to Mao would undermine the credibility of its anticommunist diplomacy in Europe. Treading water and declaring it was intent on "halting the spread of communism in Asia," it continued to aid Chiang and embroiled itself even further in Asia by sending money to France to suppress the communist-led independence movement in Indochina. Within a month after Acheson's hopeful speech Lippmann was so discouraged that he wrote Admiral Forrest Sherman that the administration had become "hopelessly committed to . . . discredited or puppet regimes."[4]

Pulled toward a new China policy by the logic of events, the administration remained paralyzed by domestic opposition from the Right. Republicans, angered by the accommodating approach to Peking, demanded that Acheson resign. These demands gained new fervor in January 1950 when former State Department official Alger Hiss, accused of spying for the Russians, was convicted of perjury, and scientist Klaus Fuchs arrested for espionage, along with two American accomplices. Acheson infuriated rightists when, after the verdict, he bravely declared: "I do not intend to turn my back on Alger Hiss." On February 9 Senator Joseph McCarthy launched an infamous career by charging that the State Department was riddled with communists. Senator Taft, pleased with the public response to McCarthy's allegations, denounced the supposedly "pro-communist group in the State Department who surrendered to every demand at Yalta and Potsdam and promoted at every opportunity the communist cause in China." Senator Wherry, a zealot of the China Lobby, went a step further by declaring that Acheson himself was a "bad security risk" who "must go."[5]

These attacks were undermining Acheson's authority and turning his congressional appearances into Roman circuses. At the beginning Lippmann had defended Acheson, describing him in February 1950, after his first year in office, as one "extraordinarily well-equipped by experience and bent of mind to be a minister of foreign affairs." But by mid-March he was no longer so sure. Acheson, in an effort to mollify his critics, had tried to demonstrate that he was even more anticommunist than they. The result was to paralyze his own ambivalent efforts to extract the United States from China's civil war. "Although he has now talked himself into a position which makes Winston Churchill an appeaser and a misguided idealist by comparison, the secretary of state is treated on Capitol Hill with less courtesy and with smaller regard for the rules of evidence than if he were a convicted horse thief," Lippmann wrote. There could be no effective foreign policy when the nation's chief diplomatist "feels he must distrust the instinct of the people instead of clarifying, guiding and rationalizing it."[6]

Even if Lippmann did not always respect the "will of the people," he heeded it. The "acid test" of a foreign policy, he had written a half-dozen years earlier, was whether it united the American people. Acheson's very definitely did not. His failure to win public support for his policies had encouraged the Republicans to blame the administration for every postwar setback from the disappointments of Yalta to the "loss" of China. The nation wondered what had happened to the bright promise of the American Century. Since few questioned the omnipotence of American power or the beneficence of American purpose, the only persuasive explanation seemed to be betrayal from within.

The problem had begun even before Acheson became secretary. In the summer of 1948, while the nation was still suffering the shock waves of the Czech coup, former communist agents Elizabeth Bentley and Whittaker Chambers told a congressional committee that spies had infiltrated the State Department a decade earlier. To Lippmann's astonishment, one of his former secretaries turned out to have been a friend of Bentley and to have filched a number of letters, none of which harbored any secrets, from his files.

The belief that the cold war reversals could be explained only by traitors and spies provided fertile ground for the Asia-firsters — confusingly labeled "isolationists." Right-wing attacks on the State Department made it clear that the "postwar isolationist movement" was under way, Lippmann wrote Alan Kirk, U.S. ambassador to Moscow, that spring. While Senator McCarthy was preaching a "military crusade against Russia," it was clear that "the men behind McCarthy are Taft, Wherry and Bridges in the Senate and their counterparts in the House." The administration was to blame for most of its own woes, Lippmann complained. It had been going to Congress and the country for three years, telling them that the Truman Doctrine was containing communist expansion. "Then the public realized that communism had not been contained in China and that it would not be contained easily in southeast Asia." The public's discontent stemmed from "this defeat which the administration has not been able to explain as a defeat or to transcend by offering a clear policy as to what is to happen after the defeat," he told Kirk. "It has been the failure in Asia which has made possible the whole McCarthy business."[7]

Although the administration was a prisoner of the China Lobby, it had the means, Lippmann learned, to discredit its tormentors. Much of the group's money came from the narcotics trade and from American aid that had been sent to Chiang and then secretly funneled back into the United States to finance the lobby's public-relations campaigns and political payoffs. In April 1950 Marquis Childs invited a number of Washington's leading journalists, including Lippmann, Edward R. Murrow, Charles Collingwood, Joseph C. Harsch and Elmer Davis, to his home to discuss how this information could be used to discredit the lobby. One nonjournalist was also invited: Dean Acheson. They disclosed details of the lobby's secret operations and told Acheson that the facts were in the Treasury's files. The administration had only to bring them into the open to be rid of its most unscrupulous enemy. Acheson listened, but would not commit himself, and ultimately never used the information. Perhaps he thought it would not work. Lippmann had another reason. "Too many people involved in the scandal were rather important Democrats," he said privately.

The evening reinforced Lippmann's suspicion that Acheson, for all his intelligence and courage, had outlived his effectiveness as secretary of state. He suffered not only from "personal vulnerability," as Lippmann had written a few weeks earlier, but from the administration's diplomatic defeats. Acheson's failure had, he charged, given the McCarthyites ammunition.[8] Unsurprisingly, Lippmann's relations with Acheson quickly deteriorated. Acheson could not hear the columnist's name without fuming, and in June Lippmann walked out of a Harvard alumni meeting in Cambridge just as Acheson was about to deliver a speech. The two men disagreed, not only on how to handle the China Lobby, but on almost everything else: the vast rearmament program being orchestrated in the still-secret document known as NSC-68, the expansion and militarization of NATO, and the German question.

One thing on which they seemed to agree was that American troops would not be sent to fight in Asia, as Acheson had indicated in his January 1950 "defense perimeter" speech. But as it turned out, the secretary had not really meant it. The test of his intentions came suddenly, on June 25, 1950, when North Korea's army surged across the thirty-eighth parallel into South Korea. The administration was caught unawares, but within hours Truman — acting on the assumption that the

Soviets had instigated the attack through their puppet regime — sent military aid to the South Koreans. He also did what the China Lobby had long demanded by ordering the Seventh Fleet to the Strait of Formosa to prevent Mao's army from invading Chiang's island stronghold.

At the same time Acheson, moving with equal dispatch on the diplomatic front, called the United Nations Security Council into session and, in the absence of the Soviet delegation, pushed through a resolution branding North Korea the aggressor. The way was now open for the United States to intervene. A United Nations army would be created — composed almost entirely of U.S. and South Korean forces, with token participation by a few other nations. Two days after the invasion, on June 27, Truman instructed General Douglas MacArthur — American proconsul in Japan and commander of U.S. forces in the Pacific — to send American air and naval units into action. On the thirtieth, with the South Korean army in full retreat and the U.S.-supported government of Syngman Rhee on the verge of collapse, Truman took the final step by dispatching American ground troops.

If the administration had been caught off guard, so had Lippmann. On the evening of the invasion he and Helen, in Maine for the summer, were at a cocktail party at Sumner Welles's. When one of the guests excitedly asked Lippmann what he thought about Korea, he waxed philosophical, citing the anomalies of that divided country and deploring the excesses of Rhee's dictatorship. "But what about the invasion?" the questioner persisted. Lippmann looked blank. As one who depended on newspapers, he rarely listened to radio or television. A bit embarrassed, he phoned his Washington assistant, Barbara Donald, and told her to monitor the news regularly for him.

The next morning he sat down to write his column. Obviously it would have to be about Korea. He was as perplexed as everyone else. Who was behind it? What did it mean? How should the United States respond? He got on the phone, called a battery of colleagues and officials in Washington, and tried to shape a picture of what had happened. Cautiously he approved Truman's initial decision to send supplies to the South Koreans and seek UN approval. As the communist armies pushed south, he grew more alarmed. Two days later he described the attack as a "naked act of aggression," and warned of international anarchy "if a wretched little satellite government in northern Korea can thumb its nose at the United Nations." Reversing his earlier position, he approved the dispatch of the Seventh Fleet to the Formosa Strait.

But he was reluctant to go further, and proposed as a "cardinal rule" that so long as the Soviets did not commit their own forces to these "borderland struggles," the United States should avoid engaging American power in theaters "not of our own choosing and where no decision can ever be had."[9] He was too late. On June 30 Truman, realizing that the South Koreans could not hold back the attack, ordered American troops into action. This momentous decision, which Truman himself later said was the "most important in my time as President," completely changed the nature of the war. For the first time American soldiers were locked in combat to prevent the extension of communism — and on a terrain never before deemed vital to America's national interest.

The public seemed to approve Truman's decision, and even Senator Taft said he would support the action. Truman was taking no chances. He circumvented the Constitution by using his powers as commander in chief rather than by seeking a war declaration from Congress. A barrier had been breached, but few seemed to realize its seriousness. "I have been very deeply depressed by the Korean affair," Lippmann wrote Joseph Alsop in mid-July about the way the whole episode had been handled. The National Security Council had not coordinated policy with State and the Pentagon. The blame lay with Truman and Acheson for "not having clarified the question of our obligation in Korea," Lippmann charged. "They knew and accepted the theory that Korea had been written off, and therefore that we were not going to be prepared to fight there." Now, having written off Korea, they had decided to fight for it after all. The right hand seemed not to know what the left hand was doing. "I am rather gloomy about the quality of the men in charge of our destiny," he complained.[10]

These men viewed the invasion of South Korea as a direct challenge to the United States. They did not seem to consider, as George Kennan later suggested, that it might have been prompted by the American decision to sign a peace treaty with Japan — a treaty the Soviets had not been allowed to join, and one that turned Japan into an advance base of American power. Nor did they consider, as others have suggested, that the Soviet-backed invasion might have been designed to challenge China rather than the United States. For them it was a test of American fortitude. To have backed away might have been, as Acheson later said, "highly destructive of the power and prestige of the United States." They also saw it as a chance to disarm critics who had accused the administration of being "soft on communism."

Yet they had not thought through the full consequences of their action. The decision to commit a land army was, Lippmann wrote John Foster Dulles in July, a "far deeper and far more momentous and much more irrevocable commitment" than the initial decision to impose sanctions and use air and naval power. Merely to push back the invaders without risking a Chinese intervention would be difficult enough. "But we have no right to count on being allowed to conduct a counter-offensive up to the 38th parallel without the intervention of at least the

Chinese." The troop commitment would be paid for dearly, he predicted. "We have given hostages to fortune which we could have been much stronger without."[11]

Dulles, interestingly, agreed. Then serving as a State Department adviser and as chief negotiator of the Japanese peace treaty, he had been in Tokyo and Seoul just a week before the invasion, and had told the South Korean parliament that if forced to defend their territorial integrity they would be "not alone." In a confidential letter to Lippmann, however, Dulles insisted that while he thought the United States should do "something" about the invasion of South Korea, he did not define what that should be, and personally "had doubts as to the wisdom of engaging our land forces on the continent of Asia as against an enemy that could be nourished from the vast resources of the USSR." Dulles underlined that he had told Pentagon officials on his return to Washington that if a land venture seemed dangerous, the State Department "could get along with something less than that." He also revealed to Lippmann that as he left Tokyo, shortly after word of the invasion came through, General MacArthur had told him that "anyone who engages the United States army on the mainland of Asia should have his reason examined."[12]

Once the administration made the decision to send in American troops, its political goals escalated. Initially its objective was to repel the invasion. By August it was to destroy the North Korean army, and by September to unify the country. On September 15 MacArthur landed his forces behind enemy lines at Inchon, and in a brilliant tactical maneuver turned the tide. Two weeks later his triumphant forces approached the thirty-eighth parallel. The original mandate had been achieved. But now the administration sensed a chance to humble the Soviets, whom it believed responsible for the invasion, and to silence its Republican critics. Restoration of the *status quo ante* was no longer enough. Truman and Acheson went back to the UN and — by short-circuiting the Security Council and marshaling a majority in the veto-free General Assembly — won sanction to seek a "unified, independent and democratic government of Korea." Containment had given way to "liberation." By the time Lippmann left for Europe in early October, the North Koreans were in full retreat and American troops were approaching the Chinese border at the Yalu River.

The administration was euphoric, but the Chinese were growing anxious. Even before Truman gave MacArthur the green light to cross the thirty-eighth parallel, Chinese Foreign Minister Chou En-lai had told the Indian ambassador — with a request to pass it on — that Peking would have to protect itself if American troops followed the South Korean army across the parallel. Acheson, in a triumphant mood, dismissed the warning as the "mere vaporings of a panicky Panikar." MacArthur, who needed no encouragement, was told to push on. By the end of November his troops approached the Yalu and he announced he would "bring the boys home for Christmas." Two days later, on November 27, the Chinese, who had for weeks been sending token forces across the border as a signal of their seriousness, moved across the Yalu in mass, trapping and destroying great numbers of American and UN forces. It was now, said an astonished MacArthur, "an entirely new war."

The day after the Chinese intervened, Lippmann returned to New York on the *Liberté*. He had not written a word about Korea since early October. Now it seemed there was virtually nothing else to write about. The administration, like MacArthur's army, was in full retreat. A badly shaken Acheson assured the Chinese they had nothing to fear from the United States. In response Chinese forces continued to push back the American and UN armies to the thirty-eighth parallel, inflicting heavy casualties along the way. MacArthur sought, and was denied, permission to bomb Chinese bases in Manchuria. The administration did not want an even wider war on its hands. Once again pressed by critics on the Right, Truman hinted at a press conference in late November that he might use atomic bombs to stop the Chinese. The suggestion brought Prime Minister Clement Attlee on a flying visit to Washington for an explanation and a disclaimer.

Through his contacts at the *New York Times* Lippmann learned that Acheson had told Attlee that the United States had no intention of fighting China on the Asian mainland, and that the secretary thought it "better to be driven out of Korea altogether than to get ourselves involved in negotiations with the Chinese communists, whom we couldn't expect to be reasonable or dependable." Acheson told the prime minister that Peking was "obviously entirely under the control of Moscow," and that if the United States recognized them, brought them into the UN and got out of Formosa, they would demand a voice in the future of Japan and of Indochina. The Japanese would then likely switch sides. Thus, according to the *Times*'s confidential report, Acheson suggested that the United States fight in Korea as long as possible, then get out and "make the government of China by the communists as difficult as possible," perhaps by an air and naval blockade.[13]

A week later, on December 12, 1950, Lippmann received a memo from James Reston to the *Times*'s editorial board revealing that the Indian ambassador had just passed on to Acheson a peace proposal from Peking offering a cease-fire in exchange for negotiations on Formosa. Reston, serving as the intermediary, presented the proposal to Acheson on December 11. The secretary's answer, he noted, was more interesting than the message itself. Acheson "astonished me," Reston reported, by saying the peace offer was merely a maneuver instigated by the Russians to prevent completion of the NATO military command and prevent the rearmament of Germany. Brushing aside the peace offer, Acheson maintained that Germany was the heart of the struggle, not Korea. Moscow was trying to divert the United States from its European plans by its "bold measures" in Asia. Even though the British and the Indians were "dancing on the fringes of appeasement," the administration would not be diverted from its objectives in Europe. The only danger, Acheson warned, was that his domestic critics might "sabotage" his policy.[14]

Lippmann had no qualms about trying to sabotage that policy because he considered much of it mistaken, and even disastrous. Laying down the gauntlet, he called for Acheson's resignation. The administration's actions, he charged, had led to "disaster abroad and to disunity at home." Acheson could not repair his fundamental mistake: "his refusal to debate the great issues, and if his real views could not command general support in Congress, his failure to resign."[15]

While Acheson was used to attacks from Neanderthals and Mc-Carthyites, a demand for resignation from one of his peers took on the air of a betrayal. Lippmann and Acheson inhabited the same social world, met at the same Georgetown dinner parties, belonged to the same clubs. Years earlier Lippmann had nominated Acheson for the Century. Each in his way incarnated the values and authority of the eastern liberal Establishment. Such an attack was a bold, and even brave, move on Lippmann's part in a town where personal loyalty often took precedence over public responsibility, let alone the demands of conscience.

Acheson's friends rallied to his defense, accusing Lippmann of having gone too far. Lippmann felt obliged to explain why he felt "very strongly indeed" that Acheson should have resigned long ago. "No man ought to be secretary of state who does not have the confidence of the substantial majority of Congress," he wrote Daisy Harriman, a Washington hostess well connected to the upper echelons of the Democratic party, and at one time FDR's ambassador to Norway. Whether Congress lacked confidence in him for good reasons or bad was "quite irrelevant," for it was "impossible to conduct foreign affairs, and especially to conduct wars, without popular confidence in the men who conduct them." A situation such as the administration faced would have been "absolutely unthinkable" in any parliamentary government. The foreign minister would have either got a vote of confidence or resigned. Simply staying in office with the majority against him was "not admirable" and made the effective conduct of government "virtually impossible." This was particularly true "in a situation like the present, where the head of the government is at once incompetent and irremovable," he underlined. Nor was the prognosis hopeful. "In my view this country is going to go either to a frightful crisis at home, or a catastrophe abroad, or both," he predicted, "unless somewhere in the system of high command there arc changes of men."

The problem with hitting Acheson was that the criticism would seem to lend aid to the McCarthyites. "Throughout this whole wretched business all my personal inclinations were and still are in his favor," Lippmann told Learned Hand. "In my job I have found myself faced with this: that it was very difficult and probably impossible to criticize his administration of the State Department without giving aid and comfort to his low-down enemies." Yet how could a man "who does not have the substantial confidence of the country" hope to perform effectively as secretary of state?[16]

Lippmann's quarrel with Acheson went far beyond the problem of bad relations with Congress and the press. The decision to send American troops above the thirty-eighth parallel and to unify Korea by force had plunged the United States into a disastrous war with China. Had the administration not been so desperate to placate its right-wing critics, it might never have made such a foolish gamble. Now it had become even more a prisoner of its critics, as MacArthur and his right-wing supporters in Congress pressed for authority to bomb China. Truman and Acheson wavered, not wanting to expand the war, yet dreading the accusations of "appeasement" from the far Right. Finally MacArthur grew so reckless in his challenge to presidential authority that in April 1951 Truman fired him for insubordination — thereby unleashing a furor that for a time shook the presidency itself. Truman and Acheson, Lippmann charged, "intending to make a limited action in support of a general principle, lost control of the situation and were sucked into a big war that they did not know how to manage and do not know how to conclude."[17]

While MacArthur had clearly overstepped his authority, it was Acheson, Lippmann reminded his readers, who was responsible for advising the President as to China's intentions, who urged that MacArthur be allowed to cross the thirty-eighth parallel and drive to the Yalu, who pushed through a UN resolution to unify Korea, who ridiculed the warnings of the Indians. Now that the scheme had backfired, he and Truman wanted to shunt off all the blame onto MacArthur. But the administration had brought its troubles on itself. Lacking confidence, it was "almost prostrate with its inferiority complex in the presence of generals, aware of its mediocrity and inexperience and its political vulnerability." Above all, it was saddled with a secretary of state who had lost all credibility and popular support. "Some day, when he retires," Lippmann wrote acidly, "I hope that Mr. Acheson will write a book explaining how he persuaded himself to believe that a government could be conducted without the support of the people."[18]

Although Lippmann thought the administration had had to make some response to the North Korean invasion, he had drawn the line at the use of troops. If this meant a communist takeover of Korea, so be it. That was preferable to distracting the United States from the far more important confrontation in Europe. "I was in favor from the very first minutes of sea and air intervention against the North Korean aggression," he later wrote Senator Millard Tydings, ". . . but I have always been unhappy about the unannounced decision, which followed a few days later, to fight a land war in Korea. Yet I do not doubt that had we refused to commit an army, but had merely used sea and air power, the North Koreans would have conquered the whole of Korea." The crucial question was the defense of Japan, and that would not have been imperiled even had the communists won. Acheson seemed to admit this when he later defended his action, not as a response to a threat against Japan, but on the nebulous ground of prestige, "the shadow cast by power." Even had it been right to put in an American army, Lippmann continued, it was a "supreme tragedy" to have crossed the thirty-eighth parallel and tried to occupy Korea to the Yalu — thereby bringing China into the war and causing seventy-five thousand American casualties. "The decision in September 1950 to press the United Nations to authorize the crossing of the thirty-eighth parallel was one of the greatest mistakes in our history," he said.[19]

A mistake, no doubt. But if the attempt to unify Korea stemmed from the premature smell of victory, the original decision to intervene rested on other grounds. It was based, not on a concern for Japan's security, but on what the administration saw as a threat to its plans for Europe. Those plans included the creation of a West German state, which had already been brought into being over Russian protests, and its incorporation into an American-run alliance. Although the administration initially denied it, by the late summer of 1950 Washington was moving to build a German army and bring it into NATO. A police force, yes, a German army, no, an agitated Lippmann wrote Dorothy Thompson that September. American policy should be devoted to "unification, elections and neutralization." The Germans had to be given a "sense of historical mission . . . some place in the world which befits their dignity and which is not necessarily to be interpreted by the Russians as Germany becoming the spearhead of the West." That place, he thought, lay as the centerpiece of a larger Europe.

While it may have been an attractive idea to him, the prospect of a reunified Germany as a great power "around which the smaller neutral states . . . and eventually the east Europeans could attach themselves" did not appeal to the Russians. It became even less appealing when Acheson in mid-September 1950 finally confirmed what many had long suspected by calling for a ten-division German army. During the October-November swing that had taken him to London, Stockholm, Oslo,

Copenhagen, Germany, Switzerland and Paris, Lippmann had tested European reactions to the plan. From his talks with German leaders, including Chancellor Konrad Adenauer, Socialist leader Kurt Schumacher, Berlin Mayor Ernst Reuter, and Adenauer's chief military adviser, he came away convinced, as he wrote in his private notes, that "nothing could be plainer or clearer than that the German army is thinking of a war of revenge and not of the defense of Europe at the Elbe river."[20]

The articles he wrote on his return were only slightly more diplomatic. The idea that the Germans would dedicate themselves to the defense of the West was an "illusion" entertained only in Washington and London, he charged. His great fear was that a rearmed Germany would lock the Red Army in central Europe and eventually trigger a war between America and Russia. "I have a fierce conviction that unless that [Soviet] withdrawal takes place within a comparatively few years, war is certain and unavoidable," he wrote James Bryant Conant, then president of Harvard and later U.S. high commissioner to Germany. As an alternative he urged that Russia and the West thin out their forces over a five-year period, during which an all-German government would be formed.[21] The administration was not interested.

The die was cast in Europe: Germany would be rearmed and brought into NATO. There would be no mutual withdrawal. Neither side trusted the other enough. Each preferred a divided Germany, and a divided Europe, to a united Germany that might join the other camp. Meanwhile the war in Korea had settled into a long and inconclusive stalemate along the thirty-eighth parallel. The *status quo ante* had been restored with one difference: the United States, by patrolling the Formosa Strait on Chiang's behalf, had become a participant in China's civil war.

It was a good time for Lippmann to take his long-planned and long-postponed leave of absence. Since the summer of 1938 he had been fiddling with a book on how men could govern themselves by humane principles in an era of totalitarian politics and rapid technological change. Envisaging it as his great work on political philosophy, he tentatively entitled it "The Image of Man." Fearing he might never finish the work unless he could devote full attention to it over a sustained period, he decided to take a six-month leave of absence from the column.

Before taking his sabbatical he wrote a three-part series, again urging a territorial settlement with the Soviets. The men in the Kremlin, he argued, had from the first days of the revolution been guided not by Marxist rhetoric but by military realities. The Soviets might have dashed Western hopes at Yalta and Potsdam for democratic governments in the areas they controlled, but they had always stuck to their word on territorial issues.

The real problem was the presence of the Red Army in central

Europe, he insisted. If that army were removed, "there would be no more Russian problem today than there had been for a century." Thus the important thing was to negotiate a military withdrawal. "When I speak of a settlement with the Soviet Union I do not mean a marriage," he underlined. "I mean a divorce. I mean the fixing of boundaries between their world and ours — the frontiers to be defined by armaments . . . an agreement to reduce the propaganda of war from, let us say, volcanic hatred to icy dislike."[22]

There was nothing novel in this prescription. But the call for a settlement, like his warnings against German rearmament, was out of key with administration policy. The announcement that he was taking an extended leave of absence, with no date mentioned for his return, prompted speculation as to whether his departure was fully voluntary. Le Monde wondered if Lippmann had been "entirely master of his own decision," and suggested that "even if the pressure of the 'war party' has not governed Walter Lippmann's decision, it is evident that the freedom of his analysis, especially during the past six years, the quiet harshness of his criticisms of adventuristic policies — in short his nature as a free man — were bound to attract hostility." Lippmann was so embarrassed by the suggestion that he had been forcefully shut off that he asked editor Beuve-Mery to print an apology.[23]

The contretemps was soon forgotten, but it revealed how much Lippmann, in the eyes of many Europeans, was viewed as the leading critic of America's cold war militancy. The fact that he spoke the language of realpolitik — military strength, spheres of influence, an Atlantic alliance — made it difficult to dismiss his attacks on a diplomacy that had seemingly lost all sight of rational objectives in an obsessive search for an ever-elusive feeling of "security."

Overtaken by Events

He was a realist and adjusted to the realities of the situation, whatever it happened to be.

— James M. Cain on Lippmann

THE second week of June 1951 Walter and Helen closed up the house on Woodley Road, packed his notes, a pile of books, and the poodles, and drove off to Maine. After more than twenty years of writing his column he was, he told his readers, going to "come up on deck for a breath of fresh air and look at the horizon." He would leave unanswered the question of whether, "the times being so critical, it is right to turn away even for a few months from the news of the day to be certain of the perennial issues of the human condition." [1] Deciding that the news could wait, he and Helen stayed in Maine all summer, and in September left their unheated camp and rented a house in the Berkshires through the fall. He did not pick up his column again until December 17.

As his sabbatical approached its end, Lippmann had made considerable progress on his book, although he would not finish it for another three years, but was dispirited at the thought of resuming the column. Although he had done well financially at the *Tribune* — averaging between sixty and seventy thousand dollars a year in flat fee and syndication profits — he wanted more time to think and to do longer projects. He had reached the age, he wrote the paper's business manager, when it seemed "foolish to accept the continued strain of being a regular columnist." He wanted to set aside the three-day-a-week column and be a "special writer," to "get away from the feeling of being a kind of one-man editorial page which is expected to comment on whatever happens to be the biggest news . . . to feel that I did not have to say something with unending regularity . . . to stop feeling that I must write, say about Iran if the prime minister has a fit, when I may be working on some articles about American education. To do that we must do away with 'Today and Tomorrow' as Conan Doyle did with Sherlock Holmes.''[2] Conan Doyle had somewhat better luck. Lippmann went back to the column in mid-December 1951 with the intention of writing only a few months longer on a regular basis. He continued for another sixteen years, although in 1955 he managed to cut back to twice a week.

By the time he resumed the column in December 1951 there was a good deal to sink his teeth into — particularly the flesh of an administration that was treading water and waiting for the merciful expiration of its term. Paralyzed by McCarthyism, Truman could not end the Korean War by negotiation on any terms the Republicans would accept. Acheson was under daily assault in Congress and the press, his policies stymied, his integrity impugned, even his patriotism questioned. The nation, resentful over the unpopular war in Korea and seeking an outlet for its frustration in a search for "communists" in high places, seemed in the grip of hysteria.

The country was ready for a change. So was Lippmann. He had been taking potshots at Truman ever since 1946, and by 1952 had become so disgruntled that he blamed Truman's reelection for everything that had gone wrong since — from McCarthyism to the rearmament of Germany and the Korean War.[3] As the 1952 elections approached — with a stalemate along the thirty-eighth parallel in Korea and the European allies blocking Washington's plans to bring a rearmed Germany into a projected European army — Lippmann would have embraced almost any Republican internationalist. This left out Senator Robert Taft, champion of the party's Old Guard, but very much included the nation's favorite war hero, General Dwight Eisenhower.

Then in Europe as NATO commander, after a brief stint as president of Columbia University, Eisenhower was everyone's candidate for President, even though no one could be sure what he stood for. He had spent his entire adult life in uniform and had never professed allegiance to any party. No matter. The very fact that he was outside the political arena added to his appeal. The country was ready for a soft-spoken, straightforward, good-natured hero, and Ike filled the bill. If for any reason the Republicans would not have him, the Democrats were eager to hand him their battered crown.

Lippmann had first met Eisenhower early in the war when Lord Halifax invited him to the British embassy to meet "a young army officer whom you will hear a lot about." After the war Eisenhower, then Pentagon chief of staff, used to ask Lippmann to his office every month or two to talk about public issues. Ike clearly had his sights on the White House. "I wasn't impressed with any of the things he had to say," Lippmann later recalled, after he had grown sour on Eisenhower, "and his political simplicity was simply astounding." Once Ike had told

Lippmann that all politics was corrupt, and that if he ever went into public life he would remain above partisanship. "You don't suppose a man could ever be nominated by both parties, do you?" Ike asked.

Four years earlier, when the Republicans had first tried to draft Ike for the 1948 nomination, Lippmann was hardly an enthusiast. "I should look upon Eisenhower's acceptance of this draft and his possible election as a very dangerous thing," he had written Lewis Douglas in 1948. Eisenhower was simply "not personally qualified" to be President. "The public legend about him is justified on his human qualities, but it takes no account of his intellectual equipment and his real experience. I have never seen anything like it," Lippmann mused. "He is not a real figure in our public life, but a kind of dream boy embodying all the unsatisfied wishes of all the people who are discontented with things as they are."[4]

But passing time — and particularly four more years of Truman — had given Ike a rosier glow. By 1952 Lippmann was ready for even an untested "dream boy." Enlisting Eisenhower to head a presidential ticket "can lead to almost certain victory by healing and uniting the nation," Lippmann told his readers in January 1952. Unlike Taft's and the isolationists', Ike's mission in politics was to "reunite the American people, to heal their divisions, to assuage the bitterness of regions, of interests, of classes and of sects." A man so respected by both parties, Lippmann explained, "offers us — for the first time in our generation — the prospect of a united nation."[5]

Lippmann was mostly worried about beating Taft, favorite of the Republican isolationists. To block the Ohioan Lippmann worked behind the scenes with Ike's promoters, particularly Senator Leverett Saltonstall. Ike should stay at NATO headquarters in Europe until nominated, Lippmann told the Massachusetts Republican, since an orthodox campaign for the nomination would work against him. "He hasn't got the political know-how to do it very well, in my view," he counseled. "All his inexperience will, I think, be exposed to the country, and the American people, we must not forget, can turn quickly against their heroes." Instead, Lippmann favored a "very aloof campaign" on Ike's part, so that, as he told Herbert Bayard Swope, Ike would not get "entangled in the little issues that are quite hot and full of politics."[6]

Lippmann went off to Europe for six weeks at the end of April, where he saw Eisenhower in Paris and gave a series of lectures at Oxford and Cambridge, later published as a small book entitled *Isolation and Alliances*. By the time he got back at the end of May, Eisenhower, Lippmann's caveats notwithstanding, had given up his post at NATO and had plunged into the fight with Taft for convention delegates. Greatly pleased by Ike's strong showing in the primaries, Lippmann was not at all troubled by his refusal to take a stand on issues. "The people, who in the end alone can elect him, will understand perfectly well why he has not had time to study all these questions," he explained to his readers. In fact, he thought it an advantage to have a man "not snarled up with all the issues that are dividing and embittering our people . . . he can come to the old controversies freshly and freely himself." Lippmann found it "deeply reassuring" that the general had left himself "entirely uncommitted for the great issues of war and peace which lie ahead of us." Normally a refusal to debate the issues was not a quality he admired. Apparently this was different.

While Ike was preparing his assault on the convention, Adlai Stevenson, governor of Illinois, was being pushed and cajoled into accepting the Democratic nomination. Stevenson claimed he did not want it — or at least not yet, not if he had to face the unassailable Eisenhower. But the party bosses told him it was now or never. In late March Stevenson, accompanied by George Ball, his former law partner, dropped by Woodley Road for dinner, advice, and, they hoped, Lippmann's blessing. "I don't want to run for President now," he told Lippmann. "I'd rather be governor of Illinois. There's no man around who can beat Eisenhower, and what's more, I don't see any good reason why anyone should want to."[7] Lippmann agreed that the governor had a point — which was not exactly what Stevenson wanted to hear.

Not until July did Stevenson make it official by becoming a candidate. Blushing and protesting feebly he accepted the Democratic nomination. A few weeks earlier Eisenhower, with a ruthlessness that belied his baby-face countenance, had outmaneuvered Taft in a battle over disputed delegates and seized the nomination. Lippmann was delighted by both conventions, and celebrated the nominations of Stevenson and Eisenhower as a "triumphant vindication of the American system." He liked Stevenson, and in the abstract thought him the better man. But Eisenhower, he was convinced, was what the country needed at the moment. Only a military hero like Ike could negotiate an end to the Korean War without being accused of "treason," he wrote. Only a Republican President could tame the blood-crazed McCarthyite wing of the party. If the Republicans lost their bid for the White House for the sixth time in a row the party would fall into the hands of its "most irreconcilable and ruthless factions."[8]

Yet as the campaign wore on, as Ike stumbled over his syntax and skirted the issues, Lippmann grew distressed by what he admitted was the "disappointing quality and the embarrassing features" of the general's performance. He was particularly bothered by Ike's handling of the Nixon affair. The general's "crusade" had been somewhat tarnished when his running mate, Senator Richard Nixon — a McCarthyite who had won notoriety during the Alger Hiss case — was revealed to be the beneficiary of a businessman's slush fund. Ike wanted to drop Nixon from the ticket, but was persuaded to let him make his defense on television.

On the night of Nixon's performance, John Miller of *The Times* of London and his wife, Madeleine, were having dinner with the Lippmanns. They watched in silence as Nixon labored to exonerate himself with weepy references to his dog Checkers and his wife's "respectable Republican cloth coat." When it was over Lippmann, who was not given to hyperbole, turned to the others and said: "That must be the most demeaning experience my country has ever had to bear." In the column he wrote the next morning he described the speech as a "disturbing experience" that was, "with all the magnification of modern electronics, simply mob law." [9]

But Ike stuck with Nixon, and Lippmann stuck with Ike. As election day approached he seemed to be endorsing a principle rather than a candidate. Although he had suggested that Stevenson "may not only be speaking in the accents of greatness, but that he may perhaps embody some of the qualities of a great American leader," he feared that if the Republicans lost they would become "wholly and irreconcilably Old Guard" and paralyze his program. Despite the "disappointment" of Ike's campaign and the "immense attractiveness" of Stevenson's promise as a leader, he believed that the "shocks and strains of the struggle will be less destructive, will probably be surmounted more successfully and sooner, if the Republicans are at the center of the struggle and have to bear the primary responsibilities." Helen, strong-minded and contrary as always, was not persuaded. She voted for Stevenson and contributed to his campaign. [10]

Ike won by a landslide margin of six million votes and 442 of the 531 seats in the electoral college. Offering Stevenson what must have been cold comfort, Lippmann told him he had "won everything that a good man could want except only the election," and to think of his losing campaign as the "big beginning." This was the wrong year for a man like Stevenson. Americans needed a consolidator, not a sophisticate. For Lippmann the finest man was not always the best man for the job. It had become imperative, as he later wrote, that the nation "collect itself, that it restore its confidence in itself, that it find a way to quiet its frayed nerves, to allay its suspicions, and that it regain its composure and its equanimity." [11]

Ike turned out to be a better tranquilizer than Lippmann would have liked. Barely four months after the inauguration he complained that Eisenhower was plagued by "weakness and indecision." Ike's view of his exalted office was "rather like that of a constitutional monarch who reigns but does not govern." To Berenson, Lippmann was even franker. "Last autumn I wrote that he did not understand the office of President and was imagining himself to be a constitutional monarch in the British, or perhaps more accurately in the Scandinavian style,'' he wrote the art historian. "But now I think he is a monarch — in the Merovingian style." [12]

The one thing Lippmann was sure Ike would do was muzzle McCarthy. He was wrong. The senator continued on his headline-hunting way, making the same fanciful charges against his fellow Republicans that he had made against the Democrats. Ike stood by silently, hoping McCarthy would somehow go away. He did not. The senator was particularly fond of attacking the State Department and had focused on some foreign service officers who had had the temerity to point out several years earlier that Chiang Kai-shek was probably doomed. The fact that they were right made them even more suspect. McCarthy was out for their scalps. Normally the secretary of state would have been expected to defend his staff — as Acheson had done. But Dulles was afraid of McCarthy, and — despite his many inspiring lectures on morality — thought silence the better part of valor. He let McCarthy pick off and destroy the careers of such distinguished diplomats as John Carter Vincent, John Service and John Paton Davies. Their only crime was that they had been right about Chiang.

Lippmann was never intimidated by McCarthy, and was a persistent critic of what he described as the senator's "cold, calculated, sustained and ruthless effort to make himself feared." In McCarthyism Lippmann saw the "seeds of totalitarianism," and scored the administration for refusing to confront an "ambitious and ruthless demagogue." McCarthy represented everything Lippmann detested and feared: the rabble-rouser who could touch primitive emotions and destroy those "mystic chords of memory, which make it possible for men to be free, and to differ, and yet to be one people." Families, communities, even nations, he wrote shortly after McCarthy first began capturing headlines, "rest finally not on law and not on force, but on a certain indispensable faith and confidence, mixed with some affection and much charity, each person for his fellow man. Without that a free society will disintegrate into a mere horde of frightened, angry, suspicious and suspected separate egos, and the last defenses will have fallen against the rise and the invasion of the barbarians and the tyrants they bring with them." McCarthy had destroyed that faith and confidence. When Senator Margaret Chase Smith in June 1950 drew up a "declaration of conscience" deploring McCarthy's methods, she went to Lippmann and got his blessing. It had little effect, however, on the Senate Republicans, for only six others were willing to sign her indictment. [13]

Though repelled by McCarthyism and sympathetic to the victims of the witch-hunt, Lippmann nonetheless wrote relatively little about the issue. This was due partly to his preoccupation with foreign affairs, partly to his insensitivity to some of the civil liberties abuses of the government's own "loyalty" program. That program, launched by Truman in 1947 to defuse Republican attacks, permitted discharge of government employees if "reasonable grounds" of their disloyalty could be shown. In 1951 Truman had broadened the program to permit dismissal if a government board found "reasonable doubt" of an employee's "loyalty." This, of course, put the burden on the employee, who was forced to prove his "loyalty," rather than on the government to demonstrate his "disloyalty." Eisenhower made dismissal even easier by establishing a category of vaguely defined "security risks" — an action that further opened the federal bureaucracy to witch-hunts. Lippmann, surprisingly, considered this action an improvement. No longer would it be necessary, he explained, to "destroy a man by branding him disloyal when, in fact, he may be an undesirable public employee because at worst he has kept bad company or is a foolish fellow."[14]

The Oppenheimer incident was a case in point. J. Robert Oppenheimer, former director of the Los Alamos laboratory that developed the atomic bomb, was accused of being a "security risk" and denied access to classified government information. A three-man government board exonerated the scientist of "disloyalty," but refused to restore his clearance on the vague grounds that his friends and behavior were questionable. Although sympathetic to Oppenheimer, Lippmann nonetheless agreed that the government had no obligation to maintain his security clearance. What offended him about the case was the "stupidity" of the administrative procedure, which had subjected the scientist to a quasi trial, and the fact that the government had made a security case from what should have been an administrative decision.

Oppenheimer, Lippmann told George Kennan, had not handled his own case well. He should not have put himself in the position "where he appears to be fighting to be retained as a high-level adviser . . . as if he hoped to compel the President to continue using him in a top job." While the security hearing was a "monstrous use of the machinery for detecting subversion," he told publisher Gardner Cowles, the real problem was how to get rid of advisers who were no longer useful. "I would not challenge the right of the administration not to employ any one of those three men," he told Cowles in referring to the parallel cases of Wolf Ladejinsky and John Paton Davies, "and if I were in their place, I think I would not employ as a high adviser in policy matters Oppenheimer." But since none of the three had been deemed disloyal, it was a "horrible proceeding to torture them in public in order to arrive at the conclusion that you don't wish to employ them any longer."[15] This seemed a reasonable position, but it ignored the fact — so critical to civil libertarians — that these men were being punished not for their actions but for their opinions. Lippmann was not particularly sensitive to this aspect of the problem.

The protracted national hysteria over "traitors" in the government did not occupy a great deal of Lippmann's attention. He did not write at all about the Dennis case, a landmark decision by Judge Learned Hand in 1950 affirming the conviction of eleven people for membership in the Communist party — a decision that was, in effect, overturned several years later by the Supreme Court when it ruled unconstitutional the "guilt by membership" provisions of the Smith Act. He wrote very little about the Alger Hiss case, except to say that it was a "pity" that Dean Acheson — who publicly defended Hiss's character — had to say anything about it.[16]

Nor, surprisingly, did he devote so much as a single column to the espionage trial of Julius and Ethel Rosenberg. Even many who believed that the Rosenbergs were guilty, as charged, of having passed atomic secrets to the Russians during World War II felt that the death sentence was excessive and vindictive. Not since Sacco and Vanzetti had a case aroused such political agitation. The trial judge, Irving Kaufman, was accused of imposing the death penalty, rather than a prison term as other atomic spies had received, because he, like the defendants, was a Jew, and wanted to demonstrate his "patriotism." All during the long months of appeals, culminating in Eisenhower's refusal to grant clemency and the ultimate execution of the Rosenbergs in June 1953, Lippmann retained his silence. Perhaps he was indifferent, perhaps preoccupied by other issues, perhaps reluctant to confront the Jewish aspect of the case. Whatever the reason, his silence was notable.

While penetrating in his critique of certain American policies — the Baruch Plan, containment, German rearmament, support for Chiang — he was always so within the self-imposed limitations of political "realism." That is, his framework for judging a policy was whether it worked, whether it was in the "national interest," whether it had public support. These were important criteria, but when put to the test they often seemed lacking. Was a policy worth trying even if it might not work? Who decides what the national interest is in any given situation? May not a policy be "right" even if the public does not initially support it?

Having only a guidepost of national interest, lacking a philosophical approach or ideological commitment, reluctant to accept the part that economic demands or imperial ambitions might play in explaining American foreign policy, Lippmann was unable to take a consistent approach to the issues he wrote about. He dealt with each situation on an *ad hoc* basis. This gave a seesaw quality to some of his arguments — as, for example, in the Dardanelles and Czech crises. Although he often criticized the administration, every administration, his criticism focused on tactics rather than goals. Indeed, he often seemed to share the goals. "The real problem of our foreign policy is not in its objectives," he could write in 1952. "On them there is fairly general agreement." Rather, the problem was the "control and administration of the policy." A critique so narrowly focused was not likely to threaten the prevalent assumptions.

To a surprising degree Lippmann went along with those assumptions. He believed that America's cold war policies were essentially defensive, that it had acquired its informal empire by "accident," and that the problem was primarily one of execution rather than conception. He criticized the policymakers, but rarely what lay behind their policies. Thus when he returned from India in late 1949 he could write that Asians need not choose sides in the cold war because they could remain sheltered by the world power balance and the "tacit protection of a friendly state which dominates the highways of the globe in order to protect the peace of the world."[17] Not for another fifteen years would he question whether that dominant state really had such "friendly" motives.

Lippmann participated in the world as an "insider," to use his own favorite word. Though he could be mercilessly harsh on those who did not pass muster, such as Truman and Acheson, he felt an insider's responsibility for making the system work. He was never alienated and was in no sense a radical. He operated entirely within the system. When, for example, he was appointed by a newsmen's committee to head the investigation of the murder of George Polk, an American journalist killed in Greece in 1948 during the civil war, he did not seriously question the State Department's contention that communist guerrillas were responsible — even though he privately recognized that discrepancies in the evidence pointed damningly toward the Greek government and the CIA.[18]

Lippmann would never have gone along with a State Department cover-up, but neither could he believe that the honorable men he knew would be capable of such an infamous action. When communists in 1952 accused the United States of secretly engaging in germ warfare in Korea, Lippmann insisted that such allegations could not be true because the "two highest responsible men in the United States government — who would have to give the orders to conduct germ warfare — have said on their word of honor that there is no truth of any kind in the charges. Both of these men happen to be old personal friends, and I believe them. If I had not believed them, I don't know just what I would have done. But I would not be writing this article."[19] Later, under the impact of Vietnam and Watergate, that trust was shaken.

Lippmann has been rightly hailed for his independence and dissent from prevailing orthodoxies during the early years of the cold war. While most of the country, including the foreign-policy establishment, was behaving as though the Red Army was about to gobble up all of Europe, along with half of Asia and Africa, and the Cominform was going to wend its insidious way into the minds and hearts of innocent American children, Lippmann preached restraint and a calculated assessment of the national interest. He warned against a containment policy that would spread American power thin, against using the atomic bomb as a political weapon, against dividing Europe by bringing western Germany into an anti-Soviet coalition, against fighting land wars in Asia, against being sanctimonious about spheres of influence, against supporting reactionary and colonial regimes in the name of anticommunism, against confusing the messianic ideology of communism with the essentially conservative foreign policy of the Soviet state. Judged by what others were writing and saying at the time, Lippmann was a model of restraint and mature analysis.

During this period he stressed the need for Americans to remember that the Soviets, too, had security interests; that within their lifetimes the Russians had suffered two German invasions and an American-aided intervention to end their revolution; that the United States also claimed a sphere of influence — one that embraced Western Europe, most of noncommunist Asia, and the entire Western Hemisphere; that the best way to deal with communism in Europe was to negotiate the withdrawal of the Red Army through a settlement of the German problem; that Western Europe was far more threatened by economic want and social unrest than by Soviet soldiers; that the containment doctrine could not preserve discredited client regimes from their own citizens; and that the greatest danger in Africa and Asia was not Soviet expansion, or even subversion, but a too-hasty collapse of the former colonial empires.

Yet if this was his general approach, it was also marked by contradictions. Although he argued that nationalism was far more powerful than ideology in the emerging nations, and that global containment of communism would lead to unending wars of intervention in support of weak client regimes, he nonetheless supported such American intervention where Western control was challenged by indigenous communists. Thus, he favored aid to the Greek monarchy, air and naval intervention in Korea (though not troops), and even support for the French in Indochina.

The communist attack on South Korea threw him off balance. Though he had insisted that the United States must not become involved in propping up reactionary Asian dictatorships, once the North Koreans invaded, he saw the issue in balance-of-power terms. That completely undercut his strictures about the danger of emphasizing ideology. In April 1950, just two months before the outbreak of the Korean War, he had warned that the United States should not finance France's war against the communist-led independence movement in Indochina. Yet by January 1952, with Washington footing most of France's military bills, he concluded that it would be a "catastrophe of enormous proportions . . . if Southeast Asia were to fall within the communist orbit." Now he decreed — without offering any compelling explanation — that the Indochina conflict had been "transformed from a French colonial war, which it was at the outset, into one of the several wars for the containment of communism." [20] He still urged a truce, but one that would keep Indochina out of what he now called the "communist orbit."

Thus, even though he continued to criticize the containment doctrine, and to repeat some of his earlier arguments about the danger of alliances with reactionaries and colonial puppets, he ended up by accepting the logic of containment in cases where balance of power was not clearly involved. His pleas for coming to terms with a revolutionary world fell by the wayside where communists seemed likely to take control. Given the choice between aiding a reactionary regime and letting it be "lost" to communism, he preferred to aid it. Whenever containment was put to the test as a policy choice rather than as an abstract doctrine, he went along with it. His only important qualification was that American troops not be sent to fight proxy wars, as in Korea. The battalions of what he once extravagantly called "Western Christendom" should not be committed until the Soviets sent in their own.

Even within Europe his argument was not consistent. Whereas until 1950 he stressed economic recovery and the neutralization of Germany, after Korea he began concentrating on Soviet military strength and the need to preserve the cohesion of the West. When Stalin in March 1952 stunned the West by offering to withdraw from eastern Germany and allow the Germans to reunite in neutrality if the allies would withdraw from western Germany, Lippmann went along with the administration's brusque rejection of the offer. Warning that an all-German election might bring about the downfall of the Adenauer government, he maintained that American and British forces could not be withdrawn from Europe "in the presence of a reunited, a rearmed, Germany bound by no European system of law or treaty, and under Russian patronage." [21] Thus, by 1952 he had accepted the logic of a divided Germany and a divided Europe in the absence of an all-European system that the Russians, and probably the Americans, would have found unacceptable.

During this period Lippmann often seemed to be less a seer than a man overtaken by events he could not fully grasp or put into place. His analysis was trenchant, his elucidation of the issues unfailingly sharp, but at times he seemed no less confused than the next man about what it all meant. His celebrated definition of a viable foreign policy as one that brought commitments and available power into balance was not of much help in deciding what those commitments should be. Nor was he aware until the mid-1960s of how important a role economic considerations and great-power temptations to hegemony played in American cold war diplomacy. The Vietnam War led him, like many other Americans, to question what he had so long taken for granted.

While he sharply challenged the globalists during the first five years of the cold war, after 1950 and until 1965 he essentially accepted the consensus, even while criticizing some of the ways it was implemented. Like the American policymakers to whom he spoke, he was concerned with global containment, even though he shunned the word, and tended to view the world in terms of a Soviet-American confrontation that he himself realized often distorted reality. The pragmatism that allowed him to approach each event with an open mind sometimes prevented him from perceiving a wider pattern. "He was a realist, and adjusted to the realities of the situation, whatever it happened to be," James M. Cain once said of him. "But the adjustments, always, were on marginal matters, not involving inner convictions." [22]

Those inner convictions — a belief in the dignity of man, in the essential contrariness of human nature, in the need to strive for the best despite the odds, in the promise of American democracy — were the mark of a humanist, a skeptic, and a man of enormous integrity. But Lippmann responded to events like a pragmatist; he did not form patterns like a philosopher. He was more like William James than he imagined, and less like Santayana than he preferred to believe. He could analyze situations with finesse and give off brilliant flashes of illumination. Yet when he tried to use these powers to mold a coherent philosophy, he stumbled — as became apparent when the book on political theory he had labored over for so many years was at last published.

◀ 38 ▶

A Private Philosophy

Let us once and for all face the limitations of democracy.
— "Political Notes," December 1911

No more than the kings before them should the people be hedged with divinity.
— *The Public Philosophy*, 1955

THE book Lippmann finished at Southwest Harbor in the late summer of 1954 had been started casually in Europe sixteen years earlier during his honeymoon with Helen. It began as a series of random thoughts scribbled on a hotel balcony overlooking the bay of Naples, under the cypresses at Berenson's villa, in a rented apartment on the Ile St. Louis. His notes reflected the pessimism of a time when the democracies seemed paralyzed by indecision and defeatism, and when totalitarian movements had captured the allegiance of what he called the "deracinated masses. . . . A civilization must have a *religion*, . . . Communism and Nazism are religions of proletarianized masses," he wrote in his notebook. "Laws which lead to monopoly and proletarianism destroy law and are a method of civilized suicide." Using the working title of "Man's Image of Man," he had, drawing a theme from the book, told a group of Catholic theologians in 1941 that the people were doomed to be unsatisfied because they had lost sight of a higher moral order, and had "accepted the secular image of man." [1]

For a time Lippmann was strongly drawn to Catholic theology, finding in its hierarchy and sense of order an antidote to a secularism that, in the guise of Nazism and communism, seemed impervious to moral restraints. Any serious thoughts he might have had about joining the Church, however, were squelched by Helen, who harbored and often expressed the anticlericalism of a lapsed Catholic. The appeal of Catholicism for Lippmann was not its ritual, its sacraments, and its promises of redemption, but rather the sense it conveyed of communion in a moral order above the whims of transient majorities and the dictates of tyrants.

Lippmann had laid aside the book in 1942 partly because of the pressures of the war, and partly because he had trouble formulating the argument. In *The Good Society* he had blamed the mass totalitarian movements on economic planning. Now, having freed himself from that misunderstanding of the problem, he believed that the "sickness of the Western liberal democracies" was imposed, not from without, "not from the machinations of our enemies and from the adversities of the human condition, but from within ourselves."[2]

After his six-month sabbatical in 1951 he continued to work on the book in Maine during the summers, and finally completed it on August 11, 1954, just six weeks short of his sixty-fifth birthday. He decided to call it *Essays in the Public Philosophy* — the use of the word *essays* giving evidence of a certain tentativeness. By the "public philosophy," he wrote Berenson a few days after finishing his labors, he meant the "natural law on which Western institutions were originally founded." Although a good part of the book dealt with the "sudden and steep decline of the Western society immediately upon the achievement of universal suffrage and the democratic control of war and peace," it was not all so gloomy. "You won't suspect me of having become some kind of authoritarian crank," he assured his friend.[3]

The disclaimer was well taken, for *The Public Philosophy* showed Lippmann in his most antimajoritarian mood. "Where mass opinion dominates the government, there is a morbid derangement of the true functions of power." The democracies had suffered paralysis and given way to authoritarianism because the people had imposed a veto "upon the judgments of the informed and responsible officials." As the people became sovereign, their governments lost authority and were unable to preserve the peace and uphold standards of "civility." The problem, in short, was that the people had "acquired power they are incapable of exercising, and the governments they elect have lost powers which they must recover if they are to govern."

His remedy was twofold: a return to a stronger executive, and a limitation on sovereignty along the lines of "natural law." A strong executive would break the stranglehold of special-interest groups upon legislatures; respect for natural law would restore the "civility" and individual liberties violated by the "Jacobin" heresy that man was bound by no higher restraints than his own ego. The "decline of the West" could be countered by adherence to that "doctrine of natural law which held that there was law 'above the ruler and the sovereign people . . . above the whole community of mortals.' "

Lippmann's argument was, as always, elegantly phrased, but even the finely wrought ardor of his prose could not conceal a disturbing vagueness. McGeorge Bundy, then a dean at Harvard, had seen the manuscript and had urged Lippmann's editor, Edward Weeks, that it not be published until Lippmann had weeded out the theological connotations of "natural law." Otherwise, Bundy warned, "it will be said that Lippmann has no logic for argument, that like Royce in the story told by Holmes, he has taken refuge in the bosom of God."[4] In early September 1954, when Weeks came to Southwest Harbor to go over the final draft, he found Lippmann tense and distraught. He had never labored so long on, or felt so anxious about, anything else he had written. Weeks told him about Bundy's comments, but Lippmann felt that he had done all he could. The book would have to stand or fall on its merits.

In mid-September he and Helen closed up the house at Southwest Harbor, sent the poodles and books off with a driver, and flew back to Washington just in time to prepare for his sixty-fifth birthday party on the twenty-third. A week later they set off for Rome on the first leg of a two-month excursion that kept them in Europe until the end of November. The first few weeks after their return were filled with send-off parties for Charles and Mary Bruggemann, who were retiring to Switzerland after his many years in Washington as ambassador, and the usual holiday activities. Then, on the day after their traditional New Year's Eve party, Walter received the first bound copy of *The Public Philosophy*.

He felt a mingled excitement and apprehension. His gloomy outlook on the "sickness" of liberal democracy, he feared, would not appeal to many readers, nor would his prescription of a "public philosophy" based on natural law. These apprehensions were soon confirmed. By the end of January, a few weeks before the official publication date, reactions started to come in, based on excerpts that had appeared in the *Atlantic*, and the bound copies that had gone out to reviewers. The responses were not what he had hoped.

A great deal was riding on this book — more than he had been willing to admit fully to himself. The lukewarm early reception by his friends, combined with his physical and emotional fatigue, overwhelmed him. On February 6, 1955, he called his old friend Carl Binger, who had moved his psychiatric practice from New York to Cambridge, and complained of insomnia and jitteriness. Two days later, on the verge of a nervous collapse, he flew to Boston with Helen. Binger took one look at him and put him into Massachusetts General Hospital. Helen — who had a revulsion to being around the sick or the dying — went off to visit Mima Porter in California. Walter stayed in the hospital for nearly three weeks, slowly recovering his strength. By the end of the month he felt well enough to leave. Helen flew back to pick him up on his release from the hospital, and together they returned to Washington. They stayed there only one night, to have dinner with journalist Joseph C. Harsch and his wife. The next morning they took a plane to California, where they spent the next five weeks in seclusion at Mima Porter's ranch in the Ojai Valley.

Harsch was among the few people who knew of Walter's collapse, and while he was in the hospital had tried to cheer him up with a long letter blaming his depression on postpartum blues. "You have distilled into that book so much of the substance of all of your mature thinking, it represents so completely all that you have fought and struggled through over many years, it so completely expresses your highest mental achievements, that you cannot now imagine ever writing another book of equal importance. This is your most perfect child and the culmination and the climax of your creative thinking. Who wouldn't have some nervous disorders at such a moment!" Harsch urged him not to consider the columns in any way less important than the books. "Your books represent only the process of perfection of the tools you need for the columns, and . . . you are now in the position of a man who is for the first time fully and finally prepared to do his best work."[5]

Bucked up by such support from his friends, and restored to his usual stoic equilibrium by a few weeks of rest, Lippmann faced the reviews of *The Public Philosophy* as they began appearing in late February. They were a mixed lot. Comments ranged from respectful to disappointed. The old argument about the "tyranny of the masses" and the call for a stronger executive struck some as a misunderstanding of the problem, others as an assault on democratic government itself. Lippmann's evocation of an undefined "higher law," with its theological connotations, actively irritated many.

The *New Republic*'s reviewer saw Lippmann's book as the work of a "badly frightened man" with a "bias against democracy"; the *Saturday Review* thought the work "eloquent but unconvincing." Archibald MacLeish was so distressed that he wrote a six-thousand-word essay accusing Lippmann of having led a "retreat from the idea of freedom." Even theologian Reinhold Niebuhr, usually prone to a dim view of democracy, found little to praise once he had tipped his hat to Lippmann's "profundity." Perhaps the hardest comment to take came from the *Nation*'s critic, who wrote that though it would "stir more thought than most books ten times its size," *The Public Philosophy* was "not the great book of distilled wisdom on the ultimate problems of political organization and human destiny for which we have been waiting."[6]

Not all the reviews were harsh. Erwin Canham found it a "magnificently lucid appeal for a return to the spiritually scientific principles" of the Founding Fathers. Berenson, who took an even dimmer view of parliaments than did Lippmann, wrote that there was "no remedy for the

situation where we are, and getting worse, unless we return to a graduated, pyramidal, i.e. hierarchical and even oligarchical society." To
please Lippmann he sent along a favorable review of the book from an
Italian newspaper, to which he added: "I recall William James occasionally pulling press cuttings about himself out of his pocket, and
shyly showing them to me, saying, 'Naturally I don't care a bit, but you
know my wife enjoys them.' " Even with mixed reviews the book had
an excellent sale of twenty-eight thousand copies in its original hard-
bound edition, briefly hit the best-seller list, and was widely translated
abroad.[7]

No words of praise, however, gave Lippmann so much pleasure as a
handwritten note from Paris in a scrawl almost as illegible as his own.
General de Gaulle, still in exile but only two years from his triumphant
return to power, had read *Le Crépuscule des démocraties,* as it was
gloomily called in French, and found it expressed exactly what he had
always thought himself. The book, he wrote Lippmann, was a treasure
house of "ideas, rare perceptions and wisdom." Elaborating on a favorite theme, the general complained that democracy had become confused
with parliamentarianism, with the "usurpation of popular sovereignty
by professional politicians" who had "neither the authority nor the confidence to deal with problems."[8] Lippmann's plea for a stronger executive liberated from the quibbling of paralyzed legislatures could hardly
have fallen on more receptive ears.

But the idea that parliaments had usurped their role and that the executive branch had become too weak to make unpopular decisions did not
sit well with Learned Hand. The jurist, then in his eighty-fourth year,
expressed his doubts that democratic government would function better
with a stronger executive, or that the "decline of the West" was due to
irresponsible popular majorities. The organized horrors of the twentieth
century — two world wars, Nazism, Stalinism, the death camps, Hiroshima — could hardly be blamed on public opinion. Natural law
seemed to him a poor refuge.

Hand's critique prompted Lippmann to a spirited reply. "Am I wrong
in thinking that the wars of this century are the first great wars waged by
governments elected by a general suffrage, and that there is a causal
connection between this and the ruinous and inconclusive character of
these wars?" Yet in attempting to explain what he meant by "natural
law" and its relation to the "public philosophy," he ended up being no
less vague than he had been in his book. "What I call the public philosophy are the assumptions which have to be accepted in order to live in
the historical, and conceivably unique and passing, political order to
which we belong." Few would quarrel with such a definition, but even
fewer would call it a philosophy.

With regard to his recent breakdown, Lippmann told Hand that it had been brought on from "trying to swim so long against the currents of public opinion with which my job is concerned. . . . Sometimes," he added, "I wish I had a profession, like law or medicine or chemistry, which has a recognizable subject matter and methods — perhaps that is what sent me off looking for a public philosophy."[9]

There was something disingenuous about Lippmann's reference to the currents of public opinion. Although he frequently had swum against them, and certainly was not afraid to challenge prevailing orthodoxies where he felt they were wrong or harmful, he had a remarkable facility for not straying too far from the main thrust of public opinion. When the dominant mood was progressivist, he was a Progressive; when it was for intervention, he was a Wilsonian idealist; when it was disillusioned, he was the skeptic of *Public Opinion* and *A Preface to Morals;* when it was for social change, he embraced FDR's experiments. Only in 1937, with the anti–New Deal diatribe of *The Good Society,* and during the early years of the cold war was he seriously out of step. Yet those aberrations did not last long. Even though he liked to think that he followed the tune of a different drummer, he was surprisingly in step most of the time.

Years later, when asked if he had even been tempted to choose a different profession, he said that he might have enjoyed being a mathematician — if he had had the talent. "I would have liked that kind of life. The precision, the elegance — there's something about it that attracts me aesthetically."[10] From an aesthetic point of view he might have enjoyed a career in which there was little human contrariness to contend with. That was the monkish side of his character. But emotionally he would have been uneasy. Mathematicians are rarely on a first-name basis with presidents, prime ministers and ambassadors; rarely are they met at airports by cabinet officials and their visits to foreign countries treated as events of state. Lippmann loved being a public figure, and when he mused about the joys of a professional life confined to the laboratory or the studio, he sounded about as convincing as a politician yearning to be relieved of the cares of office, or an actor pining for anonymity.

While the critical reception to *The Public Philosophy* disappointed him, he had long ago learned resiliency. The key to his emotional strength was that he did not look too deeply into himself, did not brood about rejection or failure. Lippmann was a complicated man, but not an enigmatic one. He was a skeptic who yearned for an overvaulting sense of order he feared did not exist — the weakness that marred *The Public Philosophy.* He was a realist who never quite suppressed his youthful romanticism and idealism — qualities that saved him from negativism and cynicism in his old age. He was a man who valued the good life, who did not compromise with what he believed, and was sure of his place in the world. Berenson, who shared certain traits with Lippmann — his discarded Judaism, his fascination with politics and access to the mighty — wrote a telling description in his diary during Lippmann's visit to I Tatti in the spring of 1953:

I study Lippmann's face and head. Rather German type, scarcely anything Jewish. When he listens his eyes take on a curious look as of a perfectly smooth deep lake. Features of hard wood. The face is of a laborer, and thinker and worrier. Dresses neatly and in good taste. Talks with a somewhat raucous voice. Scarcely any gestures. Smiles convincingly and genially. Can be good company, joking, but never *ausgelassen*. Gives clear answers to questions, and his estimates of people are decisive, never leaving you in doubt as to what he thinks of them. Vast acquaintance with dramatis personae of American politics, and sincerely tries to be fair in discussing them within the issues in which they are involved.[11]

Lippmann was at ease in his world, just as Berenson was in his own.

Five weeks of sun in southern California had restored Lippmann to health. In early 1955 he and Helen returned to Washington, where he resumed the column — which he now cut back to twice a week. Early in June they left for Maine. These summer retreats meant something very special to him. Maine was not merely a place to get away from the semitropical summer heat of Washington, but a refuge whose cool beauty and rocky austerity refreshed his spirit. Unlike many, Lippmann was not primarily drawn to Maine by the sea. Although he liked to look at the water, he did not enjoy being out in an open boat; even occasional picnics to the coastal islands were an ordeal. He would sit gripping the gunwales until his knuckles turned white, grimly awaiting the moment when the picnic party would land on solid ground.[12]

The Lippmanns' main house and the four cabins at Indian Head, two for guests, were set back from the beach looking west across Blue Hill Bay. In his private rough-planked cabin under the pines Walter did his morning writing, his solitude zealously protected by Helen. The routine was simple and unvaried: writing in the morning; tennis, golf or croquet in the afternoon — the Lippmanns were ferociously competitive — and a quiet evening with friends around the fireplace with occasional games of canasta or dominoes. When there were no guests Helen and Walter would take long hikes through Acadia National Park or on trails through the woods. "Walter," she once shouted at him as they were clambering over some slippery rocks, "look, don't think!"

Lippmann was easy, considerate, and tolerant with his friends. He would respond interestedly to anyone who knew what he was talking about. But he had trouble abiding ignorance or hypocrisy. Once on entering the Metropolitan Club he was hailed by Lewis Strauss,

Eisenhower's secretary of commerce, who said how much he admired his columns. Lippmann, who had publicly criticized Strauss, turned to him incredulously and said, "You couldn't possibly mean a word of what you're saying, and you know you don't mean it." Pomposity and pretentiousness would bring a faraway, glazed look to his eye and a retreat into silence. Those who knew him well saw a different Lippmann from the austere analyst known to the public. At his ease he could be quite witty, and even a bit malicious, in his sardonic way.

Once during an interview, when asked what he had been reading, he mentioned a philosophical book that had not yet been translated into English. He thought a moment and then said: "Give it an English title; it sounds too pretentious to say I was reading it in French." Another time, when a reader chided him for showing disrespect for historian Charles Beard by not referring to the academician as "Dr.," Lippmann replied that at Harvard, where he had gone to college, "it was considered vulgar to refer to anyone, from the president of the university down, as Doctor or Professor." All freshmen were warned at once to refer to the president as Mr. Eliot, and their professors similarly. "This may have been a Harvard affectation," he admitted, "but it used to be said that the title of doctor applied to anyone but a doctor of medicine was undignified, and that the use of such titles as doctor and professor had been spoiled by fencing teachers and chiropodists . . . I myself have thirteen degrees of doctor and I am uncomfortable when I am referred to as 'doctor' and I always avoid it." [13] A man, he thought, should command respect for his work, not his titles.

Helen always kept an eye on him in large gatherings, and whenever he seemed bored she would whisk the offending person away and bring on someone else more likely to please. Science, religion and art fascinated him as intellectual problems, but he was never comfortable with the abstract or the literary. He read some of the modern poets, like T. S. Eliot, more because he thought he should than from enthusiasm. He had little taste for music, and approvingly quoted Santayana's description of a concert as "a drowsy revery interrupted by nervous thrills." He showed no great interest in art or the work of the artists with whom he came into contact over the years. During his Village days he had known a great many, including Edward Steichen, Andrew Dasberg, Maurice Sterne (Mabel Dodge's second husband), and Marsden Hartley. In the 1930s, when the destitute Hartley sought his help, he put the artist in touch with his friend Samuel Lewisohn, the millionaire art collector and patron. But it never occurred to him to buy one of Hartley's paintings himself. For him "art" was something confined to afternoons at the Louvre, the Uffizi or the Metropolitan. Kenneth Clark, who entertained Lippmann frequently at his London home, recalled that he never once looked with particular interest at any of the remarkable pictures the Clarks owned.[14]

Although he could be immensely considerate to friends who were sick or in need, he was also, like Helen, a person accustomed to having what he wanted. He was helpless around the house, and took enormous pride in his single culinary accomplishment: the ability to make a pot of strong coffee. For most of his life he had never lived with fewer than two maids. Children, like most bad conversationalists, bored him, although he enjoyed the company of engaging young people. Susceptible to first impressions, he would form a strong judgment about someone based on a single conversation, and then later reverse himself. Also, being one who idealized people, he would turn coldly against them if they disillusioned him. Unlike Helen, he did not have a vile temper, but he was a man of powerful passions, and he kept them under control at great effort. He was also a person who cared greatly about winning and was not, some of his tennis partners believed, above a little cheating. Once when he was playing doubles with Robert Rand against John J. McCloy and Cass Canfield and the game was at match point with the McCloy-Canfield team ahead, Lippmann missed a shot that landed a foot within bounds. "Out," he called, without a moment's hesitation. His partner looked at him in amazement, then nodded his head and said, "Walter, I admire your spirit, but I don't think we can get by with that." "Oh, all right," Lippmann said with a shrug. "In."

While Maine was a welcome respite, he was always glad to get back into harness again: to writing the column, to lunches at the Metropolitan Club, to the round of cocktail parties and dinners where he could discuss high politics with public persons. By now his work habits had become etched in stone. Usually up by seven, he would peruse the morning papers — the *New York Times* and the *Herald Tribune,* the *Washington Post* — in his bedroom, and then join Helen for breakfast. By nine on the days he wrote his column, he was at his desk upstairs, scribbling away on a yellow note pad. Usually he was finished by eleven — never later than twelve — and would read the copy into a Dictaphone, punctuation marks and all. This was a system he began in the mid-1950s and stuck to because it gave him a sense of how the column sounded. While he was dressing for lunch — mostly he worked in a dressing gown or an old sweater and slacks — a secretary would type up the column in three copies. He would go over one of these copies, make a minor change or two, and then drive off to lunch with some distinguished personage while the column was being phoned or teletyped into the *Trib*'s New York office.

The talented and hardworking women who were his assistants — Frances van Schaik until 1948, Barbara Donald until 1959, and Elizabeth Farmer until his retirement in 1967 — were not secretaries (others did the typing and the chores), but people who assembled the information he needed to write his column. They went to briefings and press conferences, interviewed middle-level officials and congressmen, clipped scores of newspapers and magazines, examined new books and marked passages for Lippmann's attention, did research at the Library of Congress, and, when necessary, corrected his errors. He worked them hard, just as he worked hard himself. He insisted that every fact be documented, and always went directly to the source — for example, to the complete text of treaties and reports — rather than relying on newspaper accounts. These women served as his professional staff, just as Charlotte Wallace, who had worked for Helen when she directed the Nurse's Aide program during the war, ran the household, serving as both their social secretary and their interlocutor.

Lippmann's social life was no less regular than his work habits. After lunch he would return home for a nap and some afternoon reading, often a history book or a biography, and then take a brisk walk with Helen and the poodles. Sometimes they would go to a movie or a play in the afternoon; he was particularly fond of mysteries. At least four nights a week they went out to dinner or had guests in. Among his friends Lippmann could be charming, relaxed and an eager listener. Strangers were usually impressed by his lack of pretentiousness and his tendency to listen rather than to pontificate. Increasingly, as he grew older, he let others take the initiative and felt less of a need to dazzle. Sometimes he would be withdrawn. What those who did not know him might interpret as self-importance more often was a sign of his shyness and fear of rejection.

Helen not only protected him from disturbance during his working hours, served as his interpreter on trips, and organized his social life, but made sure he received his proper due. If chatting friends might interrupt his line of thought, she would interject, "Hush, Walter is talking." Once when they were playing tennis with Katharine and Philip Graham and some boys were shouting nearby, she stopped the game and went over to them: "Children, be quiet, Mr. Lippmann is serving." When Lippmann served, the world was supposed to sit still and watch. She also made sure that the spotlight never wandered. When they were dining in Paris with French Foreign Minister Robert Schuman and a waiter interrupted something Lippmann was saying, Helen interjected — lest someone change the subject — "Comme vous disiez, Walter . . ."

She was a dedicated Cerberus, and devoted to him. Yet she was also an extremely difficult woman, with an ugly temper that flared into sudden rages that left him hurt and shaken. Her rages would pass as quickly as they came on, but his hurt would remain. Sometimes he would sulk for days, long after she had forgotten what she had railed at him about. She was as baffled by his hypersensitivity as he was by her anger, but he was devoted to her, and he never lost the sense of wonder and gratitude that he had been able to remake his life by marrying her. They were rarely separated, and thus rarely wrote each other, although one letter remains from the fall of 1944 when he went on a wartime trip to England without her. "Dearest Creature," he wrote her on the eve of his departure by troopship from New York:

> The only good thing about being separated from you at any time is that I can write you a love letter again, and you know now that I can best say what I most mean in writing, and that in talk I become tongue-tied when I feel deeply. I love you with all my heart, completely and absolutely, and I did not even imagine until I knew you what perfect and sure love could be, and for me the reality of living with you is better than any dream.
>
> I know how preoccupied and self-centered I am so much of the time, and that I think you have understood — and if not, you must understand that this is the price we have paid for the war, and yet without you, the burden would have been unbearable, and I should have been infinitely worse than I am. Because of you we shall together yet — and soon I think — be able to live as we have hoped. I shall often think while I am traveling of all the things — accompanied by immeasurable poodles — that we want to do.
>
> I shall miss you and shall be counting the days till we are together again, darling Helen,
>
> Your,
Walter [15]

Whatever disappointment he may have felt over the reception to *The Public Philosophy* was mitigated by the emotional strength he had gained when he married Helen. Although he went off in search of natural law and transcendent values, he never again preached stoic detachment and "disinterestedness" as he had during his life with Faye. Helen, difficult and demanding though she was, had indeed — as he told her that spring night at the Rainbow Room in 1937 — opened the door to his cage.

◄ 39 ►

Waiting for an Innovator

In all men who lead multitudes of human beings there
is a bit of magic.
— To Arthur Vandenberg, Jr., November 1951

The country is waiting for another innovator.
— Article in *Life*, June 20, 1960

ONCE Ike ended the Korean War and finally stood up to McCarthy,
Lippmann felt he had pretty much exhausted his abilities. The
"mess in Washington," he wrote in June 1954, was "as great and in
some ways a more dangerous mess" than it had been under Truman.
The problem, he explained, using the argument that had dominated *The
Public Philosophy*, was that Eisenhower had not restored the executive
power that had become enfeebled under Truman. Despite his belligerent
style, Truman had caved in before his critics. The "catastrophic errors"
of his administration — leaving South Korea out of the American defense perimeter, authorizing MacArthur to march to the Yalu, giving
Chiang Kai-shek a veto over America's China policy, and rearming Germany before working out a peace treaty — were all due to its
weakness.[1]

Later Lippmann said privately that he had originally supported Eisenhower with "no particular illusion about his calibre or personal abilities or quality, but on the rather justifiably cynical or Machiavellian
ground that only the nomination of a war hero would deflect Mc-
Carthyism" and end the Korean War — although this, of course, is not
what he told his public. Neither Truman nor Stevenson could have accepted the compromise peace that Ike did without being accused of
treason by the Republicans, he pointed out. In retrospect, however, he
thought that Eisenhower's was "one of the most falsely inflated reputations in my experience. The adoration of the American people for Eisenhower I do not share. In the first place, I do not think he is a likable

man, because I think he is totally without generosity or loyalty to his friends. He showed that conspicuously in his treatment of General Marshall. He is, moreover, a man who has an embarrassing admiration for rich people, and has been willing to accept favors from the rich which no other man, not a sacrosanct war hero, would have dared as President to accept."[2]

While Ike puttered on the golf course with captains of industry, Dulles shuttled between airports rounding up "free world" allies and darkly threatening "massive retaliation" against foes and "agonizing reappraisals" of uncooperative friends. Dulles, a deeply religious man, was particularly eager to punish evildoers. In 1954 he urged Ike to drop a few atomic bombs on the Vietnamese forces that had surrounded the French military garrison at Dien Bien Phu, and to rattle the bomb at Peking for shelling two Chiang-held islands off the China coast. When Dulles patted himself on the back in *Life* for having "walked to the brink" of nuclear war in his tireless search for peace, Lippmann thought it a bit much. A foreign minister, he reminded Dulles, was "one who uses words precisely which mean genuinely what they say," while a diplomat who peddled propaganda was "like a doctor who sells patent medicine."[3]

Dulles never complained about the lecture, but neither did he change his ways. He "peddled propaganda," in Lippmann's phrase, largely because it was the only currency he had. Though he fervently denounced Truman's "cowardly" doctrine of containment (in contrast to his manly policy of "liberation"), he pursued it in practice. By "liberation" he did not mean freeing the satellites from Russian rule (as the Hungarians learned to their sorrow in 1956); he meant clucking his tongue at Soviet perfidy. When he denounced the neutrality of nations like India as being "immoral," he merely meant it might become contagious. One had to get used to Dulles's language. On the critical issues — rearming Germany, creating a European army, sticking with Chiang, supporting the French in Indochina — he was virtually indistinguishable from Dean Acheson. What he most cared about was maintaining good relations with Congress. He would not be pilloried as Acheson had been. Where this meant throwing foreign service officers to McCarthy's wolves, his celebrated sense of morality made the necessary adjustments.

With his lawyer's mania for contracts, Dulles was especially fond of treaties. Not to be outdone by Acheson, who had fabricated NATO, he put together a curious entity he called the Southeast Asia Treaty Organization. Hastily assembled in the wake of France's collapse in Indochina and the partition of Vietnam at the 1954 Geneva conference, SEATO was remarkable on many counts, perhaps above all for containing only a single Southeast Asian nation, Thailand. The other members were white

Europeans, except for Pakistan and the Philippines, which had been induced to join by the prospect of U.S. Treasury handouts. Lippmann ran into Dulles at a Washington dinner party shortly after the secretary returned from a treaty-signing ceremony in Manila.

"Foster," he asked, "what do you think you're going to accomplish with that thing? You've got mostly Europeans, plus Pakistan, which is nowhere near Southeast Asia."

"Look, Walter," Dulles said, blinking hard behind his thick glasses, "I've got to get some real fighting men into the south of Asia. The only Asians who can really fight are the Pakistanis. That's why we need them in the alliance. We could never get along without the Gurkas."

"But Foster," Lippmann reminded him, "the Gurkas aren't Pakistanis, they're Indians."

"Well," responded Dulles, unperturbed by such nit-picking and irritated at the Indians for refusing to join his alliance, "they may not be Pakistanis, but they're Moslems."

"No, I'm afraid they're not Moslems, either, they're Hindus."

"No matter," Dulles replied, and proceeded to lecture Lippmann for half an hour on how SEATO would plug the dike against communism in Asia.[4]

Though Lippmann occasionally gave lip service to such shibboleths as holding back communism in Asia, it was not a subject he thought worth much attention. As far as he was concerned, Asian communism had nothing to do with the Soviet variety, presented no particular threat to the United States, and was far less powerful a political force than nationalism. Often, with no success, he tried to point out to Dulles and his successors that even if nationalism sometimes flowed in the vessel of communism, it was nationalism that would always triumph. This did not fit into Washington's view of a world divided between "us" and "them," and certainly not into Dulles's.[5]

Lippmann was no less critical of American policy toward Europe. He had been against the expansion of NATO to include nations on Russia's frontier — on grounds that it would provoke the Kremlin and seal the division of the Continent. He had opposed the rearmament of Germany, and Washington's plan for the so-called European Defense Community designed to create an all-European army. Even though the French had originally proposed such an army — in an effort to prevent the United States from restoring the Wehrmacht — they had no serious intention of joining. Ever since the plan was first proposed by Acheson, Lippmann had been warning that it was "absurd" to expect the French to "merge their own sovereign independence in a superstate . . . certain to be dominated by Germany."[6]

Everyone in Paris — from De Gaulle to Mendès-France and Jean Monnet — had told him that EDC would never clear the French parliament. But Dulles stuck to it with the tenacity of a true believer. "My own view is that Foster Dulles's real feeling about EDC is that of a man who has sat down on flypaper and can't think what to do next," Lippmann wrote Dorothy Thompson in January 1954. "Don't you agree that the European army, far from being a means of uniting and reconciling the French and Germans, is the principal obstacle to any progress toward reconciliation?"

The French seemed to think so, and in 1954 voted down the pact. Dulles agonized but did not reappraise. Declaring that Paris had unleashed a "crisis of almost terrifying proportions," he nonetheless went along with Anthony Eden's plan to build a nonintegrated European army with British units to dilute the Germans. Dulles got his German army, but the price, as Lippmann pointed out, was the sealing of Germany's partition — a partition that had become a "vested interest not only of all the great powers of the East and the West, but also in high degree of the two Germanys themselves."[7]

Confronted in Western Europe by the thing they feared most — a re-created German army in alliance with the United States — the Russians battened down the hatches in Eastern Europe and looked abroad for ways of making the Western powers uncomfortable. They encouraged the Egyptian leader, Gamal Abdel Nasser, in his aggression against Israel, provided him with arms, and — when Dulles tried to humiliate Nasser by withdrawing promised American aid for the Aswan Dam hydroelectric project — stepped in with the money Egypt needed. Dulles, angry at Nasser for refusing to join the so-called Baghdad Pact — which Dulles had organized to prop up the monarchies of Iraq and Iran — hoped that the withdrawal of American aid would topple Nasser. Instead, it goaded the Egyptian leader into a brilliant retaliation: Nasser nationalized the Suez Canal Company, owned by a British-French consortium, and placed it under Egyptian sovereignty.

The British and the French were enraged. Although Nasser was technically within his rights, this seemed a calculated blow at their national prestige. Nothing could have demonstrated more dramatically to what depths these once-great imperial powers had sunk. Dulles, under pressure from Eisenhower to seek a peaceful solution to the problem, rushed in with a curious legal concoction he called the "users' plan," under which ships using the canal would provide their own pilots and pay the tolls not to Egypt but to the users' association. Nasser rejected this fanciful scheme and contemptuously suggested that the British apply it to foreign ships using the port of London.

With the collapse of Dulles's plan, the British and the French decided to take matters into their own hands. They would put Nasse place," and they were convinced that the United States, howe it might publicly deplore military action, would go along w

Coordinating their plans with the Israelis, who believed that Nasser was planning to attack them, the British and French plotted to seize the canal. The Israelis invaded the Sinai on October 29, 1956, and an Anglo-French force landed at Suez two days later.

Conservatives applauded, liberals deplored. Lippmann, for his part, thought it perfectly understandable. Far more concerned with British and French political sensibilities than with Egyptian pride, he refused to condemn the attack. Nasser, he explained in his first column after the invasion, was a "typical aggressor-dictator," and the assault on Suez was provoked by the Egyptian's "grandiose plans to become master of the Arab world." Even though "we may wish that they had not started," he wrote as the British and French converged on the canal from one side and the Israelis from the other, "we cannot now wish that they should fail."[8]

Some did wish it, however. Dulles was irritated at London and Paris for not consulting him in advance, and feared he had gone too far in implying that he would wink at military action. Eisenhower, determined not to tarnish his peacemaker image on the eve of the 1956 presidential elections, was livid. How dare the British and the French act on their own? He would teach them the limits of interdependence. Just as the allies were on the point of seizing the canal, Eisenhower ordered them to withdraw. And to make sure the order was carried out, he struck them at their most vulnerable point: their economic dependence on U.S. financial support.

Stunned by the American reaction, the British hesitated between a desire to retain their last shred of imperial pride and their fear that the United States would withdraw support for the faltering pound sterling and plunge their economy into chaos. They gave in. The French, abandoned by London, could not go on alone. The Israelis now had no alternative but to stop on the threshold of victory. Dulles, in a supreme irony, had saved the man he most detested, Nasser, and in doing so had destroyed the political life of Anthony Eden, the prime minister of America's closest ally. Eden, his health broken and his reputation in a shambles, resigned a few weeks later and was replaced by Harold Macmillan.

Macmillan took an apocalyptic view of the Suez affair. John Miller, then in London, lunched with him a few days after the debacle. Although he had been warned how gloomy the future prime minister was, Miller wrote Lippmann of their encounter, "even then I was not prepared for quite such a Joe Alsopian performance. He waved his hand vaguely out of the window toward St. James's Park and said: 'It's been a pretty good civilization, ours; it's a pity it's all over. You realize that by the end of 1957 Western civilization as we know it will have finished. I suppose that after some centuries of bolshevization another one will emerge. I wonder what it will be like.' ''

Western civilization somehow staggered on, but Suez left indelible marks. It destroyed Dulles's credibility with America's allies, made clear that Britain and France had only as much diplomatic independence as Washington would allow, and provided a "spectacular demonstration," as Lippmann wrote, that there were no longer any great powers in Europe. A Continent divided at the Iron Curtain and split into weak and dependent states was "unable, either by diplomacy or by force, to affirm its vital interest in the outer world." [9] From this lesson the allies drew opposite conclusions. The British, trying to play Greece to America's Rome, as Macmillan once revealingly phrased it, huddled closer to Washington and surrendered their lingering great-power ambitions. The French, battered but unrecalcitrant, moved to develop their own atomic bomb as the first step toward full diplomatic independence.

That same month of October 1956, as the Suez affair was coming to a head, the Soviet empire in Eastern Europe was rocked by a very different kind of satellite revolt. Hungarian nationalists, taking their cue from Khrushchev's denunciation of Stalin's crimes, and from the efforts of the Poles to win greater autonomy from Moscow, overthrew their Soviet puppet regime. The world watched apprehensively, wondering how much heresy the Russians would tolerate. The danger was, Lippmann wrote during the first few days of the revolt, that Hungarians might make greater demands than the Poles had won or than the Russians would tolerate. "In the interest of peace and freedom," he counseled, ". . . we must hope that for a time . . . the uprising in the satellite orbit will be stabilized at Titoism." If allowed to get out of hand the insurrection could "lead to bloody deeds in which we should be called upon to intervene, our honor being involved, though we could not intervene, knowing that the risks were incalculable." [10] His words had barely appeared in print when the new Hungarian government withdrew from the Soviet bloc and called on the West for help. This went far beyond the Polish compromise. Russian tanks rumbled into Budapest and crushed the rebellion.

The risks of an American intervention would have been, as Lippmann had said, intolerable. Neither side wanted a war. Put to the test, each would respect the other's sphere of influence in Europe. "Liberation" quietly disappeared from Dulles's vocabulary. The administration, though it had been embarrassed by the events in Hungary and had handled the Suez affair ineptly, nonetheless benefited from them politically. Nothing so rallies the people around an incumbent President as a foreign-policy crisis. With the presidential election coming hot on the heels of the Russian invasion of Budapest and the Anglo-French retreat from Suez, Ike seemed a shoo-in. He no doubt would have been anyway. Adlai Stevenson, making a second bid for the White House, seemed to have lost much of his old fervor and originality, though not his wit. Even he did not seem to think he had a real chance at the office. But Lippmann, by now convinced that four years of Ike was quite enough, thought that Stevenson might be ready to take over. He had spent the previous Thanksgiving at the governor's farm in northern Illinois and had come away, he reported to Berenson, "quite happy about him and quite reassured about his reputed indecision"; the indecision, he explained, being "simply the result of his having an open mind, his unwillingness to make snap judgments, and his capacity, which is rare in public men, for deliberating. When he has reached a conclusion, he is quite firm and decisive."

As the election approached, Lippmann offered behind-the-scenes advice to George Ball, a key Stevenson adviser, suggesting that the "right line" would be to concentrate on Dulles rather than Ike, to stress that the President had had to rescue the nation "by emergency decisions from the dilemmas and dead ends into which it has been sucked" by Dulles's brinkmanship. Stevenson, he counseled, should take the administration to task for "our militarized diplomacy," Japan's drift toward neutralism, the "alienation" of India, and Soviet "political penetration" of the Middle East.

Stepping down into the arena, Lippmann denounced the administration's policies as "hand-me-downs from Roosevelt, Truman, and the Stalinist phase of the cold war," and praised Stevenson as the spokesman for a "new generation." By the late summer of 1956 he officially advised his readers that "a voter who has been for Eisenhower can turn to Stevenson without feeling he has turned his back upon himself and made his own past look foolish."[11] A switch, in other words, was now respectable. Still, he shied away from actually switching himself. Despite his kind words for Stevenson, he refrained from formally endorsing the Democrat, and again sat on the fence. The conclusion, in any case, was foregone. Ike rolled up another triumph, yielding only seven states to the Democrats, all in the Deep South. Equally striking, the Republicans had held on to the White House while losing Congress, the first time in a century this had happened.

Though Lippmann was not sure that Stevenson was the right man for the presidency, he respected his integrity, warmed to his urbane wit, and thought he exemplified some of the best aspects of American political life. When Stevenson died of a heart attack in London in July 1965 while on a diplomatic mission, Lippmann wrote a poignant tribute. Stevenson's enemies were not men whom he had injured, for he had injured no one, Lippmann said. "His enemies were men who recognized that he did not share and was a living reproach to the new imperiousness of our power and wealth, that he was a deeply established American who had no part in the arrogance of the newly rich and the newly powerful and the newly arrived. His presence made them uncomfortable, even abashed, all the more because he was so witty when they were so hot, so elegant when they were making a spectacle of themselves."[12]

With the election safely traversed, politics was back to normal, which meant more fist-shaking at the Chinese and more squabbles over Germany. The Soviets, who had tried without success to block a West German army, were now convinced — with some reason — that the Americans would turn over nuclear weapons to the Germans. To allay these anxieties and to ease political tensions in central Europe, George Kennan — now a historian at Princeton — in the fall of 1957 gave a series of lectures over the British Broadcasting Corporation network. In these widely publicized and much-discussed talks he urged that the United States and the Soviet Union jointly withdraw their armies from central Europe and ban nuclear weapons from the area. This "disengagement" plan, which recalled Lippmann's own proposals of a decade earlier, was designed to assuage Russian fears of a nuclear-armed Germany with claims on the "lost territories," and offer the satellites hope for greater freedom from Moscow.

Enthusiastically received by many in Western Europe and the United States, the plan was pointedly ignored by the U.S. government. To Kennan's surprise even Lippmann did not support it. Lippmann believed, as he had told the former diplomat four years earlier, that Russia and the West could not withdraw their occupation forces from Germany until they had worked out a territorial settlement in central Europe. "We cannot," he elaborated, "leave the delimitation of the Eastern frontier to a bilateral agreement between a united Germany and the Soviet Union." Although Lippmann had long argued that European peace required the reunification of the two Germanys, he was now not so sure. A swing through Europe in the spring of 1958 that took him to Stockholm, Warsaw and Vienna confirmed his suspicion that Europeans on both sides of the Iron Curtain looked with apprehension on the prospect of a united Germany. The best hope, he wrote on his return, lay in "thinning out" foreign military forces in central Europe.[13]

A trip the following spring fortified his belief that now that there were two German states, "every responsible European statesman realizes that they cannot be united within any foreseeable future," as he told his readers. The partition of Germany was "regarded on both sides as not intolerable, and on the whole, preferable to reunification" under any conditions theoretically possible. By saying publicly what everyone had long known but dared not openly admit, Lippmann had cleared the air. His articles, Kennan later said, "tore to pieces" the assumptions on which his own BBC lectures had been based.[14]

Kennan and Lippmann had long differed on how to deal with the Russians. Early in 1953˙ Kennan had written Lippmann that he had been "skeptical" about the decision to recognize the Soviet government in 1933, and had thought it wrong in 1945 to allow Russia and its satellites to enter the United Nations. He would not have been opposed in principle, he told Lippmann, to a "vigorous campaign of political warfare" against the Soviet Union. This struck Lippmann as a curious position for a diplomat to take. "In general I do not like the idea of recognition to carry with it implications beyond the pragmatic rule that the government governs the area under a certain jurisdiction," he replied to Kennan. "The other view, which attaches implications of morality and political approval to the act of recognition, is inexpedient and unworkable." Was this not, he asked, a "throw-back to the kind of moralistic, legalistic thinking" Kennan himself had criticized?[15] In proposing his 1957 disengagement plan Kennan had moved much closer to Lippmann's line of thinking. But by that time such a mutual withdrawal no longer seemed feasible.

Not long after Kennan unveiled his plan, the ebullient new Soviet ambassador to Washington, Mikhail Menshikov, invited Walter and Helen to dinner at the embassy. Between the caviar and the chicken Kiev the ambassador turned to his guest and said: "You have been to other socialist countries — to Poland, to Czechoslovakia, to Yugoslavia — but never to the Soviet Union. Why have you not honored us with a visit?" Rising to the bait, Lippmann replied that he had long wanted to go, but had never been asked. "I am asking you," his genial host replied. "I would be happy to go if you can promise me one thing," Lippmann said: "an interview with Chairman Khrushchev." The ambassador assured him that nothing would be easier, and set a tentative date for the fall of 1958.

That summer in Maine Lippmann boned up on Russian history, and on his return to Washington in mid-September met a few more times with Menshikov and was briefed by Allen Dulles at the CIA. On October 15 he and Helen flew to New York for lunch at the United Nations with Dag Hammarskjöld. The secretary-general, who had seen Khrushchev several times, extended a bit of advice. "Whatever you do, don't let him think you agree with him — that bores him. He doesn't want to be bored. You must challenge and rouse him."[16] A few hours later, armed with phrase books and briefing notes, they set off for Moscow.

On arrival at the Soviet capital the next afternoon they were taken to a suite at the National Hotel that, they were assured, Lenin himself had occupied on his return from exile in 1917. Khrushchev was unable to set a definite appointment with them, and so for the next six days they met with commissars and cabinet officials, saw churches and museums, made the obligatory visit to a collective farm, attended a gala and to them inscrutable performance of *King Lear,* and took a brief trip to Leningrad. In the great fortress of the Kremlin Lippmann paid a visit to the grave of his old college friend John Reed, forever enshrined as a hero of the Russian revolution. Finally, on their seventh day in Moscow, they were told they could see Khrushchev the next morning.

Promptly at twenty minutes to eleven they were picked up at their hotel and taken in a large black Zis to the inner courts of the Kremlin palace. An officer led them to an anteroom next to the premier's office. No one was in sight: no guards, no people waiting, no secretaries carrying papers around, no newspapermen, none of the commotion usually prevalent in the waiting rooms of important officials. Entering Khrushchev's office, they found him sitting at a small desk at the end of a long, rectangular room. The desk, reminiscent of Franklin Roosevelt's, was covered with gadgets, including a large model airplane. Khrushchev greeted his guests cordially, offered them tea, made a few jokes, and then started to talk about Soviet-American sore spots, beginning with Germany. Only two other persons were present: an interpreter and an official from the foreign office. Khrushchev responded openly to questions. After the interview the Lippmanns hurried back to their hotel, where Helen transcribed her notes and wrote down everything she could remember about the conversation. These notes — four single-spaced typed pages — formed the basis of the four articles Lippmann wrote about the trip, articles that captured almost as much attention as the "cold war" series a decade earlier.

The power of Russia and China, he wrote in summing up his impressions, lay "not in their clandestine activity but in the force of their example" upon the developing states of Africa, Asia and Latin America. The West could counter that example only by demonstrating that it was possible to raise backward societies without sacrificing democracy. The Russians were convinced they could win that contest, but that the United States would resort to war to prevent them. "They cannot believe that we really think they will commit military aggression when they themselves are so sure that they must avoid a war," he explained. "So when we talk about defensive armaments they think we are deceiving them, that our military policy is to surround them in preparation for an attack on them in order to halt their revolutionary rise to world leadership." Widely reprinted in newspapers around the world, scrutinized in embassies and foreign offices everywhere, Lippmann's articles won him his first Pulitzer Prize: a special citation under the newly created category of "editorial comment." A few months later the articles were published as a small book, *The Communist World and Ours.*[17]

The death of John Foster Dulles in May 1959 and Khrushchev's visit to the United States in the fall of that year seemed to put relations between Washington and Moscow on a calmer plane. The Soviet premier's barnstorming September tour, culminating in a meeting with Eisenhower at Camp David, an appearance before the National Press Club, and an address at the United Nations — which Lippmann attended as a guest of the Soviet delegation, with a seat next to Marshal Zhukov — coincided with the more personal festivities surrounding Lippmann's seventieth birthday.

To celebrate this milestone Helen had arranged an enormous party and invited friends from New York, Boston and Maine. On September 22, 1959, the day before the event, *Washington Post* publisher Philip Graham inaugurated the celebration by presenting Walter with a Renault sedan. In the afternoon Carl and Chloe Binger arrived from Boston, and Frederick and Edith King from New York. The three couples went to lunch at the baronial home of Duncan and Marjorie Phillips, and then were taken on a guided tour of the family collection in the Phillips Gallery. That night at a gala black-tie dinner at Woodley Road, Carl Binger, sometime poet and Walter's oldest friend, composed a verse, the guests gave speeches and drank toasts, and everyone told Walter he looked twenty years younger than his age, which was in fact true.

The next afternoon the Lippmanns held a mammoth cocktail party that went beyond even their usual efforts. Their spring and fall parties marked the opening and closing of Washington's social season and had the quality of command performances. Invitations were coveted as prizes and treated as rewards. Cabinet officials mingled with diplomats, congressmen and journalists, with an occasional stage celebrity or literary personality thrown in for spice. One young man, attending a Lippmann party for the first time and not realizing quite what he was in for, stopped at the gate before a phalanx of policemen and said, "Why all the protection? Who's in there?" "Mister," the policeman said, "everybody's in there." Almost everybody was: some five hundred guests mingling in the large sunken living room and spilling over into the garden, with Helen, the renowned hostess, somehow remembering their names and introducing strangers to one another.

James Reston and Marquis Childs capped the birthday festivities by presenting Lippmann with a 238-page volume entitled *Walter Lippmann and His Times*, a *festschrift* of a dozen essays celebrating his career. Although each contributor seemed to take him to task, however gently, for one shortcoming or another, and Arthur Krock achieved the not inconsiderable feat of writing an entire essay on journalism without once mentioning Lippmann's name, the general tone was most respectful. James Reston summed it up when he wrote of Lippmann: "The point is not that he was never wrong or that he did not change his ideas and even on occasion contradict his theories, but that he provoked thought, encouraged debate, forced definition, and often revision of policies, and nourished the national dialogue on great subjects for over half a century.

. . . He has given my generation of newspapermen a wider vision of our duty."[18]

On his birthday, September 23, Lippmann was guest of honor at a luncheon meeting of the National Press Club. The room was jammed with even more people than had come to hear Khrushchev the previous week. They were honoring, not only a venerable colleague whose career stretched back to days before many of them were born, but a man still able to surprise others and renew himself. "In his late sixties that veteran of the Mabel Dodge Evenings has abandoned the conservative viewpoint of his middle years, during which time it was said he wrote like a revolving door," one chronicler wrote of him that year. "With renewed sharpness and liberalism, Lippmann has returned to the spirit of Mabel Dodge's days."[19] The tiredness and paralysis of the Eisenhower administration seemed to have revitalized him; he drew energy from its very lassitude.

It seemed fitting that Lippmann should be feted that afternoon, not by scholars or statesmen, but by his fellow journalists. Despite the books that had taken him on excursions into philosophy and morals, he was primarily a journalist. He had chosen a life of criticism and comment rather than of personal power and the lasting recognition of office. If there were times when he had wondered about the wisdom of his choice, he had long since put those doubts behind him. He stood at the pinnacle of his profession. While aware of his exalted position, he did not pull rank among his colleagues, or cut himself off from younger men who might have something to teach him. Among journalists he had a reputation for gentleness and modesty, as well as integrity. If he kept his emotional distance from people, he could also be a concerned and caring friend in time of trouble. He was, as Richard Rovere wrote, "more gracious and courteous, quicker and more willing to praise young writers than any other American of his generation, with the possible exception of H. L. Mencken." When he read an article he liked, he wrote the author a fan letter, even though he might never have heard of him. As Philip Geyelin, who later became director of the *Washington Post*'s editorial page, said: "He treated much younger colleagues as — colleagues. And he regularly paid us the ultimate compliment. He asked *us* what was going on and what *we* thought."[20]

As he rose to the applause of his colleagues that afternoon at the National Press Club, Lippmann spoke as a man who had something special to say about the work to which he had dedicated his life.

Because we are newspapermen in the American liberal tradition, the way we interpret the news is not by fitting the facts to a dogma. It is by proposing theories or hypotheses, which are then tested by trial and error. We put forward the most plausible interpretation we can think of, the most plausible picture into which the raw news fits, and then we wait to see whether the later news fits into the interpretation. We do well if, with only a minor change of the interpretation, the later news fits into it. If the later events do not fit, if the later news knocks down the earlier story, there are two things to be done. One is to scrap the theory and the interpretation, which is what liberal, honest men do. The other is to distort or suppress the unmanageable piece of news.

Last summer, while walking in the woods and on the mountains near where I live, I found myself daydreaming about how I would answer, about how I would explain and justify the business of being opinionated and of airing opinions regularly several times a week.

"Is it not absurd," I heard critics saying, "that anyone should think he knows enough to write so much about so many things? You write about foreign policy. Do you see the cables which pour into the State Department every day from all parts of the world? Do you attend the staff meetings of the Secretary of State and his advisers? Are you a member of the National Security Council? And what about all those other countries which you write about? Do you have the run of 10 Downing Street, and how do you listen in on the deliberations of the Presidium in the Kremlin? Why don't you admit that you are an outsider and that you are, therefore, by definition, an ignoramus?

"How, then, do you presume to interpret, much less criticize and to disagree with, the policy of your own government or any other government?

"And, in internal affairs, are you really much better qualified to pontificate? No doubt there are fewer secrets here, and almost all politicians can be talked to. They can be asked the most embarrassing questions. And they will answer with varying degrees of candor and of guile. But, if there are not so many secrets, you must admit that there are many mysteries. The greatest of all the mysteries is what the voters think, feel, and want today, what they will think and feel and want on election day, and what they can be induced to think and feel and want by argument, by exhortation, by threats and promises, and by the arts of manipulation and leadership."

Yet, formidable as it is, in my daydream I have no trouble getting the better of this criticism. "And you, my dear fellow," I tell the critic, "you be careful. If you go on, you will be showing how ridiculous it is that we live in a republic under a democratic system and that anyone should be allowed to vote. You will be denouncing the principle of democracy itself, which asserts that the outsiders shall be sovereign over the insiders. For you will be showing that the people, since they are ignoramuses, because they are outsiders, are therefore incapable of governing themselves.

"What is more, you will be proving that not even the insiders are qualified to govern them intelligently. For there are very few men — perhaps forty at a maximum — who read, or at least are eligible to read, all the cables that pour into the State Department. And then, when you think about it, how many senators, representatives, governors, and mayors — all of whom have very strong opinions about who should conduct our affairs — ever read these cables which you are talking about?

"Do you realize that, about most of the affairs of the world, we are all outsiders and ignoramuses, even the insiders who are at the seat of the government? The Secretary of State is allowed to read every American document he is interested in. But how many of them does he read? Even if he reads the American documents, he cannot read the British and the Canadian, the French and the German, the Chinese and the Russian. Yet he has to make decisions in which the stakes may well be peace or war. And about these decisions, the Congress, which reads very few documents, has to make decisions too."

Thus, in my daydream, I reduce the needler to a condition of sufficient humility about the universal ignorance of mankind. Then I turn upon him and with suitable eloquence declaim an apology for the existence of the Washington correspondent.

"If the country is to be governed with the consent of the governed, then the governed must arrive at opinions about what their governors want them to consent to. How do they do this?

"They do it by hearing on the radio and reading in the newspapers what the corps of correspondents tell them is going on in Washington, and in the country at large, and in the world. Here, we correspondents perform an essential service. In some field of interest, we make it our business to find out what is going on under the surface and beyond the horizon, to infer, to deduce, to imagine, and to guess what is going on inside, what this meant yesterday, and what it could mean tomorrow.

"In this we do what every sovereign citizen is supposed to do but has not the time or the interest to do for himself. This is our job. It is no mean calling. We have a right to be proud of it and to be glad that it is our work."[21]

As he finished, his colleagues rose in unison to give a standing ovation to the man whom John Reed a half-century earlier had called "our all-unchallenged Chief."

His birthday festivities behind him, Lippmann began preparing for the trip that would take him to Egypt, Iran and India. He did his homework diligently, read the reports marked by his assistant, talked with various ambassadors and government officials, and received the usual CIA briefing. On October 29, 1959, he and Helen flew to Paris and then on to Rome. This time they did not make the side trip to Florence. Berenson, frail, but faithfully keeping his diaries until the end, had died at I Tatti three weeks earlier at the age of ninety-four. Even in ill health he never lost his zest for life. "I would willingly stand at street corners, hat in hand, asking passers-by to drop their unused minutes into it," he had told Kenneth Clark not long before he died.[22]

After a few days in Rome with BB's old friend Umberto Morra, and BB's devoted companion, Nicky Mariano, the Lippmanns flew to Cairo for a round of interviews with Egyptian officials, a whirlwind two-day tour to Luxor and Aswan, and a long interview with Nasser at his home. The Egyptian leader, like his inner circle, was "attractive, intelligent, and genuinely concerned with the destiny of his country," Lippmann reported to his readers — a sharp contrast to his assessment during the Suez imbroglio three years earlier of Nasser as a "typical aggressor-dictator." While noting that Nasser and his entourage might resort "unhesitatingly and ruthlessly to the slogans and the ideologies and the war cries" to quiet the populace, he thought their hearts were devoted to raising Egypt from its poverty.[23]

After a week in Egypt they pressed on to India, which they had last seen ten years earlier. Confining their trip to Bombay and Delhi, they spent a good deal of time with Prime Minister Nehru, who persuaded Lippmann that the West should help develop India as a model for the Third World. In Iran, where they stopped off for five days en route back to Europe, they visited the Shah — who six years earlier had been temporarily chased from his throne by nationalists and then restored through a CIA-engineered coup d'etat. The Shah's opulent surroundings, attentive manners, and warnings of Soviet machinations against the "free world" did not impress Lippmann. He came away convinced that it was foolish for the United States to build up Iran as a military barrier against the Soviets. "The notion that the way to make Iran secure is to build a Maginot Line to hold back a Russian invasion until we can arrive to defend Iranian territory, is obsolete and, it is in fact, nonsense," he wrote on his return. Iran, like India, should be neutral. The Shah, whose access to the U.S. Treasury hinged on the assumption that his personal survival was vital to American interests, was most displeased by Lippmann's remarks, and later complained that they were inspired by "unfriendly elements" in the State Department.[24]

On his return to Washington early in December 1959, Lippmann fell easily into the old rhythm: writing the column twice a week, doing an occasional article, toying with some book ideas. He still wondered if it might not be a good idea to break away from the "tyranny" of the column, but of course never did anything about it. Then quite unexpectedly he was presented with a tantalizing offer. Late in March 1960 Fred Friendly, a gregarious and persuasive producer for CBS News, cornered Lippmann and asked if he would like to appear on television. "I wouldn't," Lippmann replied. He had an intellectual's contempt for commercial television, combined with an old newspaperman's suspicion of the medium. Rarely did he turn on his own set, except for an occasional political event, such as the conventions. Insofar as he had ever deigned to take notice of the medium, his comments had not been flattering. "While television is supposed to be 'free,' it has in fact become the creature, the servant, and indeed the prostitute of merchandising," he had written only a few months earlier in the wake of the TV quiz-show scandals. Television's major influence had been to "poison the innocent by the exhibition of violence, degeneracy and crime, and second to debase the public taste." The only hope for redeeming the medium, he suggested years before public television became a reality, was to set up a noncommercial government-supported network.[25]

Turning Lippmann's argument against him, Friendly countered by pointing out that the only way to improve television was for people like Lippmann to help develop its potential. After a long lunch with Friendly and CBS newscaster Howard K. Smith, Lippmann said he would think about it. Friendly pressed relentlessly, and finally Lippmann agreed to tape a one-hour interview, with the stipulation that if he was not pleased with the results, the show would never be broadcast. He also wanted to forbid commercials, but finally agreed that the few carefully chosen sponsors — no dog food, deodorants or soap — would not be allowed to break into the program. CBS sent him a check for two thousand dollars to seal the deal, taped the show on July 7, 1960, and ran it over the network on August 11.

CBS expected a few kind words from critics for being highbrow and "responsible." Instead it got a hit. Public response far exceeded anything the network had anticipated. The program was front-page news. Critics declared that television had come of age. "To have the sage of Washington up close and ad-libbing," commented the *Saturday Review,* "revealed not only his urbanity, which was to be expected, but yielded a bonus in the impression of kindliness and personal warmth never apparent in the intense concentration of his logical, impersonal prose." As the congratulatory mail poured in, CBS sent Lippmann another check for three thousand dollars and offered him a five-year contract. Pleased by his new popularity Lippmann agreed, but used his Washington lawyer, Oscar Cox, to drive a better bargain: fifteen thousand dollars a year for one program each year, and ten thousand dollars for each additional one. Altogether CBS ran six more interviews, on the average of one a year, showing the final one on February 22, 1965. When the interviews were later published in book form, Lippmann's only comment on reading the text was: "My God, what syntax!" Most viewers thought it elegant, including the Peabody Awards committee, which gave him a special citation in 1962.[26]

The interviews focused on the affairs of the day, but also at times on issues that transcended the news. In the first interview, taped in July 1960, not long after Eisenhower's inept handling of the U-2 spy plane incident and the abortion of the scheduled Paris summit meeting with Khrushchev, Lippmann was asked what qualities he thought a leader ought to have. Having reflected and written often on this question, he gave a thoughtful reply. A leader should have the "ability to see what matters in the excitement of daily events . . . to be able to see through the latest headline to what is permanent and enduring." Churchill had this "second sight," as he called it; so did De Gaulle and Theodore Roosevelt. "The ability to see which way the thing is going is the basis of great leadership. The President cannot, himself, act on everything. He has to decide. So his mind must be judicial. The function of the President is to hear the arguments of the contending factions and make a decision. And that requires not only decisiveness, as everybody says, but the ability to be judicial about it."

A second quality of leadership was to be articulate. Here Lippmann had a very special idea of how a President should make his views known, and what kind of audience he should try to reach. "He must be able to talk in a language which is not the lowest common denominator . . . but the best. What you must lead in a country are the best of the country, and they will carry it on down. There's no use of the President trying to talk down to a fellow who can just about read and write. Let somebody else do that. He must talk to the people who teach the man to read and write. And for that he requires — well, as I said, articulateness." Further, he added, the President must have sympathy, the "ability to feel for people in trouble," wherever they might be.[27]

"There are many things which people cannot understand until they have lived with them for a while," Lippmann had written three decades earlier in one of his many reflections on the art of statesmanship.

Often, therefore, the great statesman is bound to act boldly in advance of his constituents. When he does this he stakes his judgment against what the people will in the end find to be good against what the people happen ardently to desire.

This capacity to act upon the hidden realities of a situation in spite of appearances is the essence of statesmanship. It consists in giving the people not what they want but what they will learn to want. It requires the courage which is possible only in a mind that is detached from the agitations of the moment. It requires the insight which comes only from an objective and discerning knowledge of the facts, and a high and imperturbable disinterestedness.

These were, he realized, rare qualities, and it had been a long time since any American President had embodied them. But Lippmann did have a current figure very much in mind as he reflected on the qualities of leadership. General de Gaulle had returned to power just two years earlier, in June 1958, during a political crisis triggered by the insurrection against French rule in Algeria. When the civilian government in Paris collapsed and the army threatened to take over, De Gaulle stepped in and assumed power. Although some considered the general's action akin to a coup d'etat, Lippmann argued that De Gaulle had actually restored constitutional government after it became "plain as the nose on one's face that the Paris government was impotent to govern." To those who charged that De Gaulle might pave the way for fascism, Lippmann responded that this was inconceivable. "He has always been a man of extraordinary historical insight and imagination. . . . There is in De Gaulle no trace of the modern vulgar dictator." [28]

In De Gaulle Lippmann found the quality of leadership to which the French had responded in 1958, just as they had in 1940: a man who "touches the chords of memory which bind a nation together." Nations desperately needed such continuity in times of crisis. "The consciousness of a great past is indispensable," Lippmann had written on the eve of the war in 1940. "Without it, with no sense that there is an historic destiny in which Americans participate . . . this nation will never cohere." De Gaulle unquestionably had that sense of historic destiny. During the general's state visit to Washington in April 1960 Lippmann published the most glowing tribute he had ever written for any public figure. "The secret is that he is more than a great man," but truly a "genius," he wrote of De Gaulle. He was gifted with the "capacity to see beneath the surface of events, to see through the obvious and conventional and stereotyped appearance of events to the significant realities, to the obscured facts and forces which will prevail." It was a "second sight into the nature of history," bringing with it "the gift of prophesying what is going to happen because the seeing eye is already there."

Lippmann was one of the first Americans to recognize De Gaulle's special genius, among the most persistent in trying to make his countrymen realize that De Gaulle spoke for the interests of a revitalized France and a restored Europe, among the few who defended the general at a time when the White House considered him an enemy. More than any other journalist, Lippmann saw, and made others see, the historical greatness of Charles de Gaulle. "I find that almost three weeks after the fall of France," he wrote in his 1960 tribute, "I had learned enough to be able to write that 'in the misfortune of France it should be our fierce pride to be the last to forget the greatness of France. We must wish to be the first to remember . . . that France is indispensable, as indispensable to the maturity of Western civilization as Hellas was to its birth — and as imperishable.' I learned to say that only from General de Gaulle." [29]

The leadership Lippmann found in De Gaulle, along with Churchill and Theodore Roosevelt, and to a lesser extent in Wilson and even at times in FDR, had an almost mystical quality. "In all men who lead multitudes of human beings there is a bit of magic," he had written the younger Arthur Vandenberg on his father's death in 1951. "When it is working, then their other powers — such as the ability to see through an argument to the crucial issue, and to know at all times not only what they themselves are thinking, but what others are feeling, and the gift of judging what is and what is not feasible, and what has priority, and the gift of eloquence — all these become incandescent with an effective energy that in themselves they would not possess."

As the 1960 elections approached, Lippmann was looking for a leader. Eisenhower had done his work in binding the nation's wounds, and he had lingered on too long. It was time for the nation to emerge from the "complacency and the indifference of the Fifties," toward a wider vision. "As the private purposes are overcome by the impact and pressure of our public needs, the way will be opened to a wider examination of our moral condition," Lippmann wrote in the spring of 1960. "The country is waiting for another innovator."[30]

One was standing in the wings.

At the New Frontier

I have been involved in all kinds of things connected
with the formation of the new administration.
— To Allan Nevins, December 9, 1960

LIPPMANN was waiting for another innovator, not for Ike's heir apparent to seize the throne. Four years earlier he had dismissed Richard
Nixon as a "ruthless partisan . . . who divides and embitters the people." [1] His opinion about the vice-president had not changed. Among
the Republicans, Lippmann favored his summer neighbor in Maine,
Nelson Rockefeller. The plutocrat governor of New York was shrewd,
aggressive, internationalist and a friend of organized labor. Lippmann
thought he would make a fine choice. But the Republican bosses considered Rockefeller too liberal and handed the nomination to Nixon.

This drove Lippmann back into the Democratic fold, where John F.
Kennedy, the forty-two-year-old senator from Massachusetts, was pushing hard and spending freely in a no-holds-barred battle against his two
main rivals, Lyndon Johnson and Hubert Humphrey. Lippmann had
known Kennedy ever since the senator's childhood days in Washington
in the 1930s. Some of his doubts about Joseph Kennedy — with whom
he had fallen out over the appeasement issue — had carried over to the
son. John Kennedy had tried to woo Lippmann, but the columnist remained evasive and skeptical. "I had grave reservations about him, both
because of my knowledge of his father, and because of his own record
in the McCarthy affair," Lippmann later said, referring to the fact that
Kennedy had never denounced McCarthy, and that his brother Robert
had served as assistant minority counsel on McCarthy's committee. "I
couldn't possibly describe myself as an early or enthusiastic Kennedy
man."

Lippmann thought Kennedy talented, but a bit ruthless and too much
in a hurry. He hoped that Kennedy would settle for the vice-presidential
slot under Stevenson or Humphrey before making the race on his own.

This, he believed, would lessen qualms about Kennedy's Catholicism. But Kennedy had no intention of waiting. "I must tell you," Lippmann wrote him in January 1960, "that I do not look forward with any pleasure to the contest between Humphrey and you. You both will be saying and doing things that as President you would wish you hadn't had to say and do." Disturbed by Kennedy's lavish spending in the primaries, Lippmann told him that the primary system put an "excessive premium on the arts of demagogy" and gave unfair advantage to the candidate with "the most money and the general ability to manipulate blocs and organizations."[2]

Kennedy demonstrated the truth of the observation by demolishing Humphrey in a series of wild-spending primary battles. When Adlai Stevenson then decided he would not make an open bid for the nomination, Lippmann began coming to terms with the inevitable. In a television interview he taped a few days before Kennedy captured the Democratic nomination, Lippmann declared that the country needed a "new crop of young men under good leadership." Kennedy seized on these words as a personal endorsement and used them in his campaign. By mid-July Lippmann was telling his readers that Kennedy had "outgrown many of the mistakes and vacillations of his youth," and that his position was essentially the same as Stevenson's. He had proved himself to be an "unusually effective organizer and a natural leader of men." Kennedy's deft handling of the religious issue particularly impressed him. In a confrontation with Protestant ministers worried about his spiritual allegiances, Kennedy had insisted that his faith as a Catholic would not influence his decisions as an elected public official. Lippmann hailed his response as that of a "brave and truthful man."[3]

By October Lippmann's conversion was complete. It was "truly impressive," he told his readers, "to see the precision of Mr. Kennedy's mind, his immense command of the facts, his instinct for the crucial point, his singular lack of demagoguery and sloganeering . . . his coolness and courage." Adding eulogy to applause, he found in the youthful senator the "recognizable marks of the man who, besides being highly trained, is a natural leader, organizer and ruler of men." For Lippmann there was no higher compliment. His endorsement strongly influenced other journalists. But Arthur Krock, for one, was not impressed. "I may be getting old and I may be getting senile," he reportedly fumed in response to one of Lippmann's columns on Kennedy, "but at least I don't fall in love with young boys like Walter Lippmann."[4]

Lippmann's accolades notwithstanding, Kennedy barely squeezed through to victory in November, racking up a margin of only 114,000 votes out of 68,000,000 cast. But it was enough. By the time Walter and Helen returned in late November from a twelve-day tour of Brazil,

Kennedy was beginning to assemble a team. Lippmann was pleased that he leaned heavily on Cambridge academics — particularly such activist scholars as McGeorge Bundy, Arthur Schlesinger, Jr., and John Kenneth Galbraith. During the two months between the election and the inauguration a good number of politicians came to Woodley Road for tea and a chat. Among them was the President-elect.

Shortly before lunch on December 6 Lippmann got a call from Kennedy asking if he could drop by later in the afternoon. Within an hour a horde of Secret Service agents descended upon the house. They checked the entrances, grilled the servants and secretaries, and detained a man working in the garden. Kennedy arrived at four. Lippmann greeted him at the door and led him into the book-lined study off the living room. After a few moments of small talk Kennedy got down to business. He was having a problem deciding on a secretary of state. Although partial to J. W. Fulbright, he had run into flak from blacks and liberals, who considered the Arkansas senator a racist because of his opposition to civil rights legislation. Lippmann, as an old friend of Fulbright, reminded Kennedy that the senator really had no choice but to vote with the segregationists if he wanted to be reelected. "I know that," Kennedy said, "but the Africans and our own blacks will raise a terrible howl if I appoint him, even though he's probably the best man for the job." Just then the telephone rang. Helen answered and, though the caller did not identify himself, recognized Robert Kennedy's voice. After taking the call the President-elect returned to the study and said: "I don't think we're going to be able to go with Fulbright. There's too much opposition at home and abroad on the segregation issue."

They began discussing alternatives. Stevenson's name immediately came up, but Kennedy was negative. He resented Stevenson's wishy-washy role at the convention, where he had refused either to support Kennedy or to come out openly against him. At one point Stevenson's support could have been crucial, but the governor, hoping for a last-minute draft, had sat on the sidelines. Kennedy never forgot or forgave. But Stevenson still had the affection of the party's liberals, and Lippmann suggested that he be given a consolation prize — such as the ambassadorship to the United Nations. Kennedy agreed. Then Kennedy raised the name of Dean Rusk, whom he had never met, but whom Acheson and Robert Lovett were pushing. Lippmann had long known Rusk — then head of the Rockefeller Foundation and former assistant secretary of state for Asian affairs under Acheson — and considered him an unimaginative bureaucrat. "Rusk is a profound conformist," he told Kennedy. "He has a conventional mind and would never deviate from what he considered the official line. You're hardly likely to get from him the kind of original advice a President needs."

"Well," Kennedy replied, "if I can't take Fulbright, and I won't take Stevenson, and Robert Lovett doesn't want it, and you think I shouldn't take Rusk, who's left?''

"How about McGeorge Bundy?'' Lippmann shot back.

"I hadn't thought of that,'' a surprised Kennedy replied. "He's rather young, isn't he?''

"Yes,'' Lippmann retorted, "but you're a very young President.''

Lippmann never assumed that wisdom and age went hand in hand. He responded to people in terms of their intelligence, not their gray hairs, and he had had a high opinion of Bundy ever since they had tried to collaborate on rewriting *The Good Society* a dozen years earlier. When Harvard was looking for a new president to replace the retiring James Bryant Conant, Lippmann had suggested Bundy, then dean of arts and sciences.

Kennedy said he would think about Bundy, and left Woodley Road still undecided. Recounting the conversation a few days later to Allan Nevins, Lippmann seemed to waver. "For myself, I think Fulbright would do well enough under Kennedy's leadership, but I advocated his appointing Bundy and taking a chance on the fact that he was so young and not well known,'' he explained. "Now I am beginning to hope it will be Fulbright.'' But Kennedy, under pressure from civil rights adviser Harris Wofford and others, rejected Fulbright and settled on Rusk. Bundy got the influential post of special assistant for national security affairs.[5]

Two days after Kennedy's visit Adlai Stevenson came by Woodley Road. He was in an agitated state. Kennedy had told him he could not be secretary of state but could have the United Nations post. Stevenson was bitter, and thought that because of his service to the party he should be rewarded with the top foreign-affairs job. Lippmann spent the morning trying to persuade him how important it was to the nation that he go to the UN. With some reluctance Stevenson finally agreed to take the job.

Lippmann became one of the shining ornaments of the Kennedy administration. Courted and feted by the New Frontiersmen, invited to their parties, solicited for his advice, brought into their deliberative councils, he enjoyed a participation and an influence he had not known since his World War I days with Newton Baker and Colonel House. He valued that closeness, and in choosing the capable Elizabeth Farmer as his new assistant was influenced by the fact that she had worked in the Kennedy campaign and had close personal ties with highly placed people in the new administration. Lippmann would have been courted even without her, but he seemed to feel the need of her special connections.

Three days before the inauguration Kennedy's chief aide and speech writer, Theodore Sorensen, came to Woodley Road to show Lippmann the draft of the inaugural address. Lippmann thought most of it admirable, but suggested that the reference to the Soviet Union as the "enemy" be changed to "adversary." Kennedy readily accepted the change, and "adversary" it was from that time on. In his column Lippmann hailed the address as a "remarkably successful piece of self-expression" that "exemplified the qualities which the world has come to expect of the President."[6] A few years later he would deplore the speech — with its exhortation to ask "what you can do for your country" — as jingoist rhetoric.

With some reason the new team at the White House viewed Lippmann as one of their prime assets. Arthur Schlesinger, an old friend of Lippmann who had joined Kennedy's staff, served as go-between for the columnist and the President. One of his first suggestions was that Kennedy name Lippmann ambassador to France. This was a clever choice since Lippmann was not only greatly admired in Paris, but enjoyed close relations with President de Gaulle. The main argument against it, Schlesinger admitted in his memo to the President, was that Lippmann might be more useful to the administration as a friendly columnist than as ambassador. Kennedy thought so too, and never offered Lippmann the job. Nor did anyone think he would accept it, although years later he admitted privately that had anyone asked him, that was the one government post he would have enjoyed holding.[7]

Lippmann shared the exhilaration that many others felt when the Kennedy team — so eager, bright, and full of ideas — assumed power. A long era of somnolence seemed over. Slogans about "getting the country moving again" became more than empty phrases. A new energy and optimism filled the air. Before the elections Lippmann had seen the country in a negative mood, gripped by a "failure of the capacity to believe . . . that anything really matters very much and that anything is really better than anything else." But when he was asked about the nation's moral climate in April 1961, he was far more optimistic. "This is a most Presidential country," he told an interviewer. "The tone and example set by the President have a tremendous effect on the quality of life in America. The President is like the conductor of a big symphony orchestra — and a new conductor can often get different results with the same score and the same musicians. Right now there is a curious exhilaration here in Washington. There is a new generation in charge, with a new style and a new seriousness. And people are beginning to feel that we can *do* things about problems after all — that everything is possible."

Even during that period of relative euphoria Lippmann did not suspend all critical judgment. He questioned whether Kennedy, for all his energy and optimism, would be able to get his ideas through to the public and to understand its inarticulate needs. While noting that Kennedy was more politically educated and disciplined than either of the two Roosevelts, he wondered if the President had FDR's "vital gift of knowing what the masses felt."[8] The apparent lack of this quality, so critical to great leadership, was to trouble him increasingly in the months that followed.

Lippmann's close relations with the New Frontier gave him an inside track on its policies and made him a valuable interpreter to those on the outside. The Russians were quite aware of this, and in order to prepare the ground for the Kennedy-Khrushchev summit meeting, scheduled for Vienna in June 1961, decided to invite Lippmann back to the Soviet Union for an interview with the chairman. Ambassador Menshikov promised a long and uninterrupted session with Khrushchev, and set the date for early April.

Over the next few weeks Lippmann met several times with Menshikov, conferred with Charles Bohlen and other State Department officials about the American position on Germany and Laos, and was briefed by the CIA. On March 20 he lunched at the White House with Kennedy and Arthur Schlesinger, once again going over the issues. A week later he and Helen boarded the plane for Rome, en route to Moscow. No sooner had they taken their seats in the first-class section than the purser handed them a note from the Soviet ambassador. Crisis in the Kremlin: Khrushchev was at the Black Sea and wanted to postpone his meeting for a week. "Impossible," Lippmann scrawled on the note he sent back to Menshikov. Their European plans were set. He would either come to Russia on April 10 as scheduled, or not at all. When they arrived in Rome the following morning Chairman Khrushchev sent word that he would receive them as scheduled.

After a private audience with Pope John XXIII and a quick trip to Paris, they set off for Moscow, where they were greeted by U.S. Ambassador Llewellyn Thompson and taken to Spasso House, the American embassy, for a working dinner with the French, British and Swedish ambassadors. The following morning they flew to the Crimea, where they were met at the airport by the governor of the province and taken off on a tour of farms and factories, punctuated by innumerable meals and vodka toasts. Although scheduled to attend the ballet and another dinner, they rebelliously retired to their rooms and refused to budge. Recuperating on tea and toast, they went to bed early, and the next morning were driven to Khrushchev's villa at Sochi.

After passing through an iron gate they left the limousine and began walking down a long path toward the villa. Far at the other end they saw a small portly figure slowly approaching. The sleeves of his topcoat hung to his fingertips and he waddled a bit as he walked. Smiling broadly, Khrushchev gave them each a bear hug, proudly showed them around his villa, sat them down to an enormous lunch, and plied them

with an unending flow of wine and vodka. Then they moved into his office to talk, with Walter asking the questions and Helen furiously taking
notes. About an hour into the interview Khrushchev realized that Helen
was not relying on the interpreter. At his prodding she confessed she
had been studying Russian all winter and spring.

After two hours of questions and answers, mostly on Berlin, they
joined the premier for a tour of the grounds, including the gadget-
adorned swimming pool with its retractable glass doors — clearly a source
of great pride. Then he led them over to the badminton court. "Now
we play," he announced. They had expected the portly Khrushchev
to be a pushover. Instead, he was agile and swift — and no less
fiercely competitive than the Lippmanns themselves. Having trounced
the guests, Khrushchev patted them on their backs, led them to the patio
for refreshments and two more hours of conversation about the state of
the world, and then declared it was time for another meal. Although he
was supposed to be on a diet, the premier confided, he would stretch
the rules since his doctor was away for the day.

Again they entered the dining hall, its table spread with caviar,
steaming plates of meat and fowl, and bottles of vodka. Deputy Premier Anastas Mikoyan joined them for dinner, and with customary Ar-
menian exuberance led a dizzying round of toasts. He scolded the
Lippmanns for not downing their vodka after each toast, but Khrushchev took pity on them and provided a bowl into which they surreptitiously emptied their glasses as fast as the indefatigable Mikoyan could
fill them. Finally, exhausted and a little drunk, the Lippmanns begged to
be allowed to go to bed. Khrushchev gave them each a suffocating hug
and let them return to their hotel in nearby Garga.

Before going to bed Helen wrote up her notes, lest she forget something, and the next morning they flew back to Moscow. Lippmann filled
in Ambassador Thompson on the substance of the talks, and the following day they took off for London. During a brief stop in Amsterdam
they heard that the Soviets had just launched the first man into space.
Khrushchev had not dropped even a hint that such a plan was in the
works. On the long flight back to London Lippmann took out his yellow
note pad and wrote the first of his three articles on the Khrushchev interview. These articles made headlines around the world and appeared in
some 450 papers — more than double the number that usually carried
his column. They won him his second Pulitzer Prize, this time for "distinguished reporting of international affairs," and were published in
book form under the title *The Coming Tests with Russia*.

What made Lippmann's articles required reading in foreign ministries
was Khrushchev's frankness on the Berlin issue. There must be, he told
Lippmann, an all-German peace treaty and a new status for Berlin

before "Hitler's generals with their twelve NATO divisions" got atomic weapons from the United States. Without a peace treaty recognizing the new frontiers in Eastern Europe, the Soviet leader warned, Bonn would drag America into a war for recovery of the lost territories. Khrushchev was resolved to seek a solution to the German question, Lippmann concluded, even though he "dreaded the tension" and hoped for an accommodation. Despite the "relentless determination" of the Soviets to promote revolution in the Third World, they were definitely "not contemplating war" and were "genuinely concerned to prevent any crisis."[9]

On April 19, after finishing his three Russia articles and completing a social round that included a lunch at Windsor Castle, as well as the usual parties arranged by Pamela Berry and Fleur Cowles Meyer, Walter and Helen flew from London to Paris. The American papers were filled with accounts of the fiasco at the Bay of Pigs, which had taken place only two days earlier. But an even greater drama awaited the Lippmanns in the French capital. The long and agonizing colonial war in Algeria had finally spread to metropolitan France. General de Gaulle's offer to negotiate a settlement with the Algerian rebels had triggered an insurrection by the die-hard French colonialists and some army commanders. Rumors of a military coup d'etat and even an invasion of Paris hung in the air.

On April 20 Lippmann spent an hour with De Gaulle at the Élysée Palace, and that evening dined with Foreign Minister Maurice Couve de Murville and his family. They seemed tense, but guardedly optimistic. On Saturday the twenty-second Louis Joxe, De Gaulle's minister for Algerian affairs, cancelled his scheduled meeting with Lippmann because of the emergency. On Sunday the twenty-third Walter and Helen returned from lunch in Senlis with Hope and "Bunny" Carter to find the city in a state of siege. They went straight to the American embassy, where on television they watched De Gaulle plead with the French people to resist the paratroopers should there be an invasion. No one knew whether the army would remain loyal to the government or to the rebellious officers. Walter and Helen walked back to their suite at the Meurice through streets teeming with confused and frightened people. All night long their phone rang with reports that the paratroopers were about to land.

Their schedule, which as usual had been prepared months earlier, called for them to return to the United States the following day. They had no intention of changing it. When they awoke the airport was closed, but they were told it might open briefly in the afternoon. They packed their bags and hurried to Orly. In the middle of the afternoon their plane received clearance to take off. They left Paris just as De

Gaulle, rallying loyal army units, managed to crush the incipient rebellion. Not until they arrived in New York that evening did they learn that a coup had been narrowly averted and De Gaulle had saved his Fifth Republic.

That third week in April 1961 had been a dramatic one in Washington as well as in Paris. On the seventeenth a band of Cuban rebels, trained, equipped and transported by the United States, had landed at the Bay of Pigs in an attempt to overthrow the government of Fidel Castro. The collapse of their invasion attempt, followed by a hail of criticism from around the world, had left the Kennedy administration shaken. Lippmann, who arrived back in Washington just in time to watch the President go on television to explain the fiasco, had little sympathy for Kennedy's embarrassment. In a stinging column he accused the "new hands," by which he meant McGeorge Bundy, Dean Rusk and Walt Rostow, of not protecting the President from the bad advice of the "old hands," meaning Allen Dulles and Richard Bissell of the CIA, Joint Chiefs of Staff Lyman Lemnitzer and Arleigh Burke, and State Department coordinator Adolf Berle. A mistake of such magnitude could be expunged "only by the resignation of the key figures who had the primary responsibility," Lippmann charged. Some of these "old hands," such as Dulles and Bissell, were his friends. To call for their resignation was, he confessed, a "painful business, even for a newspaper writer." Kennedy gave the "old hands" a few months of grace for appearance' sake, and then sent them into retirement.[10]

Unlike Kennedy and his entourage, Lippmann had no particular animosity toward the Cuban revolution. He did not view it as a Soviet plot, or as any military danger to the United States. In the summer of 1959, after Castro had taken power from the Batista dictatorship and put through a sweeping agrarian reform program that expropriated many of the old landholders, Lippmann had reminded the Eisenhower administration that the principle of self-determination "carries with it inseparably the right of revolution." Whether or not shareholders in U.S. corporations liked it, "the old style of imperialism and overlordship is not only morally unacceptable but is practically impossible." The Castro government, already under attack on Wall Street and in Congress, sent Lippmann a letter of appreciation for his attempt to explain the revolution's aims. As the pace of nationalization increased and conservatives demanded that the United States overthrow Castro, Lippmann warned that an American intervention would be "catastrophic" for relations with the underdeveloped countries, and urged "magnanimity" toward the Cuban revolution.[11]

But his sense of magnanimity was relative to his reading of the balance of power. As Castro — in response to American pressure culminating in the revocation of Cuba's sugar quota — turned toward the Soviets for support, Lippmann began having second thoughts about the virtues of the Cuban revolution. He went along with the administration's argument that it would likely infect the rest of Latin America, and he even supported a United States embargo on trade with the island. The Russian connection swayed him, for he considered the Caribbean squarely within Washington's sphere of influence. But he drew the line at an invasion, secretly plotted and financed by the CIA without the knowledge of the American people or their representatives. "I consider it a duty of the press to expose that kind of thing to the light of day," he said on television a few weeks after the landing, "because I don't think a democracy like this should have secret training camps and secret armies and secret navies in foreign countries, all in violation of its treaties and its own laws."

In that second TV interview, taped only a month after the Bay of Pigs, Lippmann responded to those who claimed that the United States would be guilty of "appeasement" unless it sent in troops to rout communists in places like Cuba, Laos and Vietnam, or refused to negotiate over issues like Berlin. "You can't decide these questions of life and death for the world by epithets like appeasement," he replied. And then he added more softly: "I don't agree with the people who think that we have to go out and shed a little blood to prove we're virile men. This is too serious a business for that kind of thinking; and in regard to Cuba, my feeling was not only that, but also that it was illegal for us to do it, and we cannot go into the business of violating treaties. We're not that kind of country. And then behind that all lies a very personal and human feeling — that I don't think old men ought to promote wars for young men to fight. I don't like warlike old men. I think it's their business to try as best they can, by whatever wisdom they can find, to avert what would be an absolutely irreparable calamity for the world."

During that interview Lippmann muted his criticism of Kennedy, blaming the Bay of Pigs on the President's reluctance to overrule those, like the CIA planners and the chiefs of staff, who should have given him better advice. "I think that he's a man who can learn," Lippmann said. What bothered him more than the Cuban debacle, which he thought a one-shot mistake not likely to be repeated, was Kennedy's failure to mobilize public support for his legislative programs. All his life Lippmann had believed that great leaders must be great educators of their people. Although Kennedy, he had written, had "very great gifts of precise analysis and judgment . . . all the makings of a great President," to achieve real greatness he had to be "not only executive, organizer, politician and popular leader," but also a "popular teacher." Instead of inspiring the people to a sense of urgency and offering them direction, Kennedy was simply carrying on where Ike had left off. "It's like the Eisenhower administration thirty years younger," Lippmann complained, in what must have seemed the unkindest cut of all to muscle-flexing Kennedyites.[12]

Lippmann was not pulling out; but he was giving warning.

◄ 41 ►

Mythmaking

I am glad of [the Kennedy] legend, and I think that it contains that part of the truth which is most worth having.

— In the *Providence Evening Bulletin*,
November 22, 1967

ALTHOUGH Lippmann was growing a bit disillusioned, his relations with the White House remained cordial. He was in constant touch with Bundy and Schlesinger, and at the end of May lunched at the White House with the President to talk over Kennedy's forthcoming trip to Europe for conferences with Khrushchev and De Gaulle. Lippmann's advice was tactical and to the point. He told Kennedy that he could get along with De Gaulle so long as he treated France with respect, and with Khrushchev by being self-confident, and, above all, patient.

Only a few weeks earlier in his column Lippmann had warned Kennedy that he faced a series of "inglorious and unpopular rearguard actions." In confronting these tasks, Kennedy, he said, could find the answer to the question he had posed in his inaugural address. "What we can do for our country," Lippmann suggested, "is first of all to give up being too proud to go through that truly agonizing reappraisal which is needed so that we can see the realities."

That afternoon at the White House he told Kennedy he would have to make some hard compromises. In Europe he would probably have to extend *de facto* recognition to East Germany in order to defuse the dangerous Berlin issue. In Vietnam and Laos, where the United States was getting bogged down in a war against local insurgents, he would have to accept a general neutralization of Southeast Asia. Kennedy listened attentively, but spoke little and gave no hint of his own feelings. "The President was a man who understood everything very quickly," Lippmann later said, "but he was never a man to commit himself. He never said, 'I agree.' He always left an escape hatch." [1]

Kennedy went to Vienna the first week in June, still smarting from his embarrassment at the Bay of Pigs and feeling defensive. Rather than negotiating slowly, as Lippmann had advised, he tried to rush through the agenda in two days. Khrushchev was in no mood to be pushed. While agreeing to a truce in Laos, the Soviet leader remained committed to what he called "wars of national liberation" — that is, support for insurrectionary movements in developing countries — and to a new status for West Berlin. He had, he complained, waited long enough to resolve the German issue. If he did not get legal recognition of East Germany within six months, he would turn over the access routes into West Berlin to the East Germans.

Kennedy saw this as a test of will, and shortly after his return from Vienna announced a dramatic military buildup, including a fallout-shelter program. Tension mounted during the summer, until on August 12, 1961, the Soviets sealed off East Berlin and a few days later built a wall separating the two parts of the city. This stanched the exodus of East German workers to the West, but intensified the political crisis. Khrushchev then broke the three-year moratorium on nuclear testing in the atmosphere, and Kennedy followed suit. In October the East Germans began slowing Western traffic into West Berlin, while at the Wall, Soviet and American tanks maneuvered within a hundred yards of one another. War seemed very near.

Lippmann, in a search for a compromise, suggested that the United States negotiate a new accord with the Soviets to regulate the status of West Berlin. Max Ascoli, the hard-line editor of the political biweekly *Reporter,* retorted by accusing Lippmann of being a "negotiation-monger."[2] Few seemed interested in following Lippmann's suggestion. Then, at the point where the two powers appeared to have locked themselves into a showdown, Khrushchev suddenly withdrew his six-month deadline. Another Berlin crisis had been navigated, but nothing had been resolved. Tension remained high.

One lesson American strategists drew from the crisis was that the West had to speak in a single voice, both politically and militarily. This meant that the United States had to retain exclusive control over NATO's nuclear forces. However reasonable this appeared from an American point of view, others were not entirely persuaded — particularly General de Gaulle. Ever since returning to power in 1958 De Gaulle had insisted that the European allies — by which he meant France — should have a voice in American nuclear strategy. If Washington would not share control of the deterrent with its allies, he said, France would have no alternative but to build its own nuclear defense force. Although Lippmann did not agree with De Gaulle's conclusion, he sympathized with the reasoning, reminding his readers that this was "power politics as played by the masters of the game and we must not be pharisaical about it."[3]

On his return from a month-long tour of Europe in May 1962, Lippmann went to the Pentagon to talk with Robert McNamara. The secretary of defense pulled out a sheaf of charts and figures designed to demonstrate that it would be disastrous for the United States to share control of the deterrent. There could be only one finger on the nuclear trigger, McNamara insisted. The argument seemed reasonable to Lippmann, and he agreed to promote the administration's case. Two days later, on May 25, he laid down the official line in an address to the American Law Institute. The United States, he declared, "cannot and will not carry the enormous burden of the alliance, and face the catastrophic dangers of a thermonuclear war if, within the alliance, it has lost the initiative and the ultimate responsibilities on the issues of peace and war."[4] The administration was pleased with its new spokesman, but De Gaulle proceeded with his *force de frappe*.

The argument moved from the abstract to the urgent a few months later when rumors began circulating that the Russians were secretly building long-range-missile bases in Cuba. The White House assured Lippmann that these reports were untrue and were being spread by the Republicans merely to embarrass the administration before the upcoming midterm congressional elections. As it turned out, the Republicans were right. In October U-2 spy planes brought back photos confirming what the critics had charged: the Soviets were building launching platforms for missiles capable of hitting the United States. Kennedy secretly assembled a group of advisers to deal with the crisis.

The ExCom, as the group was known, met virtually around the clock, though its very existence was a closely guarded secret. Insiders, however, sensed that something was amiss, particularly when such highly visible men as Dean Acheson, Robert McNamara, McGeorge Bundy and Robert Kennedy disappeared in the middle of a dinner party, or dropped out of sight completely. Lippmann, who religiously made the cocktail party circuit, had not seen a high administration official for days. "You know," he told *Washington Post* editor Alfred Friendly at a party one evening, "something fishy is going on, and I think it has to do with Cuba." And if it was Cuba, that meant a major crisis. Friendly, his curiosity aroused, asked presidential press secretary Pierre Salinger if Lippmann's suspicions were true. Salinger denied that anything unusual was going on, but Kennedy was furious when he heard that the secret was seeping out.[5]

By this time the ExCom — after furious debate that covered every option from diplomatic pressure to invasion — had arrived at a consensus. On October 22, 1962, Kennedy went on television to announce that the Russians were building missile bases in Cuba. He had ordered the United States Navy to blockade the island and to search all approaching ships, including Soviet naval vessels, for offensive weapons. The Soviets must dismantle the missile bases immediately, he declared. This was an ultimatum — the first direct confrontation between the superpowers since the cold war began. Nuclear war suddenly seemed not a remote horror but an imminent possibility. The moment of reckoning would most likely come when Soviet ships reached the five-hundred-mile barrier Kennedy had drawn around Cuba.

As the dread moment approached, Lippmann came up with a compromise. Nuclear powers must not present one another with ultimatums. Face-saving formulas had to be devised. The solution, he suggested, lay in a horse trade: exchange the Soviet missile base in Cuba for an equivalent American base elsewhere. Not the U.S. naval base on Cuban soil at Guantánamo, as Adlai Stevenson had reportedly suggested, and certainly not West Berlin — but rather Turkey, "the only place where there were strategic weapons right on the frontier of the Soviet Union." This was a logical trade-off, since the American bases in Turkey had long been technologically obsolete. In fact, Kennedy had told the State Department months earlier to dismantle them, but Rusk had dallied because the Turks wanted to keep them.[6]

As soon as he finished his column suggesting the Cuba-Turkey trade, Lippmann drove over to the State Department to lunch with George Ball. He gave the under secretary advance warning of his plan. Ball did not try to dissuade him. The following day, October 25, Lippmann's column appeared. Neither side made any official reaction to his suggested trade. Then, on the twenty-sixth, Khrushchev sent Kennedy two messages. The first was conciliatory and implied that the Soviets would dismantle their Cuban bases. The second, which came through a few hours later, was harsher and raised the question of a swap: the Cuban bases for the Turkish ones. Wherever the Russians got the idea, Lippmann's suggestion buttressed their argument. Journalist John Scali, who had been enlisted by the Soviet embassy as an informal intermediary with the State Department, told the Russians: "Everything Mr. Lippmann writes does not come from the White House."[7]

In addition to proposing the swap, Lippmann had raised the issue of Kennedy's unusual negotiating tactics. Why, he asked in his column, had Kennedy not negotiated privately with the Russians before making his ultimatum public? Kennedy had seen Soviet Foreign Minister Andrei Gromyko on the eighteenth — three days after he had learned of the missile sites and four days before he went on television to announce the blockade. Why had he not confronted Gromyko with the evidence and given the Russians a chance to back down quietly? "This was to suspend diplomacy," Lippmann charged. "By confronting Mr. Gromyko privately, the President would have given Mr. Khrushchev what all wise statesmen give their adversaries — the chance to save face." The mood of the President's advisers, particularly such men as Dean Acheson, had made Lippmann anxious. "I have lived through two world wars, and in both of them, once we were engaged, we made the same tragic mistake. We suspended diplomacy when the guns began to shoot. In both wars as the result we achieved a great victory but we could not make peace. There is a mood in this country today which could easily cause us to make the same mistake again. We must in honor attempt to avoid it."[8]

Kennedy was not at all pleased by Lippmann's criticism or by his suggestion of a trade. Even though the Turkish missiles were obsolete, withdrawing them under pressure would set a bad precedent, Kennedy thought. And it might not go down well with the voters on the eve of the congressional midterm elections. Negotiations were at an impasse. Then, at the suggestion of his brother Robert, he decided to try a negotiating ploy. Ignoring Khrushchev's bellicose second message, he agreed to accept the terms of the first message, which implied a Soviet withdrawal in return for an American promise not to invade Cuba. But he coupled the offer with an ultimatum: dismantle the Cuban bases or the United States would destroy them. To make the pill more palatable he agreed that he would later withdraw the American missiles from Turkey — though he stressed that this would not be an official *quid pro quo*. In case Khrushchev should reject the deal, he secretly prepared for an air strike against Cuba for the thirtieth. "The smell of burning hung in the air," as Khrushchev memorably said in his message to Kennedy. Then on the twenty-eighth the Russians suddenly pulled back, agreeing to withdraw the missiles if the United States promised not to invade Cuba.

Kennedy had his victory, and Lippmann, who had had such doubts about the President's negotiating tactics, applauded it without reserve. Congratulating the President for having rejected the counsel of those who wanted a crusade rather than a settlement, he described Kennedy as having shown "not only the courage of a warrior, which is to take the risks that are necessary, but also the wisdom of the statesman, which is to use power with restraint."

On November 8, with the missile crisis safely surmounted, Lippmann went to the White House. There Kennedy showed him the secret messages he had exchanged with Khrushchev. The President seemed eager to have him understand that the Russians wanted to carry out their part of the bargain, but were having trouble with the Cubans, who wanted to keep the missiles. Mikoyan was in Havana trying to get Castro to go along with the deal. Kennedy seemed hopeful that the narrow escape of the missile crisis might help bring about greater cooperation between Washington and Moscow — an impression that was fortified when Lippmann met with Bundy and the new Soviet ambassador, Anatoly Dobrynin. The probable aftermath of the Cuban crisis, Lippmann told his readers, would be a Soviet attempt to work out a temporary accommodation with the West, beginning with a ban on nuclear testing.[9]

At their White House meeting Kennedy also impressed upon Lippmann the strategic lesson he had drawn from the missile crisis — that there must be absolute and undivided control over the West's nuclear deterrent. This was why, Kennedy insisted, he could never accept De Gaulle's demand for nuclear sharing. Drawing Lippmann into his confidence, Kennedy told him he could do his country a great service by helping the Europeans to realize the need for an American nuclear monopoly. Persuaded by Kennedy's reasoning, Lippmann agreed to talk about the nuclear issue later that month in Paris, where he was scheduled to give a major speech. On November 9 Lippmann lunched with Bundy at the Metropolitan Club, to talk about the speech and go over the nuclear argument. The following week he left for London on the first leg of a month-long trip.

On November 29 in Paris Lippmann stood before a large and attentive group of journalists who had assembled to celebrate an anniversary of the founding of the European edition of the *New York Herald Tribune*. Discussing the missile crisis, Lippmann attributed Kennedy's success to his "power to achieve a limited objective" and his "wisdom to narrow his objective to what he had the power to achieve." Here, in effect, was the classic example of Lippmann's long-standing dictum about bringing power and commitments into line. The administration had not been able to consult the European allies during the missile crisis, he explained, because surprise and spot decisions were crucial. Had the Russians been alerted before the American naval quarantine was fully in effect, they might have seized the initiative. The American journalists seemed persuaded, the Europeans not. Careful listeners might have noted that the explanation contradicted Lippmann's earlier criticism that Kennedy had suspended diplomacy by imposing the blockade before trying to negotiate with the Russians.

The Cuban confrontation demonstrated, Lippmann argued in his role as spokesman for the administration's nuclear strategy, that "the command of nuclear power to balance Soviet nuclear power cannot be divided or shared." To illustrate the point he used one of his familiar car metaphors: while the passengers might help choose the destination, "once the road is chosen . . . there can be only one driver at the wheel." European papers prominently featured Lippmann's speech as an explanation of American strategy, but it did not assuage the anxieties many of them felt about the nuclear "abdication" of Europe. Lippmann, for his part, had no qualms about the role he had played as the Kennedy administration's messenger. "My speech was as conscious an attempt as I've ever made in anything to explain the American official view," he later admitted privately. "Although I agreed with it, I took care to see that I wasn't off base, because it was a kind of official occasion where I couldn't afford just to speak my own views." Why he thought a journalist should allow himself to serve as a government emissary he did not explain.[10]

Although he had served as salesman for the administration's nuclear strategy, Lippmann nonetheless sympathized with De Gaulle's efforts to gain a greater voice for France within the alliance and more independence for Europe. Even when he disagreed with De Gaulle, he tried to understand the general's reasoning, rather than merely to dismiss it as capricious or vindictive. When, for example, De Gaulle vetoed Britain's bid for entry into the Common Market in January 1963 on the grounds that Britain was not yet ready to follow a "European" foreign policy, Lippmann — despite his own disapproval of the veto — was one of the few American commentators to take De Gaulle's objections seriously. "We are not dealing with a wicked man who can or should be slapped down," he told the administration, but with a "prophetic man who is acting as if the future . . . has already arrived." The "new reality" was that Western Europe had "outgrown the dependence upon America which began with the First World War" and would no longer accept American "leadership and dominance" in European affairs. Both Lippmann and De Gaulle, as it turned out, were premature in their supposition that Europe had outgrown its dependence on America.[11]

If during the eight years of Eisenhower Lippmann was never once invited to the White House, under Kennedy he seemed a regular fixture. He saw the President every few weeks, either at a private lunch, with Bundy or Schlesinger in attendance, or at a formal gala, where he was one of the stars invited to impress visiting heads of state. Even at these state occasions he and Kennedy invariably found a few moments for a private chat. Once when Arthur Schlesinger suggested that Kennedy invite Lippmann to some minor ceremonial event, the President replied, "No, we're doing so well with him, let's not spoil it."

Kennedy knew how to flatter journalists and use the press to his own advantage. Few Presidents had ever had a more adoring press corps. In Washington Kennedy particularly benefited from his close personal relations with Philip Graham, publisher of the *Post*. Lippmann, too, was close to Graham, and had long had ties with the *Post*, first with Eugene Meyer, the financier who bought the paper in the 1930s, then with editorial-page director Herbert Elliston. Since Meyer's son, Eugene III, decided to pursue a career in medicine rather than in journalism, Graham — who had married their attractive daughter Katharine — inherited direction of the paper. A charming, energetic, troubled man, Philip Graham was determined to turn the *Post* into an international paper to rival the *New York Times*. As part of this effort he had tried to buy the *Herald Tribune*'s news service, but had been turned down. Undeterred, Graham decided that he would start his own.

Lippmann played tennis regularly with Phil and Kay Graham, and frequently lunched with Phil at the Metropolitan Club. During one of these lunches, in late May 1962, they were talking shop, and Lippmann happened to mention that his current contract with the *Herald Tribune* was about to expire and that it was time to draw up a new one. Graham became excited. Here was a chance to strike at the *Trib* and to gain America's star columnist for his own news service. In a wild burst of enthusiasm Graham proposed an extraordinary deal. If Lippmann would sign a ten-year contract with the *Post*, Graham would guarantee him a million dollars. He need write only two columns a week for eight months a year, plus sixteen articles a year for *Newsweek* — which Graham had recently bought and wanted to make into a real rival of *Time*. Under the proposed contract Lippmann would get a flat salary of seventy thousand dollars a year, plus 90 percent of syndication revenues (as against thirty-five thousand dollars and 50 percent from the *Trib*) for additional columns. The *Post* would also throw in a New York apartment, two secretaries, a research assistant, an AP news ticker, office expenses, a limousine to ferry Lippmann around New York, and all his travel costs. As a further sweetener for a man then seventy-three years old, Graham offered to continue paying Lippmann — even if he cut down the number of his columns or stopped writing altogether — fifty thousand dollars a year, plus another twenty thousand dollars for expenses, for ten years. And on his death the *Post* would pay his widow twenty-five thousand dollars a year for ten years.

This was too much to turn down. Lippmann had long been restless at the *Trib*. He had been with the paper ever since he launched his column in 1931 and vaguely felt it was not doing quite right by him. Under the Reids he had felt some sense of loyalty to the *Trib*, but they had sold the paper to John Hay Whitney in 1957. Lippmann had stayed on with the same contract, annually earning between sixty-five and seventy-five thousand dollars in combined salary and syndication fees — not bad, but considerably less than such columnists as Walter Winchell and David Lawrence were making. The *Trib* had made a lot of money from T&T over the past thirty-one years, Lippmann decided, and he owed the new owner nothing. He would accept Graham's offer.

He instructed his New York lawyer, Norris Darrell — a Sullivan and Cromwell partner who was Learned Hand's son-in-law — to draw up the contract. Graham was elated. Pleased with himself and gloating a bit, he insisted that he, rather than Lippmann, be the one to break the news to Jock Whitney. He would rub it in. Lippmann, who did not like to be the bearer of bad tidings, was delighted to be relieved of that task.

As pleased as he was to have Lippmann as the star of the *Post*'s new syndicate, Graham was even happier to have snagged him for *Newsweek*. This was the lure, he believed, that could break *Time*'s stranglehold on the weekly newsmagazine market. He may have been right. The January 21, 1963, issue containing Lippmann's inaugural column and featuring Kennedy on the cover outsold the January issues of 1962 on newsstands by 40 percent. From that point on *Newsweek*'s circulation climbed steadily until it did rival that of *Time*.

When he first started writing for *Newsweek* Lippmann feared he would be too confined by the format of a full magazine page. He was not used to a rigidly fixed number of words. The T&T column, while usually about eight hundred words, sometimes ran a few hundred words shorter or longer. Midway through the first year he was still uneasy and asked the magazine's editor, Osborne Elliott, if there was some way to do pieces shorter or longer than a page. "I find that the articles which I have to pad out are verbose, and those which I have to cut are lifeless," he complained. "I'm so used to writing without worrying about the exact length that it cramps my style to be worrying about the target." [12] Eventually he got used to the format, although the *Newsweek* pieces tended to be mostly elaborations of his T&T columns.

The acquisition of Lippmann was a coup for Graham, but the expansion of his publishing empire made him even more manic-depressive. A man fascinated with power, Graham was emotionally fragile, given to bouts of drinking, sudden euphoria, and morbid depression. As his company grew, so did his emotional strain. He was hospitalized several times, and in August 1963 shot himself.

By the time of Graham's suicide some of the sheen had worn off the New Frontier. The great missile-crisis victory had paved the way for the nuclear test-ban treaty, which seemed a significant step forward in U.S.-Soviet relations. But the Berlin crisis lingered on, De Gaulle was becoming increasingly obdurate, and over it all hung the troublesome specter of "wars of national liberation" and the increasing turmoil in Vietnam. At home the picture was no more reassuring. On Capitol Hill a recalcitrant Congress was sabotaging Kennedy's domestic program. Civil rights, federal aid to education, tax reform were all paralyzed by a coalition of Republicans and anti-administration southern Democrats.

Lippmann blamed much of the domestic impasse on Kennedy. Elected by a minuscule majority, the President had failed to convert the country by persuasion. Although personally popular, Kennedy had "not yet won over the minds of the people," Lippmann wrote, ". . . because he has not yet conquered their hearts by opening his own." Kennedy, he explained in his May 1963 television interview, "does not ever want to force measures, as some leaders do. He's one of the boys." Politically cautious to a fault, he could not push his programs through Congress or persuade the people of their importance. "One of his two or three serious weaknesses as a public leader,'' Lippmann elaborated, ''is that he does not want to be unpopular anywhere — anywhere — with anyone; and I think that a public leader, at times, has to get into struggles where somebody gets a bloody nose, and Kennedy doesn't want that ever.''[13]

Kennedy's eye seemed to be fixed far away, halfway around the world in Indochina. He had narrowly avoided a full-scale war in Laos, and now was on the verge of making a massive American commitment to the Diem regime in Vietnam. Kennedy had been one of Ngo Dinh Diem's supporters since the early 1950s when the Catholic mandarin was tapped by John Foster Dulles as the ''free world's'' man in Vietnam. Kennedy, a founding member of the pro-Diem ''American Friends of Vietnam,'' had in 1956 declared as senator that Vietnam was the ''keystone to the arch, the finger in the dike,'' against the spread of communism. Should Vietnam fall to communism, he had warned, ''our prestige in Asia will sink to a new low.'' Thus did he link America's prestige to Diem's fate.

On entering the White House Kennedy moved to prop up Diem by dispatching a contingent of American ''special forces'' to Vietnam. At the suggestion of his academic advisers he also instituted a ''strategic hamlet'' program, which was supposed to make Vietnamese peasants secure from the rebels by herding them into fortified stockades. But the hamlet program, bitterly resented by the peasants, merely produced more recruits for the communist-led rebels. By 1963 Vietnam was in a state of chaos as the Buddhists rioted against the Catholic-dominated Diem regime. Kennedy stepped up American aid and sent fifteen thousand U.S. ''advisers'' to Vietnam. By September even he began having doubts. ''In the final analysis it is their war,'' Kennedy said in a television interview. ''They are the ones who have to win it or lose it.'' Yet he added significantly: ''I don't agree with those who say we should withdraw. That would be a mistake.'' In other words, he did not want to turn it into an American war, but neither was he willing to let the communists win. Like his key advisers, he was obsessed with the need to prove that anti-Western ''wars of national liberation'' must not succeed.

Commenting on Kennedy's statement in his column, Lippmann pointed out that the only way to cut off communist supply lines would be to bomb, perhaps even to occupy, North Vietnam — an action likely to bring China into the war. ''The price of a military victory in the Vietnamese war is higher than American vital interests can justify,'' he insisted. Assuming, like many people in the administration, that a communist victory in Vietnam would lead to Chinese domination of the area, he argued that the best way to keep Indochina out of Peking's hands was to join with other countries in seeking, as General de Gaulle had urged, a ''reunited, independent and neutral Vietnam.''[14]

Yet Lippmann, like Kennedy, was against withdrawal, or even dumping Diem in favor of a neutralist. "While I have always thought it was a mistake to become engaged in Southeast Asia," he wrote in September 1963, "while it is evident that we have made many mistakes in dealing with Diem, we must, I believe, stay with him and his family for the indefinite future." The United States should wait, he counseled, until the rift between North Vietnam and China became wider. "If North Vietnam ever becomes, like Yugoslavia, no longer the satellite and agent of a great communist power, there will be opened up possibilities of a negotiated settlement in Southeast Asia."[15] But the administration was not interested in a negotiated settlement, and indeed feared that Diem and his family might work out a secret deal with the North. On November 1 Ngo Dinh Diem was killed by his own generals — with a wink, if not open approval, from the U.S. embassy. The last symbol of political legitimacy in South Vietnam had been removed; the Americans would now take over.

Three weeks later, on November 22, Lippmann went, as usual, to the Metropolitan Club for lunch. As he and his colleague Marquis Childs were finishing their meal a waiter came over and told them that the President had just been shot in Dallas. They rushed downstairs, where they ran into Alfred Friendly, and together the three men hurried over to the *Washington Post*. The scene was chaotic: television and radios blaring, men gesticulating and shouting, women sobbing. Distracted by the noise and confusion, Lippmann went into the street and hailed a taxi. As the cab was inching through traffic up Connecticut Avenue, he heard over the radio that Kennedy was dead.

On arriving at Woodley Road Lippmann raced inside, telling Helen and Elizabeth Farmer that they must be calm. They insisted that they were calm, but he was so agitated that he seemed not to hear them. For hours he paced through the halls, glancing disconsolately at the television set, and fearful that some even more terrible tragedy might befall the nation.

Lippmann wrote no eulogy for John Kennedy. Although he was in a state of shock for days, he never publicly revealed his anxiety. His first column after the assassination was not the usual hymn of praise to the fallen leader, but a plea for the nation to purge its "hatred and venom," and to put its hopes in the "healing arts" of Lyndon Johnson. Although he had never been a particular admirer of Johnson, had in fact considered the Texan crude and rather ruthless, he was preoccupied by the need for calm and continuity.

During the terrible weeks that followed Kennedy's murder, Lippmann did not dwell on the slain President's virtues, but on the tasks that lay ahead. He felt that he must help combat the confusion and fear lest the nation succumb to anarchy and panic. When the Warren Commission later reported that Lee Harvey Oswald had acted alone in assassinating Kennedy, Lippmann supported its conclusions, stating there was "no ground on which any contemporary man, here or abroad, should question the verdict." Later, as suspicion of a conspiracy mounted, he agreed that it might be wise to reopen the case, but questioned whether the doubts would be resolved, and maintained that "we must expect to live for a long time with questions that will not be answered conclusively." While he refrained from commenting publicly in the absence of persuasive new evidence, he privately voiced his suspicion that there might have been a conspiracy.[16]

Lippmann never shared the feeling of irredeemable loss so many felt on Kennedy's death. Nor did he look back on Kennedy with sentimentality or nostalgia. "I have always seen him with his warts as well as with his best qualities," he said privately less than a year later. "I have never been able to get over the fact that on the most critical moral issue which developed between the World War and his own accession to the Presidency — namely the struggle with McCarthyism — he avoided the issue, which is perhaps a gentle and charitable way of putting it." But he admitted that Kennedy had shown "great qualities" during his last year, particularly when he called for a relaxation of tension with the Russians.

In a critical review of William Manchester's mythologizing biography of Kennedy, he wrote that "in prosaic fact" Kennedy's conduct of foreign relations was "quite fumbling" until a few months before he died, and in domestic affairs his reputation rested "not on his realistic accomplishments, for they were few and he was in deadlock with Congress, but on the right choices he made occasionally." On balance the Kennedy administration was a "very mixed collection of errors and false starts and brilliant illuminations of the future," he wrote on the fourth anniversary of the assassination. Yet as the Kennedy legend grew, it affected Lippmann, just as it did a public that yearned for an unstained hero. A "passionate multitude" all over the world believed Kennedy to have been the "herald of better things in dangerous and difficult times." This, Lippmann confessed, had given him a new respect for the mythmaking process. "I am glad of that legend, and I think that it contains that part of the truth which is most worth having. This is the conviction, for which he set the example, that a new age has begun and that men can become the masters of their fate."[17]

In the Kennedy myth Lippmann glimpsed the means by which another leader could redeem the failings of Kennedy the President.

◄ 42 ►

"A Man for This Season"

President Johnson is by instinct, temperament, conviction and experience, a man for this season.

— "Today and Tomorrow," November 3, 1964

No one during those weeks after the assassination read Lippmann's
plea for faith in the new President with greater attention than did
Lyndon Johnson. Inheriting an office he had given up hope of ever holding, surrounded by a staff that considered him a usurper, Johnson was
grateful for Lippmann's show of support.

On December 1, a few days after Kennedy had been buried and the
foreign leaders had departed, Johnson telephoned Lippmann and asked
if he could come over for a chat. Half an hour later, as darkness was
settling over the city, a cortege of black limousines pulled into the
driveway at Woodley Road. The President, flanked by his guards, rang
the doorbell. "Only Helen, he and I were there," Lippmann recalled.
"He was very affectionate to Helen, humble himself, much less boister-
ous, much more likable than I'd known him before, rather overwhelmed
with the bigness of the thing that had happened to him. He wasn't at all
frightened. I got the impression that he wanted help very much. He listened very carefully, which was not characteristic of Johnson. He
seemed to have no strong opinions of his own. He was quite humble."[1]

If humility was not normally one of Johnson's qualities, flattery was.
Wooing the influential was part of his stock-in-trade. As Senate majority
leader he had sent Lippmann notes that would have made him blush had
he thought them sincere. It was Senator Fulbright who first brought the
two men together in January 1957. The small dinner party at the Fulbrights' home had not been an unalloyed success. Johnson hid his nervousness by being boastful, Lippmann withdrew before the overwhelming spectacle of LBJ in action. Over the next few years they met several
times, the most memorable for Lippmann being a chaotic lunch on Capitol Hill in February 1959 when Johnson abandoned his guests — Lipp-

mann, Fulbright, Eugene McCarthy, Frank Church and Gale McGee — for nonstop phone calls and consultations with his aides. Yet Lippmann, unlike most northern liberals, thought that Kennedy had made a good choice in selecting Johnson for vice-president. "More than any other man in public life, more than any politician since the Civil War, he has on the race problem been the most effective mediator between the North and the South," Lippmann wrote after the 1960 Democratic convention.[2]

For years Johnson had been trying to get Lippmann to visit him at his ranch near Austin. Lippmann had long been curious about Texas, and although he had known a good many Texas politicians in his time, had never seen them on their home ground. But it was not politicians he wanted to see so much as the cattle barons, the oil millionaires and the petrochemical magnates. Late in 1961 he asked George McGhee, a native Texan who was a friend of Johnson and then an under secretary of state, to help him set up an itinerary. McGhee contacted the moguls, and Johnson set up a visit to the LBJ Ranch.

On February 14, 1962, Lippmann set off for a concentrated dose of Texas. Traveling without Helen, who had opted for the calmer pleasures of Mima Porter's ranch in California, he flew first to Dallas. There he was met by department store owner Stanley Marcus, who took him home for a lavish dinner party. The next day he gave two speeches — one to businessmen at the Republic National Bank, another to academics at Southern Methodist University. George Brown, the multimillionaire contractor, then took him off to Houston in his private plane, swooping low over the petrochemical complex and the port of Galveston so that Lippmann could get a good look. That afternoon he saw his old friend Will Clayton, and that evening was taken by William Hobby of the *Houston Post* to a dinner in his honor at the Bayou Club.

The next morning the obliging George Brown picked him up and flew him over to Austin. There he had planned to have lunch with his friends Creekmore and Adele Fath before going on to the LBJ Ranch. Lyndon Johnson, however, had other ideas, and totally unknown to Lippmann had arranged for a gargantuan stag luncheon in his honor that same day in Austin. Jack Valenti, LBJ's right-hand man, told the Faths that they would just have to cancel the little lunch they had planned at their home, to which they had invited a small group of Texas writers and intellectuals.

When Lippmann arrived in Austin late that morning, the Faths informed him of LBJ's plans and asked whether he would have lunch with them and the writers, or with two hundred bankers and politicians. "I told you I was going to have lunch with you, and I'm damned well going to," Lippmann replied. "Lyndon isn't king yet." The bankers ate with each other, LBJ stayed at the ranch, and Lippmann dined with the

Faths. He had told them he would stay until four, when LBJ had promised to send around a car to take him to the ranch. But at two o'clock, with everyone still at the table, Jack Valenti rang the doorbell and said he was ready to take Lippmann to the ranch. Lippmann replied that he was not ready to leave, and returned to his hosts and their guests. Valenti retired to the car, where he waited until four o'clock.[3]

The trip to the ranch at Stonewall took about forty minutes. As they pulled into the entry road Johnson, who was waiting there, hopped out of his car and enveloped Lippmann in one of his smothering handshake-embraces. Installing his guest in the front seat of his mammoth Lincoln Continental and Lady Bird and her secretary, Liz Carpenter, in the back, LBJ took the wheel and zoomed off in a cloud of pebbles and dust. While they were churning up the ranch roads at ninety miles an hour, Liz Carpenter busied herself at the portable bar in the backseat. "Now I think I'll just have myself a little whiskey and soda," Johnson said, screeching to a halt. Lippmann, in the spirit of the occasion, had one too. While they were sitting with their drinks, Johnson decided to liven things up a bit by pressing a horn that emitted a long, moaning sound. In a few moments a herd of cattle gathered around the car, mooing glumly at the passengers. Lippmann was delighted; it was his idea of a perfect introduction to Texas. Safely back at the ranch house they watched the cowhands, had dinner with Governor Price Daniel, and the next day, after a poolside lunch serenaded by mariachis in sombreros, LBJ and Lady Bird took Lippmann to Dallas in their plane.

While some northerners ridiculed Johnson's crudeness and exaggerated Texas mannerisms, Lippmann saw a subtle and cunning mind beneath the braggadocio. Johnson, who seemed vulnerable and insecure in the lingering shadow of Kennedy, was grateful for this sympathy and eager for Lippmann's support. He besieged the Lippmanns with invitations to dinner as though they were old friends. One afternoon in March 1964, just after Helen and Walter had returned home after walking the poodles, Johnson called to invite them to dinner that night with the Fulbrights and the McNamaras. At the table Johnson was nervous and full of complaints. Kennedy, he said, had left him with a mess in Congress and a crisis in Vietnam. After dinner he took Walter and Helen by the arm. "Come here, I want to show you something," he said. Upstairs in the presidential bedroom he pointed to a plaque affixed to the mantelpiece: "In this bedroom slept John F. Kennedy, the President of the United States, and his wife Jacqueline," with the dates inscribed. It had, Johnson said, been put there just before he moved in. To his mind it symbolized how the Kennedyites regarded him as a usurper of the office they thought belonged to them.

LBJ had some reason for his touchiness. JFK's entourage resented the fact that Kennedy's "special grace" had been replaced by Johnson's crude folksiness. They called him, with no hint of affection, "Ol' Corn Pone." With Bobby as the heir presumptive, Jacqueline as the dowager queen, and the palace guard of Harvard academics and Irish Mafiosi, they formed a kind of government-in-exile. Johnson, who had always been overimpressed by the academic credentials of Kennedy's crew, felt they viewed his administration as merely an interregnum between Kennedy dynasties. This feeling was strengthened that spring when, at a party marking Jacqueline Kennedy's first social appearance since the assassination, he believed that he was being snubbed. Embarrassed and resentful, he left the party early and asked Kenneth O'Donnell to come back with him to the White House for a drink. "No matter what they think, I am still President of the United States," he told Kennedy's former aide. "But I didn't want it this way."

Johnson found a sympathetic listener in Lippmann. The night after being shown the President's bedroom he wrote a column criticizing those nameless persons who were "speculating for their own advancement on the restoration of the Kennedy power." Warning that the Kennedy legend was a "great temptation to designing men," he urged Bobby, then still attorney general, to dissociate himself from the "organized attempt to usurp" Johnson's right to choose his 1964 running mate. The Kennedyites seemed to consider it, he said, "a kind of disloyalty to say that the King is dead, long live the King, and to go on as if the unspeakable had not happened." He reminded them that only Johnson could now turn the promises of the New Frontier into a reality: "What John F. Kennedy started will be measured in the cold calculus of history not by intentions, but by the outcome. That outcome is now the business of the Johnson administration." Nothing he could have written would have made Johnson more grateful.[4]

In May 1964, while in London on a three-week European trip, Lippmann attended a dinner party where one of the guests made a snide reference to Johnson's earthy style. An irritated Lippmann launched into a spirited defense of the President that startled the guests by its intensity. To smooth the troubled waters, host Joseph C. Harsch asked facetiously, "Isn't he called 'Ol' Corn Pone'?" "Not by me!" Lippmann bristled indignantly.

Johnson gave Lippmann, along with a handful of other favored journalists, the famous treatment: telephone calls for advice, birthday gifts, private lunches at the White House, invitations to state dinners. Once, during that honeymoon spring of 1964, Johnson summoned Lippmann to the White House for a chat. On arriving he found a chaotic scene: reporters, photographers, and cabinet officials gesticulating wildly, trade-union leaders and businessmen congratulating each other, and a puzzled contingent from the National Security Council that had come for a meeting. Above them all loomed the grinning figure of Johnson. He had just brought management and labor together to avert a nationwide rail strike, and was making the most of it before going on television to announce his victory. Suddenly he spotted Lippmann in the crowd, rushed over to put his arm around him, and announced: "This man here is the greatest journalist in the world, and he's a friend of mine!"

So it went during Johnson's first year and a half in office: bear hugs from the President, impromptu invitations to dinner with Lady Bird and the girls, regular briefings by Bundy, earnest requests for advice. Johnson was a master at such treatment, and Lippmann, even though he had had enough experience with Presidents to be wary of it, could not help enjoying such attention. He admired Johnson's powerful will, even while recognizing that it was harnessed to a drive for domination that suffocated his subordinates.

He tried to point this out to Adlai Stevenson shortly after LBJ entered the White House. Stevenson had come around to Woodley Road to express the hope that now at last, with a new President, he would be named secretary of state. Lippmann gently tried to tell him that Johnson preferred to keep Rusk, who was colorless, but also no rival. He suggested that Stevenson go to London as the American ambassador.

"Oh, Walter, I couldn't do that," replied Stevenson, who had had a bruising experience as ambassador to the United Nations. "I'm tired of being an errand boy."

"Adlai," Lippmann responded with weary patience, "if you are Lyndon Johnson's secretary of state, you'll be an errand boy."

Just as he warned Stevenson of the perils of working for a powerful man like Johnson, so he warned his colleagues of the dangers of drawing too close to public figures. "There are certain rules of hygiene in the relationship between a newspaper correspondent and high officials — people in authority — which are very important and which one has to observe," he said in his April 1964 television interview. "Newspapermen cannot be the cronies of great men. Once a man, even if you have known him more or less as a crony for years, becomes something like a governor — much less a President — it's all over. You can't call him by his first name anymore. I've known several Presidents whom I knew by their first names long before they were President, and I would never think of calling them by them when they got into the White House. I think it is advantageous for the President to be able to talk to somebody who won't exploit him, or betray him, or [to whom he can] talk his mind, and it's certainly an advantage to the correspondent to know what's really going on so he won't make a fool of himself. But there always has to be a certain distance between high public officials and newspapermen. I wouldn't say a wall or a fence, but an air space, that's very necessary."[5] The warning was well taken, but Lippmann was not applying it to himself. By the spring of 1964 the "air space" between him and Johnson was getting dangerously thin.

During his spring trip to Europe, Lippmann had spent a week in Paris talking to French officials, including Premier Georges Pompidou and Foreign Minister Couve de Murville, about the deteriorating situation in Indochina. This time he did not see De Gaulle, who was in the hospital. The general had recently incurred the wrath of the Johnson administration for having urged that Vietnam and all Southeast Asia be neutralized. Only in this way, he maintained, could the West hope to retain influence in the area, since it was clear that the Americans, like the French, could never win a military victory in Vietnam. Lippmann accepted De Gaulle's argument, but feared that no one in the administration was listening. Johnson, under the influence of such advisers as Walt Rostow and Maxwell Taylor, was pushing toward a military solution — including more American troops and the bombing of North Vietnam.

On May 19, a few days after his return from Europe, Lippmann went to the White House to see Bundy. The President's national security adviser seemed in a belligerent mood. "Well, what's the French plan?" he said as soon as Lippmann walked in the door. "I can't seem to find out, and you presumably know what it is, so tell me." Taken aback, Lippmann replied that he did not answer questions posed in such a tone, and that Bundy was clearly not in a frame of mind to listen to an explanation anyway. Bundy said he had not meant to hector Lippmann, but continued to press him. For a while they talked about Germany, where Lippmann had also been, and other issues, but then came back to the French position on Vietnam. Bundy charged that De Gaulle's neutralization plan was merely a formula for a communist takeover. "Mac, please don't talk in such clichés," Lippmann said. "We both know better than that." A Titoist regime in Vietnam, he told Bundy, would be better than anything the United States could reasonably hope for. Bundy said it would be terrible if Americans died in Vietnam only to see the communists come to power.

Lippmann drove back to Woodley Road tired and a bit shaken. Until then he had hoped that Johnson would name Bundy secretary of state in place of Rusk, for whom he had little regard. But now he was not so sure. The NSC and the White House had coarsened Bundy's method of analysis, he told Elizabeth Farmer. He decided that he would try to influence the President over the heads of his advisers.

The next morning Lippmann rose exceptionally early, went up to his third-floor study, and wrote a column praising De Gaulle's neutralization plan as America's best hope for escape from the Vietnam quicksands. "We are missing the main point and we are stultifying our influence when we dismiss the French policies as not really serious, as expressions of personal pique or personal vanity on the part of General de Gaulle, as inspired by 'anti-Americanism' and a wish to embarrass us," he insisted. The French believed that Russia and China were on a collision course, and that Peking, in order to stabilize its southern frontier, would accept neutrality for Southeast Asia. De Gaulle at least had a plan, while the administration had "no credible policy for winning the war or for ending it." For the time being, Lippmann said, Washington should continue limited support for Saigon, while pressing Hanoi and Peking for neutralization. Here was a possible escape hatch — if the President wanted it.[6]

Three days later, on May 23, Lippmann had a long talk with Fulbright about Vietnam and the neutralization ploy, and on the twenty-seventh he went back to the White House at Bundy's request. He arrived at the Oval Office to find Bundy, McNamara and Ball already there, conferring with the President. Johnson wanted to know how De Gaulle's neutralization plan could prevent Indochina from falling to the communists. There was no guarantee, Lippmann said, but neither was there any realistic alternative. But Johnson was leaning toward his advisers' view that a military victory was possible. The Americans were far stronger than the French, he told Lippmann, and the tide was turning against the communists. He shoved a pile of top-secret cables across the desk. Lippmann, having learned from the French and from returning American journalists that the war was going far worse than official reports indicated, was skeptical.

For two and a half hours they argued over Vietnam, without reaching any agreement other than that George Ball — already known as the administration "dove" — would go to Paris to talk with French officials. There was little to be optimistic about, yet Lippmann left the White House persuaded — or having persuaded himself — that though Johnson would like a military victory, he was reluctant to escalate the war. With perhaps more faith than cause, Lippmann thought that Johnson was leaving the door open for negotiations. "Unless I have been grossly and continuously misled," he told his readers, "our objective is to create a balance of forces which favors and supports a negotiated settlement in Southeast Asia."[7]

Lippmann went off to Maine, as usual, in mid-June and did not return to Washington until three months later. To celebrate his arrival back in the capital, Johnson ceremoniously presented him with the nation's highest civilian honor: the Presidential Medal of Freedom. A week later, on September 23, 1964, Johnson made another pointedly friendly gesture by coming to Woodley Road — bringing Lady Bird and Texas Governor John Connally in tow — to attend Lippmann's seventy-fifth birthday party. Johnson presented Lippmann with a gold-embossed red leather guest book, which he signed with a flourish, and then proceeded to bask in the attention of the assembled ambassadors, senators, journalists, socialites, and members of his own cabinet.

Johnson's visit to Lippmann's birthday party marked the high point of a honeymoon that was then in its tenth month and looked as though it might go on forever. With political wiles perfected from years in Congress, LBJ had pushed through almost all of Kennedy's stalled legislative program, including tax reduction, aid to urban transit, and the Civil Rights Act. The most sweeping action of its kind since Reconstruction, the rights bill guaranteed equal access to public accommodations, prohibited employment discrimination, and empowered the government to file school desegregation suits. Lippmann gave Johnson the applause he deserved, and was in fact so eager to see the rights bill passed that he abandoned his long-standing defense of the Senate filibuster.

Like most white Americans, Lippmann gave little thought to discrimination against blacks until it became a national emergency. In 1919 he had written a preface to Carl Sandburg's book on the Chicago race riots, describing the race problem, in the vocabulary of a good Progressive, as "really a by-product of our planless, disordered, bedraggled, drifting democracy" — one that would presumably be resolved when everyone was decently housed, employed, educated and guaranteed his civil liberties. Since permanent degradation of blacks was "unthinkable," and amalgamation considered "undesirable" in 1919, the solution seemed to lie in what he called "race parallelism." Such a relationship would give the black person "complete access to all the machinery of our common civilization," and yet allow him "to live so that no Negro need dream of a white heaven and bleached angels. Pride of race will come to the Negro when a dark skin is no longer associated with poverty, ignorance, misery, terror and insult."

Lippmann harbored no personal prejudice against blacks. Just out of Harvard he had tried in 1913 to get W. E. B. DuBois admitted into the Liberal Club, and in the early 1960s had seconded the nomination of journalist Carl Rowan for membership in Washington's Cosmos Club. He felt perfectly at ease with black people of his social class, such as Ralph Bunche of the UN, but he did not move in the social world where most black people lived. Once in the early 1960s he asked his friends Gilbert and Nancy Harrison if they knew any blacks. When they said yes, he asked, "Do you have them to your house socially?" And when they said they did, he replied, "How did you meet them?"[8]

During the twenty-six years from 1931, when Lippmann began writing his column, until 1957, when the riots over school integration in Little Rock became an international scandal, he devoted only ten columns to the segregation issue. As late as 1955 he could refer perfunctorily in one of his books to the "special conditions of the South." He was sympathetic to the filibuster — even when used by southern senators to block civil rights legislation — because he considered it a brake on transient majorities. During the 1930s he also thought it particularly useful as a check on FDR's pro–New Deal majority in Congress. He even supported a southern filibuster against a federal antilynching law in 1938. "If the spirit of democracy is to be maintained," he wrote, "a minority must never be coerced unless the reasons for coercing it are decisive and overwhelming." Lynching was apparently not an overwhelming reason.[9]

By the late 1940s he was ready to admit that the filibuster posed a barrier to civil rights, but was more concerned with blocking Truman's Senate majority. "The apparent struggle which he [Truman] has precipitated in Congress, ostensibly over civil rights for the Negroes," Lippmann wrote Berenson in March 1949, "really raises the gravest constitutional issues which have been presented in modern times. For if the Senatorial power to filibuster is destroyed, then the Senate can legislate by simple majorities, and our system, as Macaulay once said, will be all sails and no anchors." In his column the following day he explained that the rights of blacks "will in the end be made more secure, even if they are vindicated more slowly, if the cardinal principle — that minorities shall not be coerced by majorities — is conserved." As late as January 1961 he was warning that the civil rights of all Americans would be safer if within the Senate "we do not give absolute power to simple majorities." By concentrating on the legislative part of the problem he managed to ignore that the civil rights issue was precisely about the repression of a minority by the majority.[10]

Lippmann hailed the Supreme Court's 1954 *Brown* decision outlawing segregation in public schools. "We need not doubt," he wrote optimistically, "that the states will accept loyally the principle of the law." He felt that desegregation should not be pushed "more rapidly than local sentiment will accept it," and urged civil rights activists to concentrate on gaining blacks the right to vote in the South before doing battle on segregation. "A disenfranchised minority is helpless," he wrote during the 1957 civil rights debate. "Let it acquire the right to vote, and it will be listened to." To ease the path of southern desegregation he urged that it begin with the education of the black professional elite, and that integration of coeducational high schools not be pressed too rapidly.

After the Little Rock confrontation in 1957, to which he devoted half a dozen columns approving Eisenhower's dispatch of federal troops to ensure desegregation, he began to take the race issue more seriously. Characteristically, he saw it as a foreign-policy as well as a domestic problem. "The caste system in this country," he wrote at the time of Little Rock, ". . . is an enormous, indeed an almost insuperable, obstacle to our leadership in the cause of freedom and human equality."

Lippmann looked to southern liberals to resolve the race problem amicably. In June 1963, as Kennedy's civil rights bill was languishing in the Senate, he wrote pointedly that there was a "place in history waiting for the Southern senator who takes the lead in the dismantling of the remaining legalized discrimination." There was little doubt that he had Fulbright in mind, but the Arkansas senator remained silent, as did his southern colleagues.[11]

If Lippmann showed a notable lack of urgency regarding the race issue until the early 1960s, he was not alone. His relative indifference to legalized discrimination against blacks was striking only in contrast to his emphasis, particularly in *The Good Society* and *The Public Philosophy*, on the inviolability of the individual and the dignity of man. The passion he showed in the Supreme Court fight of 1937, for example, was not reflected in his writings on race until nearly a quarter-century later. In this issue, as in others, Lippmann's concern with the process of government made him lose sight of the human drama involved.

Not until the open defiance of race laws — beginning with the "freedom rides" in 1961, the confrontation in 1962 between the federal government and the governor of Mississippi over the right of a black student to enroll at the state university, the Birmingham bus boycott of 1963 and the mammoth march on Washington organized by Martin Luther King in August of that year — did Lippmann realize that equal rights could not be achieved by persuasion alone. Above all, the ugly incidents at Birmingham in 1963, when the police unleashed attack dogs against peaceful rights demonstrators, drove home to him the urgency of the problem. "The present rate of change will not be fast enough," he warned that spring. Given the "revolutionary condition" that existed, desegregation could no longer be a Negro movement "blessed by white politicians" in the North; it must become a "national movement to enforce national laws, led and directed by the national government." At Birmingham a "point of no return" had been reached by Lippmann, along with many others. "As one who has always opposed cloture except in extreme emergencies," he told his readers in July 1963, against the backdrop of fire hoses and police dogs, "I would now say that the present system is extreme . . . a government must be able to govern."[12]

Just as he had earlier revised beliefs he felt were no longer valid — disarmament, opposition to the welfare state — so he now rejected the most rigid barrier to majority rule. "Can the filibuster be justified?" he asked rhetorically in the spring of 1964 as nineteen southern senators tried to block the Civil Rights Act. His answer was clear and unqualified: "No more, it seems to me, than would a filibuster in time of war." The filibuster could be justified only as a device for "delaying and preventing a passionate majority from overriding a defenseless minority," he explained. "It cannot be justified morally as a device for preventing a majority from attempting to redress grievances which have been outlawed under the Constitution for nearly a hundred years." This was a powerful argument. It would have been even more powerful ten years earlier, had Lippmann used it then. But now he had been shaken by the spectacle of violence and the danger it posed to social stability as well as to the principles of American democracy.

A tone of urgency and even of moral fervor infused his columns as he spoke of civil rights legislation that would liberate Americans from the "shame of having to participate in an intolerable injustice." The fili-buster now became as dangerous as it had once been desirable. The congressional practice of "smothering and strangling, rather than of de-bating and voting," he wrote during the fight over the Civil Rights Act, "violates the basic principles of representative government." The defeat of the filibuster and the enactment of the rights bill in June 1964 was for Lippmann, as for so many Americans, an educational process.[13]

Civil rights had finally become an overriding moral issue. When a civil rights worker was murdered at Selma, Alabama, the following year, Lippmann declared it a "national disgrace." Unless the law-lessness at Selma were expunged by a "mighty national act of repen-tance and reparation," he maintained, Americans would no longer be able to face themselves. When riots broke out in the Watts district of Los Angeles in 1965, Lippmann, normally quick to reject any act of vi-olence, instead blamed the outbreak on America's "failure to make free men of the great mass of the descendants of the emancipated slaves."[14]

The historic civil rights bill of 1964 would never have been enacted without the moral fervor, the incessant cajoling, and the ruthless arm-twisting of Lyndon Johnson. He deserved enormous credit, and Lipp-mann gladly gave it to him. Indeed, as the 1964 elections approached, he turned to LBJ almost as to a savior. The alternative was not only uninspiring to him, but actually frightening. The Republicans, in a spasm of fundamentalism, had nominated Barry Goldwater, an engagingly atavistic rightist from Arizona. Lippmann, who had once said it would be a good idea for the Republicans to run an archconser-vative and get it out of their system, was not pleased when it oc-curred. He accused Goldwater of being a "radical reactionary," the mouthpiece of the "newly rich on the make." With a foreign policy that promised "victory" by bomb-rattling and a domestic program that would deny federal aid to the indigent, Goldwater was truly a unique candidate. "We all know of demagogues and agitators who arouse the poor against the rich," Lippmann wrote during the campaign. "But in Barry Goldwater we have a demagogue who dreams of arousing the rich against the poor."

Goldwater's appeal, however, lay not in his quaint economic policies, or in his homilies on self-reliance for the poor, but in his recognizing, in the senator's words, "a virtual despair among the many who look beyond material success to the inner meaning of their lives." Goldwater, without ever following through, and without even knowing how to, had nonetheless touched upon something that troubled many Americans and lay deeper than their ability to articulate. Lippmann ascribed this "despair" to the "fallen nature of man" rather than, as the Republicans would have it, to the machinations of Big Government. But he recognized that though Goldwater himself would disappear, the discontent and disaffection would remain.[15]

In this contest Lippmann had no problem making a decision. Lyndon Johnson, he declared on the eve of the balloting, "is by instinct, temperament, conviction and experience, a man for this season." Of the Republicans, who had declared that they offered a choice, not an echo, he responded: "It is Goldwater and Miller on the one hand, and Johnson and Humphrey on the other hand. Some choice." The voters agreed, and elected Johnson with the largest popular vote any presidential candidate had yet received, and an electoral majority of 486 to 52. Goldwater carried only his native Arizona and five die-hard segregationist states in the Deep South. The President had won a resounding vote of confidence with his campaign promises to end discrimination and poverty, keep a tight finger on the nuclear trigger, and never send American "boys" to die in Asia.[16]

A week after the election Lippmann flew to London on the first leg of a trip that took him to Paris, where he saw De Gaulle, Edgar Faure, Couve de Murville, and the new head of the French Communist party, Waldeck Rochet. Lippmann and Helen spent an evening with Charles Bohlen, who had become the American ambassador, and came away convinced that Bohlen could not do an effective job because he was so hostile to De Gaulle. Later Lippmann told Johnson that he ought to replace Bohlen with someone less antipathetic to the general. From Paris the Lippmanns flew on to Rome, where he met with Vatican diplomatic officials and with leaders of the Italian Communist party, including Luigi Longo and Giorgio Amendola.

Shortly after his return to Washington early in December Lippmann lunched separately with McGeorge Bundy and George Ball to report on his trip, and on December 19 went to the White House. Bundy and McNamara were already in the Oval Office when he arrived, along with McNamara's deputy, Cyrus Vance. The President was uncharacteristically silent, letting the others do the talking. What did De Gaulle really mean by his plan for a Europe "from the Atlantic to the Urals," Bundy wanted to know. Would the Europeans ultimately go along with the U.S. plan for a NATO nuclear navy, McNamara asked. What about the American bases in Europe? Lippmann explained that De Gaulle, despite his complaints about NATO, wanted the United States to keep its troops in Europe for at least another decade while the Europeans organized their own defense. De Gaulle, he insisted, should not be looked on as an adversary, but as an ally who sought a greater role for France and for Europe within the alliance. The general would never go along with the MLF, a plan hatched in the State Department during the Kennedy administration, which offered the Germans access to atomic weapons through a NATO nuclear fleet. This half-baked plan, Lippmann argued, was poisoning relations with France, creating a German appetite for nuclear weapons, and persuading De Gaulle that Washington sought to break up the new rapprochement between Paris and Bonn. A few weeks later Johnson shelved the MLF.

The main topic at the White House meeting that December afternoon was not Europe but Vietnam. Johnson pressed Lippmann for details of De Gaulle's neutralization plan, wanted to know how it could prevent the communist rebels from taking over the entire country. "This is a commitment I inherited," he complained. "I don't like it, but how can I pull out?" Lippmann could only repeat what De Gaulle had told him: that it would take a million Americans to pacify Vietnam, and that a lasting military victory was impossible. Unless the West pressed for neutralization now, De Gaulle maintained, all of Southeast Asia would eventually fall into China's orbit. Johnson would not commit himself, but as Lippmann left the White House that Saturday afternoon in late December, he realized that the President's advisers were pushing him hard toward a vastly expanded American involvement in Vietnam.

Yet Lippmann continued to hope that the President would resist that dangerous lure. A few weeks later he hailed Johnson's inaugural address, with its promise of a "Great Society" — LBJ's updated version of the New Deal — as an attempt to "open a new chapter in the annals of popular government." For the first time since the start of the Second World War the attention of the President was "not fixed upon the dangers abroad, but on the problems and prospects at home." The stage was set, he wrote, for a "correction of the great displacements of power" that brought the Russians into the heart of Europe and the Americans to the mainland of Asia. The role of the United States was to use its resources and brains to see that this "inevitable readjustment" would come about "decently and honorably."[17]

At the time he had every reason to assume that Lyndon Johnson was listening.

◄ 43 ►

Seduction and Betrayal

He misled me.

— On LBJ, May 21, 1967

IT began, like most seductions, with invitations and flattery, and it ended in recriminations and a feeling of betrayal.

Lippmann knew that Johnson wanted to go down in history as the true descendant of Franklin Roosevelt and the man who actually achieved the great reforms that John F. Kennedy had only promised. He encouraged Johnson in that ambition, underlining that the nation's domestic problems had been "sacrificed and grievously neglected" for a quarter of a century, and hailing the President as "a bold innovator, who is likely to succeed because he is deeply in touch with the great central mass of American sentiment and opinion." Rarely, he rejoiced a few weeks after the inauguration, had a new administration shown "such a coherent program, such insight and resourcefulness."[1]

LBJ soaked up the compliments, but he had something on his mind besides the Great Society: Vietnam. Even while he had been assuring the American people, during the election campaign, that their "boys" should not be sent to do the job of South Vietnamese "boys," he was secretly making plans to expand the war by bombing North Vietnam. The Tonkin Gulf Resolution, approved so casually by Congress in August 1964, provided the legal authorization in the form of a blank check. All the President needed was a pretext. It came soon enough, early in February 1965, when Vietnamese communist forces attacked the base at Pleiku, killing seven Americans. Within hours the United States retaliated by bombing military sites in North Vietnam.

Another barrier had been breached, although few realized its full meaning at the time. Lippmann was among those who misread it, defending the bombing as a "test of American will." Had the administration not retaliated, he explained, the Chinese would have labeled the United States a "paper tiger," thus backing up their view that Moscow's policy of "peaceful coexistence" with the capitalists was absurd. "President Johnson profoundly desires to avoid war, but his power to do that is not unlimited nor can he be counted on not to be provoked if the provocation is continual and cumulative," Lippmann warned.[2]

He supported the air strike on the grounds that LBJ, having now proved his manhood, could negotiate a settlement. He was sure that the Russians were pushing Hanoi toward a compromise — "The Russians have every interest in keeping the war from spreading," he told Elizabeth Farmer, "even though they will probably do things to reassure the North Vietnamese, like putting in missiles and the like, that simpleminded people here will find disturbing" — and was trying to nudge Johnson in the same direction. The retaliatory air strikes would put the United States in "a better bargaining position for a negotiation," he wrote a few days after Pleiku, adding that LBJ's "great predecessors, Woodrow Wilson and Franklin Roosevelt, never thought they could have a military solution without at the same time a diplomatic offensive." As he went over the column with Farmer he said to her of that comparison, "If Joe Alsop can needle the President, so can I."[3]

Six days later, on February 17, 1965, Lippmann went to the White House to talk with Bundy. That very morning he had written, in the column that would appear the following day, that it was time for the administration to avow openly that it sought a cease-fire and an international conference to end the war. It would be a "supreme folly" for the United States to become involved in an Asian land war, he wrote. "While the warhawks would rejoice when it began, the people would weep before it ended. There is no tolerable alternative except a negotiated truce, and the real problem is not whether we *should* negotiate but whether we *can*."[4] By "can" he meant it was uncertain that Hanoi and Peking, which he too casually lumped together, would agree to negotiate when they were so close to a military victory.

By suggesting it might be too late for the United States to negotiate the kind of settlement it wanted, Lippmann played into the administration's hands. Unknown to him, Pleiku was just the opening salvo of the administration's long-planned and carefully concealed "Rolling Thunder" offensive against the North. That afternoon at the White House, Bundy, giving no hint of the plan to expand the war, told Lippmann what he wanted to hear: that the President truly sought a negotiated settlement.

Lippmann had every reason to believe him. He and Bundy had long been on close terms. And Bundy was certainly in a position to know the administration's intentions, for he had been at Pleiku during the attack and had personally ordered the retaliation. On the day after his talk with Bundy, Lippmann taped his seventh — and, as it turned out, his final — TV interview. Although the war hawks were powerful, he told interviewer Eric Sevareid, "they're not found in the interior and at the top of the White House — that I feel sure of." War hawks wanted to knock out the industrial system of North Vietnam, even at the risk of Chinese intervention. "The President is not a war hawk," he insisted. Johnson's bombing policy was "strictly controlled and regulated," and was confined to the "rather empty country" just above the borderland of the seventeenth parallel. They were really "public relations jobs" more than military attacks, Lippmann explained, echoing what Bundy had told him. "I don't think they kill anybody . . . because what we bomb is wooden sheds."[5]

Even though he trustingly accepted Bundy's version of the bombing campaign, Lippmann began to suspect that his plea for negotiations was not making much of an impact. On March 1 a story appeared in the papers that Frank Church — one of the first senators to come out openly against the war — had cited Lippmann as an authority in urging a negotiated settlement. At a White House meeting for a key group of senators Johnson had, according to newspaper reports, glowered at the Idaho Democrat in his most intimidating manner and said, "Frank, the next time you want a dam in Idaho, you just go to Walter Lippmann for it."

The story hit the papers while Lippmann was in New York, where he had gone to deliver an address to the United Nations. Elizabeth Farmer phoned to tell him about the story, which she found amusing. But he took it with deadly earnestness. "I'm afraid they don't like me very much at the White House," he responded glumly. "I'm not angry about it — just sorry, sorry for the President. It shows how wrong his estimate of a man like Church is, that he thinks you can trade dams against questions of war or peace." As it turned out, LBJ had never made the remark about the dam; the journalist had heard the story secondhand and then garbled it. Johnson's only comment about Lippmann, Church told him when they met a few days later, had been respectful. Lippmann's reaction to the original story was more interesting than the story itself, for it showed, as his columns confirmed, that he was not a cynical man. Despite half a century of writing about politics, he was still shocked at the notion of trading off dams for war credits.[6]

The dam story was apocryphal, but it gave a true picture of the President's increasing impatience with the critics of his Vietnam policy. Early in March he complained publicly about the "folks who don't understand," a remark that led Lippmann to write a sorrowful column about the "self-delusion" of assuming a foreign policy was right if nobody dissented. "At the bottom of this self-delusion, if we search deeply enough, we shall find a visceral feeling that, as compared with foreigners, we are always right and never wrong," he wrote. "If therefore we are agreed among ourselves, none can withstand us because none should withstand us, and we shall and must prevail. This same visceral feeling has engendered the demand, which made a botch of the settlement of both world wars, for unconditional surrender as the only victory which Americans can accept.'' By expecting conformity, Johnson was evoking "visceral feelings" that would make the whole business unmanageable, Lippmann warned.

Among those provoking Johnson were journalists like Joseph Alsop, who questioned in his columns whether LBJ was "man enough" to stand up to the communists, and many of his own advisers, including Defense Secretary Robert McNamara, Saigon Ambassador Maxwell Taylor, counselor Walt Rostow, and Secretary of State Dean Rusk. "I watched Rusk on television last night," Lippmann told Elizabeth Farmer as he was recuperating from a light case of pneumonia. "He's a very intelligent stupid man. He doesn't examine his premises. His reasoning is based on misplaced historical analogies, like what happened in the 1930s or in World War II. He's like Joe Alsop in that respect. The trouble with Rusk is that he's been promoted one level too high. He would have made a good undersecretary."[7]

Johnson, disturbed by Lippmann's growing estrangement, invited him back to the White House on March 15 for lunch. The President showed him a great batch of diplomatic cables and intelligence reports, and read to Lippmann glowing accounts of American success against the Vietcong. "I don't understand why those people in Hanoi won't negotiate with me," he complained. Lippmann suggested that maybe the reason was that he had never indicated what kind of settlement he was willing to accept. "Your policy is all stick and no carrot, Mr. President," Lippmann explained. "You're bombing them without offering any incentive for them to stop fighting; in effect you're giving them a choice between destruction and withdrawal." A dark cloud crossed Johnson's face. He waved his hand impatiently and changed the subject abruptly, reading Lippmann the draft of a speech he was planning to give to Congress on Negro voting rights.

Johnson, who prided himself on his ability to manipulate people, realized he wasn't getting through. Once, in a state of exasperation, he said of Lippmann: "Every time I pull my chair nearer that guy, he pulls his chair further away." He meant it as a reproach. His long years in politics had told him that every man had his vulnerable point. With Lippmann he had tried flattery, but had not made much of a dent. Now he would take a different tack: he would be the puzzled executive humbly seeking advice from the wise elder. As the servants were bringing in dessert and Lady Bird rose to leave the two men alone, LBJ turned from a frenetic monologue that had wandered from Texas county politics to the state of his digestive system, and returned to the subject of Vietnam. "Now about that peace offensive you mentioned, Walter. Tell me just what it is you have in mind."

Seizing the opportunity, Lippmann explained why he believed the Pentagon's bombing campaign would never bring Hanoi to the conference table. The North Vietnamese would suffer, but they would take whatever punishment the Americans could inflict. The only way to get them to negotiate was to outline what kind of compromise settlement the United States had in mind. A bombing campaign without a sketch for a political settlement was simply a demand for unconditional surrender. The war could go on forever. Johnson thought a moment and then got Bundy on the phone. "Mac, I've got Walter Lippmann over here and he says we're not doing the right thing. Maybe he's right." Lippmann stayed on at the White House until four-thirty and returned to Woodley Road in an elated mood. "I made quite an impression on the President with the peace offensive idea," he told Farmer. "He asked me to think it over some more and said he'd come over and have a drink next week."

Two days later, at LBJ's request, Lippmann met Bundy for lunch at the Metropolitan Club. Lippmann elaborated his suggestion for a "peace offensive" — one that he had laid out for the public in the column he wrote that morning — and urged that the President make a declaration, something along the lines of Wilson's Fourteen Points. Since Bundy posed no objections, Lippmann felt that LBJ would soon make a major speech on the subject — one no less dramatic than Kennedy's 1963 speech calling for a reexamination of American attitudes toward the cold war. Lippmann left guardedly optimistic that the President could yet be turned around, if he could be lured away from those hawkish advisers who were pressing for a military victory.

Reports by independent journalists, particularly a devastating series by Richard Dudman in the *St. Louis Post-Dispatch*, made it clear that the air war was not slowing the communist advance and that the South Vietnamese were on the verge of collapse. The war was at a turning point. Johnson was under pressure to extend the bombing campaign, which had so far been a failure, to the heavily populated areas around Hanoi and Haiphong, and in addition to send as many as a third of a million American soldiers to fight the Vietcong. As a first step Johnson dispatched a contingent of marines to protect the American base at Da Nang. Lippmann stepped up his own campaign. "I think I wrote something that will get under their skins," he said to Farmer as he finished his article. "That's what I want." That is what he got. The nation, he wrote in his column, was on the brink of a vastly expanded war.

In order to rationalize, that is to sell, the wider war, we are being told by secretary McNamara and others that this war is a decisive test for the future. It will decide the future of "wars of liberation." This is a profoundly and dangerously false notion, and it shows a lamentable lack of knowledge and understanding of the revolutionary upheavals of the epoch in which we live. It assumes that revolutionary uprisings against established authorities are manufactured in Peking or in Moscow, and that they would not happen if they were not instigated, supported, and directed from one of the capitals of communism. If this were true, the revolutionary movements could be suppressed once and for all by knocking out Peking or Moscow. They little know the hydra who think that the hydra has only one head and that it can be cut off.[8]

A week later, on April 6, Lippmann got a message from Bundy that the President wanted to see him that afternoon. As far as the administration was concerned, Lippmann was getting to be a bit of a problem. He was not at all sympathetic to the effort to achieve a military victory, and indeed did not seem particularly concerned whether the communists even took over South Vietnam. While he was unlikely to be won over, there was at least, Bundy thought, some hope of neutralizing him.

To disarm criticism by Lippmann and others, Johnson had had his aides prepare a speech declaring his willingness to engage in "unconditional discussions" with Hanoi about a possible peace plan. Such discussions did not, of course, commit either side to any particular course of action. Talk was cheap. But the offer might assuage those critics who maintained that the administration was intent on a military solution. Lippmann was one of those critics whom Johnson most wanted to win over. On Bundy's advice he decided to try the personal approach.

That very day Bundy had sent the President a memo suggesting that he show Lippmann an advance draft of the speech. "A part of our purpose, after all, is to plug his guns," Bundy pointed out, "and he can tell us better than anyone to what degree we have done so." The only risk was the need to be "awfully careful that the language we finally use is not harder than what he sees, and for that reason it may be better to read to him from the speech and to slide gently past the words 'unconditional discussions.'" Bundy urged Johnson to ask Lippmann why he was pushing for a single Vietnam — unless that were just a way of letting the communists take over. Since he was advising negotiations, Lippmann should at least say what he expected to gain from them. Bundy also suggested that Johnson "make it clear to Lippmann that when we say we are ready to talk, we do not at all mean that we are ready for a cease-fire. The fact is that we expect our own military action to continue unless we see a prospect of a better situation in the South than we have now. Walter needs to understand this, and if he gets it straight from you, he is less likely to be objectionable about it." Lippmann, he pointed out, had a "useful tendency to think the President himself is right," even though he might believe the President's aides were wrong. Johnson would now try to make the most of that "tendency."[9]

Dusk was just beginning to fall as Lippmann drove his car past the security guards onto the White House grounds. An aide greeted him at the door and led him to an anteroom off the Oval Office. There he found the President sitting on a raised platform. To his left a sculptor stood, molding his bust in clay. Aides rushed in and out, bearing documents and messages. A television set flickered in the corner. Distant buzzers and telephones rang. It was the usual chaos that surrounded Lyndon Johnson.

"Ah, Walter," the President said as Lippmann entered the room. "You just make yourself comfortable on that sofa over there and we'll have a little talk." Lippmann took a seat, crossed his legs, and waited. "Walter, I'm going up to Baltimore tomorrow to give a speech," Johnson continued, "and I'm going to hold out that carrot you keep talking to me about. Now Mac here," he said, nodding toward Bundy, "is going to show you the speech, and I want to know what you think of it." Lippmann had barely got through the first page when Johnson started bellowing at him. "I'm not just going to pull up my pants and run out on Vietnam," he declared. "Don't you know the church is on fire over there and we've got to find a way out? There are four doors. Curtis LeMay wants to bomb Hanoi and Haiphong. You know how much he likes to go around bombing. Now I'm not going to do that. That's why I got him out of my government. Then there's the Wayne Morse way, which amounts to turning the place over to the communists. I'm sure as hell not going to do that. You say to negotiate, but there's nobody over there to negotiate with. So the only thing there is to do is to hang on. And that's what I'm going to do."

For an hour the President carried on his monologue. His listener shifted uneasily on the sofa. Finally he let Lippmann go off to another room to talk to Bundy about the speech. They went over the address point by point. Lippmann could not find the carrot. Johnson wanted Hanoi to lay down its arms, but offered virtually nothing in return. "This isn't going to work, Mac," Lippmann told the younger man. "It's just a disguised demand for capitulation. You've got to give the communists some incentive to negotiate." "Like what?" Bundy countered. "Like an unconditional cease-fire," Lippmann replied. Bundy thought a moment, then said he would see what he could do. For nearly an hour they argued over the feasibility of a cease-fire and of negotiations. Finally at seven-thirty Lippmann pleaded that he was exhausted and had to go home. Bundy was reluctant to let him leave. They shook hands, and Lippmann departed, optimistic that there might be a chance for a cease-fire after all.[10]

The next day, April 7, he flew with Helen to Boston for a checkup by his doctor, Maurice Fremont-Smith. Curiously impractical about the basics of life, he had never acquired a personal physician in Washington; every time he fell sick he saw a different doctor. That night at the home of the Fremont-Smiths, he listened to LBJ deliver his speech at Johns Hopkins University. There was something in it for everybody: hawks found grim allusions to the "deepening shadow of communist China" and the "wider pattern of aggressive purposes"; doves were heartened by a pledge to "use our power with restraint" and to engage in "unconditional discussions" with Hanoi. Yet the tone was uncompromising: "We will not be defeated. We will not grow tired. We will not withdraw, either openly or under the cloak of meaningless agreement."

Lippmann did not know quite what to make of it. Johnson spoke of negotiations, and had personally told him that the war had to be won on the nonmilitary side. But nowhere in the speech was there mention of a cease-fire. He thought he had persuaded Bundy of the need for that. But apparently he had failed. There was nothing but the vague call for "unconditional discussions." Although Lippmann tried to be optimistic, he suspected that the administration meant to do no more than disarm its domestic critics when it offered "discussions" without indicating what kind of settlement it had in mind. On his return to Washington he lunched with Dobrynin. The Soviet ambassador confirmed Lippmann's suspicion that Hanoi would never accept such a one-sided offer to negotiate. Right after lunch he went over to the White House to see Bundy and hash out the administration's policy. Bundy insisted that LBJ was not going to expand the bombing to North Vietnam's urban centers, but also made clear that he would not negotiate so long as Saigon remained so weak. That meant, Lippmann was convinced, that the war would go on indefinitely.

For months Lippmann had been trying to give the administration some basic foreign-policy lessons. It was folly to rush around the world trying to extinguish revolutions while neglecting America's own vital interests, he argued. What were those interests? "A primary vital interest is one in which the security and well-being of a nation are involved. Our security and well-being are not involved in Southeast Asia or Korea and never have been." Ever since the end of World War II the United States had been committed far beyond its primary vital interest and even beyond its military and political reach. "If it is said that this is isolationism, I would say yes. It is isolationism if the limitation of our power is isolationism. It is isolationism as compared with the globalism which became fashionable after the Second World War."

Having confronted head-on the accusation of isolationism, Lippmann explained that it was as "abnormal" for the United States to be in Saigon and Seoul as it was for the Russians to be in Berlin and Prague. The historical process was "like a geological phenomenon, like the subsiding of the earth and the return of the waters after a great upheaval."

The role of the United States was to see that this readjustment came to pass decently and honorably. "The time has come," he insisted in a gibe against the globalists, "to stop beating our heads against stone walls under the illusion that we have been appointed policeman to the human race." [11]

As his disillusion mounted, so his attack intensified. He refuted the administration's accusation that North Vietnam had committed aggression against the South. To the contrary, he maintained: the two Vietnams were never separate countries but only "two zones of one nation." The President was in "grave trouble because he has not taken to heart the historic fact that the role of the white man as a ruler in Asia" had ended in 1945. Bundy sent him a testy letter insisting that legally there were two Vietnams and thus the United States was not intervening in a civil war. [12]

The administration was particularly sensitive on this point, for it had defended its policy on the grounds that it had a "responsibility" to defend "freedom" in South Vietnam. This was, of course, the "world policeman" argument, one that the administration was particularly fond of evoking, and that recently had received powerful expression in a *Washington Post* editorial. The paper had long been hawkish on the war, and its editorial-page director, Russell Wiggins, had just written an editorial arguing that America was now in imperial Britain's shoes. Because of their enormous power and "responsibilities," great nations "must live in anguish," the *Post* editorialized. "No country can have great power and a quiet conscience."

While the editorial greatly pleased Johnson, it struck Lippmann as a globalist fantasy that failed to distinguish between vital interests and peripheral ones, between the protection of one's own nation and the attempt to impose its will upon smaller ones. "A mature great power will make measured and limited use of its power," he wrote in a deeply felt reply.

It will eschew the theory of a global and universal duty which not only commits it to unending wars of intervention but intoxicates its thinking with the illusion that it is a crusader for righteousness, that each war is a war to end all war.

Since in this generation we have become a great power, I am in favor of learning to behave like a great power, of getting rid of the globalism which would not only entangle us everywhere but is based on the totally vain notion that if we do not set the world in order, no matter what the price, we cannot live in the world safely. If we examine this idea thoroughly, we shall see that it is nothing but the old isolationism of our innocence in a new form. Then we thought we had to preserve our purity by withdrawal from the ugliness of great power politics. Now we sometimes talk as if we could preserve our purity only by policing the globe. But in the real world we shall have to learn to live as a great power which defends itself and makes its way among other great powers.[13]

In his dispute with the administration Lippmann took the pragmatic approach. He did not argue the morality of America's involvement in Vietnam because, with rare exceptions, he did not view foreign policy as a moral issue. For him it was a question of geopolitics and a cold calculation of national interest. Such a calculation made it obvious that the United States had no business fighting a land war on the mainland of Asia, that it could never win such a war and would suffer grievously if it foolishly persisted in an impossible objective.

Unlike some radical opponents of the war, Lippmann did not object to the application of American military power on principle. He cared only that it not be quixotic, irrational or self-defeating. Trained in the geopolitics of Mahan and Mackinder, weaned on Theodore Roosevelt's concept of American strength resting on a two-ocean navy, convinced that both economics and geography dictated that certain areas were more critical than others to America's vital interest, he could see no justification for an American land war in Asia. In his calculus Europe was vital, Latin America was in Washington's sphere of influence; the rest of the world, while of great interest, must inevitably be secondary.

While opposed to intervention on a global scale, Lippmann had no serious objection to a little backyard imperialism. When in April 1965 Johnson sent the marines to Santo Domingo to block a leftist coup against the U.S.-supported right-wing military regime, Lippmann initially gave his guarded support. LBJ decided to halt the rebellion, he wrote just after the intervention, on what seemed the "right ground," that "if the communists took over the government the result would be for all practical purposes irreversible." The United States, he assured his readers, did not want to restore the "old reactionary regime" of dictator Trujillo, but rather was devoted to a "popular democratic revolution" of the kind represented by Juan Bosch — the democratically elected former president who had been ousted by a military junta. How such an objective would be achieved by using the marines to aid Bosch's enemies he did not explain.

But Lippmann was less interested in what kind of government ruled the Dominican Republic than in establishing a political rule about intervention. How could the United States defend its action, he asked rhetorically. Not on the ground that it was a "global fire department appointed to stop communism everywhere," but on the "old-fashioned and classical diplomatic ground that the Dominican Republic lies squarely within the sphere of influence of the United States." It was, he underlined, "normal, not abnormal, for a great power to insist that within its sphere of influence no other great power shall exercise hostile military and political force." The fact that the Soviets were not involved in the Dominican coup did not trouble him. He wanted to make a political point: that spheres of influence were "fundamental in the very nature of international society" and not some evil impediment to a beatific "one world."

The implication was clear: if the United States had the "right" to keep other great powers or even their ideologies out of its sphere in the Caribbean, so the Chinese, by the same token, had the same right in Southeast Asia. Russia had no business mucking around in the Dominican Republic — but neither did the United States in Vietnam. "The acceptance of spheres of influence has been the diplomatic foundation of the detente in Europe between the Soviet Union and the West," Lippmann explained. "Eventually, it will provide the formula of coexistence between Red China and the United States." Two weeks later, after it became obvious that there had never been a "communist" danger in the Dominican Republic, Lippmann expressed his dismay that the marines had been used to "restore the power of a reactionary military dictatorship." There was little reason for him to have been surprised; but neither was the subject of overriding concern to him.[14]

Lippmann's attention was focused almost entirely on Vietnam. His analysis of the war tended to shift over the years. In the 1950s he saw it as the scene of an anticolonial struggle against the French, then as a battleground of great-power maneuvering, later as part of China's "orbit," and ultimately as an arena of a worldwide struggle against the white man's rule. But he never thought it an area of vital American interest. When the French in 1954 were on the verge of losing the war and wanted the Americans to step in, he decided it was time to cut losses. "There is a notion that it would be feasible for the United States alone to take over the war in Indochina and to win it," he wrote in May 1954 as Dulles and Nixon were pressing Eisenhower to take over the war from the virtually defeated French. "Cannot our aging juveniles realize that many of the countries, especially in Asia, will be opposed not only to their own involvement but to the war itself?" The United States should not even think of intervening without the full military and political support of its allies, he argued, knowing that no major ally would join such a costly and futile venture. "American military power which is on the sea and in the air can hold islands, can deny the use by an enemy of strategic points near the coast of the great continent. But it cannot occupy, it cannot pacify, it cannot control the mainland even in the coastal areas, much less the hinterland."[15]

Eisenhower ultimately decided not to intervene in Indochina when the British refused to go along and the Senate balked. The problem lay dormant until 1963, when Kennedy revived it by his determination to maintain an independent, anticommunist government in the southern half of

Vietnam. While Lippmann was not opposed to the effort in theory, he did not think it worth much of a price. As the costs mounted, so did his eagerness to have the United States pull out. A "mature great power" would, to paraphrase his words, spread its influence where it could do so safely and cheaply, and would also have the sense to know when the game was not worth the candle. In 1964 he thought the United States could, with Soviet help (given Moscow's fear of Peking's influence in Vietnam), negotiate its way out of the war through a face-saving formula based, as De Gaulle had suggested, on neutralization of all Southeast Asia. But with Johnson's dramatic expansion of the war in the spring of 1965 — by the end of the year there would be 190,000 American troops in Vietnam — he had become pessimistic even about that.

Yet he still tried to keep his lines open to the White House. He had been careful not to criticize Johnson personally, but rather the unnamed persons who gave him "bad advice." Early in May 1965, before setting off for a month in Europe, he lunched separately with Bundy and McNamara, and reported that the President's advisers, while "not warmongers and certainly not fascists," were nonetheless "seized with a grim determination" that the United States should continue its military action until Saigon started to win the war. There was, he wrote in mid-May, after seeing Bundy, "more agreement than one might suppose" between the administration and its critics. Both assumed eventual negotiations with the communist National Liberation Front. The question was what the military balance would be at the time of the negotiations. For his own part, Lippmann confessed, he saw no hope for victory, and suggested that the Americans withdraw to fortified enclaves along the coast, where they would practice a "benevolent neutrality" toward negotiations among the Vietnamese, who would "work out a deal themselves."[16]

This was hardly what the administration had in mind. It wanted to win the war, not achieve a "benevolent neutrality." But Johnson and Bundy also did not want to alienate Lippmann, so they kept assuring him that the administration would be willing to negotiate as soon as the military picture brightened just a little. By this time Lippmann had learned not to rely on the White House or the Pentagon for a true picture of what was really happening in Vietnam. He began paying more attention to critics of the war, spent the morning before going to lunch with McNamara listening to a radio broadcast of a university "teach-in" on American policy, and went out of his way to talk to journalists who had been to Vietnam and were skeptical of U.S. military "progress": Bernard Fall, David Halberstam of the *New York Times*, Jean Lacouture of *Le Monde*.

In Paris at the end of May Lippmann talked to Jacques Chaffard, an old Indochina hand, who complained that the American papers were censoring the articles he had written for *Le Monde* and *l'Express*, reprinting the part that seemed to support the U.S. position but leaving out his pessimistic conclusions. He also revealed that on his recent trip to Washington the two Bundy brothers had given him very different accounts of U.S. objectives. While McGeorge Bundy had told him that the United States was willing to hold discussions with the Vietcong, his brother William, a former CIA official who had become assistant secretary of state for Asian affairs, said that there could be no discussions until the United States had achieved a military victory. This, Chaffard said, would mean sending half a million Americans to fight for five years, and even then there could be no real settlement without the Vietcong. Jean Lacouture and Couve de Murville seconded Chaffard's pessimistic conclusions.

In a long interview at the quai d'Orsay the foreign minister told Lippmann that the war would go on for years, that the U.S. bombing would destroy both Vietnams, that the Americans would get tired and leave, and that eventually the country would fall into China's hands. De Gaulle was even gloomier. Over lunch at the Élysée Palace, the general, after plying Lippmann with questions about American policy, speculated whether the old anti-imperial America had now itself become an imperial power. The great question, De Gaulle said, was no longer Germany or the Soviet Union, and not yet China, but that of imperialism. From that lofty plateau Lippmann gently guided the general back toward a discussion of NATO and the gold standard.

Lippmann came back from Europe in a much more somber mood than when he had left. "I've been pulling my punches," he told Farmer. "I'm just going to have to take out after Johnson's foreign policy and show that it doesn't work." "That won't be hard," she said. "No," he replied sadly, "but it won't be pleasant either." He started jabbing harder. The Europeans, he reported, questioned the "wisdom and competence" of the administration's policies. They had not expected that Goldwater's recommendations about expanding the war, after being rejected by the voters, "would in such great measure be adopted by the victors." They were "shocked" by the expansion of the Vietnam War, the invasion of Santo Domingo, and the administration's "unlimited globalism." Among knowledgeable Europeans there was the "strong opinion that in the personal and unilateral exercise of unlimited power, the performance has been that of amateurs inexperienced in the use of power."[17] This was powerful stuff for Lippmann, for it was a direct attack on the President and his immediate entourage. By the time he and Helen went to Maine on June 16, following their annual giant mint julep party on the lawn, relations between Woodley Road and the White House had cooled distinctly.

All that summer at Southwest Harbor, as he watched the inexorable intensification of the war, he hammered away at the administration's policies, lamenting that it was too late to neutralize Southeast Asia as De Gaulle had earlier proposed, questioning the U.S. military presence on the Asian mainland, and warning of an unending war in Asia. He even unconsciously allowed a hint of racism to enter his argument when, in an effort to show that bombing would not force Hanoi to surrender, he observed that the Vietnamese "do not value their material possessions, which are few, nor even their lives, which are short and unhappy, as do the people of a country who have much to lose and much to live for." In an effort to find a way out short of "scuttle and run," which even he did not favor, he urged a U.S. withdrawal to fortified enclaves along the coast as a "basis of influence" while the Vietnamese negotiated, and an "honest and honorable" way out of the war.[18]

Like the administration itself he was never quite sure what the justification for the American intervention was supposed to be. He knew that arguments about SEATO "commitments" and the defense of "freedom" were just window dressing. Accustomed to thinking in geopolitical terms, he put more emphasis on the desire for Asian bases than the facts warranted. Privately he would complain that the Pentagon, having built the huge military complexes at Da Nang and Cam Ranh Bay, would never give them up. For this reason he liked the enclave theory: it offered a way to keep the bases while getting out of the war. Arguing in terms of spheres of influence, he overestimated the control Peking was able to exert over Hanoi. He saw the war too much through the lenses of Mahan, and not enough in terms of traditional great-power expansionism. He insisted that the United States could safely withdraw to its island bases and still remain a great air and naval power in the Pacific — an argument that was irrelevant to those who believed that American "prestige" required a victory in Vietnam.

His appeals, while eloquently, even fervently, argued, fell largely on deaf ears. The President still had the majority of Congress, the public and the press behind him. Open disagreement was confined to a few Senate mugwumps, such as Church, Fulbright, Morse, George McGovern, Gaylord Nelson and Ernest Gruening; a handful of liberal magazines; and a vociferous group of street protesters. Lippmann's home paper, the Post, remained one of the administration's most enthusiastic defenders. Katharine Graham, though a woman of ability and drive, had no strong feelings about the war, and allowed her paper's policy to be set by her pro-war editorial director, Russell Wiggins. Johnson was so grateful for the Post's support that he once told Wiggins, with typical hyperbole, that the Post's editorials were worth fifty divisions.

But by the fall of 1965 Katharine Graham was beginning to have her doubts. As an old acquaintance of Lippmann, she had turned to him for advice several times since the death of her husband. Just a few months earlier she had persuaded him to serve as intermediary with the *Post*'s managing editor, Alfred Friendly, whom she was dumping from his job in favor of Benjamin Bradlee. Lippmann was an old friend not only of Graham but of Bradlee, whom he had known since the latter was a boy. Bradlee's mother had been Helen's childhood friend at Chapin, while his father was the great football hero of Lippmann's Harvard class of 1910. Often while en route to Maine the Lippmanns stopped off to spend the night with the Bradlees at Beverly, Massachusetts. To help smooth the path for Bradlee, Lippmann agreed to try to persuade Friendly to step down voluntarily as the *Post*'s managing editor. That summer he invited Friendly up to Maine for the weekend, and over drinks on the terrace one evening casually suggested that Friendly get away from the tedious job of editing and return to the kind of foreign reporting he did so well. Friendly, realizing what was afoot, took the hint and went off to London as the *Post*'s correspondent, leaving his deputy Bradlee to take over as managing editor.

Having smoothed the transition at the top, Lippmann went to work on Graham to change the editorial page. Wiggins's pro-war editorials sounded like administration handouts, he told her; they were making the paper look ridiculous. "I persuaded her that decent people could no longer support the war," he recounted. He suggested that she replace Wiggins, who was due to retire in 1968, with Philip Geyelin, a political writer for the *Wall Street Journal*. Graham approached Geyelin. That summer on Mount Desert Island, where Geyelin also had a house, he and Lippmann talked it over. Lippmann urged Geyelin to take the job and to fight it out with Wiggins over the *Post*'s editorial line. Geyelin joined the paper early in 1967 as Wiggins's deputy, but did not take over the page or reverse the *Post*'s pro-war stance until Wiggins retired the following year. LBJ rewarded his favorite editorial writer by naming Wiggins as American ambassador to the United Nations.[19]

As Lippmann's frustration mounted, so did his sympathy for all forms of opposition to the war, even street demonstrations and draft-card burnings. Although he would not identify himself publicly with the antiwar demonstrators — the constraints of civility were too strong — neither would he condemn them. If the demonstrations were "self-defeating," he wrote in October 1965, they nonetheless were valuable as a "pathetic reminder" of what happened when a government stifled public debate on a vital issue. If the draft-card burners were "misguided," they should be viewed sympathetically, for they were citizens of a nation "which expects to understand what its government is doing, from a nation which is not habituated to obedience and to the idea that it must listen to its superiors and not talk back."

Lippmann, having allowed himself to be pulled into Johnson's net, was now moving over to the opposition. He had given a premonition of this a few months earlier when, in a speech to the International Press Institute in London, he had urged journalists to seek the truth and report it, however embarrassing it might be to the government of the day. Unavoidably journalists were torn, he said, between their "pursuit of the truth and their need and their desire to be on good terms with the powerful." The powerful were the chief source of news, but also the "dispensers of many kinds of favor, privilege, honor and self-esteem. The most important forms of corruption in the modern journalist's world are the many guises and disguises of social climbing on the pyramids of power," he warned. "The temptations are many; some are simple, some are refined, and often they are yielded to without the consciousness of yielding. Only a constant awareness of them offers protection."

No one was in a better position than Lippmann to know the dangers of wanting to be on good terms with the powerful. He had tried to keep his distance, but even he was not immune to the lure of privileged access to the mighty. He had allowed himself to be drawn into Johnson's web, not by any bribes or rewards, but simply because he was flattered at being called in for advice, and because he thought the administration was seriously listening to him. When he discovered that the White House was merely trying to butter him up, he was hurt and angry. He could not forgive Johnson for lying about his intentions in Vietnam and using him. Nor, in a way more difficult to admit, could he forgive himself for being used.

"He misled me," Lippmann later said of his break with the President. "The day before making his Baltimore speech, Johnson told me that the war had to be won on the non-military side. But a short time later I found that he was telling other people other things. He was either lying to me or to the others." Lippmann never set foot in Johnson's White House again after that marathon session of April 1965. LBJ became to him, as he said privately in a comment that soon got around, the "most disagreeable individual ever to have occupied the White House."[20]

Lyndon Johnson now faced a formidable adversary.

◄ 44 ►

An End and a Beginning

We shall see what I can make of it.
— "Today and Tomorrow," May 25, 1967

B Y the end of 1965 communication between Woodley Road and the White House had virtually broken down. The administration had dug in its heels and Lippmann's increasingly strident columns were dismissed as ill-informed or even "cowardly." At the end of November he and Helen flew to South America for a whirlwind three-week tour of Argentina, Peru and Chile, including the usual interviews with presidents, foreign ministers, and editors, and in Santiago, a tour through the city's slums with a Peace Corps volunteer and a visit with Socialist party leader Salvador Allende. When they returned Johnson held out an olive branch by inviting them to a state dinner for Chancellor Ludwig Erhard of West Germany. Lippmann sent his regrets. Instead of going to the White House he wrote a sharp column attacking the American military presence on the Asian mainland. "Making this artificial and ramshackle debris of the old empires permanent and committing our lives and fortunes to its maintenance means," he declared, "unending war in Asia." [1]

Others were beginning to agree with him. Fulbright used the Senate Foreign Relations Committee as a forum for dissident views on the war. Some in Johnson's entourage were beginning to drift away. Over lunch with Lippmann in February 1966 George Ball confided that he was thinking of resigning. The under secretary of state was growing tired being the administration's official dove and institutional gadfly. No one was paying any attention. Ball had hoped that the President would change course with the 1968 elections and appoint him to replace Rusk. But Johnson never had any intention of pulling back. Lippmann advised Ball to get out of the government and denounce LBJ's Vietnam policy. But resignation in protest was not in the American style. Ball lingered on until the fall of 1966 before quietly going off to Wall Street.

Part of the reason Ball and other war critics stayed on so long was that they feared being consigned to political oblivion. Lippmann had written about the problem more than four decades earlier when he had urged Wilson's secretary of state, Robert Lansing, to take his leave. Lansing's problem was that Woodrow Wilson would never tell him what he was negotiating or even with whom. Given the choice between a title and his principles, Lansing preferred the title. So had virtually everyone else, except William Jennings Bryan, one of the rare cabinet members ever to resign over a matter of conscience — when he thought that Wilson was leading the country into war by his policy toward German submarine warfare. One irrefutable principle of political life was the "almost total inability of Americans to decline an appointment or to resign a post," Lippmann wrote shortly after World War I. But if democracy were to work, men had to be able to say both no and good-bye. "What could be more disloyal than to work at cross purposes with the administration to which you belong, or to abandon your convictions about what is right?" he asked. "It is only because so few men ever resign on principle, that all resignations seem an intolerable scandal." In other countries men managed to resign without feeling they would bring disgrace upon themselves. The problem was that there was no official opposition in the American system.

One day you are at the pinnacle. The next day you are back in Lincoln, Nebraska, with nothing to do. One day your every word counts. The next day you are considering how to make a living at the bar. It is a case of everything or nothing, it or nit. And so men think twice, and then think again, and find reasons of the highest public order for not passing from greatness into obscurity. If they did not pass out of public life, but only into the opposition, perhaps they would not cling so grimly to their jobs.[2]

Nobody wanted to go to Lincoln. Or even, it seemed, to New York. When in February 1966 the Ford Foundation asked McGeorge Bundy if he wanted to be its new president, Bundy demurred. But LBJ, now grown tired of his "Harvards," as he called them, and less intimidated by them, told Bundy to take it. Eventually others went too: first Ball, then Bill Moyers, and even Robert McNamara; all left quietly, without a word of protest. Nobody wanted to be a spoilsport or seem disloyal to the team. Everybody wanted to be invited to come back and play another day — in a different administration, when bad feelings had faded, when times were happier. Troublemakers rarely got invited back. That was the American way.

By the time Bundy left, he and Lippmann were on cool terms. Lippmann felt that the younger man had used their friendship unfairly, had not been totally honest with him in explaining administration policy. "I had assumed that we were in agreement," he later said of Bundy, "but

I discovered that we weren't. It came as a great surprise to me to learn — and it slipped out only gradually — that he was much more pro-war than I knew.'' Bundy, he said, with disappointment and a touch of anger, was "very cagey, a person who, I now feel, was not in the open, not clear about where he stood.''[3] When friends feted the Bundys at a big Washington farewell dance at the end of February 1966, the Lippmanns decided that they were otherwise engaged. Helen, so quick to turn against those by whom she felt abused, and so vituperative in her denunciations, was particularly sharp in her criticism.

Lippmann by this time had virtually given up trying to influence the President or his advisers. He had become estranged from most of them, while the true believers among them discounted his criticisms as repetitive and irrelevant. They were locked into their roles just as he was into his. As his frustration mounted over his failure to make an impact on policy, or even to claim an audience within the administration, so his tone became more strident. Having tried to avoid direct personal criticism of Johnson — on his long-standing rule that you should not strike the king unless you can strike to kill — he could contain himself no longer. LBJ's conduct of foreign policy was "willful, personal, arbitrary, self-opinionated,'' he charged in the spring of 1966. By risking a war with China, the President was on the verge of making the kind of "historic mistake'' the Athenians had made in attacking Syracuse, or Napoleon and Hitler in invading Russia. "There are some wars,'' he wrote, "which must be averted and avoided because they are ruinous.''[4]

Instead of following its liberal traditions, the United States under Johnson was "playing an imperial role'' in Asia and sacrificing the promise of the Great Society. Those worst hit were the poor, many of them black, whose young men were sent off to die in Vietnam and whose needs were once again shoved to the rear. "The crude truth is that the great majority of us, for the most part white, who are safely beyond the poverty line will resist higher taxes in order to help the poor, so many of them black,'' he wrote as the war drained off tax surpluses that were supposed to finance domestic reforms. "I have been asking myself why a country which is as rich as we are today should feel itself compelled to economize at the expense of its children and its poor. There exists, I have come to think, some kind of rule which in a democratic society limits what the voters will stand for in the way of sacrifice for the public good — the public good which is not immediately, obviously, and directly to their own personal advantage.''[5]

He saw the war not only as a terrible distraction that prevented the nation from dealing with its long-neglected domestic needs, but as a dangerous temptation leading to imperialism and ruin. Where he had formerly made cool calculations of the national interest, he now began to speak of moral values and a "respect for the opinions of mankind.'' The war had become for him, as for Lyndon Johnson and many other Americans, an obsession. From the middle of 1965 he wrote about little else. When Elizabeth Farmer told him he was writing too much about the war and neglecting other issues, he agreed. "I know, I know," he said. "But I have to. What more important thing is there to write about?" He knew there was no answer to that question, so he kept on writing, hoping that somehow he could make a difference.

As he grew more and more estranged from the administration, he began listening to some of the radical critics of the war. In the spring of 1966 he talked to leftist journalist Felix Greene, who had been to Hanoi, and at the home of Bernard Fall had dinner with radical newsman I. F. Stone, just returned from Saigon. Two weeks later, when the Lippmanns gave their annual mint julep party on the lawn, they invited "Izzy" and Esther Stone — a small gesture, but one that was noticed in the tight little Washington social world, where each guest list carried a political meaning. Even more noticeable than the presence of the Stones was the absence from the party of any important administration official. Lippmann, so long an insider, was now among the outsiders.

From these dissident journalists he learned not to believe administration reports about the conduct of the war. Truthful reporting was hampered by the fact that there were few neutral observers, he wrote. Reports from American journalists were narrowly limited because they were "in the position of being able to photograph only one side of the moon." Since they could not see the war from North Vietnam, they should try to report the war they could see — the pacification of South Vietnam — as truthfully as they knew how.[6]

If reporting from the South was unreliable and reflected the Pentagon's view, reporting from the North was confined largely to the communist and the French press. For months these papers had reported that the Americans were bombing not just "wooden sheds," as Lippmann had been told, but civilian targets. Early in 1967 Harrison Salisbury of the *New York Times* went to North Vietnam and reported that American air raids had indeed destroyed homes, schools and hospitals, and killed many civilians. His dispatches were greeted with incredulity and indignation. Pro-war enthusiasts charged he had been duped by the communists. Many simply refused to believe him. Even some of his colleagues, such as James Reston, criticized him for reporting what he heard as well as what he saw.

Lippmann came to Salisbury's defense, reminding the reporter's critics that "in time of war what is said on the enemy's side of the front is always propaganda, and what is said on our side of the front is truth and righteousness." He congratulated the *Times* for printing Salisbury's articles, and, when the paper nominated the reporter for a Pulitzer Prize, wrote the committee that Salisbury had done a "great honor to the profession of journalism with singular service to his country." But the Pulitzer committee was as divided over the war as was the country. Although the judges recommended that Salisbury be awarded a prize, they were overruled by the more conservative advisory board.[7]

Lippmann had criticized other Presidents, but never in such personal and uncompromising language as he used against Johnson. He excoriated the administration for its "self-righteous use of military power," described the President's advisers as "foolish and ignorant men," and placed responsibility for the disaster on Johnson himself. LBJ could not easily "swallow the bitter pill of recognizing the fact that he is in a war which he cannot win," Lippmann wrote late in 1966. "It would take a man of noble stature and of the highest moral courage to do that. There is no reason to think that Mr. Johnson is such a man." He found "two spirits wrestling" within the breast of Lyndon Johnson: one was that of the "peacemaker and reformer and herald of a better world," the other that of a "primitive frontiersman who wants to nail the coonskin to the wall, who wants to be the biggest, the best, the first, a worshipper of what William James called the bitch-goddess success."[8]

As hope of influencing Johnson evaporated, so did Lippmann's temperance. "The root of his troubles," he wrote in the style of a Presbyterian minister, "has been his pride, a stubborn refusal to recognize the country's limitations or his own limitations. . . . Such pride goeth before destruction and an haughty spirit before a fall." The President was consumed by a "messianic megalomania" that persuaded him he could "kill mosquitoes with tanks and build a Great Society with B-52s." A new vocabulary crept into Lippmann's writing. "There is a growing belief that Johnson's America is no longer the historic America," he charged, "that it is a bastard empire which relies on superior force to achieve its purposes, and is no longer an example of the wisdom and humanity of a free society. . . . It is a feeling that the American promise has been betrayed and abandoned."[9]

Johnson liked criticism no better than any other President, and received it with worse grace than most. He rarely missed an opportunity to tell a White House visitor — be it journalist, senator or Girl Scout troop leader — that Lippmann was traitorous, irrational or senile. Finally in the spring of 1967 he struck out publicly. Lippmann had accused him of being "pathologically secretive" and of behaving as though he had the right to "manipulate the news in his own political interest."[10] The charge had been echoed by a good many other journalists, who complained even more about "managed news" under Johnson than they had under Kennedy. A few days later at a gala White House formal dinner for the president of Turkey, Johnson set aside his prepared text and indulged himself in lashing a nameless elder columnist, unfortunately "still with us," who had been wrong during his entire career. Indeed, Johnson charged, he had been against aid to Greece and Turkey when President Truman proposed it in 1947. There was little doubt whom Johnson had in mind, and the embarrassed guests tittered knowingly.

Certainly Lippmann had made mistakes during his long career, including a few big ones. Johnson had had a whole team of researchers go through all his old columns to turn up bloopers. But one thing he had not done was to oppose aid to Greece and Turkey. In answer to the accusation the culprit swiftly stepped forward, identified himself, and reprinted the original column he had written in March 1947 when Truman proposed the aid program. There he showed that he had in fact supported aid for Greece and Turkey. What he had opposed was the vague language of the Truman Doctrine, which he warned would lead to global intervention in support of weak and discredited client regimes — in other words, to what was happening in Vietnam.[11]

Johnson — his domestic programs floundering, his key aides resigning, the Republicans sharpening their knives even while supporting the war, his own party divided, an opposition group forming around Robert Kennedy, and rioters and protesters making him a virtual prisoner in the White House — struck out viciously against his critics, accusing them of prolonging the war by feeding Hanoi's hopes that the United States would withdraw. Particularly enraged by Lippmann, LBJ took out his anger in salacious jokes and sly innuendo, dragging up Lippmann's more egregious errors, and making pointed references to a "political commentator of yesteryear." Having so often bragged to visitors, "I had Walter Lippmann over today," Johnson was now goaded to a cold fury by the barbs from Woodley Road. Things got so bad that other journalists wrote stories about what they called "the war on Walter Lippmann." "If Lippmann were a less modest man," wrote *Washington Post* cartoonist Herblock, "the attention lavished on him by his chief of state would be enough to turn his head. And if he and Johnson had lived in the days of Thomas More and Henry VIII, he would have lost his head completely."[12]

Johnson was particularly fond of telling a story that presumably showed how detached Lippmann was from the real world. The story concerned Fred Friendly, who had told one of his students at the Columbia School of Journalism that in making a TV film on Vietnam protesters she should be careful to explain what the "Make Love Not War" buttons meant. "The trouble with your generation," the young woman told him, "is that you're confused about the difference between making love and getting laid." A few days later Friendly recounted the story to Lippmann. "Yes, it's a wonderful example of the generation gap," he replied. "But exactly what does 'getting laid' mean?" Friendly could not resist telling the story, and eventually it got into the newspapers in garbled form, including a girl in a tight T-shirt on a peace march, who says Lippmann doesn't know the difference between "making love and hanky-panky," and a student who asks Friendly, after hearing the story, "But who is Walter Lippmann?" Lippmann never mentioned the episode to Friendly, though variants of it had obviously come back to him. However, once as they were riding in a taxi through Central Park past a group of young people he turned to Friendly and said, "What makes you think I don't know what hanky-panky is?"[13]

The war destroyed friendships and made strange new alliances. People who had constantly lunched together no longer spoke to one another, while those who had never spoken before now became colleagues. Lippmann found himself cut off from many he had considered to be his friends. Some openly snubbed him. Administration officials and their minions in the press snidely accused him of cowardice and even of senility. A shy man in the best of times, ready to sense rejection even when it was not intended, he was wounded by these attacks. Not by what Johnson said — he was used to the vanity of politicians — but rather by the way so many friends had turned from him. Civility, the quality he valued above all, the sense of proportion that made it possible for men to differ strongly and still maintain a dialogue, had been broken.

Lippmann was so distressed that he referred in his column to the administration's "hatchet men in the Senate and in the press" who defended the war by treating dissenters as "disreputable." The whole business sickened him. He had never been treated this way before. Nor, for that matter, had he ever used such uncompromising language toward a President. He had always believed a journalist should not write until he had his passions under control, and had once warned John Miller against being unnecessarily vehement when right.[14] During his whole career he had spoken to the arbiters of power as a calm observer, one who sometimes had strong views, but who expressed them with moderation. Nothing would have been easier for him than to have continued in that vein, to have bemoaned the "anguish of power," like so many of his colleagues, and hoped for the miraculous victory that would make the whole problem go away. Instead, he allowed his passions to come tumbling out, and in his denunciation of the war recaptured the daring of the young man who, fresh out of college more than a half-century earlier, had extolled a "rebel tradition."

He began to take a far more critical view of the whole thrust of American postwar foreign policy. Having long viewed it as primarily defensive, though prone to exaggeration and globalistic excesses, he now saw the outlines of an American imperialism. When in the fall of 1967 his friend Arthur Schlesinger, Jr., published an article refuting the cold war "revisionists" and maintaining that only Stalinist "paranoia" could explain Soviet suspicion of America's motives, Lippmann took strong objection. He wrote Schlesinger that he found such an explanation "disappointing" because it neglected to take into account the "political and strategic vacuum" in Europe after the war that at once "provoked and lured Moscow and Washington to fill it. You exaggerate, I think, Soviet motives and pay no attention, as the criminal law requires, to opportunity. Furthermore," he added pointedly, "you fail to take notice of how often the search for security and the assembling of an empire are two sides of the same coin."[15] The reference to the "assembling of an empire" was not one that Lippmann would have made a few years earlier. The war, as it had for many others, had changed his interpretation of the American past.

Lippmann was not a belligerent person by nature. He found no pleasure in taking on the President in battle and in feuding with an administration whose domestic policies he admired and for which he had, at the beginning, held such high hopes. He no more wanted to be a martyr than he enjoyed being a Cassandra. Yet he kept on doggedly, indeed bravely, because he felt he had no alternative. He paid a price for his opposition: not in being cut off from the White House — he had certainly feuded with Presidents before and been roundly denounced by them — but in being snubbed and vilified by many whom he had considered to be his friends. The war did not leave many friendships unscathed.

His sense of isolation increased. The snide remarks about his age and judgment, the embarrassed encounters at his club when old acquaintances nodded curtly or averted their eyes, the all-pervasive climate of intellectual fratricide and vendetta — all these took a toll. He continued to churn out his columns, making the same attacks on the President and his advisers, the same allusions to a ramshackle American imperialism, the same laments that the war was tearing the nation apart. Lippmann began to feel, like many other dissenters, that he sounded like a broken record. There was nothing more he could say other than that the whole venture was mad. Unlike some radicals, he did not see it as a crime — his mind did not operate in such moralizing categories — but as a misguided and self-destructive obsession. He wrote on and on about the war, but with a growing sense of futility, feeling that it could not be ended so long as Lyndon Johnson remained in the White House.

He was growing tired. In the summer of 1966 he was nearly seventy-seven years old. He had been writing the column since 1931. He decided, as he had several times over the years, that it was time to stop. This time he meant it. In the years remaining to him he wanted to get away from the grind of the twice-weekly column, from being a slave to the headlines, from the poisonous atmosphere of LBJ's Washington. After one more year he would give up the column. He and Helen would embark on a new life. They would satisfy a dream that they, and particularly Helen, had had for years: they would find a villa in Europe where they would pass the summers, and spend the rest of the time in the city they had both always considered home — New York.

In July 1966 they set the plan in motion. They sold the camp at Southwest Harbor to Jane and Lucius Wilmerding, and the deanery on Woodley Road back to the cathedral from which they had bought it twenty-one years earlier. Starting a four-month leave of absence early in August, Lippmann and Helen flew to Italy to search for the perfect villa. They scoured the hills of Tuscany and Umbria for a more modest version of Berenson's I Tatti, but none was to be found. Nothing was quite the way they had imagined it would be. "We found that Florence and the region are in a state of extreme inflation and overcrowded," he wrote in his notebook. "There are no attractive places to live in that you can get at with any convenience because of the crush of traffic on narrow roads." Postponing the search until the following spring, they made their tour of the European capitals, and in early November returned to Washington. Even though the villa remained elusive, they soon found the New York base they were looking for: a seventeen-room duplex apartment at 1021 Park Avenue, near 85th Street — just a few blocks from where Walter had grown up. At $125,000 it was well within their means.

November was a month for business. Lippmann resumed "Today and Tomorrow" twice a week; conferred with Philip Geyelin about Geyelin's joining the *Washington Post;* discussed with Kay Graham, Ben Bradlee and the *Post*'s lawyer, William Rogers, the format and syndication details of the monthly articles he planned to write when he dropped T&T the following spring; and lunched with James Reston to discuss, at Reston's suggestion, the possibility of doing articles for the *New York Times.* Lippmann's column, of course, had never appeared in the *Times,* since the paper ran no syndicated material but its own. He told Reston that, although he would be pleased to appear in the *Times,* it would never be possible so long as the paper retained its syndication policy. The only alternatives in New York were the two tabloids, the *Post* and the *Daily News,* and the *Trib*'s successor, an unwieldy amalgamation with a mouthful of a title, the *World Journal Tribune.* The *WJT* seemed the best of an unlikely lot, and the *Washington Post* permitted it syndicated rights to Lippmann's articles in New York.

With business details ironed out, the Lippmanns drove to New York at the end of November, looked over their new apartment, and officially marked their entry into New York social life by attending a large dinner party of socialites and intellectuals. After dinner they went off in chauffeured limousines — along with Lillian Hellman, Isaiah Berlin and the Arthur Schlesingers — to the Plaza Hotel, where Truman Capote was giving a masked ball for Katharine Graham. Walter appeared wearing the mask of a curly-maned black unicorn.

When they got back to Washington, Lippmann officially announced that he would cease the regular column in the spring, although he would continue writing longer pieces on a periodic basis, as well as his column for *Newsweek*. The White House was delighted, while most papers expressed their regret at the imminent passing of an institution. On March 14, 1967, with his departure drawing near, his journalist colleagues at the Federal City Club gave him a farewell dinner and an award. Lippmann made a graceful speech, touched with wit, and not a little sadness. He was leaving Washington, he insisted, not "because I no longer stand very near the throne of the prince nor very well at his court. A long life in journalism convinced me many Presidents ago that there should be a large air space between a journalist and the head of a state. I would have carved on the portals of the National Press Club, 'Put not your trust in princes.' Only the very rarest of princes can endure even a little criticism, and few of them can put up with even a pause in the adulation." Rather, he was leaving, he maintained, because "time passes on" and a "change and a new start is good for the aging."

Lippmann then turned to the change in America's world role during his long career. The crucial question for Americans was "how wisely, how gracefully, how skillfully and how constructively they would adjust themselves to the reality of power and to being first among equals; to living with the fact that while we might still be the strongest power, we could not and should not wish to be omniscient, omnicompetent, omnipotent; that we were not the leader of mankind and not the policeman of the world." Rejecting the administration's analogies of Vietnam with Munich, and of the 1960s with the 1930s and 1940s, he reminded his audience that when elected in 1964 Lyndon Johnson had "told the people, and they believed him, that he would not involve them in a war in Asia," that he would deal with their problems at home. "I cannot pretend to think that such a radical and violent change of course will not affect the country greatly." Yet, he concluded, "I do not lose faith. I do not doubt that in the long run we shall find a way through the consequences of the crucial decisions which changed the course which was set by the people in the election of 1964." Lippmann, in his own subdued way, went out slugging.[16]

A few days later Helen and Walter flew to Paris for the weekend to look at houses. Having realized that an I Tatti–like villa near Florence was a dream, they, or rather Helen, had decided on France. They had heard of an old mill outside Fountainebleau that had been converted into a charming house, took one look at it, and decided on the spot to buy it. Four months a year, they thought, would be spent at the mill — which was close enough to Paris so that they could get into the city easily — and the rest at their Park Avenue duplex in New York. It seemed a perfect arrangement.

All through April and the first week in May they were guests of honor at a round of Washington parties, and on May 5 capped off the activities by giving a mammoth farewell party of their own. Several hundred people came to bid them good-bye, spilling from the long rectangular sunken living room through the French doors and into the garden. Diplomats, journalists, congressmen, the arbiters of Washington's social life were there for this very last gathering at Woodley Road — but, as evidence of Lippmann's feud with the President, not a single administration official. Lippmann always denied that he left Washington because of Lyndon Johnson. "I wouldn't give him that satisfaction," he said. "I stuck it out through the McCarthy period." Yet there was a touch of protesting too much. "I simply can't stand Washington," he explained. "It's impossible to breathe or think in this town."[17] But most of his friends were convinced that had it not been for Johnson he would have stayed on in Washington.

Perhaps not. Helen, forever restless, wanted to try something new, and Walter, usually indulgent of her moods, was more than willing to go along. On May 10 the movers came to take away their furniture. Walter and Helen flew to New York and moved into the Park Avenue duplex. On May 25 the last "Today and Tomorrow" column appeared. Entitling it "Personal Explanation," Lippmann kept it brief and unsentimental. After writing thirty-six years on a fixed schedule he had come to the conclusion, he explained, that it was time to "get rid of the necessity of knowing, day in and day out, what the blood pressure is at the White House and who said what and who saw whom and who is listened to and who is not listened to." A job like that should be done by men in their prime. He was saying good-bye to T&T, but would experiment with new forms — longer articles without fixed schedules or deadlines. "We shall see what I can make of it," he told his readers with a note of diffidence, in the last words he would write as a columnist. A flurry of accolades and tributes followed in the nation's press and abroad as his colleagues tipped their hats to the man James Reston hailed, without any fear of contradiction, as "the greatest journalist of the present age."[18]

He departed with a sense of relief, but also of melancholy. "It's a sad world I'm leaving," he told Elizabeth Farmer that last week they worked together. She knew what he meant: that he was leaving, not the world, but the daily involvement in politics that had been so central to his life ever since he had turned his back sixty years earlier on the clubman's Harvard and exhorted his classmates to interest themselves in public affairs. What his mentor Graham Wallas had called the Great Society was where he had made his life. Now he would have to find a new way of living — if he could.

If he felt anxiety over his semiretirement, he did not show it publicly. On the contrary, he seemed to look forward to his new life with optimism. The last years in Washington had been nasty. Helen had been even more short-tempered than usual, leaving him to sulk in silence, as was his nature. Close friends would have helped them escape from one another and reduce the tension that flared between them. But for all their social acquaintances, neither had a really close friend in Washington, no one to whom they could confide their anxieties or show their weaknesses. Lippmann, except for when a very young man, had never let anyone — other than Helen — really enter his life. He maintained a brave and lonely independence that he had developed in his youth and had fortified throughout a rigidly controlled life.

If he was often cross with Helen and suffered from her sharp temper, he was also dependent on her and loved her deeply. She was his companion and his protector, totally dedicated to him and his career. She had given him moments of great joy, released him from the depression of a miserable marriage, brought out his earthier and more playful side, and saved him from a melancholy that might have turned inward and destroyed his spirit. She had transformed his life, in a sense saved it, and he never ceased to be grateful to her for it.

There was no way he could say this to her directly. He would have been too embarrassed. But on her seventieth birthday, February 19, 1967, as they were beginning to prepare for their departure from Washington, he left a note on her desk:

My dear Helen,

I feel I must write you a letter on this day. For in it I can say how happy I am that I married you and how deeply and everlastingly grateful I am. Looking back, I feel as if I had never really begun to live until we set out together, and that I have known from you not only unimagined happiness, but also the secret of starting life anew.

You have been the decisive influence. But for you I would have settled down dully thirty years ago in the grooves I cut when I was young. But for you I would now be settling into a dull old age instead of feeling that we are at a new and fascinating beginning.

All my love always, my darling,
Walter

Three months later, on May 27, 1967, they boarded the S.S. *France* for Europe to begin their new life.

◀ 45 ▶

The Worst of Times

I think it's going to be a minor Dark Age.

— Interview, *New York Times Magazine*,
September 14, 1969

NOTHING worked out the way they had planned. The old mill they had bought so excitedly during their weekend trip to France in March turned out to be uncomfortable and hard to maintain. The young couple they had hired as cook and handyman were lackadaisical and inexperienced. Helen and Walter felt ill at ease in these unfamiliar surroundings. Suddenly the fact that they had actually retired to France, for at least part of the year, and had not merely rented a villa for a few months, got through to them. Helen, always impatient, grew nervous and short-tempered. She decided they had made a great mistake. They must sell the mill, she told Walter, and move to Paris. After only six nights in their new home they packed their bags, hired a car and driver, and took a suite at the Meurice. They stayed for a month, then went off to Gstaad in the Swiss Alps for the rest of the summer. With all the moving, Walter did not have either the time or the tranquillity to write any of the articles he had planned.

By mid-September they were back in New York. Even there things did not go right. The Park Avenue duplex was even bigger and harder to keep up than they had remembered. New York seemed constricting. They missed their old camp at Southwest Harbor — this was the first summer in nearly twenty-five years they had not spent in Maine — and on impulse flew back for another look. Deciding they had given up Maine too hastily, they drove around the island in the clear Indian summer light of early October to see whether the perfect house might somehow be available. In the fashionable enclave of Seal Harbor they found just what they were looking for: a large frame house with a lovely garden and a superb view of the harbor and of the Cranberry Islands. It was completely furnished — down to lamps, linen and silverware. They bought it immediately.

Having reconstituted at least a part of their former life, they settled into their New York apartment for the winter and began to enjoy the city's social life. They dined with old friends, went to Broadway first nights, and were guests of honor at a dinner given by Mayor John Lindsay at Gracie Mansion. Walter returned to his study in the mornings. Although he had given up "Today and Tomorrow," a lifetime's habit of writing could not be easily changed. In periodic articles for the *Post* syndicate and *Newsweek* he roamed over the news, dealing with civil rights, the television "wasteland," a controversial biography of John F. Kennedy, and above all, Vietnam.

"We are seeing how a war waged without hope of a military decision degenerates into savagery," he wrote of Vietnam that fall of 1967. "Perfectly decent young Americans find themselves under orders to commit acts which in the conventional wars are called atrocities." Though he had preferred to argue in terms of national interest and avoid stressing what he now called the "cruelty and the inhumanity of the actual conduct of the war," he saw popular dissent rooted in "moral revulsion." Americans were becoming "revolted and ashamed" at performing such an "uncivilized, unchivalrous, inhumane role." When pro-war critics accused him of being a "neo-isolationist," he replied: "Neo-isolationism is the direct product of foolish globalism. . . . Compared to people who thought they could run the universe, or at least the globe, I *am* a neo-isolationist and proud of it." [1]

Yet he kept his faith in politics and the possibility of change. "You have to have a new leader for the orchestra who will suddenly begin to make the rhythm go again," he told a group of college students. Long before the event, he wrote that Lyndon Johnson might decide not to run for reelection; yet he recognized that if Johnson did choose to run, no other Democrat, not even Robert Kennedy, could deny him the nomination. "He is a knowing politician," Lippmann wrote of Kennedy in the spring of 1967; "he is a young man, and he is not likely to stake his whole political future on a gamble which would almost certainly not bring him the Presidency." Even if Kennedy should decide to run, it was a well-established rule of American politics, he noted, that "when the voters are dissatisfied with the party in power, they will turn not to a dissident faction but to the other party" as the simplest way of voting for a change. Kennedy was looking further down the line, and by criticizing the war was signaling a 1972 bid for the presidency, Lippmann reasoned. "A new generation will be present then, and it is clear that Robert Kennedy cannot be with it if he shrinks from the battle now." [2]

While Kennedy stood aside, condemning the war but feeling that it was futile to take on Johnson directly, Eugene McCarthy plunged into the void and challenged Johnson for the nomination on an antiwar platform. Although Lippmann, like most people, doubted that the senator

THE WORST OF TIMES 587

had a chance, he praised McCarthy for preserving the "deepest and most cherished values of American political life." The maverick Democrat from Minnesota was, he wrote admiringly, the "defender of the American faith," one who believed that the American system of party government "shall not be held to be a fraud and a deception, that it is a valid way by which the mass of our people can redress their grievances, can express their will, and can participate in the government of the nation."[3]

As McCarthy's candidacy gathered steam, Robert Kennedy began to have second thoughts about making a try for the nomination. He had little time to make up his mind. McCarthy was fast picking up support — and campaign contributions — from antiwar Democrats. If Kennedy waited much longer, McCarthy would have the anti-Johnson delegates locked up. The first real test of McCarthy's strength would come in the New Hampshire primaries in February 1968. Kennedy felt pressed to make up his mind before the balloting, and decided to get Lippmann's advice.

On a bleak afternoon in mid-January, escorted by Arthur Schlesinger, he dropped by Lippmann's apartment. Dispensing with small talk, Kennedy quickly got down to business. Should he make his bid now, or wait until 1972? Four more years of Johnson would be a "catastrophe," he said, as would four years of Nixon. But what chance did he have for the nomination on an antiwar plank if Johnson could defuse the war issue anytime he chose — simply by calling for a cease-fire and truce talks? Lippmann listened, but did not volunteer advice. Kennedy finally asked him point-blank what to do. "Well," Lippmann replied, "if you believe that Johnson's re-election would be a catastrophe for the country — and I entirely agree with you on this — then, if this comes about, the question you must live with is whether you did everything you could to avert this catastrophe."[4]

Kennedy left still undecided, but after McCarthy's impressive showing in the New Hampshire primary, concluded that the time was ripe. He plunged into the fight, announced his candidacy, and swept a series of early primaries. Johnson, seeing the handwriting on the wall, stunned the nation in late March by announcing that he would not seek reelection. Kennedy's nomination seemed assured and his election likely. But once again an assassin's bullet changed the course of American politics.

The murder of Robert Kennedy brought the Old Guard of both parties back into control. It seemed clear that the Democrats would now nominate Johnson's vice-president and designated heir, Hubert Humphrey. The Republicans, having nothing to fear, could safely turn to the kind of conservative the party bosses wanted, Richard Nixon. Viewing what he called this "dismal choice," Lippmann urged McCarthy and Governor Nelson Rockefeller not to give up their presidential bids, to "persevere in their struggles to establish the fact that the American electorate did not acquiesce quietly and dumbly in the nullification of real choice in the election and the smothering of democratic means." There was, he insisted, "the future to be remembered."[5]

Humphrey, on winning the nomination, did a fast about-face on the war he had previously championed enthusiastically. Having now come out for a negotiated settlement, Humphrey thought he could win Lippmann's endorsement and telephoned for the expected blessing. He did not get it. Lippmann knew that Humphrey, even if he was sincere, could never get the Republicans to go along with him — or even some of the Democrats whose fate was so linked to the war. Humphrey, for all his decency, was "Lyndon Johnson's creature" and could not offer the "genuine prospect of a coherent government," Lippmann wrote. Nixon, however objectionable on other grounds, at least had no interest in continuing the war. Like Eisenhower in Korea, Nixon could end the war and blame the Democrats for having started it. For a few weeks after the conventions Lippmann tried to avoid supporting either of what he called "two uninspiring candidates." But by early October he felt he had to make a choice. "I think Nixon's whole future will be staked on getting a cease-fire and a self-respecting withdrawal of our land forces," he told his readers. "That is the best I am able to hope for. But I see nothing better in Humphrey."[6]

The country, he reasoned, was going through both a foreign-policy and a domestic crisis. The foreign-policy crisis, though difficult, could be resolved by ending the war. But the domestic crisis was so deep-rooted that it would likely continue for decades. There was no agreement on how to deal with the grievances of minorities or how to reconstruct the environment — and no willingness to pay the cost if there were agreement. Violent dissent would probably continue, and so would demands for repression. If there had to be repression it was better for conservatives to carry it out and for liberals to prepare for the "inevitable reaction against reaction." It would be a "disaster," he said, "if a man like Humphrey had to do what is against the whole grain of his nature." Nor did Lippmann deplore the need to restore "discipline and authority and self-reliance." The United States had become "by far the most violently disordered" of the world's industrial nations. Violence and permissiveness were destructive of democracy itself, he argued in repeating a conviction he had held all his life. Thus he urged liberals not to shirk the "imperative policy of the restoration of security," or to "leave the task of dealing with violence to those who do not believe in the liberal and compassionate reforms of our society."[7]

Given the candidates, the choice seemed clear. "Nixon is the only one," he told his readers a month before the election. Even though the possibility of Spiro Agnew, Nixon's running mate, as President was terrifying, a Republican victory was quite tolerable. Lippmann was convinced that this time there really was a "new Nixon, a maturer and mellower man who is no longer clawing his way to the top . . . who has outlived and outgrown the ruthless politics of his early days." Though the future was not bright in any case, it seemed to him "the better, though not the most beautiful course, that the voters should oust the party which has cost the country so much."[8] The voters did, though by a surprisingly narrow margin.

Nixon, who had tried to court Lippmann for years, was naturally delighted by the endorsement and eager to keep the columnist in his camp. In early December he invited Lippmann to his campaign headquarters at the Hotel Pierre in New York. Over lunch in a tower suite, where the two men were joined by William Rogers, the secretary of state designate, and William Scranton, governor of Pennsylvania, Nixon solicited Lippmann's advice and said that a Vietnam settlement was at the top of his agenda. Henry Kissinger, the Rockefeller protégé whom Nixon had yanked from relative obscurity to become his adviser on national security affairs, lunched with Lippmann twice that month and confirmed his impression that an early Vietnam truce was in the offing.

Feeling optimistic, Walter and Helen flew to Europe in late March for a sojourn in Ischia, Paris and Rome, and when they returned two months later, went to Maine for the summer. They had settled easily into their new home, which, in the style of Seal Harbor, bore a name rather than a number: theirs was called Ilfracombe. Among its advantages was not only the superb setting at the edge of a pine forest a few hundred yards from the water, but the proximity of old friends, like their neighbor Samuel Eliot Morison, whom Walter had known since his undergraduate days; of the club at Northeast Harbor, where Walter could drop in for lunch; and most important, of the Rockefeller estate, where he and Helen could take long walks through the woods and linger in the luxuriant gardens.

He was too old now for tennis, but he loved those walks, and the Maine woods brought him — as they had ever since the summer of 1912 when he went to the Rangeley Lakes to write his first book — solace and a sense of being at one with the physical world. For a man who could never accept the comfort of a supernatural religion, who bore the weight of the world with intellect and stoicism rather than with emotion and religious faith, the feeling of oneness with the natural world was very important. Increasingly he found, however, that long walks through the woods and up rocky paths tired him. His legs had lost their resiliency. Sometimes he would have to turn back halfway through the usual circuit and let Helen continue on alone. He would wait for her at the edge of the garden, sitting quietly on the rocky wall.

With the deadline of the column no longer pulling them back to the city, they stayed in Maine into the fall. This year there was a special reason for doing so: Walter's eightieth birthday. For the occasion Helen had invited some forty relatives and friends to Seal Harbor, including Gilbert and Nancy Harrison, Marjorie Phillips, Edward Weeks, Blair Clark, Carl and Chloe Binger, Harry and Eve Labouisse, John and Madeleine Miller, and James Reston. By the afternoon of September 23 they had all arrived by plane or car and had assembled on the patio for drinks. During the long and festive dinner that followed, Ted Weeks and Carl Binger read poems they had composed, the guests congratulated one another on how well they all looked, and Walter basked in the attention of his friends.

Lingering in Maine a few more weeks, they flew in mid-October to England, where Walter received an honorary degree at York University — the first American to be so honored — arranged by his friend Kenneth Clark, chancellor of the university. During the next few weeks in London they were lavishly entertained by their friends, including Fleur Cowles Meyer — the expatriate American journalist and hostess par excellence — who gave a party in their honor. She had gathered a dozen prominent people for dinner at her apartment in the Albany and promised several dozen more for after-dinner drinks. Among the assorted diplomats, journalists and government officials gathered around her table was the recently appointed American ambassador, Walter Annenberg. The publisher of *TV Guide* and a generous contributor to the Nixon campaign, Annenberg may not have known much about foreign policy, but, like the man who detested modern art, knew what he thought. Like many rich men surrounded by flatterers seeking his favors, he had come to assume that his opinions must be wise because they were received with such deference.

That evening the conversation at dinner inevitably turned to politics. The hostess, in an effort to draw out her guest of honor, of whom she was very fond, asked Lippmann how he felt about De Gaulle, now that the general had retired from power. This being a subject close to his heart, Lippmann launched into his usual encomiums, describing De Gaulle as one of the great men of history. Although he had been shortsighted during the recent student-led unrest in Paris, Lippmann explained, the general had a longer and more penetrating view of history than any other public man he had ever known. As Lippmann elaborated, Annenberg began to fidget noticeably. Finally he could contain himself no longer. Feeling obliged to defend the honor of the American government, which had had its share of troubles with De Gaulle, he blurted out: "Sir, you have completely misunderstood the machinations of an evil man who is a self-declared enemy of the United States!"

A deathly silence fell over the table. Lippmann looked at Annenberg with an expression of amazement that slowly turned to disdain. The guests focused on Lippmann, waiting for the withering reply they were sure would follow. A few years earlier it would have come with a cutting finality. But now he no longer had the energy for a fight. He shook his head slowly and instead turned to his hostess at his left, and said in a voice that could be heard across the hushed table: "Fleur, please excuse me, but I'm an old man who has lived through a great deal, and I cannot bear to sit here and listen to such drivel." Diplomatically she suggested that her guests retire to the living room for coffee. Walter and Helen decided they would retire completely. As they were putting on their coats, Thomas Hughes, chief political officer at the embassy, arrived as advance guard of the after-dinner contingent. As he shook Hughes's hand, Lippmann nodded in the direction of Annenberg and said: "It's a good thing you're here to take his foot out of his mouth." A moment later Helen and Walter were out the door. Annenberg, seeing them leave, said in surprise, "He didn't even say good-bye to me." [9]

Leaving London a few days later, Walter and Helen went on to Paris and Rome, and returned to New York in mid-November. They had given up the Park Avenue duplex a year earlier — Helen had decided that it was too big and hard to keep up — and had moved into an apartment at the Lowell, a discreetly fashionable hotel on East 63rd Street off Central Park. There they lived comfortably, though hardly opulently, with their Colombian cook, Maria, and their aged poodle, Candy. They tried to adjust to life in New York: dined with friends, went to the movies and the theater. That December Alan Jay Lerner invited them to the opening of his new musical, *Coco,* and their friend Drew Dudley, with his vast show-business connections, took them to Pearl Bailey's final performance in *Hello, Dolly!* They enjoyed a taste of high life, but both Helen and Walter felt uneasy in their native city. Too much had changed since they left thirty years earlier. They had grown older, the city had become noisier, dirtier and more violent. They had left more behind them in Washington than they had at first realized. Yet there was no compelling reason to go back.

Walter, who had worked under deadlines all his life, now found that time hung heavy. He went regularly to the Century for lunch, more as a way of giving a shape to the day than for any social reason. Many who used to court him when he was active now were too busy for him. Often he went to the club without a lunch date, and would take a place at the large common table with men he did not know. He wrote periodic articles for the *Post* and *Newsweek,* but with increasing difficulty and infrequency. He traveled a good deal: to Mima Porter's California ranch in February 1970, to Washington for a state dinner at the White House in honor of President Pompidou, to Europe in April and May, to Maine in June, to Princeton to receive an honorary degree, along with singer Bob Dylan and civil rights leader Coretta Scott King.

Inevitably his public voice was fading. The column had given him his clout, had made politicians and bureaucrats take notice, even when they disagreed. His power over public opinion had made him a force to be reckoned with. Now he was another elder statesman, respected and admired, but deprived of political influence. Even some of his pointed gestures went unnoticed. When Hamilton Armstrong in 1971 announced his retirement as editor of *Foreign Affairs* and his replacement by William Bundy, a key planner of the Vietnam War, Lippmann resigned from the magazine's parent body, the Council on Foreign Relations, to which he had belonged ever since it was formed in the early 1920s. Characteristically, however, he did not resign in protest, but simply let his membership lapse. This vitiated the impact of the gesture, but he did not have the energy for the in-house argument that was taking place over the appointment.

Lippmann's natural optimism battled with a conviction — inspired by the seemingly interminable Vietnam War, racial and generational conflict, technological and economic upheaval — that there was little to be optimistic about. "Are men capable of and disposed to the good life?" he wrote Nancy Blaine Harrison in 1968 on her birthday. "Or is there in almost all of us a war between good and evil, a war which is endless and decisive? The first view is the pristine idea of the American faith, and you, my dear Nancy, have been for long its truest witness. When I see you, I am sharply aware of having relapsed from the faith."[10]

When an interviewer asked him if he thought the world better than it had been when he was young, he replied that he thought it was a "much less pleasant world to live in," one in which the barbarity of modern man was incomparably greater, but also one in which certain evils had receded — where the right of human equality had gained ground. "Anything that makes the world more humane and more rational is progress; that's the only measuring stick we can apply to it. But I don't wish to imply that I think this is a great progressive age. I don't. I think it's going to be a minor Dark Age."

Yet he also considered it an age of great potential. "The absolutely revolutionary invention of our time is the invention of invention itself," he continued. "That's why this is truly the most revolutionary age that man has ever lived in. It's also the reason for the moral and psychological difficulties of our time." Although this was not the first time that human affairs had been chaotic, never before had the stakes been so high. He did not expect a nuclear war. "What is really pressing upon us is that the number of people who need to be governed and are involved in governing threatens to exceed man's capacity to govern. This furious multiplication of the masses of mankind coincides with the ever-more imminent threat that, because we are so ungoverned, we are polluting and destroying the environment in which the human race must live.

. . . The supreme question before mankind — to which I shall not live to know the answer — is how men will be able to make themselves willing and able to save themselves."[11]

He tried to focus his declining energies on that problem, to write a book on the ungovernability of mankind in an age of concurrent revolutions. He worked on it winter mornings in his little office at the Lowell, and at Ilfracombe in the summers. He scribbled in his minuscule longhand, and read his notes into a Dictaphone for the typist. Little came of it; a few shining sentences, a striking paragraph here and there. But he was too weak and tired to do more. Though his mind was still alert, it operated in fits and starts, focusing here and there like the "beam of a searchlight," to borrow the striking metaphor he had himself used half a century earlier in analyzing public opinion. In January 1971 he wrote his last article. He did not intend it to be his last; there simply were no more.

Even in the discomforts and disappointments — the "shipwreck," in De Gaulle's phrase — of his old age, he did not lose his essential hopefulness. "I have a very strong belief in the toughness of the human will to survive," he said in one of the interviews that now took the place of the articles he no longer wrote. "Man is not the frail thing that ecologists sometimes make you think he is. Men won't stand for it, they won't lie down. That's what I'd count on." When asked if he thought democracy could survive in a time of political revolution and technological and social upheaval, he responded: "Well, I believe — and this is a belief I've come to very late in life and cannot prove — that the human being, just as he somehow evolved the capacity to learn language and to speak, has acquired in the course of eons of time an inherited code of civility, I call it, by which man has learned that nobody can exercise absolute power, that power has to be exercised with some respect for the consent of other powers . . . a society won't last, will be overthrown, if that code is violated."[12]

He continued to believe, not only in the will to survive, but in a basic human decency. He remained convinced that men had the capacity, even the compulsion, to rise above their worst natures. "It is true that societies decay and that dark ages of despotism and anarchy threaten them all," he had written in the late 1930s, when there was little to be optimistic about.

But it is also true that man who relapses into barbarism recreates the civilization he did not preserve. He is a barbarian then who, it appears, must become civilized. If it were contrary to the nature of man to be civilized, he would never have become civilized at all. Or if he had only become civilized by accident, once he was decivilized again, he would stagnate forever in his barbarism. But he does not. And so it must be that the need to be civilized and the capacity are inherent in men's natures, and are reborn with each new generation.[13]

Just as he had stopped writing, Lippmann found that he no longer had the energy to take long trips. Europe was familiar and still relatively easy. But when a delegation from the Chinese mission to the United Nations came to see him in January 1972 with an invitation from Foreign Minister Chou En-lai to be the first American newsman to visit mainland China, he politely declined. Such a trip, he told the Chinese, would be too arduous for a man of eighty-two. They repeated the invitation again in March, but once again he turned it down. Instead he and Helen went to London, Paris and Vienna for two months. He preferred familiar paths.

They spent the summer of 1972 in Maine, the fall and winter in New York, and planned to return to Europe in the spring of 1973. In late March they went together to the travel agency to pick up their tickets. Walter was not feeling well and Helen sent him home in a taxi. When she returned to the hotel half an hour later she found him unconscious in his study. She called his doctor, C. Pinckney Deal, who sent an ambulance to rush him to New York Hospital, where his condition was diagnosed as a brief heart stoppage. The doctors installed an electric pacemaker, and after a week allowed him to return home. He seemed fully recovered from his seizure, and felt well enough to accompany Helen on their long-planned trip to Europe. In mid-April they flew with Candy and fifty pounds of special dog food to Switzerland, where, after a brief visit with Mary Bruggemann at Vevey, they settled in at the resort village of Bad Ragaz.

But the trip had tired him, and by the time they returned to New York at the beginning of the summer he seemed much weaker than when he had left. His memory began to fade and his sense of time became distorted. Normally lucid, if a bit withdrawn, he would momentarily become incoherent. His deterioration drove Helen into a kind of panic. She could not abide being confronted with what was happening to him. She could, of course, have hired nurses to take care of him, but the daily evidence of his physical and mental disintegration was more than she could deal with. Declaring to her friends that he needed more attention than she could provide at the Lowell, she placed him in an elegant small nursing home on Park Avenue. Walter, witnessing her obvious distress at his condition, acquiesced. For a few weeks she visited him. Then, as the summer heat began to settle over New York, she gathered Candy and Maria and went to Maine.

Whatever Walter may have felt about his imposed exile to Miss Mary James's nursing home, he never complained about it or criticized Helen for sending him there. But he did miss Maine, and as the air conditioner in his room whined away through the torrid New York summer, he would talk of the great bird that would come to take him to his refuge of pine trees and icy lakes. Finally, in August, Helen arranged to have him brought to Seal Harbor. But his presence, the constant reminder of his imminent death, proved more than she could handle. After a few weeks she sent him back to Miss James.

His ward, Jane Wilmerding, could not stand to see him in the nursing home, and brought him to live with her in Princeton. But this act of kindness was thwarted when he suffered another heart attack and had to be rushed to New York. The doctor urged Jane to let him stay at the nursing home, where he could receive constant medical attention. To the astonishment of his doctor, he recovered from the heart attack he suffered that fall, and in a few weeks seemed no worse than he had been before.

Helen, having returned to New York, visited him regularly, but with an anxiety that became almost unendurable. She sold the house in Maine and had decided that in the spring she would go to Europe — remaining there indefinitely. Her life was awful, she said, but she intended to carry through her travel plans regardless of Walter's condition. Although many thought her heartless and even cruel, she was a tormented person — torn by her feeling for Walter, and by the consuming resentment she also felt, even if she could not admit it to herself. As long as Walter was active and in full command of his faculties, a renowned public figure feted wherever he went, she was able to share his glory. But now that he had grown pathetic and infirm, the subordination that formerly seemed natural appeared a needless sacrifice.

Yet though she had made the decision to abandon him — a decision presaged by her behavior over the past year — she could not accept it easily. Racked by guilt, she wandered disconsolately around her apartment, unable to sleep, her nerves frayed, her moods fluctuating wildly from giddy enthusiasm to thoughts of suicide. On February 16, 1974, five days short of her seventy-seventh birthday — for which she had planned a party at Walter's nursing home to "cheer him up" — she died suddenly of cardiac arrest.

Since Helen was a lapsed Catholic who had embraced no other faith, the family decided to hold the funeral service at a neutral place, and chose an austere Unitarian church on upper Lexington Avenue. The day of the service, February 20, was raw and gray, with the streets lashed by an intermittent cold rain. A few minutes before two, as the service was about to begin, a large black limousine pulled up to the curb, and Walter slowly emerged from the backseat. With the help of his doctor,

C. Pinckney Deal, and Helen's nephew, Jamie Byrne, he torturously mounted the few steps into the church and began his slow passage down the aisle. The hundred people who had gathered for the service turned to watch as he laboriously proceeded, with the aid of his crutches and of the two men at his side. Shockingly thin, his fine cheekbones protruding under his flaccid skin, his black suit hanging loosely on his emaciated frame, he seemed terribly alone — a solitary and immensely courageous figure. It would have been easy for him to have come in a wheelchair, but he had spurned such assistance. For two days before the service he had practiced walking in his room so that he could manage the ordeal — the longest distance he had walked in months.

The ceremony was most austere. The minister, a modern and sophisticated man, quoted from the *Bhagavad-Gita* and Aldous Huxley, but not a line from any of Lippmann's works, although one could hardly have imagined a more fitting reading for such an occasion than a passage from *A Preface to Morals*. After the service the family and some thirty friends went back to the Lowell. Maria, weeping and muttering softly to herself in Spanish, served drinks and sandwiches. Candy, now fifteen and showing her years, wandered aimlessly from room to room in search of her mistress. Walter, however, was surprisingly lively and alert, eager to talk to people and clearly pleased by the attention he was receiving. This was the first time he had been in his apartment since he entered the nursing home, and he was savoring the experience.

Hamilton Armstrong was not at the service. He had died a year earlier, leaving his Greenwich Village house to his daughter and the four lost love letters to Helen. Gregor, who was married to a wealthy man, also received most of her mother's quite large estate. Walter, for his part, had some years earlier made out a will leaving everything to Helen — except for $50,000 each to Gregor and Jane, and $10,000 each to Maria and Charlotte Wallace — with the provision that on her death the remainder go to Harvard. As it was, Harvard got nearly all: some $750,000. Although his estate was considerable, he sometimes imagined, as his mind wandered during the last months of his deterioration, that his wealth was infinite, and he would call his lawyer, Louis Auchincloss, saying he wanted to leave him, or one friend or another, a bequest of a quarter or half a million dollars. Even trivial items took on great value, and he sought to add a codicil to his will donating Helen's address book to Harvard. Perhaps this was a way of holding on to life.

Helen's death, though it saddened him, also seemed to relieve him of a great weight. He knew that he had been a burden to her, and now he no longer had to endure her painful visits. Just as she could not bear to see him falling apart, so he had been pained to witness her distress at his condition. Rather than quickly deteriorating after her death, he seemed calmer and better. He took great pleasure in the visits of old friends, and even invited some to lunch at the Lowell, where Maria, who had remained at the apartment to take care of Candy, would serve her famous cheese soufflé. While some people who had courted him in his health neglected him in his decline, others, particularly Louis Auchincloss, Arthur Schlesinger, and the faithful Drew Dudley, regularly came to visit and to divert his mind. They brought news of the outside world, for though he had tried to read the *New York Times* in the large-type edition, he tired easily and ceased attempting to keep up with the news. Nor had he ever got in the habit of watching television. The big gray box stood unused in the corner of his room.

Some days he was animated and would sit in his chair by the window, dressed in a garish sport shirt someone had dug out of a forgotten recess of his wardrobe, and in trousers now too big for him, eager for gossip and news. His mind would wander, and distant figures, now having surmounted the broken barriers to the past, would reappear as he had known them five and six decades ago. He would muse about John Reed and Santayana, Lincoln Steffens and Teddy Roosevelt, Woodrow Wilson and Colonel House, and Mable Dodge's Pueblo husband, Tony Luhan, who, unable to express himself in words, had, on a trip to New York from Taos in the 1920s, come to dance for Walter in his living room. Often he would sit silently, seemingly lost in his thoughts, as his visitors tried to engage his mind by mentioning names of those he had known. Suddenly he would seize upon one, dredging it up from the well of the past, and make a judgment, sometimes affectionate, other times crushing. "Ah, yes," he said of a woman he had known for forty years. "She was always unhappy, and her revenge was to breed unhappiness in those around her." Or, of a man who had once been a close friend and then turned his back during the scandal over the divorce: "The first task of that man's biographer will be to enquire why he remained for so long on such good terms with his wife's lover." [14]

When Schlesinger asked him whether Richard Nixon, then suffering the full glare of the Watergate scandals, was the worst President in American history, he replied: "No, not the worst, but perhaps the most embarrassing. . . . Presidents in general are not lovable," he explained. "They've had to do too much to get where they are. But there was one President who was lovable — Teddy Roosevelt — and I loved him." To the end he remained true to his first political crush.

At moments he seemed in full possession of his mental powers, even though his body had wasted terribly. "How strange it is," he said one autumn afternoon as we sat in his room. "All my life I used to worry about being fat, and now I weigh only 120 pounds." He smiled weakly, the bones protruding from his face and the veins from his hands, not asking for pity, merely stating a curious fact. At other times that fall of 1974 he seemed very near death, sprawled on the bed, emaciated and barely coherent.

On September 23 some three dozen friends gathered at his nursing home to celebrate his eighty-fifth birthday. President Gerald Ford and West German Chancellor Helmut Schmidt sent telegrams of congratulation. He savored the moment, knowing, as his guests knew, that he would probably never see them again. A few weeks later he decided that he wanted to see the collection of his private papers and manuscripts that he had bequeathed to Yale years earlier. When well he had always been too busy. Now he had the time.

On a fine October morning he suddenly arrived in New Haven — and a campus resplendent with autumn leaves — in a chauffeur-driven limousine with Mary James and a nurse. Robert O. Anthony proudly greeted him. Anthony, a retired telephone company executive who had devoted decades of his life to assembling and cataloguing Lippmann's correspondence and printed works, proudly wheeled him through the special exhibit he had prepared at the Yale library in honor of his eighty-fifth birthday. There Lippmann, his fingers trembling slightly, leafed through the original manuscripts of long-forgotten T&T columns and of his books, through letters from Berenson and Newton Baker, photos of Faye and of his teammates on the Sachs school football and hockey teams. Then they went off to lunch at Mory's — joined by scholar Wilmarth Lewis, who had originally persuaded Lippmann to donate his papers to Yale, and Herman Kahn, director of the archives.

That same month, October 1974, the city of New York, with some prodding by Drew Dudley, honored Lippmann with its highest award, the Bronze Medallion. In an afternoon tea ceremony at Gracie Mansion the mayor, Abraham Beame, presented the award while several of Walter's friends — including Dudley, Louis and Adele Auchincloss, Arthur and Alexandra Schlesinger, Thomas and Eileen Finletter, Brooke Astor and Joan Fontaine — looked on. "You know, I was born only a few blocks from here," he said to Beame, New York's first Jewish mayor. "But my ancestors, like yours, were immigrants." It was not a remark he would have made a few years earlier. But now, with the little time he had left, he was reassembling the past.

This was his last outing. His strength failed rapidly that fall. He knew the end was near, but he did not flinch from it. Never during his last months did he show any sign of fear, or even apprehension, at his imminent death. Those who had accused him of cowardice because of his distaste for personal confrontation failed to understand his great moral courage. When he had suffered his heart attack a year earlier and had seemed about to die, he asked Louis Auchincloss, who had come to his bedside, if his will was in order. Nothing more. No complaints, no fears, no regrets. Never did he speak of prayer, or of God, or of an afterlife. To the end he was like the mature man who, as he had once written, "would take the world as it comes, and within himself remain quite unperturbed," who "would face pain with fortitude, for he would have put it away from the inner chambers of his soul."[15]

Ever since he had set out on his chosen path more than sixty years earlier he had tried to be, as he had told his mentor, Graham Wallas, "truth's pilgrim at the plough." He had done his best, he had remained true to his faith. No man could ask more of him; he could ask no more of himself. On Saturday, December 14, 1974, Walter Lippmann died of cardiac arrest. His body was cremated and his ashes were scattered, as those of Helen had been, off the Maine coast.

As he had long ago shed his Judaism and had no other religion, his friends did not know where to hold a service until Fred Friendly offered the small auditorium at the Ford Foundation. In place of a eulogy Friendly put together a short film of excerpts from Lippmann's television interviews of the early 1960s. As the lights went down and the familiar image filled the screen, his friends once again saw, not the frail, wasted figure of the past year, but the Walter Lippmann they had known: the solid frame, the fine cheekbones, the knowing smile, the relaxed air of self-confidence, the thoughtful response, the bemused flick of the hand.

Once again they saw what Mabel Dodge had seen six decades earlier in a young man fresh out of college with "a fine poise, a cool understanding, and with all the high humor in the world shining in his intelligent eyes."

Chronology

1937   August: the fateful meeting in France
       December 9: divorces Faye
1938   March 26: marries Helen Byrne in New York City; they move to Washington
1939   September 1: Germany invades Poland; World War II begins
1940   June: France surrenders
1941   June 22: Germany attacks Soviet Union
       December 7: Japan attacks Pearl Harbor
1942   August: WL meets De Gaulle in London
1946   March: Churchill's "iron curtain" speech
1947   March 12: Truman Doctrine address
       September: WL publishes "cold war" pieces in response to Kennan's "X" article
1948   February: Soviet coup in Czechoslovakia
1949   April: signing of NATO treaty
1950   June 25: North Korean attack on South Korea
1951   June–December: six-month sabbatical
1955   February: nervous collapse
1956   October: Suez crisis and Soviet invasion of Hungary
1959   September 23: seventieth birthday festivities
1960   August: first TV interview
1961   April: second visit to Soviet Union
1962   October: Cuban missile crisis
1963   January: switches from *Herald Tribune* to *Washington Post* syndicate; begins column for *Newsweek*
1965   April 7: Lyndon Johnson's Baltimore speech on Vietnam
1967   May 25: last "Today and Tomorrow" column; WL moves to New York
1971   January 11: final article for *Newsweek*
1974   February 16: Helen dies in New York
       December 14: WL dies in New York

Notes

MUCH of this book is drawn from Walter Lippmann's private correspondence, manuscripts and unpublished works at the Manuscripts and
Archives room of Sterling Memorial Library, Yale University. References are
from that source, unless otherwise indicated. Books by Lippmann are cited in
abbreviated form; full titles are in the Bibliography. Other forms of citation are:

BB	Bernard Berenson
EMH	Edward Mandell House
FF	Felix Frankfurter
GW	Graham Wallas
HBA	Helen Byrne Armstrong
LC	Library of Congress
LH	Learned Hand
NDB	Newton D. Baker
NR	*New Republic*
NYHT	*New York Herald Tribune*
OHC	Oral History Collection ("The Reminiscences of Walter Lippmann," in YLC)
RS	Author's interviews
RSC	Author's correspondence
T&T	"Today and Tomorrow" columns by WL
VF	*Vanity Fair*
WL	Walter Lippmann
YLC	Yale Lippmann Collection

Some of Lippmann's works are more readily available in various reprints
than in their original editions. Where this is the case I have, to simplify the task
of those seeking full quotations, cited the chapter number rather than the page
number of the original edition.

PROLOGUE

1. Elting Morison, ed., *The Letters of Theodore Roosevelt* (Cambridge: Harvard University Press, 1951), VIII, 872.
2. Alistair Buchan, "The Name That Opened Every Door," *Observer* (London) 12/15/74.
3. "The Scholar in a Troubled World," *Atlantic* 8/1932, Phi Beta Kappa address at Columbia University 5/31/32; also in *Essential*, 509–516.
4. *Morals*, ch. 15.

5. Tribute to C. P. Scott, editor of the *Manchester Guardian*, published as preface to *Newspaper Ideals*, pamphlet by Scott (New York: Halcyon Commonwealth Foundation, 1964), YLC.
6. "Mr. Wells Avoids Trouble," *NR* 11/7/14.
7. From an unpublished biographical fragment, 7/1/59, YLC.

1. THE ONLY CHILD

1. *U.S. Foreign Policy*, viii.
2. "A Tribute to Theodore Roosevelt," *NR* 10/27/35, also in *Essential*, 487.
3. *Morals*, ch. 13.
4. Both quotes from *Drift*, ch. 12.
5. WL–LH 9/11/27.
6. WL–Mrs. Fred Thompson 11/21/35.
7. Cited in Stephen Birmingham, *Our Crowd: The Great Jewish Families of New York* (New York: Harper, 1967), 291.

2. HARVARD '10

1. OHC 29.
2. Quote from an article Reed wrote in 1917, "Almost Thirty," *NR* 4/29/36, cited in Samuel Eliot Morison, *Three Centuries of Harvard* (Cambridge: Harvard University Press, 1936), 434–435.
3. *Red and Blue* 6/1908.
4. WL–Lucile Elsas, n.d. [1907–1908]; Carl Binger, "A Child of the Enlightenment," in Childs and Reston, *Walter Lippmann and His Times*, 21–36; WL–Elsas 5/10/08.
5. WL–Elsas, n.d. [1908].
6. Ibid.
7. *Crimson* 4/27/35.
8. "The Privileged Classes," *Harvard Illustrated* 11/1908.
9. WL–Daisy Lippmann, n.d. [1908].
10. *Politics*, ch. 6.
11. "The Footnote," *NR* 7/17/1915 (choose); "An Open Mind: William James," *Everybody's* 12/1910.
12. "George Santayana — A Sketch," *International* 8/1911; Max Eastman, *The Enjoyment of Living* (New York: Harper, 1948), 342.
13. WL–Elsas, n.d. [1908].
14. WL–BB 9/10/21; "George Santayana — A Sketch," *International* 8/1911.

3. A FRIEND OF THE MASSES

1. *Drift*, ch. 12.
2. WL–Lucile Elsas 5/3, 5/10/08.
3. "Socialism at Harvard," *Harvard Illustrated* 3/1909.
4. "That Soft Pedal," *Harvard Illustrated* 2/1915; John Reed, "Almost Thirty," cited in Samuel Eliot Morison, *Three Centuries of Harvard* (Cambridge: Harvard University Press, 1936), 434–435; WL–Elsas, n.d. [1908].
5. "In Defense of Suffragettes," *Harvard Monthly* 11/1909; "A Policy of Segregation," *Harvard Monthly* 1/1910.
6. "Harvard in Politics: A Problem in Imperceptibles," *Harvard Monthly* 12/1909; "The Non-Athletic Boy in College," *Red and Blue* 11/1909.
7. "Books and Things," *NR* 8/7/15; *Politics*, ch. 4; for a good discussion see Sugwon Kang, "Graham Wallas and Democracy," *Review of Politics* 10/1979, 536–560.
8. "The Discussion of Socialism: Politics and Meta-Politics," *Harvard Illustrated* 4/1910; OHC 40.
9. From John Reed, "The Day in Bohemia," published privately in 1913, reprinted in Mabel Dodge Luhan, *Movers and Shakers* (New York: Harcourt, 1936), 172–185.
10. Lee Simonson in *Advocate* 1/1908.

11. John Reed's account of the attack on the Institute of 1770 can be found in his manuscript "The Harvard Renaissance," YLC.
12. "Albert the Male," *NR* 7/22/16.
13. Luhan, 387.
14. Hazel Albertson–WL, n.d. [1912]; Elsas–WL 8/1, 12/4/07.
15. Lincoln Steffens–WL 2/7/10.

4. MUCKRAKERS AND SOCIALISTS

1. WL–Lincoln Steffens 5/18/10.
2. Ibid.
3. Steffens–WL 6/1/10.
4. Lincoln Steffens, *The Autobiography of Lincoln Steffens* (New York: Harcourt, 1931), 593.
5. *Politics*, ch. 1.
6. For an account of the evening see *The Greenwich* 1/4/11, YLC, and Herbert Shapiro, "Steffens, Lippmann and Reed," *Pacific Northwest Quarterly* 10/1971.
7. For Lippmann's later remarks see his unpublished interview, 8/1/63, YLC.
8. Newspaper clip file 1910, YLC.
9. Jacob Lippmann–WL 9/12/10.
10. WL–Steffens 4/17/11.
11. Caroline Dexter (secretary of Liberal Club)–WL 10/19/11.
12. "Political Notes," *International* 1/1912, 11/1911.
13. Ibid., 8/1911.
14. Ibid., 5/1912 (wisdom); *Politics*, ch. 1 (initiative).
15. "Two Months in Schenectady," *Masses* 4/1912.
16. *Politics*, ch. 3.
17. "Schenectady the Unwise," *Call* 6/9/12.
18. "The Shrewdly Good," *Call* 6/23/12; also see "A Letter on Political Action," *Call* 11/23/13, based on a letter from WL to Carl D. Thompson, a Socialist party official, 10/29/13.
19. WL–GW 7/31/12.
20. *Politics*, ch. 6; Bernard Berenson, *Sunset and Twilight* (New York: Harcourt, 1963), entry for 10/23/49.

5. A LITTLE ICONOCLASM

1. WL–GW 7/31/12.
2. WL–GW 10/30/12.
3. Alfred Booth Kuttner–WL, n.d. [1912]; the reviews were, in sequence, from the *Boston Transcript*, the *Chicago Evening Post*, the *Cleveland Plain-Dealer*, and the *Schenectady Citizen*.
4. *Politics*, ch. 2 (Tammany), ch. 6 (judgment), ch. 2 (taboo); *Imago* (Vienna), II, 4 (1913); "Freud and the Layman," *NR* 4/17/15.
5. For example, see WL–Charles Mullen 3/29/15; WL–J. G. Phelps Stokes 5/1/17.
6. Mabel Dodge, "Speculations on Post-Impressionism in Prose," *Arts and Decorations* 3/1913, 172–174; *Politics*, ch. 9.
7. Mabel Dodge Luhan, *Movers and Shakers* (New York: Harcourt, 1936), 84; Max Eastman, *The Enjoyment of Living* (New York: Harper, 1948), 523.
8. Lincoln Steffens, *The Autobiography of Lincoln Steffens* (New York: Harcourt, 1931), 654–655; also see Kaplan, *Lincoln Steffens*.
9. Luhan, 432, 119, 257–258.
10. A. A. Brill, "The Introduction and Development of Freud's Work in the United States," *American Journal of Sociology*, XLV, 322–323; Steffens, 655; WL–Mabel Dodge 7/20/15.
11. Luhan, 92–93.
12. *Politics*, ch. 4; John Reed, "The Day in Bohemia," in Luhan, 172–185; Luhan, 119.
13. David Carb–WL 9/23/10, 1/11/13.
14. WL–Lucile Elsas 5/4, 5/6/12; Lucile Elsas Emptage–RS.
15. Luhan, 432; Hutchins Hapgood, *A Victorian in the Modern World* (New York: Harcourt, 1939), 352; WL–GW 5/7/13.

6. REPUTATION

1. WL–Van Wyck Brooks 9/2/13.
2. Herbert Croly–LH 1/5/14, quoted in Forcey, *Crossroads of Liberalism*, 89–90, 178.
3. "Walter Weyl," privately printed, 1922, reprinted in *Public Persons*, 98.
4. Forcey, 176.
5. WL–Brooks 2/5/14.
6. "A Tribute to Theodore Roosevelt," *Essential*, 487–489, and in *Public Persons*, 126–127.
7. WL–Theodore Roosevelt, n.d. [1913]. Roosevelt's letter to Lippmann, along with others from prominent people, was stolen from Lippmann's files in the 1940s.
8. *Drift*, ch. 5.
9. WL–LH 6/12/14.
10. WL diary, 7/4, 7/5/14, YLC.
11. Graham Wallas, *The Great Society* (New York: Macmillan, 1914), v; WL–GW 5/12/14; WL–Audrey Wallas 8/16/32.
12. Van Wyck Brooks, *The Confident Years* (New York: Dutton, 1952), 373; Van Wyck Brooks, *Scenes and Portraits* (New York: Dutton, 1954), 217.
13. Beatrice Webb quoted in Anne Fremantle, *This Little Band of Prophets* (New York: Mentor, 1960), 193–194.
14. Leonard Woolf, *Beginning Again* (New York: Harcourt, 1964), 167–168.
15. WL–GW 7/30/14.
16. WL–FF 8/2/14.
17. GW–WL 9/7/14.

7. "AGITATION ISN'T MY JOB"

1. WL–GW 10/22/14.
2. "Force and Ideas," *NR* 11/7/14.
3. "Walter Weyl," in *Public Persons*, 98; WL–Mabel Dodge 11/20/14.
4. "Vera Cruz," *NR* 11/21/14 (unsigned), also see WL–Roy Ogden 12/8/14; OHC 155; editorial, *NR* 12/12/14.
5. "Notes for a Biography," *NR* 7/16/30; Robert Rogers–Dodge 11/12/14, in Mabel Dodge Luhan, *Movers and Shakers* (New York: Harcourt, 1936), 303.
6. Theodore Roosevelt in *Outlook* 11/18/14; Randolph Bourne–Dorothy Teall 6/14/15, quoted in Lasch, *New Radicalism*, 78; Holmes–Pollack, *Holmes-Pollack Letters: The Correspondence of Mr. Justice Holmes and Sir Frederick Pollack, 1874–1932*, edited by Mark DeWolfe Howe (Cambridge: Harvard University Press, 1941), entry for 11/7/14.
7. *Drift*, introduction (inherit), ch. 14 (science), ch. 8 (interesting), ch. 1 (muckrakers), ch. 2 (owned), ch. 3 (trust); for an interesting discussion see David Hollinger, "Walter Lippmann's *Drift and Mastery*," *American Quarterly*, Winter 1977. Lippmann argued that corporate managers, as professionals, would not be driven by the profit motive, but by pride in their work, and maintained this conviction for many years. "In the days to come," he wrote as late as 1934, "men who are about to become heads of great banks or large corporations will look upon themselves as having retired from the business of making money. . . . In the future, to make a fortune will be considered as improper for the head of a big business as for the President of the United States or the mayor of a city" ("Big Businessmen of Tomorrow," *American Magazine* 4/1934; also in *Essential*, 393–395).
8. Chamberlain, *Farewell to Reform*, 230.
9. WL diary, 7/4/14, YLC; *Drift*, ch. 9 (pedants), introduction (one party). In the summer of 1914, just before leaving for Europe, Lippmann wrote an article criticizing William English Walling for advocating income equality. "The pretense of Socialists that they alone are the agents of progress seems to me to be contradicted by the plain facts of everyday life," Lippmann charged. The poor could best be helped, not by leveling, but by providing them with the "essential decencies. . . . When they have the comforts then they are essentially free people, their struggles are no longer a matter of life and death, and the whole human problem takes on a different character" (Lippmann's review of Walling's *Progressivism and After*, NR 6/1914).
10. The magazine quote is from Lippmann's review of William English Walling's *Larger Aspects*

of Socialism, Call 5/11/13. The other quotes are from *Drift,* ch. 13 (nation), ch. 5 (unions), ch. 7 (freedom). Lippmann's faith in labor, as he wrote Theodore Roosevelt, Jr., 2/18/15, stemmed from "a belief that working men will learn industrial citizenship from the exercise of industrial power; that the only way the habit and intelligence of industrial democracy can be developed is by the increasing exercise of industrial responsibility." For an interesting comment see WL–R. C. Valentine 3/17/16.

11. *Drift,* ch. 10; WL–Upton Sinclair 5/16/14; "Upton Sinclair's Delusion," *International* 12/1911, also in *Public Persons,* 31–35.

12. WL–John Reed 3/25/14.

13. "Legendary John Reed," *NR* 12/26/14, also in *Public Persons,* 41–44. For Lippmann's break with the Socialists see WL–Charles Mullen 3/29/15, and WL–J. G. Phelps Stokes 5/1/17.

14. Mabel's account is in *Luhan,* 325–326; WL–Dodge 1/26/15.

15. "The White Passion," *NR* 10/21/16.

16. *Drift,* ch. 9; WL diary 7/4/14, YLC; Luhan, 487.

17. "Recreating Mr. Wilson," *NR* 1/16/15; "The Footnote," *NR* 7/17/15; "Life Is Cheap," *NR* 12/19/14.

18. "The White Passion," *NR* 10/21/16; "Angels to the Rescue," *NR* 1/1/16; "The Footnote," *NR* 7/17/15.

19. "Books and Things," *NR* 8/7/15; WL–O. W. Holmes 11/23/15.

8. "HYPOCRITICAL NEUTRALITY"

1. *U.S. Foreign Policy,* viii–ix.

2. "Notes for a Biography," *NR* 7/16/30.

3. WL–Robert Dell 10/26/14; "Notes for a Biography," *NR* 7/16/30.

4. "The *Lusitania,*" *NR* 5/15/15; "Pacifism or Passivism," *NR* 12/12/14; "A Cure for Militarism," *Metropolitan* 2/1915.

5. WL–Alfred Zimmern 6/7/15; see, for example, "Washington Notes," *NR* 1/15/16; WL–Dell 6/7/15.

6. "Pro-German?" *NR* 12/4/15; WL–FF 2/29/16.

7. *Diplomacy,* 7–8 (sheep), 67 (nationality), 77–78 (strong men), 62–63 (pride), 155–159 (commissions), 226 (stabilizing), 224 (isolation); see "A New Kind of War," *NR* 7/31/15, also editorial note "The Next Step," ibid.; for an interesting discussion see Forcey, *Crossroads of Liberalism,* 230–241.

8. "Uneasy America," *NR* 12/25/15.

9. Dwight Morrow–WL 12/1914, also see WL's response 1/4/15; "Washington Notes," *NR* 1/29/16.

10. WL–GW 2/21/16.

11. WL–GW 4/21/16.

12. "An Appeal to the President," *NR* 4/22/16; "What Program Shall the United States Stand for in International Politics?" *Annals of the American Academy of Political and Social Science* 7/1916, 61–70.

13. "Hypocritical Neutrality," *NR* 5/13/16; "America to Europe, August 1916," *NR* 7/29/16.

14. WL–John Reed 2/21/16 (Reed's letter to Lippmann has been lost or destroyed); WL–Reed, n.d. [1916].

15. "The Lost Theme," *NR* 4/8/16; see also "Miss Lowell and Things," *NR* 3/18/16.

16. "Mr. Wilson's Great Utterance," *NR* 6/3/16; WL–Henry Hollis 5/29/16.

17. WL–Eustace Percy 5/29/16; WL–GW 8/29/16.

18. WL–GW 12/18/15; WL–FF 1/17/16; WL–Percy 5/29/16.

19. "Integrated America," *NR* 2/19/16; for a good discussion of the relation between politics and culture, see Lasch, *New Radicalism,* ch. 5.

20. For Lippmann's reaction to TR's courting of Root, see WL–Kenneth Hunter 2/29/16; for his editorial criticizing Wilson, "Timid Neutrality," *NR* 11/14/14; for his reconsideration, "Belgium and the Western World," *NR* 3/11/16, and "Mr. Roosevelt's Afterthought," *NR* 3/25/16.

21. "A Luncheon and a Moral," *NR* 4/8/16; Herbert Croly–WL, n.d. [1916]; WL–Willard Straight, n.d. [1916].

22. WL–GW 1/12/16.

9. ELECTING A WAR PRESIDENT

1. WL–FF 2/18/16; WL–Louis Brandeis 2/18/16.
2. See FF–WL, n.d. [1916]; "Untrustworthy?," *NR* 3/11/16.
3. WL–FF 5/8/16.
4. "The Other-Worldliness of Mr. Wilson," *NR* 3/27/15.
5. "At the Chicago Conventions," *NR* 6/17/16.
6. WL–FF 6/30/16.
7. WL–S. K. Ratcliffe 6/15/16.
8. WL–Eustace Percy 7/5/16.
9. Norman Hapgood–Woodrow Wilson 8/28/16, also see WL–Joseph Tumulty 7/26/16; OHC 92; WL–GW 8/29/16.
10. WL–LH 9/4/16; WL–H. G. Wells 10/13/16.
11. OHC 89; "The Case for Wilson," *NR* 10/14/16; OHC 91.
12. "Colonel House," T&T 3/31/38.
13. WL–Mabel Dodge 12/14/16; "Peace without Victory," *NR* 12/23/16.
14. See WL–Tumulty 1/16/17; C. P. Scott–WL 3/21/17; "Notes for a Biography," *NR* 7/16/30.
15. "America Speaks," *NR* 1/27/17; unsigned editorial note, *NR* 2/3/17; "America's Part in the War," *NR* 2/10/17.
16. WL–FF 2/19/17; WL–Norman Angell 3/1/17.
17. "America's Part in the War," *NR* 2/10/17; "The Defense of the Atlantic World," *NR* 2/17/17.
18. WL–EMH 3/10/17; House diary, 3/10/17, House papers, Yale University; WL–Wilson 3/11/17.
19. WL–EMH 4/3/17; "The Great Decision," *NR* 4/7/17; WL–Wilson 4/3/17.
20. *Diplomacy*, 47; "The Great Decision," *NR* 4/7/17.
21. "The World Conflict in Its Relation to American Democracy," *Annals of the American Academy of Political and Social Science* 7/1917.
22. "An Appeal to the President," *NR* 4/22/16.
23. Randolph Bourne, "The War and the Intellectuals" and "A War Diary," in *War and the Intellectuals,* edited by Carl Resek (New York: Harper Torchbooks, 1964).
24. *Diplomacy*, 57; "A Clue," *NR* 4/14/17.

10. TO THE COLORS

1. WL–Woodrow Wilson 2/6, 4/3/17; WL–FF, n.d. [4/1917].
2. See EMH–WL 5/7/17, also House diary same date, House papers, Yale University; WL–NDB 5/7/17.
3. WL–NDB 5/10/17.
4. Mabel Dodge–Hazel Albertson 11/14/16.
5. Mabel Dodge Luhan, *Movers and Shakers* (New York: Harcourt, 1936), 310, 432.
6. WL–FF 4/23/17; WL–GW 4/23/17.
7. WL–LH 5/2/17; LH–WL 5/3/17; WL–FF, n.d. [4/1917].
8. Faye Albertson Heatley–RS; O. W. Holmes in *Adkins* vs. *Children's Hospital,* 1923; Holmes–Harold Laski 9/6/17 and 9/7/16, in *The Holmes-Laski Letters,* edited by Mark DeWolfe Howe (Cambridge: Harvard University Press, 1953).
9. "To Justice Holmes," *NR* 3/11/16; T&T 1/14/32.
10. T&T 10/22/64, reprinted in *Public Persons,* 178–180.
11. See OHC 94; War Department order, 8/15/17, YLC.
12. WL–Norman Hapgood 7/20/17; WL–Alfred Zimmern 7/13/17.
13. *Schenck* vs. *U.S.,* 1919; Max Eastman quoted in Daniel Aaron, *Writers on the Left* (New York: Avon, 1965), 53; Granville Hicks, *John Reed* (New York: Macmillan, 1936), 244; Bourne quoted in Chamberlain, *Farewell to Reform,* 300.
14. WL–Wilson 2/6/17; see WL–Charles Merz 4/11/17; WL–EMH 4/12/17.
15. WL–Louis Brandeis 10/8/17; also see WL diary 10/8, 10/9/17, YLC.
16. WL–Wilson 10/8/17; WL–EMH 10/17/17; also see WL diary 10/10/17, YLC.
17. WL diary 10/5/17, YLC.
18. WL–NDB 8/29/17; Wilson–NDB 8/22/17, Wilson papers, LC; Wilson–Benedict XV 8/27/17, Wilson papers, LC.
19. OHC 9–10, 101; WL–EMH 9/24/17.

11. THE INQUIRY

1. See WL diary 10/5, 10/7, 10/9/17, YLC; WL–NDB 5/16/18.
2. WL–FF 10/30/17.
3. *Public Ledger* (Philadelphia) 9/27/17, cited in Gelfand, *Inquiry*, 39; EMH–Woodrow Wilson 10/3, 9/20/17, House papers, Yale University.
4. EMH–Isaiah Bowman 10/27/17; WL–Wilson 11/21/17; W. A. White–WL 11/20/17; WL–NDB 10/27/17; see Gelfand, *Inquiry*, 352.
5. OHC 104–105; for Lippmann's briefing on the secret treaties see WL diary 10/11/17, YLC; Wilson–EMH 7/21/17, House papers, Yale University.
6. *NR* editorial note 12/8/17; WL–NDB 12/5/17; Wilson–NDB 12/14/17, Baker papers, LC.
7. OHC 107–111.
8. His job, he later explained, was to "take the secret treaties, analyze the parts which were tolerable, and separate them from those which we regarded as intolerable, and then develop an American position which conceded as much to the Allies as it could, but took away the poison. Each point was constructed for that purpose. It was all keyed upon the secret treaties. That's what decided what went into the Fourteen Points" (OHC 109).

WILSON'S FOURTEEN POINTS

I. Open covenants of peace, openly arrived at, after which there shall be no private international understandings of any kind but diplomacy shall proceed always frankly and in the public view.

II. Absolute freedom of navigation upon the seas, outside territorial waters, alike in peace and in war, except as the seas may be closed in whole or in part by international action for the enforcement of international covenants.

III. The removal, so far as possible, of all economic barriers and the establishment of an equality of trade conditions among all the nations consenting to the peace and associating themselves for its maintenance.

IV. Adequate guarantees given and taken that national armaments will be reduced to the lowest point consistent with domestic safety.

V. A free, open-minded, and absolutely impartial adjustment of all colonial claims, based upon a strict observance of the principle that in determining all such questions of sovereignty the interests of the populations concerned must have equal weight with the equitable claims of the government whose title is to be determined.

VI. The evacuation of all Russian territory and such a settlement of all questions affecting Russia as will secure the best and freest co-operation of the other nations of the world in obtaining for her an unhampered and unembarrassed opportunity for the independent determination of her own political development and national policy and assure her of a sincere welcome into the society of free nations under institutions of her own choosing; and, more than a welcome, assistance also of every kind that she may need and may herself desire. The treatment accorded Russia by her sister nations in the months to come will be the acid test of their good will, of their comprehension of her needs as distinguished from their own interests, and of their intelligent and unselfish sympathy.

VII. Belgium, the whole world will agree, must be evacuated and restored, without any attempt to limit the sovereignty which she enjoys in common with all other free nations. No other single act will serve as this will serve to restore confidence among the nations in the laws which they have themselves set and determined for the government of their relations with one another. Without this healing act the whole structure and validity of international law is forever impaired.

VIII. All French territory should be freed and the invaded portions restored, and the wrong done to France by Prussia in 1871 in the matter of Alsace-Lorraine, which has unsettled the peace of the world for nearly fifty years, should be righted, in order that peace may once more be made secure in the interest of all.

IX. A readjustment of the frontiers of Italy should be effected along clearly recognizable lines of nationality.

X. The peoples of Austria-Hungary, whose place among the nations we wish to see safeguarded and assured, should be accorded the freest opportunity of autonomous development.

XI. Rumania, Serbia, and Montenegro should be evacuated; occupied territories restored; Serbia accorded free and secure access to the sea; and the relations of the several Balkan states to one another determined by friendly counsel along historically established lines of allegiance and nationality; and international guarantees of the political and economic independence and territorial integrity of the several Balkan states should be entered into.

XII. The Turkish portions of the present Ottoman Empire should be assured a secure sovereignty, but the other nationalities which are now under Turkish rule should be assured an undoubted security of life and an absolutely unmolested opportunity of autonomous development, and the Dardanelles should be permanently opened as a free passage to the ships and commerce of all nations under international guarantees.

XIII. An independent Polish state should be erected which should include the territories inhabited by indisputably Polish populations, which should be assured a free and secure access to the sea, and whose political and economic independence and territorial integrity should be guaranteed by international covenant.

XIV. A general association of nations must be formed under specific covenants for the purpose of affording mutual guarantees of political independence and territorial integrity to great and small states alike.

9. Cited by Isaiah Bowman in a statement dated 10/5/39, filed with his diary, Bowman papers, Johns Hopkins University.

10. *Opinion,* 212.

11. Every word was chosen with meticulous care, Lippmann later explained (*Opinion,* 213):

The wrong done should be righted; why not say that Alsace-Lorraine should be restored? It was not said because it was not certain that all of the French *at that time* would fight on indefinitely for reannexation if they were offered a plebiscite; and because it was even less certain that the English and Italians would fight on. The formula had, therefore, to cover both contingencies. The word "righted" guaranteed satisfaction to France, but did not read as a commitment to simple annexation.

But why speak of the wrong done by *Prussia* in 1871? The word Prussia was, of course, intended to remind the South Germans that Alsace-Lorraine belonged not to them but to Prussia. Why speak of peace unsettled for "fifty years," and why the use of 1871? In the first place, what the French and the rest of the world remembered was 1871. That was the nodal point of their grievance. But the formulators of the Fourteen Points knew that French officialdom planned for more than the Alsace-Lorraine of 1871. The secret memoranda that had passed between the Czar's ministers and French officials in 1916 covered the annexation of the Saar valley and some sort of dismemberment of the Rhineland. It was planned to include the Saar valley under the term "Alsace-Lorraine" because it had been part of Alsace-Lorraine in 1814, though it had been detached in 1815, and was no part of the territory at the close of the Franco-Prussian war. The official French formula for annexing the Saar was to subsume it under "Alsace-Lorraine" meaning the Alsace-Lorraine of 1814–1815. By insistence on "1871" the President was really defining the ultimate boundary between Germany and France, was adverting to the secret treaty, and was casting it aside.

12. OHC 13, 110.

13. "The Political Scene," *NR* 3/22/19.

14. WL–NDB 2/26/18.

15. NDB to chairman of the CPI, n.d. [probably 2/1918], in Baker papers, quoted in N. Gordon Levin, *Woodrow Wilson and World Politics* (New York: Oxford University Press, 1968), 63.

16. WL–EMH 2/19/18.

17. Ibid.; also see Kaplan, *Lincoln Steffens,* 237.

18. Raphael Zon–WL 2/16/18; Kaplan, *Lincoln Steffens,* 236–237.

19. WL diary 10/9/17, YLC; Harold Laski–O. W. Holmes 1/1/18, in *The Holmes-Laski Letters,* edited by Mark DeWolfe Howe (Cambridge: Harvard University Press, 1953).

20. Ralph Hayes–WL 11/23/17.

21. "The Reminiscences of James T. Shotwell," Oral History Project, Columbia University; Bowman statement of 10/5/39, Bowman papers, Johns Hopkins University; Gelfand, *Inquiry*, 350–352.

12. CAPTAIN LIPPMANN, PROPAGANDIST

1. Heber Blankenhorn–WL 6/14/18.
2. WL–EMH 6/16/18.
3. EMH–WL 6/19/18; WL–Blankenhorn 6/19/18; "The Reminiscences of Heber Blankenhorn," Oral History Project, Columbia University, 99–100.
4. WL–NDB 6/20/18.
5. "Paul Kellogg Muckraked," *NR* 2/20/15; George Creel–WL 3/23/15; WL–Creel 3/25/15; Creel–WL 3/27/15; WL–Creel 3/29/15.
6. Blankenhorn–WL 6/21/18, telegrams.
7. War Department order 151, 6/28/18, YLC; State Department memo, 7/3/18, YLC.
8. Blankenhorn, *Adventures in Propaganda* (Boston: Houghton Mifflin, 1919), 14, 23.
9. WL–EMH 8/9, 8/15/18.
10. Arthur Murray (British Foreign Office)–William Wiseman, cable, 8/8/18, YLC; Wiseman–Murray 8/10/18, YLC; Wiseman unpublished manuscript, YLC; Gelfand, *Inquiry*, 121; Wiseman–Murray 9/14/18, YLC.
11. WL–EMH 8/9, 8/21/18; also see C. P. Scott diary, British Museum ADD 50905, 8/11–8/18/18 (pp. 103–114).
12. Woodrow Wilson–EMH 8/31/18, EMH–Wilson 9/3/18, House papers, Yale University.
13. WL–EMH 9/2/18, House papers, Yale University.
14. Wilson–Robert Lansing 9/5/18, Wilson papers, LC; EMH–WL 9/5/18; WL–EMH 10/2/18.
15. "For a Department of State," *NR* 9/17/19.
16. Blankenhorn, "Reminiscences," 110.
17. WL–Isaiah Bowman 9/10/18; WL–S. E. Mezes 9/5/18, in House papers, Yale University.
18. OHC 118; *Christian Science Monitor* 7/2/49.
19. OHC 15–17; Wilson–EMH 10/30/18, cable, House papers, Yale University.
20. WL–EMH 11/11/18.
21. Inga Floto, *Colonel House in Paris* (Arhus: Universitets forlaget, 1973), I, 64–66; Gelfand, *Inquiry*, 158–159.
22. WL–Dorothy Straight 12/1/18.
23. Ralph Hayes–NDB, n.d. [12/1918], Baker papers, LC.
24. "The Peace Conference," *Yale Review* 7/1919, 710–711.
25. Hayes–NDB 12/22/18, Baker papers, LC; also see Arthur Walworth, *America's Moment: 1918* (New York: Norton, 1977), 259, 259n.
26. Although Bowman, in his 1939 statement, said that Lippmann did go on the mission to Berlin, he was mistaken. Ernest Sutherland Bates, in an unflattering portrait of Lippmann (*Modern Monthly* 6/1933), says that shortly after Wilson's arrival in Paris Lippmann was "summarily ordered home" for reasons never revealed. "Mr. Lippmann tried in vain to obtain an interview with the President to protest against this injustice; Wilson, with his customary ingratitude, refused to see him." When I asked Lippmann if this incident took place, he denied it, and insisted that his departure from Paris had no such dramatic cause.
27. WL–D. Straight 12/28/18.
28. WL–BB 1/25/19; Harold Laski–WL 1/29/19; WL–NDB 2/7/19.

13. "THIS IS NOT PEACE"

1. Harold Laski–WL 1/29/19; see C. P. Scott–WL 1/30/19; Laski–O. W. Holmes 2/23/19, *The Holmes-Laski Letters*, edited by Mark DeWolfe Howe (Cambridge: Harvard University Press, 1953).
2. WL–EMH 3/18/19; WL–BB 3/18/19.
3. "Report of the Bullitt Mission to Russia," *Nation* 10/4/19, 475–482, cited in Kaplan, *Lincoln Steffens*, 245. For a favorable view of the Bullitt mission, see George F. Kennan, *Memoirs: 1925–1950* (Boston: Little, Brown, 1967), 80.

4. "The Political Scene," *NR* 3/22/19; Laski–Holmes 4/23/19, in *Letters*, also see Holmes–Laski 4/20/19; LH–WL 3/29/19.
5. WL–BB 5/6/19.
6. WL–William Chadbourne 5/15/19; WL–Ray S. Baker 5/19/19.
7. For the *NR*'s boast see "Who Willed American Participation?" (unsigned, but not by WL), *NR* 4/14/17; Herbert Croly–Brandeis 5/13/19, Louis D. Brandeis manuscripts, University of Louisville Law Library, quoted in Lasch, *New Radicalism*, 219; "Europe Proposes," *NR* 5/17/19, unsigned.
8. "The ABC of Alliances," *NR* 5/24/19, unsigned; *Boston Post* 5/22/19.
9. WL–NDB 6/9/19.
10. WL–Norman Hapgood 7/28/19; "Colonel House," T&T 3/31/38.
11. WL–NDB 6/9/19; WL–Raymond Fosdick 8/15/19.
12. WL–EMH 7/19/19; WL–FF 7/28/19.
13. WL–FF 7/28/19; WL–C. P. Crozier 9/16/19; also see WL–Ralph Pultizer 7/30/19.
14. WL–BB 7/16/19.
15. WL–Hiram Johnson 8/17, 8/25/19; "Mr. Wilson Testifies," *NR* 9/3/19. In 1922 Lippmann carried on a feud in the pages of the *Nation* with Ray Stannard Baker, editor of Wilson's papers, over the issue of the treaties (see *Nation* 3/29/22), and also wrote about them in 1926 in a review of a book of Colonel House's papers (see "The Intimate Papers of Colonel House," *Foreign Affairs* 4/1926). For other examples of Lippmann's reactions, see Archibald Cary Coolidge–WL 3/17/26; Sidney Mezes–WL 3/19/26; WL–Allen Dulles 2/24/36. Also see House's diary, 4/28/17, House papers, Yale University, for his discussion of the secret treaties with British Foreign Secretary Arthur Balfour.
16. See Johnson–WL 8/20/19 and WL–Johnson 9/9/19; WL–BB 9/15/19.
17. WL–NDB 7/19/19; WL–BB, n.d. [1921, probably Oct.].
18. "The Triumph of the Irreconcilables," *NR* 3/31/20 (not by WL).
19. "Liberalism in America," *NR* 3/31/19; WL–William Bullitt 1/9/20.
20. "The Intimate Papers of Colonel House," *Foreign Affairs* 4/1926; "Notes for a Biography," *NR* 7/16/30.
21. W. A. White–R. S. Baker, in *Selected Letters of William Allen White: 1899–1943*, edited by Walter Johnson, quoted in Goldman, *Rendezvous with Destiny*, 220.
22. WL–NDB 1/17/20.
23. "Leonard Wood," *NR* 3/17/20; Keynes in Richard Hofstadter, *The American Political Tradition* (New York: Vintage, n.d.), 283.
24. Editor's note, *NR* 2/4/20; WL–FF 4/7/20, also see WL–Hoover 4/8/20.
25. "Is Harding a Republican?" *NR* 7/21/20.
26. "Chicago 1920," *NR* 6/23/20; "Two Leading Democratic Candidates — McAdoo," *NR* 6/2/20; WL–Scott 6/30/20.
27. WL–F. D. Roosevelt, telegram, 7/8/20; WL–GW 8/31/20; WL–S. K. Ratcliffe 8/10/20.
28. WL–GW 11/4/20; WL–GW 3/29/21.

14. PICTURES IN THEIR HEADS

1. WL–Ellery Sedgwick 4/7/19; "What Modern Liberty Means," *Atlantic* 11/1919; "Liberty and the News," *Atlantic* 12/1919.
2. *Liberty*, 61–63 (decisions), 97 (construction), 47 (bible).
3. "A Test of the News," *NR* 8/4/20; for a good discussion, see Phillip Knightley, *The First Casualty* (New York: Harcourt, 1975), 138–170.
4. "Authority in the Modern State," *NR* 5/31/19, a review of Laski's book of the same title; Laski–O. W. Holmes 11/20/16, *The Holmes-Laski Letters*, edited by Mark DeWolfe Howe (Cambridge: Harvard University Press, 1953).
5. "The Nature of the Battle over Censorship," *VF* 3/1927; "An Anticipation of Harding," *VF* 7/1920 (both reprinted in *Destiny*); Holmes–Laski 5/12/28, in *Letters*.
6. D. M. Tucker, "Some American Responses to the Easter Rebellion," *Historian*, XXIX (8/1967), 612–613, cited in Francis M. Carroll, *American Opinion and the Irish Question* (New York: St. Martin's, 1978), 221n.

7. Edmund Wilson–Stanley Dell 2/19/21, in Edmund Wilson, *Letters on Literature and Politics* (New York: Farrar, Straus, 1977), 56.
8. Laski–Holmes 1/4/20, in *Letters*.
9. Ralph Pulitzer–WL 6/3/21.
10. WL–FF 6/24/21.
11. Edmund Wilson, *The Twenties*, edited by Leon Edel (New York: Farrar, Straus, 1975), 288; Laski–Holmes 8/14/21, in *Letters;* Philip Littell–WL 7/15/21.
12. BB–WL 3/21/38.
13. WL–Jacob Lippmann 11/8/21.
14. *Opinion*, ch. 6 (define), ch. 7 (stereotypes), ch. 9 (fact), ch. 1 (pictures), ch. 15 (dogma), ch. 24 (news), ch. 1 (fiction), ch. 20 (common).
15. John Dewey, "Public Opinion," *NR* 5/3/22; Laski–Holmes 4/5/22, in *Letters;* Holmes–Pollack 5/21/22 in *Holmes-Pollack Letters: The Correspondence of Mr. Justice Holmes and Sir Frederick Pollack, 1874–1932*, edited by Mark DeWolfe Howe (Cambridge: Harvard University Press, 1941).
16. LH–WL 5/12/22; WL–LH 5/19/22.
17. "H. G. Wells and an Altered World," *VF* 12/1920, also in *Public Persons*, 61–62.

15. A CONSPICUOUS RACE

1. Cited in Stephen Birmingham, *Our Crowd: The Great Jewish Families of New York* (New York: Harper, 1967), 294.
2. Morgenthau quoted in Goldman, *Rendezvous*, 142; Brandeis quoted in Melvin Urofsky, *American Zionism: From Herzl to the Holocaust* (Garden City: Anchor, 1975), 127.
3. Brandeis quoted in Urofsky, 129; Veblen quoted in Kazin, *On Native Grounds*, 103.
4. Randolph Bourne, "Trans-National America," in *War and the Intellectuals*, edited by Carl Resek (New York: Harper Torchbooks, 1964), 107–123, also see David Hollinger, "Ethnic Diversity, Cosmopolitanism, and the Emergence of the American Liberal Intellectual," *American Quarterly* 5/1975; Bourne, "The Jew and Trans-National America," in *War and the Intellectuals*, 124–133.
5. WL–Henry Hurwitz, 12/24/16.
6. Hurwitz–WL 1/21/15; "Patriotism in the Rough," *NR* 10/16/15, also in *Diplomacy*, 66; Hurwitz–WL 10/18/15; WL–Hurwitz 10/19/15.
7. Hurwitz–WL 7/22/20; WL–Hurwitz 7/31/21; Hurwitz–WL 2/25/22; from a manuscript in the Hebrew Institute, Cincinnati, 1/31/21.
8. *Diplomacy*, 62; Carl Sandburg, *The Chicago Race Riots* (New York: Harcourt, 1919), introduction by Lippmann, iii–iv.
9. Walter Blumenthal (associate editor of *American Hebrew*)–WL 3/3/22; "Public Opinion and the American Jew," *American Hebrew* 4/14/22.
10. For a provocative discussion of Lippmann's Jewish problem, see Heinz Eulau, "From Public Opinion to Public Philosophy," *American Journal of Economics and Sociology* 7/1956, 442–446.
11. Editors of *American Hebrew*–WL 3/10, 3/17/22; also see William A. Drake, "Walter Lippmann — A Personality," *American Hebrew* 12/5/24.
12. WL–Arthur Holcombe 6/14/22.
13. WL–Lawrence Henderson (probably 10/27/22; I have been unable to determine whether this draft was actually sent); editorial *NYW* 1/12/23.
14. WL–HBA 2/12/38; Jewish Academy of Arts and Sciences–WL 11/23/34, also 4/4/41; WL–Jewish Academy 4/3/41.
15. *Opinion*, ch. 8.

16. LORD OF THE TOWER

1. James P. Barrett, *Joseph Pulitzer and His World* (New York: Vanguard, 1941), 366.
2. Ibid., 373.

3. *NYW* 1/8/22.
4. WL–FF 2/25/22.
5. WL–BB 1/1/23.
6. WL–RS.
7. Ibid.; Arthur Krock, *Sixty Years on the Firing Line* (New York: Funk and Wagnalls, 1968), 61–62.
8. James M. Cain, "Walter Lippmann Had Style," *Washington Post, Potomac* magazine, 2/2/75.
9. WL–John Avent 5/18/22; WL–Janet Flexner 6/23/25; Cain, "Walter Lippmann Had Style," *Washington Post, Potomac* magazine, 2/2/75; WL–FF 11/26/24.
10. See Cain–WL 7/21, 7/23, 7/31/33, and WL–Cain 8/8 (telegram), 8/9/33; Cain–David Weingast 10/1/47, Cain papers, courtesy of Roy Hoopes; Cain, "Walter Lippmann Had Style," *Washington Post, Potomac* magazine, 2/2/75.
11. OHC 132–134; "Calvin Coolidge: Puritanism de Luxe," *VF* 5/1926, also in *Destiny*, 10–17; T&T 1/6/33, also in *Public Persons*, 119.
12. "Marvels and Miracles," *NYW* 5/21/24; Harry Houdini–WL 5/26/24; WL–Houdini 5/27/24; E. J. Kahn, Jr., *The World of Swope* (New York: Simon and Schuster, 1965), 246–247.
13. *NYW* 5/10/28 (radium); *NYW* 5/8/24 (Cooney); *NYW* 12/16/25 (Karolyi), also see WL–Dwight Morrow 8/11/25; on Lawrence see Mabel Dodge Luhan–WL 1/12/30, WL–Joseph P. Cotton 1/16/30, WL–Elliott Thurston 1/16/20, WL–W. W. Husband (Department of Labor) 1/27/30, WL–Luhan 1/27/30.
14. "The Mental Age of Americans," a series of six articles in the *NR*, 10/25, 11/1, 11/8, 11/15, 11/22, 11/29/22, plus two replies by WL to Lewis Terman, *NR* 1/3, 1/17/23.
15. *NYW* 2/18/26 (contempt); *NYW* 1/28/27 (Browning); T&T 4/7/36 (intolerable); T&T 4/6/32 (curiosity); T&T 12/28/35 (refugees).
16. WL talk to Graduate School of Journalism, Columbia University, YLC, also quoted in Luskin, *Lippmann, Liberty and the Press*, 81–82.
17. *NYW* 7/11/30.
18. *NYW* 2/18/25 (line); *NYW* 2/23/25 (mama); *NYW* 1/28/27 (Bible); *NYW* 2/17/31 (garbage); WL–Arthur Krock 4/3/25.
19. *NYW* 3/20/30.
20. Barrett, 85; Oswald Garrison Villard, "What's Wrong with the *World*?" *Nation* 6/25/30; James M. Cain, "The End of the *World*," *New Freeman* 3/11/31.

17. TYRANNY OF THE MASSES

1. WL–LH 9/18/23; WL–Arthur Holcombe 9/10/25.
2. *Phantom*, 20 (find time), 36–37 (voter), 65 (curtain), 77 (phantom), 70 (meddle); "Insiders and Outsiders," *NR* 11/13/15.
3. *Phantom*, 155 (herd); *Opinion*, ch. 20; John Dewey in *NR* 12/2/25; Arthur Schlesinger, Jr., in Childs and Reston, *Walter Lippmann and His Times*, 205–206; *Phantom*, 189–190 (unmanageable).
4. H. L. Mencken, "Katzenjammer," *American Mercury* 1/1926; "Political Notes," *International* 12/1911.
5. Bruce Bliven, "Atlantic's Bookshelf," *Atlantic* 11/1927.
6. *Phantom*, 58; GW–WL 12/24/25; *Phantom*, 15.
7. *NYW* 5/16/25; also see *NYW* 5/20, 5/26, 6/12, 7/1, 7/3, 7/5, 7/15, 7/16, 7/17, 7/18, 7/21, 7/24/25; WL–GW 6/11/25.
8. WL–LH, n.d. [early June 1925], also see LH–WL 6/10/25.
9. *NYW* 7/28/25, also in *Public Persons*, 74–76; "Bryan and the Dogma of Majority Rule," *VF* 3/1926, also in *Destiny*, 45.
10. *NYW* 10/27/27.
11. "Blazing Publicity," *VF* 9/1927; *Inquisitors*, 111.

18. A MUTED TRUMPET

1. J. K. Galbraith, *Ambassador's Journal: A Personal Account of the Kennedy Years* (Boston: Houghton Mifflin, 1969), 47; James M. Cain, "Walter Lippmann Had Style," *Washington Post, Potomac* magazine, 2/2/75.

2. "The Fall of President Meiklejohn," *NYW* 6/24/23, also in *Public Persons,* 67-73.
3. FF–WL 6/30/23; WL–FF 8/3/23.
4. FF–WL 8/6/23.
5. WL–LH 9/18/23.
6. WL–FF 6/11, 6/13/29, FF–WL 6/12/29; also see WL–FF 6/4/29, FF–WL 6/5/29, WL–LH 6/6/29, LH–WL 6/7/29.
7. FF–WL 6/11/24, also see FF–WL 11/8/23; "Al Smith: A Man of Destiny," *VF* 12/1925, also in *Destiny,* 1; "Behold the Leader," *NYW* 6/23/24, also see WL–Charlton Ogburn 6/12/24, WL–Philip Littell 7/18/24.
8. WL–BB 7/16/24, also see *NYW* 7/10/24; see Felix Frankfurter, "Why Mr. Davis Shouldn't Run," *NR* 4/16/24, unsigned; FF–WL 7/1/24. According to Davis's biographer, "Smith had been merely a stalking horse for the urban Catholic bosses who aimed to force the nomination not of a Catholic (they could have had Walsh, a progressive and a dry), but of a conservative and a wet." See William A. Harbaugh, *Lawyer's Lawyer: The Life of John W. Davis* (New York: Oxford University Press, 1973), 205.
9. WL editorial on Davis, *NYW* 4/4/24; FF–WL 7/18/24; also see FF–WL 7/11/24.
10. FF–WL 8/5, 8/8/24; WL–FF 8/11/24.
11. James M. Cox–WL 7/19/24.
12. *NYW* 11/1, 10/30, 10/31/24.
13. "Why I Shall Vote for Davis," *NR* 10/29/24.
14. *NYW* 11/8, 10/15/24.
15. "The Setting for John W. Davis," *Atlantic* 10/1924; *NYW* 11/6/24.
16. "The Case of Sacco and Vanzetti," *Atlantic* 3/1927, 409–432; *NYW* 8/8/27.
17. *NYW* 8/12/27; also see "The Reminiscences of Gardner Jackson," Oral History Project, Columbia University, 226, 230, 282.
18. WL–F. P. Adams 8/16/27; *NYW* 8/19/27.
19. See James P. Barrett, *Joseph Pulitzer and His World* (New York: Vanguard, 1941) 389–390; WL–Adams 8/19/27; "Patriotic Service," *NYW* 8/24/27.
20. Cain, "Walter Lippmann Had Style," *Washington Post, Potomac* magazine, 2/2/75; Amos Pinchot, "Walter Lippmann," a four-part series in *Nation,* 7/5, 7/12, 7/19, 7/26/33.
21. LH–WL 9/20/27; GW–WL 9/12/27.
22. WL–LH 9/11/27; Felix Frankfurter, *The Case of Sacco and Vanzetti* (Boston: Little, Brown, 1927); for Schwimmer case, WL–FF 6/4/29, *NYW* 6/26/29, also *NYW* 5/31/29, FF–WL 6/5/29.

19. THE MEXICAN CONNECTION

1. Faye Albertson Heatley–RS; WL–RS.
2. *NYW* 12/29/26.
3. "The Kellogg Doctrine: Vested Rights and Nationalism in Latin America," *Foreign Affairs* 4/1927; for WL's attitude also see WL–Arthur Page 10/6/24, WL–Frank Kellogg 12/18/25, 2/2/26, WL–Samuel Maginnis 2/3/26; WL–Frederick Kellogg 3/4/27.
4. *NYW* 1/14/27, also see *NYW* 1/15/27; WL–George Rublee 2/1/27, also see WL–Ralph Pulitzer 2/3/27.
5. *NYW* 4/29/28, also see *NYW* 1/8, 3/9/27; WL–Raymond Buell 4/24/28; "Empire: The Days of Our Nonage Are Over," *VF* 4/1927, also in *Destiny,* 221.
6. *NYW* 1/3/27.
7. *NYW* 10/20/27; *Harold Nicolson: Diaries and Letters 1930–1939,* edited by Nigel Nicolson (New York: Atheneum, 1966), 186; also see Harold Nicolson, *Dwight Morrow* (New York: Harcourt, 1935).
8. WL–Dwight Morrow 12/2/27; also see WL–Morrow 9/22/27, WL–Martin Egan 11/10/27, WL–William E. Borah 12/15/27.
9. *NYW* 12/16/27. The solution was only temporary; in 1938 President Lázaro Cárdenas nationalized the oil industry and expropriated foreign holdings.
10. "Church and State in Mexico: The American Mediation," *Foreign Affairs* 1/1930.
11. WL–Morrow 3/28/28; also see "Second Thoughts on Havana," *Foreign Affairs* 7/1928, WL memo in Mexico file, YLC, 4/2/28.
12. WL–Reuben Clark, 6/19/28; for WL's account see "Church and State in Mexico," *Foreign Affairs* 1/1930.

13. WL–Rublee 5/18/28; *NYW* 12/2/29, 6/6/30.
14. *NYW* 6/19/31.
15. T&T 10/6, 10/7/31.

20. MEN OF DESTINY

1. WL–H. B. Swope 1/25/27.
2. T&T 10/7/44, also in *Public Persons*, 156–158.
3. "Al Smith: A Man of Destiny," *VF* 12/1925, also in *Destiny*, 1.
4. WL–FF 7/3/28; "Tammany Hall and Al Smith," *Outlook* 2/1/28; "The Wetness of Al Smith," *Harper's* 1/1928.
5. On this issue, see, for example: *NYW* 10/3/26, WL–Al Smith 5/9/28, WL–Ellery Sedgwick 5/16/28, WL–Ralph Pulitzer 6/21/28, and also WL–Belle Moscowitz 6/26/28; *Franklin D. Roosevelt: His Personal Letters*, edited by Elliott Roosevelt (New York: Duell, Sloan, 1950), 109, quoted in Joseph P. Lash, *Eleanor and Franklin* (New York: Norton, 1971), 41.
6. WL–Moscowitz 8/2/28, also see WL–Moscowitz 6/25/28, WL–Smith 8/6/28.
7. WL–NDB 8/27/28.
8. *NYW* 4/9/24; WL–Calvert Magruder 10/9/28.
9. WL–Herbert Croly 11/21/28; also see *NYW* 9/6, 9/10, 9/26, 9/28/28, WL–C. A. Williams 11/2/27, WL–Moscowitz 9/13/28, WL–Charles Marshall 9/21/28, W. A. White–WL (telegram) 10/2/28, and *Selected Letters of William Allen White: 1899–1943*, edited by Walter Johnson (New York: Holt, 1947), 284.
10. NDB–WL 7/1/28; also see WL–NDB 7/3/28.
11. *NYW* 7/2/28; "Hoover and Smith," *VF* 9/1928.
12. "Birds of a Feather," *Harper's* 3/1925.
13. WL–Swope 10/20/28.
14. T. W. Lamont–WL 12/9/25, 1/14/28, also Lamont–De Martino 1/23/29, quoted in John P. Diggins, *Mussolini and Fascism: The View from America* (Princeton: Princeton University Press, 1972), 51.
15. Herbert Croly, "Realistic Liberalism," *NR* 11/23/27, also see "Socratic Liberalism," *NR* 12/28/27, quoted in Diggins, 231.
16. *NYW* 12/28/25; "Autocracy and Catholicism," *Commonweal* 4/13/27, quoted in Diggins, 194.
17. WL interview with Richard Rovere 6/30/64, YLC; WL–BB 4/20/29; *Phantom*, 186.
18. *NYW* 1/29, 2/1, 2/2, 2/5/22; also see *U.S. Foreign Policy*, x, 55–56; *NYW* 12/18, 12/11/24; William E. Borah–WL 12/19, 12/31/24; WL–Borah 1/1/25, 12/22/24; *NYW* 12/1/27.
19. "Borah," *Foreign Affairs* 1/1926, also in *Destiny*, 144.
20. WL–Dwight Morrow 8/11/25; WL–Borah 3/5/26; Borah–WL 3/5/26; WL–John Balderston 7/14/25; WL–Borah 7/1/26; Borah–WL 7/2, 7/9, 7/12/26; WL–Borah 7/12/26.
21. *NYW* 10/28/24, see also *NYW* 1/14/25, 1/29/26; for Lippmann's criticism of Borah's stand on the World Court, see *NYW* 1/12/28, also *NYW* 4/27, 8/7/28.
22. *NYW* 1/12/28; "The Outlawry of War," *VF* 8/1923, also in *Destiny*, 162.
23. *NYW* 1/5/29; also see *NYW* 7/28/28 and 1/16/29, and WL–Robert Wagner 1/9/29.
24. "The Political Equivalent of War," *Atlantic* 8/1928; for other comments by WL on the Kellogg pact see WL–Kellogg 7/19/28, *NYW* 12/28/28.
25. *NYW* 8/7/28, 7/25/29; Borah–WL 7/26/29, WL–Borah 7/29/29.
26. *NYW* 1/23/30, also see *NYW* 9/14/29; *U.S. Foreign Policy*, ix–x; also see *NYW* 5/16, 6/7, 6/26/30, WL–Henry Stimson 5/29/30, Stimson–WL 6/7/30, *NYW* 5/15/30.

21. THE DISINTERESTED MAN

1. *Inquisitors*, 111; "Second Best Statesmen," *Yale Review* 7/1922, also in *Destiny*, 223–241.
2. "The Causes of Political Indifference," *Atlantic* 2/1927, also in *Destiny*, 18; Norman Thomas, "Where Are the Pre-War Radicals?" *Survey* 2/21/26 (Thomas was one of many contributors to a special issue bearing this title).
3. "Free Time and Extra Money," *Woman's Home Companion* 4/1933.
4. "The Enormously Civilized Minority," *VF* 3/1928.
5. "H. L. Mencken," *VF* 12/1926, also in *Destiny*, 61–70; also see "The Near-Machiavelli," *NR* 5/31/22.

6. "Sinclair Lewis," *VF* 6/1927, also in *Destiny,* 71–92; WL–Alfred Harcourt 5/4/27.
7. Benjamin Stolberg, "Walter Lippmann: Connoisseur of Public Life," *Nation* 12/7/27.
8. "The Nature of the Battle over Censorship," *VF* 3/1927, also in *Destiny,* 93–106.
9. WL–LH 9/11/27.
10. *Morals,* ch. 1 (modernity), ch. 7 (humanists); WL–NDB 5/15/29.
11. *Morals,* ch. 15; W. A. White–Henry Seidel Canby 1/21/29, in *Selected Letters of William Allen White: 1899–1943,* edited by Walter Johnson (New York: Holt, 1947), 290–291.
12. O. W. Holmes–WL 6/14/29; BB–WL 7/11/29; Harold Laski–WL 6/11/29.
13. Charles Bennett, "Modern Morality," *Saturday Review* 5/18/29; "Faith on Easy Terms," *Commonweal* 10/16/29; Felix Morrow, "Religion and the Good Life," *Menorah Journal* 2/1930.
14. Edmund Wilson in *NR* 7/10/29; George Santayana, "Enduring the Truth," *Saturday Review* 12/7/29; also see Lippmann's response to Santayana, and Santayana's reply: "A Footnote to Santayana," *Saturday Review* 12/7/29, Santayana–H. S. Canby 1/16/30 in *The Letters of George Santayana,* edited by Daniel Cory (New York: Scribner's, 1955), 250–251.
15. *Morals,* ch. 14.
16. WL–HBA 2/8/38; HBA–WL 2/3/38.
17. "The Scholar in a Troubled World," *Atlantic* 8/1932, also in *Essential,* 515–516.

22. THE END OF THE *WORLD*

1. James M. Cain, "The End of the *World,*" *New Freeman* 3/11/31.
2. WL–H. B. Swope 9/16/25; OHC 122, also see WL's "Two Revolutions in the American Press," *Yale Review* 3/1931.
3. WL–BB 6/25/30.
4. Arthur Holcombe–WL 1/8/31; WL–Ben Dixon MacNeil 5/27/30; WL–BB 6/25/30.
5. WL–BB 12/24/30.
6. WL–NDB 2/26/31.
7. OHC 140.
8. Cain, "The End of the *World,*" *New Freeman* 3/11/31.
9. "Two Revolutions in the American Press," *Yale Review* 3/1931, 438–439.
10. WL–RS.
11. WL–BB 1/16/31; WL–NDB 3/7/31.
12. T. W. Lamont–WL 3/2/31; WL–RS, also see OHC 142.
13. *Time* 3/30/31; "The Press and Public Opinion," an address reprinted in *Political Science Quarterly* 6/1931, 161–170.
14. *Time* 3/30/31; Harold Laski–O. W. Holmes 3/23/31, in *The Holmes-Laski Letters,* edited by Mark DeWolfe Howe (Cambridge: Harvard University Press, 1953).
15. WL–LH 4/26/31; LH–WL 5/31/31.
16. WL–BB 6/28/31.
17. *New York Times* 3/28/31; Steffens–Ella Winter 9/27/31, in *The Letters of Lincoln Steffens,* edited by E. Winter and G. Hicks (New York: Harcourt, 1938); Ralph Hayes–FF 9/9/31, FF–Hayes 9/12/31, Hayes papers, LC.
18. Arthur Krock in *Vogue* 10/15/31; Beverly Smith, "The Man with a Flashlight Mind," *American* 9/1932, 16; James Truslow Adams, "Walter Lippmann," *Saturday Review* 1/7/33; cartoon in *New Yorker* 10/1/32.
19. "A Columnist Is an Editorial Writer," *Quill* 3/1951; for an interesting discussion of this issue see doctoral dissertation by Michael Schudson, Sociology Department, University of Chicago, 1977, also Schudson, *Discovering the News: A Social History of American Newspapers* (New York: Basic Books, 1978).
20. WL–J. T. Adams 1/11/33.
21. W. A. White–WL 4/19/32; "The Causes of Political Indifference," *Atlantic* 2/1927; LH–WL 5/12/22.

23. AN "AMIABLE BOY SCOUT"

1. *NYW* 1/1/31.
2. T&T 10/22/64.

3. "Hoover and Smith," *VF* 9/1928.
4. WL–Herbert Croly 3/24/30; *NYW* 6/18/30; "The Peculiar Weakness of Mr. Hoover," *Harper's* 6/1930; WL–FF 11/6/30.
5. T&T 1/5/32; WL–FF 1/21/32.
6. WL–NDB 9/10/31; T&T 2/3/32; "The Case Against the Dole," *Woman's Home Companion*, 1/1932 (demoralizing); *NYW* 11/16/26, 2/21/31; T&T 5/4/32 (menace).
7. "The Almighty Dollar," *Woman's Home Companion* 11/1931; for example, see Russell Leffingwell–WL 10/30/31; see T&T 11/24/31; WL–BB 12/24/30; T&T 5/31/33, also see 5/26/33.
8. T&T 3/29/32; WL–FF 4/5, 4/8/32.
9. T&T 5/20/32.
10. OHC 156; WL–NDB 11/24/31.
11. T&T 1/8/32; OHC 159.
12. WL–NDB 9/18/31.
13. Alfred Allen Lewis, *Man of the World: Herbert Bayard Swope* (New York: Bobbs-Merrill, 1978), 196; Heywood Broun, "It Seems to Me," 5/7/32.
14. T&T 6/7, 6/29/32.
15. T&T 7/4/32.
16. T&T 6/29/32; WL–FF 9/14/32.
17. T&T 10/7/32; Leffingwell–WL 10/27/32.
18. T&T 11/4/32; WL–Ogden Reid 11/4/32; Lawrence Winship–FF 11/5/32, YLC.
19. WL–William E. Borah 11/3/32.
20. T&T 12/30/32.
21. *Morals*, ch. 13; "Usurpers and Abdicators," *VF* 8/1922.

24. A RELUCTANT CONVERT

1. William Manchester, *The Glory and the Dream* (Boston: Little, Brown, 1974), 77.
2. WL–RS; "The Bogey of Public Opinion," *VF* 12/1931; T&T 1/17/33.
3. T&T 2/14/33 (dictatorial); T&T 2/17/33 (deny); T&T 2/24/33 (concentrate); also see T&T 2/10/33.
4. T&T 3/11, 4/6/33.
5. FF–WL 3/1/33; WL–FF 3/3/33.
6. WL–FF 3/8/33.
7. WL–FF 3/14/33; see *Roosevelt and Frankfurter: Their Correspondence, 1928–1945*, edited by Max Freedman (Boston: Little, Brown, 1968), 115.
8. *NYHT* 6/13/33.
9. WL–RS.
10. T&T 4/18/33.
11. T&T 6/29/33.
12. OHC 155.
13. T&T 7/4/33.
14. Address at Amherst College 11/11/33, YLC; "Self-Sufficiency," *Foreign Affairs* 1/1934, 215.
15. *Method of Freedom*, 8–9 (policies), 33 (laissez-faire), 35 (continuity), 59 (counteract), 80 (perversion); John Chamberlain, "The Search for a Philosopher-King," *Saturday Review* 6/9/34.
16. Lewis Gannett in *NYHT* 6/5/34; Clifton Fadiman in *New Yorker* 6/9/34.

25. TIMES OUT OF JOINT

1. WL–BB 1/9/35.
2. WL–BB 3/23/35; T&T 1/5/35; speech to Boston Chamber of Commerce 5/14/35, in *Vital Speeches* 6/3/35; speech at Harvard University 6/21/35, in *Vital Speeches* 7/1/35; also see "The Permanent New Deal," *Yale Review* 6/1935.
3. WL–John W. Davis 7/1/35.
4. WL–FDR 6/4/35.
5. WL–Armstrong 6/25/35.
6. T&T 2/5/35.

7. *NYW* 5/22/28, also see *NYW* 12/23/27 and 3/12/30; T&T 2/5/35.
8. T&T 3/16/35; WL–Stevens Warner 3/23/35.
9. T&T 7/8 (overpowering), 7/18 (victim), 8/20/35 (blanket); also see broadcast over NBC radio network 8/21/35, in *Vital Speeches* 8/26/35, and "From Walter Lippmann," *Yale Review* 9/1935; WL–Edward Sheldon 9/5/35.
10. OHC 163–165 (Lippmann apparently misremembered the date, which, according to his engagement book, was 1935, and not "shortly after the election"); WL–Sheldon 9/19/35.
11. WL–NDB 1/22/36; WL–Arthur Holcombe 1/27/36; WL–Lewis Douglas 3/16/36.
12. WL–Douglas 7/30/36; OHC 167–168; T&T 9/8/36; WL–Murray Nelson 9/23/36.
13. T&T 10/20/36; WL–LH 11/4/36; WL–Grenville Clark 11/4/36.
14. T&T 2/9, 5/20, 6/6/37; "The Rise of Personal Government in the United States," address at Johns Hopkins 4/21/37, in *NYHT* 4/22/37 and *Vital Speeches* 5/1/37.
15. T&T 2/18/37.
16. *From the Diaries of Felix Frankfurter*, with biographical essay and notes by Joseph P. Lash (New York: Norton, 1975), 59, 63.
17. OHC 166–167; "The Deepest Issue of Our Time," address at the University of Rochester 6/15/36, in *Vital Speeches* 7/1/36, also in *Essential*, 386; LH–Lessing Rosenthal 6/5/36, in *Roosevelt and Frankfurter: Their Correspondence, 1928–1945*, edited by Max Freedman (Boston: Little, Brown, 1968), 49; Kenneth Clark, *The Other Half* (New York: Harper, 1978), 90.
18. T&T 4/1/37; WL–Lucie (Mrs. Walter) Rosen 6/30/37.
19. WL–Ellery Sedgwick 4/2/36.
20. *Society*, 367; John P. Diggins, *Mussolini and Fascism: The View from America* (Princeton: Princeton University Press, 1972), 466–468.
21. For example, see Friedrich von Hayek–WL 4/6/37; *Morals*, ch. 12.
22. OHC 161.
23. Ralph Barton Perry, "The Liberal State," *Yale Review*, Winter 1937–1938; Corliss Lamont in *New Masses* 11/2/37; John Dewey, "Liberalism in a Vacuum," *Common Sense* 12/1937; Lewis Mumford, "Mr. Lippmann's Heresy Hunt," *NR* 9/29/37; Edmund Wilson, "An Open Letter to Walter Lippmann," *NR* 11/11/31.
24. T&T 12/14/37.
25. *Society*, 236; Commager, *The American Mind*, 221.
26. *Society*, 212 (epochs), x (generalizations); interestingly, this confession disappeared from later editions.

26. TREADING WATER

1. *NYW* 9/5/29; see "The Political Equivalent of War," *Atlantic* 8/1928; for a good discussion see Cary, *The Influence of War on Walter Lippmann*, especially ch. 4; *NYW* 1/23/30.
2. T&T 9/29/31; WL–Russell Leffingwell 10/22/31.
3. T&T 11/20/31.
4. T&T 12/10/31; WL–Henry Stimson 12/22/31.
5. WL–LH 2/25/32; T&T 2/26/32.
6. T&T 4/28/33.
7. Lippmann rejected an invitation to join the Jewish Academy of Arts and Sciences, and later an award from that organization, saying that he had made an "invariable rule not to accept awards or membership in organizations which have a sectarian character." See Jewish Academy–WL 10/16/34, WL–Jewish Academy 11/23/34, also Jewish Academy–WL 4/1/41, WL–Jewish Academy 4/3/41.
8. T&T 5/12/33; FF–WL 5/13, 4/28/33, also see WL–FF 5/1/33.
9. T&T 5/19/33. The key paragraphs in their entirety are:

. . . There will be some who will say that the address is merely a shrewd maneuver and that it must be rejected as insincere. I do not take this view. The truer explanation, I believe, is that we have heard once more, through the fog and the din, the hysteria and the animal passions of a great revolution, the authentic voice of a genuinely civilized people. I am not only willing to believe that, but it seems to me that all historical experience compels one to believe it. The idea that any people is intrinsically outcast has no foundation except in ignorance and cupidity. It was an intolerable idea when it was applied to the German nation and written into the Treaty of Versailles, and it is an intolerable idea when it is applied now by the Germans themselves to an integral part of their own nation. To deny today that Germany can speak as a civilized power, because uncivilized things are being said and done in Germany, is in itself a deep form of intolerance. Like all intolerance it betrays a lack of moral wisdom, in this case the moral wisdom of religious insight into the dual nature of man.

Those who have that wisdom will pass judgment upon the actions of men but never upon their whole natures. Who that has studied history and cares for the truth would judge the French people by what went on during the Terror? Or the British people by what happened in Ireland? Or the American people by the hideous record of lynchings? Or the Catholic Church by the Spanish Inquisition? Or Protestantism by the Ku Klux Klan? Or the Jews by their parvenus? Who then shall judge finally the Germans by the frightfulness of war times and of the present revolution? If a people is to be judged solely by its crimes and its sins, all the peoples of this planet are utterly damned. Such judgments can produce only the deepest kind of anarchy. The civilized judgment, on which depends all the possibilities of a decent human life, requires that men, while condemning and resisting evil deeds, should be unfaltering in their faith in and their response to the healing impulses of their fellow men. . . .

10. FF–WL 11/28/36; WL–FF 12/17/36.
11. T&T 7/23/35.
12. T&T 12/26/33; T&T 5/17/34.
13. T&T 2/2/35; WL–Peter Molyneaux 2/27/35.
14. T&T 2/2/35.
15. T&T 4/25/34; T&T 1/22/35.
16. WL–NDB 4/2/35; WL–Cordell Hull 4/2/35; WL–Hugh Wilson 7/30/35; T&T 7/23 (resolution), 7/11/35 (dream).
17. WL–H. F. Armstrong 11/9/35, also see T&T 12/17/35; "Neutrality: The Immediate Problem," delivered over radio 1/18/36, in *Vital Speeches* 1/27/36.
18. T&T 9/22/36 (fit); T&T 1/5/37 (salvation); T&T 12/12/36 (degenerated); T&T 6/6/37 (horrible); "Lippmann Protests against American Newspaper Guild Views," *New York Times* 7/22/37; OHC 172.
19. T&T 12/24/36.
20. Ibid.
21. "Rough-Hew Them How We Will," *Foreign Affairs* 6/1937, 593.
22. T&T 10/12/37; T&T 10/16, 12/2/37.
23. T&T 11/6/37.

27. A GATE UNLOCKED

1. For these negotiations see Ellery Sedgwick–WL 7/15, 9/4, 9/7, 9/22/34, and 2/27/35; WL–Sedgwick 7/17, 9/10/34, 2/26/35, 4/1, 6/30/36.
2. See Isaiah Bowman memoir, 10/5/39, filed with his diary, Bowman papers, Johns Hopkins University.
3. Ibid.
4. This account, and most of the material in this chapter, comes from conversations with Helen Lippmann, and from material furnished by her to the author and quoted with the permission of Gregor Armstrong Gamble.
5. WL–HBA 5/29/37.
6. WL–HBA 6/27, 7/2/37.
7. HBA–WL 7/19/37.
8. WL–HBA 7/9/37.
9. WL–HBA 7/2/37.
10. T&T 7/8/37; HBA–WL 7/19/37.
11. WL–HBA 7/19/37.
12. For example, see H. F. Armstrong–WL 6/25/37.
13. T&T 8/14/37.
14. *Society*, 33.

28. STARTING OVER

1. See WL–HBA 2/8/38.
2. HBA–Mima (Mrs. George) Porter 8/25/37.
3. WL–HBA 8/28/37.
4. HBA–Porter 8/29/37.
5. WL–HBA 9/1/37.
6. HBA–WL 8/31/37; WL–HBA 9/7/37.
7. WL–HBA 9/15/37; HBA–WL, telegram 9/19/37, letter 9/20/37.
8. Ralph Albertson–WL 9/20/37; WL–HBA 9/21/37.
9. *Time* 11/1/37; WL–BB 11/2/37; Arthur Graef–WL 12/17/37.
10. WL–HBA 2/13, 1/30/38; WL–BB 11/2/37.
11. WL–H. F. Armstrong 11/25/37.
12. WL–HBA 1/25/38.
13. WL–HBA 12/19/38; also see WL–BB 2/10/38, WL–Robert Hutchins 11/8/37, 2/22, 4/19/38; WL–HBA 2/11/38.
14. WL–HBA 2/18/38.
15. WL–BB 4/1/38.

29. THE PHONY PEACE

1. WL–HBA 7/31/38.
2. "Colloque Walter Lippmann," YLC; draft of "Men and Ideas," YLC; also see WL–Ellery Sedgwick 4/5/38.
3. Harold Nicolson–WL 3/8/38.
4. J. P. Kennedy–WL 3/21/38.
5. Kennedy–WL 3/28/38; WL–Kennedy 4/7/38.
6. T&T 2/24/38.
7. WL–BB 9/17/38; also see T&T 9/16, 7/28/38.
8. T&T 10/8, 10/15/38; WL–John Balderston 10/31/38.
9. Comment on Bonnet, OHC 191–193; *U.S. Foreign Policy*, 104n, 116.
10. "Let the Jews Come In," *NR* 11/23/38.
11. T&T 11/24/38; also see T&T 11/17/38.
12. See Thomas Paterson, *American Foreign Policy: A History* (Lexington: Heath, 1977), 401–405; Freda Kirchwey, "While the Jews Die," *Nation* 5/24/43; also see "A Cold Compress of Sympathy," *NR* 4/29/78. For other material on the Jews during the war, see: Martin Weill, *A Pretty Good Club* (New York: Norton, 1977); "Murder of a People," *Nation* 12/19/42; Philip Bernstein, "What Hope for the Jews?" *NR* 4/26/43; Freda Kirchwey, "A Program of Inaction," *Nation* 6/5/43; I. F. Stone, "For the Jews — Life or Death?" *Nation* 6/10/44; Arthur Morse, *While Six Million Died* (New York: Random House, 1968).
13. WL–Bruce Bliven 3/11/38.
14. WL–Nicolson 11/15 (mortal), 12/6/38 (crisis).
15. T&T 1/3/39; WL–T. W. Lamont 1/6/39.
16. T&T 4/18/39, also see T&T 4/15, 4/25/39.
17. OHC 183; WL–RS.
18. Harold Nicolson, *Diaries and Letters, 1930–1939*, edited by Nigel Nicolson (New York: Atheneum, 1966), 403 (entry for 6/14/39); OHC 186–187.
19. OHC 190.
20. In *NYHT* file, YLC, n.d.

30. TRIED AND FOUND WANTING

1. T&T 10/3/39.
2. WL–Arthur Vandenberg 10/2/39.
3. For example, see "Rough-Hew Them How We Will," *Foreign Affairs* 6/1937; John Maynard Keynes–WL 1/6/40, WL–Keynes 1/31/40; for Lippmann on the arms embargo debate see T&T 9/19, 9/23, 10/3/39.

4. T&T 10/12/39, also see T&T 10/10/39, 1/20/40.
5. Hans Kohn–WL 10/12/39; T&T 11/9/40, also see T&T 11/27/41; for WL's later view of the attack on Finland, see interview with Henry Brandon, *New York Times Magazine* 9/14/69.
6. OHC 206–207.
7. T&T 5/11/40; O. G. Villard in *Nation* 5/25/40.
8. T&T 1/12/39, 5/11/40.
9. T&T 6/15/40.
10. WL–Major General John O'Ryan 6/10/40; WL–Whitney Griswold 2/1/39, also see Griswold–WL 2/5/39.
11. T&T 1/30 (step), 2/3/40 (historians).
12. WL speech at the thirtieth reunion of the Class of 1910, 6/18/40, in *Essential*, 534–538.
13. OHC 175–176; T&T 6/18/40.
14. WL–RS; T&T 9/7 (overthrown), 9/17/40 (control).
15. WL–Wendell Willkie 7/30/40; T&T 8/8/40.
16. WL–Henry Luce 9/30/40.
17. WL–Alexander Woollcott 10/25/40; T&T 11/2/40.
18. WL–FDR 11/6/40; T&T 11/7/40.
19. T&T 12/19/40; Senate Resolution SJ Res 263, 76th Congress, 3rd session; Claude Pepper–RSC 7/18/76.
20. T&T 2/27/41.
21. "The Atlantic and America," *Life* 4/7/41, 84–88; for WL's criticism of FDR see especially T&T 4/19/41.
22. T&T 10/30/41.
23. For example, see T&T 10/8, 10/22/40; quote is from T&T 7/29/41.
24. T&T 9/20/41; also see T&T 9/18/41.
25. T&T 12/4/41.

31. PANIC AND BUNGLING

1. T&T 2/12/42.
2. "Facts Demanded on Coast Danger," *New York Times* 2/15/42, in Luskin, *Lippmann, Liberty and the Press*, 36–37; Francis Biddle–WL 2/19/42; WL–Biddle 2/20/42.
3. See John Morton Blum, *V Was for Victory* (New York: Harcourt, 1976), 155–167, and William Manchester, *The Glory and the Dream* (Boston: Little, Brown, 1974), 297–302; T&T 3/21/42; Gilbert Harrison–RS.
4. WL–John Maynard Keynes 4/2, 4/18/42.
5. T&T 12/14, 9/17/40.
6. WL–Norman Davis 1/31/42; T&T 7/16/42; T&T 11/7/42.
7. Address at French-American Club 10/28/42, YLC.
8. T&T 4/21/60, also in *Essential*, 487.
9. OHC 211–213.
10. For example, see Milton Viorst, *Hostile Allies: FDR and Charles de Gaulle* (New York: Macmillan, 1965), 122.
11. WL–Cordell Hull and WL–George Marshall 11/17/42; "Memorandum on Our Relations with Darlan," T&T 11/19/42.
12. T&T 1/19/43, also see WL–Thomas Wasson 5/29/43.
13. T&T 7/10/43; De Gaulle's comment is in *Memoirs de guerre*, vol. II, *l'Unité, 1942–1944* (Paris: Plon, 1956), 9; T&T 6/26/43.

32. REALPOLITIK

1. Henry Luce in *Life* 2/17/41; for Wallace speech 5/8/42, see John Morton Blum, *V Was for Victory* (New York: Harcourt, 1976), 269–271, and Robert Divine, *Second Chance* (New York: Atheneum, 1967), 64–65.
2. *U.S. Foreign Policy*, vii–viii (slowly), 106 (peace), 118 (victors), 152 (neutralization), 9 (balance); Taft in James T. Patterson, *Mr. Republican* (Boston: Houghton Mifflin, 1972), 289.
3. WL–J. Maritain 7/1/43; WL–Quincy Wright 7/22/43; WL–H. C. Lodge 7/1/43, in reply to Lodge speech of 6/18/43; WL–Hugh Wilson 4/8/43.

4. T&T 12/14/43.
5. *U.S. War Aims*, 164 (error), 173 (Innocence), 197 (effortless), 189 (intervention); *Life* 3/29/43; OHC 216.
6. WL–Ross Hoffman 3/15/45; for Welles-WL differences, see *Newsweek* 8/21/44.
7. T&T 10/12/44.
8. WL–Grenville Clark 9/19/44.
9. See T&T 2/5, 2/10, 4/18/44.
10. T&T 7/11/44; see OHC 230-231.
11. T&T 10/21/44.
12. J. F. Dulles–WL 10/22/44; WL–Dulles 10/25/44; T&T 3/1/45.
13. T&T 10/21/44.
14. T&T 12/2/44; WL also spoke to Stimson about the matter — see Stimson diary 11/28/44, vol. 49, Stimson papers, Yale University.
15. T&T 12/30/44; in this regard, see, for example, Joseph Alsop–WL 1/30/45.
16. T&T 1/25/44 (allied); T&T 5/18/44 (no future).
17. T&T 2/15/45; Dulles quote of 2/27/45 in Daniel Yergin, *Shattered Peace* (Boston: Houghton Mifflin, 1977), 67; T&T 4/7 (power to act), 4/5/55 (price).
18. T&T 4/7/45.

33. DRIFTING TOWARD CATASTROPHE

1. WL interview with Richard Rovere 2/5/65, YLC; T&T 1/13/45.
2. John Lewis Gaddis, *The United States and the Origins of the Cold War, 1941–1947* (New York: Columbia University Press, 1972), 170, 227; Harriman quote in Averell Harriman and Elie Abel, *Special Envoy to Churchill and Stalin, 1941–1946* (New York: Random House, 1975), 457; also see Charles Bohlen, *Witness to History: 1929–1969* (New York: Norton, 1973), 215.
3. WL–RS; T&T 4/26/45.
4. *Time* 5/14/45, cited in Gaddis, 226.
5. OHC 262; T&T 5/3/45, also see 5/8/45.
6. James F. Byrnes–WL 4/30/45; WL–Byrnes 5/10/45.
7. WL–Hans Kohn 5/30/45; WL–Ross Hoffman 7/4/45.
8. T&T 12/14/44; WL–George Fielding Eliot 6/14/45.
9. T&T 1/31/46.
10. WL–Byrnes 8/23/45 (draft copy); T&T 5/22/47, 6/1/48.
11. As historian Martin J. Sherwin has observed in his important study, *A World Destroyed: The Atomic Bomb and the Grand Alliance* (New York: Knopf, 1975): At Potsdam "not only were Soviet fears about the consequences of an American atomic bomb heightened, but on the American side, what little commitment there was among high officials for the international control of atomic energy all but vanished" (pp. 227–228).
12. T&T 9/11/45.
13. T&T 9/25/45, also see T&T 10/18/45; T&T 11/1/45.
14. T&T 12/29/45, 1/3/46, also see 1/19/46; OHC 224–225; also see James A. Nathan and James K. Oliver, *United States Foreign Policy and World Order* (Boston: Little, Brown, 1976), 57, cited in Gaddis, 241, 291.
15. T&T 2/12/46; *Business Week* 2/23/46; *Pravda* comments from "The Imperialist Plans of Walter Lippmann," Soviet Home Service, 6/12/46, YLC.
16. OHC 256; T&T 5/16/46.
17. T&T 2/26/46; James Forrestal–WL 2/26/46.
18. See *The Price of Vision: The Diary of Henry A. Wallace, 1942–1946*, edited by John Morton Blum (Boston: Houghton Mifflin, 1973), 556–557; T&T 3/7/46.
19. T&T 3/14/46; WL–D. S. Freeman 5/22/46.
20. See WL–William Mathews 3/11/46; WL–Alma (Mrs. D. P.) Morgan 3/9/46.
21. Bohlen, 252.
22. For Lippmann's reaction to the Nuremberg trials, whose verdict he hailed as a "solemn affirmation that the sovereignty of states is subject to universal law, higher than the decisions of any government and binding upon all persons everywhere," see T&T 10/1/46, and "The Meaning of Nuremberg," *Ladies' Home Journal* 6/1946.

23. OHC 248–250; also see BB–WL 5/31/40.
24. T&T 5/9/46; also see T&T 5/4, 5/7/46, WL–W. D. Rowlands 6/28/46.
25. *NYHT* 5/23/46.
26. T&T 7/20/46; also see T&T 7/16, 7/18/46.
27. WL–R. G. Swing 8/1/46.
28. Dorothy Thompson–WL 7/16/46; WL–Thompson 7/22/46.

34. SWIMMING UP NIAGARA

1. George F. Kennan, *Memoirs: 1925–1950* (Boston: Little, Brown, 1967), 583–598; Arnold A. Rogow, *James Forrestal: A Study in Personality, Politics and Policy* (New York: Macmillan, 1963), 200.
2. T&T 6/26/46; WL–Chester Barnard 6/28/46, in David Lilienthal papers, Princeton University; also see T&T 6/18, 6/20, 6/22, 11/23, 12/1, 12/31/46, WL–H. B. Swope 1/4, 1/18/47, Swope–WL 1/13, 1/20/47.
3. T&T 9/12, 9/14/46.
4. T&T 9/17, 9/19/46; T&T 4/15/47.
5. Lippmann's attitude toward Forrestal, as toward so many public men, such as Dulles and Vandenberg, was ambivalent. Although almost always generous in his obituaries of the great (William Jennings Bryan being a notable exception), he was often more critical of them in retrospect than he was during the time they held power. When Forrestal committed suicide, Lippmann wrote a touching tribute deploring the American practice whereby public men, on resigning office, were cast from the heights of power to oblivion. Forrestal, he wrote, had seen his own mistakes ''so out of their proportion in the record of his achievements, that he was exhausted — not so much by the long hours he worked as by the realization that he would never have the chance to repair his mistakes and to achieve what he had been appointed to achieve.'' In this sense, Lippmann maintained, the parliamentary system worked better, because officials could at least heckle from the back bench rather than stagnate in their rose gardens.

    Yet only two years after Forrestal's death, when an expurgated and highly flattering version of his diaries was published, Lippmann privately revealed a very different attitude than he had in his obituary. ''I knew Jim very well, personally, out of uniform, so to speak, and I admired him a lot as a public man,'' he wrote Herbert Elliston, the *Washington Post* editorial director, who had written an admiring article on Forrestal. ''But the legend is a phony — both on the score of his strength of character and of his prescience.'' It was unfortunate that the diaries had been published so soon after Forrestal's death, he said, since ''any real disclosure of what he thought from day to day, assuming he would have been willing to disclose it, which I question, would dissolve the legend completely.'' But Lippmann never put into print the doubts he expressed so forcefully in private.

    Lippmann's obituary of Forrestal in T&T 5/24/49; private attitude expressed in WL–Herbert Elliston 8/9/51, also see WL–Elliston 10/25/51.
6. Telephone conversation 11/29/46, in Forrestal papers, box 70, Princeton University; T&T 11/30/46.
7. T&T 7/5/55; for other columns on the limitations of the UN, see T&T especially 1/15/51, also 1/12/53, 6/14, 6/16/55.
8. ''A Year of Peacemaking,'' *Atlantic*, 12/1946.
9. T&T 4/8, 4/10/47 (union); T&T 3/25/47 (countermeasures); T&T 3/29/47 (Dardanelles).
10. T&T 3/15/47.
11. T&T 3/4/47 (reinforce); T&T 3/29/47 (ideological); T&T 9/7/46 (heterogenous).
12. OHC 257–258 and WL–RS. Three years later, asked when the cold war began, he said it could not be put earlier than Byrnes's visit to Moscow at the end of 1945. ''But if I had to pick a date as marking the acceptance of the whole conflict by the U.S. government, I would select President Truman's message about Greece and Turkey announcing the so-called Truman Doctrine,'' he told a reader. ''That marked the open acceptance of the idea of political warfare and was swiftly followed by the breakdown of any immediate hope of a four-power agreement about Germany and Japan'' (WL–John Hamilton 6/21/50).
13. T&T 2/11/47 (imperialism), also see T&T 2/25, 3/4, 3/6, 3/11/47; T&T 2/25/47 (liquidation), also see T&T 2/11, 2/13, 3/1/47.

14. T&T 3/20/47 (large contribution); T&T 4/5/47 (on a scale); Joseph Jones, *The Fifteen Weeks* (New York: Harcourt, 1955), 228–229.
15. T&T 5/1/47; WL–J. W. Fulbright 4/3/47.
16. Kennan, cited in Richard M. Freeland's provocative *Truman Doctrine and the Origins of McCarthyism* (New York: Knopf, 1971), 169; Charles Bohlen, *The Transformation of American Foreign Policy* (New York: Norton, 1969), 91.

In his earlier book, *Witness to History: 1929–1969* (New York: Norton, 1973), Bohlen wrote (pp. 264–265): Marshall realized that "any American plan that appeared to exclude the Soviet Union would have very little chance of being accepted in the world. He also knew that Soviet acceptance might easily kill the plan in Congress. Kennan and I . . . did not feel that the Soviet Union would accept American verification of the use of the goods and funds. Furthermore, we did not think the Soviet Union would be able to maintain its control over Eastern Europe if those countries were able to participate in the cooperative venture."

17. T&T 6/14/47; Forrestal in Daniel Yergin, *Shattered Peace* (Boston: Houghton Mifflin, 1977), 315.
18. [Kennan], "Sources of Soviet Conduct," *Foreign Affairs* 7/1947.
19. The cold war pieces appeared in T&T on 9/2, 9/4, 9/6, 9/9, 9/11, 9/13, 9/16, 9/18, 9/20, 9/23, 9/25, 9/27, 9/30, 10/2/47 (collected in *The Cold War*).
20. OHC 260; also see WL–Swope, n.d. [1950], Swope–WL 5/10/50.
21. Kennan, 358–363.
22. T&T 11/4/47; a particularly good discussion can be found in Freeland, 167–178.
23. "The Molotov Plan," *Life* 11/17/47; WL–Henry Luce 11/14/47; OHC 261–262, also see Freeland, 177–178; WL–BB 12/4/47.
24. WL–R. G. Swing 11/13/47; T&T 1/19/48.
25. WL–J. F. Dulles 11/19/47 (Ruhr) and 12/8/47, also see WL–Robert Strausz-Hupé 12/16/47; T&T 12/22/47, also see "The Rivalry of Nations," *Atlantic* 2/1948.
26. WL–Quincy Wright 11/23/48; WL–BB 12/25/47.

35. WAR SCARE

1. T&T 3/15, 3/16/48.
2. WL–Forrest Sherman 3/12/48 (unmailed draft), WL–Sherman 4/5/48.
3. WL–RS; see T&T 6/24/65, also Flora Lewis, "The Education of a Senator," *Atlantic* 12/1971, 59; T&T 1/20/48, and see Richard M. Freeland, *The Truman Doctrine and the Origins of McCarthyism* (New York: Knopf, 1971), 263–264.
4. Marshall cited in Daniel Yergin, *Shattered Peace* (Boston: Houghton Mifflin, 1977), 346–347; George F. Kennan, *Memoirs: 1925–1950* (Boston: Little, Brown, 1967), 401.
5. WL–BB 6/8/48; T&T 1/31/49; for a discussion of the Czech coup as a defensive Russian reaction see Freeland, 269–287, and Yergin, 343–350.
6. T&T 8/2/48; T&T 5/27/48; WL–J. F. Dulles 9/23/48.
7. T&T 4/27/48, also see T&T 5/3, 12/2/47, 5/14/48; T&T 6/10/48; T&T 6/3/48; WL–L. Douglas 7/9/48.
8. T&T 11/14/46; also see T&T 11/12/46, Chester Bowles–WL 10/22/46, and WL–Bowles, n.d. [1946]; *Conversations*, 20–21.
9. T&T 3/9/48; WL–L. Douglas 7/9/48.
10. T&T 6/22/48; T&T 7/19/48.
11. WL–David Wainhouse 10/30/48; T&T 10/25/48.
12. WL–Dulles 7/28/48.
13. T&T 11/4/48; see Lippmann interview with William Attwood, *Look* 4/25/61, and Lippmann interview with Richard Rovere, 6/30/64, YLC.
14. "The Diary of Eban Ayers," entry for 6/10/49, Truman Library, Independence, Missouri, postpresidential name file.
15. Bernard Berenson, *Sunset and Twilight* (New York: Harcourt, 1963), entry for 11/23/48.
16. T&T 1/3/49; WL–Sumner Welles 1/28/49; WL–R. Leffingwell 3/1/49; T&T 8/5/52.
17. WL–Dulles 5/19/49.
18. T&T 7/18/49; WL–Arthur Vandenberg 7/22/49, also see Vandenberg–WL 7/18/49.
19. Vandenberg papers, 503–504, cited in LaFeber, *America, Russia and the Cold War*, 79; WL–Vandenberg, 8/8/49; T&T 8/2/49.

20. WL–Charles Gary 7/7/49. During the war Lippmann had suggested that German remilitarization could be prevented by dividing Germany in two: an independent Rhineland, including the Ruhr and the Saar, with economic links to Western Europe, and an eastern Germany from which it would be permanently separated. See Stimson diary, vol. 49, 11/28/44, Stimson papers, Yale University.

36. ROOM AT THE TOP

1. WL–BB 12/22/49; BB–WL 1/1/50.
2. T&T 1/25/49; WL–Russell Leffingwell 12/29/49; WL–BB 12/22/49.
3. T&T 9/6, 9/8, 9/12/49.
4. T&T 1/16/50; WL–Forrest Sherman 2/16/50.
5. Cited in Richard M. Freeland, *The Truman Doctrine and the Origins of McCarthyism* (New York: Knopf, 1971), 347.
6. T&T 2/28/50; T&T 3/14/50.
7. WL–Alan Kirk 4/26/50.
8. WL–RS; T&T 3/21/50.
9. T&T 6/27/50 (aggression); T&T 6/29/50 (Seventh Fleet); T&T 7/3/50 (cardinal rule).
10. WL–Joseph Alsop 7/19/50.
11. For Kennan's comments on the Japanese peace treaty, see George F. Kennan, *Memoirs: 1925–1950* (Boston: Little, Brown, 1967), 395; WL–J. F. Dulles 7/18/50.
12. Dulles–WL 7/13/50; see Lippmann interview with Richard Rovere, 5/21/64, YLC (this story was confirmed by Morgan Beatty; see Beatty–WL 9/24/64); also see memo for WL 9/11/50 in Dulles file, YLC, and T&T 1/9/51.
13. *New York Times* internal memo, n.d. [12/1950], *Times* file, YLC.
14. Ibid., 12/12/50.
15. T&T 12/14/50.
16. Re the Century Club, see WL–LH 4/29/37; WL–Daisy Harriman 1/8/51; WL–LH 11/28/52.
17. T&T 1/9/51.
18. T&T 4/30/51; T&T 5/21/51.
19. WL–Millard Tydings 1/22/52; also see *Conversations,* 20. Yet at the very beginning Lippmann ambiguously suggested that Korea should be unified, though not militarily. "Forcing the withdrawal of the North Korean aggressors to the 38th parallel is not an end in itself," he wrote in his column of 7/20/50. "It is the means to what must be the true end for the UN and for ourselves. . . . That is to abolish the partition which has ended in war and to achieve a united and independent Korea."
20. WL–Dorothy Thompson 9/1/50; see entry in Lippmann's European diary 11/1/50, YLC.
21. T&T 12/4/50; WL–J. B. Conant 2/26/51; T&T 2/27/51.
22. T&T 6/21/51 (Russian problem); T&T 6/18/51 (divorce).
23. The allegation appeared in *Le Monde,* 6/30/51; the denial, 7/4/51. Also see *NYHT* European edition, 7/5/51, Beuve-Mery–WL 7/6/51 (misdated 6/6) and Eric Hawkins–George Cornish (*NYHT*), 7/6/51, YLC.

37. OVERTAKEN BY EVENTS

1. T&T 6/18/51.
2. WL–George Cornish 11/17/51; also see WL–Albert Stickney 11/27/51, WL–Norris Darrell 12/27/51.
3. For example, see T&T 6/17/54.
4. WL interview with Richard Rovere, 2/5/65; WL–RS; WL–Lewis Douglas 7/9/48.
5. T&T 1/10/52; T&T 3/17/52; "The Case for Eisenhower," *Look* 4/8/52.
6. WL–Leverett Saltonstall 1/11/52; WL–H. B. Swope 3/27/52.
7. T&T 6/2/52, also see 6/9/52; WL interview with Rovere, 9/16/64.
8. T&T 7/10/52; T&T 7/29/52.
9. John D. Miller–RSC 11/16/75; T&T 9/25/52.
10. T&T 10/16/52 (leader), T&T 10/23/52 (strains). Shortly after the election Lippmann gave a talk at the Massachusetts Institute of Technology. A graduate student, Francis Bator, who later worked in the Kennedy administration and collaborated with Lippmann on an article dealing with economic policy, was assigned to drive him to the airport. When Bator said he had voted

for Stevenson, Lippmann congratulated him. "It's all right for an old man like me to worry about the two-party system and such things as that," he told the student, "but men like you should be for Stevenson because he represents the best in American life." Nonetheless, for Lippmann, Stevenson was not the best man for the job. Francis Bator–RS; the incident took place 11/22/52.

11. WL–Adlai Stevenson 11/5/52; T&T 1/5/54.
12. T&T 5/21/53; T&T 8/4/53; WL–BB 3/17/54.
13. T&T 3/1/54; T&T 5/3/54 (demagogue); T&T 12/6/54 (mystic chords); T&T 5/2/50 (egos); Margaret Chase Smith–WL 6/1/50. When Daniel Lang wrote a sympathetic article in the *New Yorker* about William Remington, a government official accused of espionage, Lippmann wrote Lang — whom he had never met — a letter praising his article as a "noble masterpiece" (WL–Lang 5/24/49).
14. T&T 2/5/53.
15. T&T 6/7/54, also see T&T 4/15 and 6/3/54; WL–George Kennan 6/10/54; WL–Gardner Cowles 12/28/54.
16. T&T 2/28/50.
17. T&T 7/31/52 (agreement); T&T 10/9/52 (friendly).
18. See George Polk file in YLC, also Yiannis Roubatis and Elias Vlanton, "Who Killed George Polk?" *More* magazine 5/1977, 12–32.
19. T&T 6/26/52.
20. T&T 4/4/50; T&T 1/28/52; T&T 1/8/52.
21. T&T 4/17/51; T&T 3/20/52.
22. James M. Cain, "Walter Lippmann Had Style," *Washington Post, Potomac* magazine, 2/2/75.

38. A PRIVATE PHILOSOPHY

1. Notes for "Men and Ideas," Paris, 1938, YLC; "Man's Image of Man," *Commonweal* 2/13/42, an address delivered at the seventeenth annual meeting of the American Catholic Philosophical Association, Philadelphia, 12/29–12/30/41, reprinted in *Essential*, 162–168; also see "Education vs. Civilization," *American Scholar*, Spring 1941, an address at the meeting of the American Association for the Advancement of Science, 12/29/40.
2. *Philosophy*, ch. 1.
3. WL–BB 8/23/54.
4. *Philosophy*, ch. 1 (derangement), ch. 8 (natural law); McGeorge Bundy–Edward Weeks, n.d. [1954], RSC.
5. Joseph C. Harsch–WL 2/11/55.
6. Charles Forcey in *NR* 2/21/55; *Saturday Review* 2/19/55; Archibald MacLeish in *Yale Review* 6/1955, Lippmann rejoinder, ibid.; Reinhold Niebuhr in *New York Times Book Review* 2/20/55; Max Freedman in *Nation* 3/5/55.
7. *Christian Science Monitor* 2/17/55, also see *Time* 2/28/55, *New Yorker* 2/19/55; BB–WL 3/5/55, 2/19/57, both in *The Selected Letters of Bernard Berenson*, edited by A. K. McComb (Boston: Houghton Mifflin, 1964).
8. Charles de Gaulle–WL 5/16/56.
9. LH–WL 3/7/55; WL–LH 3/12/55.
10. "Walter Lippmann at 83: An Interview with Ronald Steel," *Washington Post* "Outlook," 3/25/73.
11. Bernard Berenson, *Sunset and Twilight* (New York: Harcourt, 1963), entry for 5/6/53.
12. See Charles Child–Weeks 3/10/77, YLC.
13. WL–RS; WL–Howard Nash 10/30/40.
14. Marsden Hartley–WL 4/21/37; WL–Hartley 4/28/37; WL–Sam Lewisohn 5/24/37; Kenneth Clark–RSC 3/12/75.
15. WL–Helen Lippmann 10/30/44.

39. WAITING FOR AN INNOVATOR

1. T&T 6/16/54.
2. WL interview with Richard Rovere, 6/30/64, YLC.
3. T&T 7/3/56.
4. WL–RS.

5. Though Lippmann often criticized Dulles's policies, this never affected their personal relations, which remained cordial and frank. On Dulles's death in May 1959 Lippmann, in his obituary, wrote that "he never forgot, as so many public men do, that after the issue which is up for debate is settled, those who took part in the debate must still live and work together. . . . He did not regard dissent as perversity, he respected debate and the practice of free journalism." Historians, Lippmann advised, should judge Dulles, not only by his policies, which were "controversial and perhaps transient," but also for his "public character and his public virtue, which were excellent and a noble example to his people." The contrast with his attitude toward Acheson need hardly be underlined (T&T 5/26/59).

6. T&T 11/3/53.
7. WL–Dorothy Thompson 1/13/54; T&T 12/14/54.
8. T&T 11/1/56; T&T 11/2/56.
9. John D. Miller–WL 12/6/56; T&T 1/29/57.
10. T&T 10/26/56.
11. WL–BB 12/3/55; WL–George Ball 11/25/55; T&T 9/28/56; T&T 8/18/56.
12. T&T 7/20/65.
13. See George Kennan–WL 1/15/53 (Kennan speech at the Pennsylvania Bar Association, 1/16/53); WL–Kennan 1/17/53; T&T 4/1/58, also see "Showdown in Germany," *Look* 5/19/53, T&T 10/22/53.
14. T&T 8/25/59, also see T&T series on Germany, 4/6, 4/7, 4/8, 4/9/59; "The Problem of Berlin," *NR* 6/1/59, also see T&T 5/11, 5/18/59; George F. Kennan, *Memoirs: 1950–1963* (Boston: Little, Brown, 1972), 255.
15. Kennan–WL 1/26/53; WL–Kennan 2/12/53.
16. WL interview with Konrad Ahlers, editor of *Der Spiegel,* held 3/7/64, YLC.
17. *Communist World,* 37. Lippmann received a citation from the Pulitzer committee rather than a regular award because at that time the rules did not permit awards to syndicated columnists (see Arthur Krock–WL 5/6/58). While chief editorial writer for the *World* during the 1920s, he had removed his name from consideration for a Pulitzer on the grounds that it would be unseemly for a person on a Pulitzer paper to receive an award (see WL–Krock 5/8/58). Nominated for a Pulitzer in 1943, he asked that his name be withdrawn (see WL–Carl Ackerman of the Pulitzer committee, 3/5/43).
18. James Reston, "The Mockingbird and the Taxi," in Childs and Reston, *Walter Lippmann and His Times,* 235.
19. Allen Churchill, *The Improper Bohemians* (New York: Dutton, 1959), 328.
20. Richard Rovere, "Walter Lippmann: Pundit and Prophet," *Flair* 1/1951. A memorial service was held for Lippmann in Washington on 1/8/75, at the Washington Cathedral. Remarks were delivered by Philip Geyelin, Katharine Graham, Gilbert Harrison, Arthur Schlesinger, Jr., James Reston, Edward Weeks, and the Reverend Paul Moore, Jr. (in YLC).
21. Lippmann's address to the National Press Club, Washington, 9/23/59, published as "The Job of the Washington Correspondent," *Atlantic* 1/1960.
22. Kenneth Clark, *The Other Half* (New York: Harper, 1978), 107.
23. T&T 12/9/59.
24. T&T 12/15/59; WL diary 12/29/59, YLC.
25. T&T 10/27/59.
26. Robert Lewis Shayon, "Today and Tomorrow on TV," *Saturday Review* 8/23/60; Oscar Cox–WL 10/17/61; *Conversations;* Peabody television award made on 4/19/62.
27. *Conversations,* 15–17 (8/11/60).
28. *Morals,* ch. 13; T&T 6/5/58.
29. T&T 6/5/58; T&T 12/14/40; T&T 4/21/60.
30. WL–Arthur Vandenberg, Jr., n.d. [11/1951]; "Why We Accept Cheating," *Look* 3/29/60; "The Country Is Waiting for Another Innovator," *Life* 6/20/60, published in *The National Purpose* (New York: Holt, 1960).

40. AT THE NEW FRONTIER

1. T&T 2/16/56.
2. From a 1964 interview with his assistant, Elizabeth Farmer, for the Kennedy Library, YLC; T&T 1/12/60; J. F. Kennedy–WL 1/19/60; WL–Kennedy 1/22/60.

3. TV interview taped 7/7/60, aired 8/11/60, in *Conversations*, 29; T&T 7/12/60; T&T 9/20/60.
4. T&T 10/18/60; for the Krock story, see David Halberstam, *The Best and the Brightest* (New York: Random House, 1972), 26.
5. WL–RS; from the private notes of Elizabeth Midgley, formerly Farmer, on her conversations with WL, RSC. Regarding Bundy as president of Harvard, see Lippmann interview with Richard Rovere, 2/6/65, YLC; WL–Allan Nevins 12/9/60.
6. T&T 1/24/61; WL–RS.
7. Arthur Schlesinger–Kennedy, 2/1/61, Kennedy papers, box 65, file 8, Kennedy Library, Boston, Massachusetts; WL–RS.
8. "Why We Accept Cheating," *Look* 3/29/60; William Attwood, "A Visit with Walter Lippmann," *Look* 4/25/61.
9. T&T 4/17, 4/18, 4/19/61; also see *Conversations*, 52.
10. T&T 5/2/61, also see T&T 4/27/61 and *Conversations*, 61–67.
11. T&T 7/23/59; Nicolas Rivero–WL 8/4/59; T&T 8/18/60, also see T&T 7/5, 7/19/60.
12. *Conversations*, 66–67 (duty of press), 69–70 (appeasement); T&T 3/7/61 (teacher); *Conversations*, 39 (Eisenhower).

41. MYTHMAKING

1. T&T 5/4/61, also see T&T 5/6/61; WL–RS.
2. T&T 10/10/61; Max Ascoli, "The Case of Walter Lippmann," *Reporter* 11/9/61.
3. T&T 5/15/62.
4. Address to the American Law Institute 5/25/62, YLC.
5. WL–RS; also Pierre Salinger, *With Kennedy* (Garden City: Doubleday, 1966), 253, cited in Luskin, *Lippmann, Liberty and the Press*, 210.
6. T&T 10/25/62.
7. Salinger, *With Kennedy*, cited in Luskin, *Lippmann, Liberty and the Press*, 211.
8. T&T 10/25/62.
9. T&T 11/13/62.
10. Address to the Anglo-American Press Association, Paris, 11/29/62, in *Washington Post* 12/2/62, also as "Cuba and the Nuclear Risk," *Atlantic* 1/1963; Lippmann interview for the Kennedy Library, 16, YLC.
11. T&T 1/31/63 (prophetic man); T&T 2/21/63 (outgrown).
12. WL–Osborne Elliott 5/23/63.
13. "Kennedy at Mid-Term," *Newsweek* 1/21/63; *Conversations*, 145–146 (5/1/63).
14. J. F. Kennedy speech, 6/1/56, from John Galloway, ed., "The Kennedys and Vietnam," *Facts on File*, New York, 1971, cited in James A. Nathan and James K. Oliver, *United States Foreign Policy and World Order* (Boston: Little, Brown, 1976), 356; Kennedy in CBS interview 9/2/63, cited in Nathan and Oliver, 360; T&T 9/5/63 (price); T&T 9/3/63 (neutral).
15. T&T 9/17/63.
16. T&T 11/26/63; T&T 9/29/64; T&T 12/1/66, also WL–RS.
17. WL interview with Richard Rovere, 6/30/64, YLC; *Washington Post* 4/8/67 (mixed collection); *Providence Evening Bulletin* 11/22/67 (legend).

42. "A MAN FOR THIS SEASON"

1. WL–RS.
2. See Lyndon Johnson–WL 8/12/57, also 9/4/57; T&T 7/17/60.
3. Creekmore and Adele Fath–RS.
4. WL–RS; T&T 3/24/64.
5. WL interview with Richard Rovere, 2/6/65, YLC; *Conversations*, 161–162.
6. Elizabeth Farmer notes 5/21/64, RSC; 5/21/64.
7. WL–RS; T&T 6/25/64.
8. Lippmann introduction to Carl Sandburg, *The Chicago Race Riots* (New York: Harcourt, 1919), iii–iv; Doris Grumbach, "The Man Who Knew Walter Lippmann," *Washingtonian* 2/1977, 70.
9. *Philosophy*, ch. 3 (conditions); T&T 2/1/38, also see 7/6/37.
10. WL–BB 3/1/49; T&T 3/3/49; T&T 1/5/61.

11. T&T 5/20/54 (Brown); T&T 7/11/57 (local sentiment); T&T 9/24/56 and 10/4/62 (stages); T&T 9/24/57 (caste); T&T 6/11/63 (senator).
12. T&T 5/28/63 (revolutionary); T&T 7/4/63 (emergencies).
13. T&T 4/16/64 (justified); T&T 6/11/64 (injustice); T&T 1/20/64 (smothering).
14. T&T 3/16/65; T&T 9/7/65.
15. T&T 1/7/64 (reactionary); T&T 9/22/64 (demagogues); T&T 8/4/64 (despair); T&T 11/3/64 (discontent).
16. T&T 11/3/64 (season); T&T 8/28/64 (choice).
17. WL–RS; T&T 1/12/65 (chapter); T&T 2/2/65 (displacements).

43. SEDUCTION AND BETRAYAL

1. T&T 2/2/65.
2. T&T 2/9/65.
3. T&T 2/1/65; Elizabeth Farmer notes 2/10/65; T&T 2/11/65.
4. T&T 2/18/65.
5. *Conversations,* 202–203 (2/22/65).
6. Farmer notes 3/1/65, RSC.
7. "Can the Question of War Be Debated?" *Newsweek* 3/15/65; Farmer notes 3/15–3/16/65, RSC.
8. Farmer notes 3/15–3/16/65, RSC; T&T 3/30/65, also see T&T 3/18/65.
9. Bundy memorandum to Johnson, 4/6/65, Johnson papers, Johnson Library, Austin, Texas.
10. WL–RS.
11. T&T 12/29/64 (isolationism); T&T 2/2/65 (time).
12. T&T 4/20/65 (zones); T&T 4/22/65 (trouble); McGeorge Bundy–WL 4/20/65, also see WL–Bundy 4/23/65, Bundy–WL 4/28/65.
13. "Anguish of Power," *Washington Post* 4/26/65; T&T 4/27/65.
14. T&T 5/4/65; T&T 5/20/65.
15. T&T 5/6/54, also see T&T 6/8/54, 5/4/61, 9/3/63, 5/21/64, 2/9/65.
16. T&T 5/13/65.
17. Farmer notes 6/7/65, RSC; WL–RS; WL diary 5/29/65, YLC; T&T 6/10/65.
18. *Newsweek* 9/13/65 (neutralize); T&T 9/30/65 (bombing); T&T 7/8/65 (enclaves).
19. WL–RS, also see Chalmers Roberts, *The* Washington Post: *The First Hundred Years* (Boston: Houghton Mifflin, 1977), 377.
20. T&T 10/26/65; address to International Press Institute, London, 5/25/65, reprinted in *Encounter* 8/1965; "Lippmann vs. Johnson," *Observer* 5/21/67, also see William J. Small, *Political Power and the Press* (New York: Norton, 1972), 196–197, and see "Lippmann to Leave Post in Capital," *Providence Journal* 12/30/66.

44. AN END AND A BEGINNING

1. T&T 12/28/65.
2. "Mr. Lansing's Book," *NR* 3/30/21.
3. WL–RS.
4. T&T 5/17/66 (willful); *Newsweek* 3/4/66 (mistake).
5. T&T 4/28/66 (imperial); T&T 7/12/66 (truth); T&T 12/29/66 (asking).
6. T&T 12/27/66.
7. T&T 1/10/67; WL–Pulitzer board 1/30/67.
8. T&T 1/3/67 (self-righteousness); T&T 12/8/66 (bitter pill); *Newsweek* 2/27/67 (spirits).
9. T&T 1/5/67 (root); T&T 11/7/66 (megalomania); T&T 1/19/67 (mosquitoes); *Newsweek* 10/9/67 (empire).
10. T&T 3/30/67 (pathologically); T&T 3/28/67 (manipulate).
11. T&T 4/6/67.
12. Herblock, *Washington Post,* "Outlook," 5/14/67.
13. Fred Friendly–RS; for variants of the story see Luskin, *Lippmann, Liberty and the Press,* 224.
14. T&T 4/26/66; J. D. Miller–RSC 11/16/75.
15. WL–Arthur Schlesinger 9/25/67; the article was "Origins of the Cold War," *Foreign Affairs* 10/1967.

16. "A Sort of Farewell to Washington," *Washington Post,* "Outlook," 3/19/67.
17. "Lippmann to Leave Post in Capital," *Providence Journal* 12/30/66, and "Lippmann vs. Johnson," *Observer* 5/21/67; Harrison Salisbury, "Final Tribute," *New Times* 1/10/75.
18. T&T 5/25/67; James Reston, "Walter Lippmann Goes Home," *New York Times* 5/26/67.

45. THE WORST OF TIMES

1. "Elephants Can't Beat Mosquitoes in Vietnam," *Washington Post* 12/3/67; WL–RS interview, *Washington Post,* "Outlook," 10/10, 10/17/71, reprinted as "The World We're In," *NR* 11/13/71.
2. Public Broadcasting Laboratory program aired 11/19/67, printed as "A New Leader for the Orchestra," *NR* 12/9/67; "1968 in the Crystal Ball," *Newsweek* 3/13/67; T&T 3/9/67.
3. "Eugene McCarthy's Mission," *Newsweek* 12/18/67.
4. Arthur Schlesinger, Jr., *Robert Kennedy and His Times* (Boston: Houghton Mifflin, 1978), 837–838.
5. "The Nation Needs a Broader Choice in Times of Crisis," *Washington Post* 7/7/68
6. "Nixon's the Only One," *Washington Post* 10/6/68 (Johnson's creature); "The Choice before Us," *Washington Post* 9/15/68 (uninspiring); "The Hard Choice," *Newsweek* 10/7/68 (cease fire).
7. "Walter Lippmann on Order and Justice," *Newsweek* 7/1/68 (reaction); "Walter Lippmann on the American Predicament," *Newsweek* 10/21/68 (imperative).
8. "Nixon's the Only One," *Washington Post,* 10/6/68.
9. WL–RS.
10. WL–RS; WL–Council on Foreign Relations 3/10/71; WL–Nancy Blaine Harrison 11/19/68.
11. WL interview with Henry Brandon, *New York Times Magazine* 9/14/69.
12. WL–RS interview, *Washington Post,* "Outlook," 10/17/71.
13. T&T 3/13/50 (from notes made in 1938–1939).
14. Louis Auchincloss–RS.
15. *Morals,* ch. 15.

Bibliography

ONE of the first questions scholars ask is why the papers of Walter Lippmann, a loyal Harvard alumnus and one of the university's Overseers, are at Yale. The answer, in brief, is that Yale asked for them and Harvard didn't. In many ways a diffident man, Lippmann did not want to be put in the position of seeming to ask his alma mater for a favor. So when Yale volunteered to house his papers, he accepted. There is another part of the story, which has to do with Robert O. Anthony, the remarkable man who turned a hobby into an unparalleled historical resource.

Anthony's hobby began modestly in the fall of 1931 when, a few years out of Amherst, he read a column by Lippmann on the death of Dwight Morrow, an Amherst trustee. Admiring Morrow and impressed by what he had read, the young man put the clipping in his desk drawer. A few weeks later he clipped another Lippmann article, and soon began saving them all and pasting them into a book. The following year he literally bumped into Lippmann at an Amherst football game, and used the opening to set up an interview. He showed his clippings to Lippmann, who was astounded. Fortified by the meeting, Anthony decided he would try to assemble every article and book Lippmann had ever written. Since Lippmann had never collected his own articles, Anthony had to start from scratch. Scouring secondhand bookstores for old editions of Lippmann's books and back issues of yellowing magazines, he gradually put together a virtually complete collection.

In 1964, at the urging of Wilmarth Lewis, a Yale alumnus and scholar of Horace Walpole, Lippmann gave some of his correspondence and original manuscripts to Yale. Two years later Anthony supplemented the gift by donating a large part of his own collection. Over the years Anthony augmented the collection until today it contains nearly everything Walter Lippmann ever wrote for publication, plus tens of thousands of letters, and original manuscripts of eighteen books. The material includes handwritten drafts for some two hundred articles, among them many unsigned pieces for the *New Republic,* and the incomplete draft of an unpublished volume written in Lippmann's declining years. Although Lippmann's editorials for the *World* during the years 1922–1931 were unsigned, proof sheets of the editorial page of each issue were later marked to indicate the author. Of the unsigned *New Republic* pieces that seem to be in Lippmann's style, many have been verified by the existence of Lippmann's handwritten manuscripts. The Anthony collection of works by and about Lippmann together with Lippmann's own collection of original manuscripts, private papers and correspondence furnish an unequaled source of archival wealth. Those collections, plus my own conversations with Lippmann, provided the basic raw material of this book.

There would be no point in listing all of Lippmann's articles, which number several hundred, or his editorials and T&T columns, which number several thousand. The researcher will readily find them listed in the collections at Yale, while those I have cited in the text are indicated in the Notes. Much of the collection has now been transferred to microfilm, and arrangements can be made with Yale for the use of the films outside the library. The entire Lippmann collection, including the private papers, is now open to researchers, along with the Anthony collection.

The bibliographical material falls into four categories: books by Lippmann, collections by others of Lippmann's works, books about Lippmann, and secondary material on the period.

I. BOOKS BY LIPPMANN

For the convenience of the reader I have divided these into two categories: first, those works written originally as books; second, those which were compiled from magazine articles, speeches and newspaper columns.

The major books are:

A Preface to Politics. New York: Mitchell Kennerley, 1913.
Drift and Mastery. New York: Mitchell Kennerley, 1914.
The Stakes of Diplomacy. New York: Holt, 1915.
Public Opinion. New York: Harcourt, Brace, 1922.
The Phantom Public. New York: Macmillan, 1925.
A Preface to Morals. New York: Macmillan, 1929.
The Good Society. Boston: Little, Brown, 1937.
U.S. Foreign Policy. Boston: Little, Brown, 1943.
U.S. War Aims. Boston: Little, Brown, 1944.
Essays in the Public Philosophy. Boston: Little, Brown, 1955.

The compilations and reprints are:

The Political Scene. New York: Holt, 1919.
Liberty and the News. New York: Harcourt, Brace, 1920.
Men of Destiny. New York: Macmillan, 1927.
American Inquisitors. New York: Macmillan, 1928.
Interpretations, 1931–1932. New York: Macmillan, 1933.
The Method of Freedom. New York: Macmillan, 1934.
The New Imperative. New York: Macmillan, 1935.
Interpretations, 1933–1935. New York: Macmillan, 1936.
The Cold War. Boston: Little, Brown, 1947.
Isolation and Alliances. Boston: Little, Brown, 1952.
The Communist World and Ours. Boston: Little, Brown, 1959.
The Coming Tests with Russia. Boston: Little, Brown, 1961.
Western Unity and the Common Market. Boston: Little, Brown, 1962.

In addition there are three works that fall outside either category. The first is a book of poems by a college friend, which Lippmann compiled and for which he wrote an introduction, *The Poems of Paul Mariett* (New York: Mitchell Kennerley, 1913); the second and third are volumes Lippmann wrote, together with William O. Scroggs, for the Council on Foreign Relations: *The United States in World Affairs, 1931*, and *The United States in World Affairs, 1932*.

2. COLLECTIONS OF LIPPMANN'S WORKS

In addition to the books cited above, there are three main collections of Lippmann's work. The most thorough of these is *The Essential Lippmann*, edited by Clinton Rossiter and James Lare (New York: Random House, 1963), which contains excerpts from both his books and articles. Although a lengthy work, this is not as good as it should be because of the editors' decision to structure the book thematically rather than chronologically, to emphasize such vague concepts as the "pattern of society" and the "tensions of constitutionalism," and to concentrate on excerpts from the books — which are readily available in any library — rather than the harder-to-find magazine articles and newspaper columns. Nonetheless, it is the only major collection covering the body of Lippmann's work, and is useful.

Gilbert Harrison has compiled two collections. The first, *Early Writings* (New York: Liveright, 1970), with an introduction and annotations by Arthur Schlesinger, Jr., contains many of Lippmann's most important pieces for the *New Republic* between 1914 and 1919. The second, *Public Persons* (New York: Liveright, 1976), is a selection of portraits, often capsule obituaries, by Lippmann of the people of his time, from William James to John F. Kennedy. Both are excellent and give a sense of Lippmann's remarkable range.

Finally there are the transcripts of his seven television broadcasts from 1960 to 1965, compiled under the title *Conversations with Walter Lippmann* (Boston: Little, Brown, 1965).

3. BOOKS ABOUT LIPPMANN

There have been a number of books assessing Lippmann's career, but none, until the present volume, has benefited from access to Lippmann's private papers. In addition to the collection of essays edited by Marquis Childs and James Reston, *Walter Lippmann and His Times* (New York: Harcourt, 1959), the reader will find a great deal of useful information in John Luskin's very readable overview, *Lippmann, Liberty and the Press* (University, Ala.: University of Alabama Press, 1972), in Hari Dam's excellent *Intellectual Odyssey of Walter Lippmann* (New York: Gordon Press, 1973), and in Anwar Syed's thoughtful *Walter Lippmann's Philosophy of International Politics* (Philadelphia: University of Pennsylvania Press, 1963). Charles Wellborn's *Twentieth Century Pilgrimage: Walter Lippmann and the Public Philosophy* (Baton Rouge: Louisiana State University Press, 1969) and Edward L. and Frederick H. Schapsmeier's *Walter Lippmann: Philosopher-Journalist* (Washington, D.C.: Public Affairs Press, 1969) are appreciative and generally uncritical. Benjamin F. Wright's *Five Public Philosophies of Walter Lippmann* (Austin: University of Texas Press, 1973) is a sharp and analytical assessment of Lippmann as a philosopher, while Francine Curro Cary's *Influence of War on Walter Lippmann: 1914–1944* (Madison: State Historical Society of Wisconsin, 1967) is a well-researched study of Lippmann's views on foreign policy through the Second World War. The informative study of David Elliott Weingast, *Walter Lippmann: A Study in Personal Journalism* (New Brunswick: Rutgers University Press, 1949), focuses mostly on the New Deal period. A fascinating examination of Lippmann's early years on the *New Republic* can be found in Charles Forcey's admirable *Crossroads of Liberalism: Croly, Weyl, Lippmann and the Progressive Era, 1900–1925* (New York: Oxford University Press, 1961), a work indispensable to any scholar of the period.

A great many magazine articles, both scholarly and general, have been written about Lippmann, and most of them can be found in the Anthony-Lippmann collection at Yale. A number of these are of considerable interest to the specialist, and some are mentioned in the Notes. Two, however, deserve special mention. The first is Richard Rovere's memoir of his relationship with Lippmann, in *Arrivals and Departures* (New York: Macmillan, 1976), pp. 124–144. The second is the audacious and thought-provoking four-part series by Heinz Eulau. In a daring exercise in psychobiography the author views Lippmann's writings in terms of his character, being generally admiring of the former and highly critical of the latter. Exaggerated and speculative, Eulau's work is nonetheless fascinating, and it is a pity that he never turned it into the book he apparently once contemplated. The four parts of the series are: "Mover and Shaker: Walter Lippmann As a Young Man," *Antioch Review*, Sept. 1951; "Man against Himself: Walter Lippmann's Years of Doubt," *American Quarterly*, Winter 1952; "Wilsonian Idealist: Walter Lippmann Goes to War," *Antioch Review*, Spring 1954; "From Public Opinion to Public Philosophy: Walter Lippmann's Classic Reexamined," *American Journal of Economics and Sociology*, July 1956.

4. SECONDARY REFERENCE SOURCES

There are hundreds of books and thousands of articles about the various aspects of American life, culture and politics during the period covered by this book, many of which I found enlightening. Rather than attempt to list them all, I will confine myself to those I found most provocative or informative.

For the entire period Arthur Link's herculean *American Epoch: A History of the United States Since the 1890s* (New York: Knopf, 1965) was an indispensable guide. For the culture of the Progressive Era I was stimulated by Henry F. May's *End of American Innocence* (New York: Watts, 1964) and by Christopher Lasch's *New Radicalism in America: 1889–1963* (New York: Vintage, 1965); for its thought, by Henry Steele Commager's *American Mind* (New Haven: Yale University Press, 1950); for their politics, by Richard Hofstadter's *Age of Reform* (New York: Vintage, 1955) and John Morton Blum's *Republican Roosevelt* (New York: Atheneum, 1966); and for their personalities, by Forcey's aforementioned *Crossroads of Liberalism*, Justin Kaplan's *Lincoln Steffens* (New York: Simon and Schuster, 1974), and Daniel Aaron's *Men of Good Hope* (New York: Oxford University Press, 1951).

For World War I and the interwar period I found most useful John Chamberlain's *Farewell to Reform* (Magnolia, Mass.: Peter Smith, 1958), Eric Goldman's *Rendezvous with Destiny* (New York: Vintage, 1955), Lawrence Gelfand's *The Inquiry* (New Haven: Yale University Press, 1963), Arthur Schlesinger, Jr.'s *Crisis of the Old Order* (Boston: Houghton Mifflin, 1957), William E. Leuchtenberg's *Perils of Prosperity* (Chicago: University of Chicago Press, 1958), and Alfred Kazin's *On Native Grounds* (Garden City: Doubleday, 1956). On the post–World War II period I benefited from Walter LaFeber's *America, Russia and the Cold War, 1945–1975* (New York: Wiley, 1976). Among the many unpublished scholarly papers on Lippmann and his times, I found of particular interest the doctoral dissertations of Michael Stockstill, "Walter Lippmann: His Rise to Fame, 1889–1945" (Ph.D., 1970, Mississippi State University), and Jackson Giddens, "American Foreign Propaganda in World War I" (Ph.D., 1966, Fletcher School of Law and Diplomacy), and the undergraduate thesis of Steven V. Roberts, "Walter Lippmann: A Gesture toward the World" (A.B., 1964, Harvard College).

Acknowledgments

I BEGAN this book at the suggestion of the late Richard Rovere, who provided some of the initial documentary material, much of which was compiled by his able research assistant, Gary Clarkson. This work could never have been undertaken without the full cooperation of Walter Lippmann, who gave me unrestricted and exclusive access to his private papers, and who made himself freely available for interviews, nor could it have been written without the remarkable work and assistance of Robert O. Anthony, whose diligence and dedication have made possible the Walter Lippmann Collection at Yale University.

Robert O. Anthony, John Morton Blum, Gilbert Harrison, Nicholas X. Rizopoulos, Arthur Schlesinger, Jr., and Martin J. Sherwin have read the entire manuscript, and I am deeply grateful for their counsel. For their helpful comments on the manuscript, I also thank Eve Auchincloss, Louis Auchincloss, Robert Divine, Frances FitzGerald, Dori Lewis, Robert Silvers, Pierre Wilkins, and Daniel Yergin.

My special thanks to the Lehrman Institute and to the John Simon Guggenheim Foundation for their financial assistance; to Beekman Cannon and the Fellows of Jonathan Edwards College at Yale for tempting me down academic byways; to the Yaddo Corporation for offering a retreat in Saratoga Springs; to the MacDowell Colony for its hospitality; to Eleanor Briggs for her generosity; and to Arne Lewis and Nancy and Reese Prosser for their kindness.

My colleagues and students at Yale, Wellesley College, the University of Texas at Austin, and Rutgers College have taught me a great deal. I feel a special gratitude to Robert Zastrow for his inspired research assistance; and I thank Michael Schwarz for his thoughtful comments; David Berreby and Peter Gibian for their assistance; Sandra Mayerson for her investigation into Lippmann's associations with Zionism in the 1920s; and Thomas Gerber, Patricia Hammel, and Thomas Slater for their insights.

The Yale University Library offered me its full cooperation, and I thank the staff of the Manuscripts and Archives Department, especially Lawrence Dowler and Judith Schiff, respectively head and chief researchist. I also appreciate the assistance of the late Louis M. Starr, director of the Oral History Research Office at Columbia University; and Erika Chadbourn, curator of manuscripts and archives at the Harvard Law School Library.

I am grateful to Louis Auchincloss for his recollections of the last days of Walter Lippmann, to Gary Clarkson for the use of his research materials, to Norris and Mary Darrell and to Gerald Gunther for permission to quote from the Learned Hand papers, to Gregor Armstrong Gamble for permission to quote from her mother's letters, to Roy Hoopes for references from the James M. Cain papers, and to Elizabeth Midgley for recollections of her years with Lippmann. I also thank John Giddens, Geoffrey Martin, Roger K. Newman, and Larry Yates for the research they shared with me. I deeply appreciate the sensitive and thoughtful copyediting of Melissa Clemence. And I congratulate Edward Weeks on enduring a long and bumpy ride with patience and optimism.

Although it would be virtually impossible to list all the people who shared their time and thoughts with me, I particularly thank George Ball, Francis Bator, Mary Bruggmann, Charles Child, Lord Kenneth Clark, Fleur Cowles, Lucile Elsas Emptage, Fred Friendly, Katharine Graham, Joseph C. Harsch, Charles Hirschfeld, Herbert Lippmann, and Jane Wilmerding.

And I sadly regret that Carl and Walter Binger, Norma Brustein, James MacGregor Byrne, Drew Dudley, Faye Albertson Heatley, Herman Kahn, John Duncan Miller, Richard Rovere, and, of course, Helen and Walter Lippmann are not here to see the final form of the work which they encouraged and to which they contributed so much.

Index

Abdullah, emir of Trans-Jordan, 454
Academy of Political Science (New York): honors WL, 276; WL speech before, 276–277
Acheson, Dean, 317, 428, 431, 440, 441, 458, 484, 523; demands for resignation of, 467–468, 469, 474, 480, 503; WL quoted on, 467, 468, 471, 474, 475, 486; quoted, 467, 471, 472, 473, 476; and Korea, 469–476; and German rearmament, 474, 476; -WL clashes, 487, (over Truman Doctrine) 439–440, 465, (over China issue) 465–467, 469, (over Korean War) 471, 474–475; as adviser to JFK, 534, 535
Adams, Franklin P., 198, 205; quoted on WL, 203; WL letters to, 229–230, 231, 232
Adams, James Truslow: quoted on WL, 280–281; WL letter to, 281–282
Adams, John, 167
Addams, Jane, 63, 97, 107, 225
Adenauer, Konrad, 489; WL meets, 463, 477
Adler, Alfred, 48
Africa, 91, 374; German colonies in, 131, 157, 330; suggested as homeland for Jews, 373; French colonies in, 397; (see also Algeria)
Agnew, Spiro, 588
Agricultural Adjustment Administration, 302, 321
Aiken, Conrad, 15, 75
Alaska, 407
Albania, 136, 375, 438
Albertson, Faye, 30; WL's courtship of and marriage to, 117–120. See also Lippmann, Mrs. Walter (Faye Albertson, first wife)
Albertson, Hazel (Mrs. Ralph), 31, 52, 118
Albertson, Ralph, 30–31, 32, 33, 117, 120, 176, 358
"Albert the Male" (WL article spoofing clubman), 29–30
Alexander, king of Yugoslavia: assassinated, 333
Algeria, 397, 400, 402; insurrection in, 518, 528
Alien and Sedition Acts (1798), 166
Allende, Salvador: WL visits, 573
Allies (World War I), 92–94, 113–114, 127, 151; and secret treaties, 126, 130–133, 135, 136, 141, 155, 160, 180; and Fourteen Points, 134–137, 149, 150, 160; and Bolshevik Russia, 135, 137, 156, 444; and "Inquiry," 144, 145; WL urges cancellation of war debts of, 253. See also "Atlantic community"; war debts and reparations
Allies (World War II): and postwar alliances, 405, 407, 414, 421 (see also spheres of influence); and second front, 408, 430; and postwar Germany, 448
Alsace-Lorraine: World War I treaties and, 131, 135, 157
Alsop, Joseph, 506, 558, 560; WL letter to, 471
Amalgamated Clothing Workers Union, 125
Amendola, Giorgio, 555
America First Committee, 379, 386, 414. See also isolationism

American Academy of Political and Social Science: WL speaks before (1917), 113
American Bar Association, 406
"American Century," 404, 425, 468
American Civil Liberties Union, 395
American Commonwealth (Bryce), 77
"American Destiny" (WL's Walgreen Lectures), 363
American Expeditionary Force, 144
American Federation of Labor, 123
"American Friends of Vietnam," 541
American Geographical Society, 129
American Hebrew (periodical), 7, 187; WL article in, 193, (quoted) 186, 191
American Inquisitors (Lippmann), 219
American Law Institute: WL addresses (1962), 534
American Legion, 299
American Liberty League, 310, 311, 312, 314, 318, 319, 326
American Mercury (magazine), 258, 259; WL offered editorship of, 342
American Newspaper Guild, 274, 337; WL's criticism of, 338
American Red Cross Commission to Russia, 137–138
America's Coming of Age (Brooks), 58
Amherst College, 117, 221, 297; WL speaks at, 307; WL offered professorship at, 342
anarchism, 157, 167, 303, 409; WL joins anarchist parade, 54; WL defends rights of anarchists (1920s), 315
Anderson, Maxwell, 198; What Price Glory?, 202
Anderson, Sherwood, 259
Angell, Norman, 75, 92; WL commissions NR article from, 110–111
Anglo-American Press Association (Paris): WL speaks to, 537–538
Annenberg, Walter, 590; WL quoted on, 591
Anthony, Robert O., 598
Anti-Comintern Pact, 336, 339, 340, 375
anti-Semitism, 376, 400; among Jews, 7, 189, 262; at Harvard, 14, 28–29, 191, (and Jewish quota) 193–195, 331; WL on, 189, 191, 192, 195, 331; German persecution / pogroms, 330–333, 369, 372–374, (death camps) 374, 430, 446; and attacks on FDR, 372. See also Jews; racism
antitrust policy. See business
"Appeal to the President, An" (WL editorial in NR), 94
appeasement, 474; pre–World War II, 340, 351, 368–369, 375–376, 413 (see also Munich accords); WL quoted on, 367, 370, 374, 530; Byrnes-Stalin agreement seen as, 426, 431; accusations of, feared, in Korean conflict, 475
Aquinas, St. Thomas, 252
Arab-Israeli conflict, 453; WL quoted on, 454

ABOUT THE AUTHOR

Ronald Steel has written extensively on American politics and foreign policy, and is the author of several books, including *Pax Americana*. Born in Illinois and educated at Northwestern and Harvard universities, he has taught at the University of Texas, Rutgers University, Wellesley College and Yale University. He lives in New York City.